PROSTITUTION, RACE, AND POLITICS

PROSTITUTION, RACE, AND POLITICS
Policing Venereal Disease in the British Empire

Philippa Levine

ROUTLEDGE
NEW YORK & LONDON

Published in 2003 by
Routledge
29 West 35th Street
New York, NY 10001
www.routledge-ny.com

Published in Great Britain by
Routledge
11 New Fetter Lane
London EC4P 4EE
www.routledge.co.uk

Library of Congress Cataloging-in-Publication Data

Levine, Philippa.
    Prostitution, race, and politics : policing veneral disease in the British
Empire / Philippa Levine.
        p.   cm.
    Includes bibliographical references and index.
    ISBN 0-415-94446-5 (hbk.)—ISBN 0-415-94447-3 (pbk.)
    1. Prostitution—Government policy—Great Britain—Colonies—History. 2. Sexually
transmitted diseases—Government policy—Great Britain—Colonies—History.
3. British—Great Britain—Colonies—Sexual behavior. 4. British—Diseases—Great
Britain—Colonies. 5. Great Britain—Colonies—Social policy. 6. Great
Britain—Colonies—Race relations. I. Title.

HQ185.A5L48   2003
306.74′0941—dc21   2003043128

CONTENTS

ACKNOWLEDGMENTS

Librarians and archivists in many countries have facilitated this research. In the United Kingdom, I owe thanks to the staff—those who catalog, those who fetch and carry, and those who advise—of the British Library, the British Medical Association, the Liverpool archives office, the National Army Museum, the Public Record Office, the Religious Society of Friends, Rhodes House (Oxford), the Royal College of Surgeons, the Sheffield archives office, University College, London, the Wellcome Institute, and the Women's Library (formerly the Fawcett Library). In Hong Kong, I owe thanks to the staff of the University of Hong Kong special collections department and the Hong Kong Public Record Office. In Singapore, my thanks go to the staff of the Public Record Office. In India, the staff at the National Archives of India in New Delhi helped me a great deal. In Australia, staff at state archives in Queensland and New South Wales were most helpful. Inspector Peter M. Guntrip of the Queensland Police Service and Nick Prins of the Department of Family Services and Aboriginal and Islander Affairs generously granted me permission to view otherwise inaccessible documents. At the Australian War Memorial in Canberra, I was made to feel fully at home. Ninette Ellis and Margaret Hoskings at the Barr Smith library at the University of Adelaide were helpful on a daily basis during my time there, as was Judy Nelson at the Mitchell Library in Sydney. In the brief time I spent at the Australian National Archives in Canberra, I was made very welcome. In the United States, I have spent many happy hours in the libraries of Florida State University, the University of Southern California, and the University of California at Los Angeles. I owe a special debt to the staff of the Close Venereology Collection at the Allen Medical Library at Case Western Reserve University.

At Florida State University, Ann Spangler and Carolyn Reynolds of the inter-library loan department worked very hard on my behalf, as have Joyce Toscan's staff in interlibrary loan at the University of Southern California, Lauren Pugh, in particular. At the University of Southern California, librarians Amy Ciccone, Susan Scheiberg, and Ruth Wallach all took an interest in my work and helped me immeasurably. Tony Farrington and Penelope Tuson, both formerly on staff at the Oriental and India Office Collections before its move from the sorely missed Orbit House location to the new British Library, were good friends and advisors. David Doughan, now retired from what was once the Fawcett Library at London Guildhall University, and Lesley Hall of the Wellcome Institute have been tremendously generous, and willingly invested their considerable intellect and energy in this project.

As this world tour implies, this was a study involving a great deal of expensive travel. Without generous funding, it would have been an impossible undertaking and I owe many thanks to the National Institutes of Health for a National Library of Medicine Award (#RO1 LM05678) and to the National Endowment for the Humanities for a Humanities Studies in Science and Technology Award (#RH-21243-95).These facilitated both extensive travel and the time off to conduct that travel and research . My research in Australia was greatly enhanced by the award of a visiting fellowship at the University of Adelaide's Centre for British Studies, and my lengthy trips to Britain were significantly helped by a Zumberge grant from the University of Southern California, as well as by research funds provided by the Deans of the College of Letters, Arts, and Sciences. I am thus in the debt of many generous institutions.

My indebtedness extends to many individuals and on a number of con-tinents. Without the help of Rick Asher of the University of Minnesota and Pradeep Mehendiratta, the director of the American Institute of Indian Studies in New Delhi, I might never have secured the necessary permissions for my work in Delhi. In India, Sumanta Banerjee, Urvashi Butalia, and Rajat Datta and family befriended me. Geraldine Forbes, Veena Oldenburg, and Barbara Ramusack made sure I knew my way around New Delhi even before I arrived there. In Singapore, Sam and Shirley Lam fed me royally, while Kate Lowe—from a distance—offered sage advice about life in Hong Kong. In Australia, Jeff and Nita Francis in Brisbane and Mary Gillard in Canberra welcomed a stranger into their homes and looked after me as if I was one of their own. Jim Hammerton, Liz Donaghue, and Marisia and David made weekends in Melbourne a pleasure whenever I could steal away. Ian Brice helped me find decent housing in Adelaide as well as providing terrific company. Jane Buckingham, Anne Cranny-Francis, and Siva Sivakumar made Sydney come alive. In Britain, Mike Hancock and Ray Parish housed me for years, as did Richard Evans and Christine Corton. I am in their debt beyond description. Adrian Levine and Jinny Fisher, and Merlin and Miranda Fisher-Levine have in recent years fed and housed me generously. Jane Mann welcomed me into her home, so convenient to the Public Record Office.

Needless to say, many scholars have also generously supported me, offering references, discussions, challenges, and support. This book bears the imprint of Alison Bashford, Derek Blakeley, Leo Braudy, Cynthia Enloe, Ian Fletcher, Raelene Frances, Deborah Gorham, Helen Jones, David Killingray, Laura Mayhall, Tom Metcalf, Tim Moreman, Ed Moulton, Carol Pursell, George Robb, Sudipta Sen, Laurie Shrage, Judy Smart, Hal Smith, Mark Stocker, Heather Streets, and Angela Woollacott, all of whom generously shared their knowledge and expertise with me. Many read sections of the manuscript and provided valued advice.

Antoinette Burton, Jim Epstein, and Doug Peers have been friends, colleagues, and coconspirators throughout. They have read this manuscript in its entirety, they have argued its points with me, and they have been a source of unending delight. Jack Wills made some dark times infinitely more bearable. I hope he knows how much his support, his honesty, and even his reprimands have meant to me. Doug Thomas and Ann Chisholm lived the final few years of this project above and beyond the call of friendship. Andras Schiff's interpretations of Bach's solo piano works kept me going throughout. But it is to Curt Aldstadt who prodded me on occasion to acknowledge other pianists, who read the manuscript and heard me talk about it for more years than he could possibly have anticipated, and who was there for me, always, that I owe my very greatest debt.

Philippa Levine
Los Angeles
January 2003

Introduction

This book has two principal themes: an archival case study of colonial policy around prostitution and venereal disease (VD) before 1918, and a more theoretical discussion of colonialism, gender, and race, and how an attention to their relationship might effect a much-needed dialogue between different forms of historical study.[1] To this end, the manuscript includes medical and military history, political and social history, and cultural and feminist history in an effort not only to understand the central importance of laws and practices around prostitution and disease control but also in an effort to integrate these widely different strands of history.

The case study focuses on the control of prostitution in British colonies, a policy ostensibly implemented to protect soldiers from the depradations of sexually transmissible diseases. Across the globe between the 1850s and the 1880s, British colonial administrators established wide-ranging legislation to stem the growing tide of VD and the attendant loss of soldier-power it entailed. Virtually every British colonial possession was subject in the mid-nineteenth century to contagious diseases (CD) regulations that identified female prostitutes as the principal source of contagion. At the heart of all this legislation lay a characteristically nineteenth-century European optimism about the effectiveness of reglementation. Women working as prostitutes, particularly those serving British soldiers and sailors, were required to register officially as prostitutes and undergo regular examinations designed to detect venereal diseases. Registration allowed them to work except when they were confined to specialized hospitals—known as lock hospitals—for treatment.[2] This system, different in detail from colony to colony, was in place by the mid-1870s throughout most of Britain's empire.

CD laws, along with other colonial health measures, have mostly been regarded as principally protecting the health of soldiers.[3] Yet a close look at the enactments suggests that a more complex set of necessities was anticipated by colonial rule, among which military health figured prominently but was by no means the sole determinant. Similar laws operated in Britain from the 1860s to the 1880s, but were neither as spatially expansive (being limited to certain garrison and port towns) nor as thoroughgoing in their impact. The existence of CD legislation across the empire allows us to make critical comparisons of these provisions not only to test the widespread assumption that they were military in intent, but also to see what other factors were at work in the making and practice of the ordinances. Unlike their domestic British counterparts, colonial CD laws looked beyond as well as at the military, justifying often intrusive measures on the grounds not just of military necessity but the need to bring to heel sexual disorder among colonized peoples. These ordinances were not just about soldiers and prostitutes, not just about the control of VD. They also tell us much about British colonialism and the culturally-specific assumptions on which it rested.

Policies around VD and prostitution were invariably controversial, and despite the delicacy of the topic surprisingly prominent in the later nineteenth century. Polite society may not have acknowledged such issues, but the need to protect soldiers and other cohorts from the depradations of gonorrhea and syphilis kept the issue before policy makers, if not wholly in the public eye, throughout this period. Though venereal diseases were largely in decline in the aggregate from the mid-nineteenth century, they were a source of considerable fear, as diseases with an openly moral as well as medical aspect. VD was seen not only as affecting individuals, but as something that would weaken the "race." Health thus became a moral and a national problem. Since VD rates in colonial settings were often higher, in part because the white community in the empire was predominantly male—and often military and unmarried—the issue came to have significant imperial overtones. The spread of disease was potentially ruinous to Britain's powerful empire as well as to its alleged racial superiority.

Little about the CD laws did not attract debate. Women campaigners bitterly resented the double standard they enshrined; only women were responsible for disease transmission and thus liable to legal and medical surveillance. Opponents also charged that the laws punished only working-class women, drawing a veil over the more discreet and hidden forms of sexual servicing exclusive to the wealthy. Regulationist laws, moreover, were not always embraced by the medical establishment, though the most common rationale offered for them was hygiene and sanitation. Indubitably and in their early years, many doctors (including some of the earliest women doctors) welcomed the idea of medically supervising the prostitute. But doubts about the efficacy of regulation grew, and by the early twentieth century many medical professionals eschewed these methods as partial and unworkable. Passed without demur through the House of Lords, and therefore with the imprimatur of the Anglican bishops, the laws caught the attention and stirred the wrath of nonconformist congregations the length and breadth of Britain. Quakers, Baptists, Methodists, and the Scottish Free Church all organized anti-CD groups, corresponding with their overseas missionaries about the sex trade and lending their weight to the considerable campaigns against the laws. Still unspeakable in polite society, these laws were nonetheless the subject of some of the most intense and ferocious debate of the later nineteenth century.

The earliest organized protests focused on the three domestic CD acts of the 1860s. Attention to colonial laws grew rapidly in the 1880s, and especially after the repeal of the metropolitan legislation in 1886. The abolitionist movement devoted to extirpating what it castigated as state encouragement of vice kept colonial CD laws in the public eye throughout the 1880s and 1890s, constantly embarrassing government and tirelessly campaigning for change. Colonial protest, not surprisingly, received much less official attention than its metropolitan cousin, but the system had vocal detractors among the indigenous population in many of the colonies where such schemes operated.

The continued colonial use of these laws in the years following domestic repeal kept the flame of controversy alive, but also reframed it in revealing ways. The colonial campaigns of the late 1880s and 1890s made imperial questions prominent in metropolitan debates, and were a constant thorn in the side of the army, the Colonial and India Offices, and colonial governors and executives. But the attention to race and to imperial prowess which CD laws in colonial settings added to the mix fueled the controversy in different directions. The arguments shifted away from the metropolitan emphasis on class and gender. The nature of empire and of Britain's colonial role in the world was, as ensuing chapters will argue, the focal point of the colonial CD debate. What kind of rule bolstered the institution of prostitution? What did the regulation of prostitution do to the much-vaunted civilizational and moral superiority of imperial British rule? In the CD controversy, we have, in effect, a valuable lens through which to examine many of the presuppositions on which Britain's political and moral assumptions of colonial power rested.

The themes taken up here will, I hope, reveal that there was nothing inevitable or natural about how Britain came to constitute itself and to rule its expanding empire. Rather, in the racial typing of its colonies, in the careful separation of British from continental European values, in the creation of values of imperial patriotism, we see both Britain's palpable success as an empire *and* simultaneously the constant work required to maintain that success. Nation and empire were fragile, in that without constant accommodation they threatened always to dissolve, yet they doggedly continued to operate and function as well as to proclaim Britain's commitment to modernity. British success at maintaining an empire suggests a degree of flexibility, but the historical record also suggests the limits of that buoyancy. By looking at one policy's fate in a variety of colonial settings, and a policy that was always under fire and imminently contradictory, we can illuminate this duality, connect it to debates in the metropolis, and examine the categories of rule in a nuanced way that can account both for local effects and global purpose. This approach allows us to offer a picture of empire as simultaneously successful and anxious, as concurrently "home" and "abroad," and as always and necessarily anything but homogenous. While many of the same debates, concerns, fears, and prejudices appear in disparate contexts, the comparative method used in this study allows us to place them historically, and to measure their sometimes differing significance and impact. Considerations around race, gender, civilization, and the like appear universal in their deployment in a variety of arenas. Different colonial contexts, however, dealt sometimes incommensurable responses. Did the colonial voice sound as one? Did indigenes respond collectively? How was difference received? These are among the questions, broadly wrought, that this project considers. Clear discontinuities between modes of rule were only sometimes paralleled by different strategies in the policies considered here. What produced commonality, and what produced difference in these instances?

For the metropole, the empire was a significant source of national pride. Elaborate exhibitions contrasted British technology with colonial backwardness. The public lapped up colonial story-telling in novels and in the press. Fashions for "oriental" decor, the popularity of travel literature, and a school curriculum which demonstrated British preeminence with a brightly colored globe all suggest how much empire was fused with the very notion of being British. The idea of Britishness, then, cannot be unyoked from the fact of empire. And central to the definition and assertion of Britishness was race as a yardstick of national identity. To be British was to embody civilization, to be born to rule, and to be *not* colonized, not enslaved, conditions fundamentally associated with nonwhiteness. Empire and metropole were not separate sites; empire itself was not a single site.[4]

But why this case study? Venereal diseases were represented as racial poison and medical authorities strenuously argued that tropical forms of the afflictions were nastier and more potent, just as colonists and explorers had long argued that tropical climes produced a distinctly un-British moral laxness. In these ways did racial distinction come to operate significantly in the contours of colonial rule, with the increasingly powerful voice of the scientific and medical communities lending their weight to justifications of racial hierarchy that, in turn, made imperial rule consistent and defensible. Yet few texts of empire even mention the controversies that erupted over regulating prostitution as a measure of disease control.

Venereal diseases, moreover, were seldom fatal though their morbidity rates were invariably high. There were many other diseases, some of them dramatically epidemic in form, where the symptoms were nastier, the prognosis grimmer, and the death toll higher. Public health in many respects owes its establishment to this fact. The venereals were not unique to the colonies, nor a product of colonial medicine. Indeed, the new tropical medicine had no interest in this disease group, since it was in no way specific to certain climates or environments. Compounding the paradox was that overall, venereal diseases were in decline from about the 1860s, precisely at the moment they captured public and medical attention. But what they had, of course, was their deep and unbreakable association with morality. The venereals conjured not only the disorder of disease but of promiscuity and licentiousness, of the dangers of untrammeled passion, the "natural" run amok. They raised issues well beyond the narrowly epidemiological, and in their alleged correspondence with prostitution lay, too, the specter of women out of control.

Race was as critical as gender. Racism was a palpable and accepted feature of life. Missionaries trudged the dockside communities of London and Liverpool hoping to bring the gospel to dark-skinned heathens allegedly in thrall to opium. In the colonies every aspect of life was regulated by racial awareness. Place of residence, occupational choice, and political representation were all governed by race. British India, in Sumit Sarkar's words, was "uncompromisingly white and despotic," while Hong Kong's British community worked to keep the colony's Chinese at a physical distance.[5] The best districts, such as Hong Kong's cool, hilly Peak district, were reserved for white residents. In the Indian hill towns the only locals permitted were luggage-toting porters and retinues of servants.[6] In Queensland, Australian Aboriginals were increasingly pushed onto reservations and Melanesian workers were heavily restricted in where they could live and work. The results were often squalid; in Singapore, James Warren notes, such spatial segregation meant severe residential overcrowding for the Chinese poor.[7]

The meaning of race in an expansionist age was multifold, and its increasingly prominent place in scientific thinking cemented its importance. More than any other ailment, venereal diseases were seen as insidious check on the march of civilization. In settler Australia, tracts warning that the "Anglo-Saxon race" would be compromised by rampant VD were commonplace in the early twentieth century. In dependent colonies, these qualms coalesced mostly around the transfer back to Britain of virulent strains of VD. Ports most especially were feared. Their putative role as centers for the dispersal of disease alongside their reputations in the west as havens for the promiscuous accelerated fears of contamination and racial mixing.

My intent in this study is not to investigate the changing meaning of race over the course of the nineteenth century, but to look rather at the effects, material and discursive, of assumptions that racial difference existed and mattered, assumptions shared by pro- and anti-imperialists, as by supporters and enemies of regulated prostitution alike. This is not to say that there were not significant differences in the racial ideologies propounded by different interest groups in the nineteenth century, but rather to argue that the fact of racial ideologies had profound implications for both the understanding and the practice of colonialism.[8] Racial identities, moreover, in the words of Vron Ware and Les Back have demonstrated an "obstinate resilience," itself an object of interest to the historian.[9]

Britain's racial consciousness in the late nineteenth and early twentieth centuries was considerable, and manifestly connected to its imperial role. At its most obvious level, racial difference seemed palpable to the British; they assumed that those they conquered and colonized were racially distinct from them and also racially inferior. That sentiment was repeatedly on display, whether in school texts that stressed savagery and primitivism or in righteous claims about the educational civilizing mission. But more was at stake for what constituted white identity, and British identity was deeply bound to colonial success. Whiteness was, as Richard Dyer argues, "a product of enterprise and imperialism."[10] And whiteness and race likewise were closely and critically tied to sex—via the body, via reproduction, via deep fears about racial dilution and racial mixing, about racial uncertainties that might destabilize the fictions of racial purity and incomparability. Colonial prostitution, and sexually transmissible diseases believed to be worse in colonial environments, struck a chord in the nineteenth-century imagination far beyond the material damage wrought by disease, and with massive and disruptive consequences for women dependent upon the sex trade for their livelihood.

It was not, however, only against the colonized that the British asserted racial and civilizational superiority.[11] British pride centered as much on a perceived distance from continental European mores as it did on separation from nonwhite peoples. A constant unease with European decadence runs through this period. Champions of prostitution regulation insisted that the British variant bore none of the offensive traits of European legislation. There were, they claimed, no *police des mœurs* in Britain, no *maisons tolérées*. Britain, according to this rhetoric, displayed a greater love for and understanding of individual liberty than the nations of the continent could ever hope to appreciate. This assertion of Britain's national greatness, exceptionalism, and moral uprightness relied on a narrative of Britain's unique and separate development.

However, reservations about Europe had to be cast differently in the colonial arena, since whiteness—shared with other European nations—was so fundamental to colonial and to national identity. Colonial officials often collapsed the terms *European* and *British* into one another, even while they continued to invoke and rely upon a hierarchical ordering of European societies that placed Britain above its continental neighbors. In colonial settings, whites were frequently called Europeans, whatever their actual origin. The association between whiteness and Europeanness underscored the potency of racial factors in these hierarchies. But while in nonwhite colonies, there was a need to assert a generic as well as a specific whiteness to separate ruler from ruled, the settler context demanded different readings. In Australia, whiteness was paramount, but class and gender worked to separate good from bad, and feckless from responsible.

Likewise in countries where the range of resident Europeans was broad (as in India), there was delineation—to ensure that the British remained uppermost in the minds of other Europeans as well as colonized subjects.

The designations *English* and *British* were also often collapsed into one another, marking an ambivalence in contemporary usage and reminding us of the colonialism within as well as beyond British shores. The empire was always *British,* but it was Englishness which proudly set Britain apart from its continental neighbors: "all within the British Isles would naturally desire to be identified with the English."[12] "The English," as Catherine Hall notes, "were confident in their assumption of dominance."[13] This celebratory invocation of a masterful Englishness obscured the fact that there were substantial numbers of non-English Britons throughout the colonies.[14] Though the terms *English* and *British* were often used interchangeably, in this period of high imperialism *English* was indubitably the preferred and more common terminology, reflecting a quite specific sense of English supremacy.

Equally prominent in these evaluative assessments was gender, more especially where women were regarded as the principal conduits of disease. The sex trade defied western sensibilities of private and public by mixing business with pleasure, and by making the workplace a site where women occupied a business role. At the same time, however, the illegitimacy of prostitution as a proper form of work, its tarnishing associations with spectacle, with unrespectability, with disease and with disorder, rendered it something to be controlled and managed. In its ambiguity lay danger, compounded by high venereal rates, the ineffectual and often toxic treatments of the period, and the growing eugenics-based fear of race suicide. It was thus commonplace to constitute prostitution as an often racialized throwback to primitivism, where passion and lust rather than reason and control ruled, positing a false notion of a metropole in which prostitution never went unchecked. Colonial officials took subject peoples to task for their supposed willingness to accommodate or to normalize prostitution. In short, the practice of prostitution became emblematic of the subject status of the colonies, a sign of damaged masculinity, of improper attitudes to sexuality, of a palpable misunderstanding of femininity, and of a tendency to brutalization and lack of reason.

The passing of CD laws coincided with a period in which British women activists were increasingly articulate about their own discontents. In galvanizing wellborn women to speak out publicly, these laws inaugurated a new era in women's activism. Women made vigorous use of comparisons between their own minority status and that of women in Britain's nonwhite colonies, often replicating the racial assumptions of imperialism.[15] The greater part of colonial social reform was aimed at the status of women, a commentary on the poor lot of women in supposedly less progressive societies. A host of alleged Asian barbarisms came under fire in this period, even as British women campaigned around their own legal, economic, and social handicaps. Colonial governments focused largely on domestic issues; since few colonial subjects exercised voting rights, women's political voice was rarely raised as an issue. Instead we see legislation around the sale of girls into domestic service or to brothels, around widow remarriage, child marriage and female age of consent, and around female infanticide. And yet, as many commentators have pointed out, the net result of the colonial presence was not increased freedom for women but often an exacerbation of existing inequalities, "the triumph of repressive measures over those favouring conciliation and reform."[16] Colonial bureaucratization and reform intensified women's marginalization.[17] Chinese women were said to be mute puppets of their powerful men, while Aboriginal Australian women are all but invisible in the official record except as the sexualized victims of male neglect, a neglect, according to white officials, most apparent among their own and among immigrant Chinese men. The Australian Aboriginals were allegedly a dirty people, the menfolk willing to sell their women for a pouch of tobacco. The Indians as a race were indifferent to moral degradation, embracing hereditary prostitution castes without hesitation. Such attitudes were common, and disclose the assumptions that molded policies with direct and substantial effects upon the lives of those they affected. For this reason, women's lives could be mapped out under the guise of protection.

Prostitution, in such an environment, could be represented as a throwback to primitivism. Colonial officials routinely argued that prostitution was normalized in nonwhite societies and held no stigma. This, they argued, was proof that subject peoples were less evolved. Alongside commonplace arguments about the cruelty with which women were treated in such societies, the treatment and role of women came to occupy a central position in imperial policy. Prostitution was by no means the sole arena in which colonial governments attempted to intervene in the social and sexual practices of local peoples, but it was amongst the most thoroughly managed of such policies. Though the contagious diseases ordinances and their successors sought to regulate prostitution mostly though not wholly amongst women who serviced a white colonial clientele, what could be done in colonial settings was distinctively more ambitious than metropolitan laws could enact. In some colonies, women worked in purpose-built brothels administered by the state. In the Chinese-dominant colonies, the brothel remained a legal and regulated institution well into the twentieth century, a practice that would have been out of the question in Britain. These significant differences in practice—between the different colonies as well as between the metropolis and the colonies—once more suggests the heterogeneity and the complexity of colonial practice, and in this instance, reveals, too, the racial workings of different policies. For in each colony, policy was shaped openly and consistently by how government and military officials understood local culture and custom.

In laws pitched as reforming measures, progress was invoked as objective and apolitical. These measures were represented as civilizing rather than subjugating. Politicians, doctors, military officials, and missionaries all laid claim to this fashioning, representing often harsh laws as in the best interests of peoples without recourse themselves to the policy arena. This is not to paint colonial societies as one-dimensional victims of a cruel colonialism; subsequent chapters will flesh out the lives and protests of those affected by these laws. But in asserting agency, we need not minimize the material facts of colonization that, for all it deplored the apparent lawlessness and looseness of societies it ruled, was itself an often violent force.

Colonial medicine was a central mechanism in the imposition of colonial power. Doctors in the colonies served mostly British needs but saw in subject populations and unfamiliar environments an expedient site for research. The pursuit of science and medicine, the final word in modern rationality, contrasted forcefully with "colonial backwardness," the reluctance to embrace the techniques and values of western medicine.[18] The apparent refusal of modernity by colonized populations, and the threat of disorder and disease it posed, coalesced in colonial understandings of how venereal disease might literally poison the body politic. And since colonialism's particular structures and demographics swelled the male population producing temporary spikes in the VD rates, the problem took on an urgency beyond, but never losing sight of, the moral. The seeming inevitability and ubiquity of VD in colonial populations, in the colonial soldiery, and exported back to Britain, strengthened the hand of medicine. Medicine claimed a central role in imperial expansion, an expression of the very project of modernity. Doctors brought the benefits of civilization to the ungrateful and the immoral.

Despite an often strident medical voice clamoring for social and medical reform, the imperial state made much of its claim to abide by the doctrine of "legal repugnancy." Legal repugnancy ostensibly committed colonial administrators to set aside local law and custom only when these conflicted with the "immutable principles of morality which Christians must regard as binding on themselves in all places and at all times."[19] The dictate seems, in practice, to have been only spottily exercised, and was continuously a source of confusion though also a useful ploy. Sheldon Amos, a long-time foe of licensed prostitution and himself a lawyer, pointed out the contradictions at stake. "The case of licensing prostitution is the only one in Christian countries in respect of which lawgivers have been so shameless as knowingly and publicly to contradict their own preferred moral code. In all other cases it is admitted that when law cannot keep pace with the promptings of morality, it must, at the least, help, substantiate, and never contradict moral maxims."[20] These lofty ideals may have been lauded by those who governed, but they were never adopted. Instead, morality, modernity, and progress were thrown into a rhetorical mix that allowed prostitution simultaneously to flourish, to be deplored, *and* to be regulated in the interests of hygiene, humanity, and the racial future.

Repugnancy in its legal wrappings was an issue of moral definition, essential to the manner in which imperial law was perceived and promulgated. David

Washbrook points out that the failure to establish customary law in India on the same independent footing as English common law "reduced the scope of judicial independence and imbued executive fiat with the sanctity of law."[21] Mrinalini Sinha has pointed out that the claims of noninterference in Indian social and religious affairs allowed government to endorse more conservative practices already in place.[22] And though the British claimed to keep the religious and secular spheres separate, the practice was "not easily implemented."[23] In Malaya, though custom and religion were ostensibly left alone by the colonial authorities, "religious law was greatly circumscribed and redefined."[24] Conversely, Hardwicke's Marriage Act, which centered legal marriage on the parish church, was not applied to the colonies.[25] This one-way approach was useful for claiming a higher moral standard for British law.

The prostitute, notes Miles Ogborn, "disordered the state and threatened the empire."[26] It was critical, therefore, that she be identified female, that she be equated with the less civilized, and that she be subject to control. Ogborn's focus is the eighteenth century, but his point is clearly pertinent a hundred and more years later, despite dramatic changes in the composition and role of Britain's empire. There is no simple formula of change over time at work here, and one of the values of the comparative colonial approach is to foreground questions about change and stasis. This study documents the changes that led to at least partial repudiation of CD methods by the early 1900s, but it will also reveal that attitudes, policies, prejudices, and practices either did not alter or continued to rely centrally on unchanging attitudes around race, gender, sexuality, and class. In an attempt to avoid too much confusion in an already ambitious undertaking, the book is therefore divided to deploy varied approaches, in an attempt to persuade readers that the false separation between different sub-branches of the discipline do our understanding of the past a disservice. The practical task of organizing such an enormity of material forced a theoretical examination of the very act of organization, evidenced in the book's unusual structure in encompassing both a diachronic and a synchronic approach. The range and scope of the materials produced a compelling need to think about how histories are processed and organized, and what effects those choices have on the stories history tells. As a result, this study draws as heavily on political, administrative, and military history as it does on cultural and social history. Part 1, narrative in form, focuses principally on medical and political history, charting the fortunes of the laws regulating prostitution and controlling disease to reveal the multiplicity of factors affecting political decision-making. Part 2 takes up the cultural themes that permeated discussions of sexuality throughout this period, and locates the ways that imperial questions shaped policy making and public opinion. In presenting arguments and methodologies drawn from such disparate branches of the discipline, my intent is to demonstrate that these forms of study can, and indeed should, coexist. I see no radical break between those categories that have come to be known as representation and reality, but would argue rather that the influence of perception has deep material consequences, and that the influence goes in both directions.[27] As Patrick Wolfe has so cogently argued: "Our goal should be a unified historical field."[28]

Part 1 introduces and follows the fortune of the legislation and of those who championed and those who opposed it. Chapter 1 offers some background on the history of the four colonies studied here. Chapter 2 details the history and operation of colonial CD laws and explores what prompted and sustained their enactment in imperial contexts. Chapter 3, also concerned with the operation of the various acts and ordinances, links their passage and practice to the triumphalism of western medicine as a key site by which modernity could be proclaimed as part of the imperial mission. Together chapters 2 and 3 suggest the links between law and medicine, and between medicine and culture, underscoring the central role medicine played in determining how race and gender were understood and controlled, both formally and informally. Chapters 4, 5, and 6, moving from the 1890s to the First World War, focus on specific moments when venereal disease, prostitution, and race were forced into the public eye. In the 1890s political activism combined with the rise of colonial nationalism kindled a new phase of antiregulationist protest focused not just on the empire but, fundamentally, on its connections with morality and civilization. This is the subject of chapter 4. Chapter 5 looks at the aftermath of the abolition of CD laws, when wary antiregulationists remained unconvinced that the compulsion in these acts had been extirpated. The controversy over regulation resurfaced during the war of 1914–1918, a conflict in which large contingents of colonial soldiers worked for their colonial masters either as laborers or as soldiers. The dispatch of large bodies of men to the various battlegrounds of the war occasioned an inevitable rise in troop VD, after years of decline. But the war, deeply implicated in wider debates about imperialism, and following a period of unusually militant feminist protest in Britain, generated larger debates around sexual behavior, gender roles, racial responsibility, and imperial rights in which VD, both symbolically and actually, was a prominent factor. Chapter 6 details these debates.

Major political and institutional events structure this chronology. At the time of the passing of the laws, Cardwell's army reforms, the Indian mutiny, the death of Lord Palmerston, and the beginnings of organized feminist activity were all topics of public concern, shaping politics and culture at mid-century. The First World War, the Boer War, Haldane's Territorial and Reserve Forces legislation of 1907, a volatile Ireland, and feminist militancy as well as the rapid growth of Indian nationalism mark out the later period. These are chronologies familiar to historians and landmarks familiar to historians of Britain and its empire. It is against this backdrop that the CD laws were enacted and operated.

Part 2 of the book dispenses with the more traditional frame that is so effective in accounting for the institutional elements at work here—when the ordinances were promulgated, how they were received, when they were abolished, and what succeeded them. Though the CD ordinances were in place in most colonies for only a few years (mostly between the 1860s and 1890s in their formal guise, at least), many of the ideas that shaped them both preceded the legislation and were remarkably tenacious even after abandonment. The chapters in Part 2 thus draw on examples from a span of some seventy years to show how the same vocabularies and ideas could be used successfully and repeatedly in a variety of contexts for imperial ends, suggesting that empire derived its fiction of stability in part from its insistence on the unchangeability of colonial knowledge. The progress of British civilization and the alleged stasis of the colonial world allowed for forms of imperial rule unthinkable in the metropole and sustained a triumphalist narrative of British conquest. These chapters underscore the fact that while enormous changes did occur in the period with which the sequential chapters deal, attitudes towards STDs and those thought responsible for spreading them—prostitute women—changed remarkably little. Indeed, these chapters are intended to show how policy and practice not only shaped but consolidated views about local societies, about sexual role, about empire and Britishness that would remain surprisingly unchanged certainly until the First World War, the temporal point at which this study closes.

Chapter 7 offers an overview of nineteenth-century thinking about commercial sex and its role and place in judgments of colonized societies. Prostitution was among the most controversial of the "social evils" so fretted about in the Victorian period. What difference did the removal of the phenomenon to distant lands make in assessments of the issue? This chapter also investigates what effects the imperial presence had on the local sexual economy. Chapters 8 and 9 connectedly explore how assumptions about racial difference and hierarchy directly affected both women themselves and assessments of femininity. In colonial settings, were white women working in prostitution considered as base as indigenous women? What did the presence of sexually available white women in the colonies signal? How were local colonized women understood in relation to imperial governance and in relation to their own social, religious, and cultural groupings? Chapter 8 looks at the lives of colonized women, and chapter 9 at those of white women in the colonies. Chapter 10 focuses on men and on the part played by masculinity in the economy and practice of prostitution and of the empire. Masculinity was integral to imperial rhetoric, and this chapter explores some of the fissures in that rhetoric by contrasting representations of racialized manhood with actual behavior and experience. Finally, chapter 11, pursuing the material effects of opinion, policy, and representation, explores the spatial aspects of the sexual economy. Where could prostitution operate and how? What were the geographical imperatives of imperialism that shaped the spaces and regulations of this flourishing if disparaged livelihood? The chapters in Part 2 thus discuss the use of race, gender, and space as policy, examining how the material and the representational worked in concert to produce and to fix certain kinds of knowledge, of working-class white soldiers or the women who serviced their sexual needs, of the allegedly profound differences and distances between ruler and ruled.

This structure allows for a disaggregation of the overly unitary categories around gender, race, and empire that obscure more than they can illuminate. In detailing opinion, attitude, and law in varied contexts and over a generous temporal range, we can more effectively appreciate how central the hierarchies around race and gender were to colonial rule, how enmeshed western medical thinking was in the expansion and the pursuit of empire, and how complex a phenomenon that empire actually was. At the same time, I hope that the forays into such differently constructed fields as military and medical history, and gender and cultural history, may persuade readers that bridges built on mutual respect and interest might deepen as well as broaden our appreciation of the complexities of our discipline.

The choice of topic—sexually transmissible diseases and prostitution—in which these comparisons are located brings together a variety of important themes including labor, sexuality, the public and private spheres, law, medicine, and the role of the military in the empire. This study details just how critical a political topic the control of VD and prostitution—not routinely of interest or significance in political history—was well into the twentieth century. It was regarded by policy makers as crucial for defense, for morality, for personal safety, for health, and as a powerful tool for knowing and containing, as well as deploring, native populations. Despite the historical silences around this topic, discussions of VD and paid sex occupied a great deal of government time and debate in all the colonies under scrutiny (and in many others) as well as in the imperial political arena in the metropolis. The contagious diseases laws, in particular, met with active and vocal protest; after the successful fight to rid the United Kingdom of such laws, opponents of state-regulated prostitution turned their attention to the colonies, fearing that their continued colonial use would serve to ease their eventual reintroduction in the domestic sphere. Colonialists in the sites studied here (and elsewhere, though not universally) put up a far bigger fight to retain these laws than did supporters in Britain, and colonial protests reveal a very significant seam of resentment against the dictate of home-based government. This clash of sensibilities between colonial and domestic politicians is intriguing, for it speaks to multiple ideas about (and responses to) the colonial project *in situ*. Even Britons who would not have dreamed of settling in the colonies where they worked and who planned to return to Britain in retirement resented deeply what they regarded as the interference of British politicians in local affairs. No simple "us" and "them" divided local peoples against a colonial presence. This study, in looking at the distinctive differences between indigenous opinion of VD and prostitution control and at colonists' views, suggests that imperialism as a practice had to negotiate literally daily in a variety of registers rather than in a simple and linear relation of opposition.

In sum, this four-colony study of venereal disease and prostitution legislation between approximately 1860 and 1918 details the fierce battles over policy associated with these twin problems that beset almost every colony Britain possessed. Simultaneously, it raises broader questions about the relationship between the metropole and the empire, between the prospect of national sovereignty and that of colonial rule, about the ways that long-standing ideas about masculinity and femininity, control and order, and promiscuity and restraint profoundly affected the course of Britain's imperial history in its most active and prominent period of rule.

Chapter I

Comparing Colonial Sites

Everything is now grand and imperial!
—William Cobbett

Colonial contagious diseases (CD) legislation operated in almost all of Britain's overseas possessions, but this book will focus principally on such laws in four important colonies. In Hong Kong, formal regulation of brothels preceded the British law, introduced first in 1857. In India, the 1864 Cantonment Act brought regulation to military zones, while the 1868 Indian Contagious Diseases Act extended it to the cities. Queensland passed a Contagious Diseases Act in 1868 and the Straits Settlements adopted its first CD ordinance in 1870.

Each of these four colonies offers a different model of colonial rule and a different demographic profile, but a shared experience of colonialism. Comparing them provides a framework that offers a nuanced reading of how colonial power operated. Different policies—and not just in the arena of VD control—were at work in each of these colonial settings, but their shared characteristics make comparison viable. All had multiethnic and racially diverse populations, were of considerable significance to Britain, were part of, or proximate to Asia, and were often and severally compared to one another by British and colonial officials. These colonies had distinctive demographic make-ups and were ruled in a variety of forms, yet they share enough population characteristics to make comparison feasible. Above all, they offer a variety of forms of colonial governance, a diversity that helps us to see the complexities within British imperialism rather than allowing all policy to be filed under a simple and homogenous heading of colonial rule. While Hong Kong and the Straits Settlements were crown colonies, settler Queensland was self-governing from the mid-nineteenth century and British India experienced a unique form of direct rule, a combination of practices inherited in part from its East India Company history and by subsequent diktat from Westminster as well as by a multilayered local white population. The Straits, moreover, had been India's fourth Presidency for a couple of decades prior to Crown Colonial status, and had, as a result, a substantial Indian population. The palpable distinctions between white settler governance and the autocracies characteristic of dependent colonies underline the racial politics at work here. Such differences in rule hint at the impossibility in talking of "empire" or of "race" in a unitary way, while the common ground of their being colonial possessions, and along a common regional axis, offers sufficient connection to make comparison workable. What do the different versions of the CD laws in these settings suggest about race, about empire, and about gender in a period in which Britain's own national sentiment was so bound up with imperial prowess?

Comparing different colonies also makes sense in this era since the movement of migrant peoples within the colonial world meant that increasingly diverse populations complicated the business of ruling subject peoples. All these colonies experienced significant migration and shared many of the same immigrant populations, not surprisingly. The Indian population of the Straits may have been larger than the Indian population of Hong Kong, but both colonies had significant pan-Asian populations by the 1870s, even if their dominant populations (either numerically or politically) were southern Chinese. Queensland, too, took in a variety of Asian migrants (predominantly from China and India) for manual work alongside a large contingent of Pacific Island labor. All these factors, these overlapping networks of population and of migration, suggest that the colonial world was a highly mobile place in which groups moved from country to country, mostly in search of work. Their presence in each of these colonies offers us a point of comparison as well as of contrast, in determining how local officials chose to label, to understand, and to control each of these diverse subject populations.

Vital to this comparative project are ideas of nation and of race, and their inextricability in the rise of the modern national/imperial state.[1] Comparative work, though it comfortably encompasses the prospect of changes in the contours and identity of the nation, has seldom put the question of nation as itself a historical category under scrutiny. Rather, comparative work often assumes rather than historicizes the idea of nation, providing what Robert Gregg calls "extra layers of cement," fixing people in "columns of transhistorical meaning."[2] In traditional comparativist readings, the nation as a fixed point of historical reference ("British" history, "Indian" history, "French" history) holds steady, even while the frontiers of the nation might change. In other words, comparative history has sometimes taken the nation to be somehow a natural as well as obvious site for historical enquiry, and thus outside and irrelevant to the analytical lens. Relatedly, as Edward Said has pointed out, comparative literature, at least, was born of imperialism, with its assumption of the sovereign western commentator privileged to view the totality.[3] This transhistorical position, in which the idea of nation is fixed and stable, the natural subject of historical investigation, necessarily relies on a notion of national difference, that nations and their peoples display certain characteristics that allow the historian to recognize them as such. The danger here, of course, is that nation and race become synonymous. The binding together of biology and politics that this association made possible served British colonial needs, as many of the following chapters will demonstrate. This preference for a universalist reading of events and hierarchies also normalized the nation-state as the proper site of politics and governance, delegitimizing tribal and communal forms of rule that were not formalized in ways understood by the colonizers. This position made the claim that colonized nations needed guidance and education before self-rule could be granted seem self-evident; "lesser" peoples needed schooling in modernity before they could be let go. This attachment to what Bill Readings has identified as an "enlightenment pattern in which local superstition is replaced by universal theory," illuminates the claims to wisdom, to universalism, and to rationality that the British claimed their colonial rule represented.[4] The nation, thus, was inextricably bound to colonialism.

Such a methodology also presupposes that nations precede empires, that the spread of colonialism can only follow from a nation's expansion. This top-down view renders imperialism a phenomenon which is catalyzed by and viewed from the metropolis. In many instances, it is an emphasis that results in a one-way reading of empire, in which ideas and policies flow from the center to the periphery. Empires, in this reading, are merely the foot-soldiers of metropolitan progress and action. My reading is a more fluid one, which contends that changes in nations are as much the product of influence from empires as from internal and domestic pressure, dissent, and debate. Certainly, an empire cannot be claimed or founded by something that has not already claimed for itself nationhood (at least, not in modern terms), but this by no means precludes the possibility that empires constitute the nation as much as they are constituted by it. This is not simply to argue that culture and politics as well as material goods move in two directions, influencing at either end, but that the identity of the nation in its modern dress is intimately linked to ideas around empire. Nations, from the eighteenth to the twentieth centuries, have seen the absence or presence of empire as a measuring stick of power and influence; the very quality of nationhood cannot thus be separated from imperialism. I would therefore argue that we cannot as historians assert a chronological and linear progression *from* nation *to* empire, but must rather engage the two as simultaneous.[5] It is to avoid this unilinear trap that Inderpal Grewal dubs her comparative stance "transnational," examining cultural "flows" rather than only marking difference.[6]

Clearly, I seek a comparative approach that can reject fixed categories and which does not assume national commonality. I am not, I would stress, ready to abandon the comparative, since it surely need not deal in universals. My comparative base specifically challenges the idea of the universal by exploring the specificities and historical contingencies that shaped the application of CD laws in the different arenas described below. As important here as recognizing the ways in which colonial power could profit from the equation of nation and race, is an insistence that we cannot speak of the colonial world, in this case the British Empire, as a single entity. Universalizing the experience and forms of colonialism would merely replicate a methodology that has served colonial power productively for many years. Instead, this study specifically and centrally compares within the spectrum of colonialism, as well as across the metropole-colony divide. Significantly different modes of colonialism clearly shaped the histories of the various colonies under study here.

Queensland

Queensland, the northeast quadrant of the Australian continent, was first set-tled by Europeans in 1824. The establishment of an isolated and harsh penal institution for repeat and serious offenders at Moreton Bay marks the start of its white history. In the far south of the colony, Moreton Bay would become the site of Queensland's capital, Brisbane, whose growth paralleled the shift in white settlement from convicts to free migrants and settlers in the 1840s. This shift lent Australian historiography its fundamental shape, one in which indigenous Aboriginal peoples had little place, classifiable neither as migrants nor as settlers.[7] Once prolific, indigenous Aboriginal communities were pushed farther and farther to the margins of this rapidly expanding area of white settle-ment. In 1859 the colony's Aboriginal population stood at around 100,000, with white settler numbers at about 30,000.[8] By the 1890s, the Aboriginal population had been reduced to less than 25,000 out of a total population of over 400,000.[9]

Gender imbalance in the colony was striking. Among Pacific Islanders, men outnumbered women ten to one. The non-Aboriginal population in 1891 was about 224,000 men and about 170,000 women, with the north more heavily male.[10] From the 1890s, a gradual balance between men and women began to emerge in the white population, but not among the migrant populations where the nature of the work and the restrictions on immigration kept the inflow predominantly male.

After separating from New South Wales in 1859, Queensland took on the typical characteristics of a settler society. Its parliament followed the bicameral model of a crown-appointed upper house (the Legislative Council, abolished in 1922) and an elected lower house (the Legislative Assembly). Legislative Council members held office for life, while Assembly members were elected to five year terms. The electorate was exclusively male until 1904. A year later, an Australia-wide federal Elections Amendment Act excluded Aboriginals, Pacific Islanders, and those of African or Asian birth from voting.

More than 50 percent of the colony was tropical, a geography with pro-found effects on the state's economic development. At 667,000 square miles, Queensland accounted for 22 percent of the total area of the continent. Though the denser and more settled areas were principally in the temperate south, the tropical north grew rapidly from the 1870s and was critical to Queensland's overwhelmingly pastoral economy. Settlement moved slowly northward in the 1870s and 1880s though sparse numbers and small frontier-style towns were dominant beyond the southeast. Sheep and cattle farming began in earnest in the 1840s. Wool dominated Queensland's exports into the twentieth century, though there was greater diversification from the 1870s.[11] The discovery of gold in 1867, as well as rich mineral veins, made mining a lucrative activity. Gold was mostly found in the north, though the earliest discoveries were at Gympie, only a hundred miles north of Brisbane. As gold faltered, tin, lead, and copper mining grew in significance. At the coast, pearling and the bêche-de-mer industry (an edible sea slug prized in some cuisines) employed considerable numbers, mostly in the Torres Strait in the far north.[12] Above all, however, it was the growth of the sugar industry that dominated northern Queensland.

Sugar was an increasingly powerful commodity in the nineteenth century, an era of rapidly increasing consumption. First grown in Queensland in the 1860s, sugar production developed quickly. The area around the coastal town of Mackay, 625 miles north of Brisbane, was the most active sugar region with plantations in the Pioneer Valley and sugar mills in Mackay. Sugar stretched all the way from a small area under cultivation immediately north of Brisbane near Caboolture to Cairns, some one thousand miles to the capital's north.

Sugar's history, of course, was inextricably tied to that of slavery, and most especially the mass and nonconsensual resettlement of Africans to the plantations of the West Indies. The abolition of slavery in British possessions in the 1830s forced sugar magnates to explore alternative forms of labor. For most of the nineteenth century, as a result, sugar was reliant on indentured labor; it remains "one of the massive demographic forces in world history."[13] Queensland's sugar plantation owners looked principally to Pacific Islanders, mainly Melanesians, for their workforce. They were aided by the depletion of the sandalwood industry in which many Pacific Islanders had found employment before the 1860s.[14] Between 1863 and 1908 (the final year of deportation, recruitment having been banned in 1904), thousands of islanders flocked to Queensland's sugar plantations under indenture.[15]

This northward agrarian expansion spearheaded by, but not exclusive to, sugar also made the north demographically distinctive, not only as a male frontier environment (a narrative that would become central in white Australia's stories of its early years) but in its considerable racial and ethnic diversity. Raymond Evans estimates the aboriginal population as 4 percent of the total and the non-European segment as 5.05 percent of Queensland's population at the end of the nineteenth century.[16] Pacific Islanders, known colloquially as Kanakas, were the largest but not the only group of migrant sugar workers. Indian, Cingalese, and Maltese labor was employed, though in smaller numbers. There were also Javanese and Japanese workers. Pearling and diving attracted Japanese as well as Aboriginal workers; while in western Australia these occupations were mainly the province of indigenous workers, Queensland employed a considerable number of Japanese divers, and had the highest Japanese population among the Australian colonies, peaking at a total of just over 3,200 in 1898.[17]

The largest nonwhite migrant group in Queensland, as elsewhere in Australia, was the Chinese. The first Chinese to arrive in Queensland came as shepherds, their presence facilitated by an Anglo-Chinese treaty of 1860 by which Chinese workers could enter into service with British subjects.[18] Numbers swelled when gold was unearthed. At its height in 1876, the Chinese made up 6 percent of the colony's population.[19] Strong anti-Chinese sentiment led the following year to a Chinese Immigration Regulation Act, modeled on existing racist legislation in New South Wales and Victoria.[20] Chinese immigration into Queensland slowed as a result, and by 1896 the population represented only 2 percent of overall numbers, about 8,500 people in all.[21] As gold fever waned, this population moved preponderantly to agriculture. A few Chinese found work on the sugar plantations but most opted for market gardening in smallholdings. It was thus a population clustered in rural and small towns, and more in northerly than southerly areas of the colony, though Brisbane had a busy Chinatown from early in its history.[22]

In some respects, the Chinese in Queensland resembled the colony's Pacific Islanders. Both were overwhelmingly male populations, concentrated in the north and involved in agriculture. Both groups labored under restrictive laws limiting their numbers and their daily lives, and both groups suffered the consequences of prejudice. The Melanesians, however, were virtually all under indenture to the sugar industry. The first recruitment from the Pacific islands to Queensland had been in 1863 for the cotton fields, but with sugar's boom, the emphasis soon shifted.[23] By 1870, about a thousand Melanesians were arriving annually in Queensland on three-year indentures.[24] The bulk of the recruits were young unmarried men, many of whom would die young; mortality rates among this group were markedly higher than in other populations.[25] Their numbers peaked in the early 1880s, following the fortunes of the sugar industry, and at this juncture there were perhaps 11,000 Melanesians in the colony.[26] Their presence was governed by a series of laws, the first inaccurately titled the Polynesian Labourers Act. Passed in 1868, it restricted laborers to three-year stays and provided for inspection of plantations. Renamed and amended in 1872 as the Pacific Islanders Protection Act, and replaced after 1880 with a wholly new law, these laws attempted to tighten recruitment practices, to curb kidnapping, to establish minimum living standards, and to restrict formally where islanders could work as well as to confine them to the sugar industry.[27] After a brief hiatus in indenture between 1890 and 1892, indenture was formally abolished in 1904, and followed by mass deportations. The 1907 Pacific Island Labourers Act, a federal law, guaranteed the cessation of the trade.[28]

During the fifty or so years that Melanesian labor maintained Queensland's sugar industry, this workforce experienced many of the same checks as indigenous Aboriginal peoples. Aboriginals, too, were limited in where they could go and how they might earn their living. Both groups were legally forbidden alcohol and those providing them with it were liable to prosecution. The Aboriginals Protection and Restriction of the Sale of Opium Act, passed in 1897, reserved considerable power to the office of the protectorate not only to control employment, movement, and access to drugs and alcohol, but also in matters of individual conscience. Marriage to a non-Aboriginal required the protector's permission, and protectors enforced savings plans on their charges, organizing compulsory deductions from wages into savings accounts they controlled. The legislation, though amended from time to time, remained in force until 1967 when the federal government acquired responsibility for Aboriginal affairs.

The 1868 act governing Pacific Islanders and the 1897 act both illuminate the poverty of racial classification. The former confused Polynesians and Melanesians while the 1897 act exempted Torres Strait Islanders on the grounds that they were a more "advanced" group than mainland Aboriginals. From 1879 those living on the islands in the Torres Strait were legally classified as Pacific Islanders and not as Aboriginals.[29] It was only after 1904 that they were, and then only gradually, brought under the aegis of the Aboriginal legislation, and reclassified as Aborigine.[30] There was always ambiguity in how formal law chose to classify Aboriginal peoples; the general trend was towards restricting the citizenship and rights of those categorized as Aboriginal.[31] In another anomaly suggestive of the plasticity of racial definition, Japanese pearlers working in Queensland's far north in the early twentieth century were exempted from the provisions of the commonwealth's White Australia policy.[32] The casual ease with which such classification and reclassification was achieved suggests how much these groups were objects of scrutiny for official Queensland.

Northern Queensland was an enormously diverse region, far more so than the settled south. The colony was "the most polyglot and multi-coloured of the Australian settlements during the pre-Federation period."[33] It was also the last segment of eastern Australia to be settled. As a result, the settlers brought with them both experience and prejudice, "not only a racial stereotype but also a stereotyped pattern of dispossessing the Aborigines."[34] It is easy to caricature the white bushmen who colonized the hot and inhospitable north as bullies and bigots, equally contemptuous of women and their nonwhite workers, but these were not sentiments unique to settlers and pastoralists. It was, after all, the predominantly southern legislature of the colony that passed not only laws restricting nonwhites but also the 1868 Contagious Diseases Act, making women the target of VD control. Attitudes among whites in southern Queensland were not that different from those in the north, and indeed it was working-class southern opposition to the use of nonwhite labor that catalyzed the north's failed attempts at secession and at annexation in New Guinea, both in the 1880s.[35] Queensland's nonwhite population may have been predominantly located in the north, but the politics of its presence reverberated throughout the colony and directly affected governing matters.

Land, labor, and race were tied together in complex ways in Queensland, and indeed in the broader Australian context. The legal basis for settlement owed its existence to the presumption of *terra nullius*. The alleged failure of indigenous Aboriginal peoples to use the land in fully productive ways undermined their claims to possession.[36] For the British, ownership of land implied productivity and responsibility as well as conferring citizenship. But maintaining the land's productivity demanded labor and the Australian colonies from their earliest history had a complicated relationship with labor. Unfree convict labor had been the basis on which the first colonies were raised. Subsequent labor needs were met by both free and indentured workers. In this duality were the seeds of inevitable conflict. Late nineteenth-century Australia was a place where white radicals and trade unionists worked hard to forge new labor relations, in which a rhetoric of the dignity and honesty of hard work reaping just rewards held out the promise of social mobility. Yet this buoyant vision of labor was largely withheld from nonwhite workers, whether Chinese, Aboriginal, or Kanaka.[37] Labor took on decidedly racial characteristics and nowhere more starkly than in northern Queensland where the burgeoning sugar industry chose cheap Melanesian labor over technology.[38] The disjunction between economics and discourse was a problem never wholly resolved.

The presence of a large class of indentured workers vitiated the claim that labor was a worthwhile form of independence, a source of pride and a watchword for self-respect. Indenture cast a shadow on the idea of free labor. Yet northern Queensland's sugar industry was wholly reliant on this source of cheap workers even while lauding the principles of independence and freedom so central to Australia's vision of its political future. The faultline that could make sense of this inconsistency was race: white workers were free laborers assured of their righteous respectability, the indentured were definitionally inferior, racially and in respect to their labor position. In similar vein, Aboriginals were often represented as unwilling workers, outside the formula of work as ennobling. And though Aboriginal-Asian labor relations appear to have been quite peaceful, the Chinese were also separated out from "good" labor either as hard taskmasters or as profiting not from honest work but from peddling opium.[39] Work thus became a racialized taxonomy in a colonial setting where new social relations for white workers were being forged.

Queensland's primary health concern was with the white population and with its ability to withstand, and to work in, tropical conditions. The Australians were also early proponents of a variety of public health measures early in the twentieth century that, elsewhere, provoked controversy as overly interventionist. Indeed the Australian medical profession prided itself on being in the vanguard of health policy. Yet the emphasis was invariably on white health. Some sixty hospitals received government subsidy by 1900, but most were loath to accept Aboriginal patients.[40] The widespread belief that the Aboriginals were a dying race encouraged a fatalistic neglect.[41] The impact of settler pastoralism on Aboriginal health was little short of devastating in its sweeping aside of traditional hunting grounds and its wholesale destruction of indigenous agriculture.[42] David Arnold has concluded that "the scale and intensity of European intervention in the period from the late eighteenth to the early twentieth centuries had a massive and probably unprecedented epidemiological and environmental impact on the peoples of Africa, Asia and Oceania," most of it negative.[43] The health needs of migrants carried equally low priority. Melanesian mortality rates between 1899 and 1903 were more than three times that of the average rate for the colony, but little was done to allay the problem.[44]

For all the rhetoric around medicine as proof of Australian advancement, only a fraction of public money was devoted to health issues. A Central Board of Health, modeled along English lines, was established in 1865, and the 1867 Medical Act policed medical qualifications. By 1891 there were 233 registered medical practitioners in the colony.[45] But most health legislation, as in Britain, was passed in response to epidemic crises. The 1872 Act was precipitated by an outbreak of smallpox, the 1884 Act by typhoid fever, and the 1900 Act by bubonic plague.[46]

Politically, as a white settler colony enjoying "responsible self-government," Queensland realistically shared little with dependent colonies where there was virtually no local representation or power. Where it did share significant characteristics was in the arena of labor need and the demographics of how that need was filled.

Straits Settlements

Not far from the northwestern coast of Australia was the crown colony of the Straits Settlements centered on the port city of Singapore. The Straits became a crown colony in 1867, though the British had a strong footing in the region by the late 1700s, acquiring Penang (also known as Prince of Wales Island) in 1786, Malacca in 1795, and Province Wellesley in 1800. Singapore was founded in 1819 when Sir Thomas Stamford Raffles formalized a treaty with the region's ruler, the Temenggong of Johore, ceding the territory to Britain. The seat of government moved from Penang to Singapore in 1832, though even before then Singapore had superseded Penang as the principal port in the region. From 1803, Penang formed the fourth presidency of the East India Company's (EIC) administration, with Singapore and Malacca added to the presidency in 1826, its trade an EIC monopoly. This was the grouping that became known as the Straits Settlements. In 1830, and with the EIC's loss of its Asian trade monopoly, the Straits was demoted to a residency of the Bengal presidency. Authority passed from the government of Bengal to the government of India in 1851, to the India Office in 1858, and finally to the Colonial Office in 1867.

With the growing recognition of both the strategic and the economic value of the region, the British stepped up their presence and their power. Over the course of the century, Britain acquired more and more control in a region formerly dominated by the Dutch and the Portuguese. The 1824 Anglo-Dutch treaty guaranteed Singapore to the British and Java to the Dutch. In exchange for recognizing Dutch lands to the south of Singapore, the British obtained the promise that the Dutch would not interfere in Malaya. Yet it was partly a fear of increasing Dutch as well as other European influence that led, in 1874, to the Treaty of Pangkor. Under its terms, residencies were established in the western Malay states of Perak, Selangor, and Sungai Ujong. Ostensibly advisory to the local rulers, the residents exerted an increasing amount of control in tax collection, law enforcement, and the like, until in 1896 their power was formalized and expanded. The Federated Malay States (FMS) formed that year and consisting of these three states plus Pahang (where a British residency was first established in 1888), reported to a resident general in Kuala Lumpur who, in turn, reported to the Straits governor. The other states in the area remained principally under Siamese influence, though those comprising the Unfederated Malay States (Kelantan, Trengganu, Perlis, Kedah, and Johore) continued to have British residencies.

While Singapore was prized mostly as a commercial port, especially after the opening of the Suez Canal in 1869, the rest of the colony also offered rich economic possibilities, aided by the port's freedom from import and export duties. The Straits had been largely insolvent during its Indian-administered years.[47] The EIC had used the territory primarily as a dumping ground for Indian convicts, and its economic potential remained unrealized. Thereafter, however, plantation crops thrived. Rubber (mainly a twentieth-century commodity), sugar, coffee, tapioca, and rice were all significant. The plantations were worked partly by Indian and Chinese indentured labor, partly by Indian convict labor, and partly by the indigenous Malay. Mining, especially for tin, was also key to the region's economic success.[48] It was an industry increasingly dominated by the Chinese merchants and workers who came to populate the Straits so considerably in these years.

The Settlements flourished economically in the latter half of the nineteenth century, trade increasing dramatically along with the tonnage of shipping at Singapore.[49] By the end of the century, over fifty lines of seagoing steamers visited Singapore regularly.[50] Banking houses and shipping companies established offices there, and wealthy Straits Chinese as well as colonialists profited handsomely. Singapore was a hugely important port, not only for local trade but as a hub for the entire region of southeast Asia. By the early twentieth century, Malaya (comprising the Straits Settlements, the FMS, and the unprotected states) boasted one of the strongest trade performances in both imports and exports of any British colony.[51]

Much of this success was premised, of course, on the supply of cheap labor that literally built the colony in much the same way as the Australian convicts had built the earliest white settlements there. Convict labor from India formed a significant percentage of the Straits manual labor force between 1788 and 1873, when convict resettlement ended. Aside from this forced migration, the Straits relied heavily on Indian indenture, on Chinese migrants, and to a lesser extent on nearby Javanese labor. Carl Trocki points out that "the entire export economy of the region came to be dominated by non-indigenous peoples," leaving natives to become "poor men in a rich land."[52] The Chinese formed the largest migrant group in the colony; the dominant Chinese group was Hokkien, the second largest was Teochew.[53] By the mid-nineteenth century, Singapore was the "focal point of Chinese immigration for the entire region."[54] From the 1870s to the 1930s, the population of the Straits increased at a ferocious rate, between 24 percent and 43 percent every decade, and well into the twentieth century this expansion was the result more of continued migration than natural increase.[55] Singapore's population rose from around 11,000 in 1824 to 81,000 by 1860.[56] By 1891, it had grown to more than 184,000, with the total Straits population at over 500,000.[57]

The migrant populations of the Straits were overwhelmingly made up of young single men, or men who had left behind families in poverty-stricken areas and to whom they remitted much of their meager earnings. Sex ratios were less dramatically unbalanced in areas of the colony where local Malay populations dominated. The imbalance reflects the changes characteristic of colonial migration. Whether in the tin mines, in the fields, or on the docks, this so-called coolie population was, until well into the twentieth century, more than 90 percent male.[58] The disproportion between men and women gradually lessened, though remaining high well into the twentieth century; there were still ten men for every woman in 1900.[59] The relatively few women migrants often worked in prostitution, though the disparaging claim that all Asian women in the colony were prostitutes was palpably absurd. Still, for women from drought or famine-affected areas of Japan and China, the living to be made in the Straits' sex trade was substantial, and the colony did support a large brothel workforce catering to the huge overseas proletariat gathered on this southern portion of the Malay peninsula. In particular, women came from Japan's stark Amekusa Island and from the southern Chinese provinces of Fukkien and Kwangtung, hard hit by agrarian poverty. As with the male migrants, their earnings were often sent back to hungry families and the wealth of the colony was not experienced by the bulk of those who had created it. Not surprisingly, these conditions spawned a high degree of violence and instability. Riots and feuds rocked Singapore and Penang on a regular basis in the later nineteenth century. Alongside the fear of Dutch influence, it was the impact of such instability on investment and profits that prompted the development of the residencies in the 1870s.

In 1877 the colonial administration established the first of what would become a chain of Chinese protectorates throughout the colony. The first was at Singapore, where William Pickering was appointed protector. Only thirty-seven when appointed, Pickering had already had a long career in China and the Straits, having joined the merchant marine in 1856 when he was sixteen. For most of the 1870s he had been Chinese interpreter to the Straits government.[60] The power of the Straits protector was never as absolute as that granted to his Australian equivalent, but the field of responsibility was nonetheless quite wide. Established initially to stem abuse of poor migrants, to suppress the so-called secret societies, and to bring "the Chinese within the control of the Administration," the protector also supervised the colony's brothels.[61] Migrant workers and brothel residents alike were obliged to assure the protectorate that they worked their trade of their own free will.

This protective legislation reflected colonial beliefs that the Chinese were a slaving nation and that workers were often coerced. Concern for their welfare, however, did not extend to political representation. As a crown colony, the Straits had as its senior official a governor appointed from London, and two nonelective legislative bodies. The Executive Council included the colony's commanding officer and six senior government officials. The Legislative Council consisted of these men plus the chief justice and four "unofficial" members not bound to support official policy. Executive Council meetings were held in camera and unreported; Legislative Council minutes were published regularly. After 1869, the Legislative Council had at least one Chinese representative among its unofficial members, usually a wealthy merchant of high standing, and often English-educated.

The creation of a separate authority in 1887 for rapidly-expanding Singapore created a limited municipal electorate. All male, this new electorate comprised less than 1 percent of the municipality's population.[62] The new municipal corporation of Singapore made sanitation and health issues a priority, though the agenda, as it had been throughout the region's colonial history, was set mostly by European needs.[63] Singapore's first hospital was a military hospital serving British soldiers. It was 1844 before the city had a pauper hospital (the Tan Tock Seng), and it was mostly privately funded.[64] A maternity hospital was founded in 1888.[65] The first hospital in the FMS was established at Taiping in 1878.[66] Western medical care competed with active and complex local therapeutic traditions, Chinese, Malay, and Indian. Even where western medicine was available, many non-Europeans chose to consult local healers. Neither they nor the western doctors were hugely effective. Mortality rates throughout the colony were high, and the fact that they were high among a youthful population suggests, as in the case of the Melanesians in Queensland, that poor conditions at work and in the living quarters of workers exacted a heavy toll. Tin mining, in particular, was noted for excessively high death rates. At between 44 and 51 per thousand of population, Singapore's overall mortality rate was higher than in Hong Kong or India.[67] And as in Queensland, mortality was race-specific. The average death rate in Singapore for Europeans between 1893 and 1925 was 14.0 per thousand. Among the Chinese it was 39.9 per thousand, and for the Malays it was 40.1 per thousand. Indian mortality was slightly better at 32.7 per thousand.[68] The figures are striking in light of the routine assumption that the tropics were particularly hard on whites used to more temperate climes. These statistics suggest precisely the opposite. Diseases such as tuberculosis and dysentery were invariably associated with poverty, and outbreaks of smallpox in Pahang in 1899 and cholera in Singapore in 1905 did little to allay European fears of allegedly dirty populations.[69] Overall, western medicine had minimal impact on the lives of nonwesterners in the colony, affecting most significantly women registered as prostitutes under the CD Ordinance.

Their numerical dominance and material success made the Chinese the focal point of colonial attention in the Straits. The existence of the protectorate, the gradual inclusion of the Chinese elite in governing circles, and the growth of a prosperous Straits Chinese population concentrated attention upon this community. But while the need to woo the elite was shrewdly manipulated, colonial opinion always painted the Chinese as cruel and business-oriented; in this context, their attitude toward sex for profit was invariably stressed. Pickering's successor as protector, G. T. Hare, published in 1894 a textbook to assist administrators learning Chinese. In it he collected what he saw as a local Chinese literature typical of the Chinese resident in the Malay Peninsula. He gathered 188 proclamations and petitions penned by local Chinese and he chose to include fully ten that dealt with matters relating to prostitution or VD.[70] Such a compilation would have been unpublishable as a language text in metropolitan Britain, but in the colonial setting Hare's declared intent of realism was well received. His choices echoed common colonial opinions about the Chinese and especially about Chinese sexuality.

Hong Kong

Many of these opinions were also common among colonists resident in Hong Kong, another Chinese-dominated British colony. Just off the southern tip of China, the tiny island that would become prosperous Hong Kong was first occupied by the British in 1841, an outcome of complex trading negotiations with China and intimately connected with the thriving sale and distribution of opium.[71] Declared a British colony in 1843, this small area of land grew with the acquisition of territory on the Chinese mainland, first at Kowloon in 1860 and then, in 1898, further into the hinterlands with the leasing of the New Territories, part of Xin'an County and the colony's only agricultural land. Hong Kong was sparsely populated before colonization; its precolonial population is routinely estimated at about 5,000 heads.[72]

Unlike the Straits, Hong Kong had no minerals and only minimal agricultural potential. Little of the land was cultivable, even after the acquisition of the New Territories, and the colony always relied on imports for its food supply. What Hong Kong did offer the British was a toehold in the China Sea and a deepwater harbor with shelter from the typhoons that regularly devastated the region. Unlike Singapore, Hong Kong was not part of a larger agglomeration in which profitable raw materials were exploited. This was a mercantile and trading colony, and also of considerable military value. Its commercial and maritime role in the region and in Britain's colonial system necessitated a large workforce, provided as in the Straits mostly by Chinese "coolie" labor. A southern Chinese labor force—young, male, and from poor areas of the Pearl River delta—dominated. Hong Kong also shipped laborers to other areas where the "coolie" was in demand.[73] Around two million Chinese emigrated through Hong Kong in the second half of the nineteenth century.[74] Money sent back by these migrants to relatives in China routinely went through Hong Kong's banking houses, enriching the colony's fiscal and commercial importance.[75] Though the greater numbers of Hong Kong Chinese were employed either in manual work or small-scale hawking and trading, the colony also developed a significant Chinese merchant community, akin to that in the Straits Settlements. These compradors quickly established themselves as a wealthy and conservative elite.[76] As Elizabeth Sinn notes, "authoritarianism was a tendency common in both colonialism and patriarchy."[77]

Aside from the Chinese, Hong Kong had a small Indian population derived mostly from Lascar seamen and Indian troops. What would later become the red-light Cat Street was named Lascar Row in early colonial days, for it was here that Indian sailors mostly lived.[78] From its earliest inception, the Hong Kong police force numbered a substantial Indian contingent, mostly Sikhs.[79] There was also a wealthy Parsi community involved in trade and as separate from the poor Indians of Hong Kong as the Chinese elite was from the coolie population.[80] A small Portuguese-Eurasian community in this rapidly growing mix remained as a reminder of the region's earlier colonial encounters.

From the small numbers of the early 1840s, the population grew to around 125,000 in the mid-1860s, all but 4,000 of whom were Chinese. Thirty years later the population had doubled again to 250,000. The 1911 census counted a little over 5,000 Europeans and Americans, some 2,500 Portuguese, almost 4,500 Indians "and others," and 450,000 Chinese.[81] An imbalance between men and women was as much a feature of the white colonial population as of immigrant workers. The colony's 1872 census showed a ratio among whites of almost five men to every one woman, and a ratio of seven to two among the Chinese.[82] As elsewhere, colonial officials routinely regarded nonwhite women migrants as prostitutes. Certainly Hong Kong's brothels were a visible feature of the landscape but this was, in part, because it was so markedly an urban colony and a physically small one at that. Invisible prostitution, which so concerned officials, existed in Hong Kong but the brothel environment was harder to conceal. This was a colony experiencing dramatic and visible growth—demographic and economic—but in a space with little room for expansion. As additional Chinese ports opened up for trading as a result of the Peking Convention of 1860, Hong Kong grew in commercial importance. Like Singapore, it was a free port, with tea, silk, and opium its main trading commodities. By the end of the century, Hong Kong's annual trade was worth around £40 million.[83] Its population grew in tandem, but it would be decades before the frontier characteristics of age and gender began to moderate.

Adding to these imbalances was Hong Kong's military and strategic importance. Sailors from both the navy and the merchant marine constantly docked in the colony's harbor, swelling the male population and providing a rich resource for the brothel industry. The barracks at Victoria housed a small but significant contingent of British soldiers, as did Singapore's Tanglin barracks. The colony's garrison commander was the governor's deputy, and a member of the Executive Council.

The colony was geographically divided, with clearly demarcated areas inhabited either by European residents or the Chinese. In 1888, a European District Reservation Ordinance reserved certain sections of the island for housing built along European lines and with considerably less density than in Chinese districts.[84] At around the same time, a Public Health bill before the Legislative Council castigated the Chinese propensity for crowded living as a health hazard. In his unsuccessful protest against the legislation, Sanitary Board member Ho Kai pointed out, with some irony, the financial consequences for poor Chinese of the colonial state's insistence on "a privy, a superb kitchen and a sumptuous backyard of 10 feet wide."[85]

As a crown colony, Hong Kong had both an executive and a legislative council, neither of them elective. The Executive Council had no Chinese members until 1926 but was unusual in the empire in having two unofficial members, a privilege secured in 1894 by the petitions of influential British residents.[86] The unofficials were outnumbered by the governor, the general officer commanding (GOC), and a further five official members, routinely the most senior men in the administration. Most of them also served on the larger Legislative Council that, until 1929, had seven official and six unofficial members. Four of the seven official members were ex-officio and overlapped the Executive Council's membership: the GOC, the colonial secretary, the attorney general, and the treasurer. The remaining three official seats were most commonly reserved for the director of public works, the secretary for Chinese affairs, and the captain superintendent of police. Four of the six unofficial members were European, two nominated by the governor and one each the choice of the Chamber of Commerce and the justices of the peace. Unlike Straits law, which was derived mostly from the Indian Penal Code, a legacy of its early EIC associations, Hong Kong's legal system was based on English common law.

The two Chinese slots on the Legislative Council were the work of John Pope Hennessy, governor from 1877 to 1882, and a champion of Chinese representation. Ng Choy, Hennessy's first nominee, joined the council in 1880. As at the Straits, the Chinese, in common with Europeans on the council, were part of a privileged elite, though when their interests diverged from that of the colonial government too far, the Chinese could be despatched.[87] Ho Kai, the first Chinese member of the Sanitary Board, was appointed to the Legislative Council in 1890, but his support for the 1911 Boxer Rebellion cost him his seat.

Hong Kong also established a Chinese protectorate, conjoint with the office of the registrar general after the mid-1850s. The registrar general/protector became an ex-officio member of the Legislative Council in 1884, and his title was later altered to Secretary for Chinese Affairs. The office oversaw emigration and immigration of Chinese workers, much as in the Straits, maintaining lists of brothel residents and in theory interviewing every new brothel resident to ensure she was not enslaved.

Health and hygiene concerns were frequently aired as urgent factors in the control of prostitution, and Hong Kong's medical and sanitary establishment was active in regulating the sex trade. The colony's sanitary board dates from 1883, considerably later than Chinese-financed hospitals. The Tung Wah hospital, founded in 1869, was closely associated with the emergence of Chinese mercantile elites in the colony.[88] Though a civil hospital already existed when the Tung Wah was founded, locals used the former only reluctantly. The alternatives offered by the Tung Wah were more attractive, for the institution provided more than just medical services. It helped families dispose of their dead, and aided those wishing to return to China.[89] Administered by local Chinese and offering Chinese treatments, the Tung Wah was legitimized and officially recognized in 1879, but remained largely untouched by western influence. It was an institution radically beyond western conceptions of the hospital's role. By contrast, Singapore's Tan Tock Seng, founded in 1844 as a Europeanized institution, was the resort of the desperate. The radical difference between these institutions highlights the historical contingency and the cultural particularity of the idea of the hospital, a theme returned to in chapter 3.

Ordinances addressing public health issues, and especially sanitation and over-crowded dwellings, became law in the 1860s and 1870s but were often stonewalled by the Chinese. On more than one occasion riots ensued as a result of health measures passed without the approval of the Chinese.[90] A serious outbreak of plague in the colony in the mid-1890s produced vigorous protests over western medical practice. Locals protested isolation tactics and state intervention in private dwellings, as well as the power of the elites.[91] It was a fight which underscored the gap between colonialists and locals. The stringent plague regulations introduced in 1894 led many laborers to leave the colony temporarily, devastating its commerce.[92]

India

In India, it was outflow rather than inflow that characterized demographic movement, though within this large landmass there was considerable internal mobility. India's diverse population contributed on a massive scale to colonial success, not only at home but through emigration. Indentured laborers traveled from India to a wide range of British colonies, often to pick up work once done by African slaves. They worked in Queensland, Hong Kong, Malaya, and the Straits, in Fiji, the British West Indies, Mauritius, a host of African countries, and anywhere else cheap manual labor was in demand. By the end of the nineteenth century, annual emigration from India stood at more than 425,000 people.[93] Immigrants were never as significant a portion of India's population as they were in the other colonies discussed here, and before direct rule the EIC had guarded the borders against immigrants closely. The British-born population in India stood at around 100,000 in 1881. European migration escalated late in the nineteenth century as Jews fled anti-Semitic violence in central and eastern Europe. Some found their way to the cities of Asia where their reception by the colonial authorities was, at best, mixed. But India in this period never experienced the high levels of immigration characteristic of our other colonies.

There was, however, nothing homogenous about those regions that over time made up British India. Immanuel Wallerstein's provocative question—"does India exist?"—makes clear the rezoning by which colonial political and economic dictates created such an entity.[94] A vast number of languages, religions, and social structures were always discernible, and with every new expansion and acquisition, the mix increased. Burma (lower Burma was annexed in 1862, upper Burma in 1886), administered by the government of India, added another complex layer of heterogeneity to the vast British holdings in the region. And while India was not a settler colony, it had a far larger white population than most dependent colonies. Its huge bureaucracy required greater numbers, and quite a few "India hands" remained in India rather than returning to Britain, a phenomenon seldom seen in other colonies. The sheer enormity of the Indian undertaking led to the creation of virtual dynasties, families who provided colonial leadership in India generation after generation. This Anglo-Indian community, segregated as it was from the population it ruled, played an ongoing role in the country until independence in 1947.

India, of course, had long experience of colonialism. The EIC had traded there since the seventeenth century, and the country had experienced foreign invasion well before then. Over the course of the eighteenth century, the direction and influence of the EIC had undergone distinctive change. Founded as a trading company by London merchants in 1600, the EIC established "factories" (warehouses and offices) across the east from the Red Sea to China. Negotiations with the Mughal empire and its successors brought the Company more and more into the Indian sphere, and its growing profitability from Indian land revenue rather than trading consolidated its presence and importance in the region. The EIC had its own army and its own civil service, all the trappings, in short, of a governing state, and by the mid-1760s was "outright ruler" of Bengal and some of southern India.[95] Under the system of dual government in the late eighteenth and early nineteenth centuries, government's role increased, and by 1833 the Company's role in India was that of "political agent for the Crown."[96] At each successive renewal of the Company's charter, the British state planted itself more firmly in a power-sharing arrangement with the company. The renewal charters of 1813 and 1833 broke the Company's trading monopoly, first in India, then in China.

In 1858, following the Indian Mutiny, administration passed directly into British government hands. The machinery of government was already in place, making the transfer of power a relatively easy business. Thus, only five years after the 1853 renewal of the EIC's charter, the Government of India Act of 1858 invested the British imperial parliament with powers over the EIC's Indian possessions. As in the crown colonies, the governor (in India, called a governor general to convey his seniority over governors of existing presidencies, and also known as the viceroy after 1877) convened both an executive and a legislative council, the former consisting of senior officials and the latter including nonofficial members. These unofficials, nominated not elected, included a few Indians. Below this structure was a complex and vast system of regional government revolving largely around the old presidential structure. Provincial governments all had governors or lieutenant governors, executive and legislative councils, and a system of departments akin to those of the government of India. Municipal councils in the large cities emerged after the passing of the Indian Councils Act of 1861. Like the structures above them, they, too, included a smattering of nonofficial Indian members.

This autocratic bureaucracy reported to the secretary of state for India in London who was a member of the Cabinet and the chief officer of the India Office. While the Colonial Office assumed oversight of all Britain's other possessions, India had its own government department in London formed out of the ashes of the old EIC and the Board of Control that had latterly supervised it. The advisory body to the secretary of state, the Council of India, also consisted of nominated rather than elected members. Nine of its fifteen members were required to have a minimum of a decade's service in India; it would be 1907 before any Indian members were appointed.[97] The India secretary could—and did—override the "quasi-independent" council, just as the governor general in India could choose to disregard the advice of his Executive Council.[98] In Francis Hutchins' words, this was "a full-fledged bureaucratic state in no direct way answerable to the people it governed."[99]

India was the most heavily militarized of the colonies compared in this study. Hong Kong may have been of fundamental strategic importance in the region, but the permanent military establishment there was always small. Not so in India where military expenditure invariably outstripped almost any other government outlay, at around £20 million annually after 1857.[100] Before 1858 there had been two colonial armies in India, the EIC's own army and that of the crown. Royal troops had been stationed in India since 1754 though in small numbers. While the post-mutiny reorganization retained the division into presidency forces (one each for Bombay, Madras, and Bengal), the ratio of Indian to British troops was drastically altered. At the time of the mutiny there were around 238,000 Indian and 45,000 British soldiers stationed in India, the bulk in the employ of the EIC. When troop reorganization under the new administration was completed in 1863, there were 140,000 sepoys, as the indigenous soldiers were called, and around 65,000 British troops.[101] It became a firm axiom that henceforth no less than 60,000 British soldiers should be stationed in India, a ratio of approximately one British for every two Indian soldiers.[102] Partly a response to the 1857 mutiny, partly a legacy from EIC days, this visible military presence was also a defense against perceived (and often exaggerated) foreign threats.[103]

The omnipresence of the soldier in India was and is a useful reminder of the military basis of colonial rule.[104] The Raj was "ultimately a despotic foreign regime dependent upon military power."[105] And tight control was maintained at the highest level. Each presidency army included serving British regiments paid for by the government of India.[106] The commander in chief in London maintained control over such issues as promotion, while more quotidian decisions were made in India.[107] Though the commander in chief in India was an "extraordinary" member of the governor general's Executive Council, most business in the period of direct rule was conducted via the military member of the council, an ordinary and regular participant though with considerable seniority. Race was a factor too. Always outranked by British officers, however junior, Indian officers could command only other Indians.[108]

The size, spread, and composition of the army had a profound economic effect, changing India's landscape and reshaping its economy. The growth of cantonments created new urban and trading environments.[109] The cantonments were surrounded by bazaars, markets from which the military drew supplies and local labor. The main bazaar was the *sudder* bazaar, supplemented by regimental bazaars that generally accompanied the regiments on the march. There were also the *lal* (or red) bazaars, also known as *chaklas,* to which registered prostitutes were usually confined.

In Hong Kong and the Straits Settlements, port trade and its concomitants were the dominant factor in the creation of wealth. In Queensland, large-scale agriculture and mining was prominent. India was more diverse. But as elsewhere, it was colonial need that influenced its development most profoundly. The Suez Canal, offering a more efficient shipping route between Asia and Europe, affected the Indian economy centrally. Though the longer shipping route via the Cape continued in use, the overland route all but disappeared. Agriculture was long established in India; cotton, jute, coffee, indigo, spices, opium, and increasingly tea were important exports. Export values increased dramatically between 1870 and 1914 and by the early twentieth century, exports to other imperial ports in Asia and Africa outstripped those to Britain.[110] India nonetheless relied heavily on imports and was a key market for British manufacturing exports.[111] By the 1880s almost 19 percent of British exports were bound for India.[112] The import of manufactured goods and export of agricultural produce reflects India's relative lack of industrialization. The huge railway growth from the 1850s—over 25,000 miles of track by 1900—was a military necessity, and was not linked, as it was in Britain, to faster-paced industrial growth. India remained largely rural even while large-scale deforestation and massive social upheaval impoverished its largely peasant population.[113]

In common with other colonies, medical provision was spotty for local people, and though hospitals and dispensaries dotted British India, they competed with local healing systems. The Sanitary Department was founded in 1864 and provincial sanitary boards began to appear from 1888. These were followed by a series of Village Sanitary Acts, though their permissive rather than prescriptive character meant that few villages actually benefited.[114] Other than during epidemics, when stringent but temporary measures were put in place, it was poor women who came most into contact with the new western medical bureaucracy, since they were the likeliest women to be identified with the trade of prostitution, and thus subject to medical surveillance.

It was not only in their dealings with doctors that Indian women experienced the impact of colonialism. The calcification of the caste system and the spread of Brahmanic values narrowed women's opportunities, with the growing attention to woman as moral scion of respectability.[115] Nationalist rhetoric mobilized frequently around gendered issues, whether the figure of the temple dancer, the role of the Hindu wife, or the pros and cons of child marriage.[116] For colonialists, the allegedly blighted position of women in Indian society signified "the degradation of India as a whole."[117]

Conclusion

These four colonies offer an intriguing mix of commonality and of difference, demonstrating the complexity of the imperial project and the central dominating ideas structuring the broader colonial enterprise. In all four colonies, British decision-making reigned supreme, even where ideas of self-governance flourished and were permitted early in the colony's history. Notions—often misconceived—about the racial characteristics of local peoples vigorously fed the ways that British colonists as well as the imperial parliament chose to deal with the disease-related and moral issues that form the basis of this study, as well as with other colonial questions. While STD policy in these various colonies shared certain cross-colonial themes and a belief in the efficacy of regulationist policy, in practice each offered rules and policies tailored by the local and the specific. The results of this local framing offer us a fascinating window into the tensions in the British Empire between local reckoning and imperial necessity, between the ideal of British moral rectitude and the practicalities of rule, and of the resulting friction not only between colonizer and colonized but between metropolitan policy making and colonial opinion at the so-called periphery.

PART I

CONTAGIOUS DISEASES LAWS

Chapter 2

Law, Gender, and Medicine

> No Government will care to deal with so contentious a subject
> unless public opinion is with it. With a fuller knowledge of all
> the facts, a robuster feeling will be developed to take the place
> of that sickly sentimentality which hitherto had paralysed
> action, and which has been the cause of so much suffering,
> and of the ruin of so many young lives.
>
> —William Hill-Climo

From the 1850s (and indeed earlier, if less formally), contagious diseases (CD) legislation was the primary, though not the exclusive, means by which prostitution was controlled. It was, in addition, the key legislation aimed at VD. While the various acts and ordinances in Britain and throughout the colonies were only one of many ways that the business of prostitution came within the arm of the law, they were almost the only way that VD came under legal scrutiny. Other than accusations of venereal infection in divorce proceedings, the law in respect to venereal afflictions was limited to an attention to the sex trade.[1] Jay Cassel has pointed out that nineteenth-century VD laws always understood disease as a by-product of prostitution; at the heart of CD legislation was the management of sexuality, and especially of the sexuality of women and of colonial peoples.[2] Common to all this legislation was that hereafter the practice of prostitution or the keeping of a brothel required registration. Emphasizing regular examination and medical detention, these laws assumed a direct relationship between sexual activity, specifically female sexual activity, and efficient disease transmission. The medical reading of the debate was overlain with presumptions about the inevitable and dangerous outcome of promiscuity, while the moral dimension was encoded within a new and increasingly technical vocabulary of medical expertise.

As we shall see, colonial CD laws differed radically from their British counterparts but these differences, I would argue, were fundamental to the shape and practice of the British laws, suggesting that distinction need not mean separation but might rather suggest symbiosis. In highlighting the relationship between politics and law, morals, medicine, and the military, the comparisons central to this study also demonstrate the state's need to assert and maintain control over sexuality in order to assure its rule.

Before the CD System

Long before the implementation of formal regulation, VD rates in the colonies were a source of political and military concern. At the Hong Kong garrison, according to *The Lancet,* before the 1857 ordinance venereal diseases "were among the most common causes of unfitness for duty."[3] Douglas Peers estimates that "upwards of 30 per cent. of European soldiers in India" were hospitalized at any one time for VD in the 1820s and 1830s.[4] Alarm over these figures was such that in the years prior to the formalized adoption of the regulation system from the late 1850s, many colonies took up and abandoned informal prostitution control, as need arose and as finances permitted. These local ad hoc arrangements seldom garnered public attention and could thus more easily disregard the politics of public approval. Military surgeons and colonial governors regulating prostitution in their own fiefdoms seldom invoked the language of reform, speaking rather to an urgent pragmatics founded on local need. Their principal enemy was cost and not public disapprobation, a situation that would change radically by the 1880s.

Most common in colonial settings were forms of regulation that tracked and treated infection, rather than discouraged business.[5] Governor Philip Dundas created a red-light district in Penang in the early 1800s, and Thomas Stamford Raffles established a lock hospital at Yogyakarta during his gubernatorial years in the Malay peninsula (1811–16).[6] It is in India, however, that we see the workings of the early system most vividly. The quartermaster general claimed that the "bazar system . . . has been in force in the Bengal presidency since the time of the Hon'ble East India Company."[7] William Burke, inspector general of hospitals for the army in India, outlined his ideal plan in 1827: a register of prostitutes; their compulsory examination fortnightly, with certification for the healthy and hospitalization for the infected; and punitive measures for women failing to appear for examination.[8] These principles would become the core of the empirewide regime enacted three decades later.

Lock hospitals at cantonments date from at least the late eighteenth century.[9] The first of the Madras hospitals, established in Trichinopoly cantonment in July 1805, must have been a fairly costly venture, with its segregated wards for women of different religions.[10] As elsewhere, the women patients received meals, treatment, and bedding at no cost; in Bengal these expenses cost the authorities "9 sonat rupees per mensem for each patient."[11] By 1823, the eighteen extant lock hospitals in the Bengal Presidency cost an annual Rs. 33, 772, including wages and building maintenance.[12]

From their earliest inception, there was lively discussion about the worth of these schemes. Abolition of the lock hospitals was already under consideration in Madras by 1809, though the EIC Medical Board granted a request to establish a new hospital at Goa in 1810.[13] In 1849, a skeptical Court of Directors "pronounced that the establishment of Lock Hospitals has been proved not to diminish the number of venereal patients."[14]

One signal criticism centered on compulsion. Burke himself felt the system had failed since "only the poorer, most wretched, and probably the most harmless class of the diseased were Sent into Hospital, while those who could afford to Soften enquiry by a bribe or by being personally favourites were allowed to remain unmolested."[15] Officials counseled that "the utmost discretion must be used in the application of anything partaking of the nature of constraint."[16] Yet in 1813, the Medical Board had urged the extension "to all the European Military Stations" of a lock hospital system in which "no patient shall, under any pretence be permitted to quit the Hospital even for the shortest period, until perfectly cured."[17] Without coercion the system could not work, but coercion by no means guaranteed success.

Hospitalizing women was not the universal choice of control. In Madras presidency, expulsion was a favored tactic.[18] At Bangalore cantonment in the early nineteenth century, infected women had their hair cut off and were then publicly expelled.[19] In other colonies, the means chosen to track prostitute women were less dramatic and ritualized, but still focused on women's mobility: the governing assumption was that knowing women's whereabouts and having the ability to register, detain, or expel them bodily was desirable. Thus, another common practice was the semi- if not fully formal establishment of *lal* (red) bazaars—the regimental or bazaar system—in which "[e]ach regiment had its quota of prostitutes whose comfort and well-being were attended to, and who were periodically inspected and in cases of sickness treated by the subordinate medical establishment."[20] The women often accompanied "their" regiments on the line of march, camping close by the barracks and enjoying a degree of protection and sometimes subventions from the regimental funds.[21] Samuel Hickson, a sergeant in the Bengal Army, remembered the "Loll Bazaar" of the early 1780s; on arrival at cantonments a committee of surgeons was ordered "to assemble on the instant, to examine the public women of the Bazar; those who are found disordered are to be sent to the Hospital at Surat.'[22]

Policies that saw the management of prostitution as the key to controlling VD laid the foundations for the widespread implementation of more formalized CD ordinances from the mid-1850s. The existence of lock hospitals and red-light districts made CD implementation easy; customized medical bases were already in place, and those detailed to oversee registration knew where to seek their clientele—in the bazaars and brothels frequented by British soldiers. All the Indian presidencies had turned buildings over to lock hospital use, and had employed local and military police in the surveillance of the sex trade at least since the turn of the century. Shortly before the formalizing legislation of the 1860s, new lock hospitals were under construction: at Secunderabad in the Northwest Provinces in 1858, in the Punjabi cantonment of Mean Mir in 1859, and in Benares in 1861.[23]

Implementing Contagious Diseases Laws

The earliest colonial CD ordinance predated its domestic cousin (the Contagious Diseases Act of 1864) by eight years. Governor Bowring, with the backing of Henry Labouchère, Palmerston's colonial secretary, lobbied energetically for Hong Kong's Ordinance No. 12, passed in 1857.[24] Initiated at the request of the naval establishment, the ordinance required brothels to register with the medical authorities and their inmates to be compulsorily and regularly examined. Unregistered women engaging in prostitution were liable to prosecution, and registered women were hospitalized if found infected. The ordinance specified brothel locality, confining brothels serving a European clientele to the east end of the town and those with a Chinese customer base to the west end. A decade on a new ordinance replaced No. 12 of 1857. It was a far cry from the British version of the law, and such was the case in most colonies.[25] The Hong Kong law applied colonywide, while British CD acts were applicable only in named military districts, eighteen by 1869. In Britain, women affected by the acts were mostly streetwalkers; brothels were never legally recognized though the acts gave them de facto status within the law. In Hong Kong, conversely, the registered brothel was the central focus. In Britain, registration depended on women's apprehension by a special detachment of constables; voluntary registration was possible, but by no means routine nor ever intended to be such. In Hong Kong, by contrast, brothel keepers were responsible for registering their workers. Written into the domestic acts was the recognition of redemption; women could move from hospital detention to a refuge or magdalen asylum for job training (invariably in domestic work) and elementary theological instruction. No such provision was entertained in Hong Kong or most other colonies. To the inhabitants of most of Britain's colonies, the domestic version of the law would have been unrecognizable. The only substantial commonality was that all the laws, colonial and domestic, used registration as a means to compulsory examination, and provided compulsory in-patient treatment for infected women. This aside, they differed widely.

Malta and Corfu followed Hong Kong in formalizing CD legislation in 1861, after two years of semiformal registration and examination. In the 1860s, VD rates were rising in almost all of Britain's garrisons.[26] Thus military areas of India came under CD control by a cantonment act (Act XXII) in 1864.[27] India's cities earned the right to pass similar legislation under Act XIV of 1868, the Indian CD Act. In 1865, Quebec and Ontario each introduced a five-year CD law, and St. Helena enacted similar legislation. After the mid-1860s, CD legislation flooded into the colonies: 1867 saw ordinances in Ceylon and Jamaica alongside a new Hong Kong law, and in 1868 it was the turn of Queensland, Barbados, and Cape Colony. The first British-administered lock hospital opened in the Japanese treaty port of Yokohama; others followed at Osaka, Yedo (Tokyo), and Nagasaki. In 1869 CD laws were passed in New Zealand and Trinidad, and in 1870 at Singapore (extended to Penang in 1872 and Malacca in 1873). In 1877 a lock hospital was established at the treaty port of Shanghai and an ordinance passed at Labuan. There were ordinances promulgated in 1878 in Victoria, and in 1879 in Tasmania. The tide slowed in the 1880s, stemmed by vigorous opposition to the domestic acts that resulted in their suspension in 1883 and repeal in 1886. Colonial repeal followed in 1888. Still, Fiji enacted an ordinance in 1882 and Cape Colony a new one in 1885. Natal's proposed ordinance of 1890 was disallowed by the imperial government.

By 1870, then, CD laws were in place in more than a dozen of Britain's colonies, in treaty ports where the British had commercial and naval interests, and in the United Kingdom. A wide range of colonies, from the plantation economies of the Caribbean to the white settler colonies of the southern hemisphere, from the European and Europeanized colonies of the Mediterranean and North America to the cluster of Asian colonies sprawled around the Indian and Pacific Oceans, adopted CD legislation. A few were exempted. Mauritius and the nearby Seychelles, acquired by the British as a result of the Napoleonic Wars, are never mentioned in the literature, and nor are early African settlements such as The Gambia, Sierra Leone and the Gold Coast, though Mauritius had been invited to pass an ordinance.[28] British Honduras, British Guiana, and the Falkland Islands all escaped CD regulation, though British Honduras may have come under the Jamaican CD ordinance before acquiring status as a separate colony in 1884. At the time of the policy reversal in 1887–1888, none of these are among the colonies reported to Parliament as having been instructed to abandon CD legislation, suggesting the laws had never been in force there.[29]

The Great Question of the Day

"The object of Contagious disease laws," wrote Charles Lucas of the Colonial Office, "is, I take it, not to put down prostitution and not directly, at least, to benefit & alleviate the condition of the prostitute but to prevent the community at large from suffering from syphilitic diseases and to prevent the spread of such diseases."[30] Justifications of and calls for the control of prostitution were contained overwhelmingly in the apparently neutral vocabulary of good medicine, emphasizing the medical and beneficent intent of the laws. Hong Kong's colonial surgeon argued in 1869 that the law's "sole object" was "restricting the extent of contagion, and curing the disease."[31] In Queensland, parliamentary supporters likewise insisted that the proposed measure was medical, not moral; its sponsors promoted the act as a public health initiative.[32] The CD system, thought India's quartermaster general, was simple common sense: "It is not the practice of prostitution that is 'legalized' but the attempts to avert its consequent and accompanying disease."[33]

Venereal diseases were cause for alarm. In 1876, the president of the American Medical Association pronounced syphilis "the great question of the day."[34] *The Lancet* thought syphilis guilty of "ravages, more incessant, more fatal, more destructive, than those of any temporary epidemic."[35] The commander in chief in India found it "impossible to persuade myself that the same penalties lie in wait for the descendants of a man who has suffered from dysentery or fever, as those which are so often bequeathed by constitutional syphilis."[36] A member of the governor general's council proclaimed the venereals "the most terrible of all contagious diseases."[37] Officers in the Indian Medical Service, according to Mark Harrison, regarded VD as a graver issue than rural sanitation provision.[38] As late as 1911, one Queensland politician declaimed that "there is nothing known to history—more appalling, more dangerous, and more terrible in its never-ending effect, to the general public than the disease of syphilis." He declared leprosy, cancer, tuberculosis, and other communicable diseases "merely trivialities" by comparison.[39]

Not everyone concurred in this frenzied rendering of VD as a cynosure of multigenerational ill-health. In Penang, the CD ordinance was temporarily suspended during a cholera outbreak in October 1882, suggesting that the management of VD was less pressing than bringing the deadly waterborne illness under control.[40] In a paper delivered before the Harveian Medical Society in London in 1866, Charles Drysdale claimed that syphilis "when not absurdly treated . . . is, in the great majority of cases, a mild disease."[41] The government of India argued that "the evil effects of fever, dysentery, and the other ordinary diseases of India" warranted more attention and funding than did those attending syphilis and gonorrhea.[42] In Britain, workhouse union returns show VD as a minor reason for admission to the poor law hospitals at a time when these were among the few medical institutions besides lock hospitals which offered treatment. In the first week of 1876, 43,548 patients were recorded as diseased, of whom 2 percent (915) were diagnosed with some form of VD. Of the deaths recorded (27, 932), 0.65 percent were attributed to VD.[43] Charles Taylor pointed out at the end of the century that, "if syphilis were a fatal or a very serious disease, the insurance officers could not have overlooked the fact; and yet they have agreed to ignore it, and accept the subjects of syphilis as first-class lives."[44] In general, venereal diseases were "less a cause of direct mortality than a source of prolonged morbidity."[45] While epidemics typically killed fast and furiously, syphilis did its job slowly and invisibly. But with high rates of contraction and the wearying and lengthy nature of treatment, venereal diseases were difficult to cure, as well as a significant source of labor inefficiency.

Sanitary Reformers and Public Health

The moral and medical ambivalences that surrounded VD allowed sanitary reformers to exclude this class of diseases from their general purview, giving them, in a sense, a way out of an invariably difficult moral issue. Far more than other diseases, the venereals were twinned with moral and religious considerations of sexual behavior. It was common currency to read venereal diseases as a zero-sum game of cause and effect, a payment for the wages of sin.[46] G. J. Guthrie, deputy inspector of military hospitals early in the nineteenth century, described VDs as "acquired through promiscuous intercourse"; almost half a century later, *The Lancet* dubbed them "the moral law thus broken."[47] Medical inadequacies in understanding the epidemiology and diagnosis of sexually transmissible diseases were exacerbated by widespread ignorance and fear. The illicit nature of these afflictions only compounded the problem. Victorian sensibilities did not silence talk of VD but they did mold it such that influential public figures could seriously argue that killer diseases such as smallpox were inconsequential by comparison. While the dramatic sweeping movement of cholera or smallpox through a population would leave more dead, clinicians and social commentators emphasized venereal afflictions as more insidious, silently stalking the unwary and rendering something more lasting than mere death—long-term intergenerational consequences.

Nonetheless, while campaigners claimed their intent as sanitary and in the interests of public health, CD enactments were invariably kept separate from other sanitary reforms, though enacted during the heyday of sanitary legislation and interest. Neither the 1866 Sanitary Act nor the 1875 Public Health Act addressed VD control. Sanitary policy makers rarely discussed VD publicly.[48] Sir John Simon, a supporter of the domestic CD acts, does not mention VD in his survey of the achievements of the sanitary lobby for "national sanitary purposes."[49] Historians have often duplicated this separation, paying less attention to nineteenth-century VD, despite its spectacular rates of infection, than to diseases with greater and more dramatic epidemic potential.[50] At the time, it seemed an obvious separation; certainly the India secretary thought so:

> There is an obvious difference between venereal diseases and the diseases ordinarily classed as infectious or contagious, which are the subject of legislation in the interests of public health in this and other countries. It is on account of this difference that the former have never been included in the same category as the diseases to which such Acts as the Public Health Act or the Infectious Diseases (Notification) Act are applicable in this country.[51]

Nonetheless venereal diseases, and most especially syphilis, became a locus of blame in the discourse of sickness and health, an originary moment of ill health passed on to the innocent. An Australian politician in 1875 declared that "most of the diseases to which the human frame was liable were attributable to" VD.[52] Many in India thought fevers there often "either much aggravated by the syphilitic taint or . . . purely syphilitic."[53] Some went further, arguing that "many local diseases have their origin in or are so marked by venereal entanglement."[54]

This persistent yoking of venereal infection to other sicknesses, and across a broad range, served to link venereology to the medical mainstream, despite its taboo status. Though sanitary reformers gave the topic a wide berth, pro-CD campaigners wielded the language of public health to considerable effect. It was public health, they argued, that was at stake, and the control of prostitution was merely a vehicle of effective implementation, almost an afterthought to the overriding medical necessities of the day. Miles Ogborn has argued that in stressing health rather than prostitution, the domestic acts could be seen as neither legitimizing vice nor overstepping governmental boundaries by poaching on the philanthropic turf of "rescue."[55] He builds a picture of the laws resting on "a combination of legal, medical and philanthropic discourses and practices."[56] In a hygiene manual for the armed services (the only venue where sanitary reform always included discussion of VD), Edmund Parkes employed the typically vigorous and no-nonsense prose of the sanitationist in his praise for domestic CD laws. "In the case of venereal diseases, the State must as much protect its citizens as from the danger of foul water, or the chances of gunpowder explosions."[57] The principle of state responsibility made the slide from treatment to legal and state control of carriers significantly easier.

The Military Stake

Tellingly, many (though by no means all) of those who campaigned to make VD a visible health issue had ties to the military. Colonial CD policies were never exclusively military, but the debate frequently focused on soldiers' health. The major fear was that "most of these infected men will, in a few years, return home to spread the contagion among the civil population of Great Britain and to transmit a heritage of misery to posterity."[58] Since soldiers were an imperial necessity, and since the assumption was that they would return to heterosexual family life in Britain, propagating the race, their freedom from constitutional disease became a deeply gendered metaphor for the health of the race and of the nation.

In the wake of the 1857 Mutiny, at the time of the 1865 Revolt in Jamaica, and with the debacle of the Crimea still stingingly familiar, Britain's military prowess was badly tarnished.[59] VD was a problem in all armies, but VD rates were higher in the British than in any of the continental European armies, and in 1859 infection rates for British troops in India rose to a staggering 359 per 1,000 of hospital admissions.[60] Disease was a significant military problem, and in unfamiliar tropical climates disease could be "a more effective killer than military combat."[61] While other and often more dramatic diseases felled the new recruits—malaria, plague, cholera, dysentery—venereal diseases were a perennial worry, prompting the Herbert Commission to dub VD "this great scourge of the soldier."[62] VD among soldiers and sailors was costly and debilitating. VD jeopardized defense strategies, undermined army discipline, and reduced troop strength. The CD ordinances were, in this context, a pragmatic attempt to deal with a problem of considerable magnitude. All the Admiralty "care about," declared one Colonial Office official, "is having some check on the communication of contagious diseases to H.M.s sailors" at Hong Kong.[63]

In Hong Kong, sailors were the main concern, passing through the port as they did in large numbers. In India it was the army, already by the early nineteenth century "one of the largest European-style standing armies in the world."[64] Charles Trevelyan thought the soldiery "the decisive consideration" in the drastic differences between colonial and domestic legislation.[65] For him, the "youth of England" were the overwhelming justification for the system, and the government of India likewise insisted that "the real importance of the sanitary question . . . consists in its bearing on the health and efficiency of the British Army in India."[66] Military needs were the "starting point of serious concern" with sanitary issues in British India.[67] "[T]he Commander-in-Chief," wrote a senior military officer with more than a hint of grandiloquence, "has instructed me to observe, that the saving of one British soldier to the service, more than repays all the lay-out involved in the establishment of Lock Hospitals."[68] Before 1900, Roger Jeffery reminds us, some 40 percent of annual health expenditure in India went to military health.[69]

The Problem of Women

John Gamble and F. B. Smith have argued that the domestic CD acts were both necessary and humane, serving the essential purpose of protecting military efficiency.[70] That women with soldier and sailor clients were solely liable to surveillance and detention is, for them as for nineteenth-century policy makers, the unfortunate by-product of a degraded occupation, the women a pawn in the larger game of imperial defense. While public representations of the CD laws were often crafted around sanitary issues, internal debate emphasized the control of women. In the colonies especially, medical and police memoranda, lock hospital reports, and internal policy discussion documents focused less on the public health aspects of the law than on the practical control of prostitution. The intemperance of rank and file soldiers or the wisdom of examining them as well as the women surfaced for occasional discussion, but the voluminous materials generated around the CD laws focused primarily on managing prostitute women. In the nineteenth century "discussions of venereal disease without reference to prostitution" were rare.[71]

Equally, considerations of prostitution were seldom without reference to VD.[72] In a late nineteenth-century report declaring the lock hospital and registration system a failure, the Army Sanitary Commission identified two factors bearing on the ineffectiveness of regulation. Ignoring the role of the client, their analysis rested exclusively on women. It was the impossibility of preventing unregistered women from selling sex and the inefficacy of the examination of women in determining the presence of disease that the commissioners identified as the reasons for failure.[73] The transmission line was clear: this was a disease which passed from women to men, and from women who were sexually active to men whose level of sexual activity was never scrutinized as closely. Transmission, then, was summarily though hardly logically linked to the selling of sex as a liveli-hood. The moral illegitimacy of the occupation, its status as nonwork, helped justify the coercive and one-way nature of legislation that at no point in its history seriously sought to question or to control male sexual behavior.

While occasional homilies deplored the behavior of soldiers or their taste in women, and certainly a measure of class-based disdain is often apparent, it is in criticisms of the women that we find most frequently outbursts of hatred, disgust, and loathing. Those involved in the day-to-day administration of CD laws denounced prostitute women fiercely, complaining of their lack of disci-pline, their duplicity, their reluctance to register, their lack of hygiene, and their cupidity. Year after year, lock hospital reports excoriated the registered women as repulsive. "The classes on the register are the lowest of the low, chiefly old, ugly, broken-down hags, deformed and scarred by disease, and dragging on a miserable existence by the aid of opium, bhang, and liquor."[74] The logic of this oft-repeated complaint was that, because the registered women were unattrac-tive (and here it is hard not to see an age-old and hackneyed complaint about "government issue" goods just below the rhetoric), men sought partners from among the unregistered, contracting disease because these were unexamined women. And yet, disease and lack of sanitation were among the complaints leveled at registered women, blurring the lines between these different groups. The message, if subliminal, was that women, sex, and disease were inevitably linked: this was a deeply gendered public health campaign in its assumptions about transmission and sexual behaviors.

"A Sick Soldier Is an Expensive Article":
The Economics of Implementation

The empire was not cheap to run, and it was by no means always a profitable or self-financing proposition. As a colonial bureaucrat points out in the section head, the cost of implementing and maintaining CD laws was of constant concern,[75] enmeshed in heated debate over the relative weight of civil and mil-itary responsibility. Questions of how to finance and who should finance the system were driven not merely by the typical parsimony of bureaucracies but by moral concerns. Antiregulationists routinely argued that CD laws not only encouraged but funded "immorality." And certainly state grants did help offset the considerable costs of maintaining a police force and a hospital, administer-ing registration, and treating the infected. In the early 1870s, Barbados received from government an annual sum of £625 for providing beds in the lock hospital and for treatments.[76] Hong Kong collected £800 per annum, while Canada and Ceylon's operating costs were met by the home government.[77] The domestic acts were funded mostly by War Office and Admiralty monies. The London lock hospital received regular payments from both departments from 1864, the funding ranging from capital grants for building to the quotidian costs of treat-ment and bedding.[78] The hospital—comparatively well-funded—nonetheless experienced "a continual financial struggle."[79] Even after the repeal of the acts, municipal authorities in areas with a large military presence successfully sought grants for the treatment of prostitutes they claimed were there to profit from the military business.[80]

The claim by local civil authorities that without military assistance they were unjustly picking up costs more properly the province of the armed forces was a charge which constantly plagued the CD system. In India especially, civil authorities were resentful of the expense. Act XXVI of 1868 (pursuant to the Indian CD Act, Act XIV of 1868) allowed for the provision of lock hospital funding from municipal funds, though the decision was always taken on an ad hoc basis. In Agra in 1870, the Municipal Committee refused to contribute. The Bombay lock hospital was forced to close in 1872, "the Municipal Corporation having refused to contribute any longer to the expense of maintaining it."[81] Madras argued that the costs associated with the act were "properly chargeable in full to the Military Budget rather than in part to Municipal Funds—the primary object of Lock Hospitals being the protection of the European soldier . . . in which the civil portion of a . . . Native community cannot be materially interested."[82] One Indian official noted:

> a general disinclination on the part of Municipalities to countenance registration and inspection beyond the limits of the soldier's range, and a decided holding back from the application of municipal funds for that purpose. If, therefore, the system is to be applied to all common prostitutes in the large centres of population adjoining the cantonments where British troops are located, the additional expense, which will be very considerable, must be borne by the Government.[83]

Yet five years later, the Lucknow Municipal Committee's request for central funding for the maintenance of the city lock hospital was refused.[84]

Funding decisions were as urgent elsewhere. The Brisbane lock hospital's funding periodically came under attack.[85] In October 1886, opponents in the Queensland legislature called into question the "tremendous amount of expense" occasioned by the establishment.[86] As the reach of the act moved north from Brisbane, expenses rose, and in the 1880s especially, parliamentary protests about cost were frequent.[87] In the late 1870s, the Admiralty contributed some £400 per annum to Hong Kong's lock hospitals, but the funds came and went. In 1888, the Colonial Office was pressing for Admiralty contributions.[88] This internal quest for funding, with the Colonial Office attempting to persuade the military of its stake in the matter, suggests that the imperial government was reluctant to formalize and make permanent funding for a policy it nonetheless stoutly defended for more than twenty years, but which it could never quite decide to anoint as either purely military or civil.

Before the Bombay Corporation abandoned the city lock hospital in 1872, it had experimented with such drastic cost-cutting measures as abolishing the post of supervisor, leaving the staff demoralized and the system in disarray.[89] Forced by government to reopen the hospital in 1880, the corporation shared the cost with the presidency government. In Calcutta, where provincial revenues were required to help the city meet its costs, some felt lock hospitals were "not worth the large sum they cost every year."[90] The skeptics included the governor general. Lord Ripon thought Calcutta's high expenditure not really justified since the city's garrison was numerically inconsequential and visiting sailors were in fact "men of the mercantile marine who receive no such special protection in any of the commercial ports at home."[91] At Hong Kong, of course, where the presence of merchant marines was much higher, the ordinance was energetically implemented. The Lucknow commissioner noted that the town's "municipality have little real interest in the registration, examination and medical treatment of prostitutes, whose services are retained for the benefit of a portion of the garrison."[92] And in Bengal the squabbles between the civil and the military wings of administration went to central government for mediation. Bengal's officiating secretary advised the central government that "if the Military Department really desire that the local civil officers should not interfere with the working of lock-hospitals in cantonments . . . the civil department should be relieved of its present responsibility in the matter."[93] His language suggests that it was a row in which the military department was already entangled, and as an antagonist towards civil participation. The Army Sanitary Commission invited the government of India in 1877 to "consider whether there is anything in the past experience of these preventive measures to justify the cost of their continuance."[94] But while the commission was disappointed with the system's efficacy, the imperial government and most colonial administrations remained committed to its continuance.

A Self-Financing System?

Proponents of regulation favored a self-financing system, funded out of fees levied on the users. Many argued that a fee base was the moral keystone which would render the system invulnerable to the criticisms of social purity activists: "I do not see why people should not pay for protection from the consequences of their own folly nor why the system should not be made self-supporting. At any rate, this seems to me to be more consistent with public morality than to pay from general revenue."[95]

No fully consistent policy was ever pursued. The ad hoc qualities of these policies suggest incoherence and injustice; women working in the trade had little choice but to comply with often arbitrary local practice, pushed and pulled by the vagaries of political change throughout the era of regulation. Moreover officials were not always wholly in control of the systems they administered. While the 1888 report of the Straits Protector of Chinese counted almost $38,000 collected in fees from the registered brothels in the previous year, his Colonial Office colleagues were under the impression that such fees had "not been levied for more than ten years."[96] Brothel fees were written into the 1867 Hong Kong ordinance at four Hong Kong dollars a month, but abandoned as unproductive in 1889.[97] Unusually, women of Chinese origin detained for treatment in Hong Kong were levied a daily hospital fee; until 1885 registered European and Japanese women were exempt. When the fees were extended to these women, they paid double the Chinese rate, presumably a reflection of their higher earning power.[98] A report in 1880 concluded that "the revenue derived from this source does not really do more than cover the expenditure."[99]

The racial distinctions in the Chinese fee system did not apply in British India or neighboring British Burma, though fee collection predated formal regulation. From 1844, each of the "Dancing girls, Cotage (sic) Women and Prostitutes" at Secunderabad cantonment paid two annas monthly, a policy discontinued in 1848 by order of the commanding officer of the station as "a door through which great extortion and injustice have been dealt out."[100] The 1864 Cantonment Act permitted fees, though in India responsibility for payment rested not with the brothel keeper, but with the individual woman, a policy reflecting how differently colonial officials imagined—and presumably experienced—the business of prostitution in different colonial settings. In the cantonments, "every registered prostitute shall be made to contribute every month to the expense of the Lock Hospital" at a rate not exceeding one rupee a month.[101] In cases of nonpayment, the cantonment authorities could sell "any moveable property of such prostitute which may be found within the limits of the cantonment."[102] At Lucknow, the civil surgeon reported that such fees funded "Assistants, Examining Daees [to examine the women], Hospital Establishment and food and medicines."[103] Despite this elaborate system, the 1868 Indian CD Act, extending regulation to the major cities, never explicitly supported a fee-based formula. "On the subject of fees the Act is silent."[104] Fees charged at the Burmese cantonments of Rangoon and Thayetmyo from 1868 were set under the terms of the 1864 law.[105]

In 1873, an internal backlash in Indian ruling circles against collecting fees from prostitutes led to an official ban on fees.[106] Yet within seven years of the ban, the government of Bengal proposed to reinstate the fee to render the act self-supporting.[107] Controversy over the efficacy and the moral wisdom of a self-supporting system continued to circulate. The Lucknow medical officer championed the abolition of fees because "[t]he women are always poor, and can ill afford to pay even so small a sum as Rs. 1 for the privileges they enjoy."[108] The Bengal lieutenant governor meanwhile thought that "prostitutes in an Indian city are notoriously a very prosperous class," and that imposing a fee would not represent a significant check on women's willingness to register.[109] More fundamental, however, was the moral furor. Important in governing circles were "the objections which would fairly be taken to Government raising a revenue from prostitution, even though the proceeds were entirely devoted to defraying the cost of working the act, and to the medical treatment of the women registered under it."[110] The abolitionist fervor that gripped activist Britain in the 1870s and 1880s had pounced upon the idea of state-sanctioned "vice," making the Indian government wary of reintroducing fees. The same sentiments prompted a Colonial Office administrator to caution that revenue derived from fees and fines not "be mixed up in the General revenue but . . . be kept distinct and any surplus funds remaining after payment of necessary expenses might be set apart for some special object—as for instance the improvement of the Hospital accomodation (sic)."[111]

Even where fees were, however reluctantly, abandoned, fines were often liberally used to help keep finances afloat and to bring women into compliance. The Rangoon hospital claimed to fund itself about 25 percent from fines and 75 percent from fees.[112] A European defendant in Hong Kong, Francesca Berger, was fined $34 in 1868 for keeping a disorderly house and for contempt of court; presumably she did not care to repeat the experience for in early 1870 we find her apparently "voluntarily submitting herself to medical examination."[113] Under the 1868 Indian CD Act, unregistered prostitution carried a one-month prison term, a hundred rupee fine, or both; failing to notify a change in residence to the local administration earned a registered woman a fourteen-day stay in jail and/or a fifty rupee fine.[114] Women and magistrates usually chose fines over imprisonment; of the fifteen women arrested in the Bengal cantonments of Darjeeling, Dum Dum, and Barrackpore in 1888, only one was imprisoned for working unregistered. And of those tried in Barrackpore the previous year, all received fines, regardless of the charges.[115]

Fines were, in a sense, the coercive complement to the general rule of providing inpatient treatment at no cost. In most instances detained women were not only exempted from all and any fees during treatment but received a small subsistence payment allowing them to provide for their own food, a far cheaper and easier arrangement for the authorities.[116]

Paying for Morality

The lock hospital, however, was only one of the expenses incurred in the brothel-based system so typical in colonial CD laws. There were administrative costs and in colonies where brothel registration was central, police costs could be high, since one of the duties of the police was to track down unregistered establishments. In Hong Kong, and to the horror of Governor Hennessy, paid informants were used to facilitate this detective work.[117]

In India, most cantonments appointed a *dhai* (literally a birth attendant, though delivering babies was not one of her standard duties in the brothels) to supervise the registered women, to ensure their attendance for examination, to keep them from accepting local custom, and to check them for signs of disease between exams. A circular memorandum from the quartermaster general in 1883 directed that "dhais should be well paid, if the [cantonment] fund can afford it, and they should be held responsible that the women under their charge consort with none but Europeans."[118] In some cases the *dhai* discharged the duties of both brothel and lock hospital attendant, a money-saving device for cash-strapped cantonments.[119]

In many cantonments, and as a means of maintaining the segregation of soldiers' women, the authorities also provided housing, often free, for registered women. Military authorities advised that any such "free quarters" should "meet the wishes of the women. Unless their comfort and the convenience of those who consort with them is considered, the results will not be satisfactory."[120] Officials at Agra cantonment in the Northwest Provinces boasted in 1884 that, "suitable accommodation has been provided, at the expense of the cantonment fund, for twenty-seven registered women in the sadr [native] bazaar, and thirty-three registered women in the European Infantry bazaar."[121] In nearby Benares, the military authorities built a house to accommodate the women rent free.[122] The Bombay medical officer reported in 1887 that "the Municipality is now building excellent pukka quarters for the branch prostitute lines at the Steamer Point."[123] In Bengal cantonments, red-light quarters (*chaklas*) were provided from the 1870s.[124] The expenses for such provision were generally met out of cantonment funds, and must have represented a significant burden on those funds. Informal arrangements were often used in small places where the acts were not in force, and these often encompassed such perks as rent-free housing for registered women in exchange for their agreement to regular medical inspection. In these circumstances, women found diseased were usually sent to the nearest lock hospital under the ordinances.[125]

At the Straits, the expenses included renting an examination room and hiring staff for lock hospital duties.[126] As elsewhere, existing hospital accommodations were adapted to lock hospital needs, though it was not long before the surgeons running these establishments complained that they had outgrown these existing arrangements. Chinese women may not have been provided with housing, but the expenses in these colonies were nonetheless substantial, funding not just medical and police expenses but also the work of the protectorates.

Colonial Officials and Local Culture

The palpable difference in the practices allowed under CD regulation was not confined to the wrangle over fiscal good management by any means. At every turn, critical distinctions marked the promulgation and implementation of the legislation in each of these colonies, and these variations on what looks nominally to be an empirewide scheme emanating from the metropole signal more than the pragmatics of local rule. In the frequent discussions of these matters in the official record, we see how colonial policy was shaped by readings of the role of women, of sexual attitudes, and of local medical and sanitation practices. In the levying of fees, Indian women were individually responsible for their payment while in dominantly Chinese areas, that responsibility fell to the brothel keepers. Such disparate practices, easily overlooked, are important, for they tell us much about how colonial officials looked at local culture, its treatment of women and of sex, and how such considerations shaped the racial grammar by which colonial difference was self-consciously punctuated. Moreover, these enactments differed not only from one another but from the domestic acts promulgated in Britain. Philip Howell points out that colonial enactments were "much more extreme forms of regulation" than the domestic variety.[127] The one thing binding colonial CD ordinances and acts together is that everywhere without exception, they differed from the three British acts.

Colonial administrators, civil and military, were keenly aware of and wedded to the need for distinctive versions of CD legislation appropriate to particular colonial settings. In white settler environments parliamentarians often claimed they had improved on the British laws, while elsewhere officials warned that applying a model intended for a western nation would be folly in the east, since "the circumstances . . . are widely different from those of England."[128] Lord Ripon in India regarded the policy there as going "far beyond the English law" in introducing "a system of registration, not only of prostitutes, but of brothel keepers, which the framers of the English measure thought extremely objectionable."[129] At the India Office, Lord Hartington thought "the course pursued in India under the Contagious Diseases Act is the opposite of that pursued in the United Kingdom," since in England the law was aimed at "small towns with large garrisons" and in India conversely at "very large cities with small garrisons."[130] This contemporary emphasis on suiting legislation to the setting is crucial to understanding colonial CD legislation.

Difference, largely imagined and even created by colonial rule itself, was read and proclaimed as natural, evidence of the advancement or stagnation of cultures ruled under the British flag. Colonial officials understood the difference in the laws to be dictated by existing differences among subject peoples rather than as something actively shaping opinion and practice. The laws were, in their eyes, less the beneficent molders of change than necessarily faulty responses to the difficulties of governing lesser peoples. If the laws fell short of English ideals, these were compromises necessary to achieve good governance in difficult, even hostile, conditions.

Registration and Race

The most striking variation in CD practices was in the registration process, and in particular on whom the onus of responsibility for registration lay. Registration in Britain succeeded rather than preceded apprehension, and was imposed upon women known to the police and medical authorities and already examined for traces of infection. Queensland's act, aimed in the first instance at Brisbane's white prostitute population, adopted the same policy. In the Christian societies of white Australia and Britain in the mid-1800s, few would choose to name their own "fall from grace."[131] Yet the hesitance of women to come forward voluntarily seemed to colonial lawmakers to offer less of an obstacle in Asian settings. While the laws implemented, on the one hand throughout India and Burma and, on the other, in the Straits and Hong Kong, were radically different from one another, they shared assumptions about the place of prostitution in these societies, and about the attitudes of women engaged in the trade. While there was a sense that no white woman, however desperate, would want to name herself as trading in sex, officials regarded self-naming as carrying little shame in eastern societies. The assumptions which routinized and normalized prostitution in settings already defined as depraved made self-registration seem uncontroversial.

But the various laws simultaneously undermined the British assumption that Asian societies were more licentious. In Hong Kong and the Straits Settlements, the laws assumed that women were coerced into prostitution. In these colonies, registration before the 1890s (when protection ordinances shorn of compulsory examination replaced the older CD ordinances) was not of individual women but of brothels. The trade was viewed as dominated so completely by the brothels that it was the allegedly wealthy and powerful keepers and not their supposedly terrorized and passive inmates on whom the burden of registration rested. While in the 1890s officials would argue that it was imperative to itemize and know each brothel inmate, in the early years of the system they argued rather that turning the spotlight on the keepers would help temper their cruelty and protect the women from the worst excesses of sexual slavery. Brothel keepers were required to display at all times a list of inmates and to keep the protector of Chinese informed of their workers' health and whereabouts. The women themselves remained, for the bureaucracy, a faceless mass. Brothel keepers were forced to acquiesce both to registration and to the payment of fees on behalf of the women and as the principal profiteers. Women were not expected to come forward individually, so closely were they said to be watched by their keepers.

In India, conversely, women were expected to register themselves. In part, this was because colonial politicians regarded local police forces as untrustworthy and corrupt bodies who would bribe women if given the power of registration. Henry Sumner Maine, legal member of the governor general's council, opposed the use of police information, "convinced that such a system could not be introduced here without a risk of grievous oppression."[132] Domestic protesters raised the question of police corruption in Britain, but lawmakers there never doubted that a well-picked corps of older married police officers could appropriately administer the acts. In India, the very possibility was considered inimical to public safety and peace of mind. "To leave it [the Indian CD Act] . . . to be worked . . . by the ordinary police, would be to leave the road open to much extortion and villainy."[133] Instead, civil and military officials in India argued that no harm would come from self-registration, for prostitution was a designated caste activity offending no indigenous mores: "prostitutes are not looked upon by the natives of India with the contempt which attaches to them in other countries. They are accepted as safeguards to society and are not themselves ashamed of their calling."[134] Self-registration was a political necessity to avoid handing the opportunity for bribery to cunning police officers, and feasible because prostitution, officials claimed, carried no stigma in the Indian context. The Indian CD Act thus rejected the English principle: "whereas [in England] . . . a superior officer of the Police . . . lays[s] an information before a Justice of a woman being a prostitute before any compulsory action can be taken in regard to her, the [Indian CD Act] makes it compulsory in the women themselves to come in for registration."[135] The principle was not singular to the law of 1868. The 1864 Cantonment Act enunciated the principle that "the onus of demanding to be registered" lay with the women themselves.[136] Not only was registration in theory not a function of police surveillance (the practice, of course, was another matter) but regulation was required legally in order to practice prostitution.

The practice caused endless trouble. Calcutta police commissioner, Stuart Hogg, issued an order to his staff in 1869 advising that police officers had no authority "to compel registration or to register . . . except *at the request* of the parties themselves (emphasis in original)."[137] Hogg cannot have been too pleased with the realization that he could not enforce compliance; his decision to remind his men of this gap between law and policing suggests the difficulties he anticipated. Hogg's caution was repaid when the Bengal High Court ruled that, since women could only be placed on the register by their own consent, they duly enjoyed the parallel right of de-registration by their own volition. The result of this faulty ultra vires law was that there was no way for the police even to maintain on the register already-registered women.[138] The law, while making registration compulsory for women engaged in prostitution, did not concede powers for the enforcement of its basic principle. In insisting on self-registration rather than state responsibility as a signal of the "Indian-ness" of the law, colonial lawmakers dug the law into an impossible hole.

One way around this chaotic situation, widely adopted in the colonies, was to register and examine only certain groups of women.[139] Superficially, this practice resembled that at work in the U.K. act where only women in designated garrison and port towns were affected. In the colonies, however, segregation and classification were racially specific. In Hong Kong, women with an exclusively Chinese clientele were of little interest to authorities. "If Chinese women for Chinese are freed from supervision their existence will be a matter of indifference to the Govt."[140] In Malacca, "all-nationalities" women, with their wider client base, were examined weekly while their "strictly Chinese" counterparts were seen only monthly.[141] Elsewhere the practice rapidly narrowed to an interest in women with a white clientele. Regulations framed under India's Cantonment Act divided "the public prostitutes in every military cantonment . . . into two classes, viz., *first,* public prostitutes frequented by Europeans; *second,* public prostitutes not so frequented . . . the rules shall be held to be applicable to public prostitutes of the first only of the two classes."[142] Local governments retained the right to extend their reach but rarely did so. The sanitary commissioner of Bengal reported in 1872 that women not taking European clients had occasionally been brought onto the register "but these are exceptional cases."[143] Calcutta's police commissioner chose to enforce the Indian CD Act only "against the commonest and most avowed class of prostitutes," for it was from these, "that he thus reached the strata of the class who most affect British soldiers and sailors."[144]

In the cantonments, local authorities tried to prohibit "all natives . . . from having intercourse with the registered prostitutes, who are only for Europeans."[145] But regulating the client base was always and everywhere an inexact science, and it was this that produced Malacca's focus on "all-nationalities" women. Authorities tried hard to segregate women into specialized groups according to their clientele, focusing their medical attention on women with white customers. But imposing segregation seldom worked. "The prostitutes set apart for the European soldiers practise their calling with diseased natives also," complained a suspicious medical officer.[146] Another worried that "[T]he second class, although they profess not to receive Europeans in their houses, seem to do so whenever they get a suitable opportunity."[147] In Kasauli cantonment in the Punjab in 1887, a two rupee fine was imposed upon "a registered prostitute of the European brothel for having sexual intercourse with a native."[148] In Hong Kong, the paid informants spent much of their time searching out unregistered brothels catering to Europeans, and in Singapore zoning followed the racial lines of the brothels and the racial geography of the city. It was the colonies rather than the law which was at fault, according to those who implemented the CD system. Were the indigenous women not indiscriminate, and were indigenous men not willy-nilly diseased, the system would have a fighting chance.

The Queensland situation was different again. Aboriginal women remained wholly outside the 1868 CD Act, and it was only as the law extended northward that Japanese women came within its embrace.[149] Queensland never attempted an official racial segregation of brothels, though police reports routinely identified brothels by the race either of the workers or their clients. Japanese-only brothels were increasingly common in the north where pearl divers and other Japanese workers congregated. And although the Queensland example may have been formally different from Asian practice in its lack of segregation, it conveyed a similarly racialized set of assumptions about how sex should be managed. The failure of racial segregation did not stop its continued use even after the acts were abandoned, and its persistence suggests how important segregation was to maintaining the appearance of racial quarantining.

Comparing the Colonial and the Domestic

As a form of protective legislation, the acts clearly protected different groups in different environments. Despite talk of extension to the civilian population in Britain, the domestic CD acts were never extended to the civil population. In colonial settings, CD laws grew quickly beyond the strictly military purview. The military barracks at Tanglin were seldom mentioned in discussions of the

Straits ordinance, and immediately after the passing of the Queensland act all discussion of the military significance of the law died. George Johnson at the Colonial Office noted a shift from enforcement in the Straits that was "more generally in the interests of the Chinese women themselves" to that in Hong Kong which served "the interests of the European males and . . . a small minority of Chinese women."[150] India, of course, had separate legislation for military cantonments and cities.

An equally crucial difference between colonial and British CD laws was in their attitudes towards streetwalking. The domestic acts tried hard to downplay brothels, for in the political and moral climate of the 1860s, it would have been folly to attempt formal brothel registration. Accusations that government was legitimizing and recognizing the right of the brothel to exist and to trade would have been swift. Streetwalking remained the definitive mark of sexual commerce, and prostitution was pathologized as the choice of individual women working largely as independents. In colonial settings the reverse principle was articulated. In Hong Kong and the Straits, in India, and in Queensland's frontier towns, the aim was to diminish if not eradicate streetwalking in favor of the more easily controlled and less openly visible brothel business. The 1867 Hong Kong ordinance specifically forbade streetwalking.[151] A Colonial Office memorandum of 1879 explicitly classified Hong Kong's law as dealing "with *brothels* not with *prostitutes*" [emphasis in original] and saw the same principle at work in the Straits.[152] In India, "the prohibition of public prostitution," as distinct from that conducted in the registered brothel, was a principal aim of the legislation.[153] One of the many conditions of registration was that business was conducted strictly indoors. Wherever the laws were in force, public solicitation was prohibited: "registered women are forbidden to solicit publicly."[154] In the Madras Presidency only officers' mistresses and concubines were eligible to be registered outside the brothel.[155]

The very different strategies for containing prostitution in domestic and in colonial Britain suggest that politicians viewed these environments quite differently. Beyond the pragmatic and material issue of what it was possible to do where, social and cultural assumptions and judgments structured policy. Whereas in Queensland, the possibility of redemption was central to CD rhetoric, the refuges and asylums to which legislators hoped women would be persuaded to pass after their lock hospital stays barely existed in nonwhite settings. Nor did legislation in the dependent colonies insist that such institutions be established when monies became available. Indeed, legislators and officials argued that such costly provision would be useless. In Britain, claimed Charles Trevelyan, the act "afforded . . . unhappy women who had lapsed from virtue," an opportunity of "shelter [from] which they might recover their place in society." But in India the "low state of morals" was such that prostitutes, inheriting a long tradition, "by no means felt degraded."[156] The Straits colonial surgeon lamented "the absence of some such home and institutions as abound in the

Mother Country, with doors always open for the reception and reclamation of the abandoned, affording an asylum from whence at a fitting time they may be able to return to society, and lead a virtuous and useful life."[157]

These piously optimistic praises of the British system were, of course, hopelessly inaccurate. The British magdalen institutions had never been particularly successful, and their minute books and annual reports tell a familiar tale of escape, resistance, and lack of response.[158] Moreover, they were far less forgiving than the Straits surgeon implies, for the abiding rule was that a woman could not return if she once left their custody.[159] And as Poor Law hospital provision increasingly picked up the treatment of impoverished VD sufferers, the treatment regimen rather than the redemptive model became dominant.[160] Yet for all the shortcomings and the failures of the redemptive program, it served to distance the moral metropolis from the wild periphery. In Britain, the door of Christian intervention remained open, even if in reality few walked through it.

Conclusion

What were the contexts which produced both this deep anxiety around VD and the particular measures with which colonial governments chose to tackle it? Philip Howell points out that this was "explicitly racial legislation."[161] While the Queensland CD Act was aimed initially at Brisbane's white prostitutes, its northerly extension often rested on racially specific anxieties. The Brisbane police inspector thought "that the extension of the Act to the various large towns of the State would be a step in the right direction especially where coloured races formed a large proportion of the population."[162] While white prostitutes needed saving from themselves, white clients needed saving from nonwhite prostitutes. The practice elsewhere may have differed from that in settler Queensland, but the racial configurations of the trade and its client base did not. White prostitutes in India or the Straits thus enjoyed certain immunities and privileges, as racial status jostled for attention alongside occupational status. For the British colonial state, it was more profitable to encourage alliance among those with racial and cultural ties than to emphasize other less equitable facets of the imperial relationship.[163] The Queensland CD Act thus differed from other colonial CD measures, claiming a closer resemblance to the domestic law, even while its champions congratulated themselves on having improved on the basic British model.

Elizabeth Van Heyningen's important point that CD legislation was "preeminently imperial legislation," concerned principally with the security of the empire, alerts us to the colonial as well as the racial questions at the heart of this policy.[164] In a period of growing imperial prowess, the condition of the army was clearly a necessary complement to the maintenance and extension of colonial rule, and it is to this connection that Van Heyningen's reading of the CD Act in the Cape Colony draws attention. Britain's military needs were seen, in many respects, as coterminous with Britain's role as an imperial power. Yet even in places where the statistics dictated a degree of urgency among a heavily infected military, policy on the ground was rarely streamlined or consensual. There was both confusion and actual dissension among colonial officials— in Whitehall and abroad—as to whether these policies were or ought to be principally military or civil, though there was general agreement that colonized peoples would benefit from their application. And, as Peter Durrans has shown, while few in the House of Commons either understood or fought vigorously on imperial questions, parliament nonetheless "remained an essential component of the machinery of imperial government."[165] Jack Cell and Arnold Kaminsky have both persuasively shown how the Colonial and India Offices respectively were, in effect, often able to override parliament's wishes, yet the relationship between metropole and periphery still occupied significant political time and attention.[166]

In this context, it is worth recalling how fully the "landscape of Victorian Britain" was "an "imperial culture" in which attempts to separate domestic from imperial considerations must surely fail.[167] While it would be a creative stretch to link the CD system to the colonial upheavals of the mid-century period, nonetheless the apparent excesses of the Indian mutiny, the Jamaican rebellion of 1865, frontier skirmishes in South Africa, and increasing unrest in the Malay states, served as reminders to the British at home, and as colonial settlers, of the distance between "civilization" and colonial peoples. Such upsetting events both unsettled colonial stability and reminded colonizers of what they saw as their superiority, if not always militarily, then evolutionarily. The empire was the principal expression of British supremacy and British good sense, worthy of defense and always in the vanguard. The military angle, important to be sure, was one facet of the overall picture but other questions and considerations were simultaneously at stake. Alexander Arbuthnot, an old India hand writing as a member of Whitehall's India Council, claimed the empire itself as reason enough to maintain the CD system. "This is essentially a matter of national interest, seriously concerning those classes of the English population from which our soldiers are taken, and demanding grave consideration from all those who regard the health of our population as a question of Imperial importance."[168] The heart of the empire itself was at risk of contamination without the *cordon sanitaire* the regulation system allegedly provided. Sir Griffith Evans urged fellow members of the viceroy's council to promote VD and prostitution control "for the safety of the Empire."[169] By the early twentieth century, VD control was a fundamental pillar of colonial public health and medical services in the civil and the military arena.[170] Nonetheless the military and the imperial do not fully overlap as concerns, and not just because the army in most places was too small and too poorly equipped to be a serious force. Many of the colonies with CD legislation were not militarily significant, but they were of imperial importance, and the empire was, in the eyes of Britain's ruling establishment and the colonists themselves, a critical factor in Britain's greatness. It was in the details rather than in the principles that dissension lay.

When John Strachey advised the government of India that "the interests of the army and of the civil population in this question are identical . . . it would be a complete mistake to suppose that they concern the European soldier only," his was more than a pious statement of whose needs the military served.[171] Henry Jordan, representing south Brisbane in the Legislative Assembly, pointed out to his fellow legislators in 1884: "though we had no soldiers in Queensland and no sailors, and, thank God, no poverty, we must needs proceed to pass an Act of Parliament."[172] Rhetorical flourishes aside, Jordan's point is important, for Queensland neither maintained nor required a standing army or a naval presence, though certainly naval contingents passed along and docked at its coast frequently.[173] While Australian versions of the CD Act closely resembled the domestic model in their redemptive features, they were never exclusively military. From their inception, all three of the Australian CD Acts were aimed at civilian populations, for as Brisbane's Health Officer warned, VD was "liable . . . to produce a puny and sickly population" unless checked by the registration system.[174] Fear of a weak and physically demoralized population was particularly meaningful in the settler context, and reorients us to the racial underpinnings of the legislation. Summing up Queensland's relations with the CD system, a civil servant there concluded in 1911 that "a factor which made the Bill necessary was immigration."[175] While the military question thus often provided initiative and a spur to action, colonial CD laws sought always to make apparent the racial-moral divides that were regarded as fundamental to the structuring of commercial sexuality and to the ways in which venereal infection could hurt a population and a nation as well as individuals. The management of sexuality, women, race, and imperial politics coalesce as organizing principles of empire, and the laws around prostitution and VD were central to that politics, and to that of modernity, as the next chapter will show.

Chapter 3

Colonial Medicine and the Project of Modernity

The veneer of civilization and the blatant blare of moral hy-
peresthetics has gone far enough. You and I, as medical men,
know to what extent this preclusion of common sense has prevented effective methods to stay the progress of this scourge
into all grades of society, has wrought misery and failure, and
is it not high time that some one should awaken the masses
from their slumbering ignorance, and, in justice to helpless
victims, teach people how to avoid the disasters of venereal
diseases!

—Robert B. Grubbs

"My heavens!" I said. I can't imagine anything further apart
than science and the veil.

—Millicent Pommerenke

The development of medicine as an elite profession in the nineteenth century
owed much to the rapidly growing prowess of science and its close association
with the idea of progress. The increasingly scientific veneer of medical research
and practice marked medicine out as a modern discipline, unencumbered by
prejudice, passion, or superstition. Medicine's place in the colonial world was
perhaps even more marked by these celebratory qualities than in the metropolis,
for in the empire medicine was invariably represented as the advance guard of
progress and enlightenment, a sign of the beneficence which would accompany
a turn to western values. Measures to tackle venereal diseases (VD) coincided
with the self-conscious rise and remodeling of the medical profession, and were
heralded as modernizing and propitious measures designed to bring safety and
comfort to the population. Public health especially developed largely in response
to the needs of colonialism, and "many sanitary officers perceived themselves to
be the vanguard not only of western medicine but of western culture in general."[1]
Doctors typified the modern distinction between superstitious prejudice and
rational good sense. Law was "held up as the harbinger of modernity," its coercive
nature justified as a necessary means to harmony and good health.[2] Contagious
Diseases (CD) laws, patently about prostitution, were represented as laws for
the public good, concerned with the health of the populace.

Complicating the medicalization of VD, however, were substantive issues beyond contagion and infection. There was never a time when shame, stigma, and moral reckoning did not shadow VD. Syphilis in particular was seen as the enemy of progress.[3] In late nineteenth and early twentieth-century Europe, its association with racial degeneration and with "primitive" peoples made VD the adversary of modernity, a disease group to be extirpated in the name of progress, the triumph of reason over passion. Modernity was central to the logic of the colonial enterprise and it projected the idea of a civilizing force on allegedly backward nations and societies. Colonial rule was represented as ultimately beneficent, and imperial medicine, deeply implicated in colonialism, was in the vanguard of the civilizing, modernizing task of rule. VD would be one of the major medico-legal battlegrounds of the nineteenth century.

Medical knowledge in almost every field was undergoing both change and, inevitably, resistance to change in this period. Such transitions were hardly unusual; we continue to witness fundamental changes in medicine and there is no Whiggish plotting of a line of progress towards enlightenment. Yet the mid and late-nineteenth century was a period of critical change. The status of the profession was rising, professional organizations carefully policed and monitored recruitment, and the state, however minimally, began to accept a responsibility for health and to consult doctors as experts. The displacement of miasmatic and humoral theories of disease by germ theory and the rise of the medical laboratory signal a slow, contested, but ultimately firm rejection of "tradition" in favor of western modernity.

Doctors in the colonies fashioned themselves as leaders of civilization, as makers of new societies.[4] They claimed a disinterested appreciation of scientific sanitation divorced from politics.[5] Painting a picture of the doctor as the selfless and dedicated wise man of his era, one author claimed that "scientists at times are apt to forget that they are a generation in advance of their age."[6] And doctors drew on this self-consciously progressive vocabulary in defense of CD regulations. We "of the Medical Profession...have the welfare of the community at heart," claimed M. Gaisford, and "being in the Public Service...so intimately connected with the bodily welfare of the soldiers and sailors upon whom the very existence of the nation depends," are duty bound to protect and defend, "the cause which we have so nearly at heart."[7] Medicine, perhaps especially in its fight against VD, shared in the colonial ideology of modernity; it was "cut from the same cultural cloth" as the broader colonial project.[8]

Colonial Backwardness

This celebration of the idea of the modern served also to highlight colonial backwardness and ignorance. Native failure was the greatest impediment to scientific progress. The failure of the regulation system was frequently represented as a sensible policy fallen victim to ignorance and willfulness.

A Character of Usefulness does seem to attach to Lock Hospital institutions, where unfortunate Females may find a refuge, and such Medical
aid as their miserable case may require, and were the habits of Asiatics
not alien to the mode of life which must be enforced in a public Asylum
these places might have proved more beneficial than they seem to have
done.[9]

It was the women who undermined and sapped the system, preventing it
from fulfilling its wholesome potential. India, Dr. McLean warned an audience
at the Netley Military Medical College in 1863, "would no more advance out
of its condition of semi-civilization than the leopard can change his spots, or
the Ethiopian his skin."[10] Resistance could be transmuted into ignorance and
superstition, and what some historians have read as political disobedience could
become nothing more than the inchoate foolishness of the native.[11]

Reluctance to submit to examination and treatment was the hallmark of this
backwardness. Lord Dufferin was much amused by the registered women in
India. "In Lord Ripon's time the prostitutes of Calcutta collectively protested to
the Viceroy against the use of "telescopes" in the medical examinations to which
they were subjected, and recommended His Excellency to consult an august
member of their sex as to the physical pain necessarily inflicted thereby."[12] His
lofty amusement at the women's mistaking the speculum for a telescope, and
at the inappropriateness of consulting a "lady" on such matters, confirmed for
him that the registered women were primitive and coarse beings.

Civilization was measured by proximity to and embracing of western medical
techniques. Chinese brothel inmates consulting local Chinese healers displayed
"national prejudices."[13] Indian sepoys were criticized for their preference for
treatment "by the bazaar quacks."[14] The "reluctance to take advantage of Hospitals is not peculiar to Chinese women but is common among other Asiatic
women"[15] A Queensland surgeon complained that he could never cauterize
venereal sores because, "I have never yet been able to get a native to submit
voluntarily to the action of the anaesthetic."[16] These preferences measured native distance from modernity. The use of local healers was proof of inferior
reasoning and of basic indifference. "The worst cases of venereal disease that
present themselves are without a doubt, aggravated by injudicious treatment at
the hands of native quacks."[17] The Japanese, thought George Newton, supervising the locks in the Japanese treaty ports, failed to take syphilis seriously, seeing
it not as a disgrace but "merely a misfortune or accident."[18]

The emphasis was on "native" irrationality. Queensland doctors spoke of a
"universal belief among the less civilised aboriginals that these venereal, as well
as other, disorders are caused by sorcery and witchcraft at the hands of an enemy, by non-observance of certain recognised rules of conduct, by the breaking
of "tabu" & c."[19] George Newton reported that antiforeign rabble-rousers exploited local suspicion to stir opposition to the regulation system. In 1871, this

whispering campaign included rumors of suicide among the registered women in Nagasaki.

> Certain interested and vile calumniators . . . diligently inculcated among the people . . . scandalous and malicious reports . . . that the examinations of the women made ostensibly for the detection of disease were in reality for the object of introducing an instrument and extracting the essential oils from the wombs, which rendered the women for ever afterwards barren; that the oils thus obtained were sent to England and sold as medicine for fabulous sums of money.
>
> Many of the prostitutes protested and stated that they would rather die than to submit to such a grievous system, and some took opium with that intention and two or three died from its effects.
>
> . . . these rumours led to . . . the still more vicious and malignant report that the most beautiful of the prostitutes were detained in the Hospital when perfectly healthy so that the native Doctors in charge of the establishment might gratify their carnal lusts.[20]

Newton's report insisted that most of the registered women were unconvinced by the rumor-mongering and comfortable with the system. Yet this malignant fairy tale of medical wickedness and beautiful victimized women contrasted an opposition wielding the tools of superstition and mythology against a system committed to modern truth. His message was that western reason finally triumphs because its enemies have only fable and nonsense as their allies. Though it is not the women whose ignorance undermines the system in Newton's scenario, his is still a story of the combat between enlightenment and backwardness, an enduring colonial tale.

Dislike of inpatient treatment was further proof of native inferiority. The chief inspector of Aborigines in Australia's Northern Territory remarked in 1916 on the "aversion of Aboriginals to medical treatment or hospital detention."[21] The medical officer at Peshawar complained that though Pathan men "bring their females frequently for inspection and medicine . . . they never consent to allow them to be in-patients."[22] It was the "ignorance, apathy and prejudice of the native population" that thwarted the potential for change.[23] Any deviation from the scientific path was a sign of obduracy and of unmodernity. The picture painted was of a ragbag of loose, inchoate sabotage. The message sent to administrators and to the British public was of ignorant, backward peoples too mired in custom and folklore to appreciate the rational ends of a system founded on the characteristically modern principles of sanitation.

Race-ing Venereal Disease

Not only were colonial peoples a bottleneck to the forward march of medical progress, but venereal diseases were themselves regarded as inimical to, and the enemy of modernity, a sign of backwardness and of the obduracy and licentiousness of the colonial world. "Native" backwardness was contrasted with rational behavior and the avoidance of "promiscuity" was said to be the best prophylaxis against VD. Even more than conditions such as malaria, the venereals were par excellence colonial diseases, revealing both personal and environmental failings.

In tropical environments, the wide variety of nonvenereal treponemal infections, passed largely by mouth or skin contact, confused diagnosis.[24] Yaws, pinta, and nonvenereal syphilis (bejel) were widespread in many regions, and their symptoms often resembled those of syphilis.[25] Bejel, relatedly, was often diagnosed as leprosy, its lesions, ulcerations, bone deformity, and disfigurement mistakenly dubbed leprotic. Nonvenereal treponemal infections were "morphologically and serologically indistinguishable" from the venereals, so doctors reliant on observational diagnosis could not distinguish between these afflictions.[26] Though tropical climate has no clinical effect on venereal diseases, the reliance on visual observation suggested a compelling link between VD and the tropics.[27] Tropical climates were seen as likelier breeding grounds for infection and contagion, and they were regarded, too, as inflaming the passions and negating caution and reason. Moreover, endemic nonvenereal treponemal diseases were associated primarily with childhood; western doctors observing seemingly syphilitic symptoms in the young frequently concluded that juvenile sexuality was uncontrolled in colonial populations. These were vital elements, of course, in the reading of VD as a measure of promiscuity, as of the reading of the tropics as less civilized and less seemly. Vice was inevitable, "especially among the Eastern peoples who do not look upon it in the same light as Christians do."[28]

While contagion theory may have refuted the notion of spontaneous origins for diseases in particular environments, the role of the tropics—as dirty, sweaty, smelly, and thus undesirable and dangerous places—in generating disease held firm. Inhospitable and unhygienic environments nourished parasites and germs. Environmentalist theories of disease were never wholly ousted, and competing theories of disease causation always rivaled one another.[29] In tropical Australia, for example, "germ theory remained wedded to environmental and climatic pathology much longer, and more intimately, than in temperate regions."[30] There was no elusive "pure" reading of VD; questions of behavior, responsibility, and culpability were too intimately tied to VD's associations with sexual promiscuity. So many beliefs were at stake in the fear of sexual activity, and the medical profession was by now so closely associated with propriety, that the melding of the medical and the moral is not at all surprising. The polarization of reason and passion, and the latter's apparent congruence with the irresponsibility of pleasure (binarized in the nineteenth century against the worth of work), confirmed medical readings of aberrant sexualities and of oversexedness as medical conditions.[31]

In the colonies such categories deepened, stressing the inherent degeneracy of tropical environments as of local peoples.[32] Many doctors firmly believed that disease acquired in the tropics was more virulent and more severe; some even argued that VD almost characterized the native. The worst cases of VD in the army, heard the Skey Committee in 1864, "are those of men who have been debilitated by tropical service."[33] At the start of the nineteenth century, one India-based surgeon thought only ten in a hundred Indians "who have attained the middle age . . . are perfectly free from [syphilis]."[34] British surgeon Berkeley Hill, on the other hand, thought syphilis more severe in cold climates.[35] Though his analysis appears superficially at odds with the tropical theory, they shared a common racial understanding, yielding the same political results. Hill saw syphilis as "less severe among the dark than the light races," implying that light-skinned northern Europeans suffered the most while tropical carriers of disease shrugged off its worst manifestations.[36] Fear of "perennial reservoirs of disease among the 'native' population" shaped the pattern of VD control.[37] VD transmission came to be seen as racially mono-directional.

> Japan has long been notorious for the large amount of disease which has existed amongst the native population and not only for the amount, but for the peculiar virulence of the disease. Moreover, for many years past, sanitary blue-books have exhibited a melancholy amount of crippling amongst our soldiers and sailors from disease contracted from the native Japanese population.[38]

Whether foreign populations had forms of VD that were "peculiarly" virulent or whether the diseases were magnified by the apparently more refined constitution of the European, these were not merely sexual but racial diseases. Venereal disease was the foreign disease, that which no one would claim as their own but which could serve as a metaphor for the imperfections and failings of those deemed its source. Native behavior thus became the faultline both of the need for colonial medical control and for the spread of painful and disfiguring diseases.[39] Indigenes were seen increasingly as "authors of their own misery."[40] Disease propensity or disposition became a negative marker against which civilization could be measured; venereal disease and its association with prostitution suggested the tempting combination of the ignorant, nonwhite, unaware woman working from cupidity and desire, the very antithesis of British claims to racial and civilizational supremacy.

Medical Understanding of Venereal Disease

J. D. Oriel has argued, somewhat rashly, that by the mid-nineteenth century syphilis was well understood in the medical profession, and that "only a few points of detail needed to be added."[41] In fact, it was 1879 before Ricord established a clinical distinction between gonorrhea and syphilis, and arguments over transmission, treatment, and the nature of the disease continued long after his work. Unsurprisingly, there was often confusion about whether a sickness was venereal in origin, as well as frequent misdiagnosis. Chancroid, in particular, was very difficult to diagnose, and many patients diagnosed with chancroid in fact suffered from other forms of VD. Leprosy could mimic certain features of syphilis, and some thought the two conditions related. The inability to distinguish competently between primary and secondary syphilis increased the potential for disease transmission by patients pronounced cured because symptomless. The typical profile of symptomless female gonorrhea also affected transmission rates before the introduction of serological tests. Some doctors regarded gonorrhea as less damaging and easier to treat.[42] James Lane of the London lock hospital claimed in 1876 that "there is no such thing as a specific gonorrhoeal poison."[43] Three years later, the gonococcus (*Neisseria gonorrhoea*) was microscopically identified as the causative organism of the disease. Medical practitioners also held some curious beliefs about contraction and transmission. One medical writer asserted in 1859 that chronic syphilis in soldiers "is entirely due to the deficient supply of pure air."[44] The colonial surgeon at Hong Kong was confident in 1879 that "self abuse will cause discharges which come under the head of venereal disease."[45] Well into the twentieth century, cautioned one venereologist, "patients whose rash is due to syphilis may sometimes arrive at the admission room of a small-pox hospital."[46] In 1882, A. G. Miller, a fellow of the Royal College of Surgeons and chief of the lock wards at Edinburgh's Royal Infirmary, defined syphilis as an "eruptive fever."[47]

While microscopy was growing in stature at this juncture, it was limited in scope, and serological tests for VD were established only in the early twentieth century. Identification of VD before then was by visual observation. Doctors looked for lesions and dermatological patterns, and faced considerable difficulty in distinguishing between viral herpes and bacterial chancres, or between syphilitic and simple soft sore (nonsyphilitic) chancres, and they frequently misunderstood genital discharges.[48] Hong Kong's colonial surgeon warned that "if all the women with innocent discharges were locked up the Hospital would always be full."[49] Yet in 1873, India's sanitary commissioner had to remind overzealous officers that menstruation was not a disease and that detaining women merely because they were menstruating was illegal. He also advised that nonvenereal forms of "uterine and vaginal disease" were not an appropriate basis for lock hospital admission.[50] His admonitions often went unheeded; some fourteen years later, the medical officer at the Bangalore lock hospital included in his statistics thirty-five women admitted to hospital for their menstrual period, presumably awaiting examination thereafter.[51] At Umballa in the Punjab, "menstruating women have their ticket taken from them and are re-examined before the tickets are returned to them."[52] There are plentiful instances of women detained for leucorrhea, one doctor in India claiming that leucorrhea constituted "the bulk of the admissions" in his region.[53] The *Indian Medical Journal* regarded leucorrhea as an early warning for gonorrhea. "Regarding what and what is not gonorrhoea in the female; given a prostitute, it should be the invariable rule that, since any discharge even a cervical leucorrhoea in such a women [sic] is liable to cause disease, every woman affected with any discharge should be admitted to Hospital for treatment."[54] Many believed that leucorrhea in women, generally a nonvenereal complaint, was the source of gonorrhea in men.[55] Even the otherwise wary Hong Kong surgeon spoke of "obstinate and acrid discharges in young recruits of the brothels, who have been overworked."[56]

Venereology seldom figured in medical school curricula. Few hospitals other than the lock and the workhouse accepted venereal patients, so students only occasionally saw VD cases.[57] Those they did see almost always manifested late sequelae, since parasyphilitic complications were the only cases most hospitals would admit.[58] Lawrence Harrison, Britain's preeminent Edwardian venereologist, remembered that in his student days in Glasgow, he saw only one case of primary syphilis, "shown to a few of us by an assistant surgeon before the patient was hurried off to the Glasgow lock hospital."[59] At the Edinburgh infirmary, students were excluded from the lock wards.[60]

Puzzling over outbreaks of VD aboard troop ships in the 1880s and 1890s, no one in authority ever formally raised the possibility that the men might be infecting one another during the long sea voyage between Britain and India. The director general of the Army Medical Department went so far as to argue that if a man's symptoms manifested after embarkation, "he cannot, in such a position at any rate, spread the disease." Conditions for acquiring VD on troop ships were, he thought, "non-existent."[61] While admission of same-sex intimacies was palpably impolitic, this reading of the human geography of transmission is not reducible merely to a horror of or unease with male-male sexual relations. It reflects, too, the instability of governing medical paradigms. The assertiveness of the claim that regulation was the modern means to stemming VD was more a rhetoric about medicine's reach than it was a practice based on evidence and experience. We cannot adjudicate a point at which disease criteria become reliable or "right" in any absolute way. Today, too, changes in attitude and technique leave all such taxonomies unstable; Sevgi Aral and King Holmes, speaking of contemporary STD reporting, warn that "data from most of the world are sketchy, at times anecdotal."[62]

The Politics of Nomenclature

These changes are perhaps most vividly understood if we chart revisions in disease nomenclature. The ever-changing taxonomy of disease construction reflects not only new medical ideas but political anxiety. The Army Medical Department constantly revised the rules governing the statistical representation of symptoms. There were changes in the classification of VD in 1870, in 1879 (defining VD as consisting only of primary and secondary syphilis, and gonorrhea and its sequelae),[63] and again in 1886. Each new categorization brought fresh protests. Medical men, though rarely speaking of it publicly, were cognizant of the instabilities of disease nomenclature.[64] Doctors complained that "under the new nomenclature [of 1870] . . . cases of Venereal affection are very apt to be lost sight of."[65] The lock surgeon at Bassein (British Burma) concurred that "all sores on young prostitutes" might be considered syphilitic "when no contra-indications are present." But experienced women, he warned, presented nonsyphilitic ulcers that it would be incorrect to enter under the head of either syphilis or of gonorrhea.[66] Since diagnosis in the nineteenth century did not involve culturing, these were unstable designations at best.[67] Moreover, and adding to the confusion, common problems such as nongonococcal urethritis, were not even recorded.[68]

The most controversial of these re-classifications was that of 1886, when penile ulcers were no longer returned under the head of primary syphilis.[69] Allying certain kinds of sores with certain sequelae was always difficult, engendering considerable debate. Hong Kong doctors complained that the form used to collect venereal statistics was inadequate. "Such a simple affection as labial abscess, for want of a proper place in it, has to be entered as 'Gonorrhoea and Primary Syphilis combined'"[70] C. H. F. Routh worried that military and naval returns obscured proper diagnosis in their pre-1886 failure to distinguish "between a truly syphilitic hard sore and a soft one," which he claimed the militia chose to include since "both incapacitate a man whose military service is needed."[71] What Routh omitted in his consideration was the political minefield in which disease taxonomy was trapped. While he worried over the clinical implications of misreading different kinds of sores, others realized the effect of these changes on the level of VD presented in the annual statistical abstracts. The Hong Kong surgeon thought the statistics were exaggerated by there being no heading other than "gonorrhea/syphilis" to itemize a labial abscess, but many recognized that these rubrics could also hide disease. "'Ulcer of the penis' is a term introduced in the new nomenclature of disease. With this any medical man can stamp out all syphilis from his returns, if he so minds, until secondaries appear."[72] Edmund Parkes, doyen of military sanitation in the 1860s, complained of the "want of uniformity" in tabulating syphilitic complaints.[73] Robert Lawson warned that in pursuing the link between primary syphilis and penile ulcers, "the practice has varied so much with different Medical officers, that the numbers of them respectively, as given in the returns, cannot be taken as trustworthy indications of the relative frequency of the two forms."[74]

This uneasiness was not confined to primary syphilis. Gonorrhea was sometimes classed not as a VD but under the head of "diseases of the urinary system."[75] More importantly, though, assumptions such as these also reflect critically on medical presumptions. Syphilis, as we have noted, was regarded as rampant in the colonies, as a serious cause of military inefficiency, and as far more devastating than gonorrhea. Moreover its moral standing was apparently far worse; naval records before 1869, according to B. A. Smithurst, "classified syphilis as a "cachectic" and gonorrhoea as a "local" disease."[76] Thus to treat syphilis was to face (and, with luck, to conquer) depravity, and not just a bodily infection. VD could be written up as serious and rampant or played down, perhaps to demonstrate the efficacy of policy or treatment, perhaps to allay public fears. Where morals, colonial fitness, and military efficiency combined, this was a potent political weapon.

The Hospital

The key site of modern medicine was the hospital, a powerful symbol of medical authority. Hospitals in the metropolis were places of treatment and knowledge-gathering, as well as authoritarian structures in which patients—overwhelmingly of modest means—occupied the lowest rung. In colonial arenas, however, the metropolitan model was unworkable, for inpatient treatment was unpopular. Colonial patients were often unwilling to stay in hospitals or would do so only if friends and kin could accompany them or visit freely. Outpatient dispensaries, cheaper to run and staffed largely by locals with a basic pharmaceutical training, were more popular.[77] Early colonial hospitals often catered largely to a European military clientele. Singapore's first hospital was located in the troop cantonment and was, before 1822, under military administration.[78] Where hospitals did attract a local clientele, it was often because, like Hong Kong's Tung Wah, they were run by locals.

While general hospital provision was erratic across the empire, the lock hospital was common, and doubtless contributed to indigenous unease with hospitals. While locks were not yoked exclusively to CD laws, they were a central feature of CD enactments around the globe. The lock hospital had a long history. The London lock hospital was founded in 1746, Glasgow's lock in 1805, and the Liverpool establishment in 1833. In the nineteenth century, wherever there was CD legislation, lock wards or hospitals compulsorily treated infected prostitutes, who could leave the hospitals only by official consent. The element of compulsion and their sometimes prisonlike qualities made them a place feared and dreaded by their most common residents, prostitute women. Strict rules always governed inmate conduct in the lock system, and punishments were meted out for shows and acts of defiance. Women sent to the Brisbane lock hospital faced solitary confinement, hard labor, and suspension of privileges and/or food for infringing hospital rules.[79] Many lock hospitals, conscious of a fractious clientele, had barred windows and bolted doors. In others, a guard was provided to prevent women from "escaping," to use the telling terminology of the day.

The first use of the word *lock* to describe an institution exclusively for the relief of VD that I have found is in 1746 when William Bromfeild established the London lock hospital on Grosvenor Place. Most authorities agree that the word *lock* derives from the French for a rag, *une loque*, highlighting the initial use of the term for leper hospitals where patients bound their sores with cloth. James Bettley claims that leper hospitals—places of isolation, as were VD hospitals—

began accepting VD patients in the sixteenth century and thus the link was born.[80] And of course, syphilitic eruptions bear a resemblance to those of leprosy. On the other hand, pursuing the Gallic thread, *un loquet* is a latch, and it is possible that the rather punitive and isolating regime promulgated from the first in hospitals serving prostitute women determined their sobriquet.[81] The military, after all, spoke of lock hospitals only in connection with treatments directed at prostitutes. Soldiers were treated in general military hospitals; only during the First World War did the Australian command isolate returning soldiers diagnosed with VD at special camps.

Lock hospitals routinely treated men as outpatients while inpatient regimens were aimed mostly at women. It would have been a fiscal impossibility to bed all male patients, since there were always so many more of them, but the policy reflects more than financial caution. Increasingly the lock was associated with prostitution, and thus with women. "The main object of a Lock Hospital is to put diseased prostitutes during the most venomous period of their career out of a position in which they can spread disease."[82]

Doctors, as we have seen, were inclined to adopt a generous view of what might constitute signs of disease in a known prostitute, and as a result, lock hospitals were often amongst the busiest of any medical institutions directed at local civilian populations, though patients were seldom confined of their own volition. Numbers varied enormously, of course, but in the period of compulsory registration and examination, detention for treatment was often conducted at a lively pace. Even before the institution of formal CD laws, the Bengal presidency reported an admissions total (in eighteen hospitals spread across the presidency) of 4,413 women in 1822, averaging 368 per month.[83] Though the figures include women admitted more than once in the course of the year, the total is still substantial. The numbers obviously reflect the size of the local population, the reach of the system, and the zealousness of local officials. Dinapore lock hospital, for example, admitted 149 women with primary syphilis and gonorrhea in 1882, 231 in 1884, and 136 in 1886. In smaller cantonments, numbers decreased correspondingly; Barrackpore, for example, admitted only twenty-four women in 1886.[84] In the first two years of the ordinance, only 188 women passed through Singapore's lock hospital.[85] The Hong Kong surgeon reported a disappointing shortfall in admissions for 1874: "only 65 against 223 in 1873."[86] Since colonial officials were convinced that Chinese women living in the colony were by and large there to earn a livelihood in prostitution, the numbers must have seemed suspiciously low. But in these colonies, not all prostitute women were even examined.

In Queensland, too, confinement was restricted to certain groups. Aboriginal women were outside the system altogether, and the Brisbane lock seems to have housed only white women. Despite the claims of outraged citizens that their city was overrun by prostitutes, admissions climbed only slowly. Brisbane's statistics include multiple admissions, giving us an admirably clear picture of the hospital's demographics. In 1868, thirty-four women were admitted, with a total of forty admissions. In 1869, 52 women were detained, with 105 admissions overall. The numbers remained steady for a decade or more; in 1877 (the last year for which statistics are available), the admissions total was 109, with 68 women held. The Brisbane authorities were nothing if not zealous; a small number of unfortunates faced five and six admissions each year.[87] In the smaller settlement of Rockhampton, admissions never climbed above thirty-one between 1869 and 1877, and here too multiple admissions were common.[88]

Since there was no uniformity in the size of the establishment, lock hospital accommodation ranged from bedding for a handful of detainees to multiple-warded establishments. In the years of compulsion, one commonly voiced complaint was of overcrowding and inadequate housing.[89] The CD exam room on Countess Street in Brisbane—next to the police stables, adjoining the Victoria barracks, and surrounded by a seven-foot high fence—was dirty, dilapidated, and in a state of disrepair, inside and out. The senior constable in charge of the premises hired "a poor woman once every three Months or thereabouts to Scrub and Wash," while he and his assistant swept and dusted weekly.[90] Across the continent, the island Aboriginal lock hospitals at Bernier and Dorre established by the Western Australian government shortly after federation, carried out much of their work in tents.[91]

At Chakrata, a third-class[92] lock hospital in northern India, "the hospital contained 20 patients (some having young children) locked in a room 33 × 9 or 10 feet, without sufficient light or air . . . Stench and dirt beyond description result from this overcrowding."[93] The Mooltan lock hospital, only four years after it had opened, was "in a very indifferent state of repair, and as scarcely deserving of the name of a lock hospital."[94] Mooltan, refurbished as an outdoor dispensary around 1895, was probably a small third-class hospital, but even larger institutions faced recurrent funding crises. Poona, in the Bombay presidency, was a large station, close by a long-standing indigenous city. Captain Dorgan, supervising its lock hospital early in the twentieth century, remembered how often his thirty-bed facility had to accommodate fifty women.[95] At Quetta, also in Bombay, before the late 1880s the same room served for both examining and housing patients.[96]

An extraordinary number of colonial lock hospitals seem to have been thrown up hastily in unsuitable accommodations, doubtless making the work more difficult and the lives of patients more uncomfortable. Many were old buildings converted to medical use. The Hong Kong lock was an old school; the frustrated colonial surgeon claimed in 1882 that it had no lavatories, bathrooms, or water-closets and that half of the building had been declared unsafe. When makeshift bathrooms were added, they further cut into the space available for housing the women.[97] Year after year, successive surgeons expressed the hope that funding for a new lock hospital at Hong Kong would allow them a better space. In 1881, the surgeon pointed out in his annual report that the lock ". . . is still in the old school-house mentioned in my report for 1880. Part of the building has now become unsafe and cannot be used."[98] The Penang lock in the Straits, opened in 1873, was a converted shed on the grounds of an old lunatic asylum, sandwiched between the civil hospital and the jail.[99] At the treaty port of Nagasaki a temple was, bizarrely, given over to lock use, while that at Yokohama was regrettably sited "in a malarious swamp."[100] At Fyzabad in the Northwest Provinces, a third-class lock hospital opened in September 1866 in what had previously been a mint.[101] These were clearly rough and ready facilities, moreso than in Britain where, while the locks suffered from underfunding, they nonetheless held to what were seen as appropriate hospital standards for the day. Less attention was paid to standards overseas.

Physical discomfort was not the lock hospital's only unattractive feature. If thought infected, a woman's hospitalization was immediate and unassailable. Even in the informal years of the system, she was "instantly confined."[102] Once detained, women were expected to conform to a stern regime. Here, the lock hospitals of white settler colonies could be more irksome because the values of bourgeois Britain were visited more directly on white inmates. In Indian and Chinese settings, indigenous women confined for treatment, but well enough to move about, could leave the hospital during the day "to go and see their friends" and receive visitors in the wards.[103] They were not expected to engage in "useful" labor and were not subject to religious instruction. In Australia, however, women experienced controls akin to those in Britain. Their lives were governed by the clock, with strict hours, allotted domestic tasks, and meager visiting hours.[104] The presumptions of education and redemption meant that women were confined, isolated from their friends, and restricted in their movements in the attempt to break them of what were seen as bad habits and bad company. A code of punishments matched the behavioral requirements, and women punished with solitary confinement or a bread-and-water diet must have wondered if they were in hospital or prison. Bad language, insufficient respect for figures of authority, destruction of property, a refusal to follow rules all brought formal and swift reprisal. In some respects, the lock hospital was barely seen as a medical environment. The Queensland health officer thought it unnecessary to seek women staff with nursing qualifications, since "the cases admitted . . . required little if any nursing."[105] He was quite clear that the matron's duties were more disciplinary than curative. She was a warder before she was a nurse.

British lock hospitals were no less spartan with their inmates.[106] The lock wards of St. Bartholomew's hospital in London were in the attic, affording "much less cubic space to the patients."[107] R. W. Johnstone noted that "it seems to be the rule" in workhouses and infirmaries, "to choose the worst ward in the house for the accommodation of the venereal cases."[108] In the early 1870s, the Glasgow lock required women to sign a contract with the hospital authorities that spelled out behavioral and sanitary boundaries, committed them to getting out of bed at a set time, attending religious services, eschewing alcohol, and emphasized that they would not leave without formal discharge.[109] The resident surgeon acknowledged the failure of the scheme, but it represented a disciplinary construct that shaped the gulf between the recipients of care and the caregivers.

Though prostitutes in the nonsettler colonies escaped the fetters of this domesticizing daily ritual, they lived instead in a more overtly prisonlike setting of bars, bolts, and guards, a constant reminder of the "salutary amount of coercion" favored by lock hospital authorities.[110] In India, in particular, where the military was so dominant, discipline was central. At Ahmedabad, "[B]ars were put on the window for the purpose of preventing the escape of patients during the night."[111] Many hospitals employed a guard to prevent women leaving without permission.[112] The Bassein lock "resembles a jail hospital, in respect to iron barred windows and patent safety locks"; escapees were kept in a punishment room for the duration of their hospital stay.[113] The lieutenant governor of Bengal advised his military officers to temper their zeal with discretion lest they drive away all the women by "rendering life utterly intolerable."[114] The secretary of state for India, Lord Hamilton, thought that were "the hospitals a little more attractive, and the discipline to the women there detained a little less rigid than it has been in the past, the success of an examination system might be secured."[115] He was motivated not by sensitivity to the women's feelings, but rather by a pragmatic need to shore up an unpopular system by tempering the rigors of its demands.

In practice, western medicine had to accommodate local need and desire in order to persuade otherwise reluctant women to accede to its demands. In one typical report, a medical officer describes the local prostitute women as "reconciled" to a regular examination schedule because they were allowed visitors while hospitalized and given a daily allowance while there.[116] Nonetheless, the associations of VD with loose morals, class disdain, and racial typing made the more disciplinarian approach the dominant one. "The general character of the measure . . . must . . . be in some degree repressive."[117]

In Britain and in Australia, the hospital was increasingly represented as a humane, safe, and entirely necessary provision of proper modernity. It was naturalized as the place one sought relief for sickness, where one consulted an expert. Attempts to persuade colonial peoples that hospitals and doctors were removed from politics, and were reliable resources, never really succeeded. Medicine's deep association with the colonial state, and the growing entrenchment of the hospital as the central site of western medicine, produced a wariness in colonial settings. CD laws imposed western medical techniques, and locals recognized such laws as imposing upon them stringent health rules designed to protect the colonists.[118] "All classes of Natives" disliked the Indian CD Act, according to the Calcutta deputy police commissioner. "They have no sympathy with it, because they consider it was introduced to benefit Europeans."[119] Locals saw few reasons to abandon the therapies and remedies with which they had grown up.

The lock was a white space though its typical inmates in colonial environs were women of color. In virtually every colonial setting the imposition of the system of regulated prostitution was the first state intervention in women's health undertaken, and quite often among the first health initiatives of any kind.[120] The governance of the lock did little to boost confidence in colonial offerings.

Disciplining the unworthy and the unclean coalesced in a policy of segregation in lock hospitals, poor houses, asylums, and the like. In Britain, it was an inflexible rule to segregate VD patients.[121] Where prostitute women were concerned, it was an easily attainable goal.[122] Outside femininity, outside respectability, outside domesticity, and doubly associated with filth—via "promiscuity" *and* disease—such women were a perfect site for medico-legal control. In nonsettler colonies, the rhetoric of uncleanliness and of primitivism allowed these modes of control to move beyond prostitute women and into the wider population. A broadly conceived notion of moral as well as physical contagion shaped such practice. Fearful of the spread of disease, authorities worried that the loose morals and tongues of prostitutes—always the largest hospitalized group of female VD sufferers—would offend or adversely affect other patients.

> If the women were mostly immoral in the sense in which certain great Empresses (sic), Actresses, Lady Noodists (sic) and Soprani are known to have been immoral, nobody would propose to put them in separate wards. But these unfortunate women can not help being offensive in their conversation to the neighbours—the necessity for their segregation.[123]

In colonial sites, officials, convinced that "respectable" women in India and China would not consent to hospital treatment, instead constructed a mimicry of "respectable" hierarchy amongst the "immoral." In addition to distinguishing between the nudist, actress or performer, and the "common prostitute" they built a class ladder within sexual commerce. The magistrate at Meerut lambasted the CD Act's "failure to recognise practically the difference in the several classes of courtesans, lumping together, as it does, the woman who answers somewhat to the *Lorette* or *Cocotte* with the commonest strumpet in the place, compelling them all to visit the same hospital, at the same time giving no more privacy to the better class women than the commonest."[124] Yet measures of segregation were everywhere in effect. Separating the guilty from the innocent, the less from the more coarse, or different racial groupings were practices that grew rather than diminished over the course of the century, culminating in such practices as quarantining and isolation wards. Segregation for venereal patients was, however, grounded more in social and sexual considerations than in epidemiology, though that is not to suggest that quarantining, for example, did not rapidly acquire nationalist and racist overtones.[125] The insistence that lock hospitals be housed in separate buildings, or at the very least in wards inaccessible to other patients, articulated anxieties with little medical basis, since the diseases were known not to be infectious. The separation was a reminder instead of behavioral boundaries and an expression of the idea that venereal patients were in a distinct category of culpability.

Treatment and Examination

Until well into the twentieth century, VD treatments were unpleasant, cumbersome, and lengthy, as well as often painful. The association of VD with profligacy and personal culpability meant that little attention was paid to rendering the treatment regimen less distressing.[126] Patient comfort was a secondary factor at best. Since many of the treatments were ineffective as well as disagreeable, sufferers not under coercion often dropped out of the purview of the medical world.

The use of mercury in the treatment of syphilis is the most widely known of the early protocols, but it was by no means the only one that patients must have dreaded. Cubebs and copaiba, also used to treat urethritis, induced nausea and vomiting. Gonorrhea therapies could be equally unpleasant. Before the 1880s, plant extracts such as cubebs, copaiba, and sandalwood oil were commonly administered for both diseases.[127] From the 1880s, gonorrhea in women was commonly treated by cervical cauterization with silver nitrate. Twice daily urethral injections of permanganate of potash (Condy's Fluid) or sulphate of copper or zinc, constituted the standard treatment for men, largely superseded after 1892 by the use of potassium permanganate, either injected or via urethral irrigation. Towards the end of the century, injections of boracic or tannic acid with glycerine were growing in favor. These remedies all tended to irritate the tissues, with silver nitrate and silver compounds causing urethral stricture and scarring of the cervical canal.[128] "More damage," thought L. W. Harrison, "was being done by the treatment than by the disease."[129] The use of potassium permanganate was no less alarming; from its application could ensue arthritis and epididymitis, inflaming the testes.[130]

Early syphilis treatments included orally administered plant extracts such as guaiacum, a wood resin from the West Indies. First used in the sixteenth century, it very often resulted in fevers. Mercury was probably the most common palliative until the introduction of arsphenamines after 1909. Closely linked to humoral pathology via its ability to induce excessive sweating and salivation, mercury had a long history in the treatment of chronic skin diseases dating back to the twelfth century.[131] For treating syphilis, it was used in a variety of ways and "suppressed rather than eradicated the pathogens."[132] There were mercurial salves and powders, it was taken orally in solution, and from the 1860s injected intramuscularly and subcutaneously.[133] Mercurial calomel solutions were also common.[134] Jonathan Hutchinson, a leading British expert on syphilis and an exponent of mercurials, claimed that "[M]ercury may be used in many different ways, and so efficient is it in all that each one has its warm advocates."[135] Detractors, seeking alternatives, began using iodides in the 1830s, especially high dosages of potassium iodide; before long the two originally competing treatments were combined.[136]

The effects of the highly toxic mercury could be dreadful, and injections of it were painful. Tooth decay, swelling of the gums and mouth, and gum ulceration were commonplace side effects induced by profuse salivation. At the London lock hospital mercury was employed as long as "the patient could bite a crust."[137] But mercury affected the entire body, not just the mouth. Patients experienced conditions ranging from hair loss and gastro-enteritic disorder to anemia and diseases of the liver and kidney. Its use was one reason why inpatient treatment for syphilis was common and often lengthy.

Some practitioners treated local manifestations rather than attempting a systemic onslaught of such virulence. It was common practice, for instance, to dust sores with iodoform powder, in part because many held to the distinction between the "true" indurated syphilitic sore and the chancroid. Labial abscesses were often opened and drained before being dusted dry. Genital warts, not understood as viral, were painted with acetic or pyrogallic acid or dusted with sulphate of iron. These were clearly less invasive and mostly less painful remedies.

In practice many western therapies resembled those in use in nonwestern healing systems in their reliance on plant and herb extracts. The salivation and sweating associated with mercurials owed much to the persistence of long-standing humoral theories, common also to Chinese medical thinking and to the Ayurvedic and the Unani Tibb systems in India (respectively Hindu and Muslim protocols).[138] Chinese healers used metals (including vermilion and cinnabar, a type of mercury), calomel, and iodide of potash in their treatment of VD, as did western practitioners.[139] Western doctors seldom acknowledged these similarities, preferring instead to dismiss nonwestern practices as dangerous quackery. The Straits surgeon repudiated local techniques: "the system of treatment adopted by the Chinese Doctors [was] calculated to aggravate."[140]

Western medical practice was proactive, seeking out VD through compulsory examination, mainly of prostitute women. Attitudes to examining soldiers were ambivalent, tinged with the distaste of the educated for the rank and file, but there was a clear sense that the treatment of such a population, even though under absolute authority, needed to be distinct from that aimed at the indigenous. Doctors certainly railed about soldiers' behavior, but they sympathized with the dislike of enlisted men for genital inspections. The Fyzabad lock surgeon wrote earnestly in 1877 of the effect of such inspections on the men; the "dangle parade" dented morale, developing "coarseness and injured modesty."[141]

No such scruples were entertained in examining registered prostitutes. In the large lock hospital at Sitapur, near the Nepalese border, '[T]he patients are made to stand or sit in a tub of water and then freely drenched by means of a syringe . . . solutions . . . are subsequently squirted into the vaginal canal, and this process is repeated several times a day."[142] Whether the treatment was comfortable for, or accepted by the patients was of no consequence. Wealthy Yorkshire woman, Anne Lister, underwent internal examination of the genital area in 1823 after contracting VD. She noted in her diary that "the handling" hurt her at the time and for a time afterwards, and she was in the hands of a private and sympathetic physician.[143] For those required by law to attend for examination, delicacy in handling was not the major consideration it was when doctors treated paying customers such as Lister.

Not surprisingly, doctors reported widespread "prejudice against inspection."[144] The Calcutta police commissioner told the government that as soon as women realized they would be compulsorily examined, they left the city, returning if at all in secret.[145] An officer in the Northwest Provinces reported that women "leave cantonment bazaars in possession of the least attractive of their sex, and fly for refuge to neighbouring cities."[146] Similar tales had Queensland prostitutes fleeing for nearby colonies where there were no CD laws, most notably New South Wales.[147] Mindful of such tales, the medical establishment at the Straits moved cautiously, familiarizing women with the CD ordinance by making house calls for the first few months.[148]

In most cases, weekly exams were the norm. The most zealous authorities experimented with daily inspections. At Fyzabad cantonment in India's Northwest Provinces, the deputy surgeon ordered daily inspections of registered women in March 1877, an order the divisional chief countermanded after only a fortnight.[149] Brothel keepers in the Chinese colonies and *dhais* in India were expected to inspect their workers for signs of disease regularly, and to report infection immediately. At Dinapore, registered women endured three different sets of overhaul—twice monthly by a doctor, every four days by a matron, and daily by the local *dhai*.[150] A circular memorandum issued by the commander in chief in 1884 instigated daily examination by the *dhai* to supplement the doctor's exams.[151]

The exam itself was an unfriendly and unfeeling affair. Even pro-regulationists were sometimes critical. "A common hard table, often without even a blanket covering it, is all that is provided for the women to lie upon. This is not even furnished with foot-rests nor is it fitted with a box containing pastes, lotions, wool and other applications for treating cases."[152] At Mean Mir in the Punjab, the table was bare, the room "primitive" and "badly lighted."[153] Women felt the effects of authority even prior to the exam. At Cawnpore, they were "assembled" an hour before the arrival of the examining doctor, "and seated in a row under the supervision of police, to prevent their cleaning themselves immediately before the examination."[154] This extraordinary level of surveillance was only possible, of course, where numbers were limited. And it was at the whim of local officials; in Brisbane where the average number of registered women between 1868 and 1877 was only eighty, such a degree of zealousness never occurred. Racial discourse left the white sex worker with a modicum of shame and feeling, and thus with the potential for reform. Antiregulationists rhetoricizing "instrumental rape" as the baseline of coerced exams, reserved their protests largely for the domestic scene.

Some doctors insisted on using the speculum for examination, while others eschewed it. One sanitary officer warned that "inspections limited to the external parts only would be of very little practical value. It is impossible for a Medical Officer to pronounce with certainty whether a woman is suffering from venereal or not, without an internal examination made with the speculum."[155] The lock hospital chief at Sitapur in the Northwest Provinces was unconvinced.

> The old dhai, who has acquired from long practice a peculiar aptitude for exposing the os, inserts the index and second finger of the right hand into the vagina in front of the anus, while she produces extension of the perineal parts downward by thrusting the same finger of the left hand into the passage under the symphysis pubis from above. In this way, as well as by a judicious manipulation of the vaginal wall, she exposes the parts so thoroughly in a few seconds as to render them obvious to an onlooker, and an amount of examination is got through in this way in a few minutes which several hours with the speculum would scarcely complete.[156]

The emphasis in his description is on speed, the claim that the *dhai's* method is both more effective and faster than the speculum. In populous colonies with high registration, doctors favored brisk methods. Stephen Fox, senior district surgeon at Perak in the Straits, boasted that he was "a quick worker . . . I felt her glands in her groin, looked at her general appearance and legs, and felt her pulse . . . in the examination of many of the women who seemed quite well I spent a short time, cases of a suspicious nature were asked to go to the hospital, where an attempt was made to examine with a speculum."[157] His colleague, Martenez Wright, also conducted examinations that were little more than nugatory. He examined "the skin of the legs, thighs, abdomen, hands and feet and inguinal glands through the clothes, and the throat if necessary," though he acknowledged that "[B]y this method I don't say I could exclude every case of venereal disease." Wright estimated that he examined about a dozen women in the course of thirty minutes.[158] Skeptics decried such methods:

> the doctors seem to have competed with one another as to the speed with which they could examine women; the record being 120 women per hour. Such a proceeding shows what a farce these examinations were. It is absurd to suppose that examining two women a minute could afford any guarantee as to the state of their health. Moreover such hasty work must have rendered antiseptic precautions impossible, with the probable result . . . that the disease was conveyed from one woman to another by the examining surgeon.[159]

The rehearsal of western beneficence and enlightenment must have been difficult to maintain in these circumstances and the doctors' complaints about inadequate funding for facilities were a shrewd way to blame parsimony rather than indifference to patient comfort or hierarchical attitudes for problems in the CD system. But at work here, too, were considerations shaped by gender, which surfaced both institutionally and attitudinally. It was women, after all, who were subject to the constraints of the system and we have already noted the contrast between medical empathy with soldierly reaction to inspection and the harsher treatment afforded the women.

The Unmodern Colonial

The legitimation of western medical prowess, Rajnarayan Chandavakar argues, required a parallel delegitimation of local medical knowledges.[160] Colonial officials were reliant upon yet simultaneously dismissive of the aid they received from local personnel. Here, too, the specter of barbarous colonial unmodernity was invoked, even where locals had been trained in western medical methods.

The Dhai

In Indian cantonments, it was common to appoint local women, known as *dhais,* sometimes as *mahaldarin* or *mahaldarni,* and occasionally as *choudhrins,* to supervise registered prostitutes.[161] The terms were used interchangeably, one *dhai* noting that, "I am sometimes called mahaldarni, sometimes dhai, indifferently. Properly the mahaldarni works in the bazar."[162] The British saw the *mahaldarni* as a hereditary prostitute or pimp (male: *mahaldar*), with a lineage stretching back to Moghul times, who procured women for the use of a regiment. The *mahaldarni,* thought the Ibbetson Commission of 1893, had in earlier eras been a spy, informing on the disobedient and the rebellious within the harem.[163] The *dhai* was the traditional Hindu birth attendant, versed in women's reproductive functions. Both (*dhai* and *mahaldarni*) lived in the women's quarters, checked their charges regularly for signs of infection, reported on their health and conduct to the medical authorities, prevented them from selling their services to men other than the white soldiers, and were responsible for ensuring women's attendance at the regular examinations conducted by the military doctors. Cantonment regulations advised that "she should be the medium of communication between the medical and other authorities and the women, for the efficient carrying out of the regulations that are laid down."[164] Typically, such women were compensated out of cantonment funds.

The British found them a distasteful group. The Ibbetson commission thought lock hospital *dhais* were "probably, without exception, old mahaldarnis, perhaps because no other class of woman would accept the post."[165] Like the largely female brothel keepers of Hong Kong and the Straits, they were seen as motivated by financial self-interest rather than the common good. India's sanitary commissioner described how the *mahaldarni* would "bind the prostitutes . . . by means of advances of money for the purchase of food, clothes, or jewelry, and . . . [then] keeps a sharp eye on their movements and takes all the care that she can that they do not escape her till they have paid her debts."[166]

The same was said of Chinese brothel keepers, ensuring the women remained indebted, so they could continue to work them profitably. But while brothel keepers in the Chinese-dominant colonies were represented as likely to conceal disease, since a hospitalized woman was tantamount to a loss of profit, the supervisory position of the *dhai* rendered her remuneration dependent on her toeing the line: "they have a direct interest in getting the girls 'passed sound' at regular intervals."[167] As an additional measure to secure the *dhai*'s fealty, some authorities fined those who did not report signs of disease among the women under their care.[168] Both the *dhai* and the brothel keeper thus walked a fine line, simultaneously figures of villainy and useful aids to the state. The army considered the *dhai* a necessity; in a circular memorandum to commanding officers in 1886, the quartermaster general noted that the "employment of Dhais...is of great importance."[169] Still, many worried about trustworthiness, regarding such women as likely to accept bribes or to overlook disease in women in whom they had a personal financial investment.[170]

The "untouchable" *dhai* was also invariably evoked in the west as the epitome of backwardness—ignorant, filthy, unscientific, superstitious. As the traditional deliverer of children in India, she was always female and because of the ritually polluting nature of the work, in both Hindu and Muslim cosmology, always of low caste.[171] These qualities mirrored the stain of her association with polluting fluids and activities.[172] Anthropological studies of south Asian birthing practices suggest that *dhais* often do work with unwashed hands, because of the impure and polluting nature of their work; thorough cleansing succeeds rather than precedes the delivery of a child to wash away the polluting fluids.[173] It is difficult to ascertain whether brothel *dhais* also attended at births, or whether the name was borrowed to describe former prostitutes now employed in surveillance. At Mhow in Bombay, "an incurable woman," a former lock patient, was employed "on small wages" to work in the hospital.[174] F. O. Mayne in the Northwest Provinces, "appointed the chief bawds of the town as dhaies or matrons" to keep a check on the other women."[175] At Lucknow, according to a military surgeon, "head prostitutes, called *Mahaldarins,* are made responsible for the special healthiness of the occupants of their own particular Mohullah or quarter."[176] But the terms *dhai* and *mahaldarni,* whether borrowed or literal, clearly connoted a woman's role in a female environment—the brothel, the zenana, the hours of labor before childbirth. With her unwashed hands and her primitive reliance on herbs and superstitions, the *dhai* was an unreliable and untrustworthy figure, excoriated for her stubborn resistance to bio-medical ways. She was, in Geraldine Forbes' lively description, transformed "into the evil witch of progressive India," becoming a symbol of "dogged resistance to change."[177]

India, however, was unusual among British colonies in the use of the *dhai* or her equivalent, just as it was unusual in training or employing in government service indigenous doctors.[178] Elsewhere use of local women in these capacities was largely eschewed. Instead, European (seldom British) women with some local language skills were brought in supervisory capacities to lock hospitals and refuges. Poorly paid and definitely not classed as ladies, they occupied ambivalent territory. Less educated than the indigenous men employed as subassistant surgeons or dressers, and proletarianized by their proximity to "soiled" women, they were nonetheless white and European. The chain of command in such situations must have been a tortuous one, for white women could not be seen to take orders from or serve local men, yet a trained cadre of native men was often a necessary feature of the system in many colonies. Indispensable as the CD system was seen to be, its administration exposed the anxieties of colonialism and of newly modernizing medicine in often striking ways.

The Native in Power

The European doctor was critical to the CD system but there was always worry about the demeaning nature of the work. Many thought it undesirable "that European medical officers should be called upon to perform a duty which must always be repulsive, and which many would consider degrading," preferring instead to appoint "a small native establishment."[179] Yet that posed problems too, and there was unanimity that local medical personnel should be trained by and invariably subordinate to white doctors.[180] "European continuous supervision is necessary."[181]

A crisis of authority lurked in these views, for British doctors found the work unalluring. This was "work which no decent medical man w[d] soil his hands with."[182] This fundament of distaste spoke to the colonial doctor as a martyr to good medicine and good politics for his willingness to soil his hands inside the bodies of low native women. Fault lay with the local society and not with the brave man of science. Unappealing as venereal work was, to turn it over to local supervision was unthinkable.

The unease over locally trained doctors was part of a broader mistrust of all local personnel. Native personnel were regarded as likely to be dishonest, a "power introduced for oppression and bribery."[183] "Native Doctors and the Police," claimed one officer, were "an engine of oppression, exaction and ill-treatment."[184] The Straits protector warned that at-risk and rescued women placed in safe custody were in jeopardy, "owing to the untrustworthiness and corruptibility of the Native attendants" employed to protect them. "Through these attendants," he argued, "the girl will be exposed to threats and blandishments which may induce her to escape from our friendly protection, and put herself at the mercy of unscrupulous people whose only object will be to gain possession of her person, for the purpose of making money by her prostitution."[185] So confident was the Cawnpore magistrate of the deceitfulness of the native that he "need not point out that the dhaie is bribable and the European doctor is not." Where "Native Doctors and dhaies" are involved, "the system will never be effectual."[186] "There is nothing to be trusted to Native doctors," remarked William Burke, "who are known to be bribed by these women not to discover their being diseased besides these doctors make considerably by their practice among them who even while under cure persist in their career of prostitution (sic)."[187]

This picture of the wretched, immoral, infecting woman as an invariable part of colonial life offered an artless contrast for the painting of the civilizing picture. The wise official and the painstaking doctor brought the model of honest enlightened modernity to the needy colonies. Officials played up the contrast between their own probity and the definitional untrustworthiness of the poor working woman. India's sanitary commissioner, accused by an antiregulation campaigner of endorsing illegal practices, defended himself in hurt tones. "I do not suppose that any reasonable person will think that I am demanding too much when I ask that Dr. Hamilton's statements and mine should be accepted as more trustworthy evidence than that based on the statements of prostitutes."[188]

Local doctors and unscrupulous women did not, though, make up the full complement in this pantheon of untrustworthiness. Hong Kong's brothel inspectors, being "men of limited education," were "certainly unable to perform the duties required of them, without efficient superintendence and instruction."[189] The Straits ordinances were jeopardized because, "worked as they must be here, by a Police Force, the lower members of which are often venal, in a community which is anything but free . . . would always" carry "a grave risk of administrative abuse."[190] In India, "any constable who is on this work above a month gets contaminated."[191] Complaints laid against non-Europeans were far likelier to be vigorously investigated and prosecuted. Two Malays at the Straits, who accused European police inspectors of accepting bribes from unlicensed women, were prosecuted and convicted.[192]

The apparently mercenary qualities of native officialdom enjoyed a long history. In the informal years of registration in India, one Mysore officer warned the quartermaster general that:

> Peons and Chuprassies were employed as Detectives or informers and as usual these functionaries made use of their power for extortion and all sorts of villainies. "I will report that women in your house are diseased and the Doctors will come to inspect them." Seldom failed of eliciting a bribe, not to bring upon even respectable women and their families, – the disgrace of such a process, the very threat was . . . sufficient to terrify the whole family into buying off such an indignity, at whatever price the rascal who used it asked.[193]

But such attitudes, commonplace though they were, revealed an instability. The potential for bribery undermined the stereotype of the promiscuous colonial unperturbed by the presence of prostitution. For the charge of bribery to be usable, it had to be shown vitiating probity. The avarice of the native doctor depended on there being a class of respectable people on whom he could prey, but the degradation of native society simultaneously belied the presence of such a class, seeing all locals, rather, as unrespectable. For one of the stereotypes to work, the other had to be cast aside.

The Brothel Keeper

Beyond the medical realm, but closely connected to it, the brothel keeper was also painted as ignorant and superstitious, immersed in unhealthy tradition, suspicious of change, and needing to be schooled in the benefits of modernity. Like the *dhais*, colonial brothel keepers were crucial to the system, for it was their task to report infection to the medical authorities. Recalling the introduction of personalized identity tickets for Singapore brothel residents, the protector remembered how angry this innovation had made the brothel keepers. "After threatening the law, riots, closing of shops, & c., and making a demonstration at the Protectorate in the shape of throwing back their license boards, dancing on the floors with wooden clogs, and howling furiously, they found they must give in, and are now reconciled to the measure as inevitable."[194] His vivid description of dancing and howling as central to their protests would have driven home to his metropolitan audience the gulf between tradition and modernity, between east and west, between proper and unmanaged women, between science and superstition. The point would not have been lost on Whitehall officials long used to decorous deputations from activist ladies politely arranging meetings with the Colonial Secretary and sending formally worded memorials as the standard form of protest. The description stands as an illuminating example of the trend, noted by Kamala Visweswaran, among colonial officials to detail not what women said, but how they spoke.[195] The emphasis on the noise rather than the substance of the protest speaks directly to Visweswaran's observation, and detracted, of course, from the idea that the brothel keepers may have advanced a rational rather than a regressive position. The small detail of footwear was also perhaps not insignificant, for it was working women in the north, far removed from parliament, who in Britain, wore clogs. While middle-class campaigning women were often seen as meddlesome and even sometimes as overstepping their boundaries, the women brothel keepers of the east, keening and whirling, were a reminder of women out of place. The greedy brothel keeper in union with others, or allied with the sinister secret societies of the Chinese colonies, was seen as the stalwart of medieval-like guilds, fighting and hindering the openness of modernity.

Colonial Dirt

As medicine's hold tightened and the critique of indigenous healers grew more vigorous, attention to the sanitary inadequacies of colonial environs also increased. While medicine and sanitation were the markers of modern civilization, local practices—and practitioners—were deemed barbarous and filthy. Indifference to prostitution and to regular washing came increasingly to be conflated; the keeping of animals in domestic residences and the overcrowding of dwellings were seen as equally unsavory. Florence Nightingale, deploring the sanitary dangers to which soldiers barracked in India were exposed, drew a connection between primitiveness and hygiene. "The bazaars are simply in the first state of savage social life . . . the real hot-beds of disease."[196] Everywhere westerners traveled, "the colonized were constructed as a collection of hygienically degenerate types."[197] There were persistent complaints about brothels "so saturated with filth that they cannot be properly cleansed."[198] "Simple sheds," thought many, were the most suitable accommodation for diseased women because they were so "often filthy."[199] George Newton deplored the "carelessness and want of cleanliness" among the women he treated in the Yokohama lock.[200] There were frequent complaints that registered women and their premises were unclean. "Lastly, I may add that the registered women are of the most loathsome, dirty, old and ugly description."[201]

Dirt and morality, filth and fever, were deeply connected. White settlers regarded areas of foreign residence as places "of poor sanitation and suspect morals."[202] The Hong Kong surgeon blamed the spread of typhoid fever in 1880 on the condition of the brothels.[203] Pathans, declared the surgeon major of the Bengal Army "are dirty in their habits," and thus more prone to VD than other sepoys.[204] The "indifferent morals of both Gurkha men and women" were "well-known" and accounted for their high rates of VD; Pathans were partial to same-sex intimacies, and therefore immoral.[205] "The Gurkha is not a clean man," remarked Meerut's deputy surgeon general while T. C. Smith, surgeon to a Gurkha division of the Indian Army, thought VD aggravated in his charges for "want of washing and other cleanliness in their persons."[206] Throughout the colonial world the same assumptions held. John and Jean Comaroff note "a persistent association of the African body with noxious organisms."[207] Brenda Yeoh, writing on Singapore, notes that "contamination, filth, and a dangerous disregard for dirt were from the municipal perspective symptomatic of Asian domestic practices."[208] Kerrie Macpherson found "virtually unanimous foreign judgments . . . that local inhabitants were dirty," in the treaty port of Shanghai, while elsewhere in China the "identification of colonial subjects with infectious diseases" by westerners was common.[209] When plague broke out in Hong Kong in the 1890s, colonial medical officers were quick to blame the dirty habits of the Chinese for the spread of the disease. At work in such observations was a suggestion that natives preferred to live in foul conditions. Colonial officials persuaded themselves that subject populations enjoyed a racial immunity unavailable to white residents. The commanding officer at Hong Kong thought locals more tolerant of filth: "[T] streets are so narrow and the houses so badly constructed and ventilated, that it would be impossible to make the buildings healthy, or habitable, except for Chinese."[210]

And no one was dirtier than the woman who sold sex. The Barrackpore lock surgeon painted a piteous picture of the stalwart medical officer overcoming his fastidious distaste for unpleasant duties. "The position in which the medical officer is placed is enough to disgust any but the most enthusiastic, and it has disgusted most of the officers in charge of lock hospitals . . . not only has he to know all about the filth of a lock hospital, but he has to write about it."[211] The selfless doctor, called upon to treat those who brought sickness upon themselves and whose diagnosis and treatment demanded a certain physical intimacy, became a common theme. Doctors bore with fortitude "patients who are often filthy," sporting "ailments that are frequently loathsome."[212] Unseemly examination would dirty a doctor's hands, making him symbolically and horrifically akin to the native midwife, invariably depicted as working with dirty hands and blackened fingernails. Hygiene operated as a key site of and for modernity, and the avoidance of hygiene became a sign of savagery.

Yet cleanliness was not always a defining characteristic of western medicine. Opponents of the CD system raised the reuse of the speculum without disinfection between patients as a factor in infection.

> One follows the other on to a table in rapid succession, exposing their persons, having a speculum pushed into their vagina, and their os and cervix uteri examined. The same hand which separated the labiae of one woman, does so to the others; the same speculum dipped into water, wiped with a small towel, and smeared with oil being, in my observation, used throughout . . . I saw nothing in these examinations to prevent the syphilitic poison of one woman being communicated almost certainly to many others.[213]

Doctors were indubitably hampered by inadequate facilities. They frequently complained that only one speculum was provided per examining room, but rather than diminishing the critique of native filth, this exemplified for doctors the derisory conditions in which they were expected to work.[214]

Locals, moreover, were indifferent to filth. "It does not appear . . . that the general health of the inmates suffers materially" from proximity to dirt.[215] "The Bengali Babu," claimed one indignant writer, reveled in his "filthy surroundings."[216] The idea that the locals were inured to filth was both critique and fear, for that same filth could have grave effects on the cleanly habits of resident or visiting Europeans. In tropical environments, the greatest terror was that while locals might escape with mild inconvenience, the colonizers would be hard-hit by tropically enhanced diseases. Yet there was a deep contradiction in this position, for many doctors and others held to the idea that there were, amongst colonized peoples, those whose extinction was inevitable. Australian aboriginals were, as we have seen, depicted in such a light but other peoples, too, were judged to be amongst the "dying races." Henry Britton, living in Fiji in the 1870s, cheerfully claimed that "the Polynesians will melt away before the sturdy descendants of the British Isles."[217]

Native recalcitrance and filth seemed horribly inevitable. When new municipal structures in the 1880s gave Indians representation on local sanitary boards, colonial doctors were horrified. "It is high time," wrote one angry surgeon, "that the disastrous attempt . . . to teach the natives of India to run in a sanitary course before they had mastered the simplest steps of hygiene, was brought to an abrupt conclusion."[218] The native needed to appreciate the benefits of sanitation before he could run his own country.

Surveillance and Hierarchy

This deep and long-standing mistrust of the locals produced a panoptical and layered mode of surveillance. The registered woman, regarded as likely to flee, to sleep with the wrong men, or to disguise signs of disease, was watched over by her own people—*dhais,* police, subassistant surgeons. In turn, these watchers, equally doubted, were themselves watched for signs of extortion or collusion by European doctors. Since many of those who sought or acquired lock hospital duties were younger men, they too felt upon them the supervisory eye of their seniors. The dizzying vertical structures of this system were clear. In all settings where the CD system operated, lock hospital rules laid out a strict chain of command.

At the Brisbane lock there were no anxieties about native subordinates since neither indigenous nor immigrant populations were regarded as capable of the work. They were seen as a class of manual workers: horse-breakers, trackers, divers, gardeners, and plantation laborers. White and European as the Brisbane hospital staff was, the lines of authority were nonetheless clearly drawn. A surgeon attended thrice weekly, while the matron and submatron were responsible for daily supervision. The matron was directly "responsible to the Dr. for the Management of the institution." She ensured treatment was given, cleanliness maintained, food properly cooked, and paperwork efficiently kept.[219] At Hong Kong, the matron of the refuge for prostitutes was specifically enjoined to obey the rules and these reminded her that she could leave the building only with prior permission.[220] The 1864 Cantonment Act in India instructed the medical officer to "exercise efficient control over the Native, Doctor, Matron and others of the hospital establishment," as well as to fulfill the requisite medical duties. His subordinate's realm was "all matters vernacular" while the matron assisted the native doctor and "might gradually be taught to apply minor details of local dressing & c."[221]

Women avoiding registration were similarly cast not as protesters, but as fettered by ignorance and uncognizant of its benefits. They were seen as the foremost reason for the system's inoperability. Year after year, medical officers complained that women evaded registration and avoided examination. Most of all, though, officials protested the effect of unregistered prostitution. "Unregistered and clandestine prostitution is rife in almost every street in the native town."[222] Clandestine prostitution, claimed many, "is prevalent in all large military stations."[223] In Singapore, officials worried that women disguised their sale of sex by adopting other occupations, especially those who visited the brothels "as hairdressers and seamstresses."[224] Women laborers invariably fell under suspicion. Clandestines in Japan were, said the lock surgeon, "pests to society."[225]

It was not the system but its recipients who made it unworkable; with cooperation and willingness, medical officers were confident the system could flourish. This rhetoric envisaged a cleaner, better, and healthier registered prostitution and a less salubrious and dangerous secret variety. The medical officer at Yokohama even claimed that clandestine "vagrant prostitution" resulted in "a more vicious form" of affliction.[226] The fissures in the system are well illuminated here, for while the brothel was unfortunate and definitionally filthy, it was always, in the vocabulary of registration, a better option than unregistered sex work, beyond control and thus filthier.

This portrait of the stubbornly grubby native made it impossible for the human face of western medicine to be its most common ambassador. Doctors and colonial officials bemoaned the need for but vigorously implemented what they saw as necessary measures of surveillance and coercion brought about by native reluctance and intransigence. As early as 1827, William Burke was recommending "confinement and punishment" for women failing to attend for examination.[227] By the 1870s, officials supported "efficient surveillance and consequent control" as "essential to the thorough working of the Act."[228] Prosecutions for evading the exam or working unregistered were instituted; at the Straits, "recourse to Magisterial coertion" (sic) was advised.[229]

Conclusion

This ambivalence between a Macaulayite vision of the compliant native trained to British specifications and the ever-present fear of a flawed assimilation was constant. Locals would and could ruin the colonial project. The use early in the twentieth century of electricity to advertise brothels became a favorite example of the misuse of progress. Frank Lenwood, of the London Mission in Benares, disapprovingly described the brothels of Lucknow as having "very brilliant" lighting.[230] Henry Champly claimed the western onlooker was blinded by the intensity of the illuminated red-light districts of the east.[231] Moral missionary John Cowen alleged that "the brilliance of electric light and dazzling display" in Singapore's brothel quarters "far outshine any other parts of the town or colony."[232] He was certainly exaggerating, since only one of the city's brothels enjoyed an electricity supply at that date.[233] But the point, made during the war years of 1914–18, articulated not only a misappropriation of progress but a disloyal waste of wartime resources. Brothels were not merely dens of iniquity but were carelessly unpatriotic.[234] Even where they embraced technology, colonial populations could not be trusted to put to good use the benefits of modern society. At one and the same time, colonial peoples both needed what modernization had to offer but could never fully grasp its benefits. The woman failing to appear for her VD check-up or reluctant to swallow western pharmaceuticals was not merely immoral in her choice of livelihood and perhaps spreading disease, but she was also thwarting progress.

This trope of the ignorant native vulgarly putting beneficence to corrupt use, shining light upon that which should not be wholly visible and delighting in the spectacle, made profligacy and abundance seem typically colonial. Western morality abided by a rhetoric of thrift and caution (even in the face of the enormous profits gleaned from the colonies). Tropical colonies were contrasted as great libertine spaces of lax behavior, abundant flora, excessive heat, and overcrowding. The streets and the bazaars were noisy and overflowing, the chatter was ceaseless, the morals as out of control as the lush forests and fruits and the intensely fertile diseases. The cordoning-off of racially and functionally segregated areas imposed the western idea of proper spheres on places seen as out of control by virtue of their luxuriant overblown nature. Technology was, in quite literal ways, ranged against nature, whether that nature was the creeping foliage or the scanty clothing of shameless locals. Thus the horror of misappropriating electric light as a device to sell sex: technology was subsumed into the dangerous nature of the colony rather than taming locals into western ways. Contamination was, in every way, a constant problem, visible in the insect life as much as in human behavior.

It was not hard in such a context, and it was common currency among colonials, to read CD control as unprejudiced, enlightened rationality, even while the reports on its workings vitriolically lambasted women's ugliness, stupidity, dirtiness, or recalcitrance. As we have seen, this concentration on the behavioral allowed the system to remain unsullied while the ignorant could be seen as seeking to bring it down.

> The effect of wider knowledge, of better habitations, better water supplies, and better facilities for ablution and general cleanliness on the gradual decline of venereal diseases in this country during the last quarter of a century, can scarcely be questioned; while to a lack of these essentials one must attribute the absence of an definitive or progressive decline during the same period in garrisons in India and the colonies, where the sanitary control of crowded bazaar populations is difficult and complicated.[235]

This starkly dichotomized view of modernity and tradition saw the colonies as static, unprogressive bastions of tradition, hostile to change and holding back progress. And as Paul Gilroy has so pertinently noted, this was a deeply racialized dichotomy.[236] The CD laws were represented as a rational and scientific approach to a problem magnified by infantile and ignorant behavior. VD control in this dress was thus more than a medical scheme to protect white soldiers from hospitalization and lengthy treatment. It became a commentary on the relationship between sexual morality and political participation. Colonial peoples, constructed as infantile, could be excluded from modern liberalism since liberty would be inappropriate and inapplicable.[237] Coercive measures otherwise inimical to visions of a beneficent modernity could, indeed had, to be applied to those with no appreciation for the liberty of the subject. And it was here that doctors, harnessing their own projects to the reach of colonialism celebrated their role as arbiters of a cleanly, a rational and, above all, a modern civilization with medical rationalism at its very heart. Modernity was at its core a colonial concept and a colonial project, forged and shaped through the implicit comparisons colonialism invited. But the hegemonic intent central to both colonial and medical policy was, of course, unrealizable. Unappreciated by subject populations, the controls deemed fundamental to the success of colonial medicine in general, and the regulation system in particular, faced constant challenges ranging from indifference to hostility to organized opposition.

For all the failures of the medical model to counter venereal diffusion and the poor showing of available treatments, this very instability also gave voice to the most potent of the arguments about colonial modernity: rational behavior as the cornerstone of the modern. Even while a new biomedical paradigm shifted towards a bacteriological reading of disease, reason as the senior partner in ideas of liberty was central to the presentation of modernity. And while medicine operated within the boundaries of that overweening notion of modernity, women and "natives" seldom displayed or appreciated it, and could thus be denied the full privileges accruing from it. This was the central dilemma of the entire colonial enterprise, reliant simultaneously on an invocation of the humane civilizing mission but requiring coercion to achieve that end.[238]

Modern medicine was not, as doctors would have it, a beneficent arm of progress brought to an unappreciatively savage set of populations. Instead what this constant and urgent need to control local populations, to make visible, and to order and cleanse their failings suggests, is that the modernity of medicine was a project produced as much by and in colonial as in metropolitan settings, and through the struggles and accommodations forced, albeit unwillingly, on doctors and officials. As Peter Fitzpatrick has so pithily advanced, "Civilization in modernity is always threatened civilization."[239] The colonies, in sum, were central to the production of modernity and in the reception of medicine as its vanguard. VD played a critical role in that process as a disease that defined native and female distance from modernity.

Chapter 4

Diplomacy, Disease, and Dissent

Although a complete stop had been put to the system in Great Britain and Ireland, yet the vast and varied dependencies of the Empire still suffered from infection derived from the evil example and encouragement of the parent state. It was unwise in the extreme for so many divisions of the great army to throw down their arms because of a successful engagement which did not end the campaign. The main stem of the moral Pupas tree has been cut down but its collateral shoots remained in the soil, and it is in the nature of such noxious vegetation to spring up and flourish whenever and wherever the quagmire of depravity shall favour its growth.

—Sheldon Amos

It is not too much to assert that the English Government in India well merits the ugly and terrible title, used in Scripture, of *whoremonger*, of which *procurer* is the gentler-sounding Latin synonym.

—Josephine Butler

From the late 1880s, controversy would dog the various Contagious Diseases (CD) acts and ordinances around the globe. While the sheer ferocity of colonial abolitionist campaigns is striking, that vigor also suggests the deep and inextricable relation between metropolitan and colonial politics, and the centrality within that politics of topics routinely excluded from the public sphere—sexuality, especially female sexuality, and sexually transmissible diseases. Though never wholly successful, the repeal campaign nonetheless revealed a vulnerability in colonial governance; governments were forced into major and often highly public political maneuverings on policies that intruded the bedroom into the boardroom. The fact that the regulation controversy was widespread and not confined only to one or two colonies underscored a liability that contemporary politicians recognized only too well. Over and over again, the regulation debates of the 1880s and 1890s were the flashpoint for tensions between metropolitan and colonial power. And the fact that public opinion about empire could be shaped by sex was an extraordinary development that repealers used to their advantage.

In June 1888 a resolution passed in the House of Commons that made it necessary for instructions to be sent to the governor general in India to dismantle

CD legislation. The repeal of the domestic acts in 1886, following their suspension three years earlier, was less the closing of a legislative chapter than the first step in a new and vigorous campaign to abolish regulated prostitution throughout the empire. Repeal activists, already angry at the widespread use of CD laws in the empire, exploited their own domestic success as well as conflicts in imperial territories to highlight this gap between domestic and colonial policy. The 1888 resolution was one segment of a larger campaign committed to destroying all regulation. While India attracted the most political attention, reformers kept a close watch on other colonial arenas, and maintained close contact with abolitionist groups in the empire.[1]

Prostitution regulation had been under attack for well over a decade, and the opposition in and out of parliament was well-organized and articulate. The political furor in the Commons was such that the system could not be left wholly untouched. Fear of parliamentary censure was a motivating factor in the wake of British repeal. The Colonial Office urged action rather than political humiliation. "I suppose as we have given way and repealed the law in England we shall not make any fight on behalf of the principle in those Colonies which are subject to control . . . If so, it may be more dignified to take a decision before the inevitable Parl[t] censure is applied to us."[2]

Shortly after home repeal, the Colonial Office sought the views of colonial governors on CD legislation. In October 1886, Edward Stanhope (first colonial secretary in Salisbury's Unionist government of 1886–1892) advised governors of the parliamentary condemnation and abolition of the domestic CD acts, requesting, "that if your Government should be of opinion that the interests of the Colony imperatively require the continuance of these laws, I may be furnished with any special reasons they may have for that opinion."[3] In several colonies, the laws had lapsed either in practice or statutorily (Canada's in 1870[4] and St. Helena's in 1879), and there was no clamor for revival. Trinidad's act was "practically inoperative."[5] At Barbados, the military and the medical authorities disagreed as to the efficacy of the system. In these colonies repeal was easily achieved, garnering little attention either locally or in Britain.

Colonial Opposition

Elsewhere, however, colonial authorities strenuously protested the prospect of losing the system they had operated, in some cases for thirty years. In Hong Kong, in the Straits Settlements, in Ceylon and in Fiji, as well as in the European colonies of Gibraltar and Malta, governors warned against abandoning the CD system. The basis of their opposition made apparent the importance of racial stratification beyond the domestic realm. The governor of Fiji highlighted the decay of the Fijian "race" and the prevalence of VD among the colony's indentured labor force.[6] The Jamaican governor sent the Colonial Office a letter from one of his military officers whose plea for retention was founded on a belief in the fundamental uncleanliness of "black men."[7] Local officials in Penang thought the "system of unrestricted male immigration" necessitated control.[8] The governor of Gibraltar argued that, "[I]t must not be lost sight of that in this colony there is a great mixture of races, viz., Spaniards, foreign seamen, Moors and Arabs who frequent the resorts of low women." Their presence increased the dangers to British naval men.[9]

The Straits and Hong Kong governors both argued that the system afforded vulnerable women a protection against outright slavery. Without the laws, cruel brothel keepers would mercilessly exploit women with no regard for their health and well-being. Though George Johnson at the Colonial Office doubted that the overworked Chinese protectors could ever make much difference to the lives of more than a handful of brothel women, others among his colleagues demurred. "We shall be accepting a terrible responsibility if ... we condemn the slave prostitutes of the Straits to the awful fate ... [of] the entire repeal of the Ordinance."[10] The need for a CD system was articulated as critically encompassing but also extending beyond the protection of imperial troops to arguments about the colonies themselves and Britain's imperial role.

The Repeal Position

Repeal activists closely monitored the colonial scene. The Baptist Missionary Society logged the presence of camp followers in India in 1872, and David Pivar argues that "anti-prostitution agitation" in India was kept alive by growing indigenous resistance and determined reformers.[11] The British, Continental and General Federation for the Abolition of Government Regulation of Prostitution, founded in 1875, included on its executive committee Calcutta activist Keshub Chander Sen, and South African repealer, Saul Solomon.[12] The Colonial Office was aware in 1879 of "commun[ication]s ... between the opponents of the Acts in England and some Person or Persons in Hong Kong."[13] In 1882, the National Association for the Repeal of the CD Acts issued a pamphlet drawing attention to Hong Kong's CD ordinance.[14] And in 1883, a deputation had met with Lord Derby (colonial secretary, December 1882 to June 1885) to urge abolition or modification of regulation.[15] Thus when antiregulation activist Josephine Butler, in an address to her followers in 1887, began by claiming that "[M]any things seem to point to the fact that we are about to enter on a second chapter of our great Abolitionist crusade," the groundwork had already been laid.[16] Both the campaigners and the politicians knew that a fight was imminent. George Johnson predicted in September 1886 that "it is certain that Parliamentary agitation will very soon be raised against the whole system in the Crown Colonies."[17] And, indeed, there had scarcely been a time when backbenchers in the Commons had not kept in the public eye the existence of empire-wide regulation. In 1887, anti-CD Liberal Harcourt Johnstone had asked the colonial secretary in the Commons about revenue raised from the licensing of brothels, and in 1881 a damning report on the working of the Hong Kong CD ordinance was a prominent and scandalous domestic news item.[18]

The Hong Kong report, occasioned by the death of two women fleeing from a CD inspector, was coterminous with the report in India of the Colvin Committee, appointed to assess the system's success in preventing VD.[19] Always controversial the imperial CD system was in strife even while the focus of opposition groups was on domestic repeal. When reformers turned their full attention on the empire, they faced a system already weakened by internal disagreement and ambivalence. While almost all senior military and medical personnel favored its maintenance, debates over funding the system dogged government officials. They were faced, too, with increasingly organized opposition within the colonies. Some of this came from powerful local religious dignitaries. Colonial bishops, backed by the bishops in the House of Lords, weighed in against regulation. The bishop of Bombay complained to the presidency governor in 1880 about the legalization of the brothel in India, a "peculiarly objectionable feature from which the English Acts are free."[20] Among the colonized, too, there was considerable opposition to what was popularly seen as the sacrifice of local women for imperial need. Rao Mandlik of the Bombay Municipal Corporation publicly blasted the Indian CD Act as "retrograde" legislation.[21]

The System in Crisis

In the 1880s, especially in India, the system was mostly shrinking rather than growing. The Bombay municipality withdrew all funding in 1872, rendering the act inoperable in the city. Calcutta suspended the act a decade later. Governor general Lord Ripon told the India secretary in 1882 that "the majority of us think that the Act had better be repealed," noting the dissent of the military members of his council.[22]

> The time has come to abandon a measure which has never in practice been a complete success, which is odious in the eyes of our Native subjects and in those of a large and influential class of Europeans, and which imposes on the taxpayers of the interior a burden which ought, if it exists at all, to be borne entirely by the inhabitants of the towns concerned.[23]

The Marquis of Hartington at the India Office, a veteran politician, disagreed.[24] Under attack, the home government was reluctant to repeal domestic CD laws which, in that same year, were the subject of a closely scrutinized Commons select committee. To repeal a major colonial chapter of the law at that moment would have been, of course, to concede defeat, signaling that metropolitan policy could be dictated by the periphery. As a sop, Hartington permitted a suspension of the Indian CD Act in January 1883.[25] But in April of that year, opposition MPs, led by James Stansfeld, secured a convincing vote against the domestic CD acts and Hartington himself announced their suspension the following month, despite the select committee's majority recommendation to maintain them. Hartington was one of only three cabinet ministers still supporting the acts, and these three were made responsible for articulating the government's response to the April vote.[26] It was Hartington and not the home secretary, William Harcourt, who made the relevant parliamentary speech, despite Harcourt's direct responsibility for administering the domestic acts. Hartington's central role suggests that the links between imperial and domestic legislation, if not yet wholly explicit, were transparent to policy makers who knew that an attention to the colonial arena would almost certainly follow domestic suspension. Hartington made no secret of his pro-CD views; writing to Bombay's governor, James Fergusson, in July 1880, he had worried that the new Liberal administration might be vulnerable on this question, as indeed it was. His own commitment was firm, however: "I have always been myself in favour of these Acts and I hope that we shall be able to maintain them both here and at Foreign Stations."[27]

In the spring and summer of 1887, Henry Holland, Stanhope's successor at the Colonial Office, instructed virtually every colony to repeal the CD ordinances. Fiji was given a temporary stay, while Hong Kong and the Straits Settlements were permitted to continue brothel registration but not the compulsory examination of brothel workers. Ceylon, which had hoped to remain untouched until the situation in India was clear, was instructed to repeal its ordinance fully in January 1888.[28] The apparent decisiveness of the Colonial Office threw repealers off the scent, at least temporarily, and it was to India that the spotlight in the later 1880s turned. It would be the 1890s before the clash between colonial and imperial governments elsewhere attracted more attention from the abolitionist campaign than did India. With its substantial troop presence, its political centrality, its separate administration, and the turmoil over the laws, India was the perfect canvas for the protesters, and the growing strength of a nationalist movement there helped light the fires of discontent.

Alfred Dyer in India

Alfred Dyer, a Congregationalist turned Quaker, had been using his publishing business for some years to publicize the scope of regulation in the colonies.[29] As well as publishing the annual reports of the British abolitionist federation, Dyer was an indefatigable pamphleteer, and in 1888 began publishing from and about India. *The Black Hand of Authority in India* accurately claimed that British authorities supported and even sometimes funded cantonment brothels. "At Deolali where the English soldier lads are taken direct on their arrival in India, my heart was deeply stirred as I stood on the border of this large camp and beheld, planted within a stone's throw of the school of the Church Missionaries, the official quarters of the licensed prostitutes."[30]

While Dyer was luridly describing the contiguity of houses of the lord and dens of iniquity, another activist in India, W. C. Madge, was bombarding the government of India with requests for information on the CD Act and on lock hospitals.[31] In Britain, memorials against the system were disrupting business at the India Office and, to a lesser extent, at the Colonial Office. Many of these were prompted by the circulation of a letter addressed to the Indian press, penned by Butler and James Stuart (a Cambridge academic and member of parliament, 1884 to 1910), calling for repeal and reminding campaigners that Ripon had supported repeal in 1882. In July 1887, the bishop of Lichfield raised in the House of Lords the question central to Dyer's pamphlet. Were there, he wanted to know, official regulations providing for prostitutes in the regimental bazaar? It was six months before the Indian government responded to official enquiries on the topic, and not without prompting.[32] Then came Dyer's next exposé. This time he sketched a map illustrating arrangements at the northerly cantonment of Bareilly, clearly showing how much closer were the tents of the "licensed harlots" to those of the East Kent regiment than was the Temperance Tent.[33] The political effect was tremendous; prorepeal parliamentarians raised embarrassing questions in the House. Throughout the early months of 1888, ministers faced regular questioning. Meetings at Exeter Hall slammed government's failure to end what the Gospel Purity Association dubbed (with the telling rhetoric of contagion) "licensed plague spots."[34]

But Dyer was saving his best weapon until last. In May 1888, he published a copy of what rapidly became known as the "infamous memorandum." Widely reprinted, this was a circular memorandum distributed throughout the army in India, signed by E. F. Chapman, quartermaster general in India from 1885 to 1889. The memo reasoned that if attractive women were supplied in sufficient number to staff the brothels and provided with "proper houses" and "means of ablution," the system would be more efficacious. Soldiers, Chapman thought, would "recognise" and appreciate such "convenient arrangements" and thereby avoid unnecessary risk.[35] The document dated from June 1886, coinciding with the final repeal of domestic CD legislation and unmistakably out of step with prevailing British opinion.

Its impact was electric. Though Chapman had not lied in his responses to Dyer's first set of allegations—the papers finally forwarded to Whitehall in January 1886—he had not mentioned this damningly frank memorandum. Other circular memoranda showed that the army had been consistent in its policy. In 1883, commanding officers were reminded that registered women were not allowed non-European clients; in 1884, Chapman urged the provision of free quarters for licensed women.[36] Indubitably, as the viceroy recognized, "many of the official circulars in existence imply that it is the duty of commanding officers to provide attractive women for the soldiery."[37]

A Colonial Unraveling

The new Conservative incumbent at the India Office, Lord Cross, was not pleased.[38] Not only did these revelations ensure uproar in parliament but the Conservatives faced almost certain defeat on the issue, which would mean repealing both the Indian CD Act and the 1864 Cantonment Act. In India, Dufferin was already pressing repeal of the Indian CD Act in March 1888.[39]

Under pressure from reformers in India, and knowing that municipal authorities were reluctant to fund the system, Dufferin counseled repeal, nonetheless
noting that "we are deeply impressed with the necessity of maintaining the provisions of the existing law which apply to our cantonments."[40] But Cross feared
that Chapman's "casuistry . . . and this miserable Circular [have] increased our
difficulties a hundredfold."[41] He told his viceroy that "questions would be asked
every week in the House as to what is being done."[42]

Cross was quite right about the extent of the political damage, but the harm
was palpably greater than in the policy arena alone. For a Liberal opposition,
mismanagement of empire was always a useful tool, and the moral questions at
stake were amplified since government had been caught lying to men of god on
a question of urgent morality. All this allowed the mainly Liberal opponents of
regulation to link their campaign to larger questions of governance, invoking
the specter of home rule as well as of whether the current Conservative administration could be trusted. In a privately circulated letter to repealers in June 1888,
Josephine Butler linked Indian nationalism and Irish home rule, warning that
the continued existence of the Cantonment Act might allow a military already
proven underhand to exercise "the same immoral tyranny as before."[43]

J. A. Godley, permanent under secretary at the India Office, had already
predicted that "the question of the Contagious Disease Regulations is a test of
the strength of the Government's back."[44] But while attention was focused so
intensely on India, the Colonial Office, Sir Henry Holland now at the helm,
was engaged in battles with both the Hong Kong and the Straits Settlements
administrations over what should replace their CD ordinances. These internal
struggles, in which Straits governor Frederick Weld was dismissed for resisting
Colonial Office orders, were not attended to with any great ardor by the antiregulationists, but in many respects they set the stage for the dramatic struggles
of the 1890s. In both colonies, the CD ordinances were replaced by Women
and Girls' Protection (WGP) ordinances. Most importantly, perhaps, the fight
between 1887 and 1889 is the first episode in what would be a decade-long battle
between Westminster and colonial governments over who had the right to legislate locally. The assumed impact of VD on military efficiency and expenditure
and the moral grounds of empire-building were huge questions in this period,
and fought primarily though not exclusively over the issues raised by the 1888
House of Commons resolution—compulsory examination and the licensing of
prostitute women.

While the protectors of Chinese and local medical officials in Hong Kong and
the Straits were unhappy about giving up the periodical examination, they saved
their loudest protests for the dangers attached to relinquishing brothel registration and licensing. Firmly convinced that prostitution was a form of slavery
against which the ordinances had provided a minimal bulwark, proregulationists painted a picture of rising exploitation and savagery alongside an inevitable
escalation in infection. Governor Weld dropped all pretence of diplomatic

language in writing to Holland in the autumn of 1887: "to abandon compulsory examination is to continue one of the gravest abuses resulting from brothel slavery."[45] He pursued much the same tactic with his Legislative Council. "I regret being the mouthpiece of the Secretary of State on this occasion, but it is my duty, as I have stated, to ask the Council to pass this measure."[46] He was rapidly replaced by the more malleable Cecil Clementi Smith, though replacing the governor did not stem the spirited opposition to repeal among the colony's white residents and Chinese elite.

In Hong Kong, Colonial Office constraints were successfully avoided for a while. The intent, with Clementi Smith in charge at the Straits, was to have the two colonies adopt the same policy, outlawing compulsion but maintaining registration.[47] The new Straits ordinance was the model for both colonies. No less angry than Weld, Hong Kong's governor, George W. Des Vœux, was more politic in his approach, sending an elaborately drafted ordinance to the Colonial Office only after publishing it locally in the *Hong Kong Gazette*.[48] Cleverly, it used much the same language as Britain's Criminal Law Amendment Act of 1885. Unlike the U.K. legislation, the ordinance did not propose a female age of consent, but highlighted children aged six to fifteen as being of special concern. The ordinance was long and detailed, with separate sections on brothel management, lock hospitals, and the powers of the registrar general, as well as procuration and abduction. It was these that persuaded the colonial secretary to preserve registration. Des Vœux's stalling tactics worked until 1890 when the Colonial Office finally compelled the colony's acquiescence.[49]

The Straits under Clementi Smith's leadership proved more amenable to imperial dictate, though in detailing his ordinance Smith informed the colonial secretary that while "everything will be done to ameliorate the condition of the women . . . this Government considers that their principal safeguard has, under your instructions, been removed."[50] Ordinance XIV of 1888 provided free voluntary treatment in lock hospitals and continued the practice of registering brothels. The definition of the brothel both at the Straits and Hong Kong was directly racial. Holland had told both governors in 1887 that "it is a matter of consideration whether this should apply to other than Chinese brothels."[51] In the legislation promulgated, exclusively non-Asian houses of prostitution were explicitly exempted from the definition of what constituted a brothel, and thus not affected by the new ordinances, upholding James Warren's assessment of the Straits legislation as "politic rather than just."[52]

Warren points out that the new law ran "roughshod over local opinion and knowledge."[53] In the Chinese colonies, in India, and elsewhere, the events set in motion by domestic repeal in 1886 and the Commons resolution of 1888, raised the question of the relationship between home and empire, and under governments of significantly different persuasion. While Salisbury's Unionist administrations (1886–1892, 1895–1902) felt the brunt of the debate, the Liberals Gladstone and Rosebery were not exempt. Indeed, the contradiction between formal Liberal rejection of regulated prostitution and its continued use in the 1880s added bitterness to the debates of the 1890s. In 1895, Josephine Butler reminded a supporter of how often the Liberals had disappointed the cause.[54] At a time of domestic electoral expansion, this controversy spoke to the place of democracy and representative government in powerful ways. Many politicians deplored the effects of the wider franchise.[55] The deeply Conservative Lord Cross wrote grumpily to the governor of Madras, Lord Connemara, of the "unreasoning democracy" spurring on the repeal movement.[56] To Lord Reay, Cross complained of "the effects that faddists amongst the constituents have upon their representatives in this Democratic Parl[iamen]t."[57] His viceroy, Lord Dufferin, loathed the "raging sisterhood who are troubling our mental purity by their obscene correspondence."[58] Feminists, radicals, and democrats were held responsible for this unwelcome controversy.

Imperial Discipline

Complicating the situation was the overwhelmingly hostile British response to repeal in the colonies. Colonial governors were consistently forced to override the majority opinions of their advisory councils, and the colonial and India secretaries found themselves frequently insisting on the need for political discipline. These were not common clashes beyond the CD controversy; it was rare for colonial and imperial administrations not to find agreement on policy. In Hong Kong's entire colonial history, there were only fifteen occasions on which the Colonial Office moved to quash an ordinance passed by the Legislative Council and signed into law by the governor.[59] The 1890s were a period of unusual tension between Hong Kong politicians and Westminster, but it was only on this issue that resentment spilled over into outright and public defiance by local politicians.[60]

In India, too, the governor was obliged to impose metropolitan decisions on his council, and governors knew that lack of cooperation was grounds for dismissal, as Frederick Weld had discovered at the Straits in 1887. Lords Dufferin and Lansdowne (viceroys respectively from 1884 to 1888, and from 1888 to 1894) were fully as occupied with attempting to smooth over dissent as was Lansdowne's successor, the Earl of Elgin.[61]

In the first instance, the Indian presidencies took much the same steps as had the Straits and Hong Kong in outlawing the compulsory examination of women but continuing registration and licensing.[62] The changes were nugatory, the military preferring to wait for the outcome of the inevitable political struggle. In May 1888, there was uproar not in India but in London, at the meeting of the Council of India, whose opinion the India secretary could, and on this occasion did, abrogate. Of the thirteen members present on 14 May, only four besides the secretary of state favored the curtailment of existing legislation. Sir John Strachey, one of the architects of the Bengal legislation, warned that the order would be "received with disapproval and regret by the Government of India and by almost every Indian authority."[63] Secretary Cross recorded that "he did not concur in the opinion of the majority and that he should send the Despatch to India."[64] Even one of the minority who assented, General Sir D. M. Stewart, thought the proposals wrongheaded. In a letter intended to alert Dufferin to the contested despatch, he argued that "if more time had been given for the consideration of the draft, I believe the opposition of the Council would have been unanimous."[65] Ripon, remembering his own former troubles on the matter, advised the governor general on the political consequences of refusal. "I hope your Government will not be induced to retain the Contagious Diseases' (sic) Act . . . resistance . . . will be in vain and will only lead to mischief."[66] But though the government of India demanded suspension of the Indian CD Act in Bombay, Madras, and Bassein, it took six weeks for the order to be implemented, and the Bombay government admitted that women were being compulsorily examined even after officials knew of the order.[67]

The new Cantonment Act of 1889 made no mention of VD. Instead, it allowed for exclusion from cantonments of "disorderly persons," means for preventing the spread of infectious and contagious afflictions by excluding suspected persons, and for the suppression of "loitering or importuning for the purpose of prostitution."[68] Its proponents argued that the new rules put VD on the same footing as other contagious and infectious diseases. Private internal memoranda suggest otherwise and senior officials deliberately sought to put repealers off the scent. Sir John Gorst, writing to Cross in July 1889, suggested amendments which he thought would evade "the virtual compulsory examination, or at least make[s] its compulsory character less obvious."[69]

Opposition remained nonetheless widespread. In the cantonments, there was fear of increased policing. Domestic activists mistrusted the willingness of the authorities to relinquish the old system.[70] Politicized Indians, restless with the closely supervised rule of colonialism, saw an opportunity to criticize the workings of empire. An editorial in *The Bengalee* welcomed the repudiation of the system but questioned colonial power.

> There is a little episode in connection with the Contagious Diseases Acts which illustrates the utter uselessness of the India Council and its complete want of power in matters where the Secretary of State has made up his mind . . . The majority were in favour of the retention of the Act. We are glad they were over-ruled, but would still further rejoice if the Council were altogether done away with, and its place occupied by a Standing Committee of the House of Commons.[71]

Reformers might have been focused on India, but other colonies were putting up a fight. The *Indian Medical Journal* noted "the battle between the Governor and the Home Authorities" in neighboring Ceylon.[72] In the Straits, miscreant governor Frederick Weld spoke openly of his support for Ceylon's governor,

Arthur Gordon, and though his defiance lost him his job, Weld enjoyed considerable local support.[73] Feelings ran high in the Legislative Council about the heavy-handed demands from the home government. Weld bitterly called himself "the mouthpiece of the Secretary of State."[74] In Hong Kong, too, repeal was "forced through a dissenting Legislative Council by the use of the official majority."[75] Official members, unlike their non-official counterparts, were obliged to support government policy.

Retaining the System

Settler colonists ignored, often to the dismay of both the Colonial Office and abolitionists, the storms raging around the CD question. Queensland maintained its law, despite local protest from women's and Christian groups. The colony's medical officer, William Hobbs, a staunch proregulationist and active politician, claimed with some pride that Queensland was unique in its "attempt to resist this disease," calling upon other Australian colonies to follow suit.[76] Queensland's would be the most tenacious of the Australian CD laws, rebuffing attempts to rescind in 1884 and 1886. In 1886 Henry Jordan, a Wesleyan missionary turned politician, brought a motion to repeal before the Legislative Assembly. "I sincerely hope that we shall not be the very last [colony] in repealing."[77] Supporters of the act stirred up racial alarm. The colony's premier, Sir Hugh Nelson, dismissed women's support of Jordan, claiming that "a very large proportion of them have not the slightest idea of the nature of the Act." And he invoked the much-feared specter of black infection spinning out of control. "Does he know," he asked of Jordan in the Assembly, "that nearly half of the black population of Australia has perished from it [syphilis], and that there are many islands in the Pacific now where scarcely a man, woman, or child is free from it?"[78] Such hyperbole carried the day. The act was never formally repealed, though beginning in 1912 its provisions were rescinded piecemeal. Some towns—Mackay in 1899, Bundaberg, more than once—did request the extension of the act to their locality, but other municipalities ignored the system, as was the case by 1900 in Maryborough and Cooktown.[79]

Evidently settler colonists, while looking to Britain itself, saw little need to attend to practice in the crown colonies. Natal attempted to pass a CD act in 1886; it was narrowly rejected in committee. At Cape Town, the CD Prevention Act (No. 39) of 1885 was deprecated by activists for its "unexampled stringency."[80] When an antiregulationist deputation met in 1894 with Sir Henry Lock (former governor of Bechuanaland), their leader, Walter McLaren, MP for Crewe, emphasized that "it was only in a few of our self-governing colonies that any traces of it [the CD system] remained."[81] This retention of CD laws in white settler lands was deeply disappointing to abolitionists, but they could not nor would not intervene against other white societies. The British abolitionist federation left regulation in settler colonies "up to the discretion of their respective governments."[82] It was a bitter pill for them to swallow, but they and their supporters argued that it was in India "that the gravest iniquities are perpetrated . . . under the sanction or by the connivance or indifference of the British authorities."[83]

The 1890s proved the most contentious decade in the system's history, even though regulation had been formally rescinded in most of the empire in the late 1880s. In many instances the entire apparatus of control was swept away, but key Asian colonies maintained many facets of the system. India, Hong Kong, and the Straits all retained the right to operate lock hospitals, though in India they were re-classified as voluntary venereal hospitals. George Johnson pointed out that at Hong Kong and the Straits "we do not propose to shut up the Lock Hospital," but that "we must I think use other means (besides compulsion) gradually to convince the women that they are free."[84] The WGP ordinances kept the system virtually intact: "the registration fee and compulsory medical examination ceased, but in other respects and as far as the provisions for the protection of inmates of brothels are concerned, the [CD] Ordinance is still being carried out."[85]

At the India Office, Lord Cross advised his viceroy in private correspondence that "you may easily keep the same restraining power without having this appearance even of 'licensing'"[86] The Indian authorities worked hard to appear willing while giving up as little control as possible. It was this sly intransigence which made India yet again a focus through most of the 1890s, and which provoked radical abolitionists who saw colonial power as ugly and autocratic. Indeed, the Friends' Association for Abolishing the State Regulation of Vice claimed that "British officials [in India] have been in the habit of exercising autocratic power."[87]

The fervent hope of governments was that by restricting the system's reach to indigenous peoples, it would find acceptance. In framing the new Cantonment Act of 1889, Dufferin and his council urged the necessity of military authority over "the mixed and frequently disreputable civil population which is attracted to our cantonments."[88] In the Chinese colonies, protectors emphasized the alleged brutalization of helpless Chinese women. And in Natal, where a second attempt at introducing a CD act was halted only by the intervention of the Colonial Office in 1890, the proregulation governor outlined a catalogue of racial ignorance and ill-health in support of the law. "These diseases were more or less common in the country districts, principally among the native and coolie Indian population . . . [the] vast number of barbarous, or semi-barbarous, people of native race . . . are ignorant of the danger . . . incapable of taking precautions against it . . . and . . . are peculiarly exposed to the evil results of its contagion."[89] In reaching for reasons to introduce or maintain the regulation of sex work, the tendency was to underline the beneficent and protective advantages offered to native populations as much as to stress their importance for military efficiency and soldierly well-being. The optimism of civilizing altruism was wielded alike by anti- and proregulationists. That reading of empire would be closely questioned in the 1890s.

Colonial Responses

Lord Cross had, with surprising naiveté, told Dufferin in 1888 that "I cannot imagine that we shall have any more trouble about the C.D. Acts & c."[90] What ensued in the 1890s, however, made the earlier debates seem mild, as wave after wave of accusation rocked the Colonial and India Offices. When the Earl of Elgin, viceroy in India from 1894 to 1898, sent an urgent telegram to the secretary of state in 1895 about this very issue, he advised: "Constitutional crisis too grave for private communication alone."[91] What brought Elgin to the brink was the range and depth of protest from organized antiregulationists on one side, and from those protesting the withdrawal of the system, on the other. And yet again, while India was the focal point for these varied hostilities, Hong Kong and the Straits also fiercely battled over these laws.

Dissatisfaction with or support for the CD system cannot be categorized simply into a neat metropole-periphery framework, as the pragmatic alliances between imperial feminists and nationalist groups demonstrate. Colonial opinion divided along class and status lines. Chinese elites mostly called for the reintroduction of the local CD ordinances.[92] The Indian press largely celebrated repeal. The *Indian Spectator* called for "a national thanksgiving" in 1888, while *The Bengalee* thought the CD Act "a scandal and a disgrace."[93] *The Pioneer*, out of Allahabad and a semi-official organ, was an unsurprising exception, predicting the "ruin of the health of the Calcutta garrison." Calcutta's *Hindoo Patriot* also favored the legislation and thought the act "smooth and successful in its working."[94]

Women affected by the laws were not shy with their opinions either. Though medical officers stressed those infrequent moments when women begged for the retention of the system, the record is full of formal complaints as well as fines for escape and noncompliance, tell-tale signs of defiance and dislike. At the Straits, there were "many" complaints, "most in the shape of anonymous letters."[95] There are a dozen or more cases in India where women formally protested registration or complained about treatment. These petitions were usually signed by groups of women and thus represent quite large numbers.[96] Significantly perhaps, not one of these petitions has survived in the archives. Relegated to the minor proceedings not sent to London, none of these petitions have endured. All that remains are indices noting their receipt. This erasure perhaps suggests official attempts to play down the volume of female protest, perhaps a lack of interest in what women, and especially poor and "unrespectable" women, had to say.

In Hong Kong and the Straits, not even records as paltry as those in India have survived. The protectors of Chinese insisted that they daily dealt with women's complaints, but in keeping with the received wisdom that the women were mute and ignorant creatures, their protests are seldom individualized in the records. An occasional case of abduction reached the courts or the desk of an official, but in these colonies, what we hear almost invariably is the voice of the protector. And that univocality made the WGP ordinances more tenable, arguing as they did that brothel women needed someone outside the system working on their behalf.

Antiregulationist Activities

In 1890, the British, Continental and General Federation renamed itself, in equally cumbersome fashion, the British Committee for the Abolition of the State Regulation of Vice in India and throughout the British Dominions. That change in nomenclature signaled the intent of Butler, Stuart, Stansfeld, and their supporters to focus on empire. They actively sought information on conditions in India, collecting evidence to support their contention that regulation and examination endured. Throughout 1891 and 1892, their supporters visited Indian cantonments and interviewed returned soldiers in Britain. Colonel Banon, a former Bengal officer, was the committee's formal paid agent in India.[97] He was convinced that "the authorities are evidently feeling their way to see how far they will be permitted to go without exposure. Their intention is, and they have gone a very long way towards it, to re-establish the old routine condemned by Parliament."[98] William Huntly, a clergyman in the Bombay presidency, had much the same to say: "To all intents and purposes the old regime is enforced."[99] Dyer and his publishing associate, Wallace J. Gladwin, sent colorful and prurient reports of infamous behavior. Gladwin and R. H. Madden, the Bombay city missionary, penned a report in 1892 entitled "Horrible Things in Bombay," full of lurid details of scantily clad women carousing with uniformed men.[100] Dyer also investigated conditions in Hong Kong, the Straits, and Shanghai, sending reports back to Quaker abolitionist groups in Britain.

As the 1880s drew to a close, controversy coalesced around the compulsory examination. Interviews with returned soldiers confirmed abolitionist suspicions, but it was the report of two American women missionaries that attracted the most attention. Elizabeth Andrew and Katharine Bushnell reached India in December 1892. On a world tour for the World Women's Christian Temperance Union, the two women had stopped in England expressly to meet Josephine Butler, with whom they developed a close rapport. Butler had always regarded Dyer with suspicion, but regarded Bushnell and Andrew as fellow devotees. She told her associates that she was "much struck with them," and with their "deep and strong convictions."[101] At her urging, the two Americans undertook to provide information on India. The medically trained Bushnell had investigated prostitution in American lumber camps in the 1880s, had worked as a missionary in China, and was no newcomer to feminist controversy. Andrew, long active in temperance circles, was the widow of a Methodist minister.[102] Convinced that they were engaged on the lord's work—"we were not ordinary detectives . . . but Christian women"[103]—and funded by the British abolitionists, they lectured in South Africa, moving around the Cape to India in the cooler season. They remained in northern India some months before moving onto New Zealand and Australia. In India, they spent time in ten of the major north Indian British cantonments, visiting hospitals and lal bazaars, interviewing officials and prostitute women to whom they also offered the message of the gospels. At the end of March 1892, they furnished the British committee with a lengthy report and with a journal of their doings. The report, much of which found its way into their published account, *The Queen's Daughters in India* (1899), outlined their charges against the government, while the journal recorded their experiences and quantified their achievements: "We have travelled 3,597 miles and have visited ten military stations . . . We have studied 637 cases of cantonment prostitutes in these stations; we have interviewed 395 persons; 11 hospital *dhais*; 18 *mahaldarnis*; 6 native physicians . . . 34 patients in Lock Hospitals, 2 district pleaders, and various other persons."[104] The sheer size of their enterprise was among the reasons their work attracted so much attention. Their basic claim was that the old system was intact and flourishing; as they would later sum it up, they saw everywhere "the iron law of the military regulation," which enslaved and terrorized countless impoverished women from "almost every part of Asia and Africa."[105] Theirs was a multifaceted condemnation, espying a sexual slave trade alongside a state sanctioning of incorrigible soldierly behavior. The commander in chief in India, George White, was bitter in his condemnation of the two investigators. They "came to India with the intention of establishing that the practice under the Cantonment Act was not in accordance with the resolution of the House of Commons."[106]

There is little doubt that Bushnell and Andrew did know what they were looking for, and that this shaped their itinerary and their activities.[107] But their assertions were verified not only by other repeal-minded travelers, but officially. John Hyslop Bell, a retired journalist paid by the British committee to investigate in India, thought "it would be impossible to break down their evidence," which he regarded as error-free.[108] More tellingly, the Earl of Kimberley (who replaced Cross at the India Office in 1892, his second stint) admitted that the women's assertions were substantially proven.[109] The governor general thought Andrew and Bushnell's "deductions" from the facts "erroneous," but did not deny the facts.[110] The volte-face of the recently retired commander in chief, Frederick Sleigh Roberts, who switched from blanket denial of the charges to a public apology to Bushnell and Andrew, made the government's position much trickier; as Kimberley remarked to Lansdowne, "Roberts really gave away your case entirely."[111]

Matters came to a head when Bushnell and Andrew returned to Britain. Ian Tyrrell has suggested that they waited to reveal their findings for tactical reasons. They had, after all, left India in the middle of 1892 but only the British committee was then privy to their report, which was not made public until April 1893. Tyrrell suggests that they may have been waiting for the Liberal party—more sympathetic to abolitionist aims, and perhaps more easily embarrassed into action on the issue—to secure a parliamentary victory in the 1892 election.[112] In the event, the election was indecisive, though Gladstone was returned to office for his final ministry. The timing, however, was more likely engineered by James Stansfeld. Stansfeld advised the executive committee (of which he was chair) that "in his opinion the time for Parliamentary action was at hand" and that he wanted to move in February of the following year for a formal committee of enquiry. With the executive's backing, he wrote to Bushnell and Andrew, asking them to be in England as "soon after Mar 1 1893" as possible, and enclosing fifty pounds towards their expenses.[113] As Stansfeld saw it, there was no point in disclosing the findings without the authors present.

Lord Elgin doubted that, as "virtuous women," they could have understood the brothel conditions they investigated.[114] Yet their testimony was clearly compelling. Kenneth Ballhatchet argues that "the thought that two respectable ladies had seen indelicate things . . . was bound to excite Victorian public opinion."[115] Tyrrell suggests that their exposure of interracial contact within a religious and feminist vocabulary gained them attention.[116] Yet none of this was entirely new. The respectable woman acknowledging an understanding of physical intimacy had been at the heart of the domestic campaign against the CD acts; by 1893, it was old hat and not particularly newsworthy. Interracial sex always excited concern, but was hardly a novel revelation by the mid-1890s though it could always be relied upon for an easy route to scandal. Likely, the women's Americanness allowed them a certain openness of expression, but their unchaperoned travel and their ability to turn their investigations into a logical and damning report which would stand up to scrutiny caught the public attention. For all their devout homilies about putting themselves in the hands of their maker, here were two doughty women who could induce reluctant rickshaw drivers to take them to the local brothel, who could walk into the office of the cantonment medical officer and demand to see his files. Damning as their findings were, their methods were exciting and their shrewd insistence on playing the part of modest women doing only their Christian duty had immense appeal. The abolitionists had plenty of other material—soldier testimony, reports from other travelers, investigators, and formal agents—to hand, but it was that provided by the two missionary women that secured the appointment of the 1893 committee of inquiry that Stansfeld himself would dominate.

Indian officials complained that John Hyslop Bell, in India at much the same time, mislead them. Bell, one complained, had made representations about himself "which I could only interpret as a desire on his part to convince me that he had no special purpose in seeking this information."[117] But no such charges would stick against the two women who had not only the sanctity of their faith on their side but could use their sex as protection from similar accusations.

George White called them naive, claiming that "the women and other natives with whom they conversed soon found out what they wished to establish and played up to them."[118] His attempts to discredit them proved hollow. The 1893 committee, and another established by the government of India to visit some of the same cantonments where Bushnell and Andrew had gathered information, both tended to confirm their allegations, and while Stansfeld's presence on the British enquiry could be held to have influenced its conclusions, that was not so for India's Ibbetson Commission. Without a doubt Stansfeld worked hard behind the scenes and it was a shrewd move to wait until his own Liberal party was once again in power. He sought and won Gladstone's support. In late March 1893 the Prime Minister congratulated Stansfeld on being "virtually . . . in sight of the goal." Moreover, Gladstone showed every willingness to make public the damning evidence of the two women, though only after the government of India had seen it.[119]

The Crisis in Hong Kong and the Straits Settlements

The first substantive clue that the Chinese-populated colonies were also disregarding, if not subverting, imperial orders came in late 1891, and from a surprising quarter. Cecil Clementi Smith, the obdurate Weld's replacement at Singapore, approved a CD system for Perak in the Federated Malay States. The colonial secretary's formal position hewed closely to that laid down in the late 1880s that protective registration remained permissible but there could be no compulsory examination.[120] Privately, Colonial Office staff discussed the bigger issue at stake: where ultimate decision-making power lay.

> It is true that in this case Sir C. Smith would have been acting literally within his powers, but not I think in a fit & proper manner, and it seems to me that without in any degree attempting to interfere in the details of administration of the Native States, the Secretary of State might with propriety & much advantage, instruct the Governor that he must not approve any new Laws in the Native States which run counter to policy which has *been deliberately adopted in the Colony under definite instructions from the Sec. of State,* without first laying the matter before the S. of State & explaining the grounds on which the Govr may think that the state of affairs in the Native States demand the application of an opposite system from that prescribed in the Colony [emphasis in original]."[121]

Over a period of some months, the Straits governor and the colonial secretary fought over the rights of colonial politicians to decide local policy.[122] Smith warned the colonial secretary that a pan-imperial policy would silence local opinion. "I must confess that it had not occurred to me that there was any desire on Your Lordship's part that the policy which had been imposed on the Colony regarding Brothels and their inmates should be extended to the

Protected Native States. It can, of course, be extended but will have to be forced on the State Councils which will be, so far as I can call to mind, an un-precedented interference with their affairs."[123] The colonial secretary, Baron Knutsford,[124] was unswayed by Smith's avowal of a rapid rise in VD rates since the abolition of the compulsory exam, and refused "sanction to any proposal for the establishment of such a system."[125]

It was Knutsford's Liberal successor at the Colonial Office, the Marquis of Ripon (August 1892 to June 1895), who bore the brunt of colonial anger. Ripon had been Indian governor general during the first round of fighting. He was also "one of the authors . . . of the first Act . . . passed in England."[126] His conversion to Catholicism and his time in India had made him reconsider his commitment to regulation.[127] By the time he arrived at the Colonial Office in August 1892, he favored neither the CD system nor the tactics of the repealers. It was not, however, an issue he could ignore, for the spat between Knutsford and Smith was but a preliminary.

In March 1893, as Stansfeld was preparing his attack on the Indian front, Ripon wrote to the Hong Kong and Straits governors that he was "of opinion that this system of registration and inspection of brothels should no longer be maintained."[128] That same day he also asked Fiji's governor to repeal one of the few CD ordinances still permitted.[129] He stressed in each case that they were "at variance with the recognised policy of Parliament, which has been followed in all other Crown Colonies and in India."[130] Ripon was ready when the inevitable parliamentary questions were fired. Stansfeld rose in the House in early 1894 and specifically pinpointed these very colonies, Hong Kong, the Straits, and Fiji.

Reaction in the colonies to Ripon's demands was predictable. Fiji stalled, while Hong Kong and the Straits protested loudly. Though all complied with the orders, they made clear they did so under duress. The acting attorney general of Hong Kong moved the second reading of the new WGP ordinance, remarking that, "we, as members of the Government, will have loyally to carry [it] through, according to the mandate of the Secretary of State."[131] While his coded distaste was hardly subtle, members without a portfolio were less constrained. One, deprecating "this ill-timed and ill-advised measure" lamented that "we are fully aware how useless would be any opposition on our part."[132] Another decried the colony's "bondage" to the home government.[133] The *Straits Times* predicted that abolishing registration "will greatly embitter the lot of the unfortunate women concerned . . . they will become practically slaves."[134] Clementi Smith asked "to be furnished with any arguments in favour of discontinuing the system of registration and inspection of brothels because I must confess that I have none of my own to bring forward in support of the proposed measure."[135] The Colonial Office was not surprised: "we were fully aware that the Members of the Council were most or all of them opposed to this Bill."[136]

The protests veered between anger at the precipitate demands of a faraway administration ignorant of local conditions, and concern about the effects of abolition. Local elites attacked not only imperial protocol but reformers too. At the Straits, prominent Chinese blamed social purity activists for the loss of local control. "Exeter Hall does not know as much of the Straits as we do here, and why have we not been consulted? . . . We cannot always be governed by English methods."[137] Frequently this tension between local rights and imperial heavy-handedness dominated, for colonialists themselves never fully agreed on what CD legislation could or did accomplish. In Hong Kong, Des Vœux claimed that "the registered women, voluntarily, and almost without exception" begged for the reinstatement of compulsory examination.[138] A year later, however, his colonial surgeon was logging a "deficit" in voluntary attendance.[139] Five years on, the surgeon suspiciously claimed six years of "ready attendance of the women at their own request."[140] Of course, when the colonial surgeon reported in 1894, the battle was on to save brothel registration, while epidemiological disaster had earlier been the more pressing case to be made. Just as disease nomenclature was politicized, women's attitudes were wielded as proof of a range of positions. Reports argued that women had no objections to compulsion. "These women entirely failed to grasp the idea of a voluntary institution for their benefit and stated that they were perfectly willing to submit to compulsory examination under the rules hitherto in force."[141] But they were used just as often to prove the failure of the voluntary system: "The Women were under the impression that it was a compulsory Lock Hospital, and immediately left the Station."[142] The story thus metamorphosed to suit current needs, but whether the narrative was of women urging the return of the regular examination schedule or turning their backs on it, suddenly the brothel inmates took on a personality and an opinion. There is little hint of slavery and coercion in descriptions of the women wantonly ignoring or clamorously pressing for the attention of western medical staff.

This slipperiness was the case, too, for claims about the rise in VD, and here, too, nomenclature played a potent role. The Straits authorities claimed a massive 300 percent rise in VD in the general population in the four years following repeal.[143] Yet only a year later, the Colonial Office noted a diminution in disease in "the last 2 years."[144] Much depended on how the counting was done. The Colonial Office noted, for example, that women's hospital admissions were rising and men's decreasing, despite the equally strong though contradictory belief that "Chinese women are very slow to avail themselves of medical treatment."[145] And what they noted as diminishing or rising was, of course, treatment, that is statistics of disease based necessarily but, of course, incompletely on who attended western medical institutions.

While the inaccuracies in quantification must leave us wary about pronouncing on the rise or fall of VD consonant upon the CD system, the insistence that the incidence of VD was fast rising was intended to promote a sense of crisis. Proregulationists argued that in not appearing to sanction vice, the authorities were sacrificing the health especially of the British soldier, but also of entire populations too immoral to mend their ways. In short, the message of the regulationists was that "native" superstition and virtuous repeal talk shared a rejection of modern rationality.

The atmosphere of crisis they induced, however, was not limited to this prospect of mass sickness, but was rapidly transferred to the tense political struggles simultaneously at play in India, Hong Kong, and the Straits. As the Legislative Councils in the two crown colonies were deploring their puppet status, government faced an even more serious revolt in India. By early 1895, the tensions over prostitution and VD control led viceroy Elgin to warn the secretary of state that, "[a]s to the Cantonments Bill, everything points to a crisis."[146]

Gladstone's resignation in 1894, after the defeat of his second Irish Home Rule bill, brought the imperialist Lord Rosebery back to power. Ripon remained at the Colonial Office, Elgin replaced Lansdowne in India, and Henry Fowler succeeded Kimberley at the India Office. Each faced a turbulent situation, made no easier by the tensions within the cabinet over imperial policy more generally. In addition, the Liberals had failed to secure Redvers Buller, their first choice, for the commander in chief in India's position and had been roundly defeated, in the same year, 1895, on the army estimates. Rosebery's aggressive policies procured dissent from such prominent anti-imperialists as Harcourt at the Exchequer and John Morley, avidly involved in anti-CD agitation.[147]

The Crisis in India

The Russell and Ibbetson inquiries both completed their reports in the summer of 1893. The former's brief was to ascertain whether extant rules and practices were consistent with parliament's dictates, while the latter investigated Bushnell and Andrew's allegations. They moved with unusual swiftness. Russell's committee, appointed in early April, produced its report on August 31, 1893. The Indian commission, chaired by Denzil Ibbetson, was appointed June 2, visited three cantonments, and issued its report before the month was out.

Ibbetson's commission retraced Bushnell and Andrew's investigations at Ambala, Lucknow, and Meerut. Ibbetson, a well-respected civil servant best known for his work on the Indian census, was joined by surgeon colonel Cleghorn, inspector general of civil hospitals, and a retired district judge, Maulvi Sami-Ullah Khan. Two military officers accompanied the commission, Lieutenant A. C. Elliott as its secretary, and Major W. B. Wilson representing the military. From the first, Ibbetson worried about the time-frame. He wrote to the secretary of the military department of the government of India the day they reached Ambala, warning him that "it is very doubtful whether the work can be done properly in the time allowed."[148] For all that, the commissioners produced a lengthy and detailed document.

Though they acknowledged instances of periodic examination and of formal payments to and provisions for the women, Ibbetson and his associates offered seamless explanations to soften these admissions. They often argued on technicalities suggesting that it was the interpretation of the rules that produced the contest between their reading and that of Andrew and Bushnell. In its deployment of class, race, and gender categories, their report painted a picture of a raucous India constantly threatening—physically, epidemiologically, and morally—at the doors of civilization. It was the troops who stood between civilization and disorder, and on whose behalf "the most comprehensive powers of minute interference and control" were rightly exercised. "The first and last consideration to which all others must give way, is the health and convenience of the troops."[149]

The commissioners conceded that at Christmas and around pay day, the British soldier might overindulge in alcohol, but military rowdyism paled next to the portrait of cantonments as perennially disordered sites necessitating "stringent sanitary precautions."[150] The absence of the "upper classes" reduced the cantonment to "a native city, with all those elements removed from it which most tend to promote stability and order."[151] The tension between the orderly precision imposed by British rule and the inherent ungovernableness of a native proletariat was constantly in danger of unraveling, however, for the reader also learned of "the docility of the uneducated native."[152] The major exception to this rule was the prostitute. While the poor Indian woman was a "mere drudge" and the woman of the "higher classes" was physically confined, the prostitute was "superior" in culture and intelligence, the product of a broader social milieu by virtue of her trade. Yet the report simultaneously argued that in servicing the British soldier, she "suffers in estimation accordingly," and "lose[s] caste."[153] Cantonment women "could hardly hope to be frequented" by "the better class of natives."[154]

The report's gendering of sexual roles was remarkably absolute in light of the colonial propensity to decry India for its more fluid approach to sexuality. The commissioners insisted that in the hereditary prostitute castes, men became pimps and women prostitutes.[155] And yet despite an insistence that this paralleled other polluting caste occupations, the report did not admit of prostitution as work, going so far as to argue that it was her lack of drudgery that set the prostitute apart among poor women.[156] The refusal to see prostitution as work, despite the comparison with trade-related castes, made it easy for the report to mention casually the loss of livelihood for prostitute women effected by the 1889 Cantonment Act. The contrast with strong advocacy for troop protection was striking. And that Ibbetson, architect of the taxonomizing census, could argue that the continued use of an older CD terminology was "a mere name, signifying nothing" must surely suggest how fragile was the establishment of these certainties even while they did damage to the daily lives of countless ordinary Indians.[157]

In the final paragraph of their report, the Ibbetson commissioners suggested that the rhetoric of repeal was thin on evidence. "A picture has been suggested, if not actually drawn, of trembling groups of miserable women . . . the ticketed and numbered subjects of the soldiers' lust . . . enslaved by debt beyond all hope of escape . . . condemned to drag on a hapless life of abject poverty and degradation."[158] The commission found "no shadow of foundation," for this vision, but their repudiation involved an act of willful forgetting. Proregulationists, too, had long traded in stock images of broken-down women forced by poverty into the beds of soldiers.

Unlike the Indian report, Russell's committee was disposed unkindly towards Indian officialdom. His was very much a report managed by a repeal-sympathetic administration. The pro-CD Kimberley told his Viceroy that this "packed" committee was the lesser of two evils. "I telegraphed to you that I had been obliged to give way to Stansfeld to the extent of appointing a Departmental Committee on which he and one of his friends are to sit. This seemed to us better than to agree to a Committee of the House, which would have been to put you on trial . . . We had really no alternative."[159]

Chaired by George Russell from the India Office, with Oliver Newmarch, military secretary at the India Office as its secretary, Stansfeld and his fellow Federation activist, Henry J. Wilson were joined by two India Council veterans, former commander in chief Donald Stewart, and Sir James Peile, formerly in the Bombay administration.[160] Inevitably the group polarized, with Stewart and Peile issuing a minority dissenting report three days after the publication of the majority report.

The majority report concluded that the will of parliament had been disregarded. Stewart and Peile, the dissenters, were caught in a bind for their alternative report shows substantial agreement between them and their colleagues in many instances. They attempted instead to highlight weak evidence or to spin dubious practices in creative ways, but even theirs was a damning blow to the government. "We have agreed that the periodical examinations after 1888 were an attempt to secure by various methods the same means of detecting disease without the old sanctions and with the substitution of motives for coercion. We have not argued that the practice was consistent with the spirit of the Resolution though we do not think it was necessarily contrary to the letter, but it was not the old system."[161]

But it was not these condemnations alone that so destabilized imperial relations. Criticism of the 1889 Cantonment Act extended beyond the already suspicious circles of reformers bent on a thorough-going dissolution of state regulation. Protests in India were equally loud. The Indian press was vocal in its criticisms, and cantonment residents, concerned that the breadth of the new regulations would act as "an engine of oppression," petitioned against the act.[162] In late 1893, Anglicans in India added their voice, claiming officials gave only "reluctant acquiescence" to the 1888 resolution.[163] The Calcutta Missionary Conference called a "Monster Meeting" in 1893, bringing together in protest "persons of all classes and ranks and of the people."[164] In Rangoon, residents petitioned the municipality about "flagrant" prostitution and "shame-less solicitation."[165]

As if this were not enough, the Army Sanitary Commission condemned the CD system as a failure in the same year.[166] But the India Office's troubles were just beginning. As in the crown colonies, colonial politicians chafed at British high-handedness. Members of the Council of India openly revolted. Arthur Godley at the India Office told Elgin in March 1894 that Kimberley had recently "to overrule the *unanimous* opinion of the Council twice: Viz., once as to the Contagious Diseases Despatch, and a second time as to the omission of cotton from the Tariff. This is a 'record.'"[167] In the preceding thirty years, the council had been overruled by the India secretary only six times.[168] 1894 would be a tumultuous year for the India Office and indeed for imperial control. Though there were other controversial issues, the most widespread and abundant dissent across the colonial landscape was over VD and prostitution control.

Military despatch 24 was sent to India under Kimberley's signature on March 1, 1894. A note in the India Office file reads "negatived Council 27/2/94."[169] Deploring the disobedience to orders and the tenacity of the out-lawed practices, Kimberley insisted in the despatch on new legislation to replace the controversial Cantonment Act of 1889. All ten members of the council voted in the negative and only Kimberley in favor of this order. But his was, by law, the binding decision, and he informed the council that "as he did not concur in the opinion of the majority, he should—under the powers conferred upon him by 21 & 22 Vict. cap. 106, Sect. 23—send the despatch to the Government of India."[170] It was only six months since he had done the same thing over the wording of a telegram to the viceroy; four members of the council formally recorded their dissent on that occasion.[171] Liberal sympathy for repeal added to the government's tenuous majority made Kimberley acutely aware of the defeat of his own views, despite his need to overrule a council with whom he fun-damentally agreed. "The late Conservative Government found it impossible to resist Stansfeld and his followers in the House of Commons, and, if they could not, with their great majority resist, you may suppose how perfectly hopeless it would be for us to attempt it."[172] His successor fared no better, as Godley reported to Elgin. "Mr. Fowler had to pass his Cantonments Despatch against the all but unanimous dissent of his Council."[173]

These episodes have attracted little attention from historians of either Britain or British India in the period, though politicians at the time recognized how much was at stake.[174] Correspondence between senior officials throughout 1894 and beyond, as well as formal debate, refer constantly to the impact of the controversy on Britain's very hold on India. Lord Reay at the India Office thought "nothing . . . more detrimental to our prestige in India than divisions in the Council . . . it is not calculated to increase the respect of the ruled for the rulers . . . the less frequently occasions arise for straining the official conscience the better."[175] Elgin adopted the same rhetoric to convince rogue members of his council of the need for unanimity. When one member hinted at resignation, Elgin argued that "the resignation of a Member of Council could not but shake the authority of the Government of India."[176]

It was not just Indian but imperial authority that was at stake. Kimberley told Elgin with palpable weariness that "hardly a day passes but that I receive numerous Resolutions passed by Associations of various kinds, and in all parts of the country, urging the amendment of the Cantonment rules."[177] Elgin responded in kind, detailing the "very considerable agitation" within India.[178] Repeal activists sought alliance with Indian nationalists. Butler and Stuart negotiated with the Indian National Congress in 1888; in return for support, Congress would monitor repeal in cantonments.[179] At its 1892 meeting, the Indian National Congress adopted a resolution against state regulation of prostitution. The issue was never high on its agenda, but the mutual support network which generated the motion rattled British officials.[180] The viceroy reported early in 1882 that "there has throughout been on the part of the Native public and press a bitterness of denunciation of the [Indian CD] Act."[181] In 1895, the dissension in the governor general's council was monitored by the Indian National Congress. "I have been told by an intelligent Native that the Congress Party hope, and not without some encouragement, to take advantage of the irritation of the Europeans [at the loss of regulated prostitution] to get them to join the Congress movement against the existing constitution of the Council."[182] Elgin sent Fowler notice of an article in the Calcutta paper, the *Amrita Bazar Patrika* "which shows clearly that the Congress Party quite understands how to turn the present attitude of Anglo-Indians to advantage."[183]

While leaders in India and Britain fretted over the stability of the imperial system, and nationalists hoped to pick up support as a result, defiant pro-CD politicians employed an almost identical rhetoric to that of government to buttress their arguments. Lyon Playfair declared that the new legislation lowered "the prestige and dignity of the Government" and that "the confidence of all classes in the government of the country is weakened." In London, Stewart told the India Council that the new legislation implied a lack of trust in the government of India.[184]

Demanding Colonial Fidelity

Members of the governor general's council were unbowed. Sir Alexander Miller's speech introducing the new bill emphasized that it was introduced "by direction of Her Majesty's Government" and that it had been "practically, though not formally drawn in England."[185] Officials at the India Office were furious. "The 'Times' of this morning publishes a Reuters telegram purporting to give a brief summary of Sir Alexander Miller's remarks . . . If the report is at all correct the tone of his speech appears to me to have been most unusual. I might use a stronger word. Any attempt to modify the decision of the House of Commons would *be a very serious matter* [emphasis in original]."[186] A week later Fowler made plain that where members felt unable to support official policy, they must resign. It was, he continued, a matter pertinent to "relations between Her Majesty's Government and the Government of India."[187] A few weeks later, he declared emphatically that "the policy is the policy of the Imperial Government and the Imperial Parliament, and that policy is not open to discussion."[188] Elgin reluctantly acceded. "I accept the position that it has been decreed by the Imperial Parliament."[189] Elgin's concern was with empire rather than VD for he shared the antiregulationist distaste for organized prostitution.[190]

Members of the council were not easily swayed. Elgin warned in August 1894 that "some of them will insist on saying that they vote under compulsion."[191] Some, he thought, were deliberately courting an official reprimand to further press their point.[192] Fowler warned that prevarication in India might force the home government to "take the matter into its own hands," a move that would have materially affected colonial governance.[193] Before the year was out, the situation was grave enough that the British cabinet met on the matter. Elgin was informed yet again "that Members of the Executive Council must, as Members of the Government here do, *vote together* in support of Government measures [emphasis in original]."[194] It could not have been an enjoyable task for Fowler to pen this letter, for he also noted that he was sending a despatch on the issue, "against which every Member of the Council voted." And though he apologized for his tone, he also warned that "with the cordial support of my colleagues, I shall immediately advise the Queen to dismiss any Member of the Council who so far forget what is due to his own position and to the position of the Viceroy as to attempt to continue a Member of a Government whose policy he is unable to support." This was so, he concluded, because "we feel here that the constitutional relations between the Viceroy and his Executive Council, and their effective action as a Government, are at stake; and we cannot consent to your Government appearing before the Legislative Council *and before the public* as a *divided* body [emphasis in original]."[195]

At the Straits and Hong Kong, it was the compliance of the official members of gubernatorial councils that was demanded. Ripon made clear that "nominated members of Legislative Councils" in crown colonies were under obligation, an opinion he shared with the beleaguered Fowler.[196] "The official members must vote for the Ordinance as is always understood to be the rule in the case of an Ord[inan]ce introduced under the instructions of the Sec. of State."[197] At the Straits, the vote was 6–5 in favor of the new ordinance, the official members heeding the colonial secretary's warnings. One of the non-official members commented on what he saw as the corralling of his colleagues by "one man, far away, not knowing the particulars."[198]

Though the Straits and Hong Kong councils grudgingly and narrowly passed the new and more stringent legislation, anger in India remained unappeased. In

January 1895, an Indian newspaper headline declared, "Legislation by mandate!" Elgin and Fowler recognized that, without changes, the bill could not pass.[199] Council debate and the judicial opinions sent to the governor general continued to raise the question of authority. One Council member pointed out that official members routinely opposed the government without invoking parliamentary wrath.[200] But as the objections gradually narrowed to individual issues of law, compromise looked possible. Various offending clauses were dropped, allowing the official members of council to save face. In February 1895, the council passed the amending legislation.

The 1895 Cantonment Act (Act V) limited the definition of contagious and infectious diseases to cholera, smallpox, diphtheria, and typhoid fever, allowing no specific mention of VD. Those suspected diseased and refusing examination could be expelled from cantonments. Examinations for VD were not specifically disallowed, but prostitutes were forbidden to reside within regimental bazaars. VD was mentioned only once in the text of the act; public health had been, in effect, reestablished on metropolitan terms with the separation of venereal from other diseases.

But as repealers constantly feared, regulation was still on the agenda. Guernsey, a crown colony, introduced regulation while New Zealand and the Cape considered but rejected its abandonment. Activists warned that moves were afoot in the Australian colony of Victoria to revive the CD Act there in 1896, and in that same year, they were quietly checking on the situation in such hitherto ignored imperial settings as Aden.[201]

Proregulation Forces

Almost immediately after the implementation of the new rules in 1895, alarm over VD began once again to grow. Newspapers, pro-CD politicians, and doctors all began to clamor for attention to what they claimed was a health problem once more growing in magnitude. Elgin had warned the new India secretary, George Hamilton, in September 1896, that the Indian military authorities were claiming heavy losses from VD, a claim made all the more urgent by Britain's uneasy relations with Russia over India.[202] Alarmist reports in the press led to parliamentary questions within a year of the new legislation. With the accession in July 1895 of Salisbury's convincingly strong Conservative government, repealers lost their parliamentary advantage. Chamberlain at the Colonial Office and Hamilton at the India Office were hostile to repealers. Indeed, Hamilton used the issue to remind the Liberals of their grinding defeat. "I should rather like to throw down, by the repeal of this Act, a direct challenge to the other party."[203]

By January 1897, the proregulationist *Times* was claiming that only 24,000 of the British troops in India were free of the venereal taint, with two-thirds of the garrison infected.[204] The government, biding its time, countered that the figures were misleading; while total aggregate troop VD admissions to hospital in 1895 were indeed 522 per thousand, that figure did not represent separate admissions or cases. "It is calculated on the latest returns that an average permanent deduction of 46 per thousand is the loss entailed by these diseases."[205]

Activists warned of "the need for our continuance and for vigilant zeal," pointing to the tenacity of the system in some parts of the empire as well as at attempts at reinstatement or introduction of new legislation.[206] Henry Wilson appointed agents to keep an eye on things in India for the British committee.[207] Activist Blanche Leppington wrote despairingly to him, "Is it all to be fought over again as from the beginning?"[208] Logging the widespread calls for reinstatement throughout that year and watching the dramas of 1897 unfold, Leppington's anxiety was not unfounded, and nor was Hamilton's glee at humiliating the Liberals.

In November 1896, Hamilton appointed a committee to consider troop VD in India. Chaired by the Earl of Onslow, parliamentary under secretary at the India Office, committee membership favored the military.[209] Hamilton kept the abolitionists off the committee by shrewdly exploiting their own rhetoric. "The representatives of the anti-Contagious Diseases party refuse to serve upon the Committee, unless they may investigate the causes of the increased disease. This is a valuable admission."[210] Onslow's fellow members were two army surgeons and James Peile, co-author of the dissenting report of the 1893 Russell committee. The Onslow committee's conclusions were published in February 1897, its chair confidently asserting that, "the feeling on the subject in England is becoming so strong that I do not anticipate much difficulty in facing Parliamentary censure if we stop short of re-establishing Cantonment brothels."[211]

The committee found substantial increase in the rate of VD, contrasting this rise with "the improvement in the general health of the troops."[212] While in a footnote they acknowledged that "the numbers of *men admitted* for any disease are not identical with the numbers of *admissions*," they still found the rates "deplorable [emphasis in original]."[213] The report demonized syphilis, noting that the syphilis wards at the army hospital at Netley had been dubbed the "Inferno" by the staff, and attaching as an appendix a graphic letter from the hospital's surgical chief.[214] Claiming that syphilis acquired abroad was more severe, the letter drew a hideous picture of the unfortunate sufferer: "utterly broken down in health, hardly able to crawl, covered with scabs and sores, with the foul odour of the disease about them, objects of disgust and loathing to themselves and all around them."[215]

Proregulation forces were delighted with the report and its impact was considerable. Journals and newspapers were filled with scare-mongering reports. *The Times* described Netley's syphilis wards as a "scene of horrors," an editorial in May 1897 declaring it was "time for action."[216] Hamilton was inundated with petitions. The Army Sanitary Commission shifted ground again, moving from its condemnation of regulation to support for controlling prostitution and expulsion of women for refusing treatment.[217]

Faltering Repeal

A plethora of memorials and petitions protested the reversal in policy. The Abolitionist Federation's petition, reprinted for parliament, boasted almost 61,500 women's signatures, and declared "hostility to every form of State regulation of immorality."[218] But the political mood had turned, and Hamilton pressed home his advantage. "I have received a large number of petitions from the more fanatical opponents of the Acts; but so far as I can judge, they have greatly lost strength; so much so that, even with the fresh provocation offered to them by the repeal of the Act of 1895, they dare not assail us in the House of Commons."[219]

The 1895 election hurt the repealers badly, and they knew that a strong Conservative majority would not serve their interests well. Butler put an optimistic face on the defeat: "I do *not* feel depressed or discouraged, tho' I fear our good cause may have to wait a while longer. The swing of the pendulum is so exaggerated, so *ludicrous* one might say, that by the very law w[h] it is obeying it is bound to swing back again as strongly." Far more worrying to her was "the *defection of women*... all about the world... publicly placing themselves on the side of the Regulationists [emphasis in original],"[220] a comment precipitated particularly by New Zealand women's support of the CD Act there.

In Britain, too, there were women who supported regulation. In an 1897 petition, British medical women called for the reinstatement of VD controls, while Isabel, Lady Somerset, president of the British Women's Christian Temperance Union, published her approval of Hamilton's position in the The Times.[221] Feminist repealers were shocked by this public breaking of the ranks. It was the final straw for Kate Bushnell and Elizabeth Andrew. Their close association with the Butlerite camp had strained their WCTU connections, and Somerset's failure to support them had rankled. They severed their ties with the WCTU in a forthright condemnation of her act.[222]

The protest movement was largely drowned out as the press and colonial booster groups joined forces with the consistently proregulation colonialists. Though *The Times* published Major C. B. Mayne's careful critique of the use of statistics to "prove" rampant VD in the Indian army, the sheer weight of the proregulation forces defeated the abolitionists in 1897.[223] Hamilton told Elgin that "the leaders of the opposite party Wilson Stuart and others frankly admit that they are nonplussed: and they do not like to move as the feeling in the House of Commons is much against them."[224]

Conclusion

The new regulations in India returned, if in a different guise, many of the powers the military had lost in 1895, but Hamilton was determined not to appear to sanction vice.[225] In repealing Act V of 1895, the new rules of October 1897 reinstated the right to expel from cantonments women refusing treatment, returned

VD to the list of contagious and infectious diseases over which control could be exercised, and allowed the prohibiting of brothels. Disorderly persons could be excluded from cantonment residence, and streetwalking and importuning were strictly forbidden.[226] The governor of Madras congratulated Hamilton on solving "the problem in the most ingenious way."[227]

Vigorous protests followed, accusing the government of reinstating compulsion using backdoor methods, but there was little the repealers could do in the face of popular support and a strong Conservative majority.[228] Jingoism and support for empire was high, and with war in South Africa on the horizon, risks to troop efficiency were unthinkable. For political consumption in India, Hamilton also reinterpreted the constitutional argument that had so dominated the earlier debate. He told Elgin that the cabinet was reluctant to be bound by the resolution of a differently constituted House of Commons, and that in fact India had been required by the secretary of state and not Parliament to acquiesce. "It would be a very dangerous admission for the Viceroy to publicly treat an abstract resolution of the House as a mandate to the Government of India & might place both you & your successors in a difficult position on some snap decision of the House of Commons."[229] This rather supported Elgin's mild protest in May 1894 that the secretary of state was going "beyond the Resolution of the House of Commons."[230]

As it became obvious that the Conservative administration favored the reinstatement of VD controls, Hong Kong and the Straits, still smarting from the changes of 1895, pressed home their advantage. Supported by metropolitan groups such as the China Association, Straits Settlements Association, and the Navy League, Hong Kong's governor urged Chamberlain to take steps for the better control of brothels.[231] Chamberlain, more cautious than Hamilton, approved only minor changes, mostly punishing procurers. No wholesale change of policy was effected as in India.

While the Indian debate raised the problem of the defiance of the military, the storms of the 1890s were just as critically about the struggle between metropolitan and colonial politicians. The leakage of sex and disease into the highest echelons of formal power was distressing, as many politicians at the time readily conceded, but utterly unavoidable. In a sense, it symbolized, too, the failure of CD laws to do their job of maintaining boundaries. The *cordon sanitaire* was breached on the ground and at Westminster, and though the repealers knew they were beaten by the end of the 1890s, they had successfully forced open the terms of the debate.

Chapter 5

Abolitionism Declawed

The blind and self-righteous Puritans of Victoria's glorious era sought to reform an innately sensuous land . . . with the appearance of the armchair martinets and evangelistic Colonel Sahibs, Jack Sepoy had need with the last of his meager coin, to smuggle in disease-ridden sluts from the filthy bazaars.

—Allen Edwardes

I fear lest Stansfeld & Co., while conscientiously no doubt, grasping at the shadow of utopian purity, may plunge us into the substantial reality of physical rottenness.

—George S. White

After the decade of controversy from 1888 to 1897, the frenzied parliamentary attention to colonial VD began to slow. Though antiregulationists revived the question regularly, keeping up a steady stream of pamphleteering and campaigning, the issue diminished in importance. The early years of the twentieth century saw a flurry of bio-medical breakthroughs affecting treatment and diagnosis of STDs, as well as a new wave of public and political anxiety over syphilis, but attention shifted largely to the domestic arena. It was the impact of a diseased or weakened British population on maintaining the empire that now moved to center stage. The grip of eugenics, growing state intervention in individual and family affairs, and demographic changes wrought by urbanization kept the dangers, especially of syphilis, in the limelight. But while the language of public anxiety was ever more alarmist, the colonies were increasingly occluded in these debates, functioning as a backdrop for nationalist sentiment and the resurgence of race talk, but uninteresting domestically in all but this respect. The result of this refiguring produced new policies in colonial settings, though they were frequently ignored in the metropolis.

Statistics and Politics

In the immediate aftermath of the debates of 1897, which had restored some powers to authorities but interdicted compulsory examination, regulationists and their foes kept careful watch. Supporters of the Contagious Diseases (CD) system anticipated rising admission rates for VD while abolitionists watched for signs that compulsion was returning. One quickly fulfilled prediction was that women would not attend examinations voluntarily. It was a widespread and cross-colony truism. From all over the colonies came reports of a substantial diminution in attendance.[1] In Hong Kong, "prostitutes ceased to attend for their weekly examinations," while in Singapore, Chinese women "wilfully left the lock hospital" in large numbers.[2] No women attended voluntarily in the Straits in 1898 or 1899.[3] At Mian Mir in the Punjab, of the eighty-one prostitutes examined in 1898–99, a mere four "offered themselves voluntarily." The remainder were summonsed under the new cantonment rules on suspicion of infection.[4] Despite the predictions of proregulationists that this mass defection would result in a rise in infections, over the long term the overall trend was a decline in VD rates. This probably had little material connection to CD legislation, but the dips and leaps in VD rates were eagerly clutched at by campaigners.

In the short term, rates varied dramatically, as the previous chapter has shown. In India, they declined. They were, according to the secretary of state, "lower in 1898 than in any year since 1887."[5] Six years later came reports of a "phenomenal and consistent diminution."[6] Even military officials proudly proclaimed the "steady annual decrease in the admission rate which began in 1896 . . . [that] has since been steadily maintained."[7] Some of the reported decrease was a political sleight of hand, a result of changes in record-keeping. A 1904 revamping of VD classification in India "had the effect of reducing the number of admissions shown in the tables—continuous treatment taking the place of frequent visits to hospital for treatment."[8] Nonetheless, the evidence of falling rates in India in the early twentieth century is overwhelming.[9] As we have seen, in the Straits and Hong Kong, however, rates rose dramatically in the short term among both civilians and the military, sufficient that James Warren has dubbed syphilis and gonorrhea "pandemic" in Singapore by 1900.[10]

Medical Innovation

By the early twentieth century, doctors had begun to question the medical value of regulation. A major international conference on VD at Brussels in 1899 criticized regulated prostitution, as did the 1911 Australasian Medical Congress. Leading metropolitan public health officers, Arthur Newsholme and R. W. Johnstone, advised the Local Government Board in 1913 that the CD acts had failed.[11] Reduced syphilis rates, claimed others, were "in no way connected with . . . the Contagious Diseases Acts."[12] Charles Bell Taylor declared the CD acts "the foulest, and at the same time, the very silliest piece of legislation the world has ever seen."[13] The 1906 committee investigating VD and scabies in the army rejected "methods of compulsory isolation and treatment," as "neither practicable nor expedient."[14]

Much of this shift in attitude was facilitated by significant biomedical changes in treatment and diagnosis. Between 1905 and 1914, medical knowledge of VD advanced considerably. In 1905, Fritz Schaudinn and Erich Hoffman isolated the syphilitic micro-organism, the spirochæte *Treponema pallidum*, demonstrating the cause of the disease. In the same year, Elie Metchnikoff and Pierre Paul-Emile Roux successfully treated syphilitic monkeys with calomel, a subchloride of mercury, which rapidly became available as an ointment. The following year saw both the development of a complement-fixation test to diagnose syphilis—the Wasserman test—and a laboratory test for gonorrhea, developed by Müller and Oppenheim. In 1909 immunologists Paul Ehrlich and Sahachiro Hata hit upon the spirochætal arsphenamine they named Salvarsan ("I save") as an effective chemotherapeutic treatment for syphilis.[15] Salvarsan, a yellow powdered form of dioxy-diamino-arsenobenzol, was a compound of 31.5 percent arsenic dissolved in distilled water and neutralized with sodium hydroxide.[16] This new generation of arsenobenzoids not infrequently led to convulsions, jaundice, and a variety of skin complaints.[17] Side effects—abdominal pain, vomiting, possible necrosis at the site of injection—could be serious. Sazerac and Levaditi's discovery in 1922 that bismuth was effective against syphilis allowed doctors to alternate the toxic arsenobenzoid with something less disagreeable than the older mercury preparations that Salvarsan had never wholly supplanted; early Salvarsan treatments were administered in tandem with a heavy metal, mostly mercury, to avoid neuro-recurrence in the form of cranial nerve palsies. Important as it was, the new treatment protocol was still hard on patients.

The reception of these new methods was mixed. Doctors were often suspicious of the new diagnostics, while social purity advocates rejected the Wasserman test and Salvarsan as antipathetic to the moral law.[18] Sir D'Arcy Power initially resisted diagnostic reliance on serum testing; "brought up in the old school . . . it was difficult to rely upon a test made by another person, however skilful and assured he might be."[19] Even where doctors embraced the new technology, and as a profession they increasingly did, cost was an impediment. In colonial settings, expense frequently occasioned an apartheid in treatment protocols, with the costlier and more effective drugs reserved for white use. In Australia, Salvarsan was widely available for treating the white population. The Queensland home secretary promoted a scheme in 1913 to allow free or reduced price Wasserman tests "for poor people."[20] Yet at Bernier and Dorre, the Aboriginal lock hospitals off the coast of Western Australia, the use of Salvarsan was at best sporadic.[21] In parts of Africa, the prohibitive cost of Salvarsan meant that well into the twentieth century patients were routinely treated instead with mercurials.[22]

Military Venereology

The state was willing, however, to invest in military health, bolstering Warwick Anderson's contention that military strategy often drove colonial disease control.[23] Throughout the controversial years of regulation one prominent argument had always been that without regulation, soldiers would return from overseas postings and infect Britain with virulent tropical variants of VD. That argument gained greater force after abolition, for "under our unprotected military system," cautioned British Burma's inspector general of civil hospitals, "the population of England is menaced with physical degeneration."[24]

The army and navy's principal concerns were wastage and efficiency, though senior officers understood the need to pay lip service to the prevailing moral climate. The loss of manpower entailed in the lengthy hospitalization for VD treatment affected both cost and military readiness. On average, a gonorrhea patient spent five to seven weeks in hospital in 1916; for syphilis the stay might rise to as much as ten weeks.[25]

Not surprisingly it was thus in the military that new treatment and diagnosis methods were first employed. T. E. Osmond, who joined the Army Medical Service in 1912, called the Military Hospital at Rochester Row in London, "the leading and most up-to-date venereal diseases hospital in the country."[26] The military boasted far better facilities than those available to civilians in the early twentieth century.[27] These were active experimental years in military venereology. Metchnikoff's new treatment received little publicity outside military circles.[28] The Wasserman test, too expensive in its early years for widespread use, was introduced into the British army in 1907, while Salvarsan was routinely used in the army and the navy from 1911.[29] In the empire, these costly new techniques were largely confined to the treatment of white soldiers.[30] In 1913, the government of India established two venereal laboratories in India, at Ambala and Poona, consolidated into a single laboratory at Poona in 1915.[31] At about the same time, the Royal Army Medical Corps expanded its venereological training. "All junior officers of the R.A.M.C. on arrival in India, undergo a short refresher course of instruction in the technique employed in the intravenous injection [of Salvarsan]. They are also made thoroughly *au fait* with the diagnosis of syphilis by the Wasserman reaction."[32]

Despite the new techniques, funding remained modest. Few hospitals were furnished with the necessary microscopes, leaving those who could to use their own private instruments.[33] The Indian government increased expenditure for equipment in 1917 and again in 1919, but it was hard to keep pace with the work, more especially with the soaring rates of VD brought about by wartime conditions after 1914.[34] But if the inevitable slippage between rhetoric and reality applied to the politics of implementation, it resonated, too, in the continued debate over the efficacy of compulsion and the targeting of prostitute women. Indubitably medical and public opinion were moving away from a reliance on reglementation though the policy was not without its proponents well into the new century.[35] As late as 1911, campaigners were informed that the India secretary "feels that the results attained by the existing system are such that any interference would not be justifiable."[36]

Support for Regulation

Abolitionist fears that the CD system might be reimposed were not wholly unfounded. Throughout the colonies, there was persistent lobbying for a return to the CD system. The Straits governor sent Joseph Chamberlain at the Colonial Office dire reports from Selangor and Perak. "What is wanted here is the Contagious Diseases Order pure and simple."[37] Singapore's municipal commission urged that "special legislation on the former lines is necessary to cope with the evil as it exists in this Colony."[38] In Queensland, the local British Medical Association (BMA) backed attempts to extend the act in the early 1900s.[39] The Cairns medical officer told the home secretary that "[I]f ever there was a town where the absence of an Act to regulate prostitution was productive of the most baleful effects on the present and rising generation it is Cairns."[40] Thursday Island requested a CD act in 1902, Mackay in 1906, and Bundaberg in 1907.[41] In British Burma, the local BMA branch demanded "[T]he registration and periodical compulsory examination of all prostitutes."[42] It was not that colonial doctors were "behind" their metropolitan colleagues in embracing an increasingly suspect system of control. Medical practice and opinion were necessarily enmeshed in cultural and political questions, and there was no "leading edge" in medicine, no pure advance in progress to which those isolated from the metropolitan institutions of research and the most well-stocked libraries were not privy.

The Colonial Office and well-placed metropolitan doctors may have been cognizant of growing public distaste for regulation and of the political damage canny abolitionists could wreak, but colonial doctors were at best uninterested, and often resentful of metropolitan opinion. They shared the widespread colonial opinion that policies imported from the metropolis failed to understand local conditions, and undermined their power locally. "Anyone acquainted with the conditions obtaining in this country," wrote the commander in chief in India in 1912, would know that "the abolition of the brothels in or near the Cantonments," was "impracticable."[43] This was less a tussle over medical knowledge (the new techniques, after all, were enthusiastically seized upon when cost permitted) than a divide mired in the political struggle between colonial and metropolitan government.

Morality, Hygiene, and Gender

In metropolitan Britain, the early twentieth century saw considerable state intervention around sexual and reproductive issues.[44] The double standard enshrined in the CD acts continued to shape policy, but sexual "deviance" came to be viewed as hereditary rather than individual moral failing. With the growing popularity of eugenics, welfare policies identified feeblemindedness and criminal tendency as likely to degrade a ruling race. Attention focused on the prostitute's helplessness rather than her willfulness and new legislation, often draconian, reflected that shift. The 1913 Mental Deficiency Act deemed illegitimate mothers in the workhouse feebleminded.[45] The Corporation of Liverpool's health committee considered a plan in 1916 to send venereally infected young women not to lock wards but to the local diocesan Association for Preventive and Rescue Work.[46] VD was closely scrutinized. Poor Law Boards campaigning for the right to detain infected workhouse inmates found support from the 1909 Royal Commission on the Poor Laws and the 1916 commission on VD.[47] The public lecture, the admonitory pamphlet, the advice manual all proliferated in the years before the war, at the same time as the criminal law increasingly regulated sexual behavior and city streets were ever more closely policed. For Britain and the settler colonies, the early 1900s was a period of repression.[48] Neither prostitution nor VD could shake off the moral taint, and a medico-moral language continued to dog both policy and opinion.[49] An Australian clergyman called syphilis the result of "the violation of Nature's laws," a "scourge" unknown "when the sexual instinct is regulated by pure love."[50] Helen Wilson, daughter of abolitionist Henry Wilson, advocated informational literature employing "a cool statement scientific in tone," yet in her own published writings was stridently moral. "The moral *atmosphere* must be *cleansed*" by the removal of inappropriate material from public display and the "removal from the centres of population of the feeble-minded, the morally defective, the unemployable—pitiful 'refuse' indeed [emphases in original]." In a "thoroughly clean moral atmosphere," she claimed, VD would dwindle.[51] Cleanliness was paramount. The minister for public health in New South Wales suggested extending federal Australian quarantining of immigrants to "the unclean who arrive by water—until the tests proclaim their purity."[52] The boundaries of the pure nation were diluted and threatened by filthy outsiders.

But in India and the Chinese colonies, the aim of the laws was quite different. Military vulnerability had been a principal concern before the 1900s; the growing concern with a civilian population and the popularity of theories about hereditary and genetic race traits focused and reshaped policy in distinct ways. Antiregulationists accepted as readily as their foes that western modesty contrasted with eastern frankness. Drafting leaflets for the newly formed National Council for Combatting Venereal Diseases in 1914, Helen Wilson asked her coauthor: "Do we want to put in the hands of a lad or young man something that will send him to the dictionary to seek the meaning of "ovary" and "egg duct"? and vice versa?"[53] English propriety, however, was irrelevant in tropical settings. Singapore undertook an aggressive wall poster campaign against VD when rates rose at the end of the century.[54] Such a campaign simply could not have been undertaken in the metropole or in settler situations for fear of offending an upright population.

Turning a Blind Eye

In many colonies, various features of the old system operated in spite of legislative fiat. In Hong Kong, an elaborate if semiofficial system of regulation had reemerged by the early 1900s.[55] Since brothels were registered, they could easily be closed for flouting regulations. Ensuring regular inspection was not difficult, despite the abandonment of the compulsory examination. It would be the League of Nations' postwar interest in the traffic in women and children that prompted drastic changes in the colony; by 1935, the system was fully dismantled.

The ordinances at the Straits allowed similarly elaborate modes of regulation. Here, too, extralegal toleration existed until the late 1920s.[56] Straits officials nonchalantly admitted the continued use of licensing. In a report in 1900, the protector of Chinese listed registered brothels by nationality, detailing each of the women working in them. European women who set up business outside the brothel zone were reprimanded and returned to work in the red-light district. In Singapore, medical examinations were institutionalized.[57] These up-beat reports conjure an optimistic picture of a well-run system of overwhelming compliance and marked success, and they do not hide the organized nature of the system from official eyes.

Despite an official blandness when responding to hostile questions, India Office officials privately acknowledged that compliance with the law had not been wholly successful after a report from India showed eighteen of thirty-nine cantonments fudging the 1897 regulations.[58] Surgeons there quietly instituted local regulation without informing the authorities. In the remarkably public forum of the *Journal of the Royal Army Medical Corps,* Captain Dorgan described the system he had implemented at Poona:

> The measures adopted were mostly in accordance with the Indian Cantonment Code; they included weekly or fortnightly examinations and detention of all suspicious cases in hospital . . . my hospital though equipped with only thirty beds [was] obliged to accommodate fifty women patients. The remaining healthy women were permitted to remain in certain specific houses, under the control of a matron responsible for their freedom from infection, and who assisted in the detention of suspects. Antiseptic lotions were provided and regularly used. Wayside prostitution was prevented rigidly, and the recognized women were zealous to report all such interference with their monopoly by outsiders, though this was a means of infection which it was long difficult to control."[59]

At about the same time, Lawrence Harrison, who would become one of Britain's most influential venereologists, comfortably defied the will of the House of Commons in his posting at Sialkot. He thought it his duty "to prevent V.D. being conveyed to the troops by the ladies of the oldest profession in the sadar bazar." Using cantonment funds, he:

> instituted daily disinfection of the ladies by the matron of the cantonment hospital, and thereby abolished venereal infection by inmates of the bazar's brothels. I may add that I was warned by the senior medical officer of the station that I was imperilling my commission and that he would not protect me if any feminist organization started a row at army

headquarters. Instead of being "broke", however, my tenure of the appointment was prolonged by Lord Kitchener, who was a decided realist in these matters, when he learnt from the P.M.O., why there was no V.D. case in the station hospital at the time of his inspection. After all, I could not see how anyone could object to the daily disinfection. It was carried out by a female nurse and we did not advertise the fact that it was being done.[60]

The commonsense tone of his admission was typical of the doctorly insistence that these were practical and efficacious applications of medical wisdom. The Foreign Office noted with approval similarly unofficial schemes run by the U.S. military in Panama, who revealed in 1918 that "we were working on the plan three months before we said anything about it to the authorities of the cities and of the Republic." Foreign Office officials applauded "what can be done in a small district by men of determination who are not subject to pressure from Parliamentary quarters."[61] Regulation may have been publicly discredited in metropolitan settings, but such behind-the-scenes comments suggest that the antiregulationists were not wholly misplaced in their skepticism.

Sometimes the authorities actually aided the flouting of the law. The government of India helpfully pointed out to local officials that, under the 1899 Cantonment Act, women "quitting hospital without permission" committed an offense punishable by expulsion, thereby offering cantonment authorities suitably coercive but legal methods of control.[62] A report in 1900 from Bareilly in Oudh showed that women could only reside in the *sudder* bazar if they agreed to "present themselves for examination voluntarily once a week."[63] Officials flagged the report, calling the practices "illegal and objectionable."[64] The medical officer insisted that the system was wholly voluntary and that the women "appear to look on the medical institution as a safeguard and readily avail themselves of the advantages it offers."[65] The cantonment magistrate concurred, adding that "[T]here is great anxiety to get into cantonments amongst these women."[66] He may have been correct. Since residence in a space where steady business could more or less be guaranteed depended on cooperation with local rules, surgeons could technically claim that women agreed to attend voluntarily. Their livelihood might depend upon it. That knowledge, to some extent, was what kept versions of the system alive. Little seems to have been done at Bareilly, for in 1910, the indefatigable James Stuart asked the India Office to respond to claims that "a modified practice" of the CD act "still prevails in India."[67] Officials concluded that such procedures "fall within the letter but outside the spirit of the regulations," and that in some places "there existed a system of examination of all prostitutes which . . . cannot be regarded as really voluntary at all."[68]

But while regulation was thus successfully perpetuated, the new dimensions of the ordinances proved harder to enforce. While VD-centered legislation had focused on women as harbingers of disease, these laws moved the spotlight, albeit unsuccessfully, to those seen as the profiteers of the flesh trade. The new twentieth-century emphasis on protection was the justification for continued brothel regulation, but had little practical effect. When the protector of Chinese removed some ten girls under sixteen from a Penang brothel in 1899, the brothel owners invoked the Habeas Corpus Act. The judge ruled the detention illegal because there was "no overt act of training for prostitution," and the girls were returned to the brothel.[69] Inevitably, officials blamed Chinese traffickers determined to beat the system. Ordinances had to be constantly amended to frustrate their "knavish tricks."[70] The overwhelming verdict of officials was that such ordinances had "been a failure" and that rescue work was "very largely a fiasco."[71] The contrast with the cheerful optimism over regulation is striking.

In India, the law on trafficking remained at best opaque. Presidency laws mostly focused on the rights of guardians rather than of those sold or trafficked.[72] The Indian Penal Code punished those prostituting minors, but there were few prosecutions and even fewer successful convictions.[73] In the early 1900s there was a flurry of judicial activity on the issue as reform organizations lobbied for change. Both the government of India and the Bengal legislature considered legislation to bolster protection of minor girls sold into prostitution, the former prompted by testimony from the Society for the Protection of Children in India and from the Calcutta police about the numbers of underage children living in the city's brothels. A four-person committee (all male, three European) appointed by the Bengal lieutenant governor recommended a rescue home be provided for girls under the age of ten.[74] Central government demurred. "A home financed by Government and managed by a nominally non-sectarian but substantially Christian society could not fail to be regarded as, to all intents and purposes, a missionary institution supported by the State."[75] Both bills failed. The same concerns surfaced when the Hon. M. B. Dadabhoy introduced an all-India bill in 1912 to outlaw the dedication of girls under sixteen to temples. "In the hands of mischief-mongers," warned skeptics, the law would be interpreted as interference with local religious custom.[76] When legislation was reintroduced in 1914, supporters stressed "emphatically . . . that the Bill is in no sense a religious measure or in any way connected with religion. It is a measure for the rescue of young girls from immoral surroundings."[77] The bill failed nonetheless.

Formal Practices

Within and outside British spheres of influence, laws to fight STDs became common in the early 1900s. Thailand passed a Prevention of VD Act in 1908.[78] In the British colony of Malta, Ordinance XVII of 1903 regulated all aspects of the brothel and instituted regular genital examination. The secretary of state for the colonies did not assent to this palpable reintroduction of a CD system, but the Maltese government went ahead anyway.[79] In 1902, the Naval Executive Officer at Wei Hai Wei sought permission to establish a regulated brothel in response to fears of a clandestine trade aimed at the navy.[80] The small island of Wei Hai Wei, off the China coast, had been leased by the British since 1898 to counter Russian annexation in the region. The request was rejected by the island's commissioner, H. Stewart-Lockhart, not least because only four sailors had contracted VD in 1902, and none of them, claimed the staff surgeon, had contracted their disease on the island.[81]

In self-governing colonies, early twentieth-century policy was often more interventionist. Australian states ushered in radical new measures. In New South Wales a 1908 law allowed detention of convicted prisoners with VD beyond the expiration of their sentence, and was used disproportionately against women prisoners.[82] In 1913, Queensland introduced compulsory notification of syphilis and gonorrhea, mandatory examination, and where necessary, segregation of sufferers. Treatment could be administered only by the medically qualified, and free treatment centers were set up. Brisbane and South Brisbane's prostitutes were required to attend for fortnightly examination, on penalty of a hefty fine up to twenty pounds.[83] Prison doctors could examine any prisoner for VD.[84] Though ostensibly a public health measure, the act also defined public soliciting as vagrancy, punishable by detention or fine.[85] Yet leaflets distributed by the department of public health stressed that "venereal disease is neither a crime nor a punishment."[86] Morals, proclaimed one speaker in the Legislative Assembly, were beside the point. The aim was "to reduce the most appalling disease known to man, if not to eradicate it."[87]

The disjunction between the public presentation of rational and sensible science and a law which clearly stigmatized the existing underclass of convicts and known prostitutes has led one historian to conclude that "the new Health Act was the Old Act—writ small."[88] Though the double standard was abandoned with respect to notification and treatment, the act echoed age-old assumptions about prostitutes as transmitters of disease. The new clinics and dispensaries were physically separated from the special clinic for prostitute women.[89] And as in the CD years, the new laws did not apply to Aboriginal peoples, despite the widespread belief that they suffered disproportionately from venereal diseases. Their employment, their social and sexual relations, their health care, and their mobility fell under strict and separate jurisdiction.[90] The new laws were, moreover, at first applied only in Brisbane, where the population though not homogenous was much less racially diverse than in the north of the state.

Women's Position

The spirited challenges to such laws organized by women across Australia had little effect.[91] Queensland, with its long-standing CD Act and its radical new legislation, was a favorite focus for protest. In 1903 Sydney feminist Rose Scott addressed a WCTU convention there, censuring the new act's degradation of women.[92] The WCTU frequently petitioned the state government, in concert with church and other women's groups, for repeal.[93] In the 1940s women's groups were still in the forefront of opposition.[94]

There was, however, another layer of women's protest against the laws, by the women most directly affected. They wrote to officials about conditions in the lock hospitals, they refused the menial duties allotted them, they swore at the staff, and they left without formal discharge. In 1897 a police subinspector complained that "the women now laugh when sent to the Hospital, as they know they can leave, or return, at their own will."[95] One report told of three patients leaving the hospital and returning with a supply of whisky.[96] Doctors complained that lock patients "have no regard for any authority in the Hospital, and if the nurses do not please them they threaten that they will write to the Commissioner."[97] The anger of women affected by the laws is not surprising. Alongside the inflexible exam schedule imposed upon them, and the irksome routine of the lock wards, the federal tax office in 1918 took action to pursue prostitutes and brothel keepers as tax defaulters.[98] Not quite fully legal in their activities, they were nonetheless liable as if their livelihood was on a par with other kinds of work.

Prostitute women themselves had few allies, even though opposition to the law could be strong. Residents feared that without antiprostitution measures, the streets would be overrun by soliciting women and prospective clients. Brisbane's newspapers claimed streetwalking was on the rise, that brothels were opening at a furious rate, and that VD was growing apace.[99] Local councils received complaints from residents who feared a drop in property prices. Yet the police divisions at West End, West Gabba, and Mowbrayton reported "no increase in brothels," while the criminal investigation branch thought the prostitute presence "no more numerous or noticeable than at any time prior to the suspension of the Act."[100]

Venereal Disease Clubs

One new twist in the system that proved popular, until scandal enveloped it in 1907, was the private brothel club movement that sprang up in the Straits Settlements in the wake of compulsory examination. The club system began in the late 1880s when colonial surgeon T. C. Mugliston contracted to examine women in the Japanese brothels on Singapore's Malay Street.[101] The arrangement was short-lived, but a series of such clubs was established in and beyond Singapore in the 1890s. Mugliston had an arrangement with the Chinese brothels from 1893.[102] Clubs proliferated thereafter, in part because a plague epidemic in Penang had increased medical inspection of brothels, rekindling the idea of medical surveillance.[103] By 1894 few Singapore brothels did not subscribe to these schemes, and by 1903 there were brothel clubs throughout the colony, operated predominantly by government doctors.[104] For the women on the examining table little changed: they were examined by the same men on the same rotation.

In principle, these were voluntary affairs in which brothel keepers contracted with a doctor for regular inspections, treatment of infected women, and hospital access when necessary. Brothels paid $1.50 each for Chinese women and $2 for Japanese, and the doctors both received the sick in their clinics and made private visits to the brothels. The doctors insisted that their involvement was at the invitation of the women, though there is no doubt that they traded on their state positions and on the familiarity of the CD system in the brothel world.[105] Throughout their existence, such clubs had the support of the Chinese protectorate. The state surgeon at Selangor, E. A. O. Travers, examined Kuala Lumpur's Japanese brothels and at the invitation of the protector, G. T. Hare, in 1899 extended the scheme to the Chinese brothels.[106] He rented space for a dispensary and a hospital offering separate wards for Chinese and Japanese women.[107] Hare also initiated the scheme at Perak, and his successor "freely admitted that without the assistance rendered by the Chinese Protectorate it could neither have been started nor carried on."[108]

At the height of his business, Travers brought in about a thousand dollars a month.[109] Such arrangements, concluded Colonial Office officials, were beyond the definition of private practice, and were "a definite and lucrative business."[110] But it was a business deeply embarrassing to the government in a host of ways. Not only did it make politicians vulnerable to accusations that the heart of the regulation system had been reestablished in underhand ways and with official sanction, but it tarnished notions of colonial duty. Government doctors were once more examining marginalized women for stigmatized diseases and worse, were engaging in "a most unbecoming fight for the business."[111] In Kinta district in the FMS, feuding between government medical officers over brothel practice became serious enough to warrant an official enquiry in 1907.[112] Dr. Duncan Cooper "entered into a profit-sharing association with two low-class Asiatic practitioners one a Chinese and the other a Japanese . . . most discreditable and highly unbecoming for a Government Medical Officer."[113]

Colonial Office staff had expressed concern when Mugliston first established his Singapore clinic. There was lively debate about whether he should be permitted to give women certificates guaranteeing their freedom from disease.[114] George Johnson, always the conscience of the Colonial Office, had warned that Mugliston's practice "was carrying on . . . practically all the machinery of the repealed C.D. ordinances," and that brothel clubs in the FMS would "differ very little from the compulsory C.D. system, except in name," since "Gov^t. Medical Officers will be mixed in it."[115] The colonial secretary had indicated to the governor in 1894 his disapproval of what he saw as indirect evasion of the imperial dictate.[116]

But while in the 1880s officials worried about whether the clubs reinstated the banished CD regulations, by the 1900s their concern focused on whether doctors neglected their government work in catering to the brothel market.[117] The doctors complained that their government salaries were low, and that their rights to private practice were due compensation for their poor official pay.[118] Civil surgeons were commonly permitted private practice to bolster their state remuneration, though there was long-standing tension over the arrangement.[119] Rather than call attention to the embarrassing proximity of these schemes to the reviled CD system, it was politic to make the debate turn on doctors' neglect of their duties. The ploy seemed largely to work. Anti-regulationists knew of the clubs, but expended little energy on protesting them.[120] In September 1907, the Straits governor forbade employees in his jurisdiction from engaging in brothel practice.[121] While public attention was directed away from the regulationist elements of the clubs, the speed with which the Straits governor ruled on the issue, before the various enquiries had even concluded, suggests that the CD debacle had not been forgotten.

The Lives of Women

Sex workers continued to be seen as the principal source of VD. As we have seen, little changed for the prostitute women of Hong Kong and the Straits. In Queensland and India, women's lives became, if anything, more difficult as a result of the changes in legislation. The new Queensland law added punitive layers to the existing system, while the new rules in India, though they folded VD into the broader category of "infectious or contagious diseases," in practice targeted the venereals. Military authorities more strictly enforced cantonment regulations and adopted "measures . . . to keep women away."[122] Officers complained that their inability to enforce rules beyond cantonment limits made a mockery of their efforts, but in practice, they maximized what was permitted in imaginative ways that directly affected the women, often exacerbating already difficult lives.[123] Loitering and solicitation were policed ever more vigorously.[124] The right to expel those suspected of disease but refusing examination began to be liberally used. Infected suspects were served an order to appear for inspection, and the diseased were hospitalized. But failure to comply resulted in removal from the cantonment.[125] Officials grumbled that women merely moved to the nearest town or village. In an attempt to prevent women moving between military locations, they reported expulsions to neighboring cantonment authorities.[126]

> The Commander-in-Chief cannot emphasise too strongly the necessity for co-operation when persons who are a danger to the community from a diseased or infected condition are excluded from a cantonment. Immediately notice must issue to neighbouring cantonments and the journeys made by such people closely watched whenever possible. Co-operative action must, in time, produce valuable results, safeguarding the soldier from the diseases which most affect his efficiency.[127]

Prostitution, Christianity, and Empire

Abolitionists never again enjoyed the political impact they had garnered in the 1880s and 1890s, but they continued to wage war against regulated prostitution.

In all corners of the empire, the agents of social purity and missionary organizations fought trafficking and sexual exploitation, but most especially it was secret and unofficial versions of the CD laws that they sought to uncover.

Far more was at stake, however, for these indefatigable campaigners than whether women were being compelled to undergo vaginal examinations or whether the state was acting as brothel keeper. These were serious evils for antiregulationists, but they were merely symptoms of a far more pernicious malaise. For antiregulationists, prostitution and its invariable concomitant, VD, were signs of a society in thrall to degradation, to lack of progress and civilization. Prostitution literally held up the advancement of Christian civilization, the core value of so much of the social purity vision. For abolitionists, the most iniquitous feature of the colonial sex trade was its sanction under British law. It was the dereliction of the duties of civilization by colonial administrations that most affronted them.

> Cairo is Egyptian, Constantinople is Turkish, but Rangoon is British. The administration of Cairo is difficult owing to its complication of authorities, Egyptian, British, and those of the various Powers. The capital of the Ottoman Empire is in a degenerate and helpless condition, like the rest of the State; Burma, by contrast, possesses an administration equal in ability to any other within our Eastern Empire.[128]

Prostitution and VD undermined not only the health of soldiers or the morals of indigenes but the very basis of imperial rule. This terror lay at the heart of social purity campaigns. Britain's role was one of uplift and enlightenment, of advance; if Britons abroad allowed the contamination of their principles, then Christianity and the Empire could not but flounder. Fears that colonial CD laws would ease their reemergence in the metropolis were strong, but even more critical was the role of Britain as an imperial, Christian, and upright power, a force for Protestant values. Butler and her followers protested regulated prostitution as Christians and imperialists. Moral rule underpinned their call for repeal. "Unless we can realise the iniquity to which this country is being committed ignorantly and against its will, we cannot hope that the Empire will endure, or that we shall continue to hold our place among the nations."[129] The supremacy of British imperial prestige was critically at stake.

The fear that retention of regulation in the colonies would pave the way for a domestic reemergence of the CD system was also a constant theme. "If these laws are allowed to be put into force once more in our Indian Provinces," asked one typical pamphlet, "what is to hinder the same thing in England?"[130] Millicent Garrett Fawcett warned that "the real force at the back of this movement is the desire, openly expressed by many of our opponents, to re-enact the Contagious Diseases Act both in England and in India."[131] One turn-of-the-century pamphlet pointed out the potent combination of cantonment legislation in India, the push for compulsory detention of patients in the lock wards of workhouse infirmaries and for disease notification, and the existence of regulation in besieged South Africa. Were regulation to return in the domestic arena, it warned, "an official standing will be given to vice—our sons will be taught thereby that it is not sinful and dishonourable—and our daughters, or at least the daughters of working men and women, will be in danger of being recruited to fill the ranks of officially-provided prostitutes."[132]

Imperial Prowess and Racial Difference

Racial ideology played an ever greater role in attitudes to VD and sexuality in the early twentieth century. Antiregulationist Maurice Gregory claimed that "Venereal Maladies have, above all others, a racial importance."[133] On the other side of the campaign, Kitchener's 1905 memorandum to the troops in India, where he was now commander in chief, warned that diseases "passed on from one race of men to another always increase in severity."[134] A 1906 select committee at the Cape recommended strengthening regulation because of syphilis, "the spread of which is helped on by coloured servants and by those of them who migrate between prostitution and service."[135] "A Public Servant" likewise concluded that since empire and morality could not be coterminous, the CD acts were a necessity. "England cannot Christianize her heathen Empire. That Empire may heathenize England, as it has already heathenized her governing class."[136] The implication that contacts with locals was a risky business, physically and morally, runs through not just Kitchener's memo but surfaces, as we have seen, over and over again in this and earlier periods, a theme shared alike by regulationists and abolitionists.

In imagining Britain's civilizing role in the tropics, abolitionists resembled their foes in seeing immutable difference and distance between the bringers of civilization and their "clients." "The uplift of Indian men and women is our only justification for being in their country at all," argued Katherine Dixon, who toured India's cantonments a number of times in the 1910s.[137] India's brothel inhabitants, she claimed, were "friendless and ignorant."[138] Violet Tempest, in a visceral display of disgust, imagined "the brown body and the black hair plastered down and reeking of rancid cocoanut (sic) oil...sucked into its heavy greasy coils," luring the soldier to danger.[139] Filth was as common a theme among antiregulation campaigners as it was among colonial doctors and army officers. John Cowen talked disgustedly of cities "polluted" by "the poison of prostitution."[140] Veteran campaigners Elizabeth Andrew and Katharine Bushnell likewise cast Chinese society as invidious and its women as helpless. Only Christianity for them was capable of raising Chinese women out of "heathen slavery."[141] Henry Wilson writing to his wife admitted that "Even now, we of the British Committee are at dead-lock as to the perplexity of the problem of what to do in the case of the Heathen Chinese in Singapore & c."[142]

For regulationists, the ability to rule in an imperial context was enormously affected by these questions around prostitution and VD. These were not minor issues, irritating but ultimately unimportant; instead they bore directly on Britain's moral stature and its physical and technological prowess. Would soldiers be fit to fight? Could western techniques conquer the severity of diseases acquired in hostile environments? Could Britain maintain its supremacy in moral terms and in its manpower? These were not idle questions, but critical issues in domestic its circles.

In the new century these were urgent considerations. Britain was at the height of its imperial prowess but aware of pressure from competing colonial powers as well as its own slow but inexorable economic decline. Significant changes in medicine catapulted syphilis, most especially, to prominence. Eugenics stressed the need to nurture, to control, and to police racial and class boundaries. The abolitionist movement struggled to define its role in relation to these new developments and, in many ways, must be deemed a failure, since extralegal methods of control continued in the colonies throughout the early twentieth century, despite its vigilance.

The issue was no longer one of central public concern. The AMSH, WCTU, and the YMCA were all determined to keep the question in the public eye; though they were successful at involving their own membership, the issue had lost its drama for the wider metropolitan population. Try as they might, the newest generation of abolitionists simply could not sustain the numbers and the popularity of the earlier campaigners. In part, this reflected changing imperial and national politics. The weakness of the Liberals in the mid-1890s and early 1900s clearly hurt the antiregulation cause. Though endlessly disappointed by Liberalism in power, the majority of activists nonetheless identified with the party's overall political philosophy, and parliamentary foes of regulated prostitution were invariably radical Liberals.

In government, meanwhile, the Unionist party faced a slew of difficult colonial questions in the wake of the Boer War: military demands for increased funding, disparagement by foreign powers of Britain's wartime conduct, internal and white settler dissatisfaction over the postwar introduction of Chinese indentured labor in South Africa. Their convincing defeat in the 1906 general election, however, left the incoming Liberals with a delicate colonial legacy, not least in Ireland. Despite an ambitious domestic agenda, Liberals continued to disappoint abolitionists with their performance on regulated prostitution in the empire. The growing militarism of the post-Boer years empowered the army to push further for regulation. The 1907 Territorial and Reserve Forces Act, creating a reserve army expressly for domestic defense and freeing the regular army for overseas deployment, demonstrates the growing strength of the military in the early 1900s. It was the "largest overhaul of Britain's armed forces since the Cardwell reforms."[143] Militarism was anathematic to abolitionists: its "sister evils" were "prostitution and alcoholism."[144]

Medical Women

In 1897, the Army Sanitary Commission had broached the possibility of utilizing "female medical assistants" in India to conduct genital examinations of women.[145] A year later, Joseph Chamberlain encouraged the Straits and Hong Kong governments to employ "one or more women Doctors to assist in the treatment of women afflicted with these special diseases, as well as of those admitted to the Government Hospitals for other diseases; in the hope of overcoming the reluctance, common among Asiatic women of all classes, to take advantage of hospital treatment."[146] Women's appointments to colonial medical posts were tied in complex ways to highly racialized ideas of imperial honor and prowess. The prospect of using white as opposed to indigenous women doctors excited the most controversy. More than local women, they trod an impossible path between medical professionalism and respectable ladyhood that detractors thought incompatible with the care of prostitutes or the treatment of sexually transmissible diseases. George Johnson at the Colonial Office argued that "it would be difficult if not impossible to get a Lady Doctor who would consent to work the compulsory (CDO) system."[147] The Lady Dufferin fund, which trained women doctors for India, was equally implacable. "The Committee decided that in no circumstances should any lady doctor attached to a hospital connected with the Association be employed on any such duty, and they expressed the opinion that any such employment would be highly injurious to the interests and work of the Association."[148]

Lord Elgin in India thought that since the women examinees were neither "modest" nor "virtuous," they would not care who examined them.[149] The commanding officer at Hong Kong claimed that, "considering that the most pure and the most virtuous women in European countries are nearly always attended by male doctors for the many internal ailments to which women are subject and which necessitate close examination and touch, I, in no way, believe that Chinese prostitutes have a stronger feeling of delicacy on this subject."[150] Curzon and his military advisers were quick to "strongly deprecate" the use of women in VD wards. The "native community," they argued, would find women's attendance offensive and their presence would negatively influence the prospects of female medical education in India.[151] And in a surprising maneuver, given the routinely antagonistic relations between government and missionaries, they argued that women's presence would compromise the medical work done by missionaries among local women. From the Straits came a volley of objections. Lady doctors would be subject to the whim of the brothel keepers who would not permit them to visit the women. "[U]nable to speak the dialects used by the Chinese prostitute," her presence would be useless. And even supposing she "surmounted these difficulties," too many such stalwarts would be required.[152] J. M. Atkinson, principal civil medical officer at Hong Kong, sent a series of spirited reports casting doubt on women's abilities to function as doctors in his colony. "Visiting Chinese brothels, would, especially during the hot summer months, be too trying for an English lady; their [sic] health would not stand it in this trying climate." The work, moreover, would be too monotonous for the "lady doctor."[153] Curzon thought "few, if any, respectable female hospital assistants would be forthcoming."[154] Atkinson concurred; since Hong Kong was so full of prostitutes, a large contingent of women would be necessary but hard to find.[155] Lord Elgin, seemingly alarmed by any employment of medical women, worried that only those likely to take bribes would be willing to undertake the "dirty" work of VD examining.[156] The reaction from colonial officials was uniformly negative and in January 1899 an internal Colonial Office memo concluded, "I suppose we must give in . . . and drop the idea for the present."[157]

Yet the very grounds of opposition revealed the many contradictions at work and the tenacious assumptions about local attitudes to western medicine. Atkinson contrasted Chinese women's reluctance to submit to European medical hands with Ceylon and India where, he claimed, the women displayed no such prejudice. But Indian officials argued exactly the opposite, that women's presence in hospitals "would be most repugnant to the feelings of the native community."[158] And this was despite petitions such as that lodged by a group of registered women in October 1881 requesting the appointment of examining female doctors.[159] Fixed as the "characteristics" of native populations were said to be, they were also malleable properties in arguing policy and practice on the ground.

Where "lady doctors" were employed, they were mostly transformed into female medical assistants, a title establishing a lesser role for them in the hospital hierarchy.[160] The arrival of or potential for women doctors complicated racial relationships, for while women could not be seen to compete with white male doctors, their racial status placed them above "native" male assistants. One route out of this dilemma, pursued most vigorously in India where western medical education was well established, was to encourage the employment of medically trained Indian rather than British women. The Indian surgeon general in 1899 urged such appointments.

> [A]s many qualified Native Medical women, married women— preferably—and not under 30 years of age . . . should be appointed to the female wards of Cantonment Hospitals; they should work under the orders of the Medical Officers in charge of the hospitals, but should be recognised as the Native Subordinates in charge of the women's wards . . . They would examine and treat, subject to the supervision of the doctor in charge, all women in or attending hospital, whether suffering from venereal or other disease.[161]

It was a debate simultaneously enmeshed in questions of sex suitability and "native" employment.

Though the "lady doctor" enjoyed some of the privileges of medical status, nurses trod a fine line with respect to status. Though some, in an essentializing gesture, saw the nurse as a humanizing influence on brutish soldiers, she still had to be kept in check.[162] Lady nurses, thought George White, might attend "theatricals" as spectators but ought not appear on stage, nor attend balls.[163] It was critical that the nurse as a member of the medical establishment and as a white woman be rendered safe from criticism and gossip.

> The amount of liberty to be accorded to the nursing sisters as to recreation, etc., is rather a delicate question ... I should be inclined to say that lady nurses should not attend balls or amusements which are likely to keep them up late at night, as it seems to me entirely inconsistent with their work in hospitals ... [they] should do nothing which unfits them in any sense of the word for their ordinary work, or which would be at all likely to bring discredit on the nursing service. An afternoon garden party or an occasional game of tennis, etc., I see no harm in, nor a drive with ladies; such recreations are necessary to health, but even these should not be too frequent, as it is not desirable that the sisters should be too much *en evidence.* I would certainly forbid them, whatever their age, riding, driving, or walking about singly with gentlemen.[164]

The Proletarian Woman

Schemes to establish matrons and police women as supervisors of other women were also characteristic of this period. Organized corps of women police were largely a product of the First World War, and were by no means always welcomed by male police.[165] The Brisbane police department, for example, rejected the idea of women police in 1915, since "we have old women in sufficient numbers in the Police Force already."[166] In the dependent colonies, abolitionists championed the use of women in rescue work, combining some medical and personal with spiritual care. The Ladies' National Association for the Repeal of the Contagious Diseases Acts suggested to the India Office in 1914 that "carefully selected and trained" Englishwomen could substitute for the police in dealing with women charged with prostitution offenses.[167] Social purity organizations advised the appointment of a Cantonese-speaking woman to the staff of the Chinese Protectorate at the Straits. The authorities mostly ignored such suggestions, dubbing them "hopelessly impractical" ideas from people "entirely ignorant" of colonial conditions.[168]

Despite the hostility to medical women, British women increasingly took up paying work in the colonies as nurses, doctors, teachers, and barmaids. Though emigration, particularly to Australasia, became substantially more acceptable in polite circles in the mid-nineteenth century, the very notion of the paid woman worker could shade into hints of prostitution, more especially in the service sector.[169] It was this fear of a connection, of a temptation and a pull as well as of native opinion that led men of the stature of Curzon to spend time fretting over the tiny number of unmarried working women in colonial employ. Since migrant women were often single, the state often stepped in, in place of a husband, to regulate their mobility and behavior.[170] Helen Kanitkar argues that restrictions on women in the colonies exceeded those in the metropole.[171] Barmaids were one group of women who particularly stirred anxiety in dependent colonies. The prototypical "good-time girl" working in an overtly male environment, the barmaid was automatically suspect. The British consul general in Portuguese Lourenco Marques thought "nine-tenths of the women so employed lead an immoral life."[172] Though their numbers were small, their presence was tied inextricably to the deep moral entanglements of sex, alcohol, and race. The government of India proposed in 1902 to prohibit employment of barmaids, and between 1902 and 1908 there were attempts to restrict and prohibit women from working as barmaids in the newly federated Australia, and in New Zealand as well as in Britain and South Africa.[173] "Whether the barmaids do or do not serve European customers," wrote Lord Curzon, viceroy of India, "yet there is nothing to prevent natives from frequenting the bars; very often they do so; the girls cannot refuse to serve them; the spectacle of service is open to the eyes of natives equally with Europeans."[174] In "the case of a Miss Matheson, of whom it is said that she became so degraded as to solicit Corringhi coolies in public houses," after working as a barmaid at the Royal and British India hotels lurked the alarming image of a white woman choosing commercial sex with indigenous men.[175] Curzon thought few barmaids "really retain their virtue," though even more importantly than the reality, he wondered, "why make public the spectacle of English girls engaged in duties which must carry with them some sense of humiliation to the native eye, and which must suggest the idea of immorality, even where the reality does not exist?"[176]

An associated fear was that of women being hired by nonwhite employers that meshed with the common vision of the sexual procurer as a foreigner. Women and Girls' Protection laws passed in Saskatchewan in 1912 and British Columbia in 1919 explicitly forbade white women from working for nonwhite employers.[177] The target in these instances was Chinese employers. In Queensland, efforts to prevent Chinese employers from hiring Aboriginal women were commonplace in the nineteenth century. Such policies strikingly parallel the rhetoric at work in the Straits and Hong Kong about protecting women from Chinese male brutality. Throughout the empire police officials closely monitored the movements of European men, and especially Jews, convinced that all such men were active in the business of procuring women for the brothels. During the First World War most especially, but even earlier, colonial officials studied closely how they might augment their powers of deportation against "undesirable foreigners."[178]

While white women employed in the colonies ran the gamut from the highly educated woman doctor to the disorderly slattern serving beer to men of all races, indigenous women workers were all potentially troublesome. In particular, the fear that all women were susceptible to men's blandishments coupled with the fear of "sly" prostitution led to limits on women's employment. Aboriginal women could work only in occupations and for employers approved by the protector, for example. In India, new rules barred women from a number of trades in cantonments.[179] The effect on their livelihood could be devastating. In 1879, the engineer at Ranikhet in the Northwest Provinces dismissed women working on a building project after some unregistered women were arrested on prostitution charges.[180] Some twenty years later, the Fort William grass cutters petitioned for the return of women's jobs, lost when the authorities suspected them of selling sex to the soldiers. Husbands and wives worked alongside one another and the male grass cutters insisted that their wives were "of good character" and that without their wages, "we cannot possibly earn enough."[181] Though the grass cutters did have their employment restored, a slew of conditions about when the women could be near the barracks, and in whose company, made their working lives the more difficult. Such restrictions had a long history. In 1871, Indian officials counseled "that the Public Works Department be required to insure that no women labourers in the Government buildings in course of erection be allowed to hut themselves within one mile of the barracks, and further that their departure from the vicinity of the works adjacent to men's quarters be secured before dusk."[182] A proposal in 1877 that women employed by the Punjab public works department be subject to registration as prostitutes was rejected, not as an unjust measure but because it would cause "the whole body of them to abandon work."[183]

Conclusion

The repeal campaign, according to its undisputed leader, Josephine Butler, was "one of the most vital movements of Christian times."[184] In many respects, Butler was right, for the anti-CD campaign had not only given feminism a new and more radical public voice but it had demanded a consideration of the deep links between home and empire. Begun to protest the domestic acts of the 1860s, the campaign rapidly moved overseas, its supporters spreading out across the empire and into continental Europe.

Though the issue stayed alive in the twentieth century, it never attracted the level of support or indeed indignation so characteristic of its late nineteenth-century manifestation. To some extent, feminist agendas had moved in different directions, but other forces were at work too. The gradual waning of Christian influences in wider society lent the rhetoric of morality an increasingly old-fashioned tone while the scientific state gave doctors greater authority bolstered by the new techniques in VD treatment. The empire, too, was changing, not only with the growing assertiveness of white settler independence but with the inescapable results of an ever more vocal nationalist lobby.

The new politics of the twentieth century raised political questions around sexuality in ways unavailable prior to the feminist attack on the CD acts in the 1880s. But that feminist rhetoric, learned so courageously in the face of virulent opposition, found itself in the 1900s curiously out of step with changing policy and opinion. After the war, attitudes perceptibly began to shift. An official committee reporting on Bombay prostitution in the early 1920s asserted flatly that "the failure of regulation under the Contagious Diseases Act all over India points to the unsuitability of the soil to such a system."[185] Such an attitude was a far cry from the insistence only a few years previously that without regulation the civilian population and the British military would be overrun with diseases that would be passed inexorably down the generations. Changes in medical opinion, a growing acceptance of state intervention in the lives of the poor, changes in attitudes to empire, and the new face of feminism all contributed to the demise of social purity feminism in the years before war engulfed the empire in 1914. Though it had little effect on entrenched prejudices about women, work, and sex, such sea changes left the abolitionist movement increasingly out of step with contemporary attitudes.

Feminist-abolitionists, furthermore, had failed to win widespread acceptance for medical women—whether as nurses or as doctors—in colonial settings. White women's presence in the colonies continued a grudging one, their main role that of civilizing and domesticating both their own menfolk and the obdurate locals. Not surprisingly, such attitudes consolidated existing myths around both race and gender, stereotypes all too often expressed in abolitionist rhetoric. The repeal movement showed little interest in the loss of livelihood occasioned by colonial attitudes to prostitution and which, in labelling native women as likely sex workers, limited their access to other employment opportunities. Indeed, the repealers saw little relationship between labor and prostitution at all.

In the winter of 1918, playwright George Bernard Shaw received a letter from the social purity group, the Association for Moral and Social Hygiene, which had recently begun a campaign intended to pressure the British government into suppressing the tolerated brothels in France, which the organization took to be a moral and sanitary threat to British troops in the western theater of war. Shaw's response to this plea for support made the point that in their own literature the AMSH acknowledged that women working in such houses were regularly expected to service twenty-four soldiers every day. Shaw reoriented the contours of the campaign in an attempt to get at the labor questions he thought central here.

> Allowing eight hours out of the twenty-four for meals and sleep and dressing, which means a working day of sixteen hours, she has to entertain three different soldiers every two hours. If her working day is twelve hours, two different soldiers every hour. Now it is clear that no woman, however abandoned or sexually insane, would submit to such

hideous drudgery except under that pressure of poverty which drives women to submit to sweating in every trade. The soldier voluntarily and for his pleasure commits a single sin against the moral code. The woman is forced to commit the same sin twice every hour to earn her bread. Had we not better begin with the care of the woman and let the soldier wait?[186]

But Shaw's impassioned plea for such considerations fell largely on deaf ears. If the abolitionist movement's attitudes to sexuality were out of step with early twentieth-century sensibilities, the same might be said of their reading of the labor market.

Chapter 6

Colonial Soldiers, White Women, and the First World War

Venus Vulgivaga slays more warriors than Mars when mad. Venus Urania remains curtained in the home, but her destroying sister, Vulgivaga, ever follows the camps and cantonments. It may be, and it is probable from evidence at hand, that the enemy sent ahead women fully loaded with those germs, gonococci and spirochetes.

—William Lee Howard

Everything depends now upon keeping the people keen about the war but if the notion which has already taken root is allowed to spread that instead of being in a sacred cause the war is a vehicle of vice and demoralisation there will arise an uneasiness amongst the soundest part of the people—that is the backbone on which you have to rely—that the war is under a curse.

—Lord Salisbury

If activists had failed to keep the issue of regulated prostitution alive in the public imagination in the early 1900s, the years between 1914 and 1918 would prove even more difficult for their cause. VD control never ceased to play a major role in the military, and the increased interest in, and panic about its spread and its potential impact on soldiers increasingly marginalized abolitionists, even while it energized debates around the relationships between morals, medicine, and politics. The outbreak of war in 1914 shifted concerns over VD back into the military arena.[1] In turn, that permitted the reintroduction of elements of the contagious diseases (CD) system to cope with the spike in VD rates occasioned by the mass movement of soldiers and by wartime conditions.

The Wars within the War

When the hostilities in Europe erupted into a full-scale declaration of war in 1914, military officials assumed that mass military deployment would send VD rates soaring. The incidence of military VD did rise during the war though not as much as predicted. Indeed, in 1917 colonial secretary, Walter Long, boasted that "the marked decrease in the incidence of venereal diseases, which has been continuous for many years in this country and in India, has not been interrupted by the war."[2] When military and civilian statistics were broken apart, however, army and navy figures were seen to be on the rise. A slight increase in incidence had, in fact, preceded the war; VD was the most constant cause of sickness among British military personnel in both 1913 and 1914, the greatest cause of "constant inefficiency in the home command."[3]

Yet even the official statistics for the war period do not show a consistent rise in infection despite the growing alarm of commentators, the press, and a number of politicians. In the early stages of the war, military admissions to hospital for VD were lower than they had been between 1911 and 1913. Admissions among British troops rose late in the war, though they never exceeded the worst pre-war figures, reaching no higher than a rate of 51.8 per 1,000 of U.K. troop strength.[4] That was not the case among Dominion soldiers whose rates were, throughout the war, significantly higher than other troops. They showed a consistently high rate of admissions for VD, seldom less than 100 per 1,000 of troop strength.[5] By 1915, 28.5 percent of Canadians serving overseas were under treatment for venereal infection.[6] Recognizing the distinction between British experience and that of the colonial allies, L. W. Harrison noted that "[O]ur overseas colleagues have pursued much more thorough methods as far as the purely material part of prevention is concerned, but have had to contend with greater incentives to incontinence than we."[7] The Australians put it more succinctly, noting that for such troops, "leave did not mean home-leave."[8]

The rhetoric of venereal disease control as a war within a war developed quickly in Britain and its colonies: "if the problem of venereal disease was important before the War it is a hundred times more so now."[9] In a rousing speech to male undergraduates at Sydney University in 1916, Professor D. A. Welsh was unequivocal that this was a "dirty war."

> In our midst are many foes by whom Australia is beset. One of the most terrible is venereal disease. While it is true that the great war is of prime importance, it is also true that the problems of venereal disease are secondary only to the problems of war, and are indeed complementary to them. Next to the war, the campaign against venereal disease is the most important thing that could engage our attention.[10]

Wartime conditions focused attention on the relationship between loyalty and morality. While Germany was the notional enemy of the allied powers, avoidable disease was close behind as a sign of disloyalty, betrayal, selfishness, and lack of moral rectitude. The marriage of morals and politics quickly emerged as a key means of representing patriotism. World War One was as much a site of moral struggle as it was a global war.

Britain deployed a huge variety of troops from its colonial possessions. Two and a half million colonial soldiers fought alongside British troops, with thousands more in noncombatant roles.[11] White Dominion countries provided about 1.3 million soldiers. Troops from nonwhite dependent colonies were regarded, however, as a risk in battle; the experience of combat both trained them in the use of powerful weaponry and exposed them to the prospect of a defeated imperial power.[12] As a result, many were organized into noncombatant labor battalions. The only nonwhite colonial soldiers who were armed were the almost one million Indian soldiers deployed on both the eastern and western fronts, of whom around 135,000 were stationed in France.[13] Despite misgivings about their suitability and loyalty, the Indians were crucial to British operations in both theaters of war. By the end of 1918, over half a million Indians had also served in noncombatant positions, in supply and transport, and in the medical service.[14] South African blacks were strictly organized as noncombatants in the South African Native Labour Contingent formed in September 1916 and in the Cape Auxiliary Horse Transport Companies.[15] A force of about 90,000 Chinese laborers was raised through the British territory at Wei Hai Wei.[16] There were also Caribbean and Fijian troops, used principally as laborers.[17]

While the problem of disciplining soldiers and retaining the loyalty of subjects was of crucial importance to the military, defining the wartime role of women was no less urgent. The "khaki fever" said to be sweeping the country conjured scenes of public display and uncontrolled behavior by girls and women anxious to offer themselves to soldiers, with or without material gain.[18] This alleged promiscuity was seen not only as an inevitable path to VD, but to an indiscriminate mixing of the races. The presence of nonwhite colonial soldiers, exotic in their foreignness and supposedly less able to resist sexual temptation, heightened both fears of and rumors about the sexual wantonness of white working-class women. These fears of potential disloyalty in two such marginal groups as colonized men and working-class women coalesced around VD and its threat to military efficiency.

In the earliest years of the war, attention to VD was focused more on military than on civilian infection. The sexual habits and leave preferences of soldiers and sailors were closely observed and potentially controversial. Juggling public opinion and political demands, soldierly interpretation of the rules, and the novelty of much medical policy, governments and military authorities never hit upon a consistent position vis-à-vis VD but veered instead between satisfying the demands of competing interests. In practice, of course, unofficial means of coping with the problem coexisted with formal policy in all the armies associated with the British war effort.

The Prophylaxis Debate

By October 1919, the British military authorities had issued more than 5 million capsules of calomel cream in their losing battle against military VD, and in the process had met with widespread hostility.[19] The debate over appropriate means of combating venereal infection was a politically sensitive one, conducted in a variety of public and professional arenas.[20] Social purity organizations rooted in feminism sided with the newly formed National Council for the Combatting of Venereal Disease (NCCVD) in opposing prophylaxis, regarded as a license for unconsidered promiscuity. Supported by feminists in the settler colonies, there were also organizations such as the British Social Hygiene Council for whom prophylaxis was the modern weapon of sanitary science that would efficiently eliminate the manpower wastage wrought by VD. Australian physician James Barrett thought the British authorities backward. "The governmental action— a lack of action—is unsound, since the man who contracts disease is severely punished, but adequate attempts are not made to prevent him acquiring it."[21] For Barrett, the inexorable logic of modern medicine was clear and simple; without a preventative policy not only was military efficiency compromised, but military logic was at fault. Governments, he thought, should be in the vanguard in encouraging modern unsentimental policy. Yet even Australian policy radicalized only under the pressure of war. Prior to the dramatic increase in VD in Egypt in late 1914 and early 1915, these diseases were dealt with "only under a veil of secrecy."[22] While proponents would later boast of Australia's farsightedness, the policy was driven mostly by need.

This tension between morality and the sanitary crystallized in the struggle over the issue of prophylactic packets to men taking military leave.[23] The prophylactic kit contained a tube of calomel ointment (for syphilis), potassium permanganate solution or tablets (for gonorrhea), and cotton swabs for their application.[24] The Germans and the Americans had experimented with kits before the war.[25] The U.S. navy began issuing calomel as a prophylactic in 1908, the U.S. army in 1909.[26] Under pressure from moral purity groups, they abandoned the practice in 1915. Dominion armies introduced the kits in 1916, though it was 1918 before the War Office agreed to their distribution among U.K. troops. Churches, social purity groups, and Dominion politicians mindful of public opinion in their own countries all opposed their issue. "Primary prophylaxis," claimed Angela Booth of the Australian Association to Combat the Social Evil, "carries with it the consent of society to sexual promiscuity; early treatment does not. Early treatment says in effect: Though you have broken the moral law, public health requires that you and others be saved from the results of your folly."[27] The AMSH sent a "strongly protesting" missive to the War Office upon learning about the distribution of packets to Australian soldiers, demanding to know whether the practice was also common in British regiments.[28]

Akin to the preventive logic of the packet, and closely associated with the idea that men were most at risk while on leave, were the blue light depots, so called for the blue light which identified them at night. Mark Harrison sees the treatment centers as "a half-way house to the distribution of prophylactic packets," but the distinction between the two was carefully maintained.[29] The War Office explicitly separated the packet and the clinic. In a 1916 despatch, they advised that men "who have exposed themselves to the danger of venereal infection should be required to attend for treatment," but also warned that the

War Office would not heed "suggestions... which would imply the adoption of any system of prophylaxis which might be said to afford opportunities for unrestrained vice."[30]

Well established in both Britain and Egypt (where they were known as lavage rooms) by the end of 1916, they offered aggressive postcoital prevention.[31] Soldiers were promised complete confidentiality, but though records were not kept, men complained that the space and layout of the clinics were too public.[32] The British Army experimented with a system allowing men to self-treat rather than attend orderly-run clinics, but such facilities were not available everywhere.[33]

The treatments on offer were neither pleasant nor comfortable, and certainly not popular.[34] They centered on penile irrigation designed to flush out infections before they could take hold. Men were required to maintain a chemical solution in their urethral canal for minutes at a time by manually closing the urethral opening. Full irrigation led to the artificial and uncomfortable filling of the bladder as the irrigating solution was washed back through the urethra and into the bladder.[35] Prostate massage—self-administered or by a medical orderly— was also common and equally unpopular.[36] Prophylaxis was the "dominating feature in the medical campaign" against venereal diseases, even though some doubted its efficacy.[37] Major B. T. Zwar of the Australian Imperial Forces (AIF) in Egypt, claimed that of three hundred patients under his care in Alexandria in 1915, "88.3%... had been infected in spite of the employment of preventive measures." He thought such methods should "occupy a subsidiary position" in VD control.[38]

The condom, though available and in some instances given free at leave time, was mentioned far less in prophylaxis debates. A more expensive preventive, it was also unequivocally linked to contraception and therefore even more morally suspect than unguents and irrigations.[39] The prominence of eugenic anxieties around race suicide and the robust pronatalist campaigns so common in Australia and in New Zealand stigmatized the condom.[40] Before the advent of family planning clinics, and at a time when information about contraception was still often regarded as obscene, military and governmental authorities were cautious about promoting or even discussing the use of the condom, despite its palpable role in disease prevention. Instead, troops were leafleted about the dangers of VD, given frequent and sometimes graphic lectures about its dangers, threatened with stoppage of pay for contracting infection, and often subject to unannounced genital inspections. Lectures explained the prophylactic kits but moralized about indulgence.

> I don't want you to be immoral but if you *will* incur danger you must not
> come back here in a filthy state, bringing disease into the barrack room.
> For the sake of your comrades, to say the least—for the sake of your
> country, your future wives and families, for the sake of almost everything
> which makes life worth living, you must disinfect yourselves.[41]

Such lectures were often halfhearted attempts to appease army chaplains rather than seriously considered productions. Edmund Burke, commanding the British Field Ambulance Service from 1915–19, characterized the educational aspect of the campaign as unenthusiastic. "Had half the organisation, support, and money expended on the Army Postal Service been given to an Anti-Venereal Service, it would have been a very profitable national investment."[42]

In practice, of course, troops responded inconsistently to these often conflicting messages. One medical officer working in a British-run hospital complained that "the men seem to think it is their duty to get V.D. They really consider it a joke altogether and laugh and rag one another about it."[43] An angry campaigner, however, pointed out that "while officially we forbid illicit relationships, practically we do not interfere with the men's 'liberties' in any way except to throw on them the whole onus of responsibility for using the means of disinfection which we provide. If they don't use those means and become infected, that's their funeral. If they do use those means, and become infected, that's their bad luck: they were officially warned to keep out of mischief anyhow."[44] Military officials already suspected that some men welcomed venereal infection since it removed them from the front.[45] Joanna Bourke claims that reluctant soldiers injected condensed milk into their penises, presumably to emulate the viscous secretions of infection.[46] The medical establishment never agreed on exactly how the preventive policies should be implemented (confusions routinely smoothed over in their postwar recollections), and the rank and file was hardly less diverse in responding. British Army logs suggest fitful enthusiasm. "The use of the outfits varies greatly in different units, e.g. one unit with a strength of 1,300 used 414 outfits in a month while another unit with a strength of 3,000 used only 31 during the same period."[47] Figures kept by the AIF show the same pattern. In some cases, not a single soldier took with him either a packet or a condom; on other occasions, every man in a unit asked for several condoms as well as a kit.[48] The German army's experience was similar: a survey conducted in 1916 found that of three hundred soldiers treated for VD, only fifty-seven had used condoms.[49] Moreover, the number of tubes of ointment in the kits varied—not only from army to army but according to the level of supplies available at any given moment.

Medical officers also acknowledged a gap between possession of the packets and proper use—or any use—of them.[50] Sir Francis Champneys had argued that "[T]he giving of the packet takes it for granted that he will use it."[51] But Alexander Godley, commander of the New Zealand Imperial Forces, found men reluctant to use the ointment as a barrier cream, since women often complained that calomel burned and blistered their vaginal walls.[52]

Race and Prophylaxis

Clinics and kits had nonetheless become part of the armory of British and Dominion troops by 1916. They were never used, though, among nonwhite

forces. The substantial soldiery culled from India, the Caribbean, South Africa, and elsewhere in the empire experienced powerfully different forms of VD control. It was not that the authorities assumed that their rates of infection would be lower.[53] Indeed, hospitals catering to wounded Indian soldiers established special VD units with substantial capacity.[54] For British West Indian regiments "disinfection on return to camp was made practically compulsory," a practice literally compulsory for black American troops in France.[55] VD among labor contingents from South Africa was lower, but that did not stop their white officers from fretting. The prescription for avoiding VD among non-white troops was to limit mobility rather than to arm individuals with the tools of prevention. Unattractive and unpopular as the therapies practiced at the blue light depots were, they acknowledged a modicum of personal freedom for British and Dominion troops never extended to other imperial soldiery. It was not until September 1919, almost a year after the end of the war, that the idea of early treatment depots for India was raised, and even then they were to be applied only in India and not made available to Indian soldiers in Europe.[56] Provision in Britain, after all, might presuppose white women as sexual partners.

Neither supporters nor opponents of prophylaxis ever doubted the good faith—or indeed, the human waywardness—of British and Dominion soldiers. It was leave in a foreign place, or temptation, or sheer human folly which led men astray and not malice or disloyalty. "Much can be done by example and precept, but human nature being what it is, it is incumbent upon us to protect from themselves those who, wherever they might be, would not respond to such an appeal."[57] Both the offer of packets and the belief in early treatment, and conversely the evocation of self-discipline, revolved around the idea that soldiers were fundamentally decent and loyal. Kits were thus offered rather than issued, and the depots were places of guaranteed anonymity.[58] Those who favored the distribution of packets publicly argued that the policy was not an encouragement to vice, but rather a fall-back position to deal with the inevitable shortcomings of human behavior. Their opponents, of course, insisted that the kits symbolized the legitimation of casual sexual encounters, rendering those shortcomings inevitable. "It is no kindness to the soldier," argued the AMSH, "to put temptation in his way."[59] There can be little doubt that had such bodies as the AMSH discovered the issue or offer of unguents, solutions, or condoms to black troops, the ensuing protests would have been more vociferous even than those aimed at Dominion and British policy. This division between the trustworthy Anglo soldier, beset by temptation but usually responsible enough in the breach, and the unstable soldiery of the tropics is palpable. Proponents of prophylaxis knew full well the furor that distribution to the latter would have stirred up, not only among their most obvious opponents but within military circles as well, where the lesser moral fiber of the nonwhite man was taken for granted.

Earlier fears of racial degeneration were exacerbated by the huge and un-abating losses of the war. White settler nations feared the loss of an entire generation of men and expressed that fear in largely racial terms. Diseased men returning would undermine and weaken the purity and health of the stock, while the best and the bravest lay dead on the battlefield.[60] Dominion opin-ion, especially in Australia and New Zealand, often depicted Britain not as the generator of new ideas or as a moral model, but as part of an older and de-caying civilization. When James Barrett criticized government's lack of logic in the matter of VD policy, his comments resonated with a school of opinion which gave pride of place to young and vigorous nations of Anglo stock. The *Australian Medical Journal* placed Australia in the vanguard of medical advance. "It is to the credit of Australia that the serious problem of venereal disease was faced at a time when other countries attempted to ignore the fact that these infections were undermining the fitness of the individual members of the community."[61] Australia in this scenario had shifted the debate from a moral to a sanitary basis, thus inheriting the mantle of modernity from the parent nation.

Ettie Rout

Australian Ettie Rout was a one-woman campaign against British indecision about prophylaxis and prevention.[62] First in Egypt, then in London, and finally in Paris, Rout campaigned ceaselessly from 1916 for a consistent and more far-reaching use of prophylaxis and early treatment regimens. A thorn in the side of military and civil officials, Rout raised money and reached into her own pocket to maintain prophylactic supplies to Anzac (Australian and New Zealand) soldiers going on leave.[63] And she did so in the name, most specifically, of racial purity. Rout's politics were a curious brew of libertarian and disciplinarian; she favored reglementation akin to the CD acts and supported notification of VD schemes, but also argued that "a free man's body is his own."[64] She wanted to separate sanitation and morality, arguing that what her supporter Lieutenant Colonel George Raffan memorably called the "well-toileted penis" should be treated in the same way as the soldier's gun.[65] "Isn't keeping 'infection' off the man just as simple as keeping 'rust' off his gun? When he has finished using his gun—he should clean it AT ONCE . . . And if he fails to vaseline his gun beforehand, and leaves it out in the rain all night, he would know that more elaborate cleaning methods were necessary, wouldn't he?"[66]

Rout was determined to bypass moral concerns which, she declaimed, would "bring the Diggers [Anzac troops] to their knees with a Bible in one hand and a Child—probably Syphilitic—in the other."[67] She constantly complained about the narrow-mindedness of the YMCA, the "English bishops," the prudish English public, and the hypocrisy of government. And underlying both her convictions and her enmities was a eugenic and racial reading of Australian purity. "Australia . . . has a much better chance of conquering the V.D. microbe.

That chance will be lost if the Returned Soldiers fail to apply the Knowledge and Experience they have gained abroad. On their failure—the Rise of the Yellow Races is staked."[68]

Over and over again in her writings, she contrasts the vigor of young Australia with Britain as old, decrepit, and potentially dangerous, contaminating healthy stock and preventing it from fighting off the "Asiatic threat." She warned of British intentions to ship "the waste products of European civilization" from England, "the cess-pool of venereal infection," where only "the Chosen Few . . . are our equals: the majority are hopelessly inferior: they are timid and feeble-minded."[69] Her greatest fear was "needless racial contamination."[70]

Rout's sentiments echoed those of the commander of the Australian forces in Egypt, Major General Birdwood, who advised his senior commanders that "it is as necessary to keep a 'clean Australia' as a 'White Australia.'"[71] The Australian League of Honour, formed within the AIF in 1917, likewise called for a purity crusade within the military for the sake of "White Australia."[72]

Race, Masculinity, and the Military

Many in and out of the military agreed with the American physician who, in 1918, claimed that "a sexless soldier is a paradox . . . The greater the maleness the greater the warrior."[73] Active heterosexuality was the demonstrable proof of the masculinity so crucial to the maintenance of the colonial enterprise,[74] but it was the tropics and the "Orient" and not Europe that was sexualized. Maintaining the fiction of racial hierarchy required distinguishing between white and black sexuality. Where colonial soldiers were quartered on European soil, those distinctions took on a greater urgency as the opportunities for racial mixing grew. Fears of racial contamination and miscegenation, of black soldiers running amok among white women, drove authorities into apartheid policies with regard to white and black soldiers, and civilians to a fear of black soldiers.

Eugenicist fears of miscegenation combined with suspicion about the rampant and violent venereal afflictions of the tropics. The latter connected in turn to the widespread myth of tropical sensuality, the unruly and greedy passions of lesser races unschooled in the disciplining of their desires. Ferocity and sexuality were seen as twin characteristics of nonwestern troops. This emphasis on the nonwhite as all body, lacking intellect or refinement but fired up with instinct, had a lengthy military history. Garnet Wolseley had argued in 1888 that the "negro soldier['s] . . . real natural pleasure" in bloodshed and "human bodily suffering" lent him a useful savagery that "went far to make up for his want of intelligence as a soldier."[75] Shelby Cullom Davis, reflecting on black participation in the 1914–18 war, reached similar conclusions half a century later. "They could not undertake missions requiring intelligence, but on the other hand, their lack of nervous system made them cool under the most trying situations, and their bravery, even to the point of rashness, was conspicuous."[76]

Nonwhite Soldiers in Europe

Nonwhite soldierly sexuality was seen as vastly different than that of the white soldier. The British Expeditionary Force (BEF) commander in France assured the secretary of state for war that "the Colour question has not been lost sight of for one minute, either by myself or by any of my officers."[77] Officers commanding the Cape Auxiliary Horse Transport (CAHT) companies in France were instructed that "no Coloured man was to be allowed to speak to a white woman."[78] The men of the 25,000-strong South African Native Labour Contingent (SANLC) were housed in closed wire-stockade compounds, forbidden fraternization with Europeans, and limited to leaves of only four hours.[79] Fear of interracial mixing was among the reasons for their disbandment in January 1918.[80]

Indian soldiers had been deployed in colonial combat prior to 1914—in China, Singapore, Hong Kong, Afghanistan, Egypt, Burma, many parts of Africa, and in the Persian Gulf—but this was the first time they had fought on or close to British soil. Novelist Mulk Raj Anand, describing their experiences on the western front, tells us that the English "did not like . . . the brown-skinned Indians to look at white women."[81] Lieutenant Colonel Evelyn Howell, censor of Indian mails on the western front, kept a close eye on the letters of Indian soldiers for sexual allusions for, were Indians allowed to conceive a wrong idea of the "'izzat' [honor] of English women . . . [it] would be most detrimental to the prestige and spirit of European rule in India."[82]

When wounded members of the Indian Expeditionary Force (IEF) were sent to convalesce on England's south coast, the War Office demanded the withdrawal of women nurses from the hospitals where the men were housed.[83] Where they were employed, "these Nurses have not to do with the dressing of the wounds & c. They see to the cleanliness and orderliness of the ward."[84] At issue here was more than just the spectacle of Indian men catered to by white women; the very physical acts of tending to wounds or feeding invalids were specifically taboo. This was a powerful corporeal threat, a hint of possible interracial mixing. For women most especially, a willingness in this regard was an instant badge of disrepute, a guarantee of inferiority. The nurse had to be protected from that stain, since she was so important a wartime symbol of feminine sacrifice and nurture.

The rules governing Indians sent to the Kitchener hospital for Indian convalescents in Brighton were "absolutely inflexible" and restricted rank and file soldiers wholly to the hospital precincts. Trustworthy Indian officers were sometimes permitted walks, in parties of three supervised by a white private of the Royal Army Medical Corps. Route marches and occasional drives around the neighborhood were the only other means by which patients might see anything beyond the hospital grounds, which were hemmed in by barbed wire reinforcements.[85]

The Unsafe Orient

Conversely, when white soldiers were stationed outside Europe, they were warned that they faced temptations greater than in the west. "Men," warned one leaflet distributed in Egypt by the Army Medical Services, "must be careful to avoid any attempts at familiarity with native women; because if they are respectable, they will get into trouble, and if they are not, venereal desease (sic) will probably be contracted."[86] Another urged soldiers to realize "that in this country prostitutes are all more or less *infected with disease* [emphasis in original]."[87] Considering the VD rates in cities such as London or Marseilles, this belief in Egypt's potentiality for infection may seem extraordinary but it held fast to the familiar refrain about the sexually unsafe Orient. In yet another leaflet men learned that "[T]he climate and conditions of life in Egypt are, unfortunately, such as to create temptations greater than those which exist at home."[88] C. E. W. Bean, official press correspondent for the AIF in Egypt, dubbed Cairo the "home of all that is filthy and beastly."[89] Some three decades later, military surgeon Robert Lees lambasted Cyprus and Egypt as lands dominated by "flies and whores."[90] This propaganda had little effect on soldiers who Suzanne Brugger describes as "queuing more than six-deep to take their turns" in the Egyptian brothels.[91] Egypt chalked up high rates of venereal infection throughout the war. The Anzacs boasted the highest rate, followed by the BEF. About 3 percent of the AIF in Egypt had VD on any given day.[92] In February 1915, the director of AIF medical services in Cairo reported to the high commissioner for Australia that over 5 percent of the men were unable to report for duty because of venereal complaints.[95]

Residence in Egypt brought together a complex of racial and sexual assumptions with sometimes violent consequences for the local population. In Port Said, the Arab Quarter was out of bounds to Indian soldiers, as much to minimize Muslim disloyalty as to keep them from buying the services of women. As a result, Indians quartered in Egypt posted much lower rates of infection than white troops.[94] For white troops, however, this was an area of supervised brothels.[95] C. E. W. Bean regretfully noticed that among the rowdy drunken soldiers, "easily the most noticeable and the most frequent offenders were the Australians."[96] Such behavior aroused concern but little was done to curb soldiers in Egypt's cities. The Australian troops were notorious for their boorish treatment of the local population.[97] Bean worked hard to put the best face on their antics, but clearly shared their low esteem of the locals. "On the whole our men, if they have erred, have erred on the side of being over familiar with any class of native who simply wants to exploit them."[98]

The Wazza Riots

On the night of April 2, 1915, a group of Australian soldiers forcibly entered a brothel at number 8 Darb-el-Moballat in what a subsequent enquiry described as "an undesirable quarter of Cairo City."[99] They threw property out of the windows, terrorizing the residents, and before long, the uproar had spread throughout the brothel district in a full-scale riot, instigated largely by men of the Australian and New Zealand forces. Bonfires were set, men applauded the flames, and moved on drunkenly through the brothel quarter. This was the first of the two Wazza riots, so named for the Wazza or Wassa district of Cairo that housed the brothels, and that, according to the commandant of the city police, was "the hot bed of these worst forms of syphilitic disease."[100] An official enquiry instituted immediately afterwards produced no substantive conclusions. Richard White has suggested that the soldiers' motives revolved around the idea of scrubbing "Pharaoh's dirty kingdom clean," though Kevin Fewster argues that "the attack on the brothels was very much a preliminary" to a deeper dissatisfaction with the military police.[101] But the second such riot, which occurred on July 31, 1915, was also in the brothel quarter, and the court of inquiry heard that "the cause of trouble was a row between four to nine Australian soldiers and prostitutes—the reason for this on the one side, the robbery of the soldiers by women, on the other side refusal to pay the women. After the altercation a number of soldiers came out into the street and whatever was said to the crowd gathering outside, it seemed to inflame them."[102] In the first riot, the committee had heard among other stories, that the trouble had begun when "three men had got a dose off a woman." It was her refusal to reimburse them for the stoppage of pay they had incurred while hospitalized which was said to have set off the violence.[103] There were certainly other issues at stake, but there can be no doubt that, in both instances, it was the brothel quarter that was targeted and brothels that were mostly damaged. Tellingly, Magnus Hirschfeld, writing about the German experience of the war, likened the Wazza riot to its "German counterpart . . . the notorious attack on the brothel in Sudan."[104] Brothels, especially in colonial environments, were fair game for inflamed soldiers.

The lack of punishment after the two Wazza riots, the inefficacy of the inquiries, the slow speed of compensatory payments to locals who suffered damage, and the military's insistence that such payments did not constitute an admission of liability, all suggest that while rioting was undesirable from a military perspective, white soldiers nonetheless enjoyed a privilege of mobility and freedom in relation to the Egyptian streets and the colonial marketplace, a privilege denied the large corps of poorly paid Indians also barracked in Egypt. On both fronts—eastern and western—distinctions were drawn within the British forces between white soldiers and the nonwhite. As Suzanne Brugger points out, "encounters with the equally abundant, but more discreet prostitutes of France and England were not taken as evidence of the natural viciousness of either the French or the English."[105] That privilege was reserved for nonwhite and colonized peoples.

Military authorities in Egypt chose to control the women of the brothels rather than their white clientele. Before the war, under the old Ottoman legal system of Capitulations, the local police had no jurisdiction over white prostitutes; only the appropriate consular authorities had any power over them.[106] Egyptian women could be sent to the lock hospital but not the Europeans; much to their frustration, the police were limited to notifying European women's venereal status to the relevant consul.[107] But by 1915, martial law had extended the regulatory powers over non-Egyptian women. All women working in the brothels were required to register and submit to regular medical examination. In Port Said, Cairo, Ismailia, and Alexandria, brothels were confined to certain districts, and women working outside those zones were subject to arrest. Unlicensed prostitutes were "vigorously pursued."[108] In Alexandria, 280 police raids in 1916 netted seventy-nine unlicensed foreign women.[109] Foreign prostitutes faced the same surveillance as local women. Their only privileges were that they were examined only by European doctors, and confined to a separate lock hospital.[110]

The Effects of War

The impact of war reached well beyond the trenches and barracks, directly affecting colonial lives. The economic consequences in British colonies were substantial. An increased demand for materials and supplies was offset by the inevitable disruptions to shipping. Colonial exports grew but prices mostly dropped, creating substantial economic volatility.[111] The cessation of trade with countries now in the enemy camp also took its toll, while Britain expected contributions to its war chest from the colonies.[112] Shortly after war was declared, borrowing in the London market was halted, cutting off one of the most important flows of capital to colonial economies.[113] Prices of many basic goods rose and, with the war effort in full swing, shortages were not uncommon as commodities were diverted to the forces. Income taxes rose too, adding to the financial strain. Sugata Bose and Ayesha Jalal estimate that India's wartime defense expenditure increased by 300 percent.[114] £146 million was contributed towards the war effort from Indian revenues.[115] While much of this differed little from Britain's own experience of war, the proportion of subsistence-level living in the dependent colonies was higher. There was little margin under normal circumstances and much less in extraordinary conditions.[116] As recruitment campaigns picked up, many rural communities felt the loss of their young men now fighting overseas. In Australia, around 50 percent of men aged eighteen to forty-five enlisted for service, about 300,000 men in all.[117] They were urged on by Australian women among whom support for the war was significant.[118]

Colonial administrations also made use of the emergency powers at their disposal to rid themselves of unwanted residents. The white prostitute whose presence was so threatening to imperial prestige was cleared out of the Singapore brothels during the war.[119] The Straits governor reported his tactics to London with obvious pride.

> After very careful consideration and discussion with the Unofficial members of the Legislative Council, who entirely agreed, I decided in December 1915, that any European prostitute who desired to leave the Colony should be given a free passage at the expense of the Colony. It was suggested to them that they should leave before the 1st July, 1916, and they were informed that the Government did not wish any other European prostitutes to enter the Colony. No threats of any kind were used . . . of the 32 European prostitutes in Singapore, 26 availed themselves of the Government's offer . . . The other six women remain in Singapore. They are said to be either kept women or to prostitute themselves secretly. The sight of European prostitutes in brothel areas is now a thing of the past.[120]

In 1916, discussions with the Japanese consul also resulted in a halt in emigration to the Straits of Japanese women working in prostitution.[121] In British Burma, the governor promised the bishop of Rangoon that the deportation of European prostitutes would be considered after the war.[122] Before the war, the Indian government had toyed with legislation to prevent the bringing into the country of European women for purposes of prostitution, but deporting those already there had always proved legally thorny. The Rangoon authorities did expel a few women in 1915, and there was some deportation from India too, but it was in Singapore that wartime powers were most enthusiastically applied.[123]

The Racial Double Standard

While enemy aliens were interned or deported, there was minimal restriction on the movement of British civilians in the region during the war. Social purity activist John Cowen visited Singapore and Burma during the war, publishing lurid accounts of their red-light districts in *The Shield*. The publication of such materials in wartime conditions was a calculated political move. His account of a thriving sex trade set amid the devastations of war fired up the protest movement. The AMSH supported Cowen to the full, not only publishing him but also inviting him to Britain in 1916 to explore the possibility of hiring him "to work for us as a Journalist in the Far East."[124] The Straits government was furious, more especially since Cowen had speciously connected a February 1915 mutiny of Indian soldiers in Singapore to the brothel industry. The AMSH demanded "immediate action" from the government to prevent "compromising . . . the British name," and in the interests of "His Majesty's forces stationed there or passing through on their way to and from the Far East."[125] No stranger to the politics of publicity, Cowen stressed the use of Singapore's brothels by British soldiers and the consequences. *Tract No. 7* in his *Tracts for Rangoon* series revealed "an enemy more fierce, cunning and cruel than the forces of Germany."[126] It was, of course, VD.

Cowen, memorably described by an official as "more zealous than discreet," cheerfully anticipated prosecution for these tracts.[127] Frequently seized by the government before distribution, they were an eccentric mix of millenarian religious fervor and titillation, peopled with mad syphilitics finding Jesus on their death beds, and dutiful soldiers cut down by the temptations of the brothel quarters. Cowen dealt in titillating hyperbole, describing Singapore as a city dominated by its brothels and luring men to their downfall.[128] But Cowen was not the only troublemaker in colonial parts. In 1916, an antiwar activist opposing conscription claimed (not entirely unfairly) that the Indian military authorities were flouting the restrictions on regulating prostitution. In a flurry of internal memoranda, India Office officials concluded that prosecution was inadvisable since it "might publish the amount of V.D. which exists and other unsavoury details."[129] VD rates among indigenous soldiers were rising in India, and had been throughout the war years, as they had among Indian soldiers stationed in Mesopotamia. Yet none of the treatment plans used among white troops were utilized. In 1917, the adjutant general in India issued instructions to commanding officers that in addition to expelling "undesirable characters" from the bazaars, there should be "a rigid imposition on offenders of all the penalties permitted by the regulations."[130] Indian Army officers, including non-commissioned officers (NCO) and warrant officers, came in for especial criticism.[131]

In August 1918, to the delight of abolitionists, the commander in chief in India issued a military order closing brothels in cantonments, under Regulation 12C of the 1915 Indian Defence of the Realm Act.[132] Abolitionists called for the extension of the measure to other colonies, most especially the Straits and Burma, but India alone followed this path. Though confined to India, these brothel closures demonstrate the drastic difference in what could be achieved domestically and imperially. Colonial law, at least in dependent colonies, had relied on the right to legalize and structure—and now to close—the brothel, options too tricky to realize in white settings. The decision of the Indian commander in chief in 1918 offers as powerful a glimpse of colonial lawmaking as the regulation of prostitution adopted in Egypt. Both understood the brothel as an entity that required legal definition and control. Both acknowledged a distinction between measures appropriate in imperial and metropolitan settings Both reflected the dominant assessment of what those measures could, might, and should be.

Enemies of the State?

While the brothel in the metropolis was not under direct attack, white proletarian women's curiosity about sex and, most dangerously, about interracial sex was a topic of great urgency. Like nonwhite colonial soldiers, white working-class women were potentially destabilizing. Joseph Maxwell spoke of "the keen feminine prospecting for shekels" in what he called the "war on the Piccadilly front."[133] His Orientalist/semitic word choice was hardly accidental; women and the "Orient" shared many of the same dangerously alluring qualities, and women, like Jews, were driven by money. Immorality was definingly proletarian as well as racially specific. Girls were regarded as developing more quickly than boys, but "this is especially true of the working class girl."[134] The upper-middle class Vera Brittain thought immorality a working-class trait; women munitions workers, overwhelmingly working class, found their morals as carefully policed as their productivity.[135] Women's mobility, their unfettered behavior on the streets, and their apparent defiance of traditional authority occasioned a fear of the disintegration of the moral and hierarchical certainties of both class and gender relations. Furthering this grim picture of a world turned upside down, print journalism and government enquiries were full of stories of innocent, ignorant, or merely reluctant soldiers who required and deserved protection from evil women. Sir Arthur Conan Doyle, well-known as a pro-imperialist and fierce patriot, wrote to *The Times* about the "harpies" of "harlot-haunted" areas of London, taking advantage of "lonely soldiers."[136] The archbishop of Canterbury claimed in the House of Lords that "we owe everything to these men."[137] Indeed, gratitude was the explanation many proffered for "the wave of emotionalism that swamped the self-restraint of so many girls and young women."[138]

More often than not, however, it was the idea of women as potential enemies that dominated. White colonial soldiers were seen as especially vulnerable. "Thousands of our boys left here and never knew the dangers of the disease, but through being fondled and idolized by women their whole thoughts have been changed by joining the army."[139] A South African temperance organizer exhorted her British counterpart to look after those white South Africans who "have gone across the water from pure and simple homes" to fight in the western theater.[140] It was, not surprisingly, Dominion officials who most vocally demanded action against VD. Walter Long (described by R. K. Webb as "a worthy but dim squire")[141] warned the War Cabinet in March 1918 that, "I have been repeatedly pressed by the Dominion Governments . . . the feeling in the Dominions, which is already angry, is likely to become most gravely exasperated."[142]

The sympathy for Dominion soldiers cut across party and class lines. Labour politician Ramsay MacDonald urged home secretary Herbert Samuel to help young men.

> A friend of mine who is working in one of the Clubs which entertains soldiers—especially Colonial soldiers—has been telling me about the numbers of women who hang about the stations . . . and their adjoining public houses to waylay men visiting London for the first time and inexperienced in consequence . . . Disease is prevalent amongst the women and theft from soldiers who do not like to complain to the police on account of the disgrace is far from uncommon.[145]

These descriptions of women's behavior were remarkably similar to portrayals of black colonials. Again and again, women "preying" on soldiers were likened to tigers. Edith Sellers described seeing "some young Colonial soldiers running for their very lives to escape from a little company of girls. One might have thought, to see them, that they had tigresses at their heels."[144] When Joseph Maxwell painted his picture of the "sensuous odalisques from a dozen nations" who sold their wares in the Egyptian brothels, he too employed the imagery of the tiger. "Hard bitten and raucous, silken-voiced and seductive, languorous as a purring cat, deceptive, decked out in blazonries like some lithe tiger moving in the gloom."[145] In talking of the Indian soldiers she sketched in France, Massia Bibikoff had similarly evoked the ferocity of the jungle creature in describing them as "dripping tigers." The Gurkha soldier, she said, had "a yellow face... his eyes... like a wild animal's."[146] The primordial passions epitomized by the feline jungle animal were contrasted with the temperate control of civilized manners. Women and nonwhite colonials had trouble containing their natural and destructive impulses; they were potentially the enemies of reason and civilization.

Defence of the Realm Act Regulations

In November 1916, the AMSH protested to the Home Office that women on remand were being examined for VD illegally, and that a London magistrate, C. K. Francis, was sentencing women convicted of soliciting to indefinite periods in infirmaries, a practice that shadowed those previously instituted by the CD acts.[147] Francis himself had written to the Home Office some eleven months earlier, about the "growing scandal" of "the great increase in the number of prostitutes" targeting soldiers. He had been advised that he could neither commit women in this way nor insist they submit to a VD test.[148] Francis was not the only member of the judiciary, however, who acted beyond his powers in such cases, though the Home Office seldom intervened. Two women arrested in Hounslow in April 1917 were subjected to medical examination while on remand, and their bail made dependent upon the results of that examination.[149] In a case before the Clerkenwell Sessions in June 1917, a woman was bound over for two years, first to the infirmary and then to a girl's home "till a situation is found for her."[150] In December, a man and a woman were jointly charged with indecency at the Marlborough Street Court. While he was fined forty shillings and released, she was remanded in custody and then sent to an infirmary. In the same month, a Westminster court magistrate offered a seventeen-year old defendant a choice between further detention and examination.[151] As a result of such misuses of the law, the AMSH established a Police Court Rota in 1918, chaired by Chrystal Macmillan, that sent observers into the magistrates' courts to report on women's cases. By 1918, most major women's organizations as well as the Salvation Army and the Penal Reform League were involved in court-watching activities designed to monitor these infractions.

Military and civil officials in the government were beset on all sides. Imperial leaders and military officials clamored for restrictions on women, while women's and social purity groups relentlessly exposed examples of regulation. Not surprisingly, however, the victory went to the men of the establishment, and over a period of some two years, government used its emergency powers under the Defence of the Realm Act (DORA) to introduce a series of restrictive regulations that recognized women as disloyal conduits of sexual infection, and men in the armed forces as their victims. *The Lancet* justified the double standard enshrined in these regulations, for "it must be remembered that a poisonous woman can poison a regiment, and it should be a point of conscience with our authorities to let nothing outweigh in their minds the meaning of this fact."[152]

Early in the war, some municipal authorities, cooperating with local military commanders, instructed businesses with liquor licenses to limit the hours that women could be served alcohol, and in Cardiff military authorities pressed for a nighttime curfew on women.[153] In February 1916, Defence of the Realm Regulation (DRR) 13A permitted naval and military authorities to prohibit those with convictions for prostitution or any association with a brothel (managing, keeping, assisting, etc.) from residing in or frequenting the vicinity of the stationed troops. Lively protests from organizations such as the AMSH had no effect. Though Ernley Blackwell at the Home Office insisted that the regulation had not been very effective, it was clearly used with some gusto.[154] In the first month of operation the coastal town of Folkestone, for example, effected thirty-seven removals under the regulation.[155] Fifteen months later, in April 1917, DRR 35C extended this restriction. Those convicted of an offense against the public order or of indecency could be notified to the police and removed from areas in which troops were stationed as well as those where munitions were handled. The regulation was careful to name neither women nor sex workers, merely those prejudicing war needs.[156] The AMSH charged that the regulation resembled the Indian Cantonment Act in using military need to justify women's expulsion from an area. Protests proved futile, and the regulation remained on the books.

These regulations were only some of the battery of weapons used in an attempt to police female behavior during the war. The Home Office briefly considered the use of DRR 27, committing an act likely to interfere with the success of His Majesty's Forces, against women alleged to have infected military men with VD. The Home and War Offices jointly discussed the likelihood of securing convictions against women for VD transmission under DRR 40C, which punished those "wilfully" maiming or injuring a member of the armed forces or reserves by disease or infirmity.[157]

Despite the use of these measures and the usual panoply of civil constraints against loitering, vagrancy, indecency, and the like, the pressure on government to reduce VD rates, especially among Dominion troops, remained intense.[158] New Zealand, Australian, and Canadian politicians pressed the British authorities. The Canadian prime minister was blunt. "I do not think Canada will ever again send men overseas to any war unless we are assured that such conditions as have met our soldiers here will not meet them again. I say unhesitatingly that if I should be Prime Minister of Canada on the outbreak of another war I would not send one man overseas if the conditions were such as have prevailed during the Progress of this War."[159] The New Zealand governor general warned Walter Long (now at the War Office) that "the feeling in New Zealand is that sufficient is not being done to deal with this matter," while the Australian governor general forwarded a resolution he had received from concerned citizens in Victoria who feared for "the moral safety of the flower of Australia's manhood."[160]

If the politics of widespread protest among middle-class activists and newly enfranchised women gave government nervous pause for thought, the imperial suit was hard to ignore. The entreaties of governors general for the maintenance of CD ordinances in faraway lands in the 1880s had been easy to dismiss when domestic controversy threatened to unseat political incumbents and protests about the return of regulation in colonial settings could be ignored. But the leaders of self-governing white settlements demanded more serious attention. It was not only that the British, along with other colonial powers, desperately needed the help of this vast imperial soldiery, but that the growing independent stature of these nations forced Britain increasingly to consider them in a different light and to rethink the source of their political relationship.

Strong pressure from the colonies of white settlement was a key factor in the promulgation of the short-lived but fiercely controversial Defence of the Realm Regulation 40D.[161] Writing to his counterparts at key ministries, Long made this abundantly clear. "As another Imperial War Conference is pending, I feel that we ought to make every effort to show the Dominion Governments that His Majesty's Government are leaving no stone unturned to remedy the evil."[162] Regulation 40D went into effect on March 22, 1918 and made it an offense for any woman with communicable VD to solicit or to copulate with a member of the British armed forces, a measure similar to that passed under the Defence of Canada Order in June 1917.[163] 40D had the backing of the War Office, Foreign Office, Colonial Office, Home Office, and Admiralty.[164] The Army Council had initially demurred, and the colonial secretary had expressed concerns over the legality of such a measure, but at the urging of the War Cabinet and with unyielding pressure from the Dominions, it passed into law. Striking as the punitive treatment of women under DRR 40D is, it is important to appreciate the singular impact of Dominion demands in shaping it. Andrew Porter has argued that in the nineteenth century, white settler countries were "hankering after self-assertion on the global scene."[165] Here they could measure their effectiveness.

It was instantly controversial for, unlike earlier regulations, 40D specifically punished only women, where 13A and 35C had retained a semblance of gender neutrality. The army's refusal to distinguish soldiers from civilian males was the excuse put forward for the regulation's sole focus on women.[166] The Home Office had unsuccessfully attempted to obscure 40D's emphasis on women; in an early draft there was no mention that prosecution was aimed at women, though officials reassured the necessary constituencies that, "though it was necessary for political reasons to create similar offences for women and men, in fact the proposed regulation would be actually operative only to deal with cases of women."[167] Privately, officials admitted that "the one-sidedness of [the] Reg^n is particularly difficult to defend."[168]

Nonetheless, the claim was made in parliament that 40D was "not one-sided" since the army exacted penalties on soldiers with VD.[169] They were liable to stoppages of pay for contracting VD, though the penalty was unevenly enforced. From 1917, Australian soldiers hospitalized for VD were denied leave of absence for a year after discharge from hospital.[170] Mostly, though, men were punished only reluctantly; there was far less enthusiasm for punishing the infected soldier than the allegedly infecting woman. Sir Bruce Seton claimed that 40D was merely the result of "the ill-advised conduct of . . . women."[171] In a climate in which the under secretary at the War Office, Ian MacPherson, could state that women "may be as prolific of 'ineffectives' and wastage of man power as German poison gas," 40D made sense.[172]

Though the regulation did not formally reinstate compulsory medical examination, the exam was the central evidence in court, making compulsion the de facto result. Since communicable VD was the essence of the charge, there was no other way for an accused woman to refute it than to undergo examination. Attempts to have the accused examined only by women doctors were trounced by the Prison Commission's claim that it would be beyond the capability of existing facilities. Instead women could choose to be examined either by a prison medical officer or by their own doctor, but in the latter case they were obliged to defray the costs of the exam themselves. Since those charged under the regulation were largely poor women, few would have had an ongoing relationship with a general practitioner, not only because fees were steep but because medical provision in working-class districts was at best spotty. Most women opted for the prison exam. One hundred and seventy-two of the 203 women prosecuted under 40D between March and October 1918 were remanded in custody for medical examination.[173] And despite recommendations that 40D hearings be held in camera, 40D prosecutions proved an embarrassingly public trial for accused women.[174] The names of the men accusing them were withheld from publication, but the women's names were published, even where their court appearance resulted in acquittal. DORA itself allowed government to dictate what the press might publish in time of war, yet in this instance chose not to invoke its substantial power. The furthest they were willing to go was a consideration in August 1918 that magistrates might request the press to refrain from publishing women's names before the result of the examination.[175] In London,

396 cases were reported to the police under 40D: 203 women were prosecuted, 171 for intercourse with a soldier while infectious. Of these, 101 were convicted, of whom half (49) pled guilty and were sentenced to three or four months imprisonment, with or without hard labor.[176] Twenty-one of the forty cases observed by AMSH court-watchers between April and August 1918 were dismissed in court; in eleven of these there was no evidence of disease.

40D's wide-open dual standard catalyzed tremendous protest. Social purity and feminist groups, temperance and church organizations (including diocesan chapters and the Church League for Women's Suffrage), and penal reform groups flooded the War Cabinet with objections. The Salvation Army and the YWCA, Liberal Associations and local Labour Party groups, the British Women's Temperance Association, the National Union of Women Workers, the Women's Freedom League, the Fabian Women's group, the National Council for Civil Liberties, trades unions and friendly societies, and even the NCCVD complained to government. The *Manchester Guardian,* the *Daily News,* and *The Nation* were critical, and more than one newspaper joined *The Herald* in pointing out that 40D had "done in the night what it failed to do in the light of day by its Criminal Law Amendment Bill," an accusation deliberately evoking the passing of the domestic CD acts of the 1860s in the early hours of the morning to avoid controversy.[177]

By October 1918—when an Order in Council extended the regulation to Allied troops—over 1,300 resolutions against the regulation had reached the Home Office, the War Office, and the Prime Minister's Office.[178] The result was a royal commission to consider its future. The seven-member commission included three women as well as the obligatory bishop, but before it could report, the regulation was rescinded. When the war ended, the committee chair advised the Home Office that only "the necessities created by the existence of a state of war" could justify so unpopular a measure, and successfully urged its abandonment.[179]

The French Dilemma

The use of DORA was only one of a series of backdoor policies which augured a return to the CD system. Another area of contention was the French tolerated brothels, long a symbol for abolitionists of all that was corrupt about regulation. The NCCVD criticized the "specious sense of security engendered by . . . municipal regulation."[180] The AMSH circulated a pamphlet in 1916 entitled *A Warning To Men Going Abroad* explaining the system of registered prostitution soldiers might encounter and exhorting them to fierce resistance to its allurements.[181] There were constant questions in the House of Commons, intended to embarrass government by pointing out that Britain applied different moral principles in the metropole and in the colonies. It was not until the spring of 1918, at the same time that 40D was enacted, that the War Cabinet placed the regulated French brothels out of bounds to British soldiers. The U.S. army had pressed the War Office in 1917, shortly after the American Expeditionary Force (AEF) disembarked in France, for help in persuading the French to abandon their licensing system.[182] The British, reluctant to tread on neighboring toes, insisted this was a matter for French law, and the Americans succeeded neither in closing down the system nor in keeping their troops from patronizing such establishments.

The U.K. military was nonetheless more actively involved in their running than the typically bland assurances of officials acknowledged. The official history of wartime medical services describes British supervision of the inspections at the Havre brothels in 1915, and even where there was no direct supervision, allied personnel worked closely with local authorities. In December 1917, Lieutenant Colonel Stewart, commanding the 15th Australian Field Ambulance, "acting on instruction" and accompanied by an Australian military police officer, an interpreter, and a local gendarme, paid a visit to the licensed houses of Boulogne, controlled by the French but frequented by the allies.[183]

The formal prohibition on the use of the licensed houses by British troops in 1918 made little difference to the soldiers; the army had made clear to the War Cabinet that it opposed any bridling of its men. But while British and white colonial soldiers might visit such establishments, nonwhite colonial personnel had less freedom. In addition to the restrictions on their movements, their lower pay and their racial status disbarred them.[184] Mulk Raj Anand's fictional portrait of the Indian soldiers looking in from outside the brothel forcefully brings home the racial inequalities that marked service in France as elsewhere in the war. "They were eager to taste this new sensation, but even as they waxed enthusiastic they were restrained by the humility of their position as sepoys who had never dared to look at a white woman with the eyes of desire. And the sense of the poverty of their pockets threatened to put all these pleasures beyond their reach."[185] Added to these barriers was the inescapable vigilance of their colonial masters, "in the phantom stares of sahibs, in the exploding voices of N.C.O.'s."[186]

Class and Sexuality

Military attitudes to the contracting of VD and of sexual behavior also betrayed a deeply class-conscious set of ideas about working-class sexuality. Alongside the rhetoric of the manly heroic soldier ran another less publicly articulated sense of the liabilities associated with the sexual habits of working-class men.[187] At the No. 9 Stationary Hospital at Havre in France, 2,700 men and 120 officers of the BEF were under treatment for VD in January 1916. The officers were housed separately, and though both they and the men were treated for syphilis with the new arsphenamine regime, officers received twelve doses while the rank and file received only eight doses. For gonorrhea cases, which comprised 65 percent of the total, the orders were "to get the men back to the firing line." As a result, medical officers treated only the symptomatic, a policy resulting in a high return rate of sufferers.[188]

In the Australian and Indian armies, the same penalties were nominally imposed on officers and men. In the Indian army, however, only Indian officers and not their white superiors were penalized. In Australia the policy was intended to symbolize the populist democracy of the young and adventurous nation.[189] "There can be no justification for treating officers differently from the men in this matter."[190] Though not treated as severely as their Indian counterparts, warrant officers and NCO's were liable to demotion if they contracted VD, but the policy was not extended to the regular officer class.[191] Unofficially officers willing to identify the woman they thought had infected them were guaranteed anonymity in any proceedings taken against her.[192] And officers often enjoyed more exclusive brothels. The French brothels segregated establishments for officers and for the ranks.[193]

Yet there was also a conscious notion that, as the mens' superiors, officers ought set an example. The Australian commander in chief sent a confidential memorandum to his commissioned officers in 1916, pointing out that "no high moral standards can be expected of the rank and file if they see even a small proportion of their Officers suffering from this incapacitating illness nor can any appeal to their moral sense or their sense of duty be entirely successful, unless the example set them by their Officers in these directions is of the highest."[194]

As VD rates rose, military authorities experimented with a variety of disciplinary measures. These, too, were class-inflected for, in making wages the punitive center of these policies, the authorities recognized that their constituency was reliant on its earnings. The AIF introduced stoppage of pay in February 1915, and by including pay allotted to soldiers' families, exposed the soldier's infractions at home.[195] The Canadian military began unannounced weekly genital inspections in 1916, docking 50 percent of pay while men remained on the sick list with VD.[196] They also experimented with giving overseas soldiers half-pay, providing the other half only when the men returned home.[197] The British borrowed from both techniques; soldiers with VD forfeited pay and lost the separation allowance payable to their wives.[198]

Citizenship, Nationalism, and Race

It was foreignness—from which the Anglo soldiers of the white settler colonies were excluded—that epitomized disloyalty in this climate ripe for xenophobia. While colonial governments were pressing European prostitutes to leave their shores, the House of Commons heard that the bulk of London's prostitutes were women of alien birth.[199] They, too, could be deported with a clear conscience. The Metropolitan Police kept a close eye during the war on London cafés "kept by foreigners" where "disorderly conduct is prevalent" and "undesirables are harboured."[200] Physician Mary Scharlieb told the *Daily Telegraph* that soldiers had a right to protection from "undesirable women, many of them foreigners."[201] Seeking to explain away the high rate of Australian VD, C. E. W. Bean intimated that the infected were "mostly old soldiers, many of them not born in Australia at all."[202] But when VD rates among the Indian troops rose, their loyalty was immediately questioned, and the disease became a mark of betrayal. "It is disappointing," wrote the Indian adjutant general, "and it must be added disgraceful that such a falling off from the peace standard of morality and efficiency should be found in war time—a time when of all others a soldier, if he be a true soldier, should make every effort to keep himself fit to render service to his king and country . . . each man who in war time allows himself to be incapacitated by such a disease is just as much an enemy to his country as one who voluntarily deserts."[203]

At stake here was the final test of citizenship, the critical question of loyalty. Careless as fighting men might be about where they sought their sexual pleasures, white colonials came willingly to lay down their lives. These were volunteer armies not coaxed with vague promises of land or power or freedom as were many of their nonwhite counterparts.[204] Judith Smart makes a convincing case for participation in the war as "a test of the new citizen nation" of Australia, federated not much more than a decade when the war began.[205] Indian activists looked to the Indian contribution to the war effort as a "turning point in the imperial relationship."[206] It was with relief that viceroy Lord Hardinge wrote to India secretary Austen Chamberlain "that the war has proved so clearly the superiority of our British over our Indian troops . . . I knew in pitting the Indians against Europeans they would not be slow to recognise their own inferiority and their absolute dependence on their British officers."[207] Disregarding the obsolete equipment issued to the IEF in France, and the parallel problems of acclimatization British troops had always faced when sent to India, Indian performance in the war thus "proved" the ineligibility of Indians for full citizenship.[208]

The "Black Horror"

The persistence of such racial differentiation would echo even after the cessation of hostilities. In 1919, the victorious French sent African troops, mainly Senegalese, to police the occupied Rhineland. The incident echoed in a wider framework many of the issues played out in Britain and its empire.

During the war the Germans had been the object of allied moral fury. Popular newspapers and magazines constantly offered up descriptions of German moral laxity in lurid and suggestive ways. Claiming the German army had reverted to the "sexual bestiality of the ape and the cave man," Australian Richard Arthur added, "I only hope that I am not doing the ape an injustice by comparing him to the Prussian officer."[209] Arnold White called the Germans "the intestinal worms of Central Europe," and warned that "[E]very father and mother in the British Empire should know the real character of the German missionaries of their Empire. The subjection of women is one of the foundation stones of the German creed, as their violation is a perquisite of their troops."[210] Germans were cruel, they were promiscuous, and they carried the "disease" of homosexuality alongside their predilection for rape.[211]

Yet the image of brutal Germany gave way to cries of French imperial cruelty when black troops were among those stationed in Germany in 1920. The French made considerable use of troops from their African colonies, introducing compulsory enlistment in 1915, and importing a considerable colonial labor force behind the lines.[212] In 1920, Senegalese, Mauritian, Moroccan, Malagasi, and other black colonial troops were part of the force sent to the Ruhr, and Germany instantly metamorphosed from a nation of brutal rapists into a people upon whom were now forced "crimes of sexual outrage and violence against women and girls."[213] Sally Marks has argued that France had no other troops it could send.[214] France certainly suffered substantial troop losses, but there would still have been a keen appreciation of what Keith Nelson calls a "subtle kind of psychological warfare" at work in sending black men to control a white population in an era of competitive European imperial power and "scientific" racism.[215] American socialist poet Claude McKay, watching the debacle from London, thought it was a smokescreen to "persuade the English people to decide which white gang should control the coal and iron of the Ruhr."[216] George Orwell, writing in 1944 when Indian troops were sent to Greece and similar protests began to be voiced, recalled the incident as "an added humiliation" for the Germans, musing that "the French may have used the black troops for that very reason."[217] It would also, presumably, have brought home to the defeated Germans their colonial as well as their military losses, more especially since, anticipating the prospect, they had actively sought to ensure that black soldiers would not form part of the army of occupation.[218]

The Germans made much political capital out of what they called *die schwarze Schande,* the black shame.[219] A medal of protest issued by the Germans at the time of the occupation showed a black soldier in profile on one side, complete with stereotypical black lips, and on the other side a German woman bound to a huge black phallus.[220] Germany's role thus shifted, and though it continued to be seen as the initiator of war, the nation also became the focus of a curious moral crusade in which black male sexuality became, once again, the principal enemy. The outcry at the use of black troops was international in scope. Socialists, feminists, and social purity groups in Europe and in white settler colonies loudly protested the stationing of black troops on the Rhine.[221] The controversy provoked questions in parliament and even affected elections in the United States in the early 1920s.[222] In her novel *Company Parade,* Storm Jameson deplored the "crime" of black troops "being used to bully Germans...under the aegis of a dirty Peace."[223] A flurry of letters passed between social purity organizers in Britain and France. Their opposition had less to do with the apparent plight of the Germans than with ensuring the safety and proper treatment of white women. "A cardinal point in all Government dealings in our Colonies is to insist on the greatest respect to all white women. All our people are agreed that to tamper with that feeling—whatever the nationality of the women—is like playing with gunpowder, and that the consequences may be far-reaching and disastrous."[224] Gone was the image of the dangerous, flirtatious, sexually active woman hounding the shy soldier. In this tale, women were innocents, repulsed by but vulnerable to the overwhelming sexuality of the invading black troops. Women's relations with black soldiers had to be seen as rape or near-rape and never as consensual, despite the paucity of evidence of violence against them by the occupying troops. Women were transformed from potential enemies of state harboring VD and uncontrollable lust to delicate creatures in constant danger of violation.

The socialist *Daily Herald,* run by George Lansbury, had been among the first newspapers to publicize the French maneuver, and with lurid headlines. On April 9, 1920, its headline read "Frankfurt Runs With Blood. French Black Troops Use Machine Guns on Civilians." The next day, it was "Black Scourge in Europe. Sexual Horror Let Loose by France on Rhine. Disappearance of Young German Girls."[225] McKay had warned Lansbury that articles critical of the French action would stir up "more prejudice against Negroes."[226] But it was for the man he called "the muckraker" (and the author of the *Herald*'s second article on the affair) that McKay reserved his greatest scorn.[227] Independent Labour Party activist Edmund Morel led the charge against the deployment of black troops by the French, publishing dramatically denunciatory pamphlets.

His notorious pamphlet, *The Black Horror on the Rhine,* was translated into Dutch, French, Italian, and Spanish, was published also in Germany, and went into eight editions. "We can say, without exaggerating, that the introduction of nearly 50,000 coloured troops in the centre of white Europe is a crime against the whole of Europe."[228] Tropical and subtropical races, Morel contended, had not the European habit of reason. In such peoples, he insisted, "the sex impulse is a more instinctive impulse, and precisely because it is so, a more spontaneous, fiercer, less controllable impulse than among European peoples."[229] Morel was quite clear about the consequences. "You cannot quarter tens of thousands of Africans, big, powerful, muscular men, with fierce, strong, natural passions...without their women folk, upon a European countryside without subjecting thousands of European women to willing, or unwilling, sexual intercourse with them. That is the bald fact which no ingenuity can set aside, or special pleading remove."[230]

For Morel, the French African troops were at one and the same time helpless victims of vindictive policy and simultaneously practitioners of a cruel and foreign sexual coercion. He had founded the Congo Reform Association and the Union of Democratic Control, and had worked tirelessly to improve conditions for black workers in West Africa and the Congo.[231] His position was that "if the women of the Rhineland are its [French policy's] helpless victims so also are the Africans whom it conscripts."[232] Robert Reinders argues that Morel's part in this crusade derived from his socialist belief in the urgency of preserving the fragile Weimar Republic.[233]

And this may also help explain why Lansbury's *Daily Herald* was so central in the campaign. Ungovernable when lust strikes them, colonial troops were nonetheless a "positively obedient instrument of... capitalist society."[234] For socialists, the Rhine scandal revealed the bankruptcy of capitalism and its colonial exploitation, but just as feminists were ultimately complicit with ideas of racial hierarchy, as we have seen earlier, the anticapitalist faction harbored similar views. For all the sympathy Morel and his cohort lavished on Africans sent by their French masters to Germany, the picture was still of a group of men in whom passion was stronger than reason, in whom ferocity would outweigh the dictates of reason and sense. And of course, these representations also resembled the charges against Germany and its "erotomania" which had been such common currency early in the war, but were now conveniently forgotten. Despite the scandal occasioned by their presence, France's black troops appear to have been a strikingly well-behaved force.[235]

The story died as it became evident that the prophecies of doom were unwarranted, though the incident rankled with the Germans for a long time. Hitler decried the "contamination" in *Mein Kampf*.[236] German sexologist Magnus Hirschfeld thought the policy a deliberate repayment of "the brutalities of the German occupation." He nonetheless deplored the consequences of what he saw as the undeniable "predilection of the black race for white, and especially blond women" combined with "race fetishism entertained by the women."[237] The sentiments matched precisely the fears that British officials had voiced about flighty women and black soldiers during the fighting.

Conclusion

The end of the war saw little change in attitudes. When Hugh Bayly offered his services as a lecturer to the NCCVD in 1918, he learned that "all reference to disinfection was taboo" and that his appointment "was conditional on agreement not to mention or recommend personal disinfection as a method of combating venereal disease."[238] Waldorf Astor's 1919 committee on demobilization and infectious diseases considered whether prophylactic packets should be made more widely available. Despite Lawrence Harrison's vigorous promotion to fellow committee members of the advantages, the committee piously concluded that the packets would "give rise to a false sense of security, and thus... encourage the taking of risks which would not otherwise be incurred."[239] In 1920, an article in the American journal, *Military Surgeon*, cautiously approved the use of prophylaxis, but still questioned its moral base. "There is little doubt in my mind that the exaggerated claims made as to the efficacy of prophylaxis in the A.E.F. did harm, by removing from many men wholesome fear of venereal disease, by giving some men the idea that illicit intercourse was sanctioned, and by causing others to lose faith in prophylaxis when they saw many of their comrades contract disease after its use."[240] When the commander in chief in India proposed to make postcoital prophylaxis compulsory for Indian and British troops in 1925, the War Office demurred, urging instead that regimental officers encourage restraint in their men.[241] A year later, however, India Office officials were advising that while the War Office would not formalize their support for prophylaxis, they would nonetheless encourage such methods "to the fullest extent" now that civilian opposition had seemingly died down.[242]

The notion that prevention potentially acted as encouragement, with its strong emphasis on personal responsibility and individual behavior, never ceased to be a common sentiment. In 1940, the AMSH campaigned against the French *maisons tolérées* in terms reminiscent of those it had used some twenty-five years earlier during the First World War.[243] In the Second World War, only soldiers posted overseas received free condoms, and it was only in foreign locations that the control of brothels was part of VD policy.[244] One physician thought the condom "should be available and free to all" but cautioned that it was "a two-edged sword. It can easily engender a false sense of security and, like the schoolboy's half-crown, is apt to burn a hole in the pocket until it is used."[245]

Yet always alongside the potential for moral lapse was the idea that men willing to lay down their life for their country were entitled to protection, and if that protection could not be in the form of sheaths and ointments, then it should focus instead on their sexual partners. Even in the Second World War, "the dominant idea was that men needed protection from women, not vice versa."[246] War may have been a male enterprise for the most part in the 1940s as in the 1910s, but it nonetheless raised the possibility that men were vulnerable to women's sexual advances. Were women not subject to control, then infection would strike soldiers "down more surely than the enemy bullets."[247] Though the interwar years had seen a greater emphasis on the protection of women, more especially when the newly formed League of Nations established an advisory committee on the traffic in women and children shortly after the end of the First World War, the onset of war in 1939 revived the idea of the dangerous, sexualized, and infecting woman again. The rhetoric of women's vulnerability, a central theme in the 1920s and 1930s, all but disappeared, at least in VD propaganda.

In the interwar years campaigns—some locally centered, others spearheaded from Britain or by the international community—had begun to take shape in various colonies around such issues as the Chinese *mui tsai* tradition, clitoridectomy in the Arab and African world, trafficking, and birth control.[248] These campaigns emphasized the vulnerability and exploitation of women at the hands of "savage" social systems, resting on the assumed contrast between the enlightened west and the colonial arena, and echoing the same sentiments that had caused outrage in Germany in 1920 and had led to the curtailing of black soldiers' freedom in wartime. The use of black troops in the Second World War, and more particularly in the American army, kept the question of race prominent.[249]

The 1939–45 war might have heralded the start of the lengthy process of decolonization among Britain's possessions, but nonwhite soldiers experienced many of the same inequities that had marked their earlier war experiences.

The "native" man supposedly servile to the dictates of his sexuality, and the poor woman eugenicists took to be mired in inherited ignorance, remained groups whose presence and whose behaviors could be wielded as malleable political weaponry. With their defective natures, they could stand as the measuring posts against which loyalty and betrayal might be marked, as the warning signs of the dangers of nonconformity, as the risk factors within rather than those beyond. Venereal diseases, those signal indices of wanton behavior, of uncivilized excess, of the dangers of temptation, were their province and their legacy.

RACE, SEX, AND POLITICS

Prostitution, Race, and Empire

> The Turks do well to shut—at least, sometimes—
> The women up—because, in sad reality,
> Their chastity in these unhappy climes
> Is not a thing of that astringent quality
> Which in the North prevents precocious crimes,
> And makes our snow less pure than our morality;
> The sun, which yearly melts the polar ice,
> Has quite the contrary effect on vice.
> —George Gordon Byron

Prostitution has always both fascinated and repelled those who read about it and those who comment on it. This mundane but mostly reliable source of income has been debated as a moral issue, an economic issue, a health hazard, and as a phenomenon defining gender relations. Opinions mostly remain deeply ambivalent, unable to reject either the idea of male sexual need or the moral strictures that dictate "proper" sexual contact. But amidst the rubble and confusion of these debates are the many men and women who work in and profit by the trade, or who constitute its clientele. In many areas of the world prostitution is big business, and has provided women with a better living than many of the other employment options open to them. And yet historically, prostitution has regularly been denigrated as work's opposite, a haven for those who will not work.

Race and Prostitution
Sexual difference characterized by nation, race, or even biology has played an immense role in the representations of prostitution, and racial imagery has been pervasive in the demarcation of sexual difference. The simultaneous exoticizing and denigrating of nonwestern countries has a long and complex history. In visual and verbal images, differences in culture, physical appearance, and lifestyle have frequently been delineated through heightened attention to sexual difference. The extent of clothing, the nature of sexual interaction, the sexual practices favored by groups became markers of considerable importance as Europeans moved around the globe encountering peoples whose lives and languages seemed so different from their own.

Journals from the South Sea voyages of the eighteenth century commented frequently on sexual encounters with local women and men, or on local sexual behaviors.[1] By the early nineteenth century, literature made full use of this simultaneity of exotic temptation and horrifying debasement. Poetry and fiction alluded frequently to the mysterious east as sensual yet coercive, while political tracts and the literature of improvement regularly used the east to represent the final word in wretchedness, the foil against which the ills of civilization might be measured and indexed. Comparing British ways to those of the east was a common and widely understood literary ploy, stretching at least from the early modern period and into contemporary representation.

It was in the nineteenth century, though, that prostitution came to be most intensely scrutinized and debased, pathologized as a significant and growing problem of social and scientific concern. Alongside the literary allusions to chastity, slavery, and desire, a plethora of sociological and medical literature delineated the prostitute. Her medical history was explored for signs of unusual physiology, her life history for clues to her motives, and her habits for patterns suggestive of danger. The changing landscape of both colonial and urban expansion alongside larger and more mobile populations increased the scope both of the sex trade and of investigations into it. The growth of cities, their physical layout, and the changing structures of entertainment in them offered new avenues for solicitation as well as greater anonymity for vendor and client alike. This growth in visible sex commerce unloosed a torrent of anxiety. In the nineteenth century, the prostitute became "the object of repeated regimes of inspection and regulation in the successive idioms of nineteenth-century morality and science," and these idioms not infrequently, as we have seen, overlapped.[2]

Organizing Prostitution

The Contagious Disease (CD) ordinances constitute the most formal articulation of a significant policy shift throughout the British colonial world in the nineteenth and early twentieth centuries. Vern and Bonnie Bullough have argued that regulation systems routinely serve "not to protect the prostitute but her customers."[3] In the imperial arena, regulation worked also to protect notions of racial hierarchy and the very power structures necessary to colonialism. It was white male sexual desire, which was thought to be heightened by prolonged exposure to the tropics or to sexually "looser" populations, that concerned the state. While prostitution between locals stood as an index of a society's lack of morals, that between the white man and the local woman, subject to intense scrutiny, was deemed inevitable if regrettable. The elaborate schemes of reglementation adopted in most of the empire focused virtually exclusively on protecting white men from the consequences of venereal disease.

Association with prostitute women was assumed less likely to result in children. Prostitutes were widely thought either to be barren from promiscuity and disease or knowledgeable about preventing conception. Children were not only potentially costly to the state but, if of mixed race, were of questionable respectability and loyalty, diluting the racial stock besides.[4] Since prostitution routinely occasioned only brief encounters between colonial men and local women, it seemed also to lack the potential intimacy of longer-term associations. As such, prostitution was less likely to threaten men's loyalties to the colonial state and to the metropolis than was concubinage. The dispassionate brevity of prostitution was regarded as easier to control, and by the mid-nineteenth century was the preferred policy for managing sexuality, especially though never exclusively in the controlled environment of the military. The irony of Britain adopting a policy it had long scorned as degrading and unchristian, as well as continental, was not lost on the foes of the system.

The prostitute fulfilled a role as the most degraded of women, a polluted and despised wretch removed from decency but nonetheless providing a "necessary" outlet. As masculine and feminine roles became more sharply defined in the nineteenth century and as fears of VD grew, the prostitute as social problem acquired a greater urgency. Weighted down with a confused medico-moral baggage tied to long-standing conceptions about gender, class, and race, prostitution symbolized difference. As such, it could also serve to yoke "lesser" populations to ideas of sexual disorder, offering a veritable commentary on the savagery and barbarism of colonized peoples. Sexual laxity became synonymous with racial primitivism, an archetype of degeneracy measuring a people's distance from the civilized world. What colonists dubbed prostitution became a concrete symbol of the need for colonial rule. Managing sexuality was more than simply protecting the health of white colonials from sexually transmissible diseases; by promoting the notion of prostitution as a primary mode of sexual contact in imperial settings, colonial authorities also defined, judged, and ordered local societies in an imperial image. Prostitution thus served state interests in complicated ways, not only in providing sexual services for colonizing men, but in offering an index of degradation.

Colonial Sexualities

Sexuality, and understandings of it, were integral to imperial as well as racial and sexual politics. Such understandings always required energetic assertions of racial and other differences as fundamental and defining. Colonial populations, after all, were heterogeneous bodies defying easy categorization. But their differing demographic profiles intersected with the managing of sexuality, affecting how sexual behaviors were defined and understood. To maintain the necessary ruling gap between colonizer and colonized, differences among colonized peoples were frequently minimized, leading to palpable misunderstandings about local practices, customs, and values. On the one hand, colonial law insisted on delineating difference in order to separate varieties of regulation appropriate to individual colonies. On the other hand, colonialists yoked together as immoral a host of distinct cultures and societies merely because they were regarded as too relaxed about sex commerce. One veteran of the Indian system, for example, claimed that only "perfect registration and compulsory periodical examination" would ensure the lock hospital's success. "But," he knew, "such a perfect registration is impossible in India without registering *every* woman and *every* man in the country, which no public opinion would ever allow."[5] Flattened in such equations were material differences in the organization of sex in the colonies as well as of satisfactory definitions of prostitution. Colonial societies were morally wanting, a common thread of concupiscence one of their defining characteristics. Skeptics saw prostitution everywhere. Australian colonists often charged that all the Japanese women in Australia were prostitutes.[6] C. P. Lucas at the Colonial Office knew that in China, "prostitution is more or less of a recognized character."[7] In India, claimed police chief S. M. Edwardes, "[I]t is hardly an exaggeration to say that the great majority of India's inhabitants . . . still regard [prostitution], and those who follow it, with tolerance and sometimes even with respect and approval."[8] A senior Punjabi official likened prostitution in India to "working in leather or exercising some or other of the less honourable crafts or occupations."[9] It was a view that saw prostitution strictly in caste terms, and as a lower-status but nonetheless accepted caste occupation. S. H. Butler in the United Provinces agreed; prostitution was customary and training began at a young age.[10] Prostitution, as colonial officials were fond of asserting, "offends no native susceptibility."[11] It was a routine part of life, and living evidence of native disorder.

The idea of the libertine east allowed prostitution to be defined as regional, with the colonies depicted as a giant brothel. The not-infrequent claims that few Chinese, Indian, or Aboriginal women could not be purchased for the right consideration buttressed the picture of a libidinous rapacious east. S. C. Bayley thought there were "thousands of prostitutes" in Calcutta alone.[12] The unchastity of Burmese women generally meant that "if not prostitutes," they were "next door to it."[13] Bengal's surgeon general warned that there were too many "phases and varieties of prostitution" to enumerate.[14] Scarcely a memoir written by a male western traveler does not include a description of the local red-light district and its inhabitants. Even where the tone is that of the experienced worldly wise raconteur who does not deny his own indulgence, his remains nonetheless the voice of the modern, observing the chaos and fleshliness of the irrational and the backward. The idea of the east as a place of passion and lust was the perfect binary foil for the west's self-representation as cool and modern and rational. Since accepted forms of prostitution could hardly be dismantled in a short space of time, they argued, and since outlets for colonial male desire were necessary, local immorality was a convenience that could be censured even while it was sampled.

The idea of the empire as a web of lust and sexual intrigue and temptation rested on an idea of sexuality as a premodern phenomenon that modernity and rationality had learned to contain and to channel. The east's problem was its failure to move beyond the primitivism of unchained nature, to contain sex within boundaries that made it productive and purposeful rather than merely sensual and pleasurable. To be natural was to be in a state of savagery, to be prerational. And yet even this depiction constantly collapsed for at the same time as colonized peoples were defined by their sexuality, they were seen simultaneously as prudish. Lieutenant Colonel H. B. Thornhill in India thought "[O]rdinary residents object and naturally object to the intrusion of the saffron-robed woman and her following into their respectable neighbourhood." Permitting brothels "would speedily be the cause of disturbances more or less serious between soldiers and fathers of families."[15] On the one hand, eastern societies were inured to prostitution and accepted it without moral judgment. On the other hand, respectable patriarchs would vigorously fight to keep it at arm's length. The simultaneity of these clearly contradictory opinions—that colonials were oversexed and that they were excessively modest—suggests a complex of anxieties among the rulers about how best to justify and to maintain British rule.

The differences that local administrators and Colonial Office staff found in the practice of prostitution in the various colonies often had more to do with prejudices about local custom than with an attention to the effects of colonialism on the local populace. Poverty was acknowledged as a substantial factor in women's turn to prostitution yet seldom connected to the effects of colonial mastery. Those who treated VD understood not only the politics behind the public reporting of disease statistics, but also that transmission and vulnerability were about more than the moral issues so wrapped up in public debate about these illnesses. Though they were often contemptuous or dismissive of indigenous populations, and more than a little fearful of the disease pool they saw there, practitioners also recognized the social dimensions affecting disease. Famine and poverty were constantly noted as major contributors to the problem and if doctors failed to link these economic issues to colonialism's grasp, they nonetheless endlessly witnessed its results. In lean years, when famine decimated rural peoples, medical officers reported that "the pangs of hunger" drove "women previously chaste" to prostitution and forced rural prostitutes "into the larger towns" seeking more lucrative custom.[16] In Agra, noted the medical officer, "scarcity of food and consequent distress" drove "large numbers of starving women . . . to practice unlicensed prostitution."[17] The press of desperate poverty, of course, forced prices down, and doctors everywhere were convinced that bad years for colonial peoples were intimately linked to a rise in military VD.

Yet for all this recognition of the demands made by poverty, moral strictures predominated. In the wealthy colony of Queensland, the preponderance in the sex trade of Aboriginal and Japanese women, and among whites, of Irish-born women, was likelier to draw comments about racial tendencies than sympathy for the economic disadvantages these women experienced. Aboriginal and Indian men were said to be careless of women's dignity, happy to trade even their wives for a small consideration. The Chinese allegedly operated slave brothels, buying and selling women cold-bloodedly for a profit.

Colonial Perversity

Jeffrey Weeks has argued that sexuality has been "a peculiarly sensitive conduc-tor of cultural influences, and hence of social and political divisions."[18] If we apply such an observation to colonial sexuality, then racial difference comes to occupy a role parallel to that of sexuality as a critical political and cultural con-duit. Race and sex as categories deployed by colonial authority to damn morally questionable societies worked invariably in tandem, inseparable in their very fashioning as well as in their material effects. Susie Tharu and K. Lalita have tracked how colonial analyses and commentaries in the nineteenth century "in-variably" alluded to sexual perversity as a defining mark of the Indian subject.[19] Sex was one of the most widely remarked upon mechanisms for measuring dis-tance from civilization, and prostitution was always central in this calculus. Race invariably influenced attitudes about sex, and vice versa. They were inseparable as categories of classification and assessment.

The damning of colonial sites as moral sinks was crucial to the overall picture of their inferiority. But the vocabulary of modern rationality was never quite enough. In Hong Kong and the Straits, the grip of the sex-slave traffic was thought to be such that "constant inspection and registration of all the 'flowery halls' becomes a necessity independent of the question of disease."[20] There was a tremendous ambivalence about who was being protected and about what could be accomplished, about whether the issue was one of hygiene or morals or civilization; it was an uncertainty compounded by the view of the colonies as endlessly and relentlessly sexual, always liable to spin beyond and outside control. And yet for all the confusion and ambiguity, the yoking of sex and the tropics remained central and fixed, unmovable as a point of definition.

Woman-Native-Prostitute

Constant in these invocations was the potential for all "native" women to be prostitutes: woman-native-prostitute was an easily assimilable equation that en-couraged regulation as an urgent and rational defense against a range of tropical dangers. The merging of blacks and prostitutes as a category, traced by Sander Gilman, suggests that race and gender were key pointers to sexuality.[21] Prosti-tution was the logical end point of uncontained desire even while it was also a necessity in the overwhelmingly male environments created by Britain's overseas expansion. One colonial medical officer reported gloomily to his superiors that it "would be as hopeful to try to 'stamp out' a 'will o'the Wisp' as to 'stamp out' venereal disease in a cantonment, by the machinery of the registration and the segregation of a few women called prostitutes, out of a multitude of unchaste women."[22] Despite this pessimism, officials from various arms of the state spent considerable time and energy on just that task, of recognizing even if never fully defining the prostitute.

The idea of prostitution as singularly female was so ingrained it barely required discussion.[23] Drafting rules for a new Indian Cantonment Act in 1890, legal writers declared, true to British law, that the masculine included the feminine, "unless there is something repugnant in the subject or context."[24] Since the principal reason for revamping the act was the late 1880s quarrel over regulating prostitution detailed in chapter 4, the rider had considerable resonance. In the context of identifying the prostitute as an exclusively female person, the idea of an overarching masculinity would be found to be repugnant. In the 1871 report on contagious diseases policy in Cape Town, the committee remarked that "a male prostitute is a character unknown."[25] Men's sexuality was motivated by desire, women's by greed. Where male prostitution could not be wholly ignored, it was presented as the province of men not fully masculine. The *hijras* of India, a eunuch community, were often cast as prostitutes. Dressed as women and often castrated, their involvement in prostitution became a vital measure of their nonmasculinity, a topic to which chapter 10 will return us.

The prostitute was female but not feminine, a separation that justified her forfeiture of a slew of rights otherwise accorded women by virtue of their sex. The prostitute's open performance of her female sexuality ran counter to contemporary notions of femininity as less sexual, domestically contained and fulfilled, and subservient to male desire. The prostitute terrifyingly represented the idea of woman in her natural state, untamed and unchained from modesty and propriety. Prostitution disrupted dominant visions of female purity and submission. Powerful as this reading of womanhood was, there was a fear that women might break out and prove something other than docile. Prostitution provided a picture of what lurked behind the necessary facade of manners and rules, made manifest in those regions of the globe yet to feel the impact of civilization. Like the crumbling civilizations or "primitive" social structures to which she was compared, the prostitute was a throwback, a reminder of the fragility and of the necessity for imperial expansion. Outside civility, she could be treated according to harsher rules. Prostitutes, thought a medical officer in India, might be "subjected to a little wholesome coercion for their own good and that of the community."[26]

In Britain, the prostitute had a similarly low status. Oxfordshire's chief constable upbraided a woman police officer during the 1914–18 war for attempting to have a distressed suspect examined for VD outside normal office hours. "He shrugged his shoulders and said, 'Oh well, you must remember it is not the same as though she were a decent woman, she is a common prostitute, and it will not hurt her to wait till the morning.' "[27] The divide between respectable and unrespectable was critical. Though officials decried the "sly" prostitute who evaded their attention, they still constantly advised one another on how to recognize the woman selling sex. And though the visual clues (scantily clad, tawdrily dressed, overly made-up) were transferred wholesale to colonial environments, officials still found themselves floundering. If, after all, the women of Asia were, whether by choice or not, already virtually all prostitutes, then how was it possible to seek a more precise classification? It was a conundrum that occupied considerable attention and debate though seldom much agreement beyond the wholesale condemnation of the Asian propensity for commercialized sex.

Vagrancy, Work, and Sex

While the prostitute herself might not always be recognizable, she was always identifiable as a vagrant, as a nonworker. The prostitute, thought London magistrate Cecil Chapman, was characteristically lazy. It was "idleness and a refusal to earn a living by honest labour," that brought her before him time and time again.[28] Noah Zatz argues that the law has been central in "suppressing sex workers' attempts to articulate their practices as a form of work and promote its (sic) interpretation as fundamentally a sexual act."[29] Concerned with contemporary legal grammars of sexual control, Zatz's point nonetheless illumines a much older and a critically important western history. Work occupied a central place for Victorians as the authentication of individual productivity and of respectability, more particularly as the influence of inherited wealth began its decline. Work defined not just respectability but also, and crucially, gender. Despite a huge female workforce confined to a narrow band of jobs, Victorian rhetoric countered the working man with the domesticated woman whose household sphere complemented his public toil. Within this value system, the woman wage earner was already walking the tightrope of "womanliness." Prostitution, while it might earn women good money, broke completely the link between profit and social approbation. Women "became the site in which questions of economics intersected with questions of morality."[30] It was an everlastingly troubled site. In colonial settings, work acquired further meaning. India, notes Francis Hutchins, was a place in which to be busy. As he points out, even the leisure activities of the English there—riding and pig-sticking, for example—were strenuous.[31] Manual labor, however, was seldom the province of whites of any class. Indenture, long abandoned in Britain, continued to supply colonial workforces into the twentieth century. Women other than whites were employed in a far wider variety of manual jobs than in Britain. All these factors affected the moral stature attached to the idea of labor; the extra layer of racial difference worked in tandem with the class valences evident in Britain to separate proletarian from bourgeois occupations. But in the colonies, natives and nonwhite migrants supplied the bulk of the labor that in Britain would be identified as working class. Work defined as manual (domestic service, agricultural work, factory labor) was almost exclusively reserved to nonwhites. Even working-class soldiers were catered to in ways unknown to them in the metropole.

The idea of vagrancy, however, remained constant as a way to define and criminalize those who refused to work. It was within the broader category of vagrancy that prostitution was understood as an alternative to "honest" work for the loose and lazy woman. The 1911 census in India classified prostitutes in the "major class of 'unproductive labour,' together with beggars, vagrants, habitual receivers of stolen goods, and cattle-prisoners."[32] Victorians could not see prostitution as work even when officials computed that women on average serviced "at least five men daily."[33] At the small lock hospital of Jellapahar near Darjeeling, the apothecary calculated that his station "required not less than twelve healthy women, being at the rate of 4 per cent. of the troops."[34] Many years later, a World War Two doctor thought that brothel workers often serviced "as many as thirty or more men in ... twenty-four hours."[35] These far-flung comments point to a task that required considerable physical stamina and long hours, but such evidence of physical effort counted for nothing. Greed, not honesty, was the motive, negating women's palpable exertions, putting them outside the hallowed work ethic.

Many believed that women supplemented other income with prostitution. Indigenous women engaged in just about any form of manual work came under suspicion. Officials in the Punjab viewed women engaged by the public works department, as well as the women grass-cutters and vendors, as a health hazard, so sure were they that these workers also sold sex to the soldiers. As a result, women laborers could be registered as prostitutes wholesale, curfews could be imposed, there were restrictions on where women could reside, and rules that only married women be employed and only "in company with their husbands."[36] The very figure of the colonial woman worker was always potentially subversive, for using the cover of legitimate work she could secretly resort to prostitution and evade notice.

A huge difference in status accrued to those whose jobs were permanent, who could display particular skills that demonstrated training and therefore staying power. The fact that women sold sex alongside working in other trades was "proof" of their lowliness, as it was an index of danger. Stability in employment—an impossibility for most working people in the volatile economies of the nineteenth century—was a marker of success and respectability. But women in the sex trade distorted the perception in treating as an occupation that which could be not classified as work, and in combining it with work that, while humble, could nonetheless be dubbed legitimate. In northern India, reported an assistant commander, "lower class" Doomnee women, working as coolies, "are not prostitutes by profession, but are mostly married; yet there is no doubt they cohabit with British soldiers."[37] Virtually every woman worker in contact with the military—"the wives of the sweepers, sellers of charcoal, sellers of fowls, sellers of butter"[38]—was available to the soldiers, according to the British, and the stress on their marital status tarnished their husbands with the brush of complicity as well. Australian Aboriginal women were similarly regarded as amenable to sexually servicing local whites, as were laundresses, seamstresses, and other working women in Hong Kong and the Straits, as well as in Britain.

But a distinction was still conjured between the British and the colonial contexts. The British woman crossed a line that at some point drew her out of the legitimate workforce to become a "fallen" woman. The British factory girl or needlewoman who also exchanged sexual favors was seen to follow a linear path of degradation that would ultimately strip her of her capacity to operate in anything other than the underworld. It was a fundamentally Christian reading of the fall from grace and it fit perfectly with lurid tales of abandonment to alcohol and narcotics, to sensuous but deadly pleasures. In Victorian literature and art, we follow the prostitute's path from the gaily lit theater, to the shadows of the street and the opium den, and finally to the workhouse, the morgue, or floating—dead—in the river.[39]

This sad narrative was seldom told of nonwhite prostitute women. They might be seen to die from sexually related disease but the tale of inevitable degradation, the decline from respectability to destitution, was irrelevant in an environment already given over to abandon, indifferent to women's vulnerability, and at best unmoved by the alleged horrors of the sex trade. The double work of women in formal waged labor and prostitution in colonial environments was represented much more as a danger to their clients than to themselves, a clear reversal of the sentimentality that often characterized metropolitan depictions of a woman's descent.

The nonworking woman in Britain was the housewife properly ensconced in family duties, or the daughter still under her father's authority, defined by the terms of marriage. In the colonies, the unoccupied woman was much likelier to be classified as a vagrant, automatically suggesting her potential for prostitution. "Where women are vagrants, prowling about the barracks of European soldiers, without being able to show that they have any honest calling or occupation, they might be arrested, it seems to me, without unduly trenching on the liberty of the subject."[40] The poor colonial woman was a worker or a vagrant while for the British woman, a third and favored option—domestic woman—might secure her moral worth.

Women's Mobility

This divide was driven, in part, by fears around mobility, conceptually so central in defining vagrancy. In the metropole, as many feminist historians have shown, women's rights to move in public spaces was always contested.[41] Even among men, mobility could be a threat to social order, and vagrancy laws existed precisely to suppress that threat. Prostitution vividly demonstrated why mobility was such a cause for alarm. Prostitute women crystallized the many dangers of mobility and its challenges to a fixed legal and social order. They often moved residence rather than conform to regulation. They exercised a choice over their living quarters and arrangements, moving when they deemed it necessary and living outside the confines imposed by respectable domesticity. Women working outside the brothel system were a danger because their mobility allowed them to locate exactly where they might find clients. Moreover, faced with examination, hospitalization, or incarceration, easy mobility meant that women could seek business elsewhere with little effort, their physical freedom undermining the system of regulation.[42] In colonial settings where migrants, whether internal or external, were central to the workforce, women tended to be more mobile than in the metropolis, driven mostly by poverty and need. It was impossible, except among the rich, to represent women as fixed by family responsibilities as the invocation of the separate spheres tried to do in the metropole. Prostitution was, thus, in a host of ways a primary challenge to the very notions of public and private, spatially, legally, and ideologically.

Mobility as excessive freedom and a social threat led to its association with criminality. In Australia, the state protectors confined and monitored the movements of nomadic Aboriginal peoples; Evans, Saunders, and Cronin have argued that the reserves on which Aboriginals were increasingly required to live explicitly served to differentiate the useless unemployed from the useful indigene, the latter defined as an Aboriginal employed by a white Australian.[43] In India, the government worked hard, though unsuccessfully, to settle the so-called criminal tribes of India; Sanjay Nigam has enumerated the powerful binaries—wild/tamed, wandering/sedentary—that shaped legislation intended to tame groups such as the Bawarias of northern India.[44] Such communities were often seen as major players in the prostituting of young women. "Many gipsy-like nomadic tribes in northern India prostitute their girls as a matter of custom," claimed Bombay's police chief.[45]

Prostitution, crime, and mobility formed a heady trio of prejudices. Women convicts transported to Australia for such nonsex related crimes as theft were branded as sexually immoral, as potential if not actual prostitutes, their lawlessness and lack of fixity the evidence of their dangerous sexuality.[46] Indian convicts banished to the penal colony of the Andaman Islands were classed as immoral. The superintendent at Port Blair informed the government of India that "locally-born children of convict parents, male and female, are, as might be expected, often not of good moral character. The girls especially are apt to become prostitutes, or at the best of loose character from an early age."[47] Linking prostitution and criminality was a useful way to strip women, and indeed vagrants generally, of any rights or moral authority. Their opinions could be discredited, their freedom compromised because, from the standpoint of the dominant moral discourse, they had abandoned their proper place in the world. Cecil Chapman recommended dealing with the prostitute, whom he dubbed "an idle and disorderly person," under the provisions of the English Poor Law. A stay in the workhouse, he predicted, would make the prostitute "hate her life more quickly."[48] Such a position broadened the fronts on which prostitution might be attacked.

Shame, Penitence, and Redemption

Equally damning and clearly connected was the frequent harping on women's lack of shame; here again a colonial-metropolitan divide operated. Refuges and asylums in Britain required true penitence among their residents, a rule that guaranteed a high rate of failure. But the narrative at work colonially often rested on the *lack* of shame and self-consciousness manifested among prostitute women, again illuminating the competing visions of native indulgence and native priggishness. The brothel woman of Hong Kong, reported a police magistrate, always blandly insisted that she had willingly chosen her occupation, a claim he said that "was very rarely true."[49] The women were, therefore, also liars. In India, one surgeon complained, the problem was that women had "no regret for the past, no desire for a higher standard of life, no self-respect."[50] The failure of such women to perform shame, a fundamental demand of Britain's magdalen asylums, marked them out as incorrigible and unreachable, precisely the language applied to those who came within the reach of vagrancy laws and of the workhouses. Running through such complaints was a fear of female independence that contradicted the prevailing idea of Asian women as helplessly enmeshed in a deviance not of their own making. These two visions competed, the one fearful of the consequences of independence, the other condemning the servitude of non-British women. This apparent contradiction bolsters Barbara Littlewood and Linda Mahood's argument that, "[T]he 'prostitute' meant different things to different people: a victim of a morally corrupt order, a conduit of disease, a source of temptation to sin, or a necessary evil."[51] This malleability allowed both the critical distinctions between colonial and metropolitan status that we have traced, and a slipperiness in the law that worked generally to women's disadvantage.

Defining the Prostitute

One of the most glaring anomalies of the legalistic nineteenth-century attention to prostitution is its signal and long-term failure ever to alight definitively on what prostitution actually was and who could be labeled a prostitute. We shall return to this theme in the next chapter to observe the contrast between this failure to define and the minute taxonomy of surveillance nonetheless inaugurated by regulation. The inability of officials ever to reach an agreement on exactly what constituted prostitution in no way inhibited either the passing of laws or the issuing of regulations designed to control the lives of those engaged in this seemingly undefinable pursuit, but it is an absence worth exploring. And seemingly, this slipperiness could affect implementation of the laws. Commenting on women taking advantage of the Indian CD Act's weaknesses to evade registration, an 1870 report noted that "the evidence of prostitution being undefined by law, the women easily evaded it."[52]

It is, however, one of the most significant features of British law in the area of sexual commerce that it has never fully defined for legal purposes what constitutes prostitution. The landmark Wolfenden report of 1957, on homo-sexual offenses and prostitution, noted that there was "no statutory definition of the term 'common prostitute,'" and did not itself propose one.[53] Offenses related to prostitution, such as soliciting, procuring, running a brothel, have been defined (although not always effortlessly), but neither in metropolitan nor colonial contexts, have lawmakers ever been willing to issue a definitive state-ment on who the prostitute is. The Metropolitan Police commissioner warned his officers in 1887 that absent "any legal opinion or decision on the subject, the Commissioner does not think that the Police are justified in calling any woman a common prostitute, unless she so describes herself, or has been convicted as such."[54] Lauren Benton's study of colonial law suggests that such vagueness was by no means limited to laws around prostitution.[55] What makes the case of prostitution interesting, however, is that this refusal or inability to define is common to both metropole and colonies, suggesting that in this arena, it was perhaps less a problem of law than a reflection of the many social and cultural anxieties circulating around sexual commerce.

Feminists have argued (and indeed still maintain) that the equivocation over defining the prostitute has allowed police and other authorities enormous ev-identiary leeway. Britain's Association for Moral and Social Hygiene pointed out in 1917 that a proposed criminal law amendment bill before the Com-mons aimed certain specific punishments against the "common prostitute" despite the fact that "[T]here exists no legal or statutory definition" of the term or of prostitution per se.[56] Activist Chrystal Macmillan excoriated the courts for their "question-begging" and informal definitions of prostitution that, she claimed, placed women "outside the ordinary law," held to different standards of evidence.[57] More than sixty years later, Carol Smart pointed out that the term *common prostitute* (a term first employed in vagrancy laws) made women liable not only, as Macmillan had also argued, to conviction on police testimony alone, but to having prior offenses aired before she was tried.[58] Conviction relied not on strict definition but on establishing a pattern of behavior and activity. The impact on women's lives could be tremendous. Officers at an East London police station kept watch on a Mrs. Smith in 1902. "She was seen on four oc-casions to take different men to her rooms and twice to well-known brothels. She was also seen frequently drinking in the company of prostitutes, therefore the evidence being sufficient her three children . . . were arrested."[59] Under the Industrial Schools Amendment Act of 1880, the children of prostitute mothers and those found in brothels were brought before magistrates for committal to industrial schools, away from their mothers, for residential training in "useful" employments.

In the colonies, much ink was spilled fretting over children brought up in unwholesome environments but government did not intervene, as it frequently did in the homes of working-class Britons. The looseness of definition that saw Mrs. Smith's children taken from her was complicated by the common view of colonial societies as inured to, and supportive of, prostitution. "What is a common prostitute?" asked a civil servant in India in a letter to one of his superiors. "The women who walk the road every evening to the west of the Cawnpore Cantonment, the coolie women and milk sellers, who are employed at the barracks in the day time, all of them married women, and by repute respectable household women, are as much common prostitutes as the most habitual professionals."[60] There was no point in defining since the definition would be too broad to be operable. Commenting on the Straits Settlements, an official at the Colonial Office scribbled a marginal note in an 1888 file, noting "there is no definition, nor can there be a good one, of the word 'prostitute.'"[61] He would doubtless have been surprised to know that his view was shared by many of the foes of regulation. In a pamphlet put out by the Federation for the Abolition of the State Regulation of Vice a dozen years later, the authors commented that "[T]here is nothing more difficult to define than solicitation."[62] Prostitution continually eluded definition—as an occupation and as an offense.

Yet solicitation was, and remains in British law, the formal basis for criminal conviction: "It will be observed by the student that the laws do not define 'prostitute'. . . . Many acts leading up to and arising out of prostitution, such as soliciting, are, however, offences."[63] In some instances this lack of precision was considered beneficial, allowing for local adjustment. A committee charged with drawing up regulations under India's first act regulating prostitution welcomed the opportunity to distinguish the public prostitute. "The line," claimed the committee, "will not be difficult to draw in practice."[64] Others argued that such haziness allowed women to avoid prosecution. "The chance of conviction . . . is becoming smaller and smaller, owing to the absence of a precise definition of the term 'common prostitute.' "[65] For many, the solution was simple. The law's vagueness invited interpretation. Hong Kong's police magistrate asserted in 1879 that "if I had trustworthy evidence that a woman offered the use of her person for a *small sum of money* (whether money changed hands or not), I should consider her a prostitute unless she could produce evidence to the contrary."[66] Calcutta's police commissioner issued a circular order to his men in 1869. "The expression 'common prostitute' is not defined in the Act but it evidently refers to all women who, in an open manner, gain their livelihood by a life of prostitution, and therefore, having no object for concealment, desire to be regarded as women of the town." Those "who do not court notoriety" remained outside his definition.[67]

The evidentiary basis on which these attempts to construct legal meaning rested were clearly deficient and wholly reliant on police testimony. It was feminists and radicals who, in Britain, questioned the trustworthiness of the police in cases such as these. In the colonies, there was a near-automatic assumption that native policemen were all unscrupulous. To render the regulation of prostitution workable, argued a senior Bengal official in 1898, "we should have to define 'common prostitute' in such a way as to get rid of the objection which the

Courts showed invariably to inferential proof, and as direct proof is for obvious reasons unattainable, this could only be done by so loosely defining the term as necessarily to place a most dangerous power in the hands of evil-disposed persons and of the police."[68] The looseness that made him wary was exactly what the lack of definition in the law brought about.

When the New South Wales legislature debated legislation around venereal disease, sex, and public morality in 1908, the distinction between the street and the brothel was constantly elided. In the parliamentary discussion on amendments to a police bill, members of Parliament used the term *streetwalking* generically, as if it accurately described all prostitution. Like all such umbrella legislation, the Police Offences (Amendment) Act dealt with a wide range of prosecutable offenses, but the politicians clearly distinguished only cursorily between the palpably *public* offenses of loitering and vagrancy (perhaps the commonest charges on which street prostitutes were arrested) and those attached to working in or keeping a brothel.[69] In this perceived connection between sex and the street was an equally casual looseness about what could be said to be prostitution. The synonymity of street and brothel was useful for rhetoric, but never prevented policing from attacking whichever seemed at that moment more politically pressing.[70]

Circling back to the paradox of work, law and public opinion tried invariably to fix prostitution as that which was not work, as that pursued by the lazy, the greedy, the intemperate, the loafer. Yet the very fixity of that negative definition tried to class prostitution as equivalent to, while always less than, work. In other words, if one was not in fruitful employ then one might be a prostitute, for prostitution was work's mirror image, profit without honor. The reality of poverty and the uncertainty of alternative employment for women ensured that this was a chimerical divide. Many women saw prostitution as one of a number of money-making opportunities.[71] "For many women 'prostitution' is not a singular identity, but merely one of a range of economic and social identities that make up their livelihood strategies."[72] Officials who saw prostitution in the women who did the laundry in Hong Kong and who cut the grass in Indian cantonments recognized this, if only obliquely.

The *Devadasi*

Perhaps the most misunderstood of local traditions was that of the Indian tradition of the *devadasi*. Attracting attention even today, the *devadasi* and similar courtesan traditions have a long history. Associations between sexuality and performance were common, the theater in Britain considered a dangerous place of assignation and stage performers barely respectable. In many environments, the pleasures of the flesh and of the performance were seen as intimately connected. In Cape Town, prostitute women engaged Malay musicians to further their trade.[73] Hong Kong's superintendent of police asserted that when the "Chinese . . . have a dinner party . . . prostitutes and singing girls [are] present."[74]

But the focus was most squarely on India where Britons believed that in certain castes girls were raised to prostitution from infancy, their occupation masked under the guise of religion. "It is horrible to think of," wrote one metropolitan commentator secure in his imperial Englishness, "but in India the ancient connection between religion and prostitution still survives."[75]

Devadasis were women dedicated to Hindu temples, literally married to the gods, beyond the reach of mortal marriage.[76] Trained in arts such as dancing and poetry recitation, they also formed sexual alliances, often long-term, with high-born men, and it was the sexual element of their lives upon which colonial attention came to rest. Britain's Army Sanitary Commission argued in the mid-1870s that "the dedication of girls to the temple service is only a cloak for the real object of making them prostitutes."[77] The surgeon general of the Indian Medical Department dubbed *devadasis* "a somewhat dangerous class of prostitutes" riddled with disease.[78] From the 1860s, convictions for dedicating girl children to "temple harlotry" under sections 372 and 373 of the Indian Penal Code became increasingly common.[79] Variations on these traditions were geographically widespread; Frédérique Marglin argues that the woman temple dancer was "a pan-Indian phenomenon."[80] Her secular counterparts, the courtesans, entertained only wealthy men and in precolonial India were often attached to the royal court. Carefully and lengthily trained in the performing arts, they were often referred to as "*nautch* girls," a term that lent its name to the campaigns devoted to banning this occupation.[81] Unquestionably colonial practice and policy helped to impoverish many of these women and to lower their standing during the course of the nineteenth century.[82] The anti-*nautch* movement gained ground in the 1910s when an official dispatch urged government servants to boycott *devadasi* performances, and when Manicekji Dadabhoy and R. N. Mudholkar introduced bills to curtail the tradition. Such campaigns threw many courtesans and *devadasis* out of work, forcing them into a more pedestrian selling of sex shorn of its connections to the performing arts.[83]

Normalizing prostitution as occupying a recognized place within the Indian proletariat made the prostitute woman the exemplar of Indian vice. "[T]he chief and almost universal amusement of the Natives is watching dances and hearing singing, and the performers are always women of immoral character brought up to the trade from their childhood."[84] It was not just the prostitute but her whole cultural milieu that made India, in colonial eyes, degraded. What the Bombay police commissioner called "sanctified harlotry" defined India, and negatively.[85] For the British, the *devadasi* was not the servant and wife of the gods, but a slave to unharnessed human desire, and a threat to Victorian readings of the marriage contract.[86] The *devadasi* was a symbol and a specter of India's fate, holding onto a crumbling status even while engaged in the "degradation" of commercial sex. The very idea that a once legitimate tradition was debased into common prostitution reflects a significant hierarchy in thinking about both sex and gender, and one which is as common in contemporary as in earlier writings on the topic. Why, after all, is the sexual service of a woman in the court of a *nawab* or in a religious temple, and accompanied by singing and dancing, more honorable than the sexual service of a women whose clients have less money and standing? In the metropole, the same question turned on the distinction between the women who serviced the wealthy and the working-class client. Certainly these were separations on which women themselves often insisted. This is hardly surprising since such distinction conferred a modicum of respectability or at least legitimation and a higher standard of living. Yet it reveals a host of class and caste prejudices. In sociological literature and in journalism, there is a stress on the tenacity of the *devadasi* tradition among "backward communities."[87] In a recent article on Delhi's *nautch* history in *The Times of India*, Abha Narain traced the degeneration of art into "crass prostitution," a narrative of debasement still widespread.[88] In an otherwise sympathetic discussion of *devadasis*, B. R. Patil claims that the profession "in its original form was free from sex and noble in character."[89] Corruption was linked to sex, a formula of which colonial authorities made good use and that continues, as Narain and Patil's work suggests, to have currency. Colonial opinion could condemn India as sexually lax, the men as ignoble, and the women as promiscuous. Indeed, the courtesan's courtly presence was a useful tool to criticize the fitness of *nawabi* rulers.[90] Even the wealthier segments of colonized societies were overly sexualized. The dinner party, the courtly gathering, and the priestly environment were clearly arenas beyond the reach of most people, but here, too, sexuality intruded indelicately.

Moral Hierarchies and Whiteness

Prostitution was as much a discourse about moral authority as it was a pragmatic if flawed solution serving the dictates of male desire. Its apparent ubiquity in female colonial populations *was* its definition, the guarantor and proof of lesser moral standing, a phenomenon that made apparent the need for the boundaries of rule. That it was a throwback to primitivism, that it was female, and that it was commonplace among the colonized attached the sex trade to categories of race, nation, and gender. "Brothels in towns in India are at present an unpleasant but real necessity."[91] Prostitution's personification of the wrongs of other peoples helped consolidate the idea that colonialism was necessary, an antidote to what a pamphlet issued to British soldiers called "queer and uncivilised countries."[92] Needless to say, those countries had frequently to be defined in ways that made them appear "queer and uncivilised." The same incentive that labeled nonwhite women potential prostitutes flattened other distinctions in colonial settings. Chris Bayly notes that "indigenous peoples" had to be created as entities in order for the very category of indigenous to acquire meaning and value.[93] The classifications were necessarily inadequate and invariably overly homogenous. John Clammer's work, for example, shows that there were at least sixteen dialect or regional groups in Singapore's Chinese community, and that similar distinctions applied to its Malay and Indian populations as well.[94] These were mostly ignored by the colonists (with the exception of caste in India, which was more misread than ignored)[95] in favor, rather, of distinguishing along racial lines. Racialization, in Satya Mohanty's analysis, involves "a dynamic process through which social groups can be bound, defined, and shaped," though in terms brought to bear from outside on those thus defined.[96] "Nation-ness," as Benedict Anderson puts it, "is assimilated to skin-colour, gender, parentage and birth-era," characteristics beyond choice and thus dubbed natural.[97] The British were natural leaders; those colonized by them were natural subordinates and mired, too, in that other and less revered naturalness, the premodern and irrational.

Central to this exercise of justifying power, though rarely acknowledged, was whiteness as the defining mark of proper rule. Richard Dyer argues that whiteness was "a product of enterprise and imperialism," insisting that colonialism was central to the process of race-making.[98] Kim Hall identifies an era of "intensified . . . interest in colonial travel and African trade" (the 1550s) with an attentiveness to racial difference.[99] These arguments suggest that whiteness was an effect of the colonial project, whether in modern or early modern periods, and certainly it was not an existing and stationary idea brought to the colonial schema. Yet to see so salient a hierarchical marker merely as *produced* by this mode of authority is perhaps to render the work it does too passive. I would argue, rather, that these categories, forms of moral, political, and economic discourse, were part of the weaponry of colonialism, less produced by it than elements of its capacity to effect its business, to do its work, necessary indices of who behaved how and who could do what.

This becomes apparent when we examine how ideas of race, nationhood, gender, and citizenship simultaneously influenced debates about political representation. Outside the settler colonies, the idea of self-governance was rejected as, at the very least, a premature notion. The attitudes of the Chinese or the Indians to women and to prostitution were held up as examples of why such peoples were far from ready for the responsibilities incumbent in government. At the very moment when prostitution was so common on governing agendas, middle-class white women in Britain and in the settler colonies were demanding their own enfranchisement, and one of their constant arguments was their own class, civilizational, and racial superiority to those with whom they shared nonvoting status.[100] When many of those same activist women took up the fight against regulated prostitution, the vocabulary of Christian morality's superiority to the heathen abandonment of women was a strong element in their campaigns. "The discourse of race was not a parallel track with the discourse of nation but part of it; the latter was saturated with a hierarchy of moralities."[101]

The talk of entitlement inherent in the demand for representation was closely tied, in the British context, to the discourse of imperialism in the latter half of the nineteenth century. Feminists campaigning for the vote alluded frequently to colonial conditions, contrasting their own situation to that of subject nations within the empire. Yet even when such comparisons were not uppermost, the very idea of enfranchisement presupposed a notion of independence. And independence was the ideal, above all others, that drove ideas both about the imperial state and about gender. Independence was what white settlers and white metropolitan women demanded for themselves; it was what nationalist campaigns in colonial countries coalesced around. Dependence marked the frailty of womanhood and the subjections of colonialism; it thus also defined colonial authority and political selfhood as a province both raced and gendered, the privileges of white manhood. Yet the demands of feminists and nationalists, and their successful incursions into white male territory, suggested that privilege could be a fragile thing and might change in definition.

Hygiene and Racism

One of the most salient and indeed misogynist areas of this privilege was the scientific establishment. The rise of scientific racism and the growing power of the logic of science and medicine were, as we have seen, characteristic of the nineteenth century.[102] It was within such a framework that prostitution was rhetorically recast as a hygiene problem to be organized through medical surveillance, and that the idea of racial hierarchy as a developmental "fact" was also seriously pursued. Colonial expansion and the growing prowess of medicine and science were intimately connected.

In such a context, it was not surprising to find confident assertions that "backward" peoples were on the verge of literal extinction, a prospect that closed down any possibility of progress. Extinction marked an inexorable decline so intrinsic that not even the beneficence of modernity could halt it. The disappearance of peoples too backward to adjust to modern life thus affirmed, if rather gloomily, the march of progress and of western civilization. As we have seen, Australian settler populations believed that indigenous Australians were dying out.[103] An official touring Queensland's outback made the sex-death-primitivism link explicit. The Kalkadoon people, he observed, were "more or less diseased with syphilis now, and fast dying out."[104] It was a commonplace attitude, found repeatedly in texts of the period and not only in Australia.[105]

Venereal diseases in these images were responsible for killing entire peoples, as well as seeding decay. Since VD was widely regarded as avoidable, this prediction also carried a message about self-destruction and irresponsibility. Doctors identified two principal forms of direct transmission: sexual contact and so-called innocent infection. This latter was reserved for such groups as infants suckled by an infected wet nurse or faithful wives whose reckless husbands brought infection into the marital bed. The very transmission, then, of these medical conditions was a moral issue with far-reaching social, political, and economic consequences. By the early twentieth century, VD's role as a racial poison had been yoked to the growingly popular "science" of eugenics.

Heritable VD would weaken racial strength, sap civilization, and potentially threaten the empire. "These diseases are poisoning the very fountain-head of our race, and are reducing ominously the already falling birth rate."[106] Health was, in this light, a highly political issue as well as a moral one, and the two were not easily separated. Drawing a boundary around these diseases, a *cordon sanitaire*, was of prime urgency. The apparent virulence of tropical forms of VD and the allegedly lackadaisical attitudes of colonial populations made mapping those boundaries a relatively easy task.

Lord Kitchener warned his troops early in the twentieth century that "syphilis contracted by Europeans from Asiatic women is much more severe than that contracted in England."[107] "Imagine," conjured a letter writer to the *Daily Telegraph* only a few years earlier,

> the terrible sadness and the blighted lives of those men, who leave home full of life and vigour, eager for the excitement and adventure only to be found in the East. When attacked by this fell disease, from which in that climate they rarely recover, obliged to drink to maintain their strength, they pass from hospital to hospital, until at last they are invalided home, shattered, worthless, drunken wretches, fit for no occupation.[108]

Responsibility lay, in these depictions, in the east and not with the soldiers. The east seduced, it lured, it tempted, sapping the west's moral strength before insatiably moving on to compromise and eat away at its physical strength. The east was sexually "inviting, but morally rotten," and nowhere was this more apparent than in the connection between pleasure and death.[109] Further complicating these intertwined readings of sex, death, and prostitution as intimately linked was the biblical understanding of sex as purely procreative. The existence of afflictions transmitted via sex cut across the notion of sex as life-giving, suggesting rather that sex had the potential to take away life. That death could come at the hands of women, who also brought new lives into the world, may go some way to explaining the stigma that attached to the selling of sex. Prostitutes both defined and challenged the very essence of womanliness and of femininity.

This constant theme of desire as a dangerous commodity invariably linked VD to prostitution as the most fundamental and damning of connections. Other forms of transmission existed, but popularly and medically, VD's originary moment was effectively located in the body of the lewd woman, tempting the man to his ugliest fate. This was a long-standing and powerful correlation and by no means limited to the west.[110] Christianity, with its gendered reading of sin, made the scapegoating of the trader in sex an easy link in the chain. The persistent presence of poor women maximizing their wage-earning potential strengthened that convergence, consolidating the class overtones that pervaded the image of the prostitute. The growing awareness of racial difference, the legitimacy of scientific racism, and the colonial economy that produced so great a demand for prostitution completed the confluence of prostitute and primitive women of "other" races.

Contextualizing Prostitution

While the sex trade was certainly not a colonial invention, the presence of an overwhelmingly male colonial population (soldiers and officials, overseers, managers and salesmen, and manual laborers from other parts of the globe) both expanded and altered local sex trades. Though they may disagree about its implications, most historians of Africa, for example, see colonial capitalism as a factor that increased prostitution in a variety of African settings.[111] Noel Loos has argued that prostitution as it was understood by the colonizers "did not exist in any really strict sense in Aboriginal society."[112] Much the same was so in India where the establishment of military cantonments gave rise to brothels specifically servicing the troops, and to casual nonbrothel liaisons between soldiers and poor local women. In the Asian colonies of Hong Kong and the Straits Settlements, brothels became more strictly racial in their client base; these were brothels proletarianized along racial lines, with the "coolie" equivalents among Chinese and Japanese women working in the cheaper brothels serving laboring men.

Streetwalking was not wholly absent in the colonies, but it occupied a less prominent role in the trade than in Britain or on the streets of the Queensland capital, Brisbane, where prostitution resembled more the metropolitan than other colonial versions. Significantly, in northern Queensland, where the population was more ethnically and racially mixed, the racially specific brothel model was more common. And while in Brisbane, brothels tended to be scattered rather than concentrated in a single red-light district, in the dependent colonies it was far more common for brothels to cluster in recognized areas. Often, the local authorities insisted upon this geography of segregation.

This expansion and alteration in the nature of sexual commerce consonant upon colonization raises questions about sexual desire and its role in the continued existence of prostitution as an occupational choice for women. R. W. Connell reminds us that sexual desire is both political and historical, rather than something that lies outside history.[113] When Richard Symanski argues that it is ultimately "male demand that drives the system of prostitution," we need to read that claim within a broad historical framework that can encompass the particularities that render sexual desire historically contingent.[114] For nineteenth-century European colonialism, male desire was a necessity for the maintenance of empire, and a powerful means to separate maleness and femaleness. But though such desire was marked as a driving force, it was female greed and native promiscuity that were seen as destructive while male desire was regarded as harnessable and productive. It was marginalized groups, already tainted, who occupied the category of risk.[115] White male desire, meanwhile, was a fact that, even now, some theorists argue, has to be catered for. In a controversial argument about contemporary prostitution, Lars Ericsson typifies an influential strand of liberal thinking, when he posits prostitution as a "socially valuable function ... decreasing the amount of sexual misery in society."[116] For Ericsson, sexual desire is as "basic, natural, and compelling as our appetite for food."[117] In short, it lies outside history, outside culture, within the realm of the biological and the timeless. In practice, of course, as both law and history amply demonstrate, sexual desire has been deeply influenced by cultural mores, by locale and prevailing value systems. It has been legislated, punished, controlled, and celebrated. The very existence of prostitution as an issue of legal concern places the question of desire under the historical and social microscope. And in the colonies, sexual desire was never a unitary notion. Different forms of essentializing distinguished natural male lustiness from the dangers inherent in colonial behaviors. Colonial sexuality was out of place, overabundant, profit-driven while the European variant was containable and ultimately productive.

Conclusion

The lengthy and complicated history of prostitution cannot be disentangled in its historical particularity from some of the most significant themes of British and British colonial history in the nineteenth and twentieth centuries. In particular, the linking of race and gender (too often dubbed "social" categories) to imperialism—generally regarded as a "political" category—demands an attention to the specifics of the historical timeframe. An active imperial policy of a distinctly masculine cast ensured a constant supply of clients for a trade deemed essential and unfortunately natural, but still evidencing a moral hierarchy in race and culture. The widespread fears around and hopes of controlling sexually transmissible diseases made prostitution a laboratory for medical surveillance; gender and class made the prostitute a vulnerable if not always obedient subject. In the ensuing chapters, we will pursue these links and show how policy around prostitution—raced and gendered as a matter of course—was never peripheral, never incidental, but always central to colonial administration and rule.

Chapter 8

The Sexual Census and the
Racialization of Colonial Women

The passions of manhood and the penalties entailed upon their gratification are causes of more broken constitutions than all other indiscretions put together. *Lues* everywhere abounds and occupies a large figure in every sick report. This is the Scylla of European life in India; the Charybdis is left-handed alliances with native females; and the "*medio tutissimus ibis*" is either through the Straits of Continence or of Matrimony.

—John McCosh

The ambivalence and difficulties that lawmakers as well as doctors experienced in actually defining prostitution did not stop them, and other figures of colonial authority, from nonetheless seeking to define those who worked in this simultaneously elusive and transparent trade. On the one hand, prostitution constantly eluded precise definition. On the other, those in the trade could be marked, enumerated, and elucidated. The sheer quantity of information about the rank, age, appearance, demeanor, medical condition, and behavior of women engaged in prostitution amounts, in effect, to a kind of sexual census akin to the growing blue-book sociology of the nineteenth century. These blue books were enormously influential; Philip Corrigan and Derek Sayer have dubbed them "the key instruments in the moral revolution of the nineteenth century."[1]

The new Victorian sociology—tracking not only the demographics of birth, life, and death but such things as economic growth, crop acreage, disease rates, and sanitary conditions—was by no means a practice confined to island Britain. The new emphasis on statistics and on expert witness, collated in a triumphant empiricism, helped guide government policy not only in Britain but throughout its colonies. By the late nineteenth century, the collection of census data was widespread, estimating population numbers and itemizing the characteristics and habits of a host of subject populations.[2]

Certainly, "instruments of control, surveillance and violence" predate the systematic employment of census-style empirical data as a weapon to control both colonial and metropolitan subjects.[3] Bernard Cohn has traced early attempts by the East India Company to gather demographic data as an aid to Indian revenue collection and more accurate mapmaking.[4] "The vast social world that was India had to be classified, categorized, and bounded before it could be ordered."[5] Gauri Viswanathan makes the point that "the state had a vital interest in the production of knowledge about those whom it ruled [and] ... a role in actively processing and then selectively delivering that knowledge ... in the guise of 'objective knowledge.' "[6] Veena Das similarly argues that this new social science was a necessary element "in the new complex of knowledge and power."[7] While India's size made the prospect perhaps a more daunting one, colonialists elsewhere in Asia and the Pacific were no less keen to know their adversities and advantages. The mapping of Australia's tropical north, Hong Kong's relation to Chinese trade, and the growth of informal British influence in Malaysia all relied on knowledge of local peoples and terrains, carefully garnered and usably classified.

The classification central to this storehouse of detail-as-knowledge was taken as a sign of progress and modernity, an index of British order, logic, and efficiency.[8] This "English epistemological authority" relied on counting as its natural mode.[9] Census-style knowledge rested on two axes: the body as the site of counting (for while household and family remained troubled and shifting concepts, the body was indivisible); and the idea of differentiation, without which the vertical hierarchies of rule had meager purchase. It was a tactic that parlayed the notion of knowledge into a distinctive justification of imperial governance.

The census and other such mechanisms did not, of course, describe so much as they fashioned, producing the very categories by which "difference" could be hierarchically explained. The typologies that resulted, while represented as factual record-keeping, were in no sense anterior to the moment. There were no a priori and immovable definitions of race, civilization, or masculinity and femininity already available to the knowledge-makers, although in its certainty their work assumed that there was. The confusion and debate over what constituted prostitution, or who might be named as a prostitute, provides a good index of the slipperiness of these categories. Value and meaning were mutable, dependent in the colonial context on both local encounter and values imported from the metropolis. Census-making of this ilk tells us much about the anxieties and the concerns of ruling elites and their desire to impose order upon that which they considered dangerously disordered. In the mid nineteenth-century, sex, with its inevitable messiness, its apparent resistance to logic, and the seeming health consequences of its unbridled forms, was an obvious area in which such strategies of containment were regarded as purposeful.

Social commentators throughout the nineteenth century devoted pages to describing the physiology and the psychology of the prostitute, her family life and education, her marital state, the date of her "fall" from grace, her penchant for or abstinence from intoxicating substances, and her recourse to other forms of money earning. When physical anthropology became a serious discipline, the prostitute was a topic of study. Fiction and art were littered with representations of the fallen woman. Colonial officials tried hard to manage and understand both the sex trade and what they understood as native sexuality by detailing every observable particular of women they regarded as prostitutes. In effect, they were making a sexual census, using much the same techniques and ideas that informed the new science of the census and social description. They counted, enumerated, and categorized, producing estimates of how many women worked in prostitution, of how many willingly registered as such, of how many presented symptoms of disease. They logged appearance, race and nationality, and religion. They measured attractiveness and they classified brothels by hygiene, clientele, and fees. British officials elusively sought knowledge of indigenous sexual conditions, but in the process actively created indigenous sexual identities.

Edward Said has dubbed Orientalism as both an anatomical and an enumerative exercise.[10] The orientalizing knowledge that marked the particulars of the sexual census was both these things. It was anatomical not just in its literal counting of bodies but also in its commitment to the sexual body as a site of disorder, and enumerative in its attempt to manage and control that disorder—epitomized by the sex trade—through detailed empirical ordering. The understanding offered by this enumerative form of regulation was a crucial form of control. Moreover, the emphasis on the indigenous woman as a sexualized being underscored the sensuality said to define and to drive the east. The fallen woman was always and everywhere eagerly chronicled by the British, in the metropole as in the colonies, but while her domestic presence "proved" her anomalousness, her apparent ubiquity in the colonies defined both her and her homeland as depraved.[11]

Striking a dominant note was race which, while underlining distinction, rested on a notion of an indifferent and homogenous mass, a body of "natives" too large and too similar to one another to count, "the infinite substitutability of the native."[12] It was "groups, rather than individuals, who were said to possess distinctive psychologies and bodies."[13] Such homogenization was directly at work in the sexual census. Unlike the social commentaries of Nathaniel Caine, William Greg, Ralph Wardlaw, and a score of mostly male writers in the metropolis, this census tabulated collective and externally observable details rather than delving into the psychological.[14] It substituted the pathology of the mass for that of the individual. The common notion of the lushness and fecundity of the "orient" made this tendency to deindividualize easy.[15] The east was simply too much of everything: "too much colour, too many faces, too much hubbub."[16]

In Queensland, the focus was on both an indigenous Aboriginal population and on others whom white settlers regarded as foreign, the Chinese, Japanese, and Melanesian islanders engaged in agriculture, fishing, pearling, and trade in northern Australia. In India and in southeast Asia, both local and immigrant populations were scrutinized, labeled, and taxonomized. This less formal, but quite palpable, census-taking approach invited attention to, and indeed was dependent upon, a careful practice of differentiation. How else were the Hindu and the "Mussulman" to be distinguished from one another? the moral from the degenerate? the clean from the dirty? the foreign from the properly English?

This contradictory impetus combined a clear dismissal of colonial populations as multitudinous and unindividual, and yet insisted on minutely refining racial categories. Characteristically it showed a disregard for divisions other than those meaningful to colonial power. Thus while certain types of "blackness" needed delineating, colonial officials were seldom inclined to respect, for instance, locally important tribal distinctions. In nineteenth-century Canada, "the European category 'Chinese' collapsed whatever distinctions people of Chinese origin made among themselves, to the service of one distinction—that of differentiating 'them' from 'whites' and white domains."[17] It was much the same wherever immigrant populations settled. A twenty-two-year old Australian woman, Annie Bowman, was described by Queensland's protector of Aboriginals as "an aboriginal half-caste girl with a Chinese father, the Chinese strain being very conspicuous."[18] Under scrutiny as a disease-carrying prostitute, and finally packed off to endure the rigors of Fraser's Island by the protector's dictate, Bowman's Aboriginal status was not qualified by tribe or region, despite the enormous differences among Queensland Aboriginals. Her blackness was made all the more threatening by her Chinese parentage, but her precise standing within Aboriginal society was irrelevant. The allegedly uncontrollable immorality that had brought her to the protector's attention in the first instance was seen by him as a product not of her *tribal* but of her *racial* status. The protector's description not only ignored the differences between Aboriginal groups (a sociology he did not even deem worth mentioning) but lumped together as racially alien the Aboriginal and the Chinese. In a recent essay, Ien Ang tells a story of her own hostile encounter with a white Australian a hundred years later in 1990s Australia, in which this very same gesture of a generalized racial exclusion takes center stage. It is Ang's contention that the ethnocentrism she encounters "is sourced precisely in the precariousness and fragility, the moot legitimacy and lack of historical density of white settler subjectivity."[19] Such instability as a necessary accompaniment to settler colonialism was equally visible in crown colonies, where a small European population constantly stressed its difference from and natural regnance over local peoples. In short, only those racial categories recognizable to the census-makers were legitimate; those that might resonate in subject populations could hardly serve the purposes of empire as conveniently and as neatly as European-inspired categories of racial difference and distinction.

Annie Bowman's fate—lonely confinement on a remote island reserved for the intractable—demonstrates vividly what Gayatri Spivak has called the "epistemic violence of colonialism" as it operated through the careful building of a body of data designed not only to manage disorder but to name it.[20] In like manner, the British census was "underpinned by hidden purposes and ideological preconceptions."[21] The attributions made by the racially cast sexual census in the colonies also served, as we have seen, to normalize and naturalize the idea of prostitution in colonial-racial settings. In this way, whiteness as a ruling norm could be distanced conceptually from unrespectable sexual practice, even while whites engaged in such activities.

Ann Stoler has persuasively argued that we need to place the management of sexuality at the core of our analysis of the operation of race and nationality in the colonial context.[22] The studied use of a census-style "Orientalist sociology," drawing on much the same methods and indeed stereotypes about the colonial body (and the colonial body politic) as did fact-grubbers intent upon demographic precision or the depth of the water table, was a crucial element in the invention of the exoticized sexualities that have been so constitutive in defining and labeling the colonized. Knowledge of sexual habits and preferences, of brothel management, and the like, was part of the way that colonialism set about constituting the need for particular forms of authority. The racially charged taxonomic care, the endless fine-tuning of the delineation of the prostitute—her race, class, caste, religion, and clientele—was drawn against the backdrop not only of legal imprecision with respect to the boundaries of her trade, but with the imprecision we have noted as to distinctions and divisions within the communities imagined, invented, and notated by census-minded colonists.

For all its dynamism and proclaimed modernity, then, the knowledge derived in this manner imposed upon colonized women a set of biological as well as cultural fixities, frozen in time. Charles Hirschman, and following him Benedict Anderson, have noted how census categories became more and more ordered over time by racial preoccupations and Sudipta Sen has noted "distinctively racial hierarchies fashioned out of the old great chain of being" in the eighteenth century, when data-gathering of this ilk was relatively new.[23] The minutiae by which prostitute women were taxonomized fixed them not only via racial characteristics but, fundamentally, by sex. As the previous chapter argued, whatever other definitions law and public opinion could *not* muster to define prostitution, it was always defined as female. While, as Hirschman has argued, "[d]irect colonial rule brought European racial theory" to the colonies, "and constructed a social and economic order structured by 'race,' " women's lives were also ordered through a reading of fixed sexual characteristics.[24]

Racial Categories

Women's sexuality was racially bound, rendering them opaque, readable, and of course, powerless.[25] When the French traveler Henry Champly wrote dismissively in the 1930s of "droves of little Yellow girls... made ready... for a lifetime of prostitution," he drew upon a common colonial representation of faceless mass helplessness.[26] Soldiers' temptations in India, according to one brigade surgeon, were actually part of a broader web applying "to service in all Oriental countries. Barbados and Gibraltar are in the same class."[27] It was a sharply different picture than that reserved for young white women similarly ensnared; to them belonged a name, a face, a personality, in short, an individualized tragedy. For the young Chinese women of Champly's description, as for the Aboriginal or Indian girls of colonial reports, the very impersonality and unnumbered enormity formed part of the racial definition and difference distancing the colonized from their masters.[28]

Even without the fears that surrounded venereal diseases in this period, prostitution was of huge importance in the maintenance of colonial order, and the greater part of interracial sexual connection between colonizer and colonized was a heterosexual prostitution in which white men purchased the sexual services of native women. The complex racial demarcation of prostitution evidenced by this sexual census-taking was one of the most noticeable ways that the anthropology of sexual commerce was cast. Definitions were important, for even while the gloomy reports of civil and military medical officers described an uphill struggle against curbing VD and bringing such women to heel, a sense of the numbers was, in many respects, also a declaration that there was some semblance of colonial control. Thomas Metcalf has made the point that various campaigns associated with what he calls the "liberal enterprise" in nineteenth-century India served to reinforce and to disseminate ideas of the Indian as different from the ruler, allowing the British to claim they were "reforming a depraved Indian society."[29] Various versions of colonial taxonomy operated similarly, identifying and labeling difference in the service of policy and governance, what John and Jean Comaroff see as a delineation designed to domesticate.[30]

The CD Ordinance (no. 23 of 1870) passed at the Straits Settlements in 1870 required that a list of brothel inmates itemizing their nationality and their age be kept. Justified as a means of keeping coercion and compulsion in check, the ordinance worked specifically from a set of assumptions about who brothel women were and what sorts of lives they led. The protectors of Chinese in both Hong Kong and the Straits Settlements often provided such information, but in all the colonies such information came too from medical officers and civil surgeons, from army men, and even from missionaries uncomfortable with what they saw as semi- if not fully official support of vice. The wealth of detail these sundry types of reports offer tell us at least as much about the observers as they do about those observed.[31]

Race, as already noted, was critical to this data and more often than not, the hierarchies it imposed were overt features of discussion as commentators compared the qualities of women of different racial background, whether critically or lasciviously, in what Ronald Hyam has termed a "ladder of erotic delight."[32] All the colonies with which we are dealing here were something of a melting pot in terms of sexual commerce, and an attention to the contemporary assessments of this variation is instructive for mapping the racial terrain of colonialism. As Richard Dyer has pointed out, "white people have had so very much more control over the definition of themselves and indeed of others than have those others."[33] The sexual census and its demographic cousin, products of colonialism, mirror Dyer's point in their imposition of British definition on local peoples, customs, and behaviors.

In British India, the range of women engaged in prostitution was enormous, though without doubt, indigenous women dominated the trade. Nonetheless, officials detailed Japanese and Baghdadi women, Europeans, a few Mauritians and "Negresses" (never defined more specifically), and Burmese women alongside indigenous women. In Hong Kong and the Straits, the bulk of the prostitute population was Chinese with a significant Japanese minority and smaller numbers of Indian and of European women, each serving men of their own racial groups. Hong Kong supported two Japanese red-light districts, one each for richer and poorer clientele, a few European women scattered around the port, and two large red-light districts staffed by local women, one catering to local men and the other to foreigners. The Japanese trading community in Singapore in the late 1890s consisted of eight dry goods stores and eighty-three brothels.[34] While Brisbane supported a significant white-operated sex trade, much of the prostitution (though by no means all of it) farther north was attributed to nonwhite women, probably accurately. Queensland's observers offered a carefully delineated racial breakdown of that trade, creating racial hierarchies akin to those elsewhere in the colonies.

The presence of white women working in prostitution will be dealt with at length in the following chapter, but we cannot pass over their presence here without distorting the hierarchies in the sexual census. Though the numbers of white women, and more particularly of British women, engaged in prostitution in the colonies was always minuscule, their presence attracted an attention wholly disproportionate to their numbers. Their presence was always heralded by alarm or distress, and police reports spent considerable time discussing, if not always effecting, their removal. Threatening as their presence invariably was, they were still the undisputed top rung of this sexual hierarchy, able to command higher payments, controlling more discriminatingly their clientele, and not infrequently represented as suitably discreet in their pursuit.

This chapter investigates how officials chose to locate those who they regarded as *below* that small coterie of white women, women marked racially by their varying distance from whiteness. Though clearly the breakdowns differ from colony to colony, depending on the local demographics, we can nonetheless see similar and racially fixed assessments at work in the creation of these grids of descending acceptability and respectability. Two factors, in particular, seem to have been operating: one, the question of mixed blood, most particularly when the mix included white; and two, the measuring of racial distance from whiteness.

Mixed race and a lack of attention to or pride in nationality had moral consequences in nineteenth-century British eyes. It was an issue of acute anxiety throughout the empire, most urgent where there was a white settler population. Queensland's Aboriginals Protection Act in 1897 carefully managed and defined the "half-caste." Mixed-race women, youngsters under sixteen, and mixedbloods living in Aboriginal communities were carefully restricted with respect to labor, residence, and sexual relations.[35] In South Africa, white settlers often distinguished between "pure" Africans and what they called the "coloureds." Feminist activist Julia Solly, an outspoken foe of South Africa's contagious diseases legislation, claimed that prostitutes at the Cape were predominantly "coloured ... that is, of mixed race, and that coloured women generally ... are not of high moral tone, thinking loosely of marriage and with very little selfcontrol of any kind."[36]

The racial ladder was carefully gradated; Japanese prostitutes, for instance, were routinely represented as superior to other nonwhite women.[37] Bombay police commissioner Edwardes regarded Japanese brothels as ranking "with the third class European houses."[38] British soldiers thought the "Japanese women were very clean, you could get baths at their houses ... and they were very rarely reported for disease."[39] Hong Kong's colonial surgeon found them "more anxious to be looked after" than Chinese women, and more dutiful in attending the regular examination.[40] The Straits surgeon agreed. The Japanese *karayuki-san* were "always ready to submit themselves to a periodical medical examination."[41] Queensland applauded Japanese malleability; Japanese brothel occupants were "clean and tidy," and conducted themselves and their business quietly.[42] Alec Dixon remembered a distinct change in atmosphere when Japanese prostitutes came to dominate the Singapore sex trade during and after World War One. "Europeans who visited those Japanese houses were surprised not to find them sordid and garish; it was shocking, they said, to discover 'fallen women' who retained vestiges of self-respect."[43] Australian memoirist, R. C. H. McKie concurred, remembering the "high-coiffured, kimono-wearing Japanese courtesans who had clean tatami-covered rooms, did not scream or throw bottles, bowed you courteously in and out, hoped you would come again, and did not mind if you only dropped in for a few minutes to drink a bottle of beer."[44]

This reckoning of the pliant quasi-respectability of the Japanese prostitute made many officials regard them as a strategic substitute for Europeans.

> [A]lthough ... European women should not be brought to India for purposes of prostitution, I have no such feelings as regards Japanese women ... On the contrary ... I consider that Japanese women are far more preferable as prostitutes because they are more cleanly and by taking care of their bodies they do not spread disease throughout the country in the same way that Burmese women do.[45]

Yet Japanese women were still drawn as visibly inferior even to the coarsest of white women. The *Cairns Post* dubbed them "prostitution machines."[46] The

Bombay police commissioner put Japanese bordellos on a par with third-class European brothels, a double-edged judgment for these poorest white brothels were commonly regarded as fearful pits of degradation. Rangoon police superintendent, E. C. S. Shuttleworth, conducting a survey of the sex trade in the cities of British India in 1917, considered the second- and third-class European houses "as bad as the first-class are good . . . they are herded together with Japanese and Indian prostitutes in a quarter of the native town." In Madras, he claimed, the Japanese establishments were "much smaller and dirtier" than their European counterparts.[47]

A brothel's clientele was as important as its residents. Mauritian women in the Indian sex trade made a living servicing poor whites and Eurasian men.[48] The yoking together of the poor and the mixed, and their servicing by a marginal migrant group of women demonstrates how brothels were ranked as much by their clientele as by their conduct and their inmates, throughout the colonies. The police sergeant at Childers was in no doubt as to the necessity of establishments serving such men in his small Queensland town. "The presence of those brothels is to be deplored, but owing to the mixed populations here, which include people of nearly all nations, some of whom are of the lowest type, the Sergt. is of *opinion that the brothels are a necessary evil here otherwise respectable women would not be safe from insult* (sic) [emphasis in original]."[49] Gail Reekie argues that the toleration of Japanese prostitutes in the colony's less urban districts was catalyzed by the presence of large numbers of unmarried Melanesian workers on the plantations.[50]

A strict segregation by race of clientele translated in many colonies into a telling ranking system. First-class brothels served only white men, and women accepting others were liable to be disciplined. The same logic applied in second-class brothels. Serving only indigenous and nonwhite foreign men, women in these brothels were punished for accepting white clients. In military environments especially, that separation was carefully policed. Though the ironies may have been lost on them, officials in many colonies had long recognized that women working in first-class brothels often faced a degree of local ostracism for their association with white men, even while their working environment ranked as first-class. Though a European clientele was first-class, humble outcast women were "the only class that would be accessible to the soldiery."[51] The colonial surgeon in Hong Kong thought that women willing to service non-Chinese men were often what he called "half-castes," women of mixed race and more likely shunned by the Chinese community.[52] Such segregation reinforced the "role of racial distinctiveness as the ideological basis of colonial society" in much the same way as it did in the formal census.[53]

Race and Hygiene

The racial-sexual hierarchy further figured native women as fixed in moral decadence. Reporting from the Malay Peninsula at the end of the nineteenth century, the resident general of Selangor district showed no hesitation in drawing direct links between race and hygiene. In his report on VD in Pahang, he excoriated the "incontinent Tamils" and the "dirty low class Chinese" for spreading syphilis, laid the origins of local gonorrhea on "Tamil women generally," and commented on the sanitary advantages enjoyed by "the cleaner and more sober Malay unfortunates and the more careful Japanese."[54] The low-caste Bombay prostitutes, thought police commissioner Edwardes, "live in great squalor" so "it is not surprising that venereal disease is extremely common and that the offering of four annas to Venus ends generally in a further expenditure of one or two rupees on quack remedies."[55]

The growing association between cleanliness and femininity fueled by Victorian readings of the domestic lent added meaning to the sanitary issues around prostitution and disease.[56] The sex trade mocked the idea of women as guardians of the sanitized and sanctified hearth. Their rejection of domesticated womanhood alongside their potential role in purveying disease brought together complex associations between race, sex, hygiene, and femininity. Hygiene became another means by which racial difference—and its effects upon sexual difference—was made visible. Dirty women were also racially marked women.

White Australians frequently alluded to Aboriginal filth, both in encampments and in terms of personal hygiene. It was a small step from this widely held opinion to the contention that "the Gins [common slang for Aboriginal women] are simply prostitutes. Wherever there is a camp there is prostitution and, more or less, venereal disease."[57] The sentiment was remarkably similar throughout the colonies. Charles Lucas at the Colonial Office claimed that 75 percent of the Chinese women living in Hong Kong were prostitutes.[58] Reports of Chinese brothels in both Hong Kong and the Straits Settlements dwelt on their filthiness, and proclaimed the civilizing success of the CD ordinances in cleaning them up. The association of dirt and disease, of disease and illicit sex, of dirt and immorality compounded the racialized reading of prostitution. A committee on VD reporting in the Straits in the 1920s claimed that, "European prostitutes set a high standard of cleanliness."[59]

Physical Categories

Commentators frequently dwelt on the physical characteristics of prostitute women. Indian officials constantly complained that "registered women are as a rule old, ugly, dirty: therefore not acceptable to British soldiers; chiefly they receive the visits of native men."[60] Lock hospital reports frequently referred to them as "old hags," complaining that their presence actively encouraged soldiers to seek out more attractive but dangerously unregistered women. The Madras lock hospital report for 1879 declared that the "registered prostitutes are, as a rule, dirty, miserably clad, and physically repulsive."[61] W. Graves wrote angrily of the women he treated at the northern Indian hill station of Naini Tal. "The registered women are of the most loathsome, dirty, old and ugly description that one cannot be surprised at any intelligent European soldier seeking and soliciting a more desirable companion when obliged to do so."[62] Some went further: "steps ought to be taken to provide a younger and more attractive class of prostitutes for the use of British troops."[63] Yet the call to people the *lal* bazaars and the cantonments with attractive women was disingenuous. Though officials constantly distinguished the reality of the unlovely woman willing to register from the unregistered enchantress, in fact few officials ever claim to have found indigenous women who fit this latter description, for as Sander Gilman has pointed out, "the nineteenth century knew that blacks had no aesthetic sensibility."[64] The English aesthetic of this era united beauty with morality and thence with race.[65] Women might be alluring but they were not beautiful in a healthy way. They were dangerous by virtue of their race as much as by their profession.

Ugliness was only one of the negative visual attributes used to damn such women. They were represented as heavily made up, as hardened, as gaudily dressed. W. N. Willis, observing the "great gaudy centre of the Babylonian quarter" of Singapore, Malay Street, described the women as "[H]eavily painted and decked out with tinselled roses in their hair, low-necked blouses, silk stockings and worked slippers, their profession is unmistakable."[66] Such commentaries, focused as they were for the most part, on nonwhite and certainly on non-British prostitutes suggest a service, a standard of hygiene, and indeed, a rate of payment, lower than those of their European competitors. They suggest too, that in many respects these shameless hoards were less amenable to European control. Descriptions of the women, the brothels, and the red-light districts abound with disapproving descriptions of colorful chaotic loudness, of unembarrassed displays of flesh, of squalid cots open to the streets, This was the common language used throughout this period to depict the conditions, lives, and appearances of women engaged in prostitution. Their trade was a mirror of the bazaars of the East and the trading posts of Australia; their living conditions reflected those of the indigenous east in general—overcrowded, unhygienic, noisy, and immoral.

Of course, many of these same complaints about painted faces and uncontrolled loudness were the stuff of class tension in Britain as well. Working-class women, prostitutes, barmaids, and others outside the sphere of respectability attracted similar criticism in the metropole. The critique of proletarian aesthetics and morals was cast in a similar language of disgust, but in the colonial setting Britons could, at least theoretically, be elevated to a homogenous set of middle-class behaviors. This willing forgetfulness of the troublesome presence of the working classes suggests the contingency of political arithmetic and definition, the taxonomies, values, and emphases shifting according to the demands of the local context and of political necessity.

The Visible and the Invisible

Troubling as all of this was to colonial English sensibilities, it provided census-makers with a useful and immediate form of visual assessment. One of the most constant sources of frustration for officials, both in the era of formal regulation and after its abandonment, was the presence of women known variously as "clandestines," "amateurs," or "sly" prostitutes. Where registration was permitted, these were women who eluded the complex of rules by which the registered were bound. In places where, and times in which registration was forbidden, they were women who chose not to reveal a public association with commercial sex but to work outside the public or official gaze. Always vilified as a fertile source of disease and infection, such women defied the law as well as the census in their concern to remain anonymous and unlabelled.

> There are of prostitute women two distinct classes—the bona fide order, who live in a recognised quarter, and sit at their doors with painted faces, lanterns, and looking-glasses inviting all comers; and the secret set . . . who do not publicly confess prostitution, but are available when called upon.[67]

In this reading, and in marked contrast to prevailing domestic British sentiment, the author constructs what is, in effect, a class of authenticated prostitutes, discernible not only via their bending to the yoke of registration, but by appearance and domicile. *Real* prostitutes are identifiable; they dress and behave in certain ways. They are yielding both to a clientele and to the state's ordering of their trade.

Secrecy, avoidance of authentication, rejection of the rules connoted trouble, a trouble located in women engaging in an occupation to which they had, effectively, no right and thus rendering ineffectual a regulatory system crucially dependent for its running on prostitutes' acceptance of the definitions that bound them. George Newton, medical officer at the British-run Yokohama lock hospital in the Japanese treaty ports, complained bitterly about the "vagrant" unregistered women who were, unless checked, "noisy" and "clamorous."[68] Women who did not look the part, women who did not advertise in the accepted and open fashion, and women who concealed their activities from the state's eye were all renegades.

Disapprobation of the sly prostitute rested on her unwillingness to declare her profession publicly and yet the unregistered woman would have to let potential clients know of her willingness. In such circumstances, it would be hard for women to hide their intentions. At the same time, colonial attitudes to prostitution were premised on the notion that the occupation carried little shame in "depraved" societies. If this was so, then the clandestine woman's reluctance could only be seen as hostility to bureaucracy or doctors and not as an index of shame. It was a division that made the definitions that structured prostitution and regulation considerably less stable.

It was with some considerable ire that the deputy surgeon general in Burma explained how this "deception" derailed the sanitary system of the CD laws.

> . . . when the matter is looked into critically it will be seen that the source of all disease is *clandestine prostitution,* and that this exists to a great

extent because the classes who seek the company of profligate females
entertain a preference for those who do homage to virtue by dropping
a veil over the revolting character of their calling, a veil which is stript
off the moment a woman is placed upon the register of a lock-hospital;
for these reports teach also that when a woman's real life is exposed, and
she is registered amongst those licensed to ply their calling without let
or hindrance, she tries every device to withdraw from her new sisterhood. . . . *Clandestine* prostitution is a very widespread vice, and it may
be classed amongst those most difficult to be suppressed or controlled by
human laws which the Legislature is ever called upon to grapple with."[69]

Queensland, as a settler colony enjoying the privileges of responsible self-
government, maintained a system of registration throughout this period. In
general, the concern of residents and officials alike was to control and render
invisible what was widely called the social evil. Neighborhood petitions complained about brothels creating upset and noise, and public servants echoed that
concern, investing more in the idea of the ordered street than in the woman evading registration. In fact, even in Brisbane with a population of almost 400,000
in 1891, the numbers of registered women clearly did not reflect the extent of
the sex trade. In 1868, the first year of the colony's CD act, 77 women were
registered with the Brisbane police; a decade later, in 1877, the number had only
risen to 115.[70] Yet these unrealistically small numbers did not raise the kind of
concern they did elsewhere in the colonies. As in the cities of India, Australian
women moved their residence and their business beyond the geographical limits
of the act. Though occasional police reports from Brisbane allude to this, overall the idea of the clandestine, and of her potential to wreak medical and other
havoc, was less shocking to Queensland sensibilities. As William Parry-Okeden,
Brisbane's commissioner of police remarked in 1899, "[G]iven that the 'Social
evil' exists and . . . must be tolerated . . . it is very desirable that, in the public interest, the doings of the persons concerned in carrying on this loathsome trade,
should be kept from being openly, flagrantly offensive and demoralizing."[71]

The situation in Queensland resembled domestic British policy more than
direct colonial rule. Australian laws around sexual commerce were in general more coercive and far-reaching than their British counterparts, but they
rested, as had the British CD Acts, on police initiative in finding and registering women who engaged in prostitution. Where nonwhite subject populations
formed the bulk of those ruled, the law relied instead on self-declaration and
self-registration.[72] Since prostitution was allegedly less morally repugnant to
"orientalized" peoples, the clandestine thus became a symbol of defiance of
the law and of the sanitary order, for her nonregistration was not attributed
to shame.[73] In white settler arenas, by contrast, she was, while still perhaps
medically dangerous, fittingly invisible. To be clandestine in white Australia was
to be respectful of the moral law; when the Geraldton police chief reported the

presence of six suspected Japanese prostitutes in his jurisdiction in 1894, he stressed that "[T]hey are never seen on the streets and there have not been any complaints of misconduct made against them."[74] These were not troublesome women.

But in India, the same invisibility constituted gross misconduct. One of the most common complaints of frustrated medical officers in India was of women, not prostitute-identified, *lurking* and *prowling* around soldiers' quarters. The language is clear in conveying the furtive subterfuge of the women's intent. "We are aware of the mischief wrought by the coolie and other women whose occupations bring them into the vicinity of the barracks."[75] Under cover of an alternative motive or occupation, such women could practice prostitution while not acknowledging it as a profession. The moral bankruptcy implied here extended beyond simply the perfidy of these always-available women, who were generally understood as seeking supplemental income.[76] Their casual morals extended further into a commentary on the colonized population; officials who complained about secret prostitution frequently described other ruses involving Indian male complicity. Local men, they charged, would pretend to be a woman's husband so that she could claim outward respectability and avoid the register.[77] Worse still, husbands might permit or even encourage their wives to seek out well-paying British customers.[78] India, then, was where the individual had urgently to be classified either as a clandestine or as a real prostitute, for healthy governance relied on policing this division.

Beyond India, too, the visible signification by which the unclean or the common woman might be known and classified was important. Queensland's white settlers might have breathed a sigh of relief that their well-mannered Japanese sex workers were not encouraging public brawls and upsets, but even where prostitution was successfully relegated behind closed doors, it was important that women in the trade were still in some way visibly marked, and thus authenticated. Clearly a painted face or a scanty outfit worked to disclose the signs of immorality but so too could a measuring and enumerating of distance from the popular conception of femininity. The stereotype of the hardened harlot, isolated from a softer, untainted femininity, found its way into this census-style knowledge of the sex trade. The protector of Chinese at the Straits thought that a "Cantonese girl of 20 years of age is often a hardened prostitute," a contrast with the soft innocent twenty-year old of Europe implied in his description.[79] Of course, the implied contrast necessitated forgetting the plethora of British literature that saw the young white prostitute in Britain as beyond help. Magdalen asylums, after all, premised their work on the divide between the truly penitent and the hardened unreachable. The rhetoric at work here normalized western women as always potentially virtuous and colonized women as their moral opposite, alien and extraneous to proper womanhood. This was a racial geography mapping the vigilantly policed bounds of colonial sexual commerce, naming and bounding women marginalized not merely by their livelihood but by their relative and carefully gradated distance from the centrally definitional and definitionally respectable English woman. This geography of racial borders was mapped through a complex taxonomy of race and ethnic distinction, what Chandra Mohanty has called a "yardstick by which to encode and represent cultural others."[80]

In the brothel-based commerce characteristic of Hong Kong and the Straits Settlements, this racialized distance was measured both through the signification of the visible and via the organization of the brothel. After the compulsory genital examination was abolished, officials in these two dominantly Chinese colonies, where brothel registration remained a legal requirement, worried about the impact not of clandestine women, but of "sly brothels." The sly brothel was, of course, one that evaded government surveillance, and it was variously represented as a busy site of infection, a place of extreme brutality employing underage workers and overworking its employees, and barely selective about its clientele.[81]

These enumerations and definitions reinforced the tendency of regulationist policies to legitimize and authenticate certain forms and features of prostitution. Brothel regulation in effect legalized indoor prostitution. The prosecution of unregistered women and of sly brothels protected pliant traders from punitive sanctions. But since the law could not offer a fully encompassing definition of prostitution, it was this ersatz sexual census that did the work of defining who would be protected, making possible police and judicial action. As Corrigan and Sayer have so cogently argued: "The centralization of knowledge requires *facts*— and the legitimation of some facts, and the methods used to collect them, against the facts—to justify features and forms of *policy*" [emphasis in original].[82] The fact, of course, was knowledge made visible and material.

The Asylum

Unlike their counterparts in Britain, hidden away behind high walls and not infrequently located on the outskirts of populous districts where they were less visible, colonial asylums for the rescued prostitute were almost always centrally located and easily accessible. And as we have seen, colonial CD ordinances lacked any interest in redemption, the very point that prompted the removal of British asylums to obscure sites. The two principal categories of magdalen asylum in the colonies were denominational refuges for women run by missionaries, and the Po Leung Kuk (PLK) societies (*bo chik on leung,* meaning protecting the young and supporting the innocent; or *bao liang ju,* protect the innocent society)[83] in the Chinese-populated colonies. In Hong Kong and Singapore, the PLK received government monies. The Hong Kong PLK was first funded in 1878 and given government approval two years later by a sympathetic governor Hennessy.[84] In its earliest days, it housed women in a ward at the Tung Wah hospital, an arrangement signaling what one historian regards as the PLK's status as "junior associate" to the powerful Tung Wah.[85] The PLK also played an important if sometimes controversial role in preventing sexual trafficking. Established by men and pledged to stamp out kidnapping though not legitimate *mui tsai* transactions,[86] its principal role in both colonies was "the protection of women and girls and . . . restoring those who had been kidnapped to their relations."[87] Women fleeing from the brothels were quite common among their residents. The PLK also instituted prosecutions against those who trafficked in women and girls. Between January 1891 and June 1892, the Hong Kong PLK successfully prosecuted sixteen kidnapping cases in the colony.[88] It was a substantial record for so underfunded an organization. The society employed two detectives and a small clerical staff until its formal incorporation in 1893, after which it received a government grant. Much of the work was done by the philanthropists who made up the committee, who themselves interviewed all the women who sought help.[89]

The Singapore PLK dates from around the same time.[90] It, too, lacked formal premises in its early years and it was 1888 before the society established a refuge. When it did so, it could house only six residents. William Pickering, Straits protector of Chinese, noted wistfully in the year of its establishment that the PLK "had not been able to do as much good as the society hoped, in consequence of the absence of a proper refuge."[91] By 1896, the home had expanded to house 120 women. The Straits government gave the PLK an annual grant of SS $2,000.[92] The Hong Kong PLK acquired new premises in 1896 with the help of a HK $20,000 subvention from the colonial government. In both colonies, it was after the establishment of these actual refuges that the societies attained more prominence as well as respectability in both the Chinese and the colonial communities. They were run largely and in both colonies by locals and on charitable donations, though the protector could and did direct women there for help.

Similar reform-based institutions in the west routinely situated themselves either outside the city or behind high walls to shield women from the lure of their old life.[93] In the colonies, the refuges relied more on strict regulations than on physical isolation, though the rules effected much the same principle. Dormitories were locked at night, and women needed permission to leave the grounds. Residents were responsible for the domestic running of the institution, including making their own clothes. Visits from locals were chaperoned and men, other than the water-carrier, the gardener, and the watchman, were excluded.[94] The rules governing the conduct of the institution and of the inmates thus mirrored western sensibilities, demonstrating predictable concerns with propriety and visibility as well as pursuing a domestic training for the women.

Laying the foundation stone of a new PLK home in Hong Kong in 1895, the colony's governor publicly proclaimed that "it would be impossible to run such an institution on European lines or under European management."[95] Yet, religion and the final destination of the residents aside, there was little to distinguish the two styles of management. His Excellency's politic disavowal was largely a bow in the direction of the Chinese elite, who Maria Jaschok identifies as the "greatest indigenous influence" on both the colonial government and the Colonial Office.[96]

Though a few women were trained and sent out as domestic servants, as in the west's magdalen houses, this was not the fate of most refuge inmates from PLK houses. Many women were returned to their families and sometimes to husbands from whom they had fled. The societies also rapidly became a source of marriage partners for Chinese laboring men. The Hong Kong PLK married 218 women between 1888 and 1892.[97] The Straits protector reported forty-four women married from the PLK in 1897.[98] The decision to allow such marriages had been taken in 1890. At a meeting of the Straits PLK committee in August 1890, the members resolved that "if any member of the Committee can find a suitable husband for any one of the girls, with her consent, and the approval of the Committee, she will be allowed to marry him."[99] Edwin Lee suggests that, in Singapore, the policy was intended to provide Chinese-born laborers with a cheaper alternative to the complex and pricey business of buying marriage partners straight from the brothel, and certainly, the demographics of the colony meant that few other women were locally available to poor men.[100]

The nature of the arrangement, which maintained control firmly in the hands of the Chinese elite who ran the PLK, "enshrined the patriarchal family."[101] Though snooty about the arrangement on class and respectability grounds, few colonial officials saw anything at odds in the provision of men with marriage partners, affirming the active male role in the transaction. One civil servant described the PLK as a "useful institution which appears to be a sort of matrimonial agency for providing market-gardeners with wives with a past."[102] Yet in the Chinese context, it was a radical solution, since women exercised a choice in the matter, their consent being necessary to the marriage.[103]

Yet for all the practicality of this approach, it proved multiply controversial. In Hong Kong, many regarded the unrespectable PLK women as undeserving of traditional wedding rites.[104] In the Straits, meanwhile, the protector, G. E. T. Hare, accused a local clergyman of using the PLK to swell his congregation. "Naturally many more Chinese would be persuaded by Mr. Cook to become Christians if they could get a wife without payment in return for their change of faith and good behaviour."[105] Hare's charge was part of a larger scandal that engulfed the PLK home in the 1890s. It spoke not only to tensions over religion but to the critical question of who was to control the PLK.

The Hong Kong and Straits governments had carefully nurtured the idea that these were locally administered institutions, though there is no doubt that without influential British support (that of Pickering in the Straits, and governor Hennessy and the registrar general, J. H. Stewart Lockhart in Hong Kong), they would have enjoyed a less stable footing. Nonetheless, they were largely

Chinese run, and from the beginning no religious training was permitted in PLK homes.[106] When a row over conversion erupted in the Straits, the PLK's managing committee consisted of the protector of Chinese and thirteen "influential Chinese gentlemen . . . The interior working of the Home is supervised by a Committee of European Ladies in Singapore."[107] It was here, according to the protector, that the trouble began. The Ladies Committee, in defiance of the rules forbidding such activity, had allowed local Christian missionaries to proselytize among the residents. Brought to book for this in 1892, they continued to ignore the rules, allowing the missionaries free rein. It was only when "certain Chinese gentlemen happened to go to the house one Sunday and found Native Chinese pastors preaching and praying," that the subterfuge was again revealed.[108] Enquiries showed that the European matron was also accompanying residents to mission services around town. She resigned when prevented from her crusade of conversion.[109] The women involved were upbraided and the regulations tightened to prevent future occurrences, though there was a range of British opinion on the topic. George Johnson at the Colonial Office, sympathetic to missionary causes, thought the protector had manufactured local antipathy to conversion, but another of his colleagues thought the whole exercise a waste of energy. "As the girls are destined to marry heathen Chinese there is not much lasting advantage in giving them a veneer of Christianity."[110]

The controversy was clearly also a struggle over who would control the PLK homes. Johnson was not wholly wrong in claiming a central role here for officers of the Chinese Protectorate. There is no doubt that they resented competing British interests and had worked out a relationship with the local Chinese elite that suited both parties. Opposition in the 1890s among PLK members to repeal of the CD ordinance is striking.[111] Local opinion while never homogenous mostly favored CD repeal, branding the acts as beneficial mainly to colonists and coercive of local women. The wealthier Chinese, however, cognizant of their privileges and themselves dismissive of the pinched lives of the local poor, were allied more closely with the pro-CD position of colonial officialdom.

Another PLK controversy, this one in Hong Kong, demonstrates the tussle over control, and shows, too, how local elites consolidated their own position within the colonial structure. In 1892, the PLK was still reliant on the Tung Wah for accommodation. The PLK committee had rejected an offer from the government of alternative accommodation the previous year because the associated rental revenue would have returned to government and not to the PLK itself. In 1892 the committee approached the registrar general seeking further government commitment. Lockhart's proposals supporting the society were opposed in the Legislative Council and an inquiry into the society was launched. Though Lockhart was its chair, the committee also numbered the PLK's most outspoken opponent, banker Thomas Whitehead. The four-member committee gathered evidence for almost a year, and though Whitehead and one other British member issued minority dissenting reports, the result was the formal incorporation of the PLK by ordinance in 1893. The new board of directors differed little from its predecessor, but as Henry Lethbridge notes, "the creation of such boards went some way towards winning Chinese support for the colonial regime."[112] Such victories as these in Hong Kong and the Straits certainly secured for the politically active Chinese merchant class a measure of influence.

PLK homes reached other regions in the last years of the century. A large asylum opened in Kuala Lumpur in 1895, and one in Perak in 1900. At Malacca the PLK, like the early Hong Kong society, maintained a ward in the general hospital.[113] Elsewhere, organizations concerned with trafficking took the PLK as their institutional model, an area where colonial governments avoided legislating.[114] Their neglect fueled a patriarchal model of philanthropy that assumed the helplessness and ignorance of women, painting them as victims in need of guidance. Though this picture did not square with the myriad rules to prevent women's escape, it was nonetheless a powerful and normative depiction of the indigenous woman.

Alongside the PLK, private missions offered Christian refuge to women. Singapore had three such homes in 1895.[115] Around 1901, a "Refuge for Chinese Women and Girls" was established in Hong Kong. "It was considered by Christian workers that a home was needed where Christian influence would be brought to bear upon the inmates."[116] In Calcutta the Women's Friendly Society limited its rescue home to European and Anglo-Indian women, a racial exclusivity reminiscent of British policy.[117] London's Magdalen hospital barred women on the basis of race: "the Committee drew the line at 'black women' but any other penitent of any class might be received."[118]

Helpless Women

Overwhelmingly, when depicting forms of native prostitution, officials and other colonial commentators ranging from disapproving missionaries to social purity advocates to man-of-the-world memoirists, called upon a vision of passivity and of helplessness even while they castigated women for their brashness, their lack of shame, and their evasiveness. Mute and choiceless, Asian and Aboriginal women were "wretched," they were "dumb" and "ignorant," though they could also be hardened. They were symbols of all that was wrong with their race.[119] In something of a self-fulfilling prophecy as regards this sexual census-making, missionary W. G. Shellabear confidently asserted that "it is clear that by far the largest proportion of women have *absolutely no voice in any matter in connection with their own lives* [emphasis in original]."[120]

Despite petitions and deputations from elite Chinese groups anxious to stem prostitution and to control their own laboring classes, colonial officials continued to claim that "in China prostitution is more or less of a recognised national institution."[121] Australian protectors represented Aboriginal society in a similar vein. "Strong and able men" lived "upon the immorality of their women."[122]

Entire societies were classified via their alleged attitudes to female prostitution and other sexual mores. The Straits colonial surgeon, Dr. Mugliston, declared that the Chinese women working in the colony "are not human beings, they are animals... partly from their being practically slaves and partly from their utter lack of education and absolute indifference. They are inferior animals." The Japanese, he judged as "more free agents than the Chinese, though not strictly free."[123] In India "the rulers' projection of the position of the Hindu woman as a singularly abject one," confirmed the need for British rule into the twentieth century.[124]

This stress on helplessness carried an interesting subset of racial, and indeed, class categories, whereby "inferior" races (and the lower classes of white men) abused not just their own kin but women of other races. The Chinese in Queensland were seen as having a deleterious effect on aboriginal health and welfare, and a major intent of the 1897 Aboriginals Protection Act was to restrict the sale of opium to Aboriginals, widely believed by white Queenslanders to be a source of significant revenue for Chinese traders. Police officials frequently alluded to the influence of the Chinese on aboriginal morals and physical well-being.[125] It was a vital part of the colonial understanding of a racialized sexual commerce that it was engineered by unscrupulous men as well as hardened or ignorant women. "The Chinese & probably Malay women also are regarded by the men as inferior beings & treated accordingly & do not exercise any independence of will, so that they have ... to be protected against their own weakness of character as well as against the brutality of the men, & of the brothel keepers of both sexes."[126] Even where white women were the object of enquiry, their "fall" was often attributed to foreigners, and especially foreign men. The British were endlessly skeptical that Indian women fabricated marriage or other monogamous attachments as a cloak for commercial sexual activity, just as they often refused to consider the courtesan or *devadasi* traditions distinct from prostitution. Whereas in British commentaries on prostitution, the stress was always on the individual and the particular life history which had led her to degradation, the census approach with its stress on numbering the whole, pathologized entire communities and peoples around sexual habit, and did so precisely by representing prostitution—a pathological aberration in western terms—as acceptable, unproblematic, and even "natural." It was the degraded and tyrannical nature of those whom they ruled that, for the British, was proof of racial distance.

This frozen tableau of abject helplessness fixing the fluid contours of prostitution into a rigid set of categorizations, was not, of course, without its contradictions. The very complaints about clandestine women and the express choice of active, almost malevolent verbs—prowling, lurking, haunting, shadowing—implied a very different slant on the sex trade, one in which the knowing assertive women made a choice to remain outside of legitimation but nonetheless to sell sex. In this alternative vision, she understood where her trade might best be plied, and demonstrated an enviable business acumen in assessing the most lucrative clientele. Officials were selective, too, in their interpretations of these women's actions. Comfortable for the most part in dismissing them as "little better than dumb animals," when the system was threatened with abandonment and women, fearful of losing their livelihood, petitioned for its continuance, the same men were happy to grant the women's voice a serious role.[127]

Equally, the common complaint that women immigrants destined for the brothels would lie in response to the protector's questions about volition and free choice, had to be brought into line with the uniform picture of brothel slavery said to dominate so completely the Hong Kong and Straits prostitution markets. Women insisting to the protector that they chose prostitution freely were said to be compliant with those they most feared or respected, their procurers and pocket-mothers, or were in so hopeless a condition of indebtedness that their assertion of agency was meaningless. Kenneth Andrew, writing about his days in the Hong Kong police force, remembered an occasion when he apprehended a woman taking eight girls to brothels in Haiphong. Even after being sent to the Po Leung Kuk, the girls continued to deny any knowledge of the arrangement, even claiming not to know one another. "We had a long argument with them," he tells us, "before we persuaded them to accept our advice and tell us the truth. It all came out in the end."[128] Describing an interview of a procurer arriving at Singapore with two women for the brothels, Hendrik de Leeuw's cynicism is vivid.

> The official questioned her. She gave him a little curtsey and prattled off her fable, smiling prettily as she talked. The gates of Singapore were opened to her. There was no effort to test the accuracy of her statements, despite the fact that there has been so much outcry in certain quarters... against the ease with which immigration officials permit themselves to be deceived by procurers.[129]

Yet once again, there were tensions within the dominant European depiction that stressed brothel slavery and helpless passivity. While many officials shared de Leeuw's suspicions about the women's seeming compliance with their brothel employers, the system simultaneously needed to retain a certain confidence about its success, if only to justify the business of brothel registration. In Hong Kong, the registrar general argued in 1882 that less supervision was required in brothels with a European clientele since women working in these institutions "so often come in contact with Foreigners to whom they can complain if they have any cause for complaint as regards their liberty."[130] In some respects, his position ran directly counter to the medical imperative of protecting white men from diseases that prompted a policy of inspecting only women servicing white men. Yet it was simultaneously a sentiment that raised the white client to a stature of potential chivalry, rescuing the unhappy woman from her fate at his own hands. It thus worked to separate the white client from the indigenous client, acting as a reminder of the cruelty and uncaringness of the latter.

Women's Resistance

For all the emphasis on passivity, women working in prostitution were simultaneously regarded as vulnerable pawns and as dishonest tricksters. Many a civil servant saw local women as playing on the chivalry of British sentiment. "The picture of the innocent village girl tilling the land accosted by the rough soldiery and ransomed by the unprincipled police is quite poetical and arcadian, but when one knows the awful specimens of female humanity who gather round a standing military camp, it cannot appear to be neither here or there (sic)."[131] While colonial officers derided their attempts to avoid classification, local women often demonstrated a shrewd understanding of the system, adopting all manner of inventive ploys to foil the registration process. One group of women in Agra successfully evaded "registration for a day or two by wearing European clothes."[132] Their ruse indicates that they understood precisely how racial-colonial classification worked against them. Petitions from individuals and groups of women complaining that they had been wrongly registered were commonplace.[133]

Nautch women, in particular, argued that the system misunderstood their place in society, and that they should not be required to register.[134] In Lucknow, the *tawa'ifs* who had once danced for the *nawabs* of Oudh fought and won the right to remain outside the new system of registration.[135] In nearby Rawalpindi, "dancing and singing women" were rarely registered under the laws.[136] In Madras, *devadasis* were not covered by the local version of the Indian Contagious Diseases Act.[137] In Meerut in the Bengal presidency, the officiating magistrate allowed the "dancers and nautch girls of the better class in the city" to remain unregistered as long as they did not accept soldiers as clients." This, he asserted, would render them "common prostitutes."[138] A Madrasi official describing "three dancing girls' houses" in the Malabar area, stressed that neither military nor low-caste men were among the women's clients. "They are, as far as prostitutes can be, rather of a respectable class."[139] Elizabeth Andrew and Katharine Bushnell also separated out the *nautch* women. "We found no Nautch girl among all the hundreds of prostitutes we interviewed who were living in Cantonments. The profession of a Nautch girl implies so much training of voice and of muscle and ensures so large an income that she feels far above the position of the degraded woman consorting with the British soldier."[140]

Such exemptions made many officials uneasy. A judge warned in 1914 that "most prostitutes would claim singing and dancing as their profession and try to disprove prostitution."[141] Rangoon police superintendent E. C. S. Shuttleworth saw Madras presidency "as the home of dancing and singing girls, and 99 per cent. of these girls may, I think, be classed as 'clandestines.'"[142] "I am not myself satisfied," wrote a police superintendent in the Madras Presidency, "that dancing girls should be permitted immunity from the restrictions which are placed upon the rest of their frail sisterhood."[143] Need, he thought, would surely induce them to accept lowly soldiers as clients.

More generally in India there was an acknowledgement of the gap between the de jure and the de facto. The law, thought the committee writing the rules for the 1864 Cantonment Act, "throw[s] the onus of demanding to be registered on the women, but it will usually be necessary in practice for the authorities themselves to take measures for preparing the register without depending on the fear of punishment forcing the women to apply for registration."[144] Lord Ripon reported to the India secretary in 1882 that twelve women were arrested daily for breach of the rules.[145]

Women often complained about the impact of the system on their livelihood. The lock hospital officer at Bassein in British Burma found women objected to registration because it reduced their potential customer base by requiring them to move to government-approved housing. "They have to move from their suitable lodgings to a place where there is less chance of getting a sufficient number of customers, the place in many cases being out-of-the-way, more especially during the rainy season."[146] In India, an officer in the Bundelkhand district received "more than one petition" from registered women, "complaining that they were not sufficiently patronized by the soldiers and asking that measures might be taken to better their trade."[147] Clearly the women understood registration as a contractual arrangement that secured them a soldier clientele in exchange for submitting to examination, that is, as a business arrangement in which they had room to negotiate. Women also contracted services with one another. The registered women at Bassein rented space in their quarters to unregistered prostitutes, as a way to increase income.[148] It was a logical arrangement, maximizing use of the premises and providing both parties with access to a living.

Others took steps to avoid the system altogether. Women often used aliases to allow them to slip through the net of surveillance. In Calcutta in the early 1870s, enterprising women dressed in men's clothes in order to gain access to the soldier's barracks where they then plied their trade.[149] Others registered but then sent "healthy friends to attend examination for them."[150] Complaints that women faked menstruation and feigned illness to avoid attendance at the exam were widespread. James Warren argues that impersonation seriously undermined the ordinance, and that the protectorate introduced photographs of the brothel workers in 1881 in an attempt to prevent this.[151] The Straits governor reported that the ordinance was "foiled by the inmates absconding and the keepers of the Brothels closing their houses and professing to retire from their occupation."[152] In Hong Kong, the authorities alleged that women boarded ships to meet sailors "under the guise of washerwomen."[153] An official in India warned that women would "don *barkhas* or Oriental veils in order to pass as respectable women, or they bribe apothecaries of Native hospital assistants to exempt them from inspection."[154] Even those unable to succeed with such ploys were not as mute, however, as the common depictions of Asian womanhood suggested. Women memorialized for examination by women doctors.[155] Some objected to exams conducted by Indian rather than British male doctors.[156] And when compulsion was outlawed in 1888, reports reached the Colonial Office that hospitalized women were leaving the Straits lock hospitals en masse.[157] Patients at the Alipore lock hospital had petitioned the Indian government in 1875, protesting the treatment they received.[158] This was evidently an unpopular locale; in 1884 a rumor "spread by some evil-disposed person" swept through the hospital that women still hospitalized at the time of Bengal's abandonment of the act would "not be allowed to leave even when cured." The day before the change in legislative policy, the inmates demanded their release.[159] Refuges and lock hospitals alike experienced continuous problems in enforcing their rules and even in keeping their inmates. Many made escape a specific and punishable offense.[160]

The existing evidence suggests that organized and formal protests were more common among women working in British India and Burma. This may well reflect on colonial record-keeping more than on the women.[161] A scandal precipitated by the death of a prostitute in Hong Kong in 1880 suggests that there, too, brothels and individual women actively eluded registration. It was in fleeing a government detective who had uncovered an illegal brothel that a woman fell to her death from the Hong Kong rooftops.[162] Though the formal record for east and southeast Asia yields less evidence of protest than the Indian, the constant worry about unregistered women and nonconforming brothels reveals that officials in Hong Kong and the Straits saw resistance around them in various forms.

In India, on occasion, women fought back using the weapons provided her by the colonial state. The Superintendent of the Calcutta lock hospital spoke of women who "employ counsel to defend them," and there were similar reports from northwest India.[163] At Bellary in southern India, one woman successfully appealed her registration to the High Court.[164] This mass of evidence implies far more than just resistance. Each occasion on which women challenged the system also contradicted the image of indigenous women as passive and biddable. In such instances, the system had to respond, either reformulating existing assumptions or finding a way to explain dissent. The often imaginative ways in which colonial women reworked their encounters with authority, on the one hand, frustrated any possibility of a smooth working for the CD system and on the other, fed colonial prejudice regarding the intransigence of the native in the face of rational systems. Yet many of their responses were clearly rational, employing the machinery of the state to the fullest: hiring lawyers and memorializing government are perfect examples. The refusal of the native to stand still long enough to be counted would, in effect, always destabilize the enumerative mechanisms that sought to contain them. Knowledge about native practice had constantly to be remade and in ways that would read palpably rational responses as anything but.

The Jewish Woman

Whether distinguishing innocence from culpability or casting doubt upon a woman's unwillingness to be named as a sex worker, racial difference was the fundamental operating matrix of this gendered colonial subjection. One powerful avenue in which we might view its operation, with all its attendant inconsistencies and contradictions, is in the thinking around and policies towards Jewish prostitution in British colonies. Jewish women, like colonized women, were often dismissed as having been tutored to lie when questioned about personal details or opinions, though they were less likely to be regarded as coerced into the sex trade.[165] Anti-Semitism had long hinted at "natural" connections between the Jew and the prostitute, via commerce and the corruption and venality it bred and disseminated.[166] European Jews were frequently cast as the lowest class of Europeans, "wholly alien to the British race."[167] Jews were conveniently classed as the bulk of Europe's prostitutes, a group likely to sully the good name of western civilization by their barbaric and degraded practices. At Shanghai, where foreign women were attracted by the lively internationalism of the city and could make a good living selling sex, the British consul general claimed that Russian Jewish prostitutes were "lower and far more objectionable" than other white women in the trade.[168] W. N. Willis, observing the Singapore sex trade, railed against "the kiss of death from a strumpet bred in Odessa." He brought to bear the full weight of his disgust on Yiddish-speaking women émigrées, disgustedly describing "[o]ne big-nosed, dark-eyed, hatchet-faced sample of the Hebrew breed."[169] Officials claimed that Jews had a near-monopoly on European prostitution in India and in Hong Kong.[170] But an attention to the chronology of this virulent anti-Semitism undoes their claim that Jews were Europe's colonial prostitutes. A Jewish presence is barely mentioned in colonial documentation prior to the mid-1880s, while the always-troubling presence of white sex workers was a constant feature of discussion around colonial prostitution well before that time. When CD ordinances were first introduced in the 1850s and 1860s, those responsible for the obligatory examinations of registered women worried about the politics and the propriety of examining local and white women together. In many cases, the latter were permitted to produce certificates of inspection from their private doctors or were visited in-house by the government doctor while local women were routinely required to attend at clinics. A European presence in prostitution thus pre-dates the mounting attention to Jews that accompanied the dispersal of the Ashkenazi Jews from the mid-1880s on.

The vicious pogroms beginning in the 1880s led to mass Jewish migration out of central and eastern Europe, and though many settled in western countries, the completion of the Suez Canal and the late nineteenth-century growth in passenger shipping brought substantial number of these Jews to other continents.[171]

The Russo-Japanese war of 1905, and of course the 1914–18 war, added to the already severe privations and to the dislocation experienced by Jews in countries such as Romania, Russia, and Austria.[172] There is no evidence that the arrival of Jewish prostitutes led to the displacement of non-Jewish Europeans in the colonies, or indeed elsewhere, but the evidence *does* suggest that Jews became the visible sign of danger and a convenient scapegoat for European peccadilloes. The escalation in attention to a Jewish presence in Asian colonies coincides with the escalation in Jewish migration and diasporic movement after the 1880s, intensifying in the early years of the twentieth century. What we see at work here is, quite literally, a category in the making.[173] The Jewishness of Jews only started to be perceived as a colonial problem at the moment of migration, despite the long-standing presence of Jews in Asia before this time. It was only when more Europeanized Jews, who might be mistaken for members of the ruling group, arrived in the colonies that police and colonial officials saw potential unrest around Jewishness.

The idea of a Jewish danger suddenly appeared at this juncture in the texts of sensational literature and of more prosaic government memoranda. Russian Jewesses "are probably almost Oriental."[174] This clear attempt to question the racial purity and racial ranking of the Jew was a common ploy. In the making of the sexual census, western and eastern Jews—the latter routinely dubbed "Asiatic Jews" to signify their *further* distance from the west, a term most commonly applied to migrant Baghdadi Jews—were invariably distinguished. Both eastern and western Jews were seen as pestilential but the distinction that was drawn between the groups ascribed greater degradation to the former who had, as westerners, further to fall.

In general, the anxiety over Jewish prostitution was stronger in India than elsewhere, though a small Jewish presence was certainly noted and deplored in the southeast Asian colonies, and especially at Singapore.[175] In India, after the mid-1880s, Jewish prostitution was a topic of constant attention in all the presidencies, though most notably in the port cities of the Bengal and Bombay presidencies, and especially in the city of Bombay itself. The greater assiduity with which Jewish women were tracked, counted, and categorized owes something, of course, to a longer-standing Jewish presence in India, but also critically to the fact that Indian Jewry comprised both a Sephardic and an Ashkenazi component, where cities such as Shanghai, Hong Kong, or Singapore tended to be home mainly to Ashkenazi migrants from the west.[176]

Though the numbers did not bear him out, and though he acknowledged that definitive statistics were unrealizable, the secretary to the government of Burma nonetheless insisted on this distinction. While "European Jewess prostitutes" were categorized as women from the servant class, "the Asiatic Jewesses would appear to come from a lower social *stratum,* to consort with bad characters generally, and to take to this mode of life as a natural means of earning their livelihood."[177] This assessment was based on six Polish Jews and seven Asiatic

Jews actually known to be working in prostitution in Burma at the time, and these small numbers suggest that the problem was more symbolic than actual. While the trade in Jewish prostitution to Argentina and South Africa was substantial, Jewish prostitution in Asia was small-scale.[178]

Still, the distinction between western and eastern Jews was invariably maintained and particular characteristics were assigned to the two groups. Jews from the west were taxonomized as hardened professionals already in the business. "Most of the Jewish Prostitutes are professional women who have come to Calcutta from Europe with some knowledge of what it is they are coming to."[179] The Calcutta police commissioner claimed that "procurers never bring young girls to this country, or women who have not acquired by experience and knowledge of the life they are intended to lead (sic)."[180]

The powerfully articulate taxonomy at work here both created and then policed the racial boundary tightly. Venal as these women were thought to be, they knew their business and they exercised volition, traits which linked them, however obscurely, to the efficient business climate of the west.[181] In contrast, the Asiatic Jew was routinely categorized as a victim, a passive and ignorant creature in the "oriental" mode. "The degeneracy of the lower class of the Asiatic Jewish community makes them an easy prey."[182] And, like their non-Jewish counterparts of Asian stock, such women lacked the professionalism of their European cousins. Eastern Jews were said to have clandestine tendencies, and to be adept at avoiding both registration and the attendant medical check-ups. They were less scrupulous about their clientele, often taking up with native men. "There are many more private than public prostitutes among this class whose attachments relate themselves to rich Indians."[183]

When the American antiregulationist missionaries Katharine Bushnell and Elizabeth Andrew toured northern India in the early 1890s, they interviewed two such women working in the *sudder* bazaar at Rawal Pindi. Pimped by a Muslim man, the two sisters allegedly told the missionary-activists that "they were expected to say that they were Mohammedans, not Jews."[184] The intent of the reporting would have been obvious to their audience. Bushnell and Andrew were devout Christian feminists, witnessing Jewish women working for a Muslim *and* lying about their religion. The prostitution of the two sisters—already a moral issue—was compounded by their association with a Muslim and by their readiness to slough off their religious affiliation in identifying themselves. And Bushnell and Andrew imply that the women are eastern Jews; they are described as hailing from Calcutta rather than from Austria or Romania.

Jewish women, then, occupied a curious position, never wholly European in habit or demeanor, always almost native, with all the negative baggage that association carried. It was a liminality not dissimilar to that which met Eurasians, S. M. Edwardes arguing that were European women to be deported en masse, "within a short time Eurasian women would open regular brothels in the place of those now managed by the Jewesses of Odessa."[185] This startling interchangeability among those of darker hue and inferior morals guaranteed that both were ranked low in this racial chain.

The deep associations that connected Jews with profit in the popular imaginary gave rise, too, to a stereotype of the Jew as the "archpimp."[186] As late as the 1930s, colonial officials were confidently claiming that the white slave "trade . . . is almost entirely in the hands of Jews."[187] The bishop of Calcutta had told the viceroy, some forty years earlier, that "the men engaged in this traffic are Jews," while in an official missive that same year, the government of Bengal saw fit to refer to "Jew pimps" in discussing legal means to remove foreign procurers from British Indian soil."[188]

Yet this colonially constructed knowledge about Jews, race, and morals undermined the sexual census even as it created it. The 1911 city census taken in Calcutta (and which counted prostitute numbers) found twenty-eight Jewish women working as prostitutes in the city out of a total of more than 14,000 recognized prostitutes.[189] An official estimate put the number of Jewish women in India in 1916 at 186.[190] The numbers had never been much higher. This was evidently a problem richer in racial symbolism and representation than in real danger, whether to British prestige or health. The presence, however slight, of women whose racial distinction from the subject population might disrupt the proper channels of sexual contact had to be marked out in order to control it more effectively. The census-making around the sex trade relied on such a knowledge, on this curious combination which overgeneralized characteristics belonging to races but, at the same time, required a carefully detailed assertion of the basis of racial heterogeneity. Thus, surveying prostitution in the presidencies, the 1917 Shuttleworth report could point out, without dissonance, that "although lists are kept up of all European and other foreign prostitutes, no attempt has been made to arrive at an estimate of the number of indigenous prostitutes."[191] Jews, part-Oriental, part-European, and wholly alien, marked out an unstable territory, more especially once their presence on British and British colonial soil became significant from the 1880s.

Jewishness mattered, then, in its many hybridities, but perhaps most of all in its racial challenge. The long-standing presence of Jewish communities both in Europe and in Asia undermined much of what cohered the imperial nationalism espoused by British power-brokers precisely at this moment when, driven by a fresh round of persecutions, the Jewish diaspora was once again on the move. Those who were neither one thing nor the other—not quite "white," not quite "native," not quite prostitutes but yet not secure in the respectable guarantees of formal marriage—made census-gathering all the harder; classification, after all, relied on being able to determine who and what someone was, on a certain measure of exactitude that hybridity defied. The claim of association had an extra dimension in colonial contexts where, like other liminal or ersatz whites, they might "pass." The need to distinguish between a variety of Jews, for the sake of European pride, cast doubt upon the very fixities disclosed by census categories. The impermissibility of hybridity in the sexual census made Jews (and indeed Eurasians) willy-nilly troublemakers.

Conclusion

Europeanness itself, then, was never anything other than ambivalent, as we shall see again in the next chapter. Whether it was an Eastern European sex trade confusing sexual propriety in Asia, or the coarseness of the low Dutch in South Africa, or poor whites in the East Indies, *proper* Europeanness was always threatened, not just by the stranger but also by the enemy within. It was to this end, as much as to the manifest Orientalism of Edward Said's analytic, that the sexual census attended in its determination to know and to classify. Evelyn Brooks Higginbotham describes the encoding of "hegemonic articulations of race into the language of medicine and scientific theory."[192] The impressionistic observations of the new colonial experts—colonial surgeons, police chiefs, magistrates—found scientific expression in the taxonomic work of the census.[193]

Edward Said has argued that "Orientals were rarely seen or looked at; they were seen through, analyzed . . . as problems to be solved or confined or . . . taken over."[194] While I think he is right in thus seeing the classification "oriental" as an evaluative one, the shift from fuzzy to enumerative description that census-making, in its various forms, represents involved both seeing *and* "seeing-through."[195] It was empirical evidence, the ethnographies of experience and witness, the informant's deposition—all heavily reliant on visual accounting ironically resonant of the visual diagnostics doctors employed in tracking VD—that lay at the heart of this classificatory method of problem-solving and policy making.

Prostitution was a critical artifact of colonial authority, a trade deemed vital to governance but urgently in need of control. This studied use of an orientalist sociology offers us a reading in which racial privilege *and* the critical place of gender stratification stand out as critical markers of colonial authority. In all of these classificatory exercises, there is an assessment of which of these outcast groups was the worst or the least offensive. Though prostitution disturbed the moral universe of the Victorian establishment, it was still considered necessary; though prostitution by white women in a colonial setting was destabilizing, such women were nonetheless and fixedly superior to their colonial counterparts. The definitional shifts that allegedly distinguished British, European, and "native" values, practices, and understandings are powerful indices of the ways that the taxonomy of language served the needs of colonization and its deep commitment to a racialized and gendered vision of the world. "Knowledge" about India was, in effect, a self-serving proposition, a colonial tool that gave political India's masters their raison d'être, a means of discerning, and indeed producing difference between white women and local women working in the sex trade. Tom Metcalf makes the point that the liberal enterprise so strongly associated with this game of delineation and detail had "the effect of disseminating more widely than ever before notions of Indian difference" and thus keeping persistent "images of Indian exoticism."[196] In turn, of course, since statistics and sociology were so closely tied to policy making in the nineteenth century, this persistent enumeration of the exotic had substantial effects on the way women (whether involved in prostitution or not) could live their lives. As Susie Tharu and K. Lalita have noted, the "sensational reports" of character and sexuality that colonial "bureaucrats, missionaries, journalists, and western commentators of various kinds" produced, put "the glare of the harsh spotlight" most profoundly on colonized women.[197]

Yet for all the attention to the abject condition of the prostituted woman, little legislation stemming the alleged trafficking of women ever made it through the imperial or colonial legislatures. Occasional bills addressing the issue surfaced in India, in the Federated Malay States, in the southeast Asian colonies, but they never came to fruition. Early in the twentieth century, the number of such bills increased but it would take the interest of the League of Nations in the 1920s before colonial governments took any concrete steps in this direction. By contrast, colonial women were subject to a slew of legislation that affected their marriageability, their childbearing and widowhood, and their age of sexual consent.[198] As was so for prostitute women, their lives were seen as evidence of an inferior but still threatening cultural divide whose fundamental axes were race and gender.

The meaning of prostitution as a gendered activity cannot be separated from its meaning as a racialized activity, a weapon wielded in the colonial context as if it were proof of the need for the civilizing mission. It was an orientalist sociology, creating and consolidating sexualities easily distinguishable from a British norm, that provided the bedrock for this exercise in epistemology as political control. The texts and reports that gradually built up these pictures of societies and peoples removed from proper and civilized behaviors served to make their inevitable instabilities recede for the colonial establishment. While it is certainly the case, as Ann Stoler and Frederick Cooper argue, that "difference had to be defined and maintained," at the same time the constant repetition of these alleged and factual truths served to make such definitions authoritative, at least in the moment and often in the face of contrary evidence.[199] Striking is the similarity of opinion among colonizers writing in the 1850s and in the 1910s. Despite the differences in the practice of colonial rule in these periods and the varied contexts in which empire operated, medical and military officers, civil servants, and others endlessly repeated scornful adages about native immorality, hygiene, and cunning. On the one hand, we may argue that this represents an endless need for consolidation; on the other, it perhaps also suggests that, within the confines of colonial knowledge, these had become authoritative positions. As the next two chapters will suggest, it was often the process of defining and containing ruling features—whiteness and maleness, in particular—that proved hardest to fix for colonial rule. Indigenes, after all, could be relegated to the unchanging map of peoples without history. White men and women posed, in some respects, the greater problem.

Chapter 9

White Women's Sexuality in Colonial Settings

We are Turks with the affections of our women; and have
made them subscribe to our doctrine too. We let their bodies
go abroad liberally enough, with smiles and ringlets and pink
bonnets to disguise them instead of veils and yakmaks. But
their souls must be seen by only one man, and they obey not
unwillingly, and consent to remain at home as our slaves–
ministering to us and doing drudgery for us.

—William Thackeray

"Bombay teems with European prostitutes, and so does Poona," heard a
Parliamentary committee in 1865.[1] At Lucknow, an unhappy abolitionist reported a "colony of European and Japanese women who obtain their living
by the Soldier."[2] Yet only 9 English women were registered as prostitutes in
Calcutta in 1875, and of the 7,000 women registered there in 1880, 65 were
European and 46 Eurasian.[3] In 1911, among the 15,000 women who earned
their principal livelihood through prostitution in the city, 28 were Jews, 80 were
Japanese, and 63 were identified as European.[4] At Lahore, both the chaplain and
the deputy commissioner estimated the city's population of foreign prostitutes
at under twenty in number, "mostly Austrian, Russian, Italian and Armenian."[5]
Rangoon's numbers were "practically negligible": two Italian women, a Spaniard
and a Rumanian, thirteen Russian Jews, and three "Arab Jewesses."[6] Numbers in the southeast Asian colonies were similarly minute. Two of the fifty-
two women treated as inpatients for VD in Singapore in the first quarter of
1898 were European.[7] In the ten European brothels operating in the city in
1900, there were thirty-seven white women. There were none in the Penang or
Malacca brothels.[8] In 1916, thirty-two European prostitutes were working in the
Singapore brothels.[9]

White Degradation

Even so slight a degraded European presence, however, was taken very seriously.
While local and indigenous prostitution was seen as normative, white prostitution occupied a more troubled zone. The dispassionate and modern control
of prostitution that contagious disease laws were intended to represent took on
new layers of meaning around both womanliness and whiteness when white

women were sexually available for cash in colonial settings. Indigenous prostitution could and did easily become a commentary on lax morals, distorted religion, and failed masculinity among colonial peoples. Practiced by white women, its dangers had less to do with the infection of British soldiers than with white prestige and the roles ascribed to women in white culture. Concern over the presence of white women prostitutes was apparent throughout the nineteenth and twentieth centuries, and police and missionaries alike kept a close eye on white sexual vendors. Late in the century, as both the white female and the Jewish presence in the colonies grew, white prostitution became increasingly worrisome.[10] By the early twentieth century, the problem seemed enormous to officials and abolitionists alike.

> The white races are at the present time the dominant and governing races of the world and anything that would lower them in the sight of the subject races should, I think, be carefully guarded against, and I do not think that there can be any doubt that the sight of European women prostituting themselves is most damaging to the prestige of the white races.[11]

The AMSH remarked with evident worry that "the toleration of European prostitutes seems to us to so closely affect the prestige of the British government."[12] The Calcutta Vigilance Committee thought "the public prostitution of any European woman, Jewess or not, brings the British Empire in India into discredit."[13] If prostitution was the faultline defining the unsuitability of colonial societies for self-governance, then its practice by Europeans raised questions around the very credentials of rule. "To guard their ranks, whites had to ensure that their members neither blurred the biological nor the political boundaries on which their power rested."[14]

Missionaries and antiregulationists were among the loudest voices expressing anxiety that "the great bulk of natives are unable to differentiate between English women and Continentals. For them, any white female is a *Mem Saheb*."[15] But these were not outlandish beliefs. The 1917 Shuttleworth report on urban prostitution in British India and Burma warned that while the "town dweller knows quite well that European prostitutes are not of the same class or race as the English woman . . . it is doubtful whether the ignorant villager who pays a visit to Rangoon is equally aware of the difference."[16] The inability of locals to appreciate the distinction between the loose and the respectable woman and that between the upright English and the sensuous European was a constant colonial dilemma. The white European prostitute needed to be distinguished from her native counterpart so that she could be tracked and identified, and because her very presence distorted the ways in which whiteness could be represented politically. In the colonial sex trade, the simplest solution to such potential misidentification would have been to forbid white women from working as prostitutes in the colonies. So pragmatic a response, however, proved rocky, foundering on who and what was white, as much as on the practical problems involved in successfully outlawing prostitution. Who could be considered white, and what distinction might hold between Englishness and Europeanness, was always precarious. The noticeable slippage in nineteenth and early twentieth century use of the terms *European* and *English* was in marked contrast to the autochthonous sexual census discussed in the previous chapter; sometimes the terms *English* and *European* appear synonymous while at others the distinction is critical, marking out and measuring a hierarchy that saw Europeans as different from and certainly less behaviorly upright than the English, though still indisputably white. To be European and especially English was to be definitionally more civilized, just as to be defined as white conferred considerable privilege. Different readings of who was "on top" were required for white settler colonies and for dependent colonies. In self-governing colonies, whiteness and Englishness were no less fissured but class played a prominent role in marking out social boundaries. In crown colonies and other dependencies where no permanent white settlement was envisaged, there was a need to represent whiteness and Englishness rather more seamlessly, less divided by class and culture than could be admitted elsewhere.[17] These differing colonial representations of race and nationality suggest that such associations and identifications were, in Theodore Allen's words, "only relative, alterable by sudden circumstance."[18]

The European Jew

The Jewish woman discussed in the last chapter became a focal point of this definitional uncertainty. Her presence, status, and racial identification were means by which, from the late nineteenth century, considerations of what the definition of *white woman* might bear became literally as well as figuratively visible. We can track shifts in racial meaning and definition through the Jew, since questions of whiteness and volition solidified as the Jewish presence grew, and alongside these was the burning question of what properly constituted whiteness. While the growth in the number of European women living in the colonies was accompanied by a sense of domestication—bringing "home" to the empire in quite literal ways—the migration of Jews seeking a refuge from the violent anti-Semitism of eastern Europe invoked very different messages. Uprooted from an already perilous and impoverished existence, Ashkenazi Jews came not with the means to establish themselves in polite society but seeking a living and a means of survival. In the Americas, in Asia, in southern Africa some turned to the lucrative business of prostitution. Though as we have seen, their numbers were not vast, long-standing anti-Semitic associations between Jews and money, the conditions that brought them to new continents, and the apparent disregard they displayed for the refinements of western culture rendered them strikingly visible. Caught between the sensibilities of whiteness and the barbarism of the locals, Jewish women stood midway between whiteness and its absence, a marginal presence but a powerful measuring stick.

Their association with the sex trade crops up frequently in the literature of outrage devoted to the topic. Ewing Ritchie's descriptions of the Jewish entrepreneurs-cum-slave drivers who he claimed sustained London's West End prostitution is typical: "What a filthy trade the Jews and Jewesses of London drive!"[19] But in Ritchie's work, as in most such articulations of anti-Semitism, the danger posed by Jewry was mitigated in part by their palpable outsider status. Few Jews, it seemed, were not visibly identifiable; whether the descriptors that accrued to Jewishness focused on the nose, on skin or hair color, or on ugliness, the Jew was depicted as different from, as standing out from the English. In colonial settings, however, such distinctions could be hard to maintain and there was an overriding fear that white Englishness would be mistakenly ascribed to Jews or other "less advanced" Europeans. The Jew in the metropole, at least discursively, was more distinctive than the Jew in the colonies.

The greater visibility of poor Europeans brought about by Jewish migration potentially eroded the stability of rulership, of fit and proper colonial governance. Jews on British soil were at the very least a nuisance, and were sometimes seen as downright dangerous.[20] Imperial prestige demanded a particular, fixed, and homogeneous reading of the constituents of European civilization. The European Jew, whose ancestry suggested a kinship with the east and whose practices stood apart from those of Christianized Europe, challenged any stable notion of the constituents of Europeanness and could thus be read as a foreigner on British soil. The fear was whether such a translation could or would hold in colonial settings where the Jew might be understood as merely another white, another European, rather than as an inferior, a masquerader not fully entitled to those designations. If Jews could be "mistaken" for whites or folded into a broadly conceived whiteness, colonialism's boundaries were under siege.

Whiteness and Class

Considerations of class proved equally pressing. The attempt to keep proletarian British women out of dependent colonies was long-standing. The service work with which they were associated, and their always imminent fall from respectability, made the category of class fundamental to the articulation of a racialized Englishness. In the metropole, those who failed to conform to a certain standard of behavior were defined as racially inferior.[21] The white British criminal woman safely located on home soil could be profitably compared to the "ignorant native" and found wanting, a point that drives home that race was as important in the metropolitan as in the colonial context. The *Cornhill Magazine* thought "criminal women, as a class, are found to be more uncivilized than the savage, more degraded than the slave, less true to all natural and womanly instincts than the untutored squaw of a North American Indian tribe."[22] G. Kerschener Knight represented prostitution in terms of racial degradation. "There is no doubt that finding herself the object of contempt and ridicule, the prostitute drifts into recklessness, and the consequence is that her self-respect is

gradually eliminated, and she becomes an alien to her race."[23] But such comparisons went unvoiced in colonial settings where it was inadmissible to compare
whites to those whom they ruled. The control of poor whites was thus a priority
of colonial governments.[24] Vagrancy laws allowed colonial authorities to define
who belonged in the European ranks. The European Vagrancy Act passed in India in 1874 embraced as European those born in settler colonies, in America, and
in Europe, and "the sons and grandsons of such persons," but excluded those
"commonly called Eurasians or East Indians." Mixed blood evidently erased
rather than enhanced what the act called "European extraction."[25] It was not
simply that the misbehavior of whites offered a poor role model to mischievous
indigenes, but that their misdeeds would stand as a challenge to the very edifice of power constructed so vocally and visibly around white racial superiority.
At work in these varying emplotments of what it meant to be white was what
Satya Mohanty identifies as a process in which culture served "to lubricate the
machinery of rule through the production of new meanings and identities."[26]

Women engaged in prostitution, however, could not be equated with respectable women married to army officers or working in mission schools and
hospitals. White prostitute women at work in the colonies occupied a racial borderland threatening to colonial rule and yet difficult to police and discipline since
control rested on knowing who was white, a question often fragmented further
into a calculus of how white was white. The European-born colonial prostitute
was both white and other, a troubling simultaneity that worried commentators.

The White Settler Context

Queensland as a settler colony offers a different perspective on the construction of a sexualized whiteness. The Queensland act was largely urban in focus,
and its principal target, like that of the British law, was the white working-class
woman.[27] The act, as we have seen, did not apply to indigenous Australian
women despite the widespread belief that they were heavily involved in prostitution and horribly diseased.[28] Controlling Aboriginal prostitution fell to the
protectors. While police and other official reports detailing commercial sexual
activity outside Brisbane invariably specified the race of the women involved
(and sometimes the race of their clients), such details were rare when Brisbane's
police filed reports. One might argue that the busier workload of the metropolitan policeman would render his reports leaner and less detailed but since allusions to racially specific areas of Brisbane such as Chinatown do show up, it is
likelier that the Brisbane officers were policing a largely white trade. Moreover,
lock hospital reports would certainly have commented on the difficulties involved in housing women of color and white women together, and the apparent
absence in Brisbane of any such difficulties suggests that the capital's sex trade
was predominantly white or that only this segment of the trade was policed with
any vigor. In a report to the Home Secretary's department in 1907, Brisbane's
commissioner of police estimated that, of women registered under the act in

Brisbane, "about 20 percent of them hailed from the Southern States, about 30 percent from the United Kingdom, France and America."[29] The other half remain unaccounted for in his reckoning, and it is likeliest that he saw them as local Queensland women, and predominantly white.[30]

Yet in the more northerly towns of the colony, police reports frequently focused on nonwhite women, especially on Japanese brothel workers. When the Mackay Town Council requested an extension of the act to their town in 1899, they did so because of "a large influx of Japanese women."[31] At Cairns the health officer argued strenuously that a multiracial environment demanded regulation.

> If ever there was a town where the absence of an Act to regulate prostitution was productive of the most baleful effects on the present and rising generation it is Cairns. We have a mixed community of many races, syphilis and gonorrhoea are rampant and the number of children that are lost to the community by premature births and deaths during the first year of infancy must total a large number per year.[32]

These early twentieth-century readings of prostitution were tied to fears of race suicide and the growing eugenic trend in which the new Australian federation was an enthusiastic participant. Degeneration increasingly replaced morality in the regulationist debate. At least theoretically, of course, the crown colonies along with the United Kingdom had, by the start of the new century, abandoned the CD acts. Queensland, alone among the colonies that concern us here, maintained the legislation for most of the twentieth century as a firewall to ensure the health of white Australia.

In the debates surrounding the passing of the Queensland act, supporters campaigned around the critical cleavage between purity and degeneration. Typical of Australian sentiment was H. P.'s letter to the editor of the *Brisbane Courier* in 1867. "If we are to become a great Colony vigorous bodies must be united to vigorous minds."[33] Prostitutes represented degeneracy and excess, threatening the healthy growth of new world settler colonialism. Such a depiction, in which whiteness and degeneration were yoked, was out of the question in dependent colonial settings where that association would undo a foundational principle of imperial rule. While compromised whiteness endangered the potential of the settler colony to grow responsibly, in nonwhite settings it wholly undermined the foundation of the colonial enterprise.

White Womanliness

In his scare-mongering racial tract of 1936, French social purity writer Henry Champly articulated the stakes for white womanliness. "What constitutes 'the White Woman' goes far beyond simply a question of colour. It embraces a whole cycle of characteristics, some of them physical, others intellectual, social and even religious."[34] For Champly, this idea of woman as racial essence was a central feature of both colonialism's strengths and its weaknesses. Without the presence of women, the colonial presence was doomed since the feminine "values" Champly endorsed were carried there, of necessity, by women.[35] Yet the colonial enterprise could be quickly destroyed through miscegenation: "no legislative action can get rid of half-breed children."[36] Building on the common idea that nonwhite men were insensibly attracted to white women, Champly's interwar version of the eugenic argument closely followed fears that had surfaced much earlier in colonial arenas.[37]

Vron Ware has commented on the pivotal role of both gender and women in conceptualizing racial difference and in organizing empire.[38] And while traditional studies of empire have perhaps overlooked this factor, contemporary colonists seldom did, as the welter of legislation, publications, and discussion in the colonial period and throughout the empire suggest. Though Champly's dire warnings of the consequences of interracial mixing date from well after the First World War, the fears he expressed have a much longer as well as a deeply complex history. Kim Hall finds women used as "the repository of the symbolic boundaries of the nation" in sixteenth-century Britain.[39] Both the presence and the absence of white women in the empire served as a rhetorical tool for the link between race and nation.

Ironically, no white woman was more prominent or more important in this debate than the woman most silenced and most marginal: the woman of compromised morals. While properly feminine white women might be seen as endangered and sometimes as meddlesome, the sexually "loose" woman was a deeply threatening and active presence liable to call into question the basis of white prestige. Policemen, civil servants, and political activists in settler and directly governed colonies alike recognized the dangers inherent in the prostitute body.

In early twentieth-century Shanghai, American, British, and European women took advantage of the cosmopolitan conditions and enjoyed a lucrative few years selling sex, despite attempts by both the British and U.S. authorities to ban them from the city. Complicating the issue was that European women working in Shanghai classified themselves as "American Girls," cognizant of the higher fees they might thus charge.[40] F. J. D. Lugard, governor of Hong Kong, thought that white women who were willing to service Asian clients "disgrace their nationality."[41] The specter hanging over Lugard's comment was, of course, that of miscegenation. Interracial sex had potential consequences deeply connected to the dilution of power. India's governor general in 1913, Lord Hardinge of Penshurst, worried that the absence of white prostitutes might "cause the more frequent resort by Europeans to Indian brothels."[42] While his worry was the inverse of that expressed by Lugard, it centered similarly on interracial sexual connection. So, too, in Queensland where the commissioner of police saw fundamental issues of sex and race at stake in the organization of prostitution. Deportation of foreign prostitutes, for him, posed a far greater threat to good

238 • *Prostitution, Race, and Politics*

governance than did careful regulation. "It is necessary and expedient there should be accessible in Districts where large numbers of coloured aliens are located, *suitable* outlets for their sexual passions. The supply by Japanese women for the Kanaka demand is less revolting and degrading than would be the case were it met by white women, and in this sense it is more 'suitable' [emphasis in original]."[43]

Prestige and Rule

Policing prostitute women, then, was about more than the need to control women's behavior and to impose middle-class standards of morality on recalcitrant populations. At stake were the long-term prospects of colonial rule, and what Ann Stoler has called the "problematic political semantics of 'whiteness.' "[44] When Hong Kong's acting registrar general went in disguise to a clandestine brothel to gather evidence for the prosecution of its keeper, the local English-language newspaper questioned his tactics. "The notion of a Magistrate, who is to sit upon the case next day, himself going to a brothel and bandying words with a China girl, is contrary to every idea of propriety."[45] But more than anything else, it was his contact with "a China girl" that they deplored.

British imperial rule rested on white responsibility. "Dare any dream that the British Government can maintain the respect and affection of the Natives of India while such open lewdness is permitted by the authorities?"[46] Policing the boundaries of white behavior was critical if imperial reputation was not to be tarnished or weakened. Prestige and reputation were about more than racial pride; the state interest in their maintenance went to the very heart of Britain's ability to maintain its colonial regnance. Mr. Justice Benson of the Madras High Court told his government's most senior civil servant that, "it is difficult to imagine anything more likely to damage the prestige of the British Government than the importation of European or American women for the purposes of prostitution." The judge recommended that both a European traffic and that in what he called "foreign Asiatic women" be "prohibited by law as opposed to the highest interests of the state."[47] Women of marginal status were thus not unimportant; the need to control their lives was at the center of colonial government policy.

European Women

At the same time there were those who, though they deplored prostitution, also saw some mitigation if the white sex trade could indeed be distanced from the English. Both in the domestic and colonial contexts, many officials represented the trade as a foreign import. London's metropolitan police commissioner, Edward Henry, who had earlier worked in India, argued in 1905 that "as there must always be prostitutes it is perhaps less demoralising to have foreigners than Englishwomen, and if you get rid of the former their places will be taken by Englishwomen."[48] E. J. Bristow argued that European (as opposed to English) women, especially Jews, were in British colonial life, a bulwark which "preserved the purity of the ruling British race."[49]

The translation of this idea of substitution in the sex industry into colonial terms demonstrates an interesting fuzziness less apparent in the domestic context where, in an era of high xenophobia, Henry's unequivocal notion of the European reprobate fell on sympathetic ears. While in Britain itself, the ascription of Europeanness could confer suspicion about morals and propriety, in the colonies that distinction was much murkier. As we have seen, Europeanness and whiteness were connected if muddily, and those classified as European were automatically representatives of a more advanced civilization and of a racially specific claim to rule.

As late as the 1930s officials were declaring that "we all agree that it is highly undesirable that any European should practice her profession in an Eastern country."[50] For many involved in the actual business of ruling, the stakes were just too high. State policy on this issue thus wavered between the idea of non-English European women as a buffer zone between the ruling English and their colonial subjects and the broader view that any degrading practice associated with whiteness was a threat to Britain's power. This latter and more alarmist reading placed much of the blame on local ignorance and lack of subtlety in distinguishing the English, a tactic that could, in some senses, leave the possibility of an unsullied English national identity intact. The idea of a native population insensible to these distinctions was a common one. Joseph Reed, the Wesleyan general superintendent in western India, was by no means a lone voice in arguing that "the off-scouring of the lowest down European races" working as prostitutes in India were "regarded by the natives as of our own nationality and religion, and are an unspeakable degradation to us as the ruling race."[51] This was certainly the position endorsed by most abolitionist activists, consistent with their contention that prostitution was a necessarily degrading pursuit for all concerned, an index of social ills. Reed's frank presumption of British preeminence was founded on a hierarchy that drew careful distinctions between Christianized and "heathen" Europe. For a Wesleyan minister to be speaking of "our" religion to the senior military commander suggests that, when it came to racial definition, varieties of protestant Christianity shared a bond denied to others. Reed was doubtless hinting here at Jewish prostitution as the problem that proper British rulership most compellingly faced.

Catherine Hall has argued that "the colonies provided the many benchmarks which allowed the English to determine what they did not want to be and who they were."[52] This sense of national belonging was given substance not just by measuring Britain's distance from colonials but from measuring the difference in British comportment in the colonies. That such a distinction was most appropriately measured by attention to sexual and especially female sexual behavior is a theme taken up by all manner of imperialist supporters. The British were not alone in their fears of racial and national dilution, more especially as eugenics gained ground. American officials complained to the British authorities in Hong Kong that "the American name suffers obloquy and injury in the Far East through the existence of what is known as the 'American girl' quarter in Hong Kong."[53] World Women's Christian Temperance Union campaigners Katharine Bushnell and Elizabeth Andrew were similarly attentive to this link between race and nation. Predicting that the Japanese slave trade they claimed to have uncovered early in the twentieth century represented the potential for "the downfall of American womanhood," they argued that "we must not allow the enslaved acquiescence in degradation of the unenlightened Oriental woman to fix the legal and social status of American womanhood."[54]

The white colonial prostitute—rarely, the pundits claimed, an Englishwoman—inhabited, then, a borderland in which she had to be distinguished both from the local and from the properly English. Despite the paltry numbers of such women, British or European, interest in them routinely remained at a high level. Missionaries and church workers were constantly offended by a white prostitute presence, as we have seen, and made frequent remonstrations to government in this regard. Travelers often commented on streets in which white women plied their trade, some disapprovingly, others adopting a man-of-the-world tone to convey a knowingness about eastern sexual mores. Officials kept a close eye on them. It was not that such women were more liable to arrest or prosecution but rather that their activities, residence, and general demeanor were observed more closely and frequently by local police, medical men, and often by military officials as well. Liesbeth Hesselink has argued that in the Dutch East Indies, "the authorities always denied the existence of European prostitutes."[55] The same cannot be said of the British colonial authorities. The actual numbers seem unimportant by comparison with the attention their presence garnered. Few commentators would have disagreed with the proposition that "it is undesirable on racial grounds and derogatory to the prestige of British rule that women of European nationalities should prostitute themselves with Indians."[56]

The Rational Prostitute

But while few contested the racial and political undesirability of their presence, these women were nonetheless still white and European. In almost all the writings about them, they retained a greater degree of rationality and of independence than was ever ascribed to their indigenous colonial counterparts. The British vice consul in Egypt just after the First World War made the distinction of race a crucial one in his account of a tour of Cairo's red-light district.

> Most of the women were of the third-class category for whom Marseilles had no further use, and who would eventually be passed on to the Bombay and Far East markets, but they were still European and not yet fallen so low as to live in the one-room shacks of the Wasaa which had

always been the quarter for purely native prostitution of the lowest class. Here in the Wasaa Egyptian, Nubian and Sudanese women plied their one shilling trade in conditions of abject squalor.[57]

A variety of pecking orders are at work in the vice consul's description, all of them critically linked to a belief in European superiority. His reading of the market in sex made the southerly Mediterranean port of Marseilles the last European rung on the downward ladder as it veers in a decidedly easterly direction. Equally, the most squalid and poverty-stricken of Cairo's sex workers are portrayed as black women from slaving regions. A similar geographic hierarchy rendered the journey east a plungingly vertical trip in R. H. McKie's description of each city as a lower rung, a more degraded "posting" for women in the sex trade.[58]

This reluctance to abandon the European prostitute wholesale was a common theme in colonial commentaries reflected, of course, in the distinction between redemptive and nonredemptive versions of CD legislation. It led to some interesting discrepancies in the rhetoric employed to talk about the problem of colonial white prostitution and in the vocabulary used to describe such women. On the one hand, white women prostitutes were routinely represented in unflattering terms as loud, coarse, and unwomanly, "foul-mouthed harridans," "sensually dressed," and "unblushing," "their only vocabulary . . . the language of filth."[59] This, of course, was a standard western narrative of prostitution, a picture of unfeminine women beyond the reaches of shame. But at the same time, in the colonial arena, these women were often simultaneously represented as practical and efficient, as coolly in charge of their own lives, however warped their existence. One well-traveled memoirist, recalling the wild days of Singapore's raucous Malay Street, was convinced that white women played heavily on their racial privilege in attracting custom. "They were shrewd enough to know that a woman who passed unnoticed in Piccadilly or the Cannebière may yet appear desirable, even beautiful, to men living in a tropical country where white women are in the minority."[60]

Fanny Epstein, a young working-class Jewish woman, disappeared from her father's house in East London in May 1891. Tracked to a Bombay brothel by the National Vigilance Association, Fanny insisted that she had been neither abducted nor coerced. The commissioner of police interviewing her, noted her "singular calm and self-possession" and her insistence that "she was entirely her own mistress."[61] This theme of white volition was widespread. In 1888, the attorney general of the Straits justified the policy of confining brothel registration "to brothels which are exclusively occupied by Asiatic women. It is considered that European women need no special protection and are able to take care of themselves."[62] A few years later, the inspector general of police investigated allegations that underage European girls were at work in Madam Laurence's brothels in Singapore. The eleven women he saw "are not merely content with their lot but are actually cheerful and light-hearted."[63] This was a markedly different story either from the European version of girls, their virginity taken from them by rape, and cut off from the world outside the brothel or from the scenario of the biddable but brutalized Asian woman with no choice of occupation. Contrary to the sensationalism of stock white trade narratives, these white prostitutes were cognizant of their actions, exercising rational choice and free will, and were not subject to the bonds of slavery so crucial to the western picture of female helplessness. They may have been prostitutes, and in the case of Epstein problematically Jewish, but they were still white and the vestiges of civilization thus clung to them.

Missionaries continued to see white prostitute women in the colonies as victims of evil men and of fleshly commerce, but their representations were constantly contradicted by police reports. Missionaries kept the police busy with allegations of a traffic in European women, but investigation invariably produced assurances from the women that they "were here of their own free will and that no pressure whatever was put upon them," and that they had worked in the trade prior to residency in India.[64] Straits officials from time to time asked their counterparts in Burma "to trace women alleged to have been forcibly removed from Burma for immoral purposes" by Chinese traffickers. "Such enquiry is generally fruitless."[65] While a few thought European women "tutored" not to disclose information (a charge frequently levied at Asian women, as we have seen), most officials took women's insistence on their own free will as an uncomplicated verity even amidst a sea of other doubts about their stories.[66] Even some social purity activists recognized that many of the women "are not girls fresh from their homes but those who have lived the life, voluntarily or under coercion, in other cities of the world."[67]

Colonial governments generally hesitated to legislate around the issue of European prostitution. In contrast to the flurry of other legislation around local prostitution, age of consent, and other sexual issues, this was a neglected topic. A senior Indian official urged the governor general in 1888 not to support any broadening of the legislation to crack down on "traffic in foreign in prostitution."

> It is shown that no offence was in these cases committed in India. The women are not under 16. What abduction took place elsewhere than in India, and by the time they reached India they had learned by experience the life they were intended to lead (sic). They can in India always extricate themselves. It is clear that there is a most immoral traffic on the Continent of Europe, but this cannot be prevented by legislation in India.[68]

Britain's consul general in Shanghai took a similar stand. Some twenty years later, he advised the Hong Kong governor that "it is the general feeling of this community that as long as women of this class are well behaved and confine themselves to the particular quarter assigned to them, they should not be in-tereferred (sic) with, but that their existence, on the other hand, should be in no way officially acknowledged."[69]

The Privileges of Race

But if public silence was the norm, private concern never died. The topic was one of constant disquiet to colonial administrations who typically deplored such women but still allowed them some of the racial privileges accruing to whites on the colonial scene. S. M. Edwardes declared that "European prostitutes are nearly always careless and unthrifty."[70] This was a stock opinion of prostitute women in the west, tied generally to their alleged love of finery and propen-sity for alcohol. Though Edwardes routinely dismissed European prostitutes in India as overwhelmingly "improvident and unbusiness-like," he noted a certain humanity nonetheless. "If anyone cares to pay a visit to the General Post Office in Bombay on the morning of the outgoing mail he will find several of these 'déclassés' (sic) sending money home to parents and kinsfolk."[71] Odessa-born Dina Goutcharoff, under surveillance by the Bombay police as a suspected white slave victim (a charge she emphatically rejected), reportedly sent money to her parents in Odessa "almost every month."[72] But debt was, of course, also a standard metaphor for sexual promiscuity, as was a questioning of hygiene, also common currency at this juncture. Police commissioner Edwardes again picked up the common thread. "These women . . . usually arrive in Bombay in-debted to somebody, and they plunge out of one debt and into another quite as light-heartedly as they submit to the embraces of a continuous succession of temporary admirers."[73] In the colonial setting, though, the simpler condem-nations of indebtedness and irresponsibility were complicated by the tangled associations between racial purity and sexual virtue. White women's prostitu-tion in the cities of the east not only defied the prescriptions of monogamy and passivity but raised the always-alarming specter of interracial sex. And yet even as they endangered the edifice of whiteness, they remained visibly part of it.

Local women emulated European ways, aware that white prostitutes enjoyed substantial privileges in the colonies. Local women were required to attend weekly genital exams at a central clinic, but European women were often entitled to home examination, and at less frequent intervals. In the earliest years of the Straits ordinance, the colonial surgeon had made house calls to all the brothels as a way of encouraging the women to accept the new system. By 1873, he found the practice too time-consuming and tiring, and consequently restricted it to white women.[74] In Hong Kong, European and American women were brought under the ordinance some twenty years after the local women.[75] Unlike the Chinese and Japanese women on the register, they were visited at home.[76] In Bengal, local women could opt for a home exam, but the monthly fee for this privilege was a substantial four rupees; few signed up.[77] In 1871, the number examined at home was "infinitesimal."[78]

Separating the Races

White women were kept in separate hospital accommodation. The four sites established to house infected women in Calcutta included "separate accommodation ... in each hospital for women of European habits."[79] In 1876, cantonment officials at the Bengal cantonment of Dinapore sought approval to build "a ward for the reception of European and Eurasian women."[80] In the early 1890s at Lucknow, "[A] number of Europeans and Eurasians ... sought admission but very naturally a large proportion of them did not care to come in as they could not be given separate accommodation."[81] When the Madrasi cantonment of Belgaum deliberated new hospital buildings in 1901, accommodations for "30 native prostitutes [and] 4 European and Eurasian prostitutes in separate rooms" were prominent in the plans.[82] In northern Queensland, Aboriginal women were often kept out of the hospitals as well as of the provisions of the CD Act. The northern protector of Aboriginals reported in 1900 that, "there has been a tendency for certain Hospital Committees to repudiate, or rather, to put obstacles in the way of, the admission of black patients, even where special lock-wards have been provided."[83]

Elizabeth Andrew and Katharine Bushnell found a white patient in the Meerut lock hospital in 1893. "This woman's pride would naturally keep her from acknowledging to a stranger that the native police had brought her in, but it is scarcely thinkable that she would 'voluntarily' confine herself in a hospital for natives ... and be under the supervision of a native physician."[84] The woman's presence in a native hospital was perfect for Bushnell and Andrew's political agenda, which centered on proving that the registration system in India had not been wholly abandoned despite the instructions of the 1888 parliament. For them no white woman could have chosen such a fate; thus an element of compulsion was clearly at work in her presence among diseased native women. And though it was not their primary purpose to dwell on the dangers of interracial mixing, the perils of colonial white prostitution—loss of control and status, shame, disease, isolation from the white community—were all too apparent in the brief notes they made on their conversation in the Meerut hospital.

This physical separation also affected the racial classification of brothels we have already noted. The 1864 Indian Cantonment Act distinguished a first class of "public prostitutes frequented by Europeans" and a second class "not so frequented."[85] Norman Miners describes the Hong Kong arrangement as having a top layer comprising brothels for Europeans "with subclasses of those with European, Japanese, or Chinese prostitutes, brothels for Indians, and brothels for Chinese (subdivided into first-class, second-class, and third-class houses)."[86] This elaborate calibration was often justified as a means of invoking propriety in an otherwise promiscuous setting. Hong Kong's colonial surgeon thought it "improper that European and Chinese women should be crowded and huddled together indiscriminately which prevents discipline amongst the women."[87] In Shuttleworth's report on urban prostitution in British India, what sets the best of the European brothels in Bombay apart is segregation. Women in the first-class houses were, he noted, "on a higher rung of the ladder of respectability," their houses cleaner, quieter, and hierarchically realized. The less salubrious, significantly, "are herded together with Japanese and Indian prostitutes in a quarter of the native town."[88] It was contact with nonwhites and with locals that brought these establishments down, the literal and figurative specter of miscegenation.

White women, moreover, generally commanded fatter fees for their services than the locals could hope to charge.[89] In some cases they were also able to enjoy a degree of police protection. In Bombay, European and Japanese houses "share . . . the executive police supervision which protects the inmates and gives them access to the Police should they be subjected to gross maltreatment."[90] Missionaries and clerics felt that the upshot of these privileges was moral disaster.

> In certain cantonment bazars white women of various nationalities are allowed a liberty and license to solicit and entice against which the ordinary powers of a cantonment magistrate appear to be of no avail . . . the result is a daily scene of debauchery on the public high road. These women are without even the restraints under which the native prostitute plies her profession . . . they are neither answerable to law, nor can any other influence be brought to bear upon them.[91]

Lawlessness was, of course, the conventional discourse of the missionary presence in the colonies; order and control were the by-words of proper conduct. For the religious constituency, it was the possibility of white women's unfulfilled rationality that was the threat and the disappointment. The possibility of appealing to the civilized vestiges assumed to remain unextinguished in white prostitutes evoked a notion of white solidarity as an ideal, even while its realization was highly unlikely. And it was this chimeric hope that white civilization could prevail that shaped the very distinctive version of the white slave trade narrative in the colonial setting.

White Slave Narratives

By the late nineteenth century, the term *white slave trade* had come to signify not the exploitation of proletarian female labor in an industrial setting, as it had earlier done, but rather the cruel coercion of innocent young women into acts of sexual commerce, or as social purity publisher Alfred Dyer so memorably put it: "slavery not for labour but for lust."[92] This powerful narrative, which gripped English-speaking nations and much of Europe in the late nineteenth and early twentieth centuries, painted a picture of fresh-faced young women snatched from their innocence and femininity to feed the cruel sexuality of powerful and unfeeling men. Stories of men lurking in the shadows with chloroform cloths at the ready, of women masquerading as kindly maternal figures to trap the unwary and lonely girl, of girls promised a career in entertainment only to find themselves imprisoned in continental brothels, all became standard fare in the popular writings of the period. Central to this lurid narrative was a dyadic representation of passive and indeed ignorant female sexuality and active male sexuality, a story of victimization, shattered dreams, and stereotypical role models of women "lacking the autonomy and coherence of the normative masculine subject."[93] Also critical was the common representation of the profiteers as foreign, frequently Jewish, sometimes French, but seldom English. The dominance of Jewish and French men in the trade and the utter absence of English men were standard features of the white slave narrative. Domestically and colonially Jewish, French, and sundry Eastern European travelers were often under surveillance as natural predators on British women. London policeman F. S. Bullock noted that:

> It is most satisfactory from a national point of view, to be able to say that scarcely any cases have come to light in which English girls have been concerned, and . . . few, if any English girls are victims of this trade . . . it may safely be affirmed that girls and women of the British race are rarely found among the victims . . . The bullies, or "souteneurs," are, almost without exception, of foreign nationality, and their occupation is repugnant to men of English race.[94]

In like vein, the Calcutta police chief described with evident distaste, "the men engaged in this nefarious calling," who were "mostly of the lowest class of continental Jews," many of whom themselves were reared in brothels.[95] In Australia the Chinese occupied this role, "English and Australian men were, by implication, above such unmanly behaviour."[96]

The scenario linked race and sex in crucial ways, writing an implicit ode to the civilized Englishman duty-bound to protect the English girl from foreign perversions. The racial-national cast that this validating description threw upon the trade played largely to the possibility of this commerce as an unwelcome foreign importation, and it placed men at the center of the story, either as the instigators and profiteers of a market in female flesh (foreign), or as women's saviors (English). The drama of the white slave trade also allowed for an enunciation of British moral exceptionalism. In the metropole, of course, the narrative of female victimhood provided the drama and tragedy of this phenomenon.[97] But such a narrative was dangerous in the colonies and in many instances colonial politicians and officials explicitly pointed to the inapplicability of an English sensibility in their province. Arguing strenuously against a call for the tightening of the laws in India, the Calcutta police commissioner in 1894 argued that introducing "the English law" in his jurisdiction would induce substantial local resentment "as an interference with the conditions of Eastern life." "It is, indeed, difficult to imagine the state of things which would ensue, if the head of the Police in Calcutta were instructed to apply his hand vigorously to enforce such provisions as those set forth in the English enactment."[98]

The familiar storyline of the hapless and properly passive white woman sexually enslaved against her will could not and did not work in the colonial context. As the Women and Girls' Protection Ordinances in the southeast Asian colonies suggest, and as the insistence on a prostitute caste in India demonstrates, the idea of total passivity was the province not of "civilized" whites but of ignorant "natives" in thrall to the sexual savagery of their own menfolk and their "barbaric" cultures. "Chinese prostitution is essentially a bargain for money and based on a national system of female slavery; whilst European prostitution is more or less a matter of passion, based on the national respect for the liberty of the subject."[99] Native women exercised no choice, while European women, however defiant of the constraints of femininity and distanced from proper society, entered such work of their own volition. This was a far cry from the tales of slavery and coercion to which a white public thrilled in Australia and New Zealand, in Britain, Europe, and the United States. A Straits committee declared that while "Europeans and Japanese women . . . come here avowedly to practice their profession and are willing to submit to the consequences thereof," their Chinese counterparts "have absolutely no voice in any matter in connection with their own lives."[100] Colonial Office civil servants concurred. "If these wretched women were responsible persons & able to take care of themselves they might be left to themselves, but being as they are little better than dumb animals . . . we ought to do something for them."[101]

While local women were born, sold, or otherwise forced into the trade, western women were magically transformed in the colonial arena into shrewd businesswomen appreciative of the market, rationally considerate of the need of the state to examine and otherwise regulate them; in short, women who according to the colonial police, "give . . . very little trouble."[102] Even Helen Wilson, a stalwart abolitionist-feminist, grudgingly acknowledged that Bombay brothel keeper Mrs. Caroline Goldenberg was "said to be a very capable and business-like person."[103] While in the metropolitan context women such as Goldenberg would have been condemned, shunned, and even harassed, their imperial presence called for a curious reworking of standard narratives around sexual commerce, and especially around the idea of the white slave traffic. White women prostitutes could be loud and uncouth and perennially in debt, but they were simultaneously in control and rational. And while they posed an indubitable problem for imperial respectability, for female behavior, and for the easy racial divides of imperial rhetoric, they were still firmly European. Since some locals would read them, problematically, as members of a ruling race, and since they palpably were not native, they had to be seen and treated separately even if their occupation and demeanor separated them from other whites.

Not surprisingly, the Australian white slave narrative was the metropolitan version, full of tales of white girls abducted into brothels by seedy and cunning foreigners. Flora Harris of the Queensland National Council of Women inquired of the police commissioner in 1917 as to a "traffic in coloured women for immoral purposes," since her organization thought it likely that women of many races were procured in a sexual slave trade.[104] But such an interest was rare in the pursuit of this narrative in Australia where, as in Britain and in New Zealand, the white slave trade became a feminist and social purity rallying cry. Ross Barber has argued compellingly that its period of greatest exposure in Queensland came in the wake of women's failure to raise the age of consent in the 1890s.[105] And certainly the issue gathered steam a little later in Australia than in Britain and in crown colonies where Jewish migration from the 1880s lent white proletarians in the empire a greater visibility. White slave stories were a marvelous warning as to the dangers of allowing foreigners on Australian soil. The accent on the whiteness of the traffic's purported victims deflected "the gaze from the trade in Aboriginal women's bodies."[106]

Flora Harris deplored the dangers to women, "so often ... the fairest and healthiest daughters of a nation."[107] This was a narrative reserved specifically for a white and Anglo version of the story, and it is in marked contrast to the continual insistence of crown colony officials that it was weak and flighty women, the scourings of the white race, who sought work—and voluntarily— in the brothels of the east. Australia's version was far closer to the American, British, and European script that stressed passivity and weakness as exemplars of a pure femininity, and not as corruptions of an ideal. So much was the victim narrative inapplicable in the colonial context that superintendent Shuttleworth roundly declared in 1917 that "the 'White Slave' traffic as known in Europe is not existent in India."[108]

Police officials in island Britain and in Australia, as well as in nonwhite colonies, almost always played down allegations of white slavery. Their inquiries invariably concluded that the women in question were involved in the trade prior to arriving on their shores. The Queensland commissioner of police reassured his counterpart in South Australia in 1913 that "there is not the slightest foundation in fact for such allegations," though that did not prevent his police department, and others in Australia, from keeping close track of mobile young working-class women.[109] In the Straits, too, there were no cases to prosecute. A Straits government official reported to the colonial secretary in 1912 that "it is doubtful whether there is a single innocent white girl brought for immoral purposes in a year. The Police have not heard of such a case."[110] Yet in 1912, as a result of the passing of the Criminal Law Amendment Act (often referred to as the White Slave Trade Act), London's Metropolitan Police established a white slave trade unit. The unit instituted few prosecutions, but clearly had political significance. "This is a political question, & it may be that Gvt may find it necessary to deal with it in order to put an end to an agitation, however ill-founded, both in & out of Parlt."[111]

The discourse of the white slave trade clearly linked race, sexuality, and the position of women in powerful ways, with its emphasis on white vulnerability. Henry Champly, never one to mince words, insisted that the white slave trade "means the *prostitution of white women for Coloured men* [his emphasis]."[112] Focused on the eastern caravan, Champly played the race card to its fullest while extolling the particular feminine values of the white woman. Women who defied the proper role of woman, who challenged racial separation, risked both their personal safety and their place in society.

The idea of a white slave trade was a culturally specific notion with little documentable evidence to prove its existence or otherwise. Teresa Billington-Greig, writing in 1913, distanced her brand of feminism from that of the social purity advocates in her firm belief that there was little more than fiction, hearsay, and cheap journalism in the allegations of a traffic in women.[113] More recently Mariana Valverde, assessing English Canada's moral reform campaigns, has called white slavery an "invention" that consolidated and perpetuated racial and class assumptions about prostitution and female sexuality.[114] Yet neither contemporary officials nor historians subsequently investigating the colonial sex trade of this period doubted the existence of a criminal trade in the buying and selling of women, whether in China, South America, Africa, or India.[115] There was a human trade route from Europe both to South America and to the East, with the Egyptian ports of Alexandria and Port Said as the "turnstile" of the Asian-European sex routes.[116] In addition, a lucrative trade within Asia ensured a supply of local women for brothels throughout the east, but colonial authorities showed reluctance to intervene even when they were willing to implement legislation aimed at the putative white slave trade. Despite constant badgering by both religious and feminist campaigners and bills such as those introduced in 1912 to the viceroy's Legislative Council to combat the sale of young women, no such legislation was ever seriously considered.[117] The contrast in what was deemed politically expedient is startling; the common theme of lesser morals as a barometer of savagery held good in colonial legislation.

In Argentina, argues Donna Guy, white slavery gave Europeans a way of distinguishing white women's prostitution from that of indigenous women, excusing the former as hapless victims, an interpretation dramatically at odds with what we see in Britain's colonies.[118] While the staking of a national claim, to which Guy points, reverberates powerfully in Asian and Pacific colonial settings, the varied terrains of British colonialism complicate the picture. Thus European women working in Asian sex markets acquired a patina of ersatz professionalism and personal volition, while in Australia, as in Britain, European women involved in prostitution could, when necessary, be depicted as helpless victims. At stake was the way that race and gender categories fed different varieties of power and policy, malleable stories to be reworked in keeping with a variety of settings.

Race and Class

Valverde's class reading of the white slave trade narrative in anglophone Canada adds an enriching and complicating category to the flexible and unstable stories we have so far traced. Carolyn Martin Shaw sees white prestige in the colonies "built on middle-class morality and discipline," clearly a foundation with no room for women's prostitution, the "paradigmatic working-class female vice."[119] Lori Rotenberg has argued that the career prostitute defied class boundaries since as a contractor she worked outside the proletarian labor market.[120] Rotenberg's rigid distinction between the worker, the petit bourgeois, and the professional fails to place the prostitute in either the gendered or racial terms critical to opening up the category of class meaningfully. Conditions of work alone cannot serve as a satisfactory process of identification, more especially in the hybrid conditions that pertained in the empire. Class took on new meanings in colonial contexts with their regionally distinct and differently operating maps of social status. Poor or delinquent white colonials were not simply described by their behavior; the racial marker was critical because of the taint to white prestige that might follow from their actions.[121] Derek Hopwood realistically notes that some of the British "who fetched up in Egypt . . . could not have done much to burnish the imperial reputation."[122]

Few colonies, particularly the more populous, did not have a small white working-class presence.[123] For working-class white women—very much the minority in this militarily and commercially dominated arena—job opportunities were certainly no more adventurous than in the domestic setting. Prostitution was only one in a small and poorly paid range of options, and was often more profitable than other available work.[124] Women engaged in prostitution were automatically deemed to be working class. In Queensland, prostitutes were assumed to be the "daughters of the working men of the colony."[125]

Governing such connections were racially inflected ideas of evolution and degeneracy that, again, were handled dissimilarly in different colonial settings. White prostitutes in Australia could be excoriated as "the very sweepings of the old country," but such sentiments could be perilous in colonies where the "old country" was held to be at the pinnacle of civilization.[126] Certainly paupers and deviants everywhere were liable to an often punitive and always isolating institutionalization, what Raymond Evans has described in the Queensland context as a "brandishing and literally banishing" policy.[127] The punitive aspects of this were long-lived; Kay Saunders and Helen Taylor have documented a class-fueled separation of venereally infected women in Queensland as late as the Second World War, which branded working-class women as prisoners and middle-class women as patients.[128] But women often challenged the system, just as they did in the dependent colonies. Police and hospital officials constantly complained about their lawlessness while hospitalized, how they smuggled alcohol onto the wards or managed to get past guards to attend a dance, arriving back late and inebriated. By the early twentieth century, women were vocal in their criticisms of the organization of lock hospitals. Ten of the thirteen lock ward patients at the Brisbane general hospital sent a letter around 1916 to the chief doctor cataloguing their many grievances.

> We are put in here and left till its (sic) convenient for the Dr to call & see us. The Dr. is supposed to be here at 3:30 and rarely gets here before five o'clock, he has already disappointed us twice . . . None of us girls are in a position to wait here the Drs convenience (sic). We are bundled in here quick & lively and as to the treatment we receive we could do the same (& in fact improve on) at home. Another thing we girls are all strong & want plenty of food not starvation diet. There are 13 girls here & we get enough food for about six.[129]

Clearly these were women undeterred by their situation and ready to fight for their rights. Still, women falling into the categories of unfortunate and fallen bore the brunt of political righteousness, and their condemnation as stubborn throwbacks diluting the promise of the new world was part of Australia's national narrative of progress.

Migration and Mobility

Women prostitutes were out of place, removed from home in literal and metaphorical ways by their travels. Mobility could, in itself, be cause for suspicion. Two women were reported to the Foreign Office in 1915 as "typical white slave traffickers" bound for Britain on a ship from Rio de Janeiro. Queried on arrival at Falmouth, they were found to be "dealers in ladies' clothing," who frequently traveled between Britain and South America.[130] "Both women," reported the investigators at the Home Office, "are said to be immoral but no evidence could be obtained that they engaged in the White Slave Traffic."[131] No evidence linked the women to human trafficking other than their port of embarkation and their status as single women travelers. Still, they remained under suspicion and were dubbed immoral.

In nonwhite colonies this tension between female vulnerability and female threat had a powerful legislative impact. The potent idea that white women were objects of insatiable desire for black men led to countless tales of threat and rape.[132] While the narrative stress was clearly on the need to protect the properly helpless woman (a stereotype endlessly contradicted, of course, in novels and memoirs), the underlying message was that the empire was no place for women, that their defenselessness was a direct result of an inappropriate assumption of properly male territory, that of travel, migration, and empire. Ann Stoler reminds us that one neglected context of the white slave trade panic was the increasing emigration of women, not all of whom were accompanied by a male protector.[133] The potential independence implicit in women's solo migration was an important factor determining how such women were viewed.

An attention to mobility in an age of growing migratory practices, and more generally migration as a phenomenon, brings together conceptually some of the class and labor questions circulating around the white woman prostitute working in the empire. Migration cannot be read merely as a description of movement which separates an obvious and definable *home* from an adventure-some, sometimes intimidating, and possibly lucrative *away*. Migration carries with it, rather, valences around gender, class, race, and nation expressed in this period quite frequently in the prostitution debate, and especially in the white slave trade panic. Edward Bristow's observation that "motion was at the heart of the white slave trade" was certainly apparent in the watchful eye of police forces across the British globe.[134]

The fact of movement, and certainly of voluntary migration, cut across traditional ideas of womanliness and carried with it both the possibility of compromised morals and a potential for liberation and independence. Campaigners in the mid-nineteenth century worked hard to improve the image of female migration and though Australia still labored under the burden of a convict past, it was to white settler colonies and to the U.S. that British women were encouraged to move. In such places, the white newcomer came quickly to acquire a birthright, losing the stigma of migrancy, transferred instead to nonanglophone immigrants.[135] Earl Lewis's study of how European immigrants to America "defined themselves in relation to blacks," tells us much about how migrancy fosters or follows particular racial hierarchies.[136] Queensland with its diverse racial mix offered similar opportunities in which white migrants could privilege their own rights to settlement over those of both an indigenous black population and the Asians and Pacific Islanders who flocked to the fishing, agriculture, and mining opportunities offered by colonial settlement. Queensland's increasingly restrictive migration laws foreshadowed Australia's white-only Immigration Act of 1901, an act which also barred entry to prostitutes.

Since women were not real or proper migrants unless they came as wives, their deportation on grounds of immorality was rarely contentious. In the early twentieth century, such deportations were viewed as a valuable if not always strictly legal measure. The English prostitute "if found is 'induced' to leave India, [an] unwritten law known far and wide."[137] Missionary John Cowen told the AMSH in 1916 that the practice was widespread in India; W. N. Willis claimed "the British, very properly, deport all British prostitutes from Singapore."[138] These claims were somewhat optimistic, for in practice, the number of such deportations was quite small, partly because there were few British women engaged in commercial sex in the colonies and partly because, by their own admission, the authorities had little legal muscle in acting. But the declaration of intent was significant; Cowen and Willis saw the promise of such deportation as one of the few government measures worth celebrating. Women's rights to mobility and to a choice of occupation had to be secondary to the needs of the colonial state, and different scripts were written for how women could and could not behave in particular colonial environments. The European prostitute working in Singapore or Calcutta, always on what Catherine Hall calls the "troublesome margins," was in the metropole either victim or disgraced, but in the colonies she was a hardened professional; women's roles followed patterns determined as much by racial and class considerations as by gender.[139] Colonial need threw up wildly competing ideas of womanliness and female role. The white prostitute was an ugly necessity as long as she was not English, she was a major threat to the capacity of whites to maintain colonial rule, she was a shrewd entrepreneur, as well as a victim of male cruelty, she was a hiccough on the evolutionary ladder, and she was lastly a prophecy of women's independence. This amazing discursive malleability should warn us against an overly unitary reading of colonial practice or indeed of female prostitution.

The Promise of Home

White women occupied startlingly different roles in different contexts. The *Australian Star* described a nineteen-year old white woman removed from a Chinese-run brothel as "a silly, homeless, helpless creature."[140] This emphasis on feminine frivolity and ignorant passivity was a safe representation in Australia since this was a dominantly and increasingly white environment. In a crown colony setting, however, silliness might tarnish too greatly notions of white firmness and power, thus even women who were elsewhere dubbed ignorant or giddy had to be cast in a way that would not question white superiority.

Ultimately what distinguished and separated the white prostitute from the indigenous was, that in one form or another, there was for the former a strong and powerful notion that a return "home" was a possibility. Home in this context had a whole range of meanings, from the forcible deportation of women who crossed the line, to ideas of rehabilitation into proper and thus domestic femininity, to release from hospital into suitably subservient and feminine occupations. These powerful associations worked as much to differentiate proper and improper as they did to underline the important distinctions between metropole and colony. But it was here, in the possibility of narrative closure, perhaps through repatriation or rehabilitation, that the white prostitute was ultimately managed. While colonial CD enactments spoke of the uselessness of redemption in barbarous societies, white women's attachment to these laws was always partial, largely privileged and, most of all, always offered the possibility of the return to "civilization" unavailable to local women routinely seen as hopelessly enslaved to brothel owners or local men. The trope of home merged into that of femininity and both fed on imperial-national typing that particularly and necessarily linked Englishness and morality as civilizing notions. Indeed white women living in

Britain but married to "Asiatic" men took on unseemly masculine qualities as a result of their "freedom from Englishness."[141] The stereotype of the mixed race family as a feckless and improper unit underlines these women's distance from home.[142] The Eurasian woman in India, likewise, had shifted away from the civilizing influences of whiteness. Kipling's description of brothel inmate "Mrs D.—, widow of a soldier, mother of seven children," sums up typical attitudes to women of mixed descent.

> . . . a rather pretty, slightly-made Eurasian . . . whatever shame she may
> have owned she has long since cast behind her. A shapeless Burma-native
> trot. . . . calls Mrs. D.—"Memsahib." The word jars unspeakably. Her life
> is a matter between herself and her Maker, but in that she—the widow
> of a soldier of the Queen—has stooped to this common foulness in the
> face of the city, she has offended against the white race.[143]

In 1913, the Home Office entered into an agreement with the National Vigilance Association whereby "a lady visitor" from the association visited "alien prostitutes" in Holloway prison both to help the women and to gather information about them. When such women were deported from Britain, the Home Office allowed these lady visitors to accompany deportees on their journey home, and to deliver them to "ladies of the local committee" when they reached their destination.[144] The plan reveals more than just the increasing use of deportation as a weapon in early twentieth-century immigration laws. The return to good influence—residing at home—assumes again the opportunity for rehabilitation; Britain's foreign prostitutes came largely from nearby Europe rather than from farther afield. And the specifics of women as chaperoning companions—instead of policemen—speaks to the same picture of a feminized and white potential for redemption.

Kay Anderson has shown how European migrants moving to western Canada were automatically assumed to have created or arrived in a new home, while Chinese migrants continued to be figured as outsiders and aliens.[145] Conversely, when white women settled in nonwhite colonies, they were expected to recreate western notions of home in a hostile and antithetical environment not only as a means of bolstering middle-class images of feminine domesticity as a crucial part of the civilizing mission, but as a sign and symbol of permanence. While their sojourn itself might only be temporary, as was the case for whites in the dependent colonies, the creation of the home environment was a way of signaling British permanency as colonial rule and as civilization. Sending "alien" prostitutes *home*—whether they were deported from Britain or from its colonies—was a cleansing mechanism, a domesticating way of ensuring that the visible woman was a woman who belonged, not as an indigene but as a member of a ruling race. Donna Guy sees similar associations at work in nineteenth-century Argentinian white slave trade rhetoric. "To keep women in their homelands and under the control of their families, reformers assured single women that they would be safe from sexual exploitation if they remained immobile and dependent."[146] Home was a guarantee of safety, a bulwark of civilization, and a proper womanly place.

Lock hospital rules in Australia and Britain worked with much the same script, inscribing a domestic vision of proper working-class womanly behavior. Far less attention was paid to the language, conduct, and occupations of nonwhite women sent to lock hospitals than to white inmates in dominantly white settings. Indeed, nonwhite women received gratuities during treatment and were not expected to perform the wide variety of domestic tasks assigned to white lock residents. The latter were assigned sewing and laundry duties alongside Bible readings in a vain attempt to instill in them middle-class versions of womanhood. Though conditions were clearly irksome in the lock wards, as evidenced by the many escapes and protests, the intent was clearly to replicate, in typically clumsy institutional form, the proper duties of home as the woman's environment.[147]

The possibility of redemption, however unlikely, was never abandoned in the typing and in the treatment of white and especially of English women. They were invariably seen as further along the evolutionary road, however outrageous their deeds.[148] In the white context, home was, ultimately, the only possible closure for the linear narrative of fallenness.[149] Since white women prostitutes in colonial settings could not merge back into the local community as it was always suggested indigenous women could, their only possible salvation was through repatriation. In practice, of course, local women engaged in prostitution in many of the colonies were not welcome back into their communities if they left prostitution; the high proportion of young Hindu widows and the social shunning of Chinese women servicing Caucasian men is well-documented. But colonial officials held onto a fiction of native degradation, as we have seen, which argued for the normative status of prostitution in many colonial settings. The white woman in a nonwhite setting, however, could neither be part of the community nor fail to stand out in her whiteness. She faced only two possibilities: death, or rehabilitation to proper whiteness. The more pessimistic western commentator, mapping the journey east as the downward path, fell easily into a script in which no return was possible.

> The Europeans nearly all arrive by the same route, viz., Odessa, Constantinople, Cairo and Port Said. After a few years in Bombay or Calcutta, with an occasional interlude perhaps in one of the larger Indian cantonments they flit to Colombo and the Far East, where the sorry pilgrimage eventually closes.[150]

Conclusion

This was not merely a cartographical route-map but a moral mapping, a narrative of hopelessness and degradation, in which distance from home was an effect of and a pointer to shame and to death. Only rescue and deliverance—with all their Christian associations—could intervene to avert such an ending.

> What makes the recruitment of white women for prostitution so excep-
> tionally an evil in India is the circumstance that the obstacles to rescue
> work are so formidable. A foreign woman cannot abandon her profes-
> sion and merge in the general population. She cannot, like the Kanjar
> woman, find a place ready for her in her community or caste when she
> ceases the active pursuit of her profession. The white woman who comes
> to the country as a prostitute can only be saved by repatriation.[151]

Merged here are the legal meaning of repatriation and the Christian idea of redemption. The profoundly different ways in which class-inflected readings of gender worked in different racial contexts demonstrates the tremendous impor-
tance of establishing appropriately distinctive boundaries for differently situated colonial locations. Ann Stoler has argued that neither sexual promiscuity nor restraint were "abstract characteristics" attributable to behavior, but that they were instead "post-hoc interpretations contingent on the racialized class and gender categories to which individuals were already assigned."[152] That assign-
ment to a type, in the case of women working in the sex trade, took on a certain urgency if white European women, however degraded, were to be distinctively identified as somehow superior to their nonwhite counterparts in the trade. If the message of British paramountcy held steady, it did so only because it was able, if only sporadically and unevenly, to effect these adjustments.

Chapter 10

"Not A Petticoat In Sight": The Problem of Masculinity

> Good Heavens! a white European Man, standing on his two
> legs, with his two five-fingered Hands at his shackle-bones,
> and miraculous Head on his shoulders, is worth something
> considerable, one would say!
>
> —Thomas Carlyle

One of the most striking—and in Britain, the most controversial—aspects of CD legislation was the focus it placed upon the inspection and treatment of women while ignoring any surveillance of men. This was the double standard so vilified by opponents of the laws who argued that the policy enshrined a license for men that relied on the control of women. CD enactments looked only to control women; men, whether as carriers or recipients of disease, were curiously excised from the texts of these laws. Though absent, other than as enforcers or administrators, men were nonetheless central to the legislation, since the commonest defense of the policy was their protection. Yet colonial CD legislation, for all its textual emphasis upon women, relied crucially on distinguishing among men—native or European, manly or effeminate, courteous or cruel, decent or dishonorable. Who, after all, was the right client for a first- or a second-class brothel?

Not all men, in the colonial reckoning, were created equal, and alongside the hierarchies of race and class that distinguished among them, there was also a constant, if never very tidy, accounting of who was and was not properly masculine and properly manly. Masculinity, a crucial preoccupation in the empire, connoted more than simply a distinction between the good Englishman and the bad indigene. Class and race evaluations often overlapped with assessments of behavior in critical ways, constructing masculinity "across male groups as well as between men and women."[1] Ideas around men, manliness, and masculinity form an important backdrop against which to contextualize the particulars of colonial CD enactments. The contradictory attempt to argue that imperial conquest was a natural expression of masculinity, which in turn required a condemnation of those manifestations of masculinity that did not fit the colonial bill, profoundly influenced the state's understanding of why regulated prostitution was necessary. CD laws relied on particular readings of what was masculine and feminine. This investigation of the role of men and masculinity will argue that what appeared natural was part, rather, of a pedagogy of sexual and social order that changed to suit contemporary needs.

Categories of Manhood

Just as officials set about creating a minutely detailed taxonomy of the prostitute woman, they laid out in similar fashion the different categories of manhood. Race, caste, religion, region, and sexual preference were among the typical markers employed in this classificatory exercise. The marked differences in CD ordinances in the various colonies relied for their logic as much on colonial assessments of local men's standing and behavior as they did on the typing of women engaged in the sex trade, for colonialism materially affected an area's demographics and relied on a ranking of local men.

In Britain, the imperial century was also one in which women's and men's lives—especially in the middle classes—diverged more sharply than ever before. The idea of separate spheres, though less frequently its practice, governed popular perception of how the sexes ought to behave. And with this greater attentiveness to the performance of sex roles came considerable debate about what constituted proper masculinity or femininity, a debate in which class played a vital role. Encouraged by the growth of the connected doctrines of nationalism and eugenics, masculinity and femininity came to act as tropes of health and respectability.

John Tosh has shown how bourgeois conceptions of manliness relied heavily on a combination of the qualities of courage, independence, and self-discipline.[2] These values were transmitted to younger men in a variety of forms: in their school regimen, in the adventure stories so popular at the turn of the century, and in organizations such as the Boy Scouts. In all these educative avenues, the colonial experience figured prominently as a place where one's manliness could be forged and tested in rigorous but heroic conditions. The unity of moral and physical valor stood in stark contrast to colonial surrounds and peoples. While Englishmen walked tall and proud and were honest and fair in their dealings, the locals were frequently depicted as stunted and unhealthy, or sly and greedy; it was easy for such stereotypes, already a stock-in-trade of British schooling, to spill over into the constitution of "proper" masculinity. Influenced critically by imperial considerations, ideals of masculinity also served to shape the contours of imperialism.[3] The "exemplary colonial identity" was "at once manly, white, and civilized."[4] Civilization itself was defined by both gender and racial difference.[5]

Christopher Bayley sees "moral independence" as the touchstone of British colonial rule, a corollary of financial independence and a measure of suitability for leadership.[6] These all became specific measures of manhood.[7] "If there is any discourse that joins the triumph of rational bourgeois man in colony and metropole, it was that which collapsed non-Europeans and women into an undifferentiated field, one in which passion and not reason reigned."[8] Neither women nor those unable or unwilling to throw off the yoke of colonial rule were, by definition, independent.[9] As a physical and a moral state, independence spelled both manliness and Britishness through the exclusion of women and of colonial subjects. While women were literally not men, some men were not manly, defined not by "their difference from femininities, but by their difference from other masculinities."[10]

But in excluding from manliness those governed by colonial rule lay the specter of millions of unmasculine men, outsiders to manhood by virtue of their colonial dependence. Masculinity was associated with vigor and progress, so the unmanly man implied decline and degeneration.[11] The codes governing masculinity as a pillar of empire demanded not only keeping women at a distance from the centers of power, but disciplining men such that the proper man and the dissipated unmanned could always be distinguished from one another. Their difference necessitated constant performance and constant reiterations of definition.

The critical differences in individual colonies further loosened the moorings of this seemingly definitive masculinity featuring the decent chap of countless adventure stories and rose-tinted memoirs. An invocation of masculine prowess and superiority was, in some ways, of more critical consequence in Queensland and India than in the "coolie" colonies of the Straits and Hong Kong. India and Queensland housed greater numbers of white men for whom much was at stake. In the Australian context, Judith Allen insists, "masculinism [is] a political position."[12] Greater attention was thus paid to these issues in the more heavily white colonies, more time spent in formulating policy that would sustain the stability of this representation and that would continue to represent the frontier as a place of male freedom.[13] This chapter will reflect, to some extent, that uneven attention, with greater emphasis on India and Australia than on Hong Kong and the Straits Settlements.

Settler Men and "Natives"

In Queensland and elsewhere in Australia, the ethos of settler success was built on a characteristic sentiment of white male camaraderie. Though the physical hardships and back-breaking work required in a frontier economy were, in fact, shared with wives and sisters and with hired aboriginal and foreign workers, the narrative of masculinity beating the odds was irresistible.[14] In the Straits and Hong Kong, an overwhelmingly Asian labor force worked in equally taxing conditions to secure the dizzying success of these port colonies. They did so, though, as employees, dependent on overseers, employers, and the colonial state for their livelihood. In Australia, the dominant myth was that men's efforts gained them independence, that masculinity was a prerequisite for settlement. The Chinese laborer content to work merely for wages could thus be represented as lacking in the drive and ambition of the man making himself and improving himself in the acquisition of property, the material manifestation of his manliness. This was the increasingly dominant mid-nineteenth century discourse of the "white middle-class man as master, as superior in essence and for all time, to inferior blacks."[15]

The racial profile of Queensland's male labor force complicated the cozily simple picture sustained by mateship as the core of settler values, but the idea of self-governing settlership—with its connotations of independence—depended fundamentally on racial differentiation. Settlerhood, in many senses, came to define a version of masculinity that allowed for a radically different implementation of CD legislation than was the case in the dependent colonies. "Low" white men certainly complicated the Queensland picture, but it was the nonwhite man, indigene or migrant, who was most represented as failing in his masculinity. A wide-ranging, often contradictory, set of practices was associated with him, and signaled his inferiority. The kinds of ethnographies that dominated racial and ethnic classifications were a self-fulfilling practice that used the idea of a proper English masculinity as the measure by and against which colonial subjects were both classified and disciplined.[16] In the first instance, as we have seen, the very dependence implied by the colonial relation was taken as a mark of weakness. Though by no means universal in its application, the idea of effeminacy still powerfully shaped assumptions about a host of colonial peoples. While the allegedly effeminate Bengali is the most written-about, many other groups were similarly classified.[17] The slim stature and relative hairlessness of east Asian men was sometimes seen as proof of their feminized nonmanliness; this view necessitated, of course, that their abilities as manual laborers in rigorous conditions be overlooked. So, too, the recently liberated slaves of the British West Indies. Though prized for their field labor, Thomas Carlyle found them pretty and glossy, traits, as Catherine Hall points out, more readily associated with femininity.[18] Subject men were akin to women, defined by subjecthood and weakness, unfit to govern, and unsuited for power.[19] The conflation of moral and physical prowess is palpable in such formulae: stature, hairiness, and prettiness became more than physical descriptors—consolidating and justifying, rather, the strength of an easily differentiated imperial masculinity.

The "coolie" populations of Hong Kong and the Straits Settlements were regularly depicted as brutish users of the cheapest prostitutes while their wealthier compatriots were said to keep women in domestic as well as sexual slavery. The coolie—so fundamental a source of colonial labor—was both wealth creator and stubborn problem. The Straits protector of Chinese, W. A. Pickering, thought Chinese laborers "conversant with an extraordinary state of immorality which cannot be well named in European Christian society."[20] Pickering's tone of hushed indignation probably indicates same-sex liaisons regarded as common in eastern societies, but he was equally sure that these men formed the bulk of the city's brothel customers. Worse even than same-sex relations was a fluid sexuality embracing a variety of partners and behaviors.

It was no different elsewhere in the colonies. Purdah signified Indian men's indifference and neglect of their women's health.[21] A commissioner in India's Northwest Provinces told tales of cowardly Indian men.

> When I was Magistrate at Banda, in 1858, after the re-occupation of the district, the male inhabitants of the city of Banda had mostly fled, leaving the female of their families without any means of subsistence. Meanwhile the troops . . . were quartered actually in the Native houses of the town. The natural result was that the women universally prostituted themselves.[22]

These criticisms often went hand in hand with an insistence on the child-ishness of the native who could be lured and persuaded by baubles.[23] The widespread use of the term "boy" in speaking of adult men drove home the central place of discipline in colonial relations. Underutilization of resources was another common "proof" of native inferiority; *terra nullius* assumed Aboriginal mismanagement of agriculture, while in India the reformulation of property profoundly altered farming, and with it, social relations on the land. Conforming to European notions of the organization of space had devastating consequences for local peoples, but these changes, in the name of progress and development, were part of the ways in which the stewardship of colonialism fed the idea of the native as incapable child in need of guidance and education.

This trope of childishness was ultimately unsustainable, for the qualities of innocence and purity that Victorians saw in children were not amongst the traits said to distinguish adult colonials. Colonial men were routinely regarded as unable to exercise self-discipline over the sexual body, something white infants were taught early on. And in this inability to control the sexual urge lay not only a fertile source of disease transmission but a neglect of the proper avenues of male life. Syphilis sapped "the strength of manhood of the natives."[24] Sexuality was overwhelmingly the mark of this hybrid adult-child, and the sexual characteristics associated with colonial men were always negative.

It was always foreign men who, for example, were associated with and seen to profit from prostitution. Reports of colonial trafficking and procuring, sinister kidnapping, and buying of young girls from impoverished villages abounded. "It is well known that . . . agents . . . travel throughout Gujarat, Central India, Rajputana and other districts, picking up superfluous and unwanted girls of tender age for a small sum . . . and then selling them at a profit to brothel keepers in the large cities and towns."[25] "Gangs of lawless men" were said to extort protection money from the Straits brothels.[26] Even the native customer was worse than his European counterpart. Describing the notorious cages in which Bombay's Falkland Road prostitutes touted for business, the local police commissioner explained that bars were installed to prevent women "from being overwhelmed by a low-class male rabble, ready for violence on the smallest provocation."[27]

These male connections to prostitution condemned native men in multiple ways. Those whose activities could not be subsumed under the rubric of childishness could be alternatively disposed of as cruel or amoral. Alongside the tarnishing association with both a female and a commercial sexuality, the connection to illicit sex removed men from the sphere of proper work, a corollary to their apparent underutilization of their land's resources, and their lack of properly-directed ambition. Men engaged in prostitution were soiled by association, unmanned and unmanly.

Male Cruelty

Cruelty to women was a hallmark of the scarred unmanliness of the colonial male. Nancy Paxton has remarked on the disappearance of "the figure of the English man as rapist . . . from nineteenth-century discourse," leaving the field open for foreigners.[28] The "cruel and vengeful" eastern man was a long-standing stereotype discernible in pornographic literature, in slave trade narratives, and in fiction as well as in official reports. The dangers native men apparently posed to European women hindered female emigration and mobility. In the mid-nineteenth century, accounts of Indian brutalities in the 1857 mutiny fueled such fears. W. J. Shepherd's pious but nonetheless titillating account of the "trials" of English women "now placed in the power of a horde of savages, brutes whose tongues emitted venom and abuse at every move," is typical of the flood of outraged horror stories produced in the aftermath of rebellion.[29] Popular British accounts dwelt on the sadism, brutality, and deviance of the rebels evidenced by their disrespectful treatment of unprotected white women, proof to the British that Indian men lacked the essential qualities of manliness and independence.[30] Australian captivity narratives are equally suffused with white fears of aboriginal men, and the notorious 1926 White Women's Protection Ordinance in Australian-controlled Papua, which made rape or attempted rape of a white woman a capital offense, drew on much the same fears of nonwhite male sexuality.[31]

Queensland historians have noted that the rape of Melanesian women in the colony excited far less public attention than did assaults on white women.[32] Yet cruelty to nonwhite women was often held up as emblematic of the savagery of native men, unappreciative of proper masculinity's attachment to a sex-stratified chivalry. Daisy Bates, a white woman living among western Australia's aboriginal peoples, described the annual trek of "practically every boy [Aboriginal] who had a woman" to "trade her with the Asiatics" when the pearling season ended.[33] The "ordinary native," asserted an official in India in 1872, saw nothing wrong in selling his daughter into brothel work.[34] Chinese and Malay culture afforded men savage license. "Chinese and probably Malay women also are regarded by the men as inferior beings and treated accordingly . . . they have in these cases to be protected . . . against the brutality of the men."[35] The procurer, like the greedy brothel keeper eager to exploit hapless women for profit, was typical of the man of cruelty.

The sentiment that colonized women needed protection from their own menfolk formed a rationale for CD and related legislation. The claim that sexual slavery was fundamental to Chinese culture prompted Hong Kong and Straits officials, as well as Europeans resident in the colonies, to demand the maintenance of brothel regulation for the sake of their vulnerable inmates. These were all convenient yardsticks for adjudging native men as effeminate, cowardly, and unmanly in their treatment of women; CD legislation, by contrast, was held to guarantee women enlightened protection in a modern idiom. British colonial rule was cast as protecting women, a role that left little room for colonialism to acknowledge its own part in producing at least some of the conditions it so deplored.

In 1836, an administrator in western India expressed horror at living among those "who look upon infanticide[,] suttees[,] tuggee[,] and hijeras [eunuchs] without apparently a feeling of horror."[36] With the exception of *thuggee* (gangs of ritual stranglers), the practices that shocked him related in some way to sexual cruelty or deviance. What Francis Hutchins calls "extreme sexuality" became a defining racial characteristic. Unnerved at the prospect of a greater male potency in the east, colonists instead saw oversexedness as decadent and depraved, reserving the trait of manliness for those exhibiting a restrained sexual aggression.[37] Reporting on the *mui tsai* system of domestic servitude, the Hong Kong governor's secretary connected its existence to a variety of sexual practices. Support for the buying and selling of servant girls, he claimed, was widespread among "intelligent Chinese" who "look upon this system as the necessary and indispensable complement of polygamy, as an excellent counter remedy for the deplorably wide-spread system of infanticide, and as the natural consequence of . . . an over-populated country."[38] His position explicitly pinpoints a series of relationships between an overly active sexuality—polygamy and over-population—with brutality, infanticide, and the enslavement of impoverished girls. The proximity of the two systems, the vulnerability of women, and the calculated greed of men, stood as a wholesale condemnation of practices originating in barbarous Asian sexual activity.

Sexuality and Masculinity

The theme of the oversexed native frequently acted as a link to the spread of VD. One Queensland protector detailed the range of "deviant" sexual behaviors he saw as producing a devastating cycle of contagion: "group marriage . . . the drinking of seminal fluid . . . the right of sodomy over one's younger brothers-in-law, the eating of the dead . . . the inter-tribal system of barter [of women]."[39] This inventory of degradation set the native apart from his masters. This was the catalogue of his "moral weaknesses."[40] The oversexed native was also the polygamist, the masturbator, the whorer, and the sexually fluid. Bengali men's effeminacy was the result of sexual enervation, early marriage, and masturbation.[41] "Coolie" men in the Straits and Hong Kong were not only frequent brothel visitors but were content to marry women they might formerly have hired there.[42] It was a contagion beyond merely the spread of sexually transmissible diseases; at stake here was the gap between the seemliness and restraint of British culture and the greed and profligacy of native cultures. And the threat to order was at its worst when cultures mingled, each deepening the other's proclivities.

In these representations, the nonwhite man—oversexed, cruel, effeminate, barbarous—stands in stark contrast to modern manhood with its emphasis on reason and restraint. "The cult of masculinity rationalized imperial rule by equating an aggressive, muscular, chivalric model of manliness with racial, national, cultural, and moral superiority."[43] It was a formula with considerable staying power. In the Second World War, physician Robert Lees praised British troops for their responsible use of prophylactic centers. But the ragbag of men from "backward" regions—"Greeks, Cypriots, French coloured troops and South-African non-Europeans"—was, he contended, "habitually promiscuous," spreading disease in their wake.[44] One feature of being modern, of being part of an "advanced" civilization was an appreciation that VD prevention was desirable.

In attempting to pin down what rendered the colonial different from his master, it was necessary to establish a litmus test for proper masculinity. The disciplinary potential of this exercise policed the boundaries of white masculinity as carefully as it did those of nonwhite masculinity. In colonial literature, in medical texts, in pamphlets aimed at the military, and in private correspondence, it was clear that, though no formal definition of the manly man was forthcoming, few questioned that there was an identifiable male sexual nature. Even in Ronald Hyam's fluid reading of colonial male sexuality, in which men move without remorse between same-sex and opposite-sex partnerings, there is a base-line notion of the male sex drive as a natural condition, rather than as a product of historical and cultural circumstance.[45] In the nineteenth-century literature, while there was endless debate over the relationship between sexual release and general health, the idea of an urgent, driving, male sexual urge was taken as a given, a descriptor of normalcy.[46] This was a long-standing assumption, so built into ideas about behavior and sexuality that it was an unchallengeable truth, used to bolster a range of policies and practices and by authorities in many fields. One retired captain recalled an army medical officer in colonial Ceylon who, instructed to sign a "misconduct return" listing soldiers who had contracted VD, retorted "Misconduct, do you call it? I call it human nature." According to the narrator, the return was ever after "known in the Garrison as the 'human nature' Return."[47]

Men's memoirs of a colonial past, military or otherwise, frequently depicted the move east as the threshold to men's initiation into adulthood via the brothel, in a kind of sexual *Bildungsroman*.[48] Somerset Maugham's upright young Scot, Neil MacAdam, in the short story of that name, spends a brief period in Singapore on his way to a posting in Malaya. An old hand, not insignificantly married to a Japanese woman, encourages Neil to take his pick in the local brothels but, as is the unfaithful (and foreign) wife of his employer, is rebuffed by MacAdam's Calvinist discipline. Ultimately it is not the debauched captain with his knowledge of the Singapore red-light district who undoes Neil's ethics but a woman bent on taking his virginity, itself a reverse of the more usual narrative of male defloration of young women. Even more importantly, perhaps, this incarnation of female evil is determined to undermine MacAdam's strong sense of male companionship.[49]

Maugham's partnering of the male sex drive and of homosociality is critical in the colonial context. When memoirists conjured up brothel scenes in Calcutta or Cairo, they invariably depicted the streets crowded with groups of carousing male friends, egging one another on. Sex was a wayside stop in an evening of fun in most memoirs, just as soldiers remembered the comradely queuing for service and its inevitable jostling and teasing more than they recalled the always brief sexual servicing this camaraderie preceded. Thus when the military and the medical specialists asserted, as they predictably did, that men will be men, the seldom-acknowledged emphasis was always on this group spirit rather than on individual pathology. Masturbation, solitary in nature, was a more alarming prospect than the use of commercial services. It was,

> an indisputable proposition that men will be immoral . . . Nature lays a demand on men to exercise all their physiological functions. . . . For a young man who cannot marry, and who cannot attain to the high moral standard required for the repression of physiological natural instincts, there are only two ways of satisfaction, viz., masturbation and mercenary love. The former, as is well known, leads to disorders of both body and mind; the latter to the fearful dangers of venereal.[50]

This linking, in Joseph Alter's words, of "sex and identity with questions of power and authority" consolidated empire as a masculine enterprise.[51] And the sociability that was so fundamental to this literal performance of masculine sexuality endorses Rosalind O'Hanlon's point that masculine attributes needed the "recognition and affirmation of other men."[52]

The Queensland frontier was another such homosocial environment. The rural foundations of the colony's economy, the scattered nature of the population outside the urbanized southeast, the high numbers of non-Europeans employed in the agrarian sector, and the unusually large population of unmarried men combined to produce conditions in which prostitution flourished and camps of men lived together for long stretches. These were fertile conditions for this combination of homosociality and heterosexual display, more akin in many ways to the lifestyle of British soldiers in India than to the urban population of Brisbane.[53] Like the soldiers in cantonments, camps of men in rural Queensland relied in large part on locals and on foreign merchants (mainly Chinese) for their goods and services, looked for sex from local black women, and frequently characterized the lives they themselves led as unsuitable for white women. Masculinity was simultaneously description, celebration, and performance, a means of making the best of uncomfortable and isolated conditions.

But this picture of the healthily unbridled white man forced ideas about sexuality into racial categories; when indigenous men frequented brothels this was evidence of their inherent disgustingness, while for whites a nod and a wink at infidelity or nonprocreative sex were standard. Edward Walter Hamilton, twice Gladstone's private secretary, received a cheerful letter in 1887 from a friend traveling in India. After an account of his part in luring "a bride of 3 weeks" into marital infidelity, he assured Hamilton that "things get pretty warm in the Hills during the season."[54] It is not without significance that writing man to man, Hamilton's correspondence highlighted the sexual exploits of the colonizers; he would doubtless have concurred with Ronald Hyam's opinion that "[R]unning the empire would probably have been intolerable without resort to sexual relaxations."[55] At any rate, his tone vindicates Hyam's assertion that "[S]exual opportunities were seized with imperious confidence."[56] The sister of three brothers seeking colonial betterment in India wrote to another sister, describing the easterly colonies: "No wonder so many women come to ruin in these colonies . . . The place reels with vice and drunkenness."[57]

The dangers of the colony were by no means exclusively physical, and it was the moral environment which most concerned critics. Soldiers were surrounded by unchastity; in India it was "a female population who do not know the meaning of the word chastity and the majority of whom are affected by the worst type of disease."[58] It was women who spelled men's downfall, but in complicated ways. Many blamed the lack of home restraint for soldierly incontinence, seeing men's civility as dependent on a womanly presence.[59] "Withdrawn from the preservative, purifying and softening influences of every *Womanly* connection, he is amongst *Men* always [emphasis in original]."[60] Women were both the guardians of proper manhood, and its destroyer. Unrestrained, men would "satisfy their unfortunate cravings" and "especially in a tropical climate, amongst an alien population."[61] As late as the 1940s Robert Lees was comfortable describing colonial Cyprus as "a land where half-a-crown bought a bottle of brandy, a woman and gonorrhoea."[62] Women were a Protean force, offering peace, solace, and the civilized inhibiting of men's baser nature on the one hand, and on the other, temptation, disloyalty, and death.

Abena Busia has suggested that white men's sexual license in colonial contexts was tethered only "when they begin to disrupt the British social order."[63] Such a reading allows for more fluid readings of masculinity in which differing contexts and contingencies produced different expectations, and we can trace these different and sometimes competing readings. In the following pages, we shall look at the soldier, the sailor, the settler, the laborer, the pimp, and the homosexual. We shall see how different colonial settings and situations required radically different rules and how, despite contradictions, colonial officials still managed to cobble together a notion of proper masculinity sufficient to sustain the CD policy, in which white men's protection at native and female expense remained paramount.

Military Masculinity

The importance of the military in any appreciation of colonial power cannot be overestimated. Armies were "the ultimate expression of colonial rule."[64] W. R. Mansfield, Indian commander in chief in the late 1860s, told his viceroy that British troops were "the bullion deposit on which the security of the Indian Empire and therefore of the civilization of the country reposes . . . the real demonstration of British power."[65] Mansfield's avowal of the visible and physical impact of the soldiery was, for all the solidity it implied, equally invested in the symbolic role of that presence; the British army was both the literal and the symbolic reminder and guarantee of the colonial presence. His choice of a fiscal metaphor suggests the centrality of military expenditure to political debate in this period. Despite constant arguments over the funding of the CD system, "in financial terms . . . the army was by far the most important element of the colonial state."[66] The British soldier in India was "an enormously costly import," to whose upkeep government allocated far more of its funds than were directed to other key budgetary arenas.[67] "The saving of one British soldier to the service," claimed the adjutant general in India, "more than repays all the out-lay involved in the establishment of Lock Hospitals."[68]

Over the course of the nineteenth century, military expenditure shifted away from the navy in favor of the army, at the same time as there was major imperial expansion. The empire was indubitably "the most consistent and most continuous influence on shaping the army as an institution."[69] This fiscal change was coincident with a slow but decisive thawing of metropolitan attitudes towards the soldiery. Aided by a raft of military reforms from the 1850s as well as by a growingly jingoistic assertion of national identity, the soldier's image improved radically over the course of the century, a change linked closely to the Crimean War.[70] Joany Hichberger has argued that before the 1850s, veteran soldiers were imagined as Chelsea Pensioners or as physical cripples.[71] As the soldier's rehabilitation as a guarantor of order intensified, the cripple was reborn as the soldier constitutionally undone by VD.

> Syphilis . . . assumes a horrible, loathsome and often fatal form through which in time, as years pass on the sufferer finds his hair falling off, his skin and the flesh of his body rot, and are eaten away by slow, cankerous and stinking ulcerations; his nose first falls in at the bridge and then rots

and falls off; his sight gradually fails and he eventually becomes blind; his voice, first becomes husky and then fades to a hoarse whisper as his throat is eaten away by foetid ulcerations which cause his breath to stink.[72]

This vivid description of the sufferer literally falling apart from casual sex was intended to dissuade the soldier from risky behaviors. The image of the wholesome and brave defender of the motherland was valuable in encouraging nationalism and as a recruiting tool.[73] George Hamilton remarked to Lord Curzon during the South African war of 1899–1902 that the "defects and faults" of soldiers had to be downplayed, "otherwise you will make the army unpopular and stop recruiting."[74] It was only privately that officials acknowledged a more diverse and less sunny reality. The "European soldier . . . influenced by lust and drink" was a ferocious being whose wrath no locals would willingly incur.[75] In public, meanwhile, the focus was on national unity.

Saving the Soldier

Public support for the CD system rested on a championing of the British soldier, and soldiers were frequently presented as sacrificial lamb on the altar of unyielding social purity. Newspaper editorials as well as their letter columns were full of such sentiments. The *Saturday Review* thought antiregulationists condemned "the innocent to bear the penalty of his offences," while a correspondent in the *Daily Telegraph* championed the right of "our young soldiers" to "be saved from a horrible life and a premature and disgraceful death."[76] A decade earlier, the commander in chief praised the refusal of civilians in the government of India "to sacrifice the health of their soldiers at the bidding of the Exeter Hall school."[77] Viceroy Dufferin spoke disparagingly of those "who would . . . allow disease and death to be propagated wholesale throughout the British Army."[78] This idea that soldiers needed to be saved both from the jaws of death and the clutches of uncomprehending faddists was a powerful one, and abolitionists found themselves forced to reframe their position to account for their apparent disregard of soldiers' well-being. In the *Contemporary Review,* Blanche Leppington of the Abolitionist Federation praised soldiers for their devotion and discipline, blaming instead the authorities who failed the men by continuing to provide licentious and trying environments. The fault, she counseled, "is less in Tommy Atkins than in his masters."[79]

This debate around soldiers and VD had implications for the ways in which military masculinity could be signified. In important respects it rendered the soldier a passive creature buffeted by the forces of political interest, incapable of understanding his environment, and all too easily harmed by women. On the one hand, the soldier was imagined as the epitome of the manly man, risking his own life in the service of others, putting duty before pleasure and knuckling under to military discipline and obedience. But the furor over venereal disease dictated that he be seen in this context as a passive creature subject to political whim as well as physical temptation. It was a theme that allowed for the distinct possibility that women could unman the soldier in a host of ways. The prostitute woman was his undoing because she put temptation and lust in his path, passed onto him grave diseases, and literally embodied his promiscuity and lack of fidelity. The respectable woman unthinkingly supportive of the antiregulation campaign sealed the soldier's death warrant in her disavowal of the licensed brothel. VD and women alike were potential destroyers of men's masculinity. VD undermined the soldier as a physical asset, erasing his fighting potential and limiting his ability to produce heirs. If physical performance was as significant a mark of masculinity as R. W. Connell argues, it was women who rendered men vulnerable, such that "the performance cannot be sustained."[80] The body's inability to function in a properly masculine way was produced by women, a paradox whereby sex itself rendered men impotent.

Venereal disease was not the only danger women posed. Military loyalty was also under threat. In the American revolutionary army, according to Walter Blumenthal, "amongst those who deserted were many who were accompanied by women."[81] Women's disruption of the homosocial nature of army life was a palpable danger to discipline and loyalty. Alongside the more obvious economies of scale involved in limiting marriage among soldiers, fidelity and loyalty were key features of the army regimen, closely associated with the insistence on absolute obedience. Women were not only incapable of manly activity but could actively work to nullify it and, as one surgeon argued, that was so "in all Oriental countries."[82]

Sex and Marriage

This threat to soldierly compliance, and to the particular reading of masculinity associated with it, emerged powerfully in the colonies in relation to marriage. In pre-mutiny India, 12 percent of crown troops were permitted to marry; in 1872, 11 percent of the strength was married.[83] In Britain, by 1867 around 7 percent were allowed to marry, though the expansion of the colonial military and the introduction of shorter enlistment periods may have reduced the percentage who actually did so.[84] An 1898 report informed parliament that between 4 percent and 7 percent of rank and file soldiers were permitted to marry.[85]

Many saw nonmarital sex as an inevitable by-product of the discouragement to marriage, a view that consolidated men's (hetero)sexual nature, especially among the young.[86] A surgeon in the Northwest Provinces reported that "the army being now composed of much younger men, with a smaller proportion of married men, and very few old soldiers, is rapidly becoming a mere 'venereal' army . . . composed of men in whom the passions are stronger, and among whom a greater extent of disease is to be looked for than among the men of a few years back."[87] Many championed marriage as a civilizing and stabilizing force in men's lives; it was "the remedy which God himself had provided."[88] More

secular commentators argued that soldier marriage was the civilized alternative to institutionalized prostitution.[89] The low incidence of VD among Indian
sepoys was often traced to their higher marriage rates, since it was commonly assumed that monogamous sexual relations would reduce VD rates. "Many of the
artillery-men keep women . . . each man so kept apart from prostitutes reduces
the liability of the disease."[90]

Military Prostitution

With low rates of marriage and an increasing official disapproval of concubinage,
military prostitution was regarded as inevitable wherever soldiers gathered. The
military presence had a powerful hand in shaping local sexualities, especially paid
sex. "Where white men visited and settled, brothels and grogshops followed."[91]
The connection between sex and alcohol was perhaps nowhere more apparent than in military settings, the boredom and limitations of the soldier's life
helping to produce the circumstances for a particularly bawdy and boisterous
performance of male "nature." Cynthia Enloe has made the point that military
prostitution is quite distinct from other paid sex, "in that there are explicit steps
taken by state institutions to protect the male customers without undermining
their perceptions as sexualized men."[92] In other words, prostitution was a necessary and a convenient provision to bolster masculinity, and if it was necessary
to shape it to privilege the client overtly, that was a political necessity.

Disease and Hygiene

Such performing of the masculine urge, however, resulted in high venereal rates
at all military stations. As noted in earlier chapters, the statistical reports of VD
are by no means reliable, and different documents sometimes offer contradictory
findings on this point. Notwithstanding the need for caution, white British
troops in the nineteenth century were clearly prone to these infections, and the
state saw itself as justified in seeking means to reduce sickness and wastage from
this source. Their need to retain a notion of manliness as a central quality of
soldiering made the regulation of prostitution seem a logical and a practical
strategy.

As the numbers of troops stationed abroad rose, so for the most part did
statistics tracking their rates of VD. Peaking in the mid-1890s, hospital admission rates paint a picture of a runaway problem. In the 1870s, Indian admission
rates had hovered around 200 per thousand of troop strength. They climbed
into the 300s by the late 1880s, and reached an extraordinary 522 per thousand
in 1895.[93] In the mid-1890s, Gibraltar, the West Indies, South Africa, Mauritius,
Ceylon, Egypt, Hong Kong, and the Straits Settlements all had rates over
200 per thousand, with domestic troops only marginally lower at 194.6 per thousand in 1893.[94] The figures are horrifying even taking into account a degree of
clinical unreliability and the inevitable political doctoring they underwent. Yet

soldiering was an unhealthy occupation more generally in this period.[95] In the first half of the century, military mortality rates were considerably higher than in the population at large; it was contagious and infectious diseases, especially respiratory complaints, that pushed the figures so high.[96] In the wake of the Crimean War, sanitary conditions in the army received considerable attention. Newspapers called for reform, and government commissions were appointed to investigate. They laid much of the blame on the living conditions of soldiers. The military canteen was criticized as a squalid and degrading environment.[97] The overcrowding of barracks, their lack of facilities and poor ventilation were well-known, and these were issues attacked by sanitary reformers.[98]

With the massive expansion in colonial overseas postings, it was also easy to posit the colonial environment itself as an unhealthy influence, physically and morally. Tropical climates and debilitating diseases were among the colonial enemies soldiers encountered, as were the "densely populated" native areas so productive of filth and contagion.[99] The common allusions to filth and overcrowding associated with native living space began, later in the nineteenth century, to replace concerns about the inadequacy of barrack accommodations.

The Soldier's Failings

At the same time, the class failings of the average military recruit were an equally well-rehearsed complaint, opening up another chink in the armor of masculinity. George White wrote with some distaste to the bishop of Lucknow about "men who, like our soldiers, are a class under little religious or moral instruction."[100] He would doubtless have concurred with the unflattering description offered by the commanding officer at Hong Kong. Sailors arriving in port there, he reported, immediately go on "a spree, when they get drunk and become riotous, and finish with a visit to the police office."[101] The laxity of tropical living unloosed "already acquired habits of licence," undoing the good effects of domestic proximity to civilizing influences.[102]

Rank and file soldiers were "the least privileged and most restricted" among colonial white populations.[103] Drawn largely from the casual unskilled poor in Britain, often attracted by the promise of uninterrupted wages, the army was overwhelmingly working-class in composition, comprised of "the poor and the powerless."[104] The protection the CD ordinances offered was both from the depradations of women and from self-inflicted damage. "The animal passions of man are said to be strongly developed in these classes, while moral or religious restraints are small."[105] Bombay-based missionaries R. H. Madden and Wallace Gladwin painted a lurid picture of the red-light antics of soldiers, "uniformed representatives of the power and prestige of the British Government," busily drinking, fornicating, and frolicking in full view of the local population.[106]

In Hong Kong, the attorney general reported "the treacherous conduct of men who have deliberately had commerce with women with the ulterior purpose of swearing against them."[107] The medical officer at Jhansi lock hospital in the Northwest Provinces thought the men thoroughly unreliable in identifying women who have given them a disease. He thought that, as a result, "the prostitutes stand more in danger of infection from the men than the men from them."[108] And at the turn of the century, India secretary Hamilton was appalled by what he saw as the casually brutal treatment of locals meted out by "ignorant . . . careless and clumsy" soldiers.[109]

This ambivalence, crystallized so well in the gap between public and private talk about soldiers, was widespread and affected CD implementation as well as military policy more broadly. Though the soldier mistreated the local and accused the wrong women of transmitting disease, medical officers also complained when men refused to divulge women's identities. In the 1820s, the military health authorities had considered withdrawing soldiers' spirit rations until they named the guilty female party.[110] In the CD era, their successors regarded it as "useless to expect the soldier to point out the woman from whom he contracted disease."[111] Men were thought to shield the culprits and to be reluctant to inform on unregistered women.[112] Antiregulation activist Joseph Edmondson elaborated a complex theory for men's seeming collusion with the women, which blamed the system itself for debasing men's honor.

> There is a certain refinement of corruption brought about by the regulation system itself . . . Many men, seeing the way in which others rush in to take advantage of the regulations, seeking something "less common" outside the *cordon* and having found it, they try to keep it select, and to prevent its becoming known to the sanitary officers. They therefore aid the women in their evasion, and between the two the administrators are outwitted and checkmated at every turn.[113]

Frank Richards, in his graphic memoir of soldiering in the early twentieth century, paints a related picture of soldiers aligning themselves with the local women against their pimps and keepers, an image of sympathetic if rough men, with an innate appreciation of justice but still seeking a bargain.[114]

This was not quite how the authorities saw soldiers. In Hong Kong, the CD police used paid informers armed with marked currency to circumvent soldier unreliability, a practice vigorously opposed by governor Hennessy.[115] Former soldier Frank Richards also acknowledged violence against locals alongside his tale of working-class chivalry to prostitute women.[116] Yet the authorities shied away from punishment for these sorts of infractions. Despite Curzon's determination to clamp down on soldiers raping and assaulting Indian women and appropriating or destroying local property, one Madrasi newspaper remarked bitterly on the leniency with which soldierly misdeeds were treated. "[T]hey seek to gloss over the matter and let him escape without the least consideration for the injured Hindus."[117]

The New Soldier

The Army Enlistment Act of 1870 had introduced a short-service option of six years followed by a six-year term in the reserves as part of the package of reforms introduced by Cardwell (and opposed by India's commander in chief, Frederick Roberts) at the War Office.[118] Short service replaced enlistment periods of ten to twelve years introduced in 1847 as an alternative to unlimited recruitment that had kept men in the service often for upwards of twenty years. The effect of this change was to make the army significantly younger, a change seen by many as a source of military failing. In matters sexual, the young were said to be "peculiarly exposed to temptation."[119] Youth and soldiering were a devastating combination.

> Short service sends a constant stream of youths untainted by these diseases into the Army every year, and returns them in so many instances with constitutions so shattered, or so affected with communicable disease, as not only to impair their future health and wage-earning power, but to be a source of danger to the community from which they came, and to which they return.[120]

This focus on an axis of age and class as productive of trouble brought about a fascinating recuperation of the old soldier in military circles. While public opinion was swinging away from the former image of the soldier as a riotous drunken sot, holding him up instead as an exemplar of "moral manhood," the complaints and excuses about age turned the old soldier into a figure enriched by the wisdom of experience.[121] "The soldier of long service was all round a better man because a better Christian, than the soldier of the present time."[122] Perhaps more compellingly, "older and more experienced men" knew the dangers of VD transmission.[123] Frederick Roberts even thought that "[I]n former days the better specimens of old soldiers used undoubtedly to exercise a considerable moral and restraining influence on their younger comrades . . . Now, there are but few old privates, and the period a man has to serve in the ranks is so short, that it tends to make him regardless of the consequences."[124] This reinvention of the old soldier as a solid and reliable force rather than a man fleeing creditors or suitors implied that class disadvantages could be overcome by discipline to produce properly manly specimens. But the alternative and parallel discourse about class contradicted its optimism with its insistence on the naturally intemperate habits of working-class men.

The Demon Drink

This contradiction was perhaps most conspicuous in changing attitudes towards alcohol, and its relation to sexual activity. The teetotal man was an anomaly in the hard-drinking world of the colonial expatriate. At the same time, the loosening effects of alcohol, its undoing of inhibitions, opened the gates to disease through indiscriminate fornication. Intemperance, claimed the anti-alcohol lobby, filled the venereal wards.[125] Soldiers drinking local brews lost their ability to discriminate: they could, in their cups, be "successfully solicited by the lowest class of prostitute women, with inevitable result of disease contract (sic)" or even "not know with whom they had cohabited, being under the influence of drink."[126] Few soldiers were capable of "the high moral standard" associated with abstinence, but "when the reasoning powers and recollection are obscured by alcohol," men were particularly vulnerable to the allurements of prostitute women.[127]

Of course, "refined" men could hold their drink while the rough descended into their natural wild state; it was an argument that worked at the class and at the racial level. White settlers were invariably convinced that the "savage" Aboriginal could not hold his drink as well as the white man. Alongside disease and more especially sexually transmissible diseases, it was alcohol that was said to be guaranteeing the extinction of Aboriginal peoples. The native and the working man alike were identifiable by their inability to drink hard and at length without becoming troublesome.

The nineteenth century in Britain, and in settler colonies as well as in North America, was a time of growing hostility to alcohol. Religious, feminist, and welfare campaigners pointed to the physical and spiritual misery liquor strewed in its path, and the temperance pledge became a watchword of serious respectability. The principles of temperance reached military circles quite late, and for much of the century alcohol formed part of a soldier's rations, and hard drinking one of his chief recreations. There were concerns that local liquor lacking the imprimatur of the colonial state or the military command was a riskier product, but no one writing about the nineteenth-century British army, whether overseas or stationed in the metropole, can ignore the centrality of drink to the soldier's life.[128] Ken Hendrickson points out that at the Aldershot garrison in southern England, alcoholic frolics accounted for a substantial proportion of court-martials in the early 1860s.[129] An early nineteenth-century army officer declared that "an old Indian soldier and a great drunkard, are synonymous terms."[130] The proximity of the Hong Kong barracks to areas peopled by Chinese was thought to make soldiers there particularly susceptible. It was a constant complaint that in every colony hawkers sold locally brewed concoctions close to barracks in defiance of ordinances to the contrary. In a dispatch to the governor general in the early 1860s, the India Office urged "the strictest precautions to prevent the soldier from getting access, by surreptitious means, to the more fiery and deleterious spirit to be found in the Native bazars."[131]

Yet alcohol was not simply an index of lawlessness amongst soldiers, since a soldier's pay included money for a daily beer ration.[132] Until 1854, men were entitled to a daily ration of spirits.[133] Attempts to reduce alcoholism in the second half of the nineteenth century returned to the practice of providing men with a ration of liquor to dissuade them from drinking under less controlled conditions.

But even paying the soldier more in monetary wages was problematic. "It is largely because he has so much money which he does not know what to do with, that he indulges so freely in drink and whore-mongering. If you are going to give him an extra 6d. a day, I do not hesitate to say that the increase of pay will find its early correlative in increased syphilis and intoxication."[134] Abolitionists, at least privately, expressed similar sentiments. The "Beer and Beef over fed Tommy" scattered his earnings, and presumably his semen, with abandon around the red-light districts of the colonies.[135]

By the end of the century, as army temperance organizations grew, military authorities considered strategies for "weaning" the men from drink. An 1897 General Order in India spoke of "the influences that have been used to wean [soldiers] from excess," and in a letter to a cleric the commander opted for the same verb, describing means by which "to wean men from debauchery."[136] His predecessor in office also invoked this metaphor, writing to a fellow officer, "[My] object is to wean men from the canteen."[137] Such language served to reinforce the gap between the inferior men of working-class provenance whose drinking and whoring endangered the boundaries of masculinity and of empire, and those able to control their appetites and their finances. Such comments bring together a number of themes: the temptations offered by conditions in colonial settings, working-class lack of restraint, and faulty masculinity indulging to excess traits managed properly by the well-bred. The gravity of soldierly responsibilities, according to Lord Curzon, could not be underestimated. Running through his plea for sobriety was the message that the British must not, under any circumstances, become indistinguishable from those whom they ruled.

> But how can the drunkard set an example . . . ? Where are our boasted civilisation and our superior ethics . . . ? If we are to measure our own responsibility by that of the millions whom we rule, what becomes of our right to rule, and our mission? It is, therefore, officers and soldiers, not for mere grounds of abstract virtue, nor for the sake of the discipline and reputation of the Army, nor for your own individual good alone that I have stood here to plead the cause of Temperance, but because the British name in India is in your hands just as much as it is in mine, and because it rests with you before God and your fellow men to preserve it from sully or reproach.[138]

The cause Curzon espoused centered on an organization founded in 1862 as the Royal Army Temperance Association. By 1893 it had ten colonial branches, five of them in India.[139] Despite viceregal support and the praise of commander in chief White, who spoke in an interview of the "magnificent work" of the organization, colonial membership in 1892–3 stood at a mere 819.[140] Nor were its members invulnerable to temptation; at Cannanore, "good character men and members of the Army Temperance Association constituted the majority of men affected with venereal diseases."[141] Privately even proponents of restraint saw little success in these activities. An Army Health Association (motto: "Keep Thyself Pure") report in 1894 concluded that "the growth of temperance has not been accompanied by the prevention of the growth of disease."[142]

Education

Military education on VD and on the dangers of alcohol consisted largely of lectures on the moral and physical consequences of indulgence. A War Office memorandum issued in 1898 instructed officers to promote "a cleanly and moral tone amongst the men," to punish immorality, and to warn of the effects of excess.[143] The commander in chief urged men to heed advice from experts and from "blameless" men, and doctors pressed for more "sanitary education."[144] Though skeptics dismissed the efficacy of education as "a far-off *utopia* [emphasis in original]," little else was permitted.[145] At Subathu cantonment in the Punjab:

> the Officer Commanding spoke to the men repeatedly on parade about the danger they ran in contracting syphilis, and appealed to their moral sense concerning the obligation they were under not to throw extra work on their comrades, by rendering themselves unfit for duty through venereal disease. He also threatened to place the bazar out of bounds, if his men became diseased through association with the prostitutes living there, and he encouraged his men to put their money in the regimental Savings Bank, instead of squandering it amongst prostitutes.[146]

Such a mix of threats and cajoling are reminiscent of the schoolroom and the chapel, but spoke, too, to the ideals of manly responsibility both towards comrades and in terms of thrift. The contrast between saving and squandering had moral and physical resonances, more especially in an era where spending was a term connoting male ejaculation.

Education had as limited an appeal as the temperance message for most soldiers. The White Cross Society, though "given a free hand . . . does not influence a large number of men."[147] Old soldiers interviewed by Charles Allen remembered missionaries and welfare people, as well as the army itself, handing out literature urging restraint to men embarking on overseas stints. "[T]he troops stuffed it in their pockets and never read it."[148] Abolitionists heard similar stories. Kitchener's regime in the early 1900s encouraged the active distribution of leaflets "pointing out the evils and dangers of impurity." They were not well received. "Many of the men, after receiving theirs, would not even read them but placed them in a bundle on his (sic) bed, & told him (sic) to throw them away."[149]

Indeed not a few soldiers regarded venereal disease as a token of belonging and of experience. A surgeon at the army's main metropolitan hospital at Netley echoed a common medical concern when he remarked that a dose of VD carried "little feeling of shame" for soldiers.[150] An infantry man in the Royal East Kent regiment recalled the occasional distribution of religious tracts and being "marched to church once a week." None of this had an effect, for "with these exceptions everyone followed his own sweet will as far as Military discipline would permit without any moral or spiritual influence whatsoever." He commented moreover that "to be able to boast of a frequent connection with [prostitutes] was considered to be a most manly thing by a great many of the men."[151] Soldiers, in short, had their own code of manliness, not always corresponding to that of their masters.[152] Drawing, ironically, on long-standing images of male behavior, soldiers made whoring and drinking part of their manly code, part of the culture associated with soldiering not as a colonial enterprise per se, but as a working-class male occupation.

The "Dangle" Parade

Army and defense authorities wrestled with the question of genital inspections for soldiers as a result both of these attitudes and of the vociferous criticism of the one-sidedness enshrined in CD enactments. Weekly genital examination of soldiers was abandoned in 1859.[153] The Skey committee appointed in 1864 to consider military and naval VD had considered its reintroduction; Henry Storks, the pioneer of CD legislation in the Ionian islands and at Malta, favored inspection for married as well as single men.[154] The practice unsurprisingly was revived in the colonies far earlier than in Britain. Sailors at the China station were examined prior to taking leave at least from 1869.[155] In August 1876, the quartermaster general in India ordered the examination of registered women and "of every unmarried soldier on the day of his arrival at a new station from the line of march."[156] In 1880, he reminded those in command that the exams were "to be conducted with the utmost decency."[157] There is every likelihood that these orders were implemented only sporadically for in 1887 the quartermaster general issued further orders, and medical reports began, for the first time, to detail military acquiescence.

> It should be a standing rule that all bodies of troops are subjected to special examination on entering a command, or before leaving it; that troops returning to their Cantonments from Divisional Camps should be medically inspected, and that arrangements should be made for the medical examination of details at rest-camps upon the line of Railway.[158]

For a brief period, hospital and medical reports were careful to indicate conformity with the rules, and "frequent venereal parades" became common.[159] At Dum-Dum cantonment in the Bengal presidency, troops underwent inspection every Saturday, and on arrival and departure.[160] But at some point in the following decade, the practice lapsed once more. Following the controversies over regulation and rising VD rates, there were high-level discussions about the efficacy of such methods between the commander in chief and the War Office. Those on the ground in India favored a limited system of inspection but Lord Lansdowne (an ex-viceroy with experience in the CD controversy) at the War

Office was less sanguine. Commander in chief George White and Edwin Collen (late secretary of the military department of the Indian government and military member of the viceroy's council) supported limited inspection, exempting married men, those with no history of VD, and those "two years clear of treatment for it."[161] The War Office rejected any "return to the old system under which all soldiers were periodically inspected without regard to decency, or to the feelings of the men themselves."[162] Repeatedly the sticking point with genital inspections—known by the men as "dangle" or "short arm" parades—was a reluctance to offend or upset the men, a sensibility striking in its contrast to the most frequently expressed opinion of women's attitudes to such exams. For the men of the army the exam was always represented as "painful to their self-respect" and "injurious to morale."[163] Such a practice was "as degrading to the soldier as it was revolting to the inspecting officer."[164] Degrading was a term used over and over to describe these exams, and generally in the context of their tendency to work against "the elevation of character which it is so desirable to encourage among the men."[165]

This issue locked the civil and military authorities into some deeply contradictory thinking about soldiers and masculinity as well about womanliness. Domestic medical practice in the fee-paying sector took for granted that intimate examination would distress the well-born woman while CD legislation assumed prostitute women to have forfeited the privilege of such dismay and to be, in any case, indifferent to discomfort or humiliation. Yet soldiers, so long cast in the image of carousing roustabouts, became in the face of such an ordeal modest and shy, even if in need of moral uplift. The fear that inspections would "develop coarseness and injure modesty" was not quite compatible with the practical fear of concealment which was a key criticism of inspection.[166] Men "conscious of moral rectitude" (a far cry from older representations of the rogue soldier) were surely not the same men as those who, receiving a "warning that they will be inspected ... will find a means of concealing most forms of venereal disease in their earlier stages."[167] Policy makers moved uneasily in the 1890s between seeing their rank and file as modest men of sensitivity and as sly fornicators skilled at hiding their symptoms. Women subject to inspection, meanwhile, were simply vectors to be stopped rather than educable and sensible beings.[168] And yet, as other chapters have shown, deception and cunning as a kind of inverted agency were attributed to indigenous women prostitutes by many an official, a characterization that further destabilized the already slippery representations of the soldiers, sometimes shy, sometimes wily.

Ultimately practical considerations won the day. A General Order in India at the end of 1898 reiterated the existing inspection system still on the books. Married men and those two years clear of treatment were exempted and the recently cured were checked weekly "for so long as may be expedient."[169] The new system spread quickly to encompass all British soldiers stationed overseas, and was everlastingly unpopular.[170]

Punitive Strategies

Stopping the pay of soldiers admitted to hospital with VD was a controversial strategy, so much so that during the passage of the 1870 Army Act, "this question was not allowed to be discussed."[171] Such a punitive course had been briefly used from 1873, and was favored by the government of India and by social purity missionaries.[172] But sympathetic medical officers allegedly subverted the policy by returning new instances of disease as relapses, since these did not affect men's pay.[173] The strategy was debated again in the stormy 1890s in the midst of furious political argument and rising military VD admissions. By 1896, it was under consideration at both the War and India Offices, both of which recognized its role in the concealing of disease.[174] The viceroy and the commander in chief lobbied for pay deductions unless the affected soldier "could prove that the disease was contracted under circumstances not the result of his own immorality," and urging that the principle be applied to the entire British army.[175] The War Office was "strong against it."[176] Nonetheless, when the stoppages were reintroduced, authorities claimed great success. A 1909 report on military VD rather dubiously claimed that loss of pay was "one of the most important factors" in the drop in admissions.[177]

In other areas of disciplinary concern, the authorities did not shy from imposing fines, cancellations of leave, additional and irksome workloads, and even corporal punishment on soldiers. Yet Lord Lansdowne argued in 1897 that, "if the knowledge of the awful condition to which many of their comrades have been brought has had no effect in keeping men from acts of immorality which led to disease of this description, they are not likely to be discouraged by fear of a small daily fine during their detention in hospital."[178] The knowledge that even registered women sought to conceal disease meant that not imposing pay stoppages could have only minimal effect on disease rates. Other less publicly acceptable reasons surely lay behind this decision; the fear of the alternative sexual outlets to which men might have recourse; the determination to maintain, however informally, a system of military prostitution; an acknowledgment of the impossibility of preventing such contacts; and an unwillingness to muzzle this expression of a soldier's heterosexual masculine prowess.

Preventive Strategies

The alternatives posited to punishment devolved largely on attempts to divert men's attention from sex to physical forms of recreation that would sublimate their sexual energies.[179] Boredom was seen as a major catalyst for debauchery, so intensifying the creation of facilities for off-duty amusement. Though an occasional angry officer thought that "the injudicious action of purity associations and would-be reformers" did untold damage "in constantly keeping unclean subjects before the soldier's (sic) minds," official policy centered instead on a public-school ethos of competitive sport.[180] Though the General Order issued for Indian troops in 1898 acknowledged that "mental occupation and reading" met with army approval, and though Frederick Roberts listed gardens and workshops alongside gymnasia in his suggestions for "rational employment and amusement," most recreational policy targeted physical exertion.[181] "Hard exercise and manly games" underlined the ideal physical condition to which soldiers should attain and glorified fitness and muscularity as the male ideal.[182] Moreover the focus on sport assumed that fatigue would act "as a deterrent to sexual indulgence."[183] The inculcation of team spirit alongside physical exertion was intended to uplift men morally and thus not only lure them from the brothels on a purely bodily basis, but replace sexual with "healthier" pursuits.

The prevalence of short service amplified by the class assumptions that working-class men required educating in the principles of proper manhood made this school ethos the more compelling. This version of masculinity rested on the idea of the soldier as young and in need of guidance. Yet it sacrificed none of the key ideas of physical prowess and homosociality; instead it reoriented them in ways familiar to the historian of middle-class mores. The links between manliness and soldiering were too important to be abandoned because of public opinion or activist critique, but they needed to be cast in a framework that could sustain the notions of masculinity to which the politics of colonialism owed so much. The soldier, after all, was the bulwark against a great range of perceived enemies. His loyalty could not, in an age of empire, be risked, and indeed the rhetoric of regulation often hinted jingoistically at the betrayal of those who attacked the CD system. The soldier, reimagined for public consumption as dutiful, brave, manly, and loyal was everything that the "faddy fanatics" were not.[184]

Troop Mobility

Military policy and imperial prowess alike stressed the importance of soldier mobility. Troop visibility was a key strategy, a demonstration of power and strength, and even of numbers.[185] The instructions to Indian native police not to "interfere with European soldiers" visiting the brothels was part of the same structure of power.[186] "Few will hold it advisable to make already irksome and monotonous lives doubly irksome, thus driving men to drink."[187] At one level, soldiers needed protection from the local environment (whether from diseases, dishonest merchants, or plain malcontents), but they were also the most numerically dominant symbol of colonial power and their presence dramatized and manifested that authority in important ways and on a daily basis. It was "quite impossible" to confine soldiers to barracks as a VD preventive.[188] The army did everything it could to avoid confining soldiers. "Every possible measure, short of placing close restrictions on the mens' movements, was taken to prevent the increase of disease."[189]

There was a material relationship between travel and mobility, between power and race.[190] This insistence on soldiers' mobility spoke both to the consolidation of a male public sphere beyond the home, and to its construction as an outdoor and unconfined space. The recreational emphasis on sport and games saw the outdoor as a masculine sphere, a point O'Hanlon presses home as a mark of martial masculinity in an earlier era.[191] Mobility spoke both to the power of the military and to that of masculinity. While laws aimed at the local populace sought consciously to restrict mobility—criminal tribes legislation in India, aboriginal protection laws in Australia, residential zoning in Hong Kong— soldierly mobility was a fundamental declaration of European male freedom.

The Rhetoric of Soldiering

In promoting VD control, military rhetoric focused on a robust and rational common sense, encouraging and promoting a no-nonsense practicality in the effort to reduce VD admissions. If a certain heartiness of tone is sometimes detectable in the literature, its context is a thorough repudiation of emotionalism and sentimental morality in favor of practical problem-solving. In the greater imperial scheme, the antiregulationist party was sacrificing the paramountcy of military efficiency and thus the empire, for the sake of minor principle. It was, then, another twist on the ever-malleable conceptual model of manliness, for while abolitionists argued that state-sanctioned prostitution degraded both clients and vendors, the common-sense rationalism offered masculine logic as the counterweight to emotion. Since nature made men's instincts mostly unstoppable, the practical outcome of abolition would be to make the army vulnerable. Secretary to the Admiralty, Clarence Paget, explained that the policy was "only in the pounds, shillings and pence interest."[192]

In his influential manual of military hygiene, Edmund Parkes acknowledged that preventive treatment for VD might strike some as "an offence against morality," but felt that "we must deal with things as they are."[193] It was a common and long-standing line of defense.

> Nothing is more certain than that the vast majority of young Englishmen have neither the tradition, the sentiment, nor the habit of sexual continence. Those who join the army are subjected to a discipline a great part of which secures the supreme development of a healthy body. They are fed regularly, they are kept in perfect health by sufficient but not undue exercise. They are surrounded by an atmosphere of virile activity that may and often does make them heroes, but that does not make them puritans. For most of them marriage is impossible, and to tell the truth, undesirable. Imagine these men transported to the sensuous East, where virtue and vice, in our northern sense of the words, have no significance. Consider the old habits and the new opportunities, and the result seems to us tragically inevitable.... Overwhelming evidence shows that the English soldier in India pays an appalling penalty for behaving precisely as the vast majority of men under similar conditions would behave."[194]

Those dealing with troops translated these sentiments into practical suggestion. Major General Whitfield at the Hong Kong garrison recommended the government build suitable houses for rent "to the most respectable women of this class."[195] In India, one military surgeon wanted the opportunity to impress upon his men "the comparative respectability and safety of intercourse with a recognised registered agent."[196] In one respect, these suggestions appear radical in the context of nineteenth-century sensibilities, but they reflect more accurately the conservatism which John MacKenzie argues is fundamental to military organization.[197] This seeming ease in talking about sex as "a matter of practical politics" obscured the ways in which such policies upheld ideas of masculinity as the guarantor of empire.[198]

The Officer Class

Rank and file soldiers were the principal focus of concern in the relationship between military discipline and sex, but the role of officers was crucial as purveyors of the "right tone." Statistics of officer VD were seldom maintained, and officers were frequently exempt from compulsory inspection. They were in a far better position to seek private and confidential treatment if affected, one of the numerous privileges accorded their class and rank. Even after the abolition of the purchase of commissions in 1871, the officer corps was at the very least an upper-middle class enclave, and evidence suggests that it may have become more rather than less exclusive after the Cardwell reforms.[199] Since the dominant reading of masculinity lent well-born men a self-discipline allegedly absent in those under their command, there was no need to bother officers with inspections and penalties for VD since the assumption was that they were less liable to contract disease. Officers were neither routinely examined for, nor liable for disciplinary action if infected, unlike the corps.[200]

Nor, when questions were asked in the imperial parliament about the failure to abandon regulated prostitution, were officers ignoring this dictate much disciplined. The government of India took the position that "over-zealous" and "well-meaning" officers were protecting their men, arguing that when officers ignored orders, they were motivated by the best of intentions.[201] There was considerable reluctance to punish disobedient officers, and it was only when members of parliament sympathetic to the abolitionist cause raised the issue at Westminster that anything at all was done. The India Office was questioned in the Commons in September 1893 on its "intention of calling to account the officers" violating the parliamentary will.[202] Nine days later, the secretary of state sent a telegram to his viceroy: "You will doubtless call to account all officers concerned who are proved to have allowed practices inconsistent . . . [and] in contravention of orders."[203] As a result, a number of officers were asked to justify their command. Some made the dubious claim that they simply didn't know there were registered women in residence. Others admitted minor infractions in practice but none saw themselves as seriously out of step with the rules.[204] The government, of course, could not afford to overlook this disobedience entirely, but were reluctant to impose more than nugatory punishments. Anything beyond censure, advised the government of India, would be inappropriate. The Bombay commander in chief made it clear that unless forced to do so, he would not "move any more in this matter." Indeed, he thought officers had been placed in "a somewhat embarrassing position," and had done their best to interpret shoddily composed laws.[205] Faced with this closing of ranks, the government of India rather wearily detailed for parliament who had and had not been censured, insisting that "[A]n expression of our dissatisfaction" was duly conveyed to the guilty.[206] And there the matter rested.

Indigenous Soldiers

Discomfort with officers flaunting the rules, however, was perhaps less irksome than the palpable and constant fact of low VD rates among Indian soldiers. In the aftermath of 1857 native soldiers were envisaged as dirty, savage, and unintelligent. Their low VD rates, however, had to be explained in terms that did not put at risk the alleged superiority of the British soldier. How was a superior western masculinity to be asserted in the face of the seemingly matchless self-discipline of native troops? The contrast was quite striking. At Dum-Dum, 374 European soldiers and 40 Indian soldiers were hospitalized for VD in 1868 and 1869. At Dinapore the numbers were 319 Europeans and 18 Indians, and at Allahabad 396 Europeans and 30 Indians.[207]

All manner of explanations, often contradictory, sought to minimize this powerful divide between an apparently more continent local soldiery and the excesses of their British counterparts. The more positive interpretations stressed that the men did not drink, that they refrained from commercial sex because of caste obligations, were better able to find less risky encounters, were fed a less stimulating diet than their European counterparts, or were older and thus more sedate.[208] The surgeon general and the viceroy both thought Indian soldiers a generally temperate grouping, mellowed by marriage and age.[209] And since many men supported families with their pay, another common argument was that, "he has little margin out of his pay to spend on pleasure."[210] Local men, "except the Rajpoots, keep their wives in the regimental bazaar," and thus did not frequent the public women.[211] The Madras army formally permitted wives to accompany regiments, and in the Bengal army, spouses were authorized to live in the regimental bazaar.[212]

The sense of responsibility sepoys demonstrated in respect of family obligations was dented, however, by the assumption that they avoided brothels only for lack of funds.[213] Driving home the racial distance between sepoys and white soldiers, the commander in chief informed the viceroy in 1889 that "99 out of every 100 of sepoys" were married, and "when with their regiments, keep women, or what they term *lance wives.*"[214] He was thus able in one clever sentence to explain away lower VD rates and still suggest the sexual excesses of native men.

Negative theories explaining the contrast in VD rates between Indian and British soldiers were certainly as familiar as positive ones. Medical officers suspected the sepoys of dishonesty, of malingering, and of counterfeiting disease in order to collect a tidy pension and retire.[215] Some claimed that men chose male-male encounters over visits to women and thus avoided infection.[216] Circumcision as a prophylactic among Muslim troops was a favored explanation.[217] There were claims that men found ways to conceal disease, used local healers, or self-treated.[218] The Dinapore cantonment magistrate thought it "a most remarkable circumstance that there should apparently be so little venereal disease among the native troops." Since he thought them unlikely to be living with their wives, he found the matter even more puzzling.[219]

Inevitably, this drive to justify became enmeshed in martial race theory not new after 1857 but certainly at its zenith. The template for this distinction between the warrior and effeminate "races" of India had been written much earlier, but the administrative and military structure after 1857 encouraged the dominance of race and caste recruitment.[220] After reorganization, the allegedly warriorlike north Indians (Sikhs, Punjabi Muslims, Gurkhas, and Rajputs) comprised 56 percent of enlisted Indians.[221] Martial race theory perpetuated differences between white and black soldiers and between martial and effeminate indigenes. But while some Indian peoples were considered natural fighters, senior military officials strongly doubted they had leadership abilities. In an interview he granted in 1894, in part to skewer a proposal to provide more complete officer training for Indians, the commander in chief praised the native troops as "proud magnificent men, and thoroughly loyal." But on the question of their potential to command, he was adamant: "the native officer lacks initiative to be trusted with anything more than a company."[222] The *Saturday Review* had made much the same argument a few years earlier in relation to the armies raised by Indian rulers in the princely states. They lacked competent leadership and were uneven in quality.[223]

Commander in chief Roberts, one of the most enthusiastic proponents of martial race theory, thought poorly of native troops as a body.[224] Many regarded such troops as childish and simple.[225] The British, claims David Omissi, believed martial Indians to be stupid.[226] Certainly, the policy of recruiting among those without access to much education gave the British more semblance of control over their recruits. Under the provisions of the 1878 Arms Act, Indians but not Europeans or Eurasians were required to pay a license fee for the possession of arms, playing on fears of a popular uprising by well-armed and ferocious peoples.[227] The *Saturday Review* pondered the implications for the colonial state of "the existence of hundreds and thousands of armed and partly disciplined men, not actively friendly."[228] A too effective or a badly disciplined force could spell substantial damage, a powerful reason so many in the senior echelons of the military opposed training Indian leaders and lobbied for the use of colonial troops only as laborers in the 1914–18 war. Garnet Wolseley, one of Britain's most admired late nineteenth-century soldiers, published a damning essay on "The Negro As A Soldier" in 1888, and though his focus was on the African command with which he was most familiar, his dismissive comments are typical of those used against nonwhite soldiers more broadly. While "the savage" lacked intelligence, was riddled with disease, and enjoyed human suffering, the Anglo-Saxon craved "manly sports" that had developed in him a "bodily strength" unmatched by any other nation.[229]

It remained an embarrassment that Indian soldiers displayed such distinctively lower rates of so stigmatized and reviled a clutch of diseases than did whites, for it pointed to the intolerable conclusion that the natives were somehow less "otherly" than the British troops themselves. But all such explanations, as Joseph Alter points out, rested and were reliant upon "a single theory of sexual power: aggressive virility or a lack thereof."[230] The disparity in VD rates, however awkward, could be turned instead into a critique of native women and native customs. The native woman was always close to prostitution, and when VD admissions among the Bengal sepoys rose to 3.98 percent of total admissions in 1878, authorities determined that "the only conclusion to be drawn is that *the disease exists among the married women* [emphasis in original]."[231] This was familiar territory, the common condemnation of colonial women as widely diseased and sexually untrustworthy, of greedy men selling their womenfolk to the highest bidder, and of a general laxity in respect to monogamy and formal marital arrangements. Marriage could not be wholly shrugged off, even where it did not enjoy the benefit of clergy, but at the same time, the oversexedness attributed to the native could also not be overlooked. And in the condemnation of indigenous women was always the implied lack of proper control their men exercised over them. In the British imagination, as we have seen, indigenous male control of women was either nonexistent or overly brutal, never at the right pitch.

Sailors in Port

Sailors shared with soldiers worryingly high rates of VD. Women's admissions to hospital in Rangoon rose "during the shipping season, when there are a large number of sailors in port."[232] At Hong Kong, naval rates of VD were higher even than army rates.[233] Yet far less attention was paid to naval than to army VD other than at the Japanese treaty ports administered by the navy's China Station. Some of this may reflect the growing dominance of the army as nineteenth-century defense policy was linked increasingly to colonialism.[234]

"Jack on shore," according to military surgeons, was even less likely than his army counterpart to attend to questions of hygiene or to act cautiously. On leave, his first two stops were "the liquor shop and afterwards the public brothel."[235] He was, moreover, victim to "very inefficient treatment till he reaches port again."[236]

That the sailor never stayed long in one place may point to the central reason why sailors figured low in practical priorities. Army men stayed in a single place for longer, they were more visible and more permanent, and the effects of VD transmission could thus be more easily connected to their presence. The brief presence of sailors ashore, however riotous, made such connections difficult to maintain. Naval VD was mostly regarded as an internal health problem while the soldierly variety had potential long-term political implications. Sailors could be policed less both in their behaviors on shore, and in their performance of masculinity, because theirs was a temporary and often a fleeting presence, while soldiers stood as symbols of the permanence and solidity of imperial rule by their long-term presence.

Nonmilitary Masculinities

But masculinity was not the sole province of army and navy. Manliness was important with or without a military presence. While competing versions of masculinity were at work in different colonial settings, shared precepts made racial and colonial difference a key element in the envisioning of proper white masculinity. In Queensland, its presence was made manifest in similarly physical activities—conquering the bush and rendering it profitable, training restive natives, surviving rigorous conditions. This racialized imperial masculinity was of substantial significance in Australia, where CD acts, cast initially as military necessities, went into force just as the presence of substantial troops in the Australian colonies was phased out. The last regular British regiment left Australia in 1870 and, according to John Mordike, "defence received scant attention" thereafter.[237] Local forces were not meaningfully developed until the 1880s. Moreover, the Queensland CD Act coincided with the colonial government's complaints about the burden it shouldered in maintaining the naval settlement of Somerset at the top of Cape York for control of the Torres Strait. In this instance, colonial politicians demanded less and not more naval presence.[238] In practice, this was a law aimed primarily at civilians. Parliamentary opponents of the law asked: "Where are our soldiers and sailors in Queensland? Who are the people who needed to be protected here?"[239] There were, of course, none, but there was an act purportedly for their benefit.

Government Men

Figures of civilian authority were required to adopt behaviors appropriate to a ruling class. The senior civil servant was expected to be a gentleman, and the public school and Oxbridge background most typical of this class ensured he was already immersed in a "masculine culture and space."[240] Like other government departments, the Colonial and India Offices ingrained in their staff ideas of continuity and conservatism. Brian Blakeley has shown how alike in background and values senior Colonial Office staffers were, and the cohesiveness this offered was central to the smooth running of both the home and overseas civil establishments, even after the Northcote-Trevelyan reforms of the 1850s.[241] When the first few women were employed as telegraph operators in the British civil service in the 1870s, they were confined to a segregated workroom so as not to disturb the pattern of work in an all-male environment.

Just as officers in the army enjoyed freedom from the tyranny of VD checks, colonial surgeons fought for the related right to maintain confidentiality in their dealings with government servants. Were embarrassing conditions to become public knowledge, men's sense of self, their masculine bearing, would be undermined.

> A Medical Officer is often greatly exercised in his mind as to how to word a Medical Certificate so as to inform the Government of the disease or illness of an official without hurting or wounding the feelings of the latter.... Of course in the vast majority of instances the Medical Certificate is for some slight illness of common occurrence ... and no one cares who sees it or through how many officers or Clerks' and Subordinates' hands it passes. But it may be far otherwise. An official may be found to have something really the matter with him, which he does not care for all the "world and his wife" to know about.[242]

As a result, doctors hid diagnoses of VD among senior British officials behind technical language: "for instance, a man suffering from Bubo is described as suffering from Adenitis which to the average lay mind conveys but little meaning."[243]

The considerations shown to those of gentlemanly stature did not extend to police officers, however. Colonial police were frequently subject to regular VD inspections and were assumed to buy sex from the same women as did soldiers.[244] As in Britain, the police force was largely proletarian, and in the dependent colonies it was common to import men from other colonies for police work. Of the 168 men in Hong Kong's first police force, 46 were Indians, mostly Sikhs.[245] It was this Asian contingent, and not colonial European policemen, who underwent compulsory VD checks.

Working Men

In white settler zones the question of labor and its relation to manliness found its most complicated expression. This was a vexed issue in tropical north Queensland. A region never worked by convict labor, it was the "only tropical community in which whites were numerically dominant."[246] As the acreage under sugar grew, the importation of Pacific Islanders swelled alongside high white immigration to the colony.[247] Gold and minerals, outback farming and plantation-grown fruits, and deep-sea fishing made tropical Queensland a place in which physical hardship and manual labor were inextricably linked, symbols of a harsh male environment. The ratio of men to women only began to even out in the 1890s, as more settled prosperity turned the towns of the north into properly administered municipalities. North Queensland in 1876 numbered about 22,000 men and around 5,600 women.[248] And in the sugar town of Cairns, while half the town's male population was non-European in 1901, only 9 percent of its female population was non-European.[249]

Unlike crown colonies, white and nonwhite men in northern Australia alike engaged in manual labor, though seldom in the same jobs. In the Straits or India, manual work was almost exclusively the domain of nonwhites and a symbol of their lesser status. On the settler frontier the boundary was less clear-cut, for here, labor was the hard-working white man's badge of honesty and devotion. The brotherhood of toil, with its romanticization of an outdoors and physical reading of masculinity, had to exclude the labor of non-white migrants and of Aboriginals. The indentured "coolie" was written off as a mercenary worker. The line between white and "colored" labor in contexts such as Queensland had to be vigorously demarcated in ways that left whites as controllers, directors, and overseers of labor. It was a thinking similar to that which insisted that Indian soldiers required white leadership, since Indians possessed the physical but not the mental capacities for soldiering.

In the Queensland context, work could become either an emblem of honor or of servility. It was the slipperiness between these two potentialities that made the assertion of white masculinity all the more critical. Aboriginals were dismissed, on the one hand, as lazy, though their bush skills and horsemanship were prized by settlers, and many were employed as police trackers in the Native Police force in the colony. This reliance on nonwhite labor—whether in the Queensland canefields or at the Hong Kong docks—was unsettling, but in tropical climates widely regarded in the nineteenth century as unsuitable for white exertion, class, climate, and race meshed in producing a race-specific workforce.[250] Medical and public opinion alike saw tropical climes as unsuitable for permanent white settlement.[251] Climate was as much moral as physiological, and was thought to have a potentially degenerative effect on mind and body.[252] That the tropics enervated the "white constitution" was a constant concern, and made the esteem that attached to the idea of honest work a less than stable construct.

In Australia, collective articulations of masculinity gelled around strong trades unions and the vision of a racially homogenous democracy. Northern Queensland's plantation-style economy was out of step with this vision, and the powerful labor movement looked unfavorably upon its indenture-dominated work practices. The manly worker was a citizen who knew his rights as an employee. Free labor was undermined by indenture, and white racism made white workers reluctant to work with, or in the same jobs as the nonwhite man. "The white man will not work alongside the coloured . . . and thus where coloured labour is employed, ordinary work becomes dishonourable in his eyes."[253]

In Queensland, these differences had direct consequences. Samuel Griffith, elected Queensland premier in 1883, pledged to restrict nonwhite labor in the north. He halted the importation of Melanesian laborers, though in 1892 they were once more permitted to work in the sugar industry, though not for long. Emergent nationalism made white success in the north a pressing concern, as did the restrictions on nonwhite immigration imposed by the White Australia policy of 1901. In the years following federation, medical research "proved" that the exclusion of pathogenic peoples could make the tropics safe for white laborers and settlers.[254] The sugar industry became the focal point for a part-medical, part-political debate over the suitability of white labor in tropical climes. Overlaying the environmental question that taxed public health officials were sensitive issues of status. What sort of white workers would want to undertake jobs long associated with "inferior" races? How would the transition from unfree to free labor be managed in a plantation context? Complicating this tropical conundrum was the related fear of "racial degeneration in the torrid zone."[255] What would it mean for much-vaunted white superiority if white workers were found to be *unable* to withstand the strenuous work in the field done for so many years by "lesser" peoples? That question would dominate tropical medicine in Australia in the early years of the twentieth century, for white work in the tropics was vital once the system of indentured labor was abandoned.[256] White failure in this situation would destabilize ideals of masculinity as tough, strong, and able to endure, and on white masculinity as the best and definitive version of maleness.

Rogue Males

This whitening of Australia, in making the tropics safe, necessarily prompted a rethinking of the parameters of masculinity. The disfranchisement of Aboriginals effected in 1902 made material their distance from citizenship, one of the more concrete concerns of western masculinity. The strength of organized labor and the celebration of white western democracy produced in the Australian context a strongly articulated masculinity visible in physical strength, fraternal loyalty, and political canniness. With Aboriginals and Asians pushed to the unenfranchised margins, the failed white—explained in eugenic vocabulary in terms of racial degeneracy—became the target of disapproval less in imperial and more in national terms, and as a commentary on the contours of proper white masculinity. The poor white, the vagrant, the unemployed, and the diseased were threats not to the empire but to the nation in its incarnation as product of masculine effort. As Raymond Evans has argued, the "mateship" so characteristic of Australian culture was not extended to such men, for admission to the fraternity was restricted to those who were "originally strong and capable . . . There could be no workable mateship with a madman or incapacitated cripple."[257] In like manner, it was poor men who were mostly prosecuted for transgressing state laws around mixed-race coupling and not those who, in other respects, fitted the definitions of proper masculinity the new nation demanded.[258]

Disreputable white men became targets of disapproval for their betrayal of propriety. The unfit white man was frequently represented as a man associated with the sex trade. The pimp and the procurer were the antithesis of manliness in their alleged exploitation of women and in their association with a female and unrespectable trade. The male brothel keeper was proof of unmanliness, a virtual slave master, treating his women workers as commodities, forcing them to work even when sick, and undermining the effective operation of CD legislation: "even diseased women are forced to carry on their trade, or they would be beaten or turned out to starve."[259] Women keepers were, with a cruel logic, seen as defeminized; the men were unmanned. Their rejection of the chivalry towards women that was a basic building block of ideas of masculinity (despite the vigorous and unceasing brothel trade) marked them as depraved. The pimp, a stock figure of what was commonly called viciousness, was counterposed, alongside the vagrant and the pervert, against "healthy masculinity."[260] The revival of flogging in the early twentieth century was designed, as Angus McLaren has argued, to discipline those whose misdemeanors implied their failure "to live up to newly created standards of masculinity."[261]

Robert Fitt, a Queensland man, was convicted of keeping a brothel and sentenced to twelve months' imprisonment with hard labor. Mr. Justice Lilley was satisfied that Fitt "had not the excuse—if indeed it were any at all, which he could not admit—of being a man without means of earning a living. He . . . could have earned an honest livelihood; but he preferred to keep and harbour women leading the most abandoned life women could live."[262] When Fitt petitioned for release in early 1878, the police report noted that he "ill-treated his wife."[263] Fitt was again brought to court in 1892, this time on vagrancy charges, and the sergeant's report claimed that he had known Fitt for seventeen years, "during which time . . . he has never known him earn an honest shilling."[264] The association of prostitution and vagrancy underscored the refusal to countenance prostitution as work. In the white settler context, Fitt epitomized the man gone astray; unwilling to work an honest job, a wife beater and general maltreater of women, and profiting from their sexual labors. His vagrant status connected class and masculinity in creating a vision of the proper man.

In the crown colonies, different representations dominated. In a statement prepared for the government of India on trafficking in 1902, the Bombay administration named twelve male suspects: Lieble Rabichovsky, Jacob Hirsch, Misha Pohakoff, Lazar Aronson, George Coplemaniz, Fraim Greenberg, Peter Jacobson, Yacob Bileas, Isaac Silberman, Lazar Finkelstein, Maisha Valeniteh, and Ivan Nakardyapollo. Unlike other reports, this one did not need to point out the obvious—and doubtless satisfying—fact that these were not Englishmen, but European Jews. The Jewishness of pimps was not routinely left as a hint or a suggestion; it was a central fact that separated the pimp from the Englishman, and thus from the proper manly man. In nineteenth-century Britain, Jews were characterized as "not man enough to be rough," their lack of organized criminality a bizarre form of demasculinization.[265] The Jew's existence highlighted the unambiguous virtues of English manhood. According to the Calcutta police commissioner, the problem was Jews reared in brothels—a female environment.[266] The pimps in Lahore district were largely "Russian Jews," a type dubbed with considerable distaste as "the Jew procurer" by S. M. Edwardes.[267]

The church, too, indulged in anti-Semitic stereotyping. The bishop of Calcutta was sure that "the men engaged in this traffic are Jews who have no status or lawful occupation."[268] The Calcutta Missionary Conference likewise thought it was "mostly German and Roumanian Jews" who dealt in women.[269] Jewish men from eastern Europe certainly were involved in the global sex trade at this time, and for the same reasons that European Jewish women worked in prostitution. In general, they worked with Jewish women rather than across national or race boundaries, and sometimes husband and wife teams turned procuring into a family enterprise.[270] In a climate of prevailing anti-Semitism, it was inevitable that their presence would be logged so decisively: "a Jewish pimp was a political as well as a social fact."[271]

Even when Jews were not highlighted as the heart of the trade, there was always an insistence on pimping and procuring as definitively un-English. Foreign traffickers were "the riff raff of Europe."[272] Such men are "almost without exception, of foreign nationality, and their occupation is repugnant to men of English race."[273] In an Edwardian pamphlet full of stories of girls lured into the business, those responsible for the women's downfall were invariably depicted as foreigners. More often than not the tales related involved young English women whisked abroad and European girls stranded in London by unscrupulous foreign men.[274] Jews, foreigners, and natives were represented as pimps and procurers content to live cruelly off the degraded labor of women.

Beliefs that asserted British paramountcy and clung to a vision of respectable but hearty manliness (and indeed gentlemanliness) as its most vital component were central tenets of British imperialism. The foreigner whose lifestyle or religion set him apart from that system of beliefs was a danger to Britain's rightful hold on empire. The foreigner was not just foreign, but in his non-Englishness demonstrated traits proving his unfitness to rule. They "spend their day in carousals, which they interrupt only to visit their victims in order to extort their gains from prostitution."[275] Drunk, lacking proper employment, and supported by women, the presence of foreign men made a mockery of manliness, and this was in many respects their most singular crime.

In many instances they broke no laws, to the frustration of their enemies. Even when they crossed the line of legitimacy, pimping was a notoriously difficult area in which to prosecute and successful convictions were rare.[276] Deportations were rare (though this may indicate that the traffic was greatly exaggerated by scaremongers) and sentences were generally light. Thirty men were deported from Bombay for procuring in 1903, twenty in 1904, two in 1905, and twenty-nine in 1909.[277]

Homosexuality

Same-sex activity among men was perhaps the most threatening of all unmanly practices, a danger to family, nation, and empire. Homosexuality was castigated as unnatural and unmanly, resulting in physical manifestations of depravity. It was a useful tool for emphasizing colonial unmanliness and distance from a comprehension of proper manhood. The India secretary told his viceroy, Lord Curzon, in 1901 that he was not at all surprised to learn that "so considerable a proportion of the Chiefs of India are addicted to unnatural vices."[278] "The great preponderance of males" added to the "Eastern" propensity for "vice" made the Straits Settlements "especially prone to . . . nameless horrors."[279] Same-sex activity among men became a means to censure a whole range of social and cultural conventions from the veiling of women to the perversity of hot climates.[280]

The existence of male prostitution was authoritative proof of the unwholesomeness of the colonized world. In Ceylon's capital, Colombo, "on any night there may be seen in public places a number of boys from 14 to 18 years of age . . . waiting to be spoken to."[281] Similar "evil" beset India.[282] Norman Chevers knew of "at least a hundred houses of ill-fame, registered and taxed, which are tenanted by *Men* only," as well as of a thriving "Up-country" business in "unnatural prostitution regularly carried on by Eunuchs."[283] At the China Station, and especially at Hong Kong, "they are addicted" to male prostitution.[284] Same-sex activity was both an unnatural crime and something associated with less evolved peoples.

Yet supporters of regulated prostitution had argued that without access to prostitution in colonial environments, men's natural urges were such that they would choose sex with one another over celibacy. It was a historical "fact" that "the vice of homo-sexualism has invariably made its appearance among collections of male human beings deprived of access to women."[285] William Pickering, protector of Chinese in the Straits during the CD years, thought regulated prostitution a vital defense against homosexuality where there was a large male population of laborers.[286] Lai Ah Eng argues that a similar fear motivated Raffles' unwillingness to ban prostitution in Singapore's early days.[287] Would, asked a Straits committee in 1899, plantation laborers denied access to women turn to "worse, because unnatural, forms of vice?"[288] A "strictly confidential" memorandum to commanding officers throughout British India in 1904 warned that "there is little doubt that in some natures if feelings are completely suppressed they may become perverted in the direction of more serious vice."[289] Hotter climates loosened the moral fibers of civilization. When a homosexual scandal broke out in London in 1889, involving several prominent young men, one of Lord Curzon's friends marveled that "[T]hese things are almost incredible in a country where men are not corked up like soldiers in a camp."[290]

Same-sex practices were, like VD, a contagion, though even harder to regulate. George Hamilton was ready to acknowledge "unnatural vices" in lesser cultures, but he feared the consequences of their spread. "If a taint of this kind once gets in amongst young men and boys, it is almost impossible to eradicate it."[291] Though the commonest dismissal of same-sex activity was its unnaturalness, the argument that without opportunities for heterosexual connection men would turn to homosexual connection rested on a masculinity expressed directly through the sex drive.

The argument that men's sexual urges were part of what made them properly masculine opened up a space for nonheterosexual behaviors as an expression of male sexuality per se. Thus, alongside the common association of natives and male-male couplings, there was a strong strand of reasoning that abandoning regulated prostitution would result in mayhem. "The absence of prostitutes in cantonments where large numbers of young unmarried soldiers are living would probably lead to such offences as criminal assaults, rape and unnatural crime."[292] Within months, probability apparently became fact. Elgin's military advisers were, in 1894, logging "an increase in unnatural crimes."[293] Two years later, Elgin still believed "there is only too much reason to believe that there is . . . an increase in the number of unnatural offences."[294]

The homosociality so central to imperialism blurred the situation further. The British empire was an "intensely homosocial but also intensely homophobic culture."[295] As Eve Sedgwick notes, the boundary between a "man's man" and being physically interested in another man is always a tenuous one.[296] The practice of colonial masculinity often involved men seeking sex in groups, speaking of and boasting about sex to their peers, and representing sexual conquest as a metaphor for political conquest. It would be surprising, given the centrality of sexual imagery and talk in so male an environment, if there were not some degree of blurring between homosociality and homoeroticism.[297]

Conclusion

Masculinity, then, for all its invocations of strength, determination, toughness, and independence was at its center a fragile thing, part of "the fantasized fiction of imperialism as masculine triumph over feminized colony."[298] Masculinity, the non-fictional version, was prey to disease and environment, to class and to race, to women, and indeed to the "wrong" sort of men.[299] The theme of protection so central to the rhetoric of CD enactments applied as much to the idea of masculinity that constantly required policing and protection. The soldier abroad was "assailed" by moral dangers.[300] His protection was "absolutely necessary to maintain our army in an efficient condition."[301] Officials and other carriers of the imperial flag were troubled by mental stress and potential breakdown brought on by tropical conditions; their vulnerability was their proof of civilization, for neurasthenia was a white condition.[302] But it was far more than soldiers and administrators who needed protection. At stake was imperial power, whether from "pestering" women, unnatural sexual relations, miscegenation, or the inability of whites to achieve dominance over tropical landscapes.[303] Just as protective CD ordinances saved "the young and foolish," the protection of manliness from the instability of its own construct was a vital concern of empire.[304] The instigation of protectorates was certainly about the policing of aberrant masculinity—the protection of "proper" masculinity, in effect—as much as it was about protecting allegedly helpless women. Joseph Bristow has argued that "imperialism staked . . . a high claim on a specific kind of masculinity to perpetuate its aims." He also points out that this version of manliness was found more frequently in story books about colonial heroism than on the ground.[305] The unstable and slippery nature of constructs of masculinity were made more, not less, uncertain by the empire where pride in strength, the celebration of a heterosexually inflected homosociality, and new racialized modes of gendered exclusivity prevailed. If the colonial experience was meant to be the testing ground for the real man, cut off from domestic influence in all its meanings, it was also the place in which such politics were mapped and remapped not by the vicissitudes of climate or of local culture so much as by imperialism's own insistence on a hierarchy of authority that left no room for sexual fluidity.

What we see in these multiple and contradictory imaginings, of course, is discourse in action, and highly motivated and situated discourse at that. The maintenance of an idea of masculinity that could sustain colonial rule required impossible explanation, generating contradiction after contradiction. The sexual urges apportioned men had to be somehow divided between the cruel and lustful variety associated with the native man and that of the British. Yet the commonest descriptions of soldiers, even after their public recuperation, drew them as unruly, undisciplined, childish, unschooled, and excessive, a series of traits akin to those associated with indigenous men. Soldiers were simultaneously defenders of British liberty *and* libertines. Faced with genital inspections, however, they enacted a modesty more readily associated with women. And those inspections were only a crucial instrument of civilizing medical authority when applied to women or soldiers. Officers, naturally chivalrous by virtue of their class position, nonetheless needed shielding from the possibility that the rank and file might learn of their superiors' struggles with VD. And when regular soldiers shielded prostitute women from the glare of the system, theirs was but a parody of the model of civilized relations between the sexes, and not the real thing. Meanwhile, indigenous men were children but they were oversexed; they were brave but they were never loyal. And native women, depicted as likely diseased and thus always dangerous, were nonetheless a factor in the lower venereal rates displayed by nonwhite soldiers. All these categories then were fissured. Most striking is the reasoning, favored by men from a variety of backgrounds and positions, that male "nature," left to run its "natural" course would – presumably naturally—turn to unnatural acts.

Eve Sedgwick makes the point that the word *homosexual* entered the language at a time when "power relations between the genders and the relations of nationalism and imperialism . . . were in highly visible crisis."[306] While these discourses are evidence of political anxiety, they are also devices of enablement, making possible and shoring up the very issues that Sedgwick identifies as in crisis. Nationalism, colonialism, the separation of the spheres were all ideas (and indeed materialities) that were hotly contested and differently understood by varied constituencies. However slippery, however ambiguous, the discourses outlined here, even in their contradictoriness, worked to fix, to maintain, and to contain such ideas. The constructedness of that which imperial culture posed as natural is readily apparent in these representations. And when, in 1919, the influential Australian doctor Richard Arthur wrote of venereal disease as threatening the "very future of Australia as a virile, white nation," it is the ties that bind race, sexuality, and the medico-moral apportioning of masculinity and femininity that are so vividly crystallized in his statement.[307]

Chapter II

Space and Place: The Marketplace of Colonial Sex

> The Suddar Bazaar was on the right of the main road leading to Agra. Opposite the centre of it, on the left of the road, and standing on its own, was the Protestant Church. It was possible on a Sunday evening to stand in the road outside the church and hear, on one side, the parson with his monotonous clerical voice preaching about the spiritual joys of life, and on the other side, the shrill and equally monotonous cries of the girls in the brothel advertising its material joys.
>
> —Frank Richards

Many of the fears circulating around the colonial sex trade were nebulous, resting on always evanescent attempts at definition, whether of race or civilization, of gender, or of propriety. There were, though, palpable material concerns, and one such key set of worries centered on spatial and geographical questions. Where prostitution might take place and how visible and public it could and should be became tremendously important issues. The location of brothels, where prostitutes could live and work, and who needed protection from these sites posed a considerable challenge. In an era of regulation, this attention to spatial detail was more than incidental, for if the prostitute was to be examined and interrogated, she had also to be placed as much in literal as in metaphorical ways within the colonial landscape.

The Idea of Home

This attention to the geographical highlighted the critical distinction, itself spatial, between home and colony. Ideas of Englishness and Britishness were spatially rooted in a long-standing myth of English soil as beneficently abundant but never overly fecund, of the English lifestyle as "clean, orderly, methodical."[1] English space was the polar opposite of colonial spaces, which were invariably too crowded, hopelessly messy, loud, and unordered. The image of a chaotic east and a well-regulated harmonious Britain was a potent one. White settlers anxious to recreate British landscape and scenery abroad took for granted the inferiority of what they found when they left home. For colonizers, there were ordered spaces—Britain and places resembling it—and those requiring ordering, the native spaces.

The notion of home was a complex one, and always political. Home's most potent meaning in the nineteenth century was familial, celebrating the private sphere, the nurturing gentle hearth of private life removed from the bustle of public office and business. For those who went abroad, however, home invited comparison with the alien features of foreign soil, a contrast with familiarity and belonging. Home typifying security and warmth acquired new meanings beyond the private and public sphere. "To the European inhabitants, this familiar, rational, self-contained environment contrasted with the unhealthy, mysterious, possibly dangerous, teeming indigenous city."[2] Domesticating colonial space was an ideal that could never be realized, but which had to be constantly sought.[3]

Sexual commerce upset western boundaries of public and private. Prostitutes, contemptuously dubbed "public women" for their apparent disregard of such borders, were the conduit via which infection and disease invaded the safe space of home. That it was women, the traditional guardians of home, who violated the boundaries only exacerbated the problem. Women's work in the sex trade disrupted a whole range of cultural mappings: the distinction between home and work, between business and pleasure, between femininity and malleability, between public and private. Both the colonial experience and prostitution profoundly disrupted the mental and physical maps of Victorian and Edwardian Britain, for while public and private were inevitably blurred spheres even in the metropolis and palpably did not reflect the lives of many men and women, the need in colonial settings to rigidify and intensify such sentiments and boundaries—and the contradictions that invariably surrounded them—offers a window into the tensions that always beset colonial control.

Gender and Space

Feminist geographers and cultural critics have rightly insisted that spatial questions are fundamentally gendered. The "links between the gendered body and the national landscape" are central to the assumptions Englishmen and women made about the zenanas of the east or the contours of the Asian bazaar.[4] "In the discourse of the British colonial enterprise, gender, always itself a racialized category, is inseparable from geography."[5] The British claimed that the gendered segregation of women in purdah was oppressive, but nonetheless stoutly defended the "strict segregation" along racial lines typical of colonial patterns of residence and settlement.[6]

Simon Ryan has pointed out that, as in so many other arenas, modern states have assumed a universal and shared definition of what space is, and how it should be used.[7] In colonial contexts, this universalizing tendency was used to justify expropriation of land, as in Australia, or its reallocation, common throughout the colonies, with dramatic consequences for local populations. But this application of an allegedly common understanding of space also affected women's mobility and freedom. The geography of colonial relations had long-lasting impact on the lives of women engaged in prostitution, as well as on the structures of the colonial marketplace of sex. In drawing up a geopolitical map of colonial sexuality through such instruments as the sexual census—spatially plotted and drawing on the idea of sexuality as rooted in nature—colonial administrators mapped the contours of colonial prostitution within a geography that logged culture, religion, and class as well as obviously spatial considerations such as place of birth.

Landscape and Colonization

Space, and the need to order it, were of constant concern in colonial settings where "crooked natures" inhabited "crooked lanes."[8] Unordered space was potentially dangerous, suggesting contagion and dissent. Military order was of prominent concern, and military encampments of various kinds became emblems of both order and of the potential failure of order. Though some cantonments were established in the vicinity of large towns, others actually served to create new towns as locals flocked to provide the services and businesses demanded by a standing army.

> A cantonment consists of an area varying from 10 to 15 miles square, with European troops varying from 2,000 to 5,000 and with a native population of from 20,000 to 50,0000 or more, devoted exclusively to trading with or labouring for the troops and supplying their necessities. It is highly migratory in its habits; no member of it has a settled home in the cantonment, or intends to remain there; and it is probably not composed of an especially orderly or moral class. Males preponderate in the proportion of 15 men to 10 women. . . . It is obvious that order in such a community could be maintained only by somewhat drastic measures. The case has been met by investing the Cantonment Magistrate with despotic powers.[9]

Community and order were natural partners, rejecting the non-European setting as improperly constituted. Eastern spaces were disorderly in their layout and their buildings, in their lack of attention to safe sanitation, and in their morals. "[T]he barracks in Hong Kong form practically part of the city of Victoria [modern day Hong Kong island], and . . . men need only overstep that line to find themselves in a locality devoid of restraint."[10] Restraint and respectability signified the properly constructed location, military or civil, where the private did not spill into the public, where commerce did not mingle indiscriminately with residence, and even the streets boasted an orderliness utterly lacking in the east. Jean and John Comaroff, analyzing missionary narratives in nineteenth-century Africa, note an identical tendency to contrast the "uncouth" lands where missionaries traveled with "the small-scale tidiness, the nice demarcations, of the British model of spatial order."[11]

Sex in the Streets

The conduct of the sex trade was a vital component in assessing the orderliness of a location, for the presence or congregation of soliciting women always and everywhere connoted a threat to public order. The situation was made more complex by the tensions between the more open and the less visible forms of the trade. Streetwalking was emblematic of prostitution, with its rude intrusion into public spaces, its refusal to hide business behind closed doors. Typical portrayals of the prostitute woman invoked the streetwalker, although she represented only a small portion of a mostly less visible industry. Consistently regarded as the most offensive segment of the sex trade, streetwalkers were frequently the chief target of police action. "Street prostitution is ... totally corruptive of public decency."[12] Colonial doctors argued that streetwalking increased VD rates.

> ... the women left their residences in the Bazar and took to practising their trade in the vicinity of the Barracks, on the public roads, and often in empty bungalows. ... Control became almost impossible and admissions into Hospital immediately increased. The women's conduct became so offensive that several respectable inhabitants complained to the Police Inspector, who treating the matter as a public nuisance, caused the Magistrate to issue a prohibitory order on them, and thus relegated them to their recognized residencies, bringing them under supervision again, the natural result being their attendance at Hospital as usual.[13]

But while the streetwalker was always a problem, in the colonies the chief mischief-maker was the clandestine prostitute, working outside the registered brothel. She operated in secret, rejecting registration and the brothel, preferring open-air solicitation of custom. The British streetwalker was *too* public, but the "clandestine" was insufficiently so. She used the public sphere as a backdrop to conceal and to keep private her unregistered and therefore illegal activities. The link between public prostitution, loss of control, and rampant disease were located in a tidy geographical space in which the brothel, still an offense to propriety, was nonetheless more easily controlled than outdoor prostitution.

The Brothel

Almost everywhere, the brothel and indoor commerce dominated the sex trade. Colonial conditions certainly restructured the trade in sex, but the brothel often predated British rule.[14] It was when the British introduced Victorian notions of the public and the private to the colonies, however, that the brothel became an object of state scrutiny. Brothels had to be removed when they surfaced in the wrong location—near "good" areas, schools, and colleges, or in busy thoroughfares and expensive residential areas. Brothels had to be restricted to certain locales. They did not properly belong in the public eye for the business they conducted was of a private nature. Scores of commentators expressed distaste at Asian disregard for these proprieties. Hong Kong policeman, Kenneth Andrew, remembered the Wanchai brothels as "very public" because the women sat "in full view of the passers-by in the street outside."[15]

The Wesleyan mission in India took great exception to conditions in the Lucknow cantonment, prompting the quartermaster general to demand "a full and complete" report from the commanding officer.[16] The Wesleyan superintendent charged that the "finest thoroughfares" in the cantonment bazaar were given over to the temptations of the flesh. "Houses on both sides of the road have been rented and modified to meet the needs of this class. The women are allowed to expose their persons, and call to men persistently from the courtyard of their houses, and soliciting on the public thoroughfare is common."[17] The cantonment magistrate thought the problem mitigated by the fact that "the locality is not one that is usually occupied by persons of the better classes." Women's confinement to less desirable neighborhoods lessened the offense. Though the magistrate would have preferred that "these women . . . be moved to some less public locality," they were better off out of sight of the people who mattered most, the cantonment's respectable European residents.[18]

In northern Queensland the local police praised the Japanese brothels in Cairns because, "a stranger coming to town would have to seek them before he would find them . . . they are not prominent to public view."[19] But in Childers, further south, the brothels were too close to a school and to "private and business houses."[20] In Singapore, "the red light districts served as a 'natural' form of boundary maintenance," with the regulated brothels limited to the less salubrious districts.[21] In keeping with his hierarchically racial assessment of India's urban sex trade, E. C. S. Shuttleworth praised Calcutta's European brothels for their "well hid" location in the suburbs, while casting scorn on the "rampant" indigenous practice of "advertisement by sitting at doors and windows and balconies and . . . both by voice and gestures."[22] The too-public locale of the native woman was mirrored by her unwomanly loudness and her shameless touting of her wares; she appreciated neither the feminine space of domesticity nor the feminine virtues of modesty and soft-spokenness.

Mistresses and Kept Women

The mistress who served only one client, known in Hong Kong as a "protected" woman, was not classified as a common prostitute, degraded by servicing multiple customers.[23] In Bombay, the Commissioner of Police was instructed "not to interfere with or attempt to register women in the position of mistresses of wealthy persons, or kept women."[24] Neither politicians nor the military would risk alienating the wealthy, whatever their race or nationality. It was not merely because the kept woman was frequently the consort of richer men that she enjoyed certain privileges, but that her arrangements guaranteed a level of privacy which the brothel, and certainly the street, could never emulate; what set mistresses apart from the women of the brothels and of the streets was that they were hidden from the public gaze, despite the blasphemous parody of marriage in their sexual arrangements. Richard Symanski notes that in British law the distinction made between legal prostitution and illegal soliciting encodes "a difference between social status and behavior, between those who do and do not have easy access to private spaces."[25] Spatial privilege organized sexual commerce in ways which colonial officials appreciated. The rules of the 1864 Cantonment Act were "only applicable to *public* prostitutes. There are prostitutes to whom the term 'public' is hardly appropriate" [emphasis in original].[26] The distinction between the woman paid by one man and the woman reliant on multiple and impersonal partnerings to earn a living was carefully preserved.

The reality in the colonies was that a mistress was likely to fulfill housekeeping and domestic as well as sexual duties, although in Hong Kong the protected woman seems likelier to have been set up in a separate household, and significantly in a neighborhood on Hong Kong Island "neither exclusively European nor exclusively Chinese."[27] As a woman not quite abandoned but not quite respectable, a district known to be racially mixed was an obvious location, an apparently "natural" pairing of an ambiguous geography and an ambivalent status. Nonetheless the enduring notion of a mistress as a woman kept in luxury and idleness helped maintain a distinction between her and the prostitute.

Mixing Business and Pleasure

While the mistress could, however unrealistically, be represented as living domestically, the brothel occupied more ambivalent territory. It was, after all, fundamentally a site of male leisure and female labor. Women came to the brothels to earn a living, while for men they were a source of sex and female company. But the brothel crossed many more boundaries too. They were, of course, seldom purpose-built; to speak of a brothel is to describe activities and not a space. Arguments about location and suitability are a posteriori positions related to moral tenets, and do not derive from any inherent spatial "fact". Most brothels were converted residential buildings and therefore close to family dwellings. This discomfiting proximity of the brothel to the home sparked lively debate over siting.[28] While such arguments were never a colonial monopoly, they were amplified in such settings, because the key and oppositional western sites of home and workplace, of private and public, had little prior historical meaning. Since the home was so central a mark of Victorian tranquility, its transformation into a site so antithetical to domestic gentility was jarring. Home and work were not to be mixed in ideal Victorian settings and nor could marital procreational and paid recreational sex. The brothel—looking like a home, acting like a business—was at the heart of the debate.

The failure to observe the proper boundaries and proprieties of domesticity and work, the indiscriminate mixing of the two with its deleterious sanitary effects, evidenced the moral failure of subject peoples. The constant British complaints in south and southeast Asia about overcrowding and lack of sanitation in the cities and in the villages, and the filth that was seen as endemic to the Aboriginal camps of Queensland, spoke to this same sentiment. In colonies all over the empire, public health regulations in the late nineteenth and early twentieth centuries defined the proper home and its functions, separating animals and humans, thinning out the numbers considered appropriate per house in the name of hygiene.[29] In Hong Kong, for example, the Order and Cleanliness Ordinance of 1866 forbade the unlicensed keeping of animals in dwelling-places.

It was an indiscriminate mixing of the spheres that was always the most harmful. In Hong Kong's brothels, even the kitchen had literally permeated the bedroom, to the horror of the inspecting surgeon. "I've a pretty good stomach and don't stick at trifles, but I found the inspection of these places acted as a very unpleasant emetic. The girls' rooms, near the kitchen, nearly all had ventilating openings into the kitchen."[30] In Singapore, the contiguity of commerce and residence was under fire by the late nineteenth century, the verandah the principal site of conflict between residents and the municipal authority. In India, too, "extension platforms and verandahs in front of shops" were seen as unsavory examples of the Asian mixing of private and public spaces.[31] In tropical arenas, the verandah was both a place of business opportunity and a space for socializing, the two less categorically separated than in the west. This improper mixing and mingling confounded the spatial mappings desired by colonial authorities. "[A]ll life is lived in public. Here a barber clips his customers. Next door, a couple are getting married. Further on, a woman is having a baby. . . . When it is a question of satisfying an entirely private necessity, the person concerned leaves his house and plants himself politely at the corner, just where the throng is thickest."[32]

Brothels, of course, were sites where business and pleasure were critically linked as the best means to profitability. Attempts to keep the women from doorway and verandah soliciting were constant. In Rangoon in British Burma, policing policies pushed brothel residents literally indoors. "European and Japanese prostitutes are now kept behind swing doors quite hidden from the users of the streets."[33] The verandah lost the battle in this instance. More noteworthy, perhaps, is that it was white and "almost" white women who the Burmese authorities here sought to control and to hide away, a group whose presence in public was clearly more troubling.

Typically the brothel served as both home and workplace for women, for brothels were actual places of residence, and not just houses distorted to "improper" use. In progressive-era North America, when a wave of antiprostitution sentiment swept the country, municipalities restricted where prostitutes could live as well as where they could conduct their business, a policy that survives in regulated systems even today. Similar geographies were at work in the colonies. The four Indian Cantonment Acts of the 1890s directly affected where women could live. Those suspected of harboring disease and refusing genital examination could be expelled from cantonments; they could neither live nor work within an area defined by the cantonment magistrate. Since the prostitute had both defiled and desanitized the home by turning it into a brothel, she could be ejected summarily from the comforts deserved by and reserved for those who respected proper boundaries. The 1897 Aborigines Protection Act similarly allowed Queensland officials to monitor both the workplace and residence of Aboriginal women, specifically as a check against immorality.

Female Spaces

The west had its own versions of sexual segregation in the linking of domesticity and femininity, but the brothel fit neatly into neither the western nor the eastern forms. The brothel was a paradox definitive of colonial immorality. "A brothel is not a brothel as in Europe, where girls live as one family, but in this country prostitution is considered of so little importance that chaste women and prostitutes reside in separate rooms adjoining each other in the same house and are even on intimate terms."[34] Of course, similar patterns of residence were easily discernible in western cities, where the greater toleration by the poor of prostitutes in their midst was an index of weak moral standards among the proletariat.[35] Yet these comments are nonetheless revealing. European women living in brothels apparently acknowledged the importance of family and thus sought to re-create the brothel as home by living as a family. For their colonial counterparts, work and home were not distinct, and nor were the divisions between the respectable and the outcast. White prostitutes withdrew into familial and private arrangements but colonized women, unversed in these delicate sensibilities, lived their lives unencumbered by such considerations and unmoved by propriety.

It was not only in the promiscuous entanglement of home and work that the brothel symbolized disorder. The brothel was also a strange distortion of the idea of a women's space, a geography that fascinated and repelled colonists. Despite the zenana's association with elite groups, like the brothel it spoke to the idea of a secret and sexually mysterious east.[36] Invariably eroticized in western culture, the links between the zenana and the brothel go deeper than merely the whiff of a hitherto untasted sexuality.[37] It was in India more than in our other three colonies that the practice of purdah was commonest. It was practiced mostly among the wealthy in the north, northwest, and east.[38] These were also areas with a significant British military presence, and therefore, too, a substantial prostitute population, setting the stage for comparison between these two versions of female space.

Zenana inhabitants and brothel residents alike were regarded as idle women, corrupted by their distance from useful and fulfilling occupations.[39] Women in the brothels were palpably earning a living, and often a hard one at that, but their activities could not be admitted as work without tarnishing work as a source of virtue and moral uplift.[40] The brothel—where male leisure rather than its necessary counterpart, female labor, was the dominant personification—evoked the twin evils of sex and idleness, and of course their connectedness. Idleness, lack of employment, doing nothing were, in metropolitan terms, evidence of degeneration and immorality. Inderpal Grewal has argued that the zenana offered the British a useful means of representing the distinction between British industriousness and Asian laziness, an invariably eroticized torpor.[41] The stigma attached to unemployment in Britain translated in the east into a pathology where the zenana and the brothel—though at opposite ends of the spectrum of respectability—evidenced a host of improper attitudes. Colonial systems of hygiene "privileged openness, visibility, ventilation, boundaries, and a particular spatial differentiation of activities."[42] One of the most constant criticisms of the zenana was that it was sunless and airless.[43] The brothel similarly was a place of the night, where sunshine and the wholesomeness of fresh air did not belong and could not penetrate. Life in the brothel was lived at night when the respectable slept, disrupting the normative diurnal rhythms. Airlessness in the vocabulary of Victorian health was synonymous with insalubrity, uncleanliness, and, of course, contagion. These were insanitary and pathogenic environments, "a gendered space of confinement and infection."[44] Such attitudes have been slow to die; in 1968, Paul Scott could write comfortably in the second novel of his *Raj Quartet* of the *burkha*-wearing woman as a "walking symbol of inefficient civic refuse collection," her dress an "unhygienic head-to-toe covering."[45] Separate women's spaces defied both proper hygiene *and* respect for the diurnal distinctions that regulated good behavior and separated work and leisure, home and workplace, good and bad habits.[46] The zenana's threat to colonial rule lay in its impenetrability, a place uncolonized.[47] Designated unmodern, colonial efforts at entering it were often justified on sanitary grounds.[48]

Sanitation and Regulation

Sanitation was another way that the brothel was brought under control and made visible. Ironically, the brothel was one of the few colonial sites inhabited by locals where an active sanitation program was attempted. Mostly the pressing health and sanitation problems faced by indigenes were secondary to the needs of European residents.[49]

The brothel acted in its liminality as a *cordon sanitaire* dividing the clean and the dirty. As a quasipublic institution, it could be regulated and sanitized without disturbing the basic divide between public and private. Medical and military authorities cleansed and ordered the brothel, even while deploring its existence. In parts of British India, the authorities built or considered building brothels over which supervision could be better exercised.[50] "In Japanese towns brothels are confined to particular localities which are strictly defined and surrounded by high fences or deep canals, for the purpose of enabling order to be the more stringently enforced."[51] In Hong Kong, the most noxious of the brothels were closed by state order in the early 1870s, as likely breeding grounds in a typhoid outbreak. The consequences were grounds for optimism. Inspecting the regulated establishments in 1874, the colonial surgeon found "a wonderful change has been effected; the houses look clean, light and airy for the most part."[52] Unlike the typical quarters of the east, these brothels were conforming to western standards of cleanliness, making them acceptable even while their business undercut basic notions of hygiene and of decency.

The Indian Cantonment Act of 1864 allowed the local magistracy "to make special rules for the maintenance in a state of cleanliness of all houses occupied by registered prostitutes within the limits of the cantonment, and for the provision therein of a sufficient supply of water and of proper means of ablution."[53] "In every room in the brothels," at Fyzabad, "a permanent brickwork stand has been erected, the height of a man's hips, and on this stand the basin is kept ever ready with water. Soap is always present, and a towel is kept on a nail close by."[54] In the Patna district, provision had been made by the 1870s for water to be available in the bedrooms of the brothels.[55]

Even after formal regulation of prostitution ended, sanitary arrangements continued to be deemed legitimate. Indeed, the commander in chief encouraged "the provision of suitable ablutionary arrangements in the quarters of all professional prostitutes . . . without a system of enforced registration."[56] A nod in the direction of hygiene became one of the chief means by which the control of the brothel, as of other local and disorderly spaces, could be undertaken.

Marking Sexual Spaces

Colonial officials experimented with various methods for identifying the brothel, versions of the familiar symbol of the red light as well as a form of control. In Hong Kong and the Straits Settlements, brothel workers were issued tickets that served as an identity card. By the late nineteenth century these tickets included the woman's photograph.[57] The ticket system was seen as a check against brothel slavery and was almost everywhere part of a broader system of literal visibility that required photographs to be kept on file, and women's names to be displayed on the walls of the brothel where they worked. The military command in India considered adopting a practice used by the occupying British troops in Egypt in 1882, marking the houses of diseased women with a warning sign.[58] In some cantonments, women's rooms bore their registration numbers for purposes of identification.[59]

But these forms of control seemed destined to fail in the unmodern spaces, crowded and complicated, of the east. "In garrisons in India and the Colonies . . . the sanitary control of crowded bazaar populations is difficult and complicated."[60] The built environment of the east symbolized and manifested all that was wrong with colonial subjects. "Hidden from the British gaze, the bazaar-dwellers spread disease and deceit, elude justice and practice secret arts."[61] Left invisible, colonials would undermine the principles and practices of empire.

It was vital for colonial rule that British and native spaces be distinct, and that respectable and dangerous environments be clearly separated, just as it was necessary to distinguish among prostitute women. This spatial segregation, the cordoning-off of ordered spaces from those requiring order, ensured the pristine nature of the former. The sights and sounds of the native city had consciously to be ignored, and white spaces had to be fervently maintained.[62] By-laws in the 1890s restricted Indians not engaged on porterage from the hill station malls at certain times. Hard as they tried to re-create an English landscape in these towns, it was only topography that "made the Indian inhabitants of the hill stations 'invisible' by dint of their lower elevation."[63] Aboriginal camps in remote areas of Australia effected similar removal from sight of offending populations. An increasing number invariably drifted into the territory of white domesticity. In Hong Kong and in Singapore, cities limited by the vagaries of the terrain, there were clear areas of white and of nonwhite settlement—the latter also often racially distinctive with separate Japanese, Chinese, and Indian areas.

Entitlement to residence had far-reaching consequences for women in prostitution. Their association with disease and loose morals made them constant targets. They could be expelled or required to submit to all manner of regulation in the name of good order and health. Prior to the formal regulation of the sex trade, military authorities in particular had championed their right to expel "bad characters" from regimental proximity.[64] During the CD years, police and medical authorities dictated, though seldom successfully, where the trade was allowable. The chief secretary of Bengal argued that to dictate women's residence "would be a measure quite foreign to the national practice in Great Britain," and that it might stir up local discontent.[65] Yet in cantonments restrictions were commonplace. At Bareilly, for example, "prostitutes are not allowed to reside in cantonments except in one specified portion of the sudder bazaar, where little or no inconvenience is likely to be caused to the general residents."[66]

After regulation was banned, the physical constraints on women's mobility were, if anything, exacerbated as colonial governments experimented with alternative controls on VD. Wide-ranging new powers of expulsion from Indian cantonments, promulgated primarily to replace the lost powers of full-scale regulation, significantly affected women from the 1890s. And in an unusual inversion of these restrictions, the new federal government of Australia considered legislation that would allow only licensed whites to live in certain parts of the Northern Territory, a policy catalyzed by the spread of VD among Aboriginal peoples.[67]

The *Cordon Sanitaire*

Feminists condemned the red-light district as "an abatoir of virtue" but many saw such areas as what English sanitarian Edwin Chadwick called "the architectural barriers of decency," better under supervision than left in a potentially infective state which might ooze out of the indecent and into the decent.[68] The *cordon sanitaire* protecting the white population from dread disease was a central guiding principle. Though the racial architectures used to erect the boundary differed according to colony, the principles of isolating the orderly from the disorderly, the clean from the dirty, held steady. The *lal* bazaars and red-light districts needed to be close to the quarters of their customers for convenience, but not too close, and certainly not located in European-populated neighborhoods. In the Straits, the Penang Advisory Board warned that the lack of a recognized brothel quarter would jeopardize respectable neighborhoods.[69] As the commanding officer at Cawnpore argued, giving registered women their own place in the bazaar would "bring them under better control than can be exercised . . . when they live scattered about the bazars."[70]

Prostitution belonged in the native space by virtue of being neither western nor modern. But as a woman's space that defiled femininity, it had to be relegated to the physical world of commerce. Its segregation from residential districts was not only to sharpen the distinction of respectable and unrespectable, but to separate the *business* of sex from the place of feminine domesticity.

> Those who voluntarily adopt prostitution as their trade cannot reasonably complain if they are placed under greater restrictions and disabilities than persons engaged in respectable occupations, and fortunately for our soldiers, black as well as white, and indeed for those who are obliged to live in military stations, the discipline necessarily maintained in them renders it comparatively easy for the authorities to keep the disorderly classes who elect to reside in cantonments under control. In the present Bill [the new Cantonment Act of 1890, then under consideration and passed late in 1889] power is taken to ensure the greatest possible amount of decorum in the conduct of prostitutes.[71]

Prostitutes were cast here as women exercising choice and free will, choosing disorder and danger as their lifestyle. Unlike the victim status often accorded the Chinese prostitute, George White saw her Indian counterpart as a free agent, a trader in the bazaar, whose occupation should be subject to the same restrictions as other trades deemed noxious or dangerous. It was the bazaar or native space, a masculine space, which was the core of disorder, and within that space the distortion of proper female behavior was inevitable.

The Indian context—the most markedly military of our colonies—operated rather differently from elsewhere, especially in cantonments. Not surprisingly, therefore, in practice the authorities offered women a barter: access to the bazaar (and thus a soldier clientele) in exchange for an agreement to undergo regular genital examination. The exchange, a precursive echo of the exchange of sex for money, was largely unaffected by the abolition of formal compulsion. Under the Cantonment Acts of the 1890s, the prospect of expulsion on suspicion of disease worked much as the compulsory examination had done in tethering women to supervision regardless of legal compulsion.

Sex in the City

Prostitution was often seen as more difficult to control in the anonymous space of the city. The new Australian federal government, considering means to combat venereal diseases in the early twentieth century, mapped disease statistics directly onto the city. "Venereal diseases are town diseases. Great towns suffer more than small towns, and small towns more than country districts."[72] It was a commonplace opinion that reflected the widespread idea of the city as a place of danger, both physically and morally. Sexual diseases were, of course, a perfect symbolic means for demonstrating how the physical and the moral might damagingly mesh. The city was a place of density and anonymity, a place of assignation and secrecy, and though the Australian government's assessment of venereal disease's urbanity necessarily ignored the shape of the Queensland VD debate, it squared well with colonial fears of the native city as a place of debauchery and strangeness.

The failure of the Australians to see the inutility of this position in regard to Queensland conditions stems, however, from similar ideas. The idea of the city as a more dangerous environment inevitably focused the Queensland spotlight on Brisbane as the largest city in the state, in both the colonial and subsequent period. Brisbane's sex trade was always represented as different in kind from that in the state's more northerly regions. Prostitutes in Brisbane were seen, even if inaccurately, largely as white women while those elsewhere were almost always seen to be Japanese or Aboriginal, always *outside* the framework of what had come to be counted as Australian. And since the overriding assumption was that venereal and other diseases were in any case killing off the Aboriginal population, the problem could be separated out racially and coordinated geographically.

Obviously in nonsettler locations, the opposite was seemingly the case, that the alleged problems of indigenous prostitution and disease were paramount in the minds of administrators. But as we have seen over and over, that was true only insofar as it was crucial to protect the European population from the dangers wrought by prostitution and disease. In Hong Kong, the colony was synonymous with the city, and as a small landmass, the other urban questions— of overcrowding and sanitation—melded sometimes imperceptibly into general complaints about the unsavory conditions of an urban Chinese population. Though such straightforward synonymity was not as obvious in the Straits outside Singapore, certainly the legislative practices in the city itself were seen as part and parcel of the broader problem of making hygienic the districts of nonwhite settlement. Even elsewhere in the Straits, the emphasis tended to be on the larger towns and their brothel culture, where uncoincidentally, the local administrators and colonial medical staff were also to be found. The city, then, in these contexts occupied much the same prominence as Australian administrators awarded it in a more aggressively "modern" arena.

In India, the major cities were densely packed before the arrival of the British, and urban culture was perhaps less directly affected by colonial rule than was rural India, or towns contiguous to the British cantonments. The growth of the cantonments confused the picture, for these were towns in their own right, in which thriving trade and business grew, and populations gathered. While one old India hand described cantonments rather idealistically as "pockets of orderliness and tidiness," William Lee-Warner, as experienced an Anglo-Indian politician as one might find, thought "the cantonment is not a part of the district which is separated from other parts of the district by a Chinese wall. It is a mere arbitrary division."[73] David Arnold, from today's perspective, sees the deliberate location of cantonments outside the main towns as a policy designed to facilitate their "segregated or enclavist nature."[74] Either way, it was impossible to draw wholly successful divisions between ordered and chaotic spaces. The quartermaster general pointed out in 1875 that "a mixed jurisdiction where civil and military native populations are in juxtaposition renders the rules inoperative."[75]

Nowhere was this failure more apparent than in the working of the Indian CD Act of 1868. Police and medical officers despaired as women moved outside city limits to avoid registration, as they did in Britain's scheduled districts. Everywhere the law was in force, women who could do so moved to places unaffected by the law, and plied their trade in increasingly mobile ways, to the despair of law enforcement and medical officials. The government of India and provincial governments alike were queasy about increasing the areas under control, unwilling to push too hard on the good will of the local population, and uncomfortable about the increasing departure from principles of individual liberty. In any case, extending the boundaries of the registration system resulted only in a leapfrogging pattern, which had the effect of removing women from tight supervision. Pushed to the edges of the cantonment or into adjoining villages and towns, women were lost to the supervisory intent of the laws.

> Rules of this kind in Military Cantonments will . . . be almost inoperative unless they are extended to the country beyond Cantonments, to at least as great a distance as a soldier is likely to walk for the purpose of meeting a prostitute; and if the Cantonments are put under Regulation, while the bazars and country round them remain unregulated, the consequence will be that the prostitutes will leave Cantonments and live outside.[76]

The failures of the laws revealed how porous the boundaries of white and native habitation were, despite the state and the military's efforts. The governor general explained to the India secretary that:

> [C]antonments . . . are, in many cases, in point of area and population, virtually large cities, and the attempts to exclude these women would involve an altogether uncalled for amount of interference with their private life, and would moreover have the effect of compelling them to reside on the confines of cantonments, where the most ordinary sanitary precautions such as are compulsory on all residents of cantonments could not be enforced, and where soldiers visiting the women would be less within the reach of military discipline.[77]

Women frequently chose to settle in less coercively managed environments. In Brisbane "a stampede of women of doubtful reputation" out of the city followed the introduction of registration.[78]

The partial—and it had been no more than partial—administration of the act in the city of Brisbane had the effect of driving infected females who were afraid to go up for inspection in Brisbane into the neighbouring country towns, and thus spreading the disease. Doctors in Toowoomba [said] . . . there had been cases directly traceable to either women who were registered in Brisbane and had cleared out, or to women who had come from Sydney, and who, on finding they had to register in Brisbane, had gone to Toowoomba or Warwick."[79]

The Sydney authorities resented the alleged influx of diseased women moving south to evade registration and plying their trade, instead, in the New South Wales capital. Though in 1878, Sydney's inspector general of police could list for Parliament only eighteen such women logged by his officers, he thought nonetheless, "there may be many more" from Queensland.[80] The myth of a disturbing plenitude, more commonly associated with the teeming east, nonetheless exerted a certain dread power when prostitute women were its subject.

The theme of diseased women removing themselves from government scrutiny was a familiar grievance throughout the empire. Hong Kong and Straits officials complained about unregistered brothels. In India and Australia, it was the new technology of transport which helped women undermine the regulatory system—by hopping on a train. In the late 1880s, the Bombay surgeon general called for the extension of the Indian CD Act beyond Bombay's limits to the suburb of Bandra. "Cheap railway fares exist between these two places, and . . . women on finding themselves diseased, resort to this suburb to evade the Police, coming into Bombay at night by the trains."[81] This defiant trick was evidently much used; almost twenty years earlier, the same complaint was made in India's northwest, where women avoided registration in Cawnpore, "when . . . to avoid interference [they] retired temporarily to other places, for which they have every facility by the East Indian and Oudh railways."[82]

Women could be secreted to the margins but there they would be harder to control. Brought to a more central location, they would be more visible but, as a result and more valuably, they would also be more malleable. Brothel districts, a reality in most large cities and not just in the colonies, were simultaneously safe and unsafe. They were safe because they were recognized and thus under some restraints; but they were unsafe not only because they were peopled with "bad characters" but because they represented the prospect, the imminence, of unbridled transgression, a place simultaneously both public *and* secretive.

Racial Tensions

The classification of brothels into first, second, and even third class categories effected another sort of segregation, ensuring that the same women did not service both local and European men. Racial mixing in the sex industry was regarded as a potent force for violence. Commander in chief, George White, thought an inattention to segregation would "be most injurious to the peace of any cantonment . . . British soldiers naturally prefer establishments where they will not meet native men. . . . Were the two races of men to meet at the same house, there would be constant breaches of the peace, destruction of property, and probably ill-treatment of the women."[83] Racial resentments did indeed flare in the brothels. Fighting was reported during World War One "between coloured men, the crew of an overseas boat and the prostitutes" in a Brisbane brothel."[84] At Secunderbad, the cantonment magistrate regarded "any . . . interference by the Native Police with European soldiers as 'unadvisable.'"[85] Social purity activist, John Cowen, thought wartime Singapore the most virulently intolerant of the British colonies.

> Nowhere is race hatred more bitter than in the brothel quarters, and in no brothel quarters more than those of Singapore. Here English, German (before the war), Dutch, Mahomedan, Ceylonese and others, jostle each other in the streets and rival one another in the brothels. Soldiers or sailors, and other Englishmen, educated or uneducated, who enter a brothel and find "niggers" there, at once proceed to turn them out. The Dutch visitors from Java and Sumatra do the same, even more peremptorily, and the Germans are always said to have been the most provocative of all. The "niggers" may be educated Malay or Indians youths, who feel themselves superior to the drunken English soldier or sailor, but give way if the latter are in force . . . racial animosity is bred and fostered day by day and night by night in the brothels.[86]

The message is clear: that the physical and sexual separation of the races in brothels was imperative, and that the dangers posed by the brothel were broad in scope, encompassing not just disease, infection, and immorality but the potential for more immediate bodily harm. That the women offering their services were of a variety of races was, it seemed, a lesser issue. Good order, hygiene, and peacability were achieved by separating male customers, potentially violent, into racially specific spaces and by directing prostitute women into racially distinct service.

Violence could take more unusual forms too. In the mid-1890s, sixteen men and five women from the Bombay Mission organized a spate of Midnight Missions, very loosely derived from those in London's theater district that offered women night time shelter. If in exchange they were obliged to sit through a sermon or to hear out a proselytizer, this was no more than many other recipients of Christian charity endured in exchange for food, shelter, or clothing. The Bombay version, however, offered little in the way of respite and succor to the women, and instead seemed designed to provoke violence. Gathering in front of the brothels on Cursetji Sukhlaji Street in the heart of Bombay's red-light district, the missionaries "parade themselves at either end of [the street] from 9 p.m. to past midnight, accosting all (chiefly Europeans) men who enter the street either walking or driving, on the assumption that they do so with the intention of visiting a brothel."[87] This aggressive intervention was not appreciated by the workers or by their customers. The outsiders were verbally and, on occasion, physically abused. Customers made carnal suggestions to women missionaries, provoking fighting. Though loathe to interfere, the police feared a serious eruption of violence.

This radical and vaudevillian protest—which, the police implied, owed something to the presence of American missionaries—had no lasting effect on the siting or presence of brothels, but it highlights the bodily and spatial issues at stake here. The missionaries defiantly and deliberately violated the public and private divide. Their strident and confrontational activity revealed a fundamental corruption; that privacy cloaked the decidedly secular exchange of money for an act revered as the sacrosanct moment of marital union not in deference to Christian sentiment, but to protect the purchaser's identity. Driving home their point, the Midnight Missionaries augmented their deliberately obnoxious and vulgar presence at the brothel gates by disclosing the identity of white customers, publishing "the names of certain Europeans who some time ago visited the street" alongside "plain hints . . . regarding other gentlemen."[88] Small wonder the police feared some greater dispute.

The Principle of Isolation

Many of the questions about where to site brothels were equally pertinent in establishing lock hospital facilities. Should these offensive if vital institutions be visible or invisible? Should they be located in convenient central places or pushed to isolated spots in keeping with the intent to isolate their inmates? Could they share accommodation with nonvenereal medical cases? In these ways the political geographies governing lock hospital policy were similar to those focused on the brothel. There were, of course, diverse opinions, often reflecting what administrators hoped the hospitals might accomplish. In Britain and Australia, their intent was reformatory as well as medical; much pious ink was spilled on the religious and moral work carried on within their walls. Elsewhere, consonant with the assumptions that rescue was a less urgent or necessary claim on the state's resources, lock hospitals functioned exclusively as medical centers treating VD. But the lock hospital—a vital cog in the machinery of regulation—was fundamentally a place of segregation and isolation, an inpatient treatment center that in cordoning off from the community those deemed dangerous, held out the promise of hygiene and safety. Danger lay not only in infective status, however, but in gender and in race. Women in both Britain and the colonies were mostly treated on an inpatient basis, while male patients were typically handled primarily as outpatients, despite the grueling nature of VD treatment. In the colonies, outpatient dispensaries treated most of the nonprostitute patients who sought western remedies. Prostitutes, considered a graver public health problem, were admitted to the locks as a matter of course. Prostitute women were regarded as needing the additional discipline of a hospital regimen alongside medical treatment.

The champions of philanthropic regimes saw isolated sites as more appropriate to the hospital's mission of removing women permanently from harmful and unhealthy surroundings. The medical lobby thought venereal hospitals, as shameful establishments, should remain hidden from public view. At Cannanore, the lock hospital was "objectionably situated in proximity to the main road, and the patients are exposed to the observations of the passers-by."[89] Such a concern for the patients was perhaps less common than the fear that prostitutes tainted their environs.

In reality, practical and moral considerations competed in situating lock hospitals. No medical imperatives demanded the isolation of venereal patients. In many areas the pull of an isolationist policy was strong, invoking in literal ways the creation of the *cordon sanitaire*. Dorre and Bernier Islands, off the western Australian coast, became venereal reserves for the isolation of Aboriginal venereal disease sufferers sent under duress between 1908 and 1919, when the hospitals were returned to the mainland.[90] The Queensland protectors were hopeful that Queensland would follow suit, establishing a hospital on Fitzroy Island.[91] This isolationist philosophy was also prominent where VD sufferers were non-European, a means to ensure that disease did not move into the white population easily. Though it shared an element of compulsion with other policies, the isolationist approach depended fundamentally on the assumed ability to dominate a subject population in direct and profound ways. Under such laws, as in most CD legislation, refusal to cooperate constituted a punishable offense.[92]

There was no consistent policy across or even within colonies. In India, doctors recognized that without the constant and close contact that hospitalized patients demanded with their kin, they would eschew western treatments. When a new lock hospital was planned in Toungoo in British Burma, one surgeon thought it made sense to build it "in the vicinity of the houses of ill-fame."[93] The old lock hospital was "badly situated . . . at the extreme end of the Native town, and at a considerable distance from any other public building, such as the jail or dispensary, or police station, and . . . therefore free from any and all supervision." Escapes were frequent.[94] Visibility was a critical component, for an inappropriately located lock hospital arguably facilitated escape.

Venereal hospitals were not, though, an acceptable part of the routine medical establishment. Colonel Little in Burma thought it inappropriate for lock hospitals to be merely wards within general hospitals, "on grounds of propriety, morality and discipline." The lock had to be "a separate institution, in a retired position."[95] Lock hospital patients were to be invisible. Ferozepore in the Punjab set aside a prostitute's wing in the native cantonment hospital, after legislation forbade the older compulsory lock system. The doctors boasted that the inmates had "no access to the main building, and are not ever seen by the other patients."[96] Locks were commonly located close to lunatic or leper asylums, or jails. The Penang lock was on the grounds of what had been the local insane asylum, sandwiched between the hospital and the jail. The new lock built in Brisbane in 1900 was on the gaol reserve, also used by the Department of Insanity.[97] Frequently associated with other contagious or fearsome complaints, locks were also coupled to criminality, and relegated to a spot conveniently near the local lock-up.

Architecture, space, and living arrangements took on a moral cast. When Aboriginals rejected the prospect of confinement, and Indian women demanded the right to have their kin visit them at the lock hospital, the western critique of an improper indigenous understanding of how public and private *ought* to operate was never far away. If the system failed, it was not because the system was flawed, but that it ran afoul of the unmodern and unhealthy habits and practices of the locals, resistant to the health and tidiness of segregation, unmoved by filth, and ignorant of the separation of the public and the private. While mobility and freedom were basic entitlements for the wealthy, they augured criminality in the poor. The denizens of the red-light district thus found themselves restricted not just by poverty but by occupation in where they could work, reside, or otherwise even be present. The *cordon sanitaire* protecting the white, the wealthy, and the respectable was an ever-present constraint on indigenous mobility.

Policies of Containment

Prostitution was widely regarded as out of hand when evidence of its workings became visible outside the de facto zones in which it was legalized or tolerated. In Hong Kong, complaints reached the authorities in the late 1870s about a brothel on Wellington Street, a location "necessarily passed through by European ladies ... [and which] contains moreover the chief place of worship of a large Roman Catholic community, the residence of the Roman Catholic bishop and a College for the education of youth." The CD exam rooms were situated opposite a French convent.[98] Reports of a "very serious scandal" in Rangoon in the 1890s were prompted by brothels brazenly opening "in respectable parts of the Town."[99] And in northern Queensland, the Cairns Town Clerk worried that "these women occupy places in our public and important thoroughfares."[100]

As a result, measures to contain the women and the brothels were common. Formal and informal directives about place of residence were employed. The chief secretary of Bengal, arguing that to dictate women's residence "would be a measure quite foreign to the national practices in Great Britain," also worried that such a measure would stir up local discontent.[101] Yet restrictions were still commonplace. At Bareilly in India, for example, "prostitutes are not allowed to reside in cantonments except in one specified portion of the sudder bazaar, where little or no inconvenience is likely to be caused to the general resident."[102] Controlling brothels, their placement, and their inmates was a necessary corollary to ensuring European safety and peace of mind. The right of Europeans to live unharmed and untainted was overriding, and as a result, it was "common" women whose rights and movements had to be restricted. While there were areas and streets Europeans chose not to use, subject populations and especially unrespectable women were governed by far more formal and coercive restrictions.

After the mid-1890s, the Indian cantonments came under scrutiny as abolitionists monitored the army's obedience to the parliamentary will, and as officials on the ground experimented with alternative policies of VD and brothel control. Section 10 of the newly amended Cantonment Act of 1895 (Act V, which replaced Act XIII of 1890) forbade the residence of known prostitutes in the regimental bazaar, a policy that often resulted in women being evicted from their homes. Lord Lansdowne had insisted in 1893 that "it is absolutely necessary unless further inroads are to be made upon the health of our army, to maintain some supervision over women of this class, and to retain the power of expelling them from cantonments when they are known to be diseased and refuse to submit to treatment in hospital."[103] Despite the political fall out from the CD system, that supervision was retained. The Secunderabad surgeon reported in 1901 that seven women who had refused examination upon suspicion of disease had been expelled from the cantonment under Section 203 of the Cantonment Code.[104] Kitchener, when commander in chief, urged "a rigid adherence to the rules" including "expulsion from the cantonment of such as will not be treated."[105] The military attended, too, to who entered the cantonment; a 1907 report boasted that a decrease in VD rates had been effected in part by a "strict *policing of cantonments* to prevent the ingress of undesirable women [emphasis in original]."[106] When the cantonment laws were amended yet again in 1909, section 215 of the Cantonment Code allowed for the removal of disorderly persons while section 214 made loitering for the purpose of prostitution an offense punishable by up to eight days in jail or a substantial fine of fifty rupees.[107] These rules had a tremendous effect on women's ability to earn a living, and on where they might reside.

India's military context made for a very visible form of containment, but even where formal laws did not restrict prostitute mobility, it was invariably native women whose freedom was expendable. As late as the Second World War, Aboriginal women mixing with African-American troops stationed in Australia's far north were removed forcibly from their homes to curb such associations.[108] Though the policy was a failure, and such evacuations were not repeated, the willingness of state and military authorities to relocate marginal women is striking.

Less dramatic and more piecemeal policies were continually on the table for discussion. In India proposals that the huts of women laborers not be allowed near barracks, and that the women leave the military vicinity before sundown, materially affected women's working conditions and comfort.[109] Nighttime curfews were a favorite way to restrict the sex trade. At Nowshera in the Punjab, the prostitutes' walled enclosure was locked nightly at 10 o'clock.[110] Hong Kong's colonial surgeon proposed passes for registered women allowing them "to be out in certain parts of the town at certain hours of the evening."[111]

Practical restraints on women's physical liberty were often accompanied by a seemingly unironic concern for broader notions of liberty as a governing principle. Even while promulgating rules about where women might go and when, colonial officials worried, in the case of Chinese women, that the Protectorate might have "failed to make these women realize that they are 'free.'"[112] The surveillance exercised by the colonial authorities was represented as the best means to ensure the liberty of the subject. In practice women were constantly the subject of either prohibition or of permission for their choice of residence, their movements in their own country, and around the towns in which they lived and worked. In 1888, women prostitutes in Wellington cantonment in south India were "cleared out."[113] In Quetta, in the Bombay presidency, the prostitutes' quarters were peremptorily closed late in 1895.[114] In Poona, healthy women were permitted to remain in certain specific houses, a practice that found favor with many medical and military officers reluctant to abandon all supervision.[115] In such cases, women could choose to surrender mobility in exchange for the opportunity to maintain both residence and livelihood, a stark choice for poor Indian women, akin to the migrations that brought Japanese and Chinese women desperate to earn a living to brothels all over Asia in the wake of famine.[116]

In 1876, a case in the High Court at Calcutta put to the test the rights of the colonial authorities to control the movements of local women and men. In April 1875, Rughbur Singh was seized by regimental police while visiting the house of Mussamut Doolaro, a registered prostitute, "who was one of those specially meant to be visited by the British soldier only, and not by Natives," in the Patna cantonment of Dinapore.[117] After a scuffle in which Singh managed temporarily to evade his captors, he was arrested and convicted for obstructing his lawful apprehension for a punishable offense. He successfully appealed his sentence of two months' rigorous imprisonment before the Patna Sessions Judge, but had meanwhile escaped from custody again, and was re-arrested at Doolaro's residence. Re-tried, he was sentenced to a lengthy ten month confinement, while Doolaro received a two month sentence for harboring him. Singh appealed again. The case reached the High Court in December 1875. The bench ruled that "Singh was in the first instance arrested and confined absolutely without warrant of law," and that he had committed no offense.[118] The ruling, which freed both Singh and Doolaro, resulted in a flurry of legal opinions intended to clarify what rules commanding officers might enforce in cantonments. In September 1876, the quartermaster general notified commanding officers of their right to issue prohibitory notices with respect to cantonment land, and of their right to exclude natives "from places where soldiers live, provided that such exclusion be for the welfare of the soldiers."[119]

Ironically, the Singh case strengthened the hand of military commanders in supervising the residence and lives of prostitutes working in military districts. The right to reside in the cantonment was duly linked to the agreement to be registered as a prostitute and thus to abide by cantonment regulations that frequently included the agreement not to entertain local men as Doolaro had done, though there is no evidence that her visit from Singh was sexual in nature or intent. Zealous officers sometimes sought to extend these powers by introducing a system for tracking women as they moved from district to district in search of new customers. The Cawnpore magistrate recommended in 1870 that for every registered woman "a very detailed descriptive roll [be] made out and whenever she moves from one town to another, a copy of this roll should be sent after her."[120] Too cumbersome to be adopted, the suggestion nonetheless demonstrated that colonial officials had no hesitation in organizing surveillance of local peoples. What was at stake here was the use of boundaries and the rights to mobility.

While rank and file soldiers experienced restrictions consonant with military discipline, the army, as we have seen, shied away from circumscribing the troops, principally for strategic reasons.

> The Commander-in-Chief, whilst most desirous of supporting measures having for their object the prevention and treatment of the disease, does not wish to restrict the troops to the limits of cantonments. He holds it to be of importance that the native population should be accustomed to the unrestricted circulation of British soldiers in towns and other places. The country generally and the towns of India cannot, in his opinion, be closed against our soldiers, whose familiarity with the neighbourhood of cantonments in which they reside is an important advantage in case of disturbance.[121]

Limiting native movement was preferable, and while restrictions were stepped up during crises such as outbreaks of epidemic disease, even in ordinary times local peoples were far likelier to find their mobility restricted than were colonists. At least as early as the 1830s, when Lord Bentinck tried to bring the practice of *thuggee* under colonial control, Indians experienced such limitations. Elsewhere—whether as a result of the work of protectorates or of openly racial residential and other forms of physical segregation—such restrictions were no less irksome. Women on whom suspicion of prostitution fell were, not surprisingly, among the most restricted.

The Geography of Race and Class

Control of prostitution depended on control of women's movements, as well as their place of residence, and the mode in which they conducted their work. Just as the case against Rughbur Singh, found in the *chakla* at Dinapore, had focused on who had rights to be where, the question of women's ability to move freely and practice prostitution was of urgent interest to colonial authorities, civil and military. While, on occasion, this boundary-checking had its humorous moments—as when a woman "believed to have been a source of much mischief, was found in the lines, living in a rum-barrel" in Muttra cantonment—mostly it devolved into attempts at strict residential and social segregation in the classification of brothels as European or native.[122]

An 1880 commission described "the social gulf which to the present day practically separates all classes of Chinese in Hong Kong from the corresponding classes of foreign residents, a gulf which remains unbridged by mutual sullen consent."[123] This social gulf was a geographical as much as a social fact, resulting in urban overcrowding for the poor.[124] Inevitably, this class geography was mapped onto prostitution. European women in colonial cities could establish houses in "better" neighborhoods and charge higher sums for their sexual services, while women willing to register in cantonments were often recipients of government-provided facilities, accepting restrictions on their freedom in exchange. In Singapore, the police tended not to interfere with brothels in richer areas, and their wealthier clients could choose the more expensive option of an overnight stay; in poorer brothels—smaller, more crowded, reliant on fast turnover—short and cheaper service was the norm.[125] For the greater number of colonial women engaged in prostitution, this spatial economy translated into squalor and constraint.

> The inmates of brothels licensed for the use of foreigners are, on the average, a decidedly inferior class of women, the refuse in fact of the brothels licensed for Chinese. . . . Consequently these brothels for foreigners are resorted to chiefly by the lowest class of Hong Kong residents, principally soldiers, and form the chief resort of the seafaring population passing through the Colony. These brothels, therefore, shade down in regular gradation from houses which will not admit any but officers, to brothels for coloured men, and the lowest class patronised by the privates of the infantry.[126]

In practice, colonial contexts created and indeed enforced a new kind of marketplace for sex, formalizing economic and racial divides within the brothel system.

Migration

As a result of these multifarious divisions, the patterns of migration and settlement wrought by colonization were gendered in critical ways. Women's mobility posed multiple threats to empire—the spread of disease, the growth of immorality, the specter of women cut loose from constraints. A high degree of mobility was necessary to imperial growth, but it brought with it undesirable consequences. It was the problems allegedly caused by unrestricted immigration in nineteenth-century Australian colonies that, along with a substantial dose of eugenically inflected racism, catalyzed clamor for restriction after federation. One opponent of New South Wales' 1908 Prisoner's Detention Act thought the legislation would "allow any diseased man or woman from India to come in without examination," that is, that it was aimed at the wrong people in its emphasis on the Australian-born rather than the immigrant.[127] Tamils from south India moving to Rangoon for work were castigated as "perhaps the most filthy and loathsomely lascivious races to be found in the world . . . frequently saturated with venereal diseases . . . accompanied or followed by an army of prostitutes . . . [of] characteristic greed."[128] But the labor demands of colonialism depended on such mobility, even while the moral and medical failings of migrants were feared. Women more than men were in the spotlight because, as migrants, they were often outside or away from their proper sphere of home. While the zenana was an improper form of home by western lights, it did at least enclose women; the brothel, and the work of prostitution, magnified the particular dangers—moral and physical—of women's mobility. The prostitute woman, mobile in her trade, epitomized the dangers of female migration.

Missionary Florence Garnham visited Fiji's plantations in 1918 as the representative of Australian women's groups, alarmed by reports of the depraved conditions among indentured Indians there. She found "life in the lines . . . unspeakably corrupt."[129] More worrisome even than the exposure of the young to unchaste behavior, Garnham feared that "immorality is not left behind but carried, as a disease might be, wherever the time-expired worker next moved."[130] Even in the feminist Garnham's view the prostituted woman laborer was circumscribed in terms of her contagion, a source of disease both literally and metaphorically. Indentured women lived the western contradiction. They were necessary as workers and as mothers but they represented the tensions between work and domesticity, between maternity and sexuality, and between enlightened modernity and vicious premodernity. And as migrant women, they stood as a worrying symbol of what would ensue from female mobility and migration.

The migration of men carried its own moral dangers. The movement of single men to towns in search of work occasioned by the disruptions of the colonial economy fed the demand for paid sex and companionship in various forms and throughout the empire. This large pool of single men was massively amplified by a mostly bachelor military population held together in part by a vision of masculine prowess on and in both the battlefield and the bedroom. The maleness of imperial expansion and the belief in male sexuality as an aggressive natural force fed the notion that the provision of women for male use was necessary. Male migration and female migration were thus complexly related, and though by no means all migrant women worked in the sex industry, demand and supply certainly worked to give those who did an added incentive to mobility, another defiance of proper femininity.

Conclusion

In the defiance of the separate spheres lay the threat of immorality. Visibility and its attendant spatial concerns were fundamental to the organization of sexual commerce. Managing sex in colonial sites was always unstable and complex, for the imperial project relied on actual sexual availability alongside an ethos of sexual respectability. The brothel needed to be both spectacular and secretive, vulgar and discreet, available but controlled, inviting but off-limits. Sex was a guarantor of certain kinds of stability, but it simultaneously disrupted deeply held sensibilities. Colonial space was always potentially sexual, revealing both the failings of the locals and of the masculine penetrativeness of the colonizing force. The geography of colonial relations had a long-lasting impact on the lives of women engaged in prostitution, and on the structures of the colonial marketplace of sex; and the empire, as Anne Godlewska and Neil Smith remind us, was as much geographical as it was historical.[131]

As Susan Morgan has pithily noted, "in the politics of culture, 'where' is as complex and incoherent a category as 'who.' "[132] The spaces occupied by the zenana and the brothel became sites of interest and anxiety, sites that, if left uncontrolled, would taint if not immobilize the *cordon sanitaire* that so fundamentally required their visibility and their concreteness, as evidence of their conformity to colonial rule. There was a quite specific set of physical and geographical anxieties collected around prostitution, and they were magnified during the years of regulation. These anxieties were formulated largely around visibility, which posed dilemmas for which no satisfactory resolutions really existed. Vagrancy laws, loitering ordinances, and the attack on streetwalking all demonstrated fundamentally physical and geographical anxieties around where women were and how visible they were.

For the brothel to be properly controlled, it needed to be visible, yet its business was something officials always hoped they could at least partially conceal. The sentiment of propriety worked not only against the fundamental principles of surveillance but also against business practice. If the brothel were to succeed as a bulwark against VD, it had to be sufficiently visible to attract customers, even while it needed from the moral perspective to be separated from the mainstream. The brothel was a potentially more private location for sexual commerce than the street (traditionally excoriated as the site of public sex) unless and until the clients or vendors spilled out onto the streets—in brawls, in merriment, or simply to drum up customers—or until it was located inappropriately near schools, churches, or wealthy residences. Such considerations constantly undermined attempts to maintain the sex industry without controversy. Laws regulating prostitution all sought to unveil and uncover women by listing them on registers, issuing them with tickets, keeping their photographs on file, posting their names in the brothel, but meanwhile they intended to keep the sex business from spilling over into the world of acceptability and respectability.

All this was done in the name of rational efficiency, exposing the brothel's unhygienic potential to the unsentimental glare of science and good government. The brothel, like the slum, was one of "the impossible edges of modernity," a place colonialism could not do without, but that it nonetheless rejected.[133]

In rendering prostitution and carnality visible, regulation and related policies created a public space for a private act, for a trade that authorities regarded as better off behind closed doors. The moral element of spatiality created a dilemma about who exactly could or should see and track who. The too-visible brothel invited even while it could be watched and disinfected. Sex, though it had to be represented as marginal, was in fact central to colonial rule. The marketplace of colonial sex had to be maintained but how to achieve that, and still preserve the hard geographical boundaries by which "civilized" morality was defined, recognized, and sustained proved inevitably an impossible endeavor.

Epilogue

Escalating fears of the grim and racialized consequences of venereal disease swept across Britain, among other countries, in the second half of the nineteenth century. Blamed mostly on women working in the sex trade, these fears coalesced around sexual and racial difference. In an age of colonial expansion, where heightened attention to such differences and to their relation with political participation and civic responsibility were so key, these fears were frequently magnified in colonial contexts. The differing and allegedly more dangerous environments offered by a largely tropical and semitropical empire facilitated the use of measures far more draconian and far broader in intent than those attempted in Britain. As we have seen, contagious diseases laws in the empire not only preceded in some instances those promulgated at home, but almost always embraced a greater level of surveillance, casting the net far wider than merely those women thought to service a military clientele. While the laws came under fire by the late 1880s, producing tremendous controversy and a potent fear of imperial instability, the opinions and data that had bolstered their passing remained remarkably inflexible. While regulation as a practice lost more and more support over the years, the assumption of a direct link between promiscuity and disease, and between sexual desire and racial characteristics, remained stable. Doctors writing early in the twentieth century were just as likely to blame the filth and loose morals of natives for the spread of disease as were their counterparts sixty and seventy years earlier. The sexual fecundity of the tropics, the fear of contagion, the associations between race and sex changed very little from the mid-Victorian period and into the First World War.

During that war, colonial and female loyalty as well as regulatory systems of controlling venereal disease and prostitution were, yet again, put to the test. And just as had been the case in the 1880s and 1890s, British and colonial opinion clashed significantly, for it was Dominion pressure that catalyzed the draconian regulationist measures in the spring of 1918. While in the stormy abolitionist era of the 1890s, the imperial government got its way in legal terms, if not always in practice, the tables were turned, to some extent, by wartime pressures. White settler demand saw the brief return of regulation naming women as active transmitters of disease. The long-standing notion that female activity was invariably dangerous rather than productive was paralleled, of course, by suspicions of nonwhite colonial subjects as unstable and unmodern, a point also driven home by the inequalities in the freedoms allowed and opinions of the colonial soldiers called to battle during the war.

But the language of war had even greater purchase. By homogenizing women as the source of VD, dirt as the vector of disease, and disease as an assault on humankind, doctors had at their disposal even in noncombat times and environments, an aggressive vocabulary of battle and of war. The greater vulnerability of British troops abroad to disease more than to combat made military metaphors potent. As medical knowledge grew increasingly surefooted, this triumphalist vocabulary was ever more apparent, but it acted too as a warning signal of the need for constant vigilance—against tropical contagion, prowling women, and the empire as it were, of the senses.[1] Colonial doctors could style themselves as frontline troops, taming a climate hitherto untenable for European settlement. Their close association with the military lent the metaphor added force. But at stake in what was commonly articulated as a "war" against VD were a host of linked concerns and anxieties, by no means limited to the improved efficiency of Britain's colonial military.

From the moment at which serious attempts at formal regulation surfaced in imperial politics in the 1850s, severe tension between the realms of private and public was in play. Antiregulation activists were blamed for bringing indelicate matters to public attention, and they in turn accused officials of encouraging rampant male sexuality by selling the idea of safe nonmarital sex to men who might otherwise remain untempted. In colonial contexts, the issues were magnified by fears around racial difference (so often represented in sexual terms) and by an anxiety that certain forms of sexual license would loosen the imperial hold. The more open and more public place that Britons thought sexuality occupied in colonized societies might not always have been an accurate assessment, but it nonetheless deeply influenced the contours of policy in this arena. But for a society so embedded in maintaining a public-private divide as the basis for morality and order, the need to legislate around sex precipitated by colonialism was a deeply troubling urgency.

The refusal of government to recognize the impossibility of segregating public and private, alongside their failure to countenance sexual issues as meaningfully political rather than wholly pragmatic, offers us a new perspective for reading colonial politics. The governing assumptions that matters such as VD, sexuality, and prostitution belonged in a private, and preferably unspoken space made for a deep contradiction in the public arena that was not easily resolved. The need, driven (though not exclusively) by the military, to legislate in sexual arenas required justifying the intrusion of sex—a private matter—into public spaces. Indeed, the fundamental defense offered for the regulation of prostitution was that sex workers violated the natural separation of the two spheres by shifting what belonged in the private into the public. Despite the language of sanitation, of military necessity, of studied neutrality, the removal of sex to the public arena undermined representations of what constituted the public sphere, and once that definition became unfocused, the contradictions multiplied. Women behaved like men, people of color tried to pass as white, colonial politicians questioned imperial edict. Sex disturbed the fabric of the public realm profoundly, and the colonial VD/CD controversy, despite its neglect by historians, was no minor incident easily dispatched and silenced. On the contrary, it was one of the most vigorous of late nineteenth-century campaigns, even if the antiregulationists' victories were short-term and piecemeal.

Much of this, of course, was relevant to domestic as well as to colonial versions of the acts and of the debates. In the colonial context, however, the racial and sexual difference that was said to underline the difference between colonizer and colonized also permitted broader and more thorough forms of regulation and sexual surveillance than allowable in the metropolis. Colonial backwardness and unmodernity held back the propitious benefits of western attention. The failure of colonial subjects at every level to respect the public-private division named them as a problem; the very fabric of their customs and cultures were seen as inimical to and subversive of imperial rule. It was not just sex out of place that made colonial settings so disturbing; it was that sex out of place was definitional of colonial culture. The endless arguments that naturalized prostitution, promiscuity, and homosexuality as central to Chinese, Indian, Arabic, "Oriental", and Aboriginal societies were definitive of what made these places ripe for colonial governance, unworthy of self-rule, and inferior to their colonial masters. Colonial danger meant that sex had to be brought into the public sphere, for the failure to exercise control over native sexuality would threaten the success of colonial rule. It was on these grounds that colonial politicians, mindful of their fragile situation in colonial settings, so vigorously denounced the decision of imperial government to get out of the business of managing sex late in the nineteenth century. Such surveillance, they contended, was vital to colonial rule and to their lives as colonial masters. If, after all, they were given the task of ruling, then for the home government to disregard their views and needs was tantamount to questioning their abilities to sustain empire appropriately.

It was a theme that would, a century later, come back to haunt the imperial government. On January 1, 2001, Britain's Privy Council overturned laws that criminalized consenting homosexual acts between men in five of its remaining dependent territories. Repeal was pushed through by an Order-in-Council, because the territories in question—Anguilla, the British Virgin Islands, the Cayman Islands, Montserrat, and the Turks and Caicos Islands—refused to abandon anti-gay laws despite a decade of appeals from the imperial government in London. In all five of the territories, the British government knowingly took action against the wishes of local politicians and officials, overwhelmingly hostile to any decriminalization of male homosexuality. The British claimed that the existing laws had to be abandoned because they violated commitment to the European Convention on Human Rights, to which British membership of the European Union bound them.

Dissension in these colonies was long-standing and widespread, and not just among officials. In the Cayman Islands, a pamphlet entitled *Sexual Sins* was widely distributed in churches, and many churches also spearheaded petition drives to protest Britain's plans.[2] The five territories finally conceded their powerlessness in the face of Britain's determination. Yet the incident, which was reported only superficially for the most part, reflected not only a difference in values but a vast gulf in political power. The agriculture minister of Montserrat called the British decision an affront to local opinion. "It's the attitude," he claimed, "typical of colonialism."[3]

Though the Caribbean dissenters framed the controversy in contemporary anticolonialist terms, the incident nonetheless echoes the battles between Britain and its recalcitrant colonies over the regulation of prostitution in the 1880s and 1890s. Over and over, as we have seen, government in London rode roughshod over the contrary opinion of colonists. Those colonists claimed that metropolitan opinions and values were irrelevant in their territories, and resented what they saw as the high-handedness and arrogance of British insistence on centralized imperial paramountcy. Governments likewise clashed repeatedly with church leaders as well as missionaries, on how far morals and law needed to coincide. *Sexual Sins,* with its Biblical quotations and righteous ferocity, closely resembled the fiery denunciations of abolitionists for whom government was little more than the largest and most powerful of the sexual procurers of its day.

A hundred years or so after the controversy over the CD laws, the last remnant of the British Empire thus found itself once more embroiled in a tussle focused on questions of sexual morality. What lessons might we draw from this recrudescence of colonial tension over matters sexual? Seemingly, though twentieth-century governments have increasingly intervened in the sphere of personal conduct, the discursive boundaries of private and public remain as unresolved as they palpably were in the 1880s and 1890s. In 1986, another former British Caribbean territory, Trinidad and Tobago, was occupied with drafting a Sexual Offences Bill. Faced with public uproar over the possibility of decriminalizing homosexuality, the executive took the unusual step of convening a select committee whose deliberations remained private.[4] It is surely not coincidence that this atypical step of making private a routinely public procedure was invoked in an instance where issues of allegedly private morality were at stake. The always-porous, always-unstable boundaries between public and private are never more apparent than when public institutions take on questions they themselves regard as belonging in and to the private.

The apparent conservatism of the periphery, whether seeking to continue the surveillance of women prostitutes or to maintain criminal sanctions for homosexual acts, speaks to a pattern in dependent colonial relations that represents colonial thinking as less progressive and modern than metropolitan, a difference with potential material consequences as well. It was, after all, a rhetoric of unreadiness that shaped Britain's insistence that so many of its colonies were not ready for self-rule. Present-day ministerial frustrations at Caribbean obduracy contrast the modernity of sexual tolerance with the backward-looking conservatism of the colonies. The issue at stake may be at sharp odds with that which dominated a century ago, but the relations we glimpse in both instances between colony and metropolis are far from dissimilar. Far harder, in a sense, to resolve than traditional political, diplomatic, and economic concerns, sexual questions muddy the waters. In the nineteenth century, government asserted its stand as sanitary; at the end of the twentieth century, it was adherence to human rights which politicians invoked to justify their intervention. Sexuality per se took a backseat to bigger, broader principles of allegedly greater significance, In the end, whether government's stand is a regressive or a progressive one on the particular issue at stake, neither at the end of the nineteenth or of the twentieth century can established politics countenance sex as a proper matter for politics. Evelyn Hammonds has argued that "[s]exuality has become one of the most visible, contentious, and spectacular features of modern life in the United States during this [the twentieth] century."[5] In that sexuality can and has been named more freely than in the past—and perhaps more polymorphously if not always perversely—the observation is an accurate one. I would argue, however, that contentions around sexuality, whether in the United States, the British Empire, or a host of other arenas, have a far longer and equally spectacular history which predates the twentieth century, and which has changed surprisingly little. The rage over the CD acts documented here, the level of disruption their existence engendered, the attendant policies that clustered around them, surely suggest that sexuality, deeply entwined with fears around race and contagion, occupied a key role in politics well before the dawn of the twentieth century. Jeffrey Weeks and Frank Mort have both rightly insisted that the state has played a crucial role in defining, in categorizing, and in managing sexuality, and that we ignore that politics at our peril.[6] Yet even given the increasing interventionism traced here, and apparent in other sexual arenas in which the state has become involved, a pervasive uneasiness has invariably shrouded governmental debate and action in these areas. In general, while the management of sexuality has indubitably affected the lives of many women and men, governmental policies around this issue more often than not fail in their intentions.

The CD controversy at the core of this study is in many respects one such study in failure. Palpably, the form of reglementation central to the VD system that identified women as the major source of transmission, was doomed to failure, but its failure was larger than simply the illogic of a preventive scheme shaped by a double standard of sexual morality. The system could not meet its goals and intentions; not only was it based on a faulty premise, but those affected found ever more creative ways to sabotage it. Moreover, the system faced massive dissent, ultimately producing tensions in colonial rule grave enough for the governor general in India to predict constitutional crisis in the 1890s. Historians of empire have mostly chosen to ignore how far the tensions over the abandonment of CD legislation pushed the imperial government to the brink, and on several occasions.[7] That the topic precipitating such a crisis was concerned with lowly prostitute women and diseases impossible to name in polite circles is important. Prostitution, race, disease, and politics remain as inextricably bound with one another today as they did in the high Victorian era. Their combined ability to bring governments to political crisis point should not surprise us; it should perhaps orient us rather to fruitful new avenues for historical investigation.

The case of the remaining dependent territories does not, however, exhaust the contemporary resonances of the debates and controversies discussed in these pages. The association between sex and disease so central to this study has proven a tenacious myth, emerging yet again in the late twentieth century around AIDS. Press reports about AIDS suggest new forms of both racial and sexual marginalization alongside older assumptions about promiscuity and especially about prostitution, both represented as dangerous practices. In the past decade or so, emphasis has shifted from the characterization of AIDS as an affliction of gay men to a subtly racialized representation focused on nonwhite regions of the world. AIDS has become, in one sense, an emblem of racial disadvantage but also a problem indelibly associated with unmodern peoples whose unrestrained behaviors put the larger population at risk. The intertwining of race and sex so palpable in these associations is depressingly reminiscent of the nineteenth and early twentieth-century debates around colonial sexuality and its relation to VD. Not only does the politics of sex remain an impossible conundrum for governments, but the hierarchies endlessly proclaimed around both race and sex continue to exert tremendous power, no less damaging though differently packaged than that so critical in colonial contagious disease policy.

Abbreviations Used in the Notes

AAC	Australian Archives, Canberra
ADM	Admiralty Papers (Public Record Office)
AMSH	Association for Moral and Social Hygiene Papers (Women's Library)
AWM	Australian War Memorial, Canberra
BALC	Josephine Butler Autograph Letter Collection (Women's Library)
BGF	British Committee of the International Abolitionist Federation Papers (Women's Library)
BL	British Library, London
CAB	Cabinet Papers (Public Record Office)
CO	Colonial Office Papers (Public Record Office)
FHL	Friends' Association for Abolishing the State Regulation of Vice Papers (Friend's House, London)
FO	Foreign Office Papers (Public Record Office)
HC	House of Commons
HJW	Henry J. Wilson Papers (Women's Library)
HKPRO	Public Record Office, Hong Kong
HO	Home Office Papers (Public Record Office)
IAF	International Abolitionist Federation Papers (Women's Library)
JEB	Josephine Butler Collection (Women's Library)
LLH	London Lock Hospital Papers (Royal College of Surgeons)
LRO	Liverpool Record Office
MEPO	Metropolitan Police Papers (Public Record Office)
ML	Mitchell Library, Sydney
NAI	National Archives of India, New Delhi
NAM	National Army Museum, London

NSW   New South Wales
NSWSA   New South Wales State Archives, Sydney
NSWPD   New South Wales Parliamentary Debates
NVA   National Vigilance Association Papers (Women's Library)
NWP   Northwest Provinces
OIOC   Oriental & India Office Collections (British Library)
PP   Parliamentary Papers
PRO   Public Record Office, London
QPD   Queensland Parliamentary Debates
QSA   Queensland State Archives, Brisbane
RAMC   Royal Army Medical Corps Papers (Wellcome Institute, London)
RCS   Royal College of Surgeons
RH   Rhodes House, Oxford
SCA   Sheffield City Archives
SP   *Sessional Papers*
WI   Wellcome Institute, London
WL   Women's Library (formerly Fawcett Library)
WO   War Office Papers (Public Record Office)

Notes

Introduction

1. I have chosen to use, for the most part, the older term *venereal disease,* or *venereal diseases* rather than the contemporary term, *sexually transmissible diseases* (STDs). I do so since this is the historically specific term used at the time.

2. The locks were specialist hospitals dedicated to the treatment and eradication of VD. Women admitted for treatment for VD might be treated for other sicknesses simultaneously, but were never admitted for problems regarded as nonvenereal.

3. David Arnold, *Colonizing the Body: State Medicine and Epidemic Disease in Nineteenth-Century India* (Berkeley: University of California Press, 1993), 64; Mark Harrison, *Public Health in British India: Anglo-Indian Preventive Medicine 1859–1914* (Cambridge: Cambridge University Press, 1994), 2; J. B. Harrison, "Allahabad: A Sanitary History," in *The City in South Asia: Pre-modern and Modern,* ed. Kenneth Ballhatchet and John Harrison (London and Dublin: Curzon Press; Atlantic Highlands, NJ: Humanities Press, 1980), 170; Roy Macleod, "Introduction," in *Disease, Medicine, and Empire: Perspectives on Western Medicine and the Experience of European Expansion,* ed. Roy Macleod and Milton Lewis (London: Routledge, 1988), 6; Radhika Ramasubbhan, "Imperial Health in British India, 1857–1900," in *Disease, Medicine, and Empire,* 40.

4. Within Britain itself, the meaning of empire was always contested; see Andrew S. Thompson "The Language of Imperialism and the Meanings of Empire: Imperial Discourse in British Politics, 1895–1914," *Journal of British Studies* 36, no. 2 (1997): 150.

5. Sumit Sarkar, *Modern India 1885–1947* (Basingstoke: The Macmillan Press, 1989), 1; Kate Lowe and Eugene McLaughlin, "Sir John Pope-Hennessy and the 'Native Race Craze': Colonial Government in Hong Kong, 1887–1882," *Journal of Imperial and Commonwealth History* 20, no. 2 (1992): esp. 224–7.

6. Dane Kennedy, *The Magic Mountains: Hill Stations and the British Raj* (Berkeley: University of California Press, 1996); J. E. Spencer and W. L. Thomas, "The Hill Stations and Summer Resorts of the Orient," *Geographical Review* 38, no. 4 (1948): 637–51.

7. James F. Warren, "Rickshaw Coolie: An Exploration of the Underside of a Chinese City outside China, Singapore 1880–1940," in *At the Edge of Southeast Asian History* (Quezon City: New Day Publishers, 1987), 74.

8. Douglas A. Lorimer, "Race, Science, and Culture: Historical Continuities and Discontinuities, 1850–1914," in *The Victorians and Race,* ed. Shearer West (Aldershot, Scolar Press, 1996), 12–33.

9.   Vron Ware and Les Back, *Out of Whiteness: Color, Politics, and Culture* (Chicago: Chicago University Press, 2002), 2.

10. Richard Dyer, *White* (London: Routledge, 1997), 13.

11. For a sustained discussion of the belief in Anglo-Saxon exceptionalism, see Catherine Hall, *Civilising Subjects: Metropole and Colony in the English Imagination, 1830–1867* (Chicago: University of Chicago Press, 2002).

12. Stephen Heathorn, " 'Let us remember that we, too, are English': Constructions of Citizenship and National Identity in English Elementary School Reading Books, 1880–1914," *Victorian Studies* 38, no. 3 (1995): 398–9.

13. Catherine Hall, "The Economy of Intellectual Prestige: Thomas Carlyle, John Stuart Mill, and the Case of Governor Eyre," *Cultural Critique* 12 (1989): 186, n. 33. Bill Schwarz quotes a revealing speech of Churchill's made in 1940, in which he remarks "when I say 'English' I really mean British." (Schwarz, "Conservatism, Nationalism, and Imperialism," in *Politics and Ideology,* ed. James Donald and Stuart Hall (Milton Keynes and Philadelphia, PA: Open University Press, 1986), 181.

14. Andrew Porter, "Introduction: Britain and the Empire in the Nineteenth Century," in *Oxford History of the British Empire:* vol. 3: *The Nineteenth Century,* ed. Andrew Porter (Oxford: Oxford University Press, 1999), 19.

15. Antoinette Burton, "The Feminist Quest for Identity: British Imperial Suffragism and 'Global Sisterhood,' 1900–1918," *Journal of Women's History* 3, no. 2 (1991): 46–81; idem, "The White Woman's Burden: British Feminists and 'The Indian Woman,' 1865–1915," in *Western Women and Imperialism: Complicity and Resistance,* ed. Nupur Chaudhuri and Margaret Strobel (Bloomington: Indiana University Press, 1992), 137–57; idem, *Burdens of History: British Feminists, Indian Women, and Imperial Culture 1865–1915* (Chapel Hill, NC: University of North Carolina Press, 1994).

16. Malavika Kasturi, "Law and Crime in India: British Policy and the Female Infanticide Act of 1870," *Indian Journal of Gender Studies* 1, no. 2 (1994): 189.

17. Kumkum Sangari and Sudesh Vaid, *Recasting Women: Essays in Colonial History* (New Delhi: Kali for Women, 1989), esp. 5–9.

18. For stimulating discussions of colonial medicine, see Warwick Anderson, "Where is the Post-colonial History of Medicine," *Bulletin of the History of Medicine* 72, no. 3 (1998): 522–30; David Arnold, "Introduction: Disease, Medicine, and Empire," in *Imperial Medicine and Indigenous Societies* (Manchester: Manchester University Press, 1988), 1–26; John and Jean Comaroff, *Ethnography and the Historical Imagination* (Boulder, CO: Westview Press, 1992); Philip D. Curtin, *Disease and Empire: The Health of European Troops in the Conquest of Africa* (Cambridge: Cambridge University Press, 1998); Macleod and Lewis, *Disease, Medicine, and Empire;* Shula Marks, "What is Colonial about Colonial Medicine? And What has Happened to Imperialism and Health?" *Social History of Medicine* 10 (1997): 205–19; Megan Vaughan, "Health and Hegemony: Representation of Disease and the Creation of the Colonial Subject in Nyasaland," in *Contesting Colonial Hegemony: State and Society in Africa and India,* ed. Dagmar Engels and Shula Marks (London: British Academic Press/German Historical Institute, 1994), 173–201; Sheldon Watts, *Epidemics and History: Disease, Power, and Imperialism* (New Haven, CT: Yale University Press, 1997).

19. Elfed Vaughan Roberts, Sum Ngai Ling, and Peter Bradshaw, *Historical Dictionary of Hong Kong and Macau* (Metuchen, NJ and London: The Scarecrow Press, 1992), 127.

20. Sheldon Amos, *A Comparative Survey of Laws in Force for the Prohibition, Regulation and Licensing of Vice in England and Other Countries* (London: Stevens and Son, 1877), 14.

21. David Washbrook, "India, 1818–1860: The Two Faces of Colonialism," in *Oxford History of the British Empire,* 3, 407.

22. Mrinalini Sinha, *Colonial Masculinity. The "Manly Englishman" and the "Effeminate Bengali" in the Late Nineteenth Century* (Manchester: Manchester University Press, 1995), 141.

23. Thomas R. Metcalf, *The New Cambridge History of India:* 3: 4: *Ideologies of the Raj* (Cambridge: Cambridge University Press, 1994), 36–7.

24. Carl A. Trocki, "Political Structures in the Nineteenth and Early Twentieth Centuries," in *The Cambridge History of Southeast Asia:* vol. 2: *The Nineteenth and Twentieth Centuries,* ed. Nicholas Tarling (Cambridge: Cambridge University Press, 1992), 99.

25. Persis Charles, "The Name of the Father: Women, Paternity, and British Rule in Nineteenth-Century Jamaica," *International Labor and Working-Class History* 41 (1992): 11. On

Hardwicke's Marriage Act, see Miles Ogborn, "This Most Lawless Space: The Geography of the Fleet and the Making of Lord Hardwicke's Marriage Act of 1753," *New Formations* 37 (1999): 11–32.

26. Miles Ogborn, *Spaces of Modernity: London's Geographies, 1680–1780* (New York: The Guilford Press, 1998), 47.

27. For further discussion of this position, see Ania Loomba, *Colonialism/Postcolonialism* (London: Routledge, 1998), 29.

28. Patrick Wolfe, "History and Imperialism: A Century of Theory from Marx to Postcolonialism," *American Historical Review* 102, no. 2 (1997): 407.

Chapter 1

1. Prasenjit Duara, *Rescuing History from the Nation: Questioning Narratives of Modern China* (Chicago: University of Chicago Press, 1995), esp. 17–33.

2. Robert Gregg, "Preface," *Inside Out, Outside In: Essays in Comparative History* (Basingstoke: Macmillan; New York: St. Martin's Press: 2000), x.

3. Edward W. Said, "Secular Interpretation, the Geographical Element, and the Methodology of Imperialism," in *After Colonialism: Imperial Histories and Postcolonial Displacements,* ed. Gyan Prakash (Princeton, NJ: Princeton University Press, 1995), 21–39.

4. Bill Readings, *The University in Ruins* (Cambridge, MA: Harvard University Press, 1996), 93.

5. Antoinette Burton, "Who Needs the Nation? Interrogating 'British History,'" *Journal of Historical Sociology* 10, no. 3 (1997): 231–2; Catherine Hall, *Civilising Subjects: Metropole and Colony in the English Imagination, 1830–1867* (Chicago: University of Chicago Press, 2002), 8, 12.

6. Inderpal Grewal, *Home and Harem: Nation, Gender, Empire, and the Cultures of Travel* (Durham, NC: Duke University Press, 1996), 17–19.

7. Jane M. Jacobs, *Edge of Empire: Postcolonialism and the City* (London and New York: Routledge, 1996), 23.

8. Henry Reynolds and Dawn May, "Queensland," in *Contested Ground: Australian Aborigines under the British Crown,* ed. Ann McGrath (St. Leonards, NSW: Allen and Unwin, 1995), 171.

9. *Handbook for Queensland, Australia* By Authority of the Agent-General for the Government of Queensland (London: Lake and Sison, 1893), 17; Reynolds and May, "Queensland," 181.

10. John Anderson, *The Colonial Office List for 1897 comprising Historical and Statistical Information respecting the Colonial Dependencies of Great Britain* (London: Harrison and Sons Ltd., 1897), 205.

11. Reynolds and May, "Queensland," 169; Bill Thorpe, *Colonial Queensland: Perspectives on A Frontier Society* (St. Lucia: University of Queensland Press, 1996), esp. 125; Duncan Waterson and Maurice French, *From the Frontier: A Pictorial History of Queensland to 1920* (St. Lucia: University of Queensland Press, 1987), 55.

12. Details of the work involved in these industries can be found in Athol Chase, "'All Kind of Nation': Aborigines and Asians in Cape York Peninsula," *Aboriginal History* 5, no. 1 (1981): 7–19.

13. Sidney W. Mintz, *Sweetness and Power: The Place of Sugar in Modern History* (New York: Penguin, 1986), 71.

14. Tom Harrisson offers a lively account of the transition from sandalwood to sugar indenture in *Savage Civilization* (New York: Alfred Knopf, 1937), 144.

15. Mark Finnane and Clive Moore, "Kanaka Slaves or Willing Workers? Melanesian Workers and the Queensland Criminal Justice System in the 1890s," *Criminal Justice History* 13 (1992): 141. See, too, Donald Denoon with Marivic Wyndham, "Australia and the Western Pacific," in *The Oxford History of the British Empire:* vol. 3: *The Nineteenth Century,* ed. Andrew Porter (Oxford: Oxford University Press, 1999), 553.

16. Raymond Evans, "'The Owl and the Eagle': The Significance of Race in Colonial Queensland," *Social Alternatives* 5, no. 4 (1986): 21; Mark Finnane and Stephen Garton, "The Work of Policing: Social Relations and the Criminal Justice System in Queensland 1880–1914, Part II," *Labour History* 63 (November 1992): 45.

17. Andrew Markus, *Australian Race Relations 1788–1993* (St. Leonards, NSW: Allen and Unwin, 1994), 112; Waterson and French, *From the Frontier,* 5.

18. Luke Trainor, *British Imperialism and Australian Nationalism: Manipulation, Conflict and*

Compromise in the Late Nineteenth Century (Cambridge: Cambridge University Press, 1994), 84.

19. Ross Fitzgerald, *From the Dreaming to 1915: A History of Queensland* (St. Lucia: University of Queensland Press, 1982), 235; Waterson and French, *From the Frontier*, 5.

20. On anti-Chinese sentiment, see especially Raymond Evans, Kay Saunders, and Kathryn Cronin, *Race Relations in Colonial Queensland: A History of Exclusion, Exploitation and Extermination* 3rd ed. (St. Lucia: University of Queensland Press, 1993), 309; 353.

21. Fitzgerald, *From the Dreaming*, 225; Waterson and French, *From the Frontier*, 5. Howard Markel and Alexandra Minna Stern demonstrate an equivalent process in Chinese immigration into America in "Which Face? Whose Nation? Immigration, Public Health, and the Construction of Disease at America's Ports and Borders, 1891–1928," *American Behavioral Scientist* 42, no. 9 (1999): 1322.

22. Markus, *Australian Race Relations*, 73.

23. Fitzgerald, *From the Dreaming*, 236.

24. J. C. R. Camm and John McQuilton, ed. *Australians: A Historical Atlas* (Broadway, NSW: Fairfax, Syme and Weldon, 1987), 152; Finnane and Moore, "Kanaka Slaves or Willing Workers?" 144.

25. G. C. Bolton, *A Thousand Miles Away: A History of North Queensland to 1920* (Brisbane: Jacaranda Press, 1963), 241; Fitzgerald, *From the Dreaming*, 246.

26. Bolton, *A Thousand Miles Away*, 140; Camm and McQuilton, *Australians*, 153; Fitzgerald, *From the Dreaming*, 248.

27. Fitzgerald, *From the Dreaming*, 244–7; Markus, *Australian Race Relations*, 87.

28. For a more detailed history of these laws, see Robert A. Huttenback, *Racism and Empire: White Settlers and Colored Immigrants in the British Self-Governing Colonies, 1830–1910* (Ithaca, NY: Cornell University Press, 1976), 288–90.

29. Regina Ganter and Ros Kidd, "The Powers of Protectors: Conflicts Surrounding Queensland's 1897 Aboriginal Legislation," *Australian Historical Studies* 25 (1993): 550–1.

30. Ganter and Kidd, "The Powers of Protectors," 551; Reynolds and May, "Queensland," 196.

31. Marilyn Wood, "Nineteenth Century Bureaucratic Constructions of Indigenous Identities in New South Wales," in *Citizenship and Indigenous Australians: Changing Conceptions and Possibilities*, ed. Nicolas Peterson and Will Sanders (Cambridge: Cambridge University Press, 1998), esp. 51.

32. Denoon and Wyndham, "Australia and the Western Pacific," 564. On the angry reaction of the Japanese to the White Australia policy, see Huttenback, *Racism and Empire*, 281–4 and 303–4.

33. Finnane and Garton, "The Work of Policing," Part 2, 45.

34. Noel Loos, *Invasion and Resistance: Aboriginal-European Relations on the North Queensland Frontier 1861–1897* (Canberra: Australian National University Press, 1982), xviii.

35. There was already a long history of white working-class opposition to nonwhite labor: see K. M. Dallas, "The Origins of 'White Australia,'" *Australian Quarterly* 23 (1955): 46.

36. Wood, "Nineteenth Century Bureaucratic Constructions of Indigenous Identities," 39. *Terra nullius* was overturned by the landmark Mabo decision of 1992, *Mabo vs. Queensland* [No. 2] [1992] 175 CLR 1. For a detailed discussion of active Aboriginal land management, and white misunderstanding and ignoring of it, see Dawn May, *Aboriginal Labour and the Cattle Industry: Queensland from White Settlement to the Present* (Melbourne: Cambridge University Press, 1994), esp. chapter 1.

37. Evans, Saunders, and Cronin, *Race Relations in Colonial Queensland*, 18.

38. Trainor, *British Imperialism and Australian Nationalism*, 39.

39. On labor relations between Asians and Aboriginals, see Chase, "All Kind of Nation."

40. *Handbook for Queensland*, 53; Ross Patrick, "Health Administration 1860–1910," in *People, Places and Policies: Aspects of Queensland Government Administration 1859–1920*, ed. Kay Cohen and Kenneth Wiltshire (St. Lucia: University of Queensland Press, 1995), 248.

41. On the dying races, see Patrick Brantlinger, "'Dying Races': Rationalizing Genocide in the Nineteenth Century," in *The Decolonization of Imagination: Culture, Knowledge and Power*, ed. Jan Nederveen Pieterse and Bhikhu Parekh (London and New Jersey: Zed Books, 1995), 43–56; Patricia Jacobs, "Science and Veiled Assumptions: Miscegenation in W.A. 1930–1937," *Australian Aboriginal Studies* 2 (1986): 16.

42. Stephen J. Kunitz, *Disease and Social Diversity: The European Impact on the Health of Non-Europeans* (New York: Oxford University Press, 1994), 51.

43. David Arnold, "Introduction: Disease, Medicine and Empire," in *Imperial Medicine and Indigenous Societies* (Manchester: Manchester University Press, 1988), 5.
44. Bolton, *A Thousand Miles Away*, 241.
45. *Handbook for Queensland*, 53.
46. Patrick, "Health Administration," 258–9.
47. C. M. Turnbull, *A History of Singapore 1819–1988* 2nd ed. (Singapore: Oxford University Press, 1989), 48.
48. Robert E. Elson, "International Commerce, the State and Society: Economic and Social Change," in *The Cambridge History of Southeast Asia*: vol. 2: *The Nineteenth and Twentieth Centuries*, ed. Nicholas Tarling (Cambridge: Cambridge University Press, 1992), 147–48.
49. Wong Li Ken, "Commercial Growth before the Second World War," in *A History of Singapore*, ed. Ernest C. T. Chew and Edwin Lee (Singapore: Oxford University Press, 1991), 41–65; Turnbull, *A History of Singapore*, 76; Anthony Webster, *Gentlemen Capitalists: British Imperialism in South East Asia, 1770–1890* (London and New York: Tauris Academic Studies, 1998), 169; 194.
50. Anderson, *Colonial Office List for 1897*, 227.
51. Michael Havinden and David Meredith, *Colonialism and Development: Britain and its Tropical Colonies, 1850–1960* (London: Routledge, 1993), 107–11.
52. Carl A. Trocki, "Political Structures in the Nineteenth and Early Twentieth Centuries," in *Cambridge History of Southeast Asia*, 2, 114.
53. Edwin Lee, "Community, Family and Household," in Chew and Lee, *A History of Singapore*, 246.
54. Turnbull, *A History of Singapore*, 58.
55. Brenda S. A. Yeoh, *Contesting Space: Power Relations and the Urban Built Environment in Colonial Singapore* (Kuala Lumpur: Oxford University Press, 1996), 35.
56. A. J. Stockwell, "British Expansion and Rule in South-East Asia," in *The Oxford History of the British Empire*, 3, 377.
57. Anderson, *Colonial Office List for 1897*, 227.
58. *Extract from the Chinese Protectorate Report Summarising Regulations Concerning Brothels and the Protection of Women and Children up to August 1936*, 16, RH. MSS. Ind. Ocn. s. 306. box 1, file 6; W. Peacock, *Annual Report of the Protector of Chinese, Straits Settlements, for the Year 1914* (Singapore: Government Printing Office, 1915), 1, WL, JEB, box E2/4.
59. "Report of Chinese Protectorate," 16, RH, MSS. Ind. Ocn. s. 306. box 1, file 6; Lee Poh Ping, *Chinese Society in Nineteenth Century Singapore* (Kuala Lumpur: Oxford University Press, 1978), 94. Hong Kong's ratios were always closer together. Even as early as 1865, when men dominated substantially in the colony, they were approximately 63 percent of the population, according to Jung-Fang Tsai in *Hong Kong in Chinese History: Community and Social Unrest in the British Colony, 1842–1913* (New York: Columbia University Press, 1993), 47.
60. On Pickering, see R. N. Jackson, *Pickering: Protector of Chinese* (Kuala Lumpur: Oxford: Oxford University Press, 1965).
61. David Gray, *The Chinese Problem in the Federation of Malaya* (Malaya: Chinese Secretariat, Federation of Malaya, 1952), 2, RH. MSS. Ind. Ocn. 320, file 2. On protectorates in Malaya, see Trocki, "Political Structures," 113.
62. Yeoh, *Contesting Space*, 60.
63. Lenore Manderson, *Sickness and the State: Health and Illness in Colonial Malaya, 1870–1940* (Cambridge: Cambridge University Press, 1996), xiii.
64. Lee Yong Kiat, *The Medical History of Early Singapore* (Tokyo: Southeast Asian Medical Information Center, 1978), 23; 83; Manderson, *Sickness and the State*, 15; Turnbull, *A History of Singapore*, 63.
65. Lenore Manderson, "Shaping Reproductions: Maternity in Early Twentieth-Century Malaya," in *Maternities and Modernities: Colonial and Postcolonial Experiences in Asia and the Pacific*, ed. Kalpana Ram and Margaret Jolly (Cambridge: Cambridge University Press, 1998), 32.
66. Manderson, *Sickness and the State*, 15.
67. Turnbull, *A History of Singapore*, 113.
68. Brenda S. A. Yeoh, *Municipal Sanitary Surveillance, Asian Resistance and the Control of the Urban Environment in Colonial Singapore* (Oxford: University of Oxford School of Geography Research Papers, 1991), 6.

69. "Medical Report on Pahang, 1899," PRO, CO273/262 (33384); Turnbull, *A History of Singapore*, 114.
70. G. T. Hare, *A Text Book of Documentary Chinese Selected and Designed for the Special Use of Members of the Civil Service of the Straits Settlements and the Protected Native States* (Singapore: Government Printing Office, 1894).
71. G. B. Endacott, *Government and People in Hong Kong 1841–1962: A Constitutional History* (Hong Kong: Hong Kong University Press, 1964), chapter 1.
72. John M. Carroll, "Chinese Collaboration in the Making of British Hong Kong," in *Hong Kong's History: State and Society Under Colonial Rule*, ed. Tak-Wing Ngo (London: Routledge, 1999), 18; H. J. Lethbridge, *Hong Kong: Stability and Change, A Collection of Essays* (Hong Kong: Oxford University Press, 1978), 52.
73. Hui Po-Keung, "Comprador Politics and Middleman Capitalism," in *Hong Kong's History*, 34.
74. Tsai, *Hong Kong in Chinese History*, 24.
75. Po-Keung, "Comprador Politics," 34.
76. Nigel Cameron, *An Illustrated History of Hong Kong* (Hong Kong: Oxford University Press, 1991), 104; Carroll, "Chinese Collaboration," 13–29; Kate Lowe and Eugene McLaughlin, "Sir John Pope-Hennessy and the 'Native Race Craze': Colonial Government in Hong Kong, 1887–1882," *Journal of Imperial and Commonwealth History* 20, no. 2 (1992): 231; Po-Keung, "Comprador Politics," 37; Tsai, *Hong Kong in Chinese History*, 9.
77. Elizabeth Sinn, "Chinese Patriarchy and the Protection of Women in Nineteenth-Century Hong Kong," in *Women and Chinese Patriarchy: Submission, Servitude and Escape*, ed. Maria Jaschok and Suzanne Miers (London and New Jersey: Zed Books, 1994), 165.
78. For the history of Cat Street, see Jeffrey Hantover, *Gambling Dens and Licensed Brothels: A Brief History of Cat Street* (Hong Kong: Casey Co. Ltd., 1992).
79. G. B. Endacott, *A History of Hong Kong* (London: Oxford University Press, 1958), 113, 161; Elizabeth Sinn, *Power and Charity: The Early History of the Tung Wah Hospital, Hong Kong* (Hong Kong: Oxford University Press, 1989), 27. Sikhs joined the Singapore police force from 1881.
80. Endacott, *A History of Hong Kong*, 70; Lethbridge, *Hong Kong*, 177–8.
81. David Faure, ed. *Society* (Hong Kong: Hong Kong University Press, 1997), 49.
82. Norman Miners, *Hong Kong Under Imperial Rule 1912–1941* (Hong Kong: Oxford University Press, 1987), 191.
83. Endacott, *Government and People*, 120.
84. Faure, *Society*, 46–7.
85. *Sessional Papers*, August 1868 to September 1887, 404–5, quoted in Faure, *Society*, 87. On racial segregation in the colony, see Lowe and McLaughlin, "Sir John Pope-Hennessy and the 'Native Race Craze.'"
86. Miners, *Hong Kong Under Imperial Rule*, 126.
87. Chan Lau Kit-ching, *China, Britain and Hong Kong, 1895–1945* (Hong Kong: The Chinese University Press, 1990), 7.
88. Lethbridge, *Hong Kong*, 60.
89. Lethbridge, *Hong Kong*, 63; Sinn, *Power and Charity*, 71; Endacott, *Government and People*, 105.
90. Tsai, *Hong Kong in Chinese History*, 52.
91. Endacott, *A History of Hong Kong*, 219, 244; Mary P. Sutphen, "Not What, but Where: Bubonic Plague and the Reception of Germ Theories in Hong Kong and Calcutta, 1894–1897," *Journal of the History of Medicine and Allied Sciences* 52, no. 1 (1997): 89–90.
92. Sutphen, "Not What, but Where," 93.
93. David Northrup, "Migration from Africa, Asia, and the South Pacific," in *Oxford History of the British Empire*, 3, 92.
94. Immanuel Wallerstein, "Does India Exist?" in *Unthinking Social Science: The Limits of Nineteenth Century Paradigms* (Cambridge: Polity Press, 1991), 130–4.
95. P. J. Marshall, "The British in Asia: Trade to Dominion, 1700–1765," in *The Oxford History of the British Empire*: vol. 2. *The Eighteenth Century*, ed. P. J. Marshall (Oxford: Oxford University Press, 1998), 503.
96. Vincent A. Smith, *The Oxford History of India* 4th ed. (Delhi: Oxford University Press, 1958), 526. See, too, H. V. Bowen, "British India, 1765–1813: The Metropolitan Context," in *Oxford History of the British Empire*, 2, 530–51.

97. Robin J. Moore, "Imperial India, 1858–1914," in *Oxford History of the British Empire*, 3, 426.
98. Judith M. Brown, *Modern India: The Origins of An Asian Democracy* (Delhi: Oxford University Press, 1985), 91; Arnold P. Kaminsky, *The India Office 1880–1910* (New York: Greenwood Press, 1986), 39; Moore, "Imperial India," 425.
99. Francis G. Hutchins, *The Illusion of Permanence: British Imperialism in India* (Princeton, NJ: Princeton University Press, 1967), 129.
100. Moore, "Imperial India," 442.
101. Brown, *Modern India*, 95; Thomas R. Metcalf, *The Aftermath of Revolt: India, 1857–70* (Delhi: Manohar Publications, 1990), 297.
102. David Omissi, *The Sepoy and the Raj: The Indian Army, 1860–1940* (Basingstoke and London: Macmillan, 1994), 132; Edward M. Spiers, *The Army and Society 1815–1914* (London: Longman, 1980), 135.
103. In the late nineteenth century, the notion of a Russian threat gripped many. It led not only to close attention to the Afghan-India border as a potentially vulnerable spot, but to the British leasing of Wei Hai Wei (1898) off the north China coast to counter Russia's annexation of Port Arthur.
104. P. J. Cain, and A. G. Hopkins, *British Imperialism: Innovation and Expansion 1688–1914*, vol. 1 (London: Longman, 1993), 330.
105. Moore, "Imperial India," 444.
106. The three presidency armies were amalgamated into a single service in 1893.
107. Brian Robson, ed. *Roberts in India: The Military Papers of Field Marshal Lord Roberts 1876–1893* (Stroud, Glos.: Alan Sutton for the Army Records Society, 1993), xv.
108. Omissi, *The Sepoy and the Raj*, 155; Douglas M. Peers, "Privates off Parade: Regimenting Sexuality in the Nineteenth-Century Indian Empire," *International History Review* 20, no. 4 (1998): 832. See, too, Stephen P. Cohen's invaluable study, *The Indian Army: Its Contribution to the Development of a Nation* (Delhi: Oxford University Press, 1990).
109. For more on cantonments, see T. Jacob, *Cantonments in India: Evolution and Growth* (New Delhi: Reliance Publishing House, 1994).
110. Moore, "Imperial India," 441.
111. Sugata Bose and Ayesha Jalal, *Modern South Asia: History, Culture, Political Economy* (Delhi: Oxford University Press, 1997; London and New York: Routledge, 1998), 100; Brown, *Modern India*, 96; Cain and Hopkins, *British Imperialism*, 333; Moore, "Imperial India," 441.
112. Ronald Hyam, *Britain's Imperial Century, 1815–1914: A Study of Empire and Expansion* (Basingstoke: The Macmillan Press, 1993), 35.
113. Bose and Jalal, *Modern South Asia*, 79; Richard H. Grove, "Colonial Conservation, Ecological Hegemony and Popular Resistance: Towards a Global Synthesis," in *Imperialism and the Natural World*, ed. John M. MacKenzie (Manchester: Manchester University Press, 1990), 32–6; Peter Marshall, *The Cambridge Illustrated History of the British Empire* (Cambridge: Cambridge University Press, 1996), 70.
114. Mark Harrison, "Towards A Sanitary Utopia? Professional Visions and Public Health in India, 1880–1914," *South Asia Research* 10, no. 1 (1990): 35.
115. Dagmar Engels, "History and Sexuality in India: Discursive Trends," *Trends in History* 4, no. 4 (1990): 29; Rosalind O'Hanlon, *A Comparison Between Women and Men: Tarabai Shinde and the Critique of Gender Relations in Colonial India* (Madras: Oxford University Press, 1994), 10–12; Tanika Sarkar, "The Hindu Wife and the Hindu Nation: Domesticity and Nationalism in Nineteenth Century Bengal," *Studies in History* n.s. 8, no. 2 (1992): 228.
116. Uma Chakravarti, "Whatever Happened to the Vedic *Dasi*? Orientalism, Nationalism and a Script for the Past," in *Recasting Women: Essays in Colonial History*, ed. Kumkum Sangari and Sudesh Vaid (Delhi; Kali for Women, 1993), 27–87; Partha Chatterjee, "Colonialism, Nationalism, and Colonialized Women: The Contest in India," *American Ethnologist* 16, no. 4 (1989): 622–33; Geraldine H. Forbes, "The Politics of Respectability: Indian Women and the Indian National Congress," in *The Indian National Congress: Centenary Hindsights*, ed. D. A. Low (Delhi: Oxford University Press, 1988), 54–97; Mrinalini Sinha, "Gender in the Critiques of Colonialism and Nationalism: Locating the 'Indian Woman,' " in *Feminists Revision History*, ed. Anne-Louise Shapiro (New Brunswick, NJ: Rutgers University Press, 1994), 246–75.
117. Lata Mani, *Contentious Traditions: The Debate on Sati in Colonial India* (Berkeley: University of California Press, 1998), 2.

Chapter 2

1. Gail Savage, "'The Wilful Communication of a Loathsome Disease': Marital Conflict and Venereal Disease in Victorian England," *Victorian Studies* 34, no. 1 (1990): 35–54.
2. His one exception to this rule is Scandinavia. Jay Cassel, *The Secret Plague: Venereal Disease in Canada 1838–1939* (Toronto: University of Toronto Press, 1987), 89.
3. "Contagious Diseases in China," *The Lancet* (14 November 1868): 645.
4. Douglas M. Peers, "Soldiers, Surgeons and the Campaigns to Combat Sexually Transmitted Diseases in Colonial India, 1805–1860," *Medical History* 42 (1998): 138.
5. The early Australian colonies used the criminal law to control prostitution, an unusual tactic hardly ever used in nonwhite colonies, and presumably feasible only because the bulk of the population was de facto classified as criminal. See Milton Lewis, "Sexually Transmitted Diseases in Australia from the Late Eighteenth to the Late Twentieth Century," in *Sex, Disease, and Society: A Comparative History of Sexually Transmitted Diseases and HIV/AIDS in Asia and the Pacific,* ed. Milton Lewis, Scott Bamber, and Michael Waugh (Westport, CT: Greenwood Press, 1997), 251.
6. Brendan O'Keefe, "Sexually Transmitted Diseases in Malaysia: A History," in *Sex, Disease, and Society,* 156; Anke Van Der Sterren et al., "A History of Sexually Transmitted Diseases in the Indian Archipelago," in *Sex, Disease, and Society,* 212; John Ingleson, "Prostitution in Colonial Java," in *Nineteenth and Twentieth Century Indonesia. Essays in Honour of Professor J. D. Legge,* ed. David P. Chandler and M. C. Ricklefs (Clayton, VIC: Centre of Southeast Asian Studies, Monash University, 1986), 123.
7. E. F. Chapman to Secretary to Government of India, Military Department, 5 May 1888, OIOC, L/MIL/3/980.
8. Memorandum on the Health of Europeans, 9 June 1827, OIOC, F/4/1079.
9. See Peers, "Soldiers" for policy in India prior to the CD system. For western India, see Judith Whitehead, "Bodies Clean and Unclean: Prostitution, Sanitary Legislation, and Respectable Femininity in Colonial North India," *Gender & History* 7, no. 1 (1995): 47. For Madras, see J. J. Frederick, Secretary, Army Sanitary Commission, 4 March 1873, OIOC, V/24/3677; M. Sundara Raj, *Prostitution in Madras: A Study in Historical Perspective* (Delhi: Konark Publications PVT Ltd., 1993), 23. For Bengal, see Bengal Military Consultations, 21 September 1807, OIOC, P/22/35 (21).
10. 8 September 1805, OIOC, F/4/200 (4502); Raj, *Prostitution in Madras,* 140.
11. OIOC, P/22/35(21).
12. Military Letter from Bengal, 31 January 1824, OIOC, F/4/835 (22253); Lock Hospital Returns for 1828, 31 July 1829, OIOC, P/33/31, Bengal Military Consultations.
13. Medical Board, 1 May 1809, OIOC, F/4/345 (8032); OIOC, F/4/379 (9490).
14. Adjutant General to Government of Madras, 10 July 1849, OIOC, F/4/2341.
15. Burke to Colonel Casement, Secretary to Government of India, Military Department, 21 April 1832, OIOC, F/4/1338 (53031). Peers, "Soldiers," addresses Burke's change of heart.
16. Public Letter to Madras, 24 April 1847, OIOC, F/4/2341.
17. Military Letter, 19 November 1813, OIOC, F/4/486 (11710).
18. Madras Judicial Consultations, September 1839, OIOC, P/325/65.
19. Raj, *Prostitution in Madras,* 25.
20. Surgeon General and Principal Medical Officer, British Forces in India to Secretary, Government of India, Military Department, 14 May 1877, OIOC, P/1203; C. B. Mayne, *How Far Past Legislation Has Proved Effective in Securing the Health of the Troops in India, With Suggestions as to Future Legislation on This Important Subject* (London: Horace Marshall, 1897), 5.
21. Military Department no. 81, 18 May 1888, OIOC, L/MIL/3/139; E. F. Chapman, Quartermaster General to Secretary to Government of India, Military Department, 5 May 1888, OIOC, P/3248.
22. Samuel Hickson to unnamed cousin, December 24, 1781, f. 79, Letters and Papers relating to Samuel Hickson, vol. 1, OIOC, Mss. Eur B. 296/1.
23. J. Strachey, President, Sanitary Commission, Bengal to Secretary to Government of India, Military Department, 21 March 1864, and no. 157, 24 March 1866, OIOC, P/438/27; Adjutant General to Military Department, 6 June 1859, OIOC, P/191/29.
24. Henry Labouchère, Baron Taunton (1798–1869) was colonial secretary from 1855 to 1858.
25. Henry Lethbridge claims the ordinance was "patterned" on the U.K. acts ("Prostitution in Hong Kong: A Legal and Moral Dilemma," *Hong Kong Law Journal* 8, no. 2 [1978]: 153), and

Norman Miners sees it as "modeled" on them: *Hong Kong Under Imperial Rule 1912–1941* (Hong Kong: Oxford University Press, 1987), 191. I depart from this view.

26. Alan Ramsay Skelley, *The Victorian Army At Home: The Recruitment and Terms and Conditions of the British Regular 1859–1899* (London: Croom Helm, 1977), 53.

27. The Cantonment Act and its many successors were not exclusively concerned with questions of sex or disease. The 1864 Act was a broad umbrella act intended to address hygiene issues in the military cantonments.

28. Sheldon Amos, *A Comparative Survey of Laws in Force for the Prohibition, Regulation and Licensing of Vice in England and Other Countries* (London: Stevens and Son, 1877), 407.

29. HC, *SP*, 1887, 347, *Contagious Diseases Ordinances (Colonies);* HC, *SP*, 1887, 196, *Contagious Diseases Acts (Egypt);* HC, *SP*, 1887, 20, *Contagious Diseases Ordinances (British Colonies).* With thanks to David Killingray for invaluable advice on Britain's West African colonies in personal correspondence, April 1998.

30. C. P. Lucas to Frederick Meade, 6 May 1879, PRO, CO129/184 (6690).

31. Dr. Murray, Colonial Surgeon, PRO, CO129/296 (4718).

32. *QPD*, Second Series, 1868, VI, 16 January 1868, 853–5, esp. Hon W. Wood. B. A. Smithurst points out that the bill's sponsors saw the legislation as a public health measure: "Historic and Epidemiologic Review of Venereal Disease in Queensland" (MD thesis, University of Queensland, 1981), vol. 1, 69.

33. Quartermaster General Major General E. B. Johnson to H. K. Burne, Secretary to Government of India, 22 October 1873, sent to the Secretary of State for India by Government of India, 2 January 1874 as Enclosure to OIOC, L/MIL/7/13809. The identical phrase was rehashed by a later incumbent, E. F. Chapman, writing to the Government of India, 2 August 1877, OIOC, L/MIL/3/977.

34. J. Marion Sims, "Presidential Address," *Transactions of the American Medical Association* 27 (1876): 102.

35. *The Lancet* (19 March 1863): 327, quoted in Kerrie L. Macpherson, "Conspiracy of Silence: A History of Sexually Transmitted Diseases and HIV/AIDS in Hong Kong," in *Sex, Disease, and Society,* 86.

36. Minute of Frederick S. Roberts, 15 May 1884, OIOC, P/2261 (also in OIOC, L/MIL/17/5/1615/3).

37. *Proceedings of the Council of the Governor General of India, 1897* (Calcutta: Office of the Superintendent of Government Printing, 1898), 8 July 1897, 317, OIOC, V/9/30.

38. Mark Harrison, "Towards A Sanitary Utopia? Professional Visions and Public Health in India, 1880–1914," *South Asia Research* 10, no. 1 (1990): 35.

39. Queensland, *Official Record of the Debates of the Legislative Council and the Legislative Assembly,* 1911–12, vol. 108, Hon. B. Fahey, 13 September 1911, 931.

40. O'Keefe, "Sexually Transmitted Diseases in Malaysia," 157.

41. Dr. Drysdale [probably Charles R.], *Prostitution Medically Considered with some of its Social Aspects* (London: Robert Hardwicke, 1866), 32.

42. Lord Ripon to Lord Hartington, 16 January 1882, OIOC, L/E/7/3 (230), and reprinted in HC, *SP,* (200) 1883, *Copy of, or Extracts from Correspondence between the Government of India and the Secretary of State in Council upon the Subject of the CONTAGIOUS DISEASES ACTS and their Repeal,* 16 June 1882, 64.

43. HC, *SP,* (260) 1877, *Workhouse Unions, England and Wales (Diseases): Returns of the General Diseases and Venereal Diseases from the Workhouse of each Union in England and Wales, during the First Week in January 1876,* 17.

44. Charles Bell Taylor, *The Soldier and His Masters: From A Sanitary Point of View* (London: Kelvin Glen and Co., 1898), 8.

45. Ivor Felstein, *Sexual Pollution: The Fall and Rise of Venereal Diseases* (Newton Abbot and London: David and Charles, 1974), 21.

46. Dorothy and Roy Porter, *In Sickness and In Health: The British Experience 1650–1850* (London: Fourth Estate Press, 1988), 72.

47. G. J. Guthrie, *Observations on the Treatment of Venereal Disease Without Mercury* (London: G. Woodfall, 1817), 2; *The Lancet* (15 January 1853): 63.

48. Examples of those who excluded VD as a topic for discussion might include Alexander P. Stewart and Edward Jenkins, *The Medical and Legal Aspects of Sanitary Reform,* 2nd ed. (London: R. Hardwicke, 1867) and Henry W. Rumsey, *Laws Affecting the Public Health in England* (London, n.p. 1870). Rumsey notes in his single paragraph on syphilis (9) that it

is a disease "no less formidable than smallpox" but discusses the implications of this no further. In their survey of public health in nineteenth-century Britain, Elizabeth Fee and Dorothy Porter stress environmental issues as the principal concern of the famed Chadwick survey of 1842: clean water, efficient sewerage and drainage, clean streets and thoroughfares, and control of industrial effluents. Fee and Porter, "Public Health, Preventive Medicine and Professionalization: England and America in the Nineteenth Century," in *Medicine in Society: Historical Essays*, ed. Andrew Wear (Cambridge: Cambridge University Press, 1992), 252–3.

49. John Simon, *English Sanitary Institutions Reviewed In Their Course of Development, and in Some of their Political and Social Relations* (London: Cassell, 1890). Simon was medical officer of health for the City of London Corporation from 1848. He was appointed medical officer of the Board of Health in 1855. The department was moved to the Privy Council in 1859 as a result of changes made in administrative structure by the 1858 Public Health Act.

50. Good examples are Philip D. Curtin, *Death by Migration: Europe's Encounter with the Tropical World in the Nineteenth Century* (Cambridge: Cambridge University Press, 1989) where VD is mentioned only at 156, and Radhika Ramasubbhan, "Imperial Health in British India, 1857–1900," in *Disease, Medicine, and Empire: Perspectives on Western Medicine and the Experience of European Expansion*, ed. Roy Macleod and Milton Lewis (London: Routledge, 1988), 38–60, which devotes only a footnote to VD. David Arnold also notes this neglect of VD in "Sexually Transmitted Diseases in Nineteenth and Twentieth Century India," *Genitourinary Medicine* 69, no. 1 (1993): 3. Arnold is, of course, one of a growing number of historians who have studied VD at length. I am indebted to Alison Bashford for pointing out to me in private correspondence that this separation is also reflected in the surprisingly different historiographies of sanitary reform and VD control.

51. Henry H. Fowler to Governor General, India, 29 November 1894, OIOC, L/MIL/7/13854.

52. *Report of Proceedings in New South Wales Legislative Assembly, Sydney Morning Herald*, 8 December 1875, 4, (Mr. Farnell).

53. *Transactions of the Seventh International Congress of Hygiene and Demography*, vol. 11. *Indian Hygiene and Demography* (London: Eyre and Spottiswoode, 1892), 65.

54. William Hill-Climo, "The British Soldier in India and Enthetic Diseases," *United Services Magazine* 15 n.s. (1896–7): 375.

55. Miles Ogborn, "Law and Discipline in Nineteenth Century English State Formation: The Contagious Diseases Acts of 1864, 1868 and 1869," *Journal of Historical Sociology* 6, no. 1 (1993): 37–8.

56. Ibid., 39.

57. Edmund A. Parkes, *A Manual of Practical Hygiene Prepared Especially for Use in the Medical Service of the Army* (London: John Churchill and Sons, 1864), 451.

58. Lord Lansdowne to India Secretary, Lord Cross, 4 February 1891, OIOC, L/MIL/7/13834.

59. Freda Harcourt, "Disraeli's Imperialism, 1866–1868: A Question of Timing," *Historical Journal* 23, no. 1 (1980): 95.

60. Curtin, *Death by Migration*, 156; Officers of the Royal Army Medical Corps, *A Manual of Venereal Diseases* (London: Oxford Medical Publications/Henry Frowde/Hodder and Stoughton, 1907), 1–3; Arnold, "Sexually Transmitted Diseases," 3.

61. Peter Burroughs, "Imperial Defence and the Victorian Army," *Journal of Imperial and Commonwealth History* 15, no. 1 (1986): 62.

62. HC, *SP*, 1863, (3184), XIX, *Report of the Commissioners appointed to enquire into the Sanitary State of the Army in India*, 126.

63. Unsigned, undated memo, 1879, PRO, CO129/186 (12523).

64. Sugata Bose and Ayesha Jalal, *Modern South Asia: History, Culture, Political Economy* (Delhi: Oxford University Press, 1997; London and New York: Routledge, 1998), 68; Mark Harrison, *Public Health in British India: Anglo-Indian Preventive Medicine 1859–1914* (Cambridge: Cambridge University Press, 1994), 72.

65. *Proceedings of the Council of the Governor General of India, 1864* (Calcutta: Military Orphan Press, 1865), 105, OIOC, V/9/8.

66. Government of India to Secretary of State for India, 27 March 1888, OIOC, P/3195.

67. J. B. Harrison, "Allahabad: A Sanitary History," in *The City in South Asia: Pre-modern and Modern*, ed. Kenneth Ballhatchet and John Harrison (London and Dublin: Curzon Press; Atlantic Highlands, NJ: Humanities Press, 1980), 170.

68. Adjutant General to Secretary, Government of India, Military Department, 18 March 1859, OIOC, P/273/101.

69. Roger Jeffery, *The Politics of Health in India* (Berkeley: University of California Press, 1988), 68.

70. John Gill Gamble, "The Origins, Administration, and Impact of the Contagious Diseases Acts from a Military Perspective," (Ph. D. diss., University of Southern Mississippi, 1983): F. B. Smith, "The Contagious Diseases Acts Reconsidered," *Social History of Medicine* 3, no. 2 (1990): 197–215.

71. Jean M. Kehoe, "Medicine, Sexuality and Imperialism. British Medical Discourses Surrounding Venereal Disease in New Zealand and Japan: A Socio-historical and Comparative Study," (Ph. D. diss., Victoria University of Wellington, 1992), 65.

72. Mary Poovey, "Speaking of the Body: Mid-Victorian Constructions of Female Desire," in *Body/Politics: Women and the Discourses of Science*, ed. Mary Jacobus, Evelyn Fox Keller, and Sally Shuttleworth (New York: Routledge, 1990), 30.

73. *Selections from Despatches Addressed to the Several Governments in India by the Secretary of State in Council* (London: Eyre and Spottiswoode for HMSO, 1894), 453. Enclosure (Army Sanitary Commission memorandum, 11 December 1893) to Military Despatch no. 25, Earl of Kimberley to Governor General, 1 March 1894, OIOC, V/6/331; also at OIOC, P/5016 (1778).

74. *Fourth Annual Report on the Working of the Lock Hospitals in the Northwest Provinces and Oudh for the Year 1877* (Allahabad, n.p.,1878), Report of Bareilly Lock Hospital, 18, OIOC, V/24/2290.

75. W. M. Muir, Inspector General of Hospitals and Principal Medical Officer to British Troops in India to Secretary to Government of India, Military Department, 31 December 1869, OIOC, V/24/3675.

76. PRO, ADM1/6418; HC, *SP*, 1886, 247, *Contagious Diseases Ordinances (British Colonies)*.

77. HC, *SP*, 1886, 247, *Contagious Diseases Ordinances (British Colonies)*.

78. House Committee Minute Books, LLH, RCS.

79. T. J. Wyke, "Hospital Facilities for, and Diagnosis and Treatment of, Venereal Disease in England, 1800–1870," *British Journal of Venereal Diseases* 49 (1973): 78.

80. Advisory Board for Army Medical Services, *First Report: The Treatment of Venereal Disease and Scabies in the Army* (London: HMSO, 1904), 5.

81. *General Report on the Administration of the Bombay Presidency 1871–2* (Bombay: Bombay Secretariat Office, 1872), 480, OIOC, V/10/283.

82. Major General H. Marshall, Secretary to Government of Madras, Military Department to Officiating Secretary, Government of India, Military Department, 26 May 1868, OIOC, P/435/62.

83. C. A. Elliott, Officiating Secretary to NWP Government to A. O. Hume, Officiating Secretary to Government of India, 10 December 1870, NAI, Home Department, Public Consultations A, Proceedings 1870.

84. Letters between Chief Commissioner of Oudh and Officiating Secretary, Government of India, Home Department, 1876, OIOC, P/1002.

85. *QPD*, Legislative Assembly, *Votes and Proceedings* 1879, Report of W. Hobbs, Medical Officer to Colonial Secretary, 10 March 1879, 3.

86. *Official Record of the Debates of the Legislative Assembly* 1886, vol. 50, Mr. McFarlane, 6 October 1886, 1122.

87. Enid Barclay, "Queensland's Contagious Diseases Act, 1868—'The Act for the Encouragement of Vice' and some Nineteenth Century Attempts to Repeal It, Part 1," *Queensland Heritage* 2, no. 10 (1965): 31.

88. Minute, 2 April 1878, PRO, CO129/183 (4062); Minute of G. W. Johnson, 23 November 1888, PRO, CO129/239 (22188).

89. *Report of Prostitution Committee, Bombay*, 1921, OIOC, V/26/803/4.

90. Memo of J. M. Cuningham, Sanitary Commissioner, Government of India and Surgeon General, Bengal Presidency, 4 August 1880, f. 461, Diary no. 111, Ripon Papers, LXXXIV, BL, Add. Ms. 43, 574.

91. Ripon et al. to Secretary of State for India, 16 January 1886, OIOC, P/1851.

92. Commissioner, Lucknow Division to Secretary, Chief Commissioner, Oudh, 20 November 1875, OIOC, P/1002.

93. R. L. Mangles, Officiating Secretary, Government of Bengal to Secretary, Government of India, Military Department, 25 January 1877, OIOC, P/1003.

94. HC, *SP*, [C. 2415], 1879, *Report on Sanitary Measures in India in 1877–78*, vol. 11;

Memorandum of the Army Sanitary Commission on the Report on Lock Hospitals of the Madras Presidency for 1877, 196.

95. Colonial Office Memorandum, illegible initials, 27 November 1879, PRO, CO129/186 (17899).
96. *Annual Report on Chinese Protectorate, Singapore and Penang, 1887* (Singapore: Government Printing Office, 1888), 24, PRO, CO273/152 (12665); memo (author unknown, probably George Johnson) to John Bramston, 21 January 1887, PRO, CO273/149 (1927).
97. Memo, signature illegible, 16 May 1931, PRO, CO129/533/10 (28460).
98. *Hong Kong Legislative Council Sessional Papers, 1887* (Hong Kong: Government Printer, 1888), Colonial Surgeon's Report for 1886, Enclosure no. 2, 305.
99. March 1880 draft of a proposed Colonial Office reply to a letter from Lord Stanley of Alderley, PRO, CO129/191 (4096). There is no indication in the file of whether this was ever sent.
100. Officer Commanding, Secunderabad to Adjutant General, 17 June 1848; and Order of Captain Morgan, Superintendent of Police, 28 November 1844, OIOC, F/4/2341.
101. *Special Committee's Exposition of the Lock Hospital Rules* (Strachey Committee), 14 August 1865, 94; confirmed in *Cantonment Regulations framed under Act XXII of 1864* (Calcutta: Superintendent of Government Printing, 1881), 54, OIOC, L/MIL/17/5/1828; reproduced in HC, *SP*, 1887,C. 61, LXII, 903.
102. HC, *SP*, 1887, LXII, 903 (C.61), *East India (Contagious Diseases Acts)*. Extracts from Rules and Regulations for Military Cantonments in Madras Presidency, chap. V.
103. Memorandum of F. Douglas, Civil Surgeon, Lucknow, 2 February 1864, OIOC, P/438/27.
104. Deputy Commissioner, Lucknow to Secretary to Chief Commissioner, Oudh, 16 February 1872, and quoted by H. J. Sparks, Officiating Secretary to Chief Commissioner, Oudh to Officiating Secretary, Government of India, 17 June 1875, NAI, Home Proceedings of the Government of India, Sanitary Department A, April 1875.
105. R. Hope Pilcher, Junior Secretary to Chief Commissioner of British Burma to Officiating Secretary, Government of India, 31 October 1878, OIOC, P/1338.
106. Quartermaster General, Circular Memorandum no. 80, 30 September 1873, OIOC, L/MIL/3/980, and printed for parliament, HC, *SP*, 1888, 107, *East India (Contagious Diseases)*, 5. The policy was almost certainly India-wide despite later claims that it applied only to Bengal by the Bengal surgeon general, J. Fullarton Beatson, in a letter to the officiating secretary of the government of Bengal, Judicial Department, 16 May 1877, OIOC, P/1003, and by the quartermaster general, E. F. Chapman writing to the secretary to the government of India, Military Department, 5 May 1888, OIOC, L/MIL/7/13822. The Lucknow division commissioner, however, writing to the secretary of the chief commissioner of Oudh on 20 November 1875 opined that it was the government of India and not the government of Bengal who prohibited the collection of fees, OIOC, P/1002. The NAI Home Proceedings of the Government of India, Sanitary Department A for August 1875, speaks of an order issued by the government of India military department, no. 129 of 4 September 1873, prohibiting fees. The Circular Memorandum was actually issued 30 September 1873.
107. HC, *SP*, 1883, (200), *East India (Contagious Diseases Acts)*. Government of India, Home, Sanitary Department to Secretary of State for India, 16 June 1882.
108. Report from Lucknow, n.d., 1877, OIOC, P/1203.
109. Colman Macaulay, Officiating Secretary to Government of Bengal, Judicial and Political Department to Secretary, Government of India, Home Department, 3 February 1879, OIOC, P/1338.
110. Government of India, Home Department, Sanitary to Secretary of State for India, 16 June 1882, HC, *SP*, 1883, (200), *East India (Contagious Diseases Acts)*, 65.
111. Memo, initials illegible to Frederick Meade, 20 January 1873, PRO, CO273/65 (2546).
112. J. M. Cuningham, Sanitary Commissioner, Government of India to Secretary, Government of India, Military Department, 11 May 1875, NAI, Home Proceedings of the Government of India, Sanitary Department A, August 1875.
113. John Pope Hennessy to Michael Hicks-Beach, Colonial Secretary, 18 March 1879, PRO, CO129/184 (6691). For more on Berger, see Susanna Hoe, *The Private Life of Old Hong Kong: Western Women in the British Colony 1841–1941* (Hong Kong: Oxford University Press, 1991), 141–4.
114. *Bills, Objects and Reasons, 1868*, OIOC, L/P& J/5/10.
115. Lock Hospital Reports, Bengal, for 1888 and 1887 respectively, OIOC, L/MIL/7/13903.
116. *Rules under Clause 7, s. 19. Act XXII of 1864*, OIOC, P/1003.

117. Minute of Governor, April 1879, PRO, CO129/203 (20349).
118. Quartermaster General's Circular Memorandum no. 69, 26 November 1883, OIOC, P/3248, and at OIOC, L/MIL/3/980.
119. See, for example, Lock Hospital Reports for Central Provinces, 1886–8, Pachmarhi Report, 15, OIOC, L/MIL/7/13908.
120. Circular Memorandum no. 42, 12 July 1883, OIOC, L/MIL/3/980.
121. *Tenth Annual Report on the Working of the Lock Hospitals in the Northwest Provinces and Oudh for the Year 1883* (Allahabad, n.p.,1884), 6, OIOC, V/24/2290.
122. Ibid., 12.
123. Bombay Lock Hospital Reports, 1887, OIOC, L/MIL/7/13905.
124. J. Fullarton Beatson, Surgeon General, Indian Medical Department to Officiating Secretary to Government of Bengal Judicial Department, "Memorandum on the Working of the CD Acts in Bengal Proper, 16 May 1877," OIOC, P/1003.
125. See, for example, the policies described in Major C. H. Le Mesurier, Commanding at Jutogh to J. W. McNabb, Deputy Commissioner, Simla, 15 August 1874, NAI, Home Proceedings, Sanitary A, October 1874.
126. Administrator (signature illegible) to Kimberley, Colonial Office, 21 November 1871, PRO, CO273/51 (12747).
127. Philip Howell, "Prostitution and Racialised Sexuality: The Regulation of Prostitution in Britain and the British Empire before the Contagious Diseases Acts," *Environment and Planning D: Society and Space* 18 (2000): 328–9.
128. Memo, C. P. Lucas to Frederick Meade, 6 May 1879, PRO, CO129/184 (6690).
129. Minute, 21 October 1880, f. 470, 1880, Ripon Papers, LXXXIV. Diary no. 111, BL, Add. Ms. 43, 574.
130. India Office to Governor General, 26 October 1882, OIOC, L/P& J/7/92 (2090/1884).
131. Barclay, "Queensland's Contagious Diseases Act, part 1," 27.
132. *Proceedings of the Council of the Governor General in India, 1868* (Calcutta: Office of the Superintendent of Government Printing, 1869), 27 March 1868, 218, OIOC, V/9/10.
133. C. S. Bayley, Secretary, Government of Bengal to Secretary, Government of India, Home Department, 30 July 1877, OIOC, P/1003.
134. Minute, 1 July 1893, OIOC, L/MIL/7/13843.
135. S. C. Bayley, Officiating Additional Secretary, Government of Bengal to Government of India, Home Department, 20 January 1868, *Annual Report of the Administration of the Bengal Presidency* (Calcutta: Bengal Secretariat Office, 1868), 184, OIOC, V/10/29; also at P/435/52 (381).
136. India Military Consultations, November 1865, OIOC, P/192/38 (70).
137. Circular Order no. 43, 20 September 1869, OIOC, P/674.
138. Colman Macaulay, Officiating Secretary, Government of Bengal to Government of India, Home, Revenue and Agriculture Department, 26 July 1880, OIOC, P/1664.
139. Timothy Gilfoyle has noted that regulation systems invariably registered only a minority of those practicing prostitution: "Prostitutes in History: From Parables of Pornography to Metaphors of Modernity," *American Historical Review* 104, no. 1 (1999): 134–5.
140. Memo, signature illegible, probably John Bramston, 29 April 1879, PRO, CO129/186 (17899).
141. *Annual Medical Report for the Straits Settlements, 1887*, 2, PRO, CO273/152 (11275).
142. *Rules under Clause 7, s. 19. Act XXII of 1864*, ss. 2 and 3, OIOC, P/1003.
143. Resolution on Sanitary Commission Report, 7 November 1873, OIOC, P/525.
144. *Annual Report of the Administration of the Bengal Presidency* (Calcutta: Bengal Secretariat Office, 1872), 208, OIOC, V/10/47.
145. *Lock Hospital Reports for Central Provinces, 1878*, 5, OIOC, V/24/2295.
146. *Fourth Annual Report . . . 1877*, Bareilly report, 16, OIOC, V/24/2290.
147. Lock Hospital Reports, Bengal 1886–90, Report for Barrackpore, 1887, OIOC, L/MIL/7/13903.
148. Lock Hospital Reports, Punjab 1887–90, Report for 1887, 1, OIOC, L/MIL/7/13906.
149. When a VD ordinance was passed in Papua in 1918, it followed the principle of the Queensland legislation in being inapplicable to "natives . . . owing to the existence of sufficient powers" already enjoyed. AAC, Series A1, 1919/4034, Commonwealth of Australia, Home and Territories Department, Papua Health (Venereal Diseases) Ordinance 1918.
150. Memo of G. W. Johnson, 23 November 1888, PRO, CO129/239 (22188).

151. Hong Kong Ordinance no. 10 of 1867, s. 30.

152. Undated, unsigned memo, 1879, PRO, CO129/186 (12523).

153. *Special Committee's Exposition of the Lock Hospital Rules*, 91, OIOC, L/MIL/17/5/1828.

154. *Fourth Annual Report . . . 1877*, 8, OIOC, V/24/2290.

155. Raj, *Prostitution in Madras*, 38.

156. *Proceedings of the Council of the Governor General of India, 1864* (Calcutta: Military Orphan Press, 1865), 105, 30 March 1864, comments of Sir Charles Trevelyan, OIOC, V/9/8.

157. W. M. Clarke (Visiting Surgeon), *Report on the Working of the Contagious Diseases Act from December 1st 1869 to December 31st, 1870*, n.p, PRO, ADM/1/6197.

158. Archival records of resistance abound. See, for example, PRO, ADM/1/6498 (31); ADM/1/6292 (34) and (56) and (85), all from the years in which the metropolitan CD laws operated. See too Linda E. Merians, "The London Lock Hospital and the Lock Asylum for Women," in *The Secret Malady: Venereal Disease in Eighteenth-Century Britain and France*, ed. Linda E. Merians (Lexington: University of Kentucky Press, 1997), 140; Philippa Levine, "Women and Prostitution: Metaphor, Reality, History," *Canadian Journal of History* 28, no. 3 (1993): 479–94; idem. "'Rough Usage:' Prostitution, Law, and the Social Historian," in *Rethinking Social History: English Society 1570–1920 and Its Interpretation*, ed. Adrian Wilson (Manchester: Manchester University Press, 1993), 266–92.

159. James Bettley, "Post Voluptatem Misericordia: The Rise and Fall of the London Lock Hospital," *London Journal* 10, no. 2 (1984): 169; RCS, LLH, "Rules for Asylum Patients," 1890; M. A. Waugh, "Attitudes of Hospitals in London to Venereal Disease in the 18th and 19th Centuries," *British Journal of Venereal Diseases* 47 (1971): 148; M. A. Crowther, "The Later Years of the Workhouse 1890–1929," in *The Origins of British Social Policy*, ed. Pat Thane (London: Croom Helm, 1978), 51. Asylums and refuges in England did not allow women readmission. Irish refuges, according to Maria Luddy, did: "'Abandoned Women and Bad Characters': Prostitution in Nineteenth Century Ireland," *Women's History Review* 6, no. 4 (1997): 497; idem. "Prostitution and Rescue Work in Nineteenth-Century Ireland," in *Women Surviving: Studies in Irish Women's History in the 19th and 20th Centuries*, ed. Maria Luddy and Cliona Murphy (Dublin: Poolberg Press, 1990), 74.

160. For the treatment of VD in the workhouse system, see A. Fessler, "Venereal Disease and Prostitution in the Reports of the Poor Law Commissioners, 1834–1850," *British Journal of Venereal Diseases* 27 (1951): 154–57.

161. Howell, "Prostitution and Racialised Sexuality," 331.

162. Memorandum: Contagious Diseases Act of 1868, n.d, QSA, HOM/J80.

163. Luke Trainor, *British Imperialism and Australian Nationalism: Manipulation, Conflict and Compromise in the Late Nineteenth Century* (Cambridge: Cambridge University Press, 1994), 1.

164. Elizabeth B. Van Heyningen, "The Social Evil in the Cape Colony 1868–1902: Prostitution and the Contagious Diseases Acts," *Journal of Southern African Studies* 10, no. 2 (1984): 173.

165. Peter J. Durrans, "The House of Commons and the British Empire 1868–1880," *Canadian Journal of History* 9, no. 1 (1974): 19. For a different view of parliamentary interest in colonial questions, see Trainor, *British Imperialism*, 95.

166. John W. Cell, *British Colonial Administration in the Mid-Nineteenth Century: The Policy-Making Process* (New Haven, CT: Yale University Press, 1970); Arnold P. Kaminsky, *The India Office 1880–1910* (New York: Greenwood Press, 1986).

167. Antoinette Burton, "Recapturing *Jane Eyre*: Reflections on Historicizing the Colonial Encounter in Victorian Britain," *Radical History Review* 64 (1996): 60. For further discussions of the view that the metropolitan and the imperial cannot be separated, see Frederick Cooper and Ann Laura Stoler, ed. *Tensions of Empire: Colonial Cultures in a Bourgeois World* (Berkeley: University of California Press, 1997); Mrinalini Sinha, *Colonial Masculinity: The "Manly Englishman" and the "Effeminate Bengali" in the Late Nineteenth Century* (Manchester: Manchester University Press, 1995); and Catherine Hall, "Rethinking Imperial Histories: The Reform Act of 1867," *New Left Review* 208 (1994): 3–29.

168. Note by Sir Alexander J. Arbuthnot, 7 May 1888, OIOC, L/MIL/7/13819.

169. *Proceedings of the Council of the Governor General of India, 1895* (Calcutta: Office of the Superintendent of Government Printing, 1895), Hon Sir Griffith Evans, 24 January 1895, 38, OIOC, V/9/29.

170. Maryinez Lyons and Megan Vaughan both offer interesting rationales for the marked colonial public health interest in syphilis in early twentieth-century Uganda; see Vaughan, *Curing*

Their Ills: Colonial Power and African Illness (Stanford, CA; Stanford University Press, 1991), 132–9, and Lyons, "The Power To Heal: African Medical Auxiliaries in Colonial Belgian Congo and Uganda," in *Contesting Colonial Hegemony: State and Society in Africa and India*, ed. Dagmar Engels and Shula Marks (London: British Academic Press/German Historical Institute, 1994), 205–6.

171. J. Strachey, President, Sanitary Commission, Bengal to Secretary to Government of India, Military Department, 2 May 1864, OIOC, P/438/27.

172. Queensland, *Official Record of the Debates of the Legislative Assembly*, 1884, vol. 44, 21 November 1884, 1523.

173. Kay Daniels argues that the passing of the 1879 CD Act in the southerly island colony of Tasmania was prompted by naval interests; see "Prostitution in Tasmania during the Transition from Penal Settlement to 'Civilized' Society," in *So Much Hard Work: Women and Prostitution in Australian History*, ed. Kay Daniels (Sydney: Fontana/Collins, 1984), 58–9. See too Mary Murnane and Kay Daniels, "Prostitutes as 'Purveyors of Disease': Venereal Disease Legislation in Tasmania, 1868–1945," *Hecate* 5 (1979): 6.

174. *QPD*, Second Series, 1867, vol. 5, Hon William Hobbs, 19 September 1867, 148.

175. Home Secretary's Department, General Correspondence, 1911, *Contagious Diseases Act of 1868*, QSA, HOM/J80.

Chapter 3

1. Mark Harrison, "Towards A Sanitary Utopia? Professional Visions and Public Health in India, 1880–1914," *South Asia Research* 10, no. 1 (1990): 21; E. Richard. Brown, "Public Health in Imperialism: Early Rockefeller Programs at Home and Abroad," *American Journal of Public Health* 66, no. 9 (1976): 897.

2. Sudhir Chandra, "Whose Laws? Notes on a Legitimising Myth of the Colonial Indian State," *Studies in History* 8, no. 2 (1992): 187.

3. In communist China, conversely, syphilis was seen as a peculiarly modern affliction, symbolizing the decline of civilization. See Frank Dikötter, *Sex, Culture, and Modernity in China: Medical Science and the Construction of Sexual Identities in the Early Republican Period* (Honolulu: University of Hawaii Press, 1995), 132.

4. Rajnarayan Chandavarkar, "Plague, Panic and Epidemic Politics in India, 1896–1914," in *Epidemics and Ideas, Essays in the Historical Perception of Pestilence*, ed. Terence Ranger and Paul Slack (Cambridge: Cambridge University Press, 1992), 214; Harrison, "Towards A Sanitary Utopia?," 21–2.

5. Gwendolyn Wright, writing on French colonialism, notes the claims of colonial professionals across the board to an apolitical stance: *The Politics of Design in French Colonial Urbanism* (Chicago: University of Chicago Press, 1991), 7.

6. "Clinical Notes," *The Indian Medical Journal* n.s. 8, no. 13 (July 1888): 353.

7. M. Gaisford, "Some Remarks on the Contagious Diseases Act and Its Working in Indian Cantonments," *Proceedings of the N.W. Provinces and Oudh Branch of the British Medical Association* 2, no. 13 (June 1883): 219.

8. John and Jean Comaroff, *Ethnography and the Historical Imagination* (Boulder, CO: Westview Press, 1992), 216.

9. Governor General's Minute, Military Department, 27 December 1831, OIOC, F/4/1338 (53031).

10. *Lecture delivered by Dr. McLean at the opening of the Military Medical College, Netley, October 1st 1863*, n.p., n.d.

11. Satadru Sen, "Policing the Savage: Segregation, Labor, and State Medicine in the Andamans," *Journal of Asian Studies* 58, no. 3 (1999): 769.

12. Dufferin to Cross, 29 June 1888, OIOC, Mss. Eur. F.130/11A, f. 115; also in OIOC, Mss. Eur. E.243/24.

13. Minute of G. W. Johnson to J. Bramston, 23 November 1893, PRO, CO129/259 (12527).

14. T. E. P. Martin, *Sketch of the Medical History of the Native Army of Bombay for the Year 1871* (Bombay: Education Society's Press, 1872), 141, OIOC, V/24/3103; see too *Medical and Sanitary Reports of the Native Army of Bengal for the Year 1872* (Calcutta: Office of the Superintendent of Government Printing, 1874), 26, OIOC, V/24/3109.

15. Minute, G. W. Johnson, 27 May 1893, PRO, CO273/187 (4922). An internal office memo, 22 November 1897, (signature illegible) describes Johnson as an "expert" on the topic, PRO, CO129/276 (17234).

16. Report of the Northern Protector of Aborigines for 1900, 1 January 1901, n.p., QSA, COL/1452 (04884).

17. Appendix to Report of a Committee assembled at Calcutta under the Orders of the Government of India, 14 January 1881, 19. Evidence of Dr. Reilly, Resident Medical Officer, Chandney Dispensary, OIOC, L/E/6/66 (19054).

18. George Newton, *Medical Report of the Yokohama Lock Hospital for 1869* (Yokohama: *Japan Gazette* Office, 1870), 14, PRO, ADM125/16 (804).

19. Report of the Northern Protector of Aborigines for 1900, QSA, COL/1452 (04884).

20. George Newton to Sir Henry Kellett, 1 July 1871, PRO, ADM125/16 (804).

21. Chief Inspector of Aborigines, January 1916, AAC, Series A3/1, NT1916/608.

22. Peshawar report, Cantonment Hospital Reports, Punjab Command 1894–1896, OIOC, L/MIL/7/13915.

23. Surgeon Colonel R. Harvey, Indian Medical Service, quoted by A. E. Grant in *The Indian Manual of Hygiene* 1 (Madras, 1894): ciii–civ, quoted in turn in David Arnold, "Public Health and Public Power: Medicine and Hegemony in Colonial India," in *Contesting Colonial Hegemony: State and Society in Africa and India*, ed. Dagmar Engels and Shula Marks (London: British Academic Press/German Historical Institute, 1994), 136.

24. Milton Lewis, "Sexually Transmitted Diseases in Australia from the Late Eighteenth to the Late Twentieth Century," in *Sex, Disease, and Society: A Comparative History of Sexually Transmitted Diseases and HIV/AIDS in Asia and the Pacific*, ed. Milton Lewis, Scott Bamber, and Michael Waugh (Westport, CT: Greenwood Press, 1997), 250; P. Ariyaratne De Silva and Michael G. Gomez, "The History of Venereal Disease and Yaws (Parangi) in Sri Lanka," *Genitourinary Medicine* 70, no. 5 (1994): 349; Deborah Pellow, "STDs and AIDS in Ghana," *Genitourinary Medicine* 70, no. 6 (1994): 418.

25. Judy Campbell argues, for instance, that the Australian colonists mistook nonvenereal treponemal infections for syphilis among Aboriginal peoples: "Smallpox in Aboriginal Australia, 1829–31," *Historical Studies* 20, no. 81 (1983): 537.

26. Kenneth F. Kiple, "Syphilis, Nonvenereal," in *The Cambridge World History of Human Disease* (Cambridge: Cambridge University Press, 1993), 1033. See, too, Sheldon Watts, *Epidemics and History: Disease, Power, and Imperialism* (New Haven, CT: Yale University Press, 1997).

27. O. P. Arya, A. O. Osoba, and F. J. Bennett, *Tropical Venereology*, 2nd ed. (Edinburgh: Churchill Livingstone, 1988), 7.

28. Internal Colonial Office memorandum, author unknown, 15 June 1887, PRO, CO273/144 (8517).

29. Bridie J. Andrews, "Tuberculosis and the Assimilation of Germ Theory in China, 1895–1937," *Journal of the History of Medicine and Allied Sciences* 51, no. 1 (1997): 120.

30. Warwick Anderson, *The Cultivation of Whiteness: Science, Health and Racial Destiny in Australia* (Carlton South: Melbourne University Press, 2002), 81.

31. See, for example, Harry Oosterhuis, "Medical Science and the Modernisation of Sexuality," in *Sexual Cultures in Europe: National Histories*, ed. Franz X. Eder, Lesley A. Hall, and Gert Hekma (Manchester: Manchester University Press, 1999), 221–41; Alan Hunt, "The Great Masturbation Panic and the Discourses of Moral Regulation in Nineteenth and Early Twentieth Century Britain," *Journal of the History of Sexuality* 8, no. 4 (1998): 575–615.

32. For discussion of the medical racialization of disease, see Melbourne Tapper, *In the Blood: Sickle Cell Anemia and the Politics of Race* (Philadelphia, PA: University of Pennsylvania Press, 1999), Keith Wailoo, *Dying in the City of the Blues: Sickle Cell Anemia and the Politics of Race and Health* (Chapel Hill, NC: University of North Carolina Press, 2001); and Nancy Rose Hunt, *A Colonial Lexicon: Of Birth Ritual, Medicalization, and Mobility in the Congo* (Durham, NC: Duke University Press, 1999).

33. Evidence of Thomas Longmore, professor of military surgery, Army Medical School, Netley, Skey Committee Report and Minutes of Evidence (1864), 42, PRO, WO33/17A (0274).

34. William Ingleden to James Anderson, Physician General, 23 September 1808, OIOC, F/4/345 (8031).

35. M. Berkeley Hill, *Syphilis and Local Contagious Disorders* (London: James Walton, 1868), 34.

36. Ibid., *Syphilis*, 35.

37. David Arnold, *Colonizing the Body: State Medicine and Epidemic Disease in Nineteenth-Century India* (Berkeley: University of California Press, 1993), 89.
38. "Contagious Diseases on the China Station," *The Lancet* (19 June 1869): 859.
39. Brenda S. A. Yeoh, "Sexually Transmitted Diseases in Late Nineteenth- and Twentieth-Century Singapore," in *Sex, Disease, and Society*, 177.
40. Arnold, *Colonizing the Body*, 42–3.
41. J. D. Oriel, *The Scars of Venus: A History of Venereology* (London: Springer-Verlag, 1994), 39.
42. Mary Anne Jebb, "The Lock Hospitals Experiment: Europeans, Aborigines and Venereal Disease," *Studies in Western Australian History* 8 (1984): 76.
43. Michael A. Waugh, "History of Clinical Developments in Sexually Transmitted Diseases," in *Sexually Transmitted Diseases*, ed. King K. Holmes, Per-Anders Mårdh, P. Frederick Sparling, and Paul J. Wiesner, 2nd ed. (New York: McGraw Hill, 1990), 9.
44. "C," *The Army in Its Medico-Sanitary Relations* (n.p., 1859), 17.
45. Annual Report of Colonial Surgeon, 1879, PRO, CO 129/203 (20349).
46. Norman Moore, "Opening Address with Special Reference to the Prevalence and Intensity of the Disease in the Past and at the Present Day," in *Syphilis: With Special Reference to (a) Its Prevalence and Intensity in the Past and at the Present Day, (b) Its Relation to Public Health, (c) The Treatment of the Disease. A Discussion* (London: Longmans, Green and Co., 1912), 31.
47. A. G. Miller, " 'Four And a Half Years' Experience in the Lock Wards of the Royal Edinburgh Infirmary," *Edinburgh Medical Journal* 28 (1882): 392.
48. John Thorne Crissey and Lawrence Charles Parish, *The Dermatology and Syphilology of the Nineteenth Century* (New York: Praeger, 1981), 84.
49. Annual Report of Colonial Surgeon, 1879, PRO, CO129/203 (20349).
50. J. M. Cuningham, "Note on the Working of the Rules for the Prevention of Venereal Disease among European Troops in the Bengal Presidency in 1873," OIOC, P/945 (339).
51. *Annual Report on the Military Lock Hospitals of the Madras Presidency for the Year 1887* (Madras: Government Press, 1888), Bangalore, 9, OIOC, L/MIL/7/13904. The Sabathu lock hospital in the Punjab also detained menstruating women: see *Report on Voluntary Venereal Hospitals in the Punjab for the Year 1887* (Lahore: Civil and Military Gazette Press, 1888), 3, OIOC, L/MIL/7/13906.
52. *Report on Voluntary Venereal Hospitals in the Punjab for the Year 1888* (Lahore: Civil and Military Gazette Press, 1889), 2, OIOC, L/MIL/7/13906.
53. *Fourth Annual Report on the Working of the Lock Hospitals in the Northwest Provinces and Oudh for the Year 1877* (Allahabad, n.p.,1878), Report of Naini Tal, 70, OIOC, V/24/2290.
54. "Lock Hospital Examinations," *The Indian Medical Journal* n.s. 8, no. 9 (March 1888): 119.
55. *Fourth Annual Report . . . 1877*, Report of Naini Tal, 70, OIOC, V/24/2290.
56. Annual Report of Colonial Surgeon, 1879, PRO, CO129/203 (20349).
57. T. E. Osmond, "Venereal Disease in Peace and War with some Reminiscences of the Last Forty Years," *British Journal of Venereal Diseases* 25, no. 3 (1949): 101; J. L. Fluker, "Personal Reminiscences of a Venereologist before Penicillin," *International Journal of STD & AIDS* 1 (1990): 443.
58. R. W. Johnstone, *Report on Venereal Diseases* (London: HMSO, 1913), 20.
59. L. W. Harrison, "Those Were the Days! or Random Notes on Then and Now in VD," *Bulletin of the Institute of Technicians in Venereology* n.d. ?(1950s) 1. With thanks to Lesley Hall for generously providing a copy of this obscure article. Ambrose King makes reference to this incident but offers no citation in "The Life and Times of Colonel Harrison," *British Journal of Venereal Diseases* 50 (1974): 391.
60. Robert Lees, "The 'Lock Wards' of Edinburgh Royal Infirmary," *British Journal of Venereal Diseases* 37 (1961): 187. In private correspondence, Douglas Peers has pointed out that George Ballingall, who taught military surgery at Edinburgh early in the nineteenth century, included a section on the venereal diseases in his textbook on military surgery, and that many a doctor serving in the colonial service would have been trained under his aegis. Nonetheless, Ballingall was an exception and venereology remained the Cinderella of the medical school curriculum well into the twentieth century.
61. Minute by Director General, Army Medical Department, 16 January 1888, OIOC, L/MIL/7/15559; Minute by Director General to Secretary of State for War, 24 August 1888, OIOC, L/MIL/7/15557.

62. Sevgi O. Aral and King K. Holmes, "Epidemiology of Sexual Behavior and Sexually Transmitted Diseases," in *Sexually Transmitted Diseases*, 19.
63. HC, *SP*, 1894 (509), 2, OIOC, L/MIL/7/13845.
64. W. M. Frazer, for example, points out that in metropolitan Britain in the 1840s, the term *fever* encompassed typhoid, typhus, and a host of other "febrile conditions" with little distinction evident: *A History of English Public Health 1834–1939* (London: Bailliere, Tindall, and Cox, 1950), 41.
65. *Report on Measures adopted for Sanitary Improvements in India from June 1872 to June 1873* (London: HMSO, 1873), 70, OIOC, V/24/3677.
66. Report on Bassein Lock Hospital for 1873, 15, OIOC, V/24/2296.
67. R. Basu Roy, "Sexually Transmitted Diseases and the Raj," *Sexually Transmitted Infections* 74, no. 1 (1998): 21.
68. Ibid., 21.
69. *Annual Report on the Military Lock Hospitals of the Madras Presidency for the Year 1886* (Madras: Government Press, 1887), 5, OIOC, L/MIL/7/13904; Surgeon General W. A. Thomson, Principal Medical Officer, British Troops to Secretary to Government of India, Military Department, 13 August 1890, OIOC, L/MIL/7/13834; HC, *SP*, 1894 (509), L/MIL/7/13845.
70. *Hong Kong Legislative Council Sessional Papers, 1887* (Hong Kong: Government Printer, 1888), Enclosure no. 2, Report on the Lock Hospital, 8 February 1887.
71. C. H. F. Routh, *On the Difficulty of Diagnosing the Syphilitic Disease in Women and the Nature of Its Contagion* (London: T. Danks, 1883), 6.
72. D. Blair Brown, "The *Pros* and *Cons* of the Contagious Diseases Acts as applied in India," *Transactions of the Medical and Physical Society of Bombay* n.s. 11 (1888): 96.
73. Edmund A. Parkes, *A Manual of Practical Hygiene Prepared Especially for Use in the Medical Service of the Army* (London: John Churchill and Sons, 1864), 450.
74. Robert Lawson, "Observations on the Variation in the Prevalence of Venereal Affections in this Country," *Medical Times and Gazette* (7 January 1871): 7.
75. *Medical History of the European Troops in the Bombay Command for the Year 1885* (Bombay: Education Society's Press, 1886), n.p, OIOC, L/MIL/7/15558.
76. B. A. Smithurst, "Historic and Epidemiologic Review of Venereal Disease in Queensland," (MD thesis, University of Queensland, 1981), 16. Early feminist doctor Louisa Martindale is also at pains to make this distinction in *The Prevention of Venereal Disease* (London: Research Books Ltd., 1945), 29.
77. On dispensaries, see Mark Harrison, *Public Health in British India: Anglo-Indian Preventive Medicine 1859–1914* (Cambridge: Cambridge University Press, 1994), 88; and Roger Jeffery, *The Politics of Health in India* (Berkeley: University of California Press, 1988), 87.
78. Lenore Manderson, *Sickness and the State: Health and Illness in Colonial Malaya, 1870–1940* (Cambridge: Cambridge University Press, 1996), 15.
79. *Government Gazette*, 1 May 1886, 1613–14, QSA, COL/A360 (3279).
80. James Bettley, "Post Voluptatem Misericordia: The Rise and Fall of the London Lock Hospital," *London Journal* 10, no. 2 (1984): 167.
81. Henry Burdett offers both theories, that of the term as descriptive of restraint and of lepers' rags: *Hospitals and Asylums of the World: Their Origin, History, Construction, Administration, Management and Legislation*, vol. 4 (London: J. and A. Churchill, 1893), 307. The abolitionist-feminist periodical *The Shield* advanced both these theories and another in which a mysterious Dr. Lock appears as a founder of the first of the metropolitan lock hospitals. The journal warns that no evidence whatsoever exists for this latter supposition! ("Lock Hospitals," *The Shield* 12, no. 113 (February 1910): 10); Gregg S. Meyer, "Criminal Punishment for the Transmission of Sexually Transmitted Diseases: Lessons from Syphilis," *Bulletin of the History of Medicine* 65, no. 4 (1991): 553. Michael Waugh argues that the name derived from the Loke, the leper house: "Attitudes of Hospitals in London to Venereal Disease in the 18th and 19th Centuries," *British Journal of Venereal Diseases* 47 (1971): 147.
82. Max F. Simon to Colonial Secretary, 17 April 1895, PRO, CO273/203 (8688).
83. Statement of Medical Board to Secretary to Government of Bengal, Military Department, n.d. ?1824, OIOC, F/4/835 (22253).
84. Annual Report on the Dinapore Cantonment Lock Hospital for 1887; Annual Report on Cantonment Lock Hospitals at Barrackpore and Dum-Dum for 1886, OIOC, L/MIL/7/13903.

85. Annual Medical Returns, *Proceedings of the Legislative Council of the Straits Settlements, 1875* (Singapore: Government Printing Office, 1876), lxxiii.
86. Annual Report of the Colonial Surgeon, 1874, n.p, PRO, CO129/189 (13163).
87. Statistics of Brisbane Lock Hospital, 1868–1877, QSA, COL/A268 (4353).
88. Statistics of Rockhampton Lock Hospital, 1868–1877, QSA, COL/A268 (4353).
89. Cramped conditions were certainly not unique to the lock hospitals. Raymond Evans in "The Hidden Colonists: Deviance and Social Control in Colonial Queensland," in *Social Policy in Australia. Some Perspectives 1901–75*, ed. Jill Roe (Stanmore, NSW: Cassell Australia, 1976, 74–100) offers a glimpse of the same problems in the wing housing those designated as lunatics at the Brisbane Gaol. Since in the early years of the colony there was no asylum, and the general hospital was as unwelcoming to psychological imbalance as to prostitution, the gaol became their home. Institutions for the "undeserving" poor, whether places of incarceration or treatment, were frequently overcrowded, as they remain even now. Staff at such places were faced daily with the often severe and even sometimes dangerous consequences of this, and residents suffered both bodily and mentally.
90. Senior Constable Timothy Sullivan, Moreton District to Sub-Inspector of Police, 31 October 1892, QSA, A/45367; and miscellaneous police correspondence, 1892, QSA, A/45367.
91. Jebb, "The Lock Hospitals Experiment," 79.
92. The classification of lock hospitals as first, second, or third class rested on assessments of military strength. First-class hospitals were those at stations with more than one British infantry or cavalry wing with artillery, and with "Native Cavalry or Infantry." Circular Memorandum 117, 8 November 1867, OIOC, P/435/52.
93. *Eighth Annual Report on the Working of the Lock Hospitals in the Northwest Provinces and Oudh for the Year 1881* (Allahabad, n.p., 1882), 21, letter (author unspecified) to Surgeon General of NWP, 26 March 1882, OIOC, V/24/2290.
94. E. McKellar, *Medical and Sanitary Report of the Native Army of Bengal for the Year 1873* (Calcutta: Office of the Superintendent of Government Printing, 1874), 149, OIOC, V/24/3110.
95. J. Dorgan, "Prevention of Venereal Disease," *Journal of the Royal Army Medical Corps* 11, no. 2 (1908): 124.
96. Report on the Working of Quetta Lock Hospital for the year 1887, OIOC, P/3195.
97. Extracts of Minutes, Executive Council, 2 October 1882, PRO, CO129/203 (20349); Colonial Office minute, 18 July 1882, addressed to Frederick Meade, PRO, CO129/206 (12623).
98. Annual Report of the Colonial Surgeon for 1882, 192, PRO, CO131/11.
99. Report on the Lock Hospital at Penang, *Proceedings of the Legislative Council of the Straits Settlements, 1875* (Singapore: Government Printing Office, 1876), lxxxv.
100. George Newton to Kellett, 23 January 1871; *Report of the Yokohama Lock Hospital*, 13, PRO, ADM125/16.
101. *Medical and Sanitary Report of the Native Army of Bengal for the Year 1874* (Calcutta: Office of the Superintendent of Government Printing, 1876), 103, OIOC, V/24/3110.
102. Thomas Williamson, *The East India Vade Mecum or, Complete Guide to Gentlemen Intended for the Civil, Military, or Naval Service of the Hon. East India Company*, vol. 2 (London: Black, Parry, and Kingbury, 1810), 424. With thanks to Doug Peers for sharing this reference with me.
103. HC, *SP*, 147 (1894), Enclosure 3 in no. 17, P. B. C. Ayres, Colonial Surgeon, Hong Kong to Colonial Secretary, 26 April 1893 (also in CO129/259 (12527)).
104. Evans, "The Hidden Colonists," 91; Mary Murnane and Kay Daniels, "Prostitutes as "Purveyors of Disease": Venereal Disease Legislation in Tasmania, 1868–1945," *Hecate* 5 (1979): 8.
105. J. Espie Dods, Government Health Officer to Under-Secretary, Home Department, 21 August 1903 and 20 October 1911, QSA, COL/A360 (13092/04545).
106. This is one of the few instances where I disagree with Douglas Peers's argument in "Soldiers, Surgeons and the Campaigns to Combat Sexually Transmitted Diseases in Colonial India, 1805–1860," *Medical History* 42 (1998): 137–60. He claims (147) that British lock hospitals "lacked the blatantly coercive character of their counterparts in India." My own research suggests otherwise; see "Women and Prostitution: Metaphor, Reality, History," *Canadian Journal of History* 28, no. 3 (1993): 479–94; and "'Rough Usage:' Prostitution, Law, and the Social Historian," in *Rethinking Social History: English Society 1570–1920 and Its Interpretation*, ed. Adrian Wilson (Manchester: Manchester University Press, 1993), 266–92.

107. F. Oppert, *Hospitals, Infirmaries, and Dispensaries: Their Construction, Interior, Arrangement, and Management with Descriptions of Existing Institutions and Remarks on the Present System of Affording Medical Relief to the Sick Poor* (London: John Churchill and Sons, 1867), 116.

108. Johnstone, *Report on Venereal Diseases,* 21.

109. Alexander Patterson, "Statistics of Glasgow Lock Hospital Since Its Foundation in 1805—With Remarks on the Contagious Diseases Acts and on Syphilis," *Glasgow Medical Journal* 6 (December 1882): 408.

110. General Officer commanding Hyderabad Subsidiary Force, Secunderabad to Government of Madras, Military Department, 27 November 1858, OIOC, P/273/101.

111. Cantonment Hospitals and Dispensaries Reports, 1900–1901, Ahmedabad Report, 2, OIOC, L/MIL/7/13920.

112. See, for example, *Report on the Working of Quetta Lock Hospital for the year 1887,* OIOC, P/3195; *Eighth Annual Report . . . 1881,* report for Roorkee, 16, OIOC, V/24/2290; 19 November 1813, OIOC, F/4/486; McKellar, *Medical and Sanitary Report of the Native Army of Bengal;* Mooltan, 149; Ferozepore, 150, OIOC, V/24/3110; *Medical and Sanitary Report of the Native Army of Bengal for the year 1874,* Barrackpore and Alipore, 10, OIOC, V/24/3110.

113. Report on Lock Hospitals in British Burma for the Year 1877, 28; 35, OIOC, V/24/2297.

114. Extract from Proceedings of the Government of Bengal, Medical, 21 June 1877, OIOC, P/1003; C. A. Elliot, Officiating Secretary to Government of the NWP expressed similar sentiments in a letter to local government, 6 July 1870, NAI, Public Consultations A, Proceedings, 1870.

115. Hamilton to Elgin, 4 June 1897, OIOC, Mss. Eur. C.125/2, f. 258, also in OIOC, Mss. Eur. F.84/15.

116. Cantonment Hospitals and Dispensaries' Reports, 1899–1900, Belgaum hospital report, f. 4, OIOC, L/MIL/7/13919.

117. John Strachey to Secretary, Government of India, Military Department, 2 May 1864, OIOC, P/438/27.

118. Jeffery, *Politics of Health,* 100; Maneesha Lal, "The Politics of Gender and Medicine in Colonial India: The Countess of Dufferin's Fund, 1885–1888," *Bulletin of the History of Medicine* 68 (1994): 65; Sandhya Shetty, "(Dis)Locating Gender Space and Medical Discourse in Colonial India," *Eroticism and Containment: Genders* 20 (1994): 192; K. N. Panikkar, "Indigenous Medicine and Cultural Hegemony: A Study of the Revitalization Movement in Keralam," *Studies in History* n.s. 8, no. 2 (1992): 288.

119. *Report of a Committee assembled at Calcutta under the Orders of the Government of India, 14 January 1881,* evidence of J. Lambert, Deputy Commissioner of Police, 22, OIOC, L/E/6/66 (1054).

120. Maneesha Lal makes this point for India but it holds good elsewhere in the colonial world as well: "The Politics of Gender," 32.

121. Frederick W. Lowndes, "The Liverpool Lock Hospital, Its Origin and History; Statistics of Recent Years," *Liverpool Medico-Chirurgical Journal* 11 (July 1886): 297; *The Lancet* (15 January 1853): 63.

122. For a discussion of how this was achieved in Queensland, see Evans, "The Hidden Colonists," and Lynette Finch, *The Classing Gaze: Sexuality, Class and Surveillance* (St. Leonards, NSW: Allen and Unwin, 1993).

123. Memorandum, Edward Fairfield, 24 May 1895, PRO, CO273/203 (8688).

124. W. C. Plowden, Officiating Magistrate, Meerut to M. H. Court, Commissioner, Meerut Division, 18 July 1870, NAI, Home Department, Public Consultations A, Proceedings, 1870.

125. Alison Bashford, "Quarantine and the Imagining of the Australian Nation," *Health* 2, no. 4 (1998): 387–402; Howard Markel, *Quarantine! East European Jewish Immigrants and the New York City Epidemic of 1892* (Baltimore, MD: Johns Hopkins University Press, 1997).

126. J. E. Ross and S. M. Tomkins, "The British Reception of Salvarsan," *Journal of the History of Medicine and Allied Sciences* 52, no. 4 (1997): 402.

127. Helena Whitbread, ed. *I Know My Own Heart: The Diaries of Anne Lister (1791–1840)* (London: Virago, 1988), 162; Osmond, "Venereal Disease in Peace and War," 101.

128. Miller, "'Four And a Half Years' Experience," 402.

129. Harrison, "Those Were the Days!" 5.

130. Osmond, "Venereal Disease in Peace and War," 101.

131. Elizabeth A. Ross, "Victorian Medicine in Penang," *Malaysia in History* 23 (1980): 87; Osmond, "Venereal Disease in Peace and War," 81.

132. Lewis, "Sexually Transmitted Diseases in Australia," 252.
133. Waugh, "History of Clinical Developments," 9.
134. Whitbread, I *Know My Own Heart*, 162.
135. Jonathan Hutchinson, *Syphilis* (London: Cassell and Co., 1887), 50.
136. Waugh, "History of Clinical Developments," 8.
137. Skey Committee Report and Minutes of Evidence (1864), 335, evidence of Edward Cutler, Consulting Surgeon to the London Lock Hospital, 26 May 1865.
138. For a description of these indigenous practices, see Panikkar, "Indigenous Medicine and Cultural Hegemony," 284.
139. H. MacFarlane and G. E. Aubrey, "Venereal Disease among the Natives of Hong Kong," *The Caduceus* 1, no. 1 (1922): 22–3; Minutes of Evidence of Straits Committee on the Prevalence of Venereal Diseases, 1899, evidence of Mr. M. Wispauer, Medical Hall, Singapore, 59, PRO, CO882/6; Kerrie L. Macpherson, "Conspiracy of Silence: A History of Sexually Transmitted Diseases and HIV/AIDS in Hong Kong," in *Sex, Disease, and Society,* 88.
140. *Proceedings of the Legislative Council of the Straits Settlements, 1875* (Singapore: Government Printing Office, 1876), Annual Medical Reports of the Civil Hospitals for 1873, lxxiii.
141. *Fourth Annual Report . . . 1877*, Fyzabad report. 97, OIOC, V/24/2290.
142. Ibid., Sitapur report, 103.
143. Whitbread, I *Know My Own Heart*, 288.
144. M. Macauliffe, Deputy Commissioner, Montgomery to Commissioner and Superintendent, Mooltan Division, 27 February 1878, OIOC, P/1338.
145. Commissioner of Police, Calcutta to Secretary, Government of Bengal, 8 March 1871, NAI, Agriculture, Revenue and Commerce Department Sanitary Proceedings, August 1871, no. 628.
146. M. Macauliffe, Deputy Commissioner, Montgomery to Commissioner and Superintendent, Mooltan Division, 27 February 1878, OIOC, P/1338.
147. Edmund Fosbery, Inspector General of Police, New South Wales to Principal Under Secretary, NSW, 20 December 1884, NSWSA, NSW 5/5300; Superintendent of Police, Metropolitan District, Sydney to Inspector General of Police, NSW, 24 August 1906, NSWSA, NSW 5/5300; report of Sergeant Robert Dell, Brisbane Police, to unknown recipient, 21 December 1911, QSA A/21955.
148. G. W. Johnson to J. Bramston, internal minute, 23 November 1893, PRO, CO129/259 (12527).
149. Commissioner, Fyzabad Division to Secretary to Lieutenant Governor, NWP and Chief Commissioner for Oudh, 21 March 1877, OIOC, P/1003.
150. Annual Report on the Dinapore Cantonment Lock Hospital for 1887, OIOC, L/MIL/7/13903. The matron, like the *dhai,* was probably an indigenous woman, perhaps with a modicum of training or experience.
151. Circular Memorandum 1054, 16 February 1884, OIOC, L/MIL/3/977; also at OIOC, L/MIL/3/980; and at OIOC, L/MIL/7/13814.
152. "Lock Hospital Examinations," 118.
153. *Report on Voluntary Venereal Hospitals in the Punjab for the Year 1887*, 2, OIOC, L/MIL/7/13906.
154. *Fourth Annual Report . . . 1877*, 2, OIOC, V/24/2290.
155. Sanitary Commissioner, Punjab, 10 August 1868, OIOC, P/435/62.
156. *Fourth Annual Report . . . 1877*, Sitapur Report, 104, OIOC, V/24/2290.
157. Fox's response to allegations against him, report of triumvirate hearing the charges, February 1908, PRO, CO273/339 (9181).
158. Evidence of Martenez James Wright in case against Stephen Fox, report of triumvirate hearing the charges, February 1908, PRO, CO273/339 (9181).
159. G. W. Johnson to Charles P. Lucas, 18 March 1898, PRO, CO129/286 (28461).
160. Chandavarkar, "Plague, Panic and Epidemic Politics," 214.
161. The transliterated spelling varies: *dhai* is the commonest variant but the records sometimes show alternatives such as *dai, da'i* or *dhaee. Mahaldarni,* according to Denzil Ibbetson, was from the Persian.
162. *Report of the Special Commission appointed to Enquire into the Working of the Cantonment Regulations regarding Infectious and Contagious Diseases* (Simla: Government Printing Office, 1893), Statements and Notes, Testimony of Mehr-ul Nissah, Dhai, Cantonment General Hospital, Ambala, 7 June 1893, xii.
163. *Report of the Special Commission,* s. 39.

164. *Cantonment Regulations framed under Act XXII of 1864 and Act III of 1880* (Calcutta: Superintendent of Government Printing, 1887), 95.

165. *Report of the Special Commission,* s. 42.

166. Surgeon Major General W. R. Rice, Sanitary Commissioner, Government of India to Secretary, Government of India, Military Department, 6 June 1894, OIOC, P/4383.

167. Lansdowne to Kimberley, 23 May 1893, OIOC, D558/6, B33.

168. Lieutenant General M. Beresford, Commanding Mysore Division, Bangalore to Adjutant General, 25 October 1858, OIOC, P/273/101; Surgeon H.M. 104th Regiment to Officiating Major of Brigade, Bareilly, 9 July 1863, OIOC, P/438/27.

169. Circular Memorandum, 17 June 1886, WL, JEB, D1/4.

170. Indrani Chatterjee, "Colouring Subalternity: Slaves, Concubines and Social Orphans in Early Colonial India," in *Subaltern Studies X: Writings on South Asian History and Society,* ed. Gautam Bhadra, Gyan Prakash, and Susie Tharu (Delhi: Oxford University Press, 1999), 67–8.

171. Santi Rozario shows how in contemporary Muslim-dominated Bangladesh, ideas about the pollutant nature of childbirth are still in force ("The Dai and the Doctor: Discourses on Women's Reproductive Health in Rural Bangladesh," in *Maternities and Modernities: Colonial and Postcolonial Experiences in Asia and the Pacific,* ed. Kalpana Ram and Margaret Jolly (Cambridge: Cambridge University Press, 1998), 149). Her work is a useful reminder that South Asian readings of pollution have force outside the Hindu cosmology.

172. Lal, "The Politics of Gender and Medicine," 47–8; Shetty, "(Dis)Locating Gender Space," 189; Rosemary Fitzgerald, "A 'Peculiar and Exceptional Measure': The Call for Women Medical Missionaries for India in the Later Nineteenth Century," in *Missionary Encounters: Sources and Issues,* ed. Robert A. Bickers and Rosemary Seton (Richmond, Surrey: Curzon Press, 1996), 184.

173. Rozario, "The Dai and the Doctor," 146.

174. Circular Memorandum no. 51, 23 August 1872, OIOC, L/MIL/3/980.

175. F. O. Mayne, Commissioner, 4th Division to C. A. Elliott, 20 August 1870, NAI, Home Department, Public Consultations A, Proceedings, 31 December 1870.

176. Surgeon H.M. 104th Regiment to Officiating Major of Brigade, 9 July 1863, OIOC, P/438/27.

177. Geraldine Forbes, "Managing Midwifery in India," in *Contesting Colonial Hegemony,* 154; 171. Birthing attendants in rural Malaya were also sometimes cast as witches. See Lenore Manderson, "Shaping Reproductions: Maternity in Early Twentieth-Century Malaya," in *Maternities and Modernities,* 31.

178. Jeffery, *Politics of Health,* 86.

179. J. Strachey, President, Sanitary Commission for Bengal to Secretary, Government of India, Military Department, 2 May 1864, OIOC, P/438/27.

180. Before 1892, appointment to the Indian Medical Service was restricted to those who held British medical qualifications, and the entrance examinations were held only in London; see Roger Jeffery, "Doctors and Congress: The Role of Medical Men and Medical Politics in Indian Nationalism," in *The Indian National Congress and the Political Economy of India 1885–1985,* ed. Mike Shepperdson and Colin Simmons (Aldershot: Avebury/Gower, 1988), 163). In the Straits, local men could train as subassistant surgeons and dressers through bonded apprenticeships. It was 1887 before the Hong Kong College of Medicine for Chinese opened, offering tuition in western skills. The first such training school in India, the Native Medical Institution in Calcutta, dated from 1822.

181. *Fourth Annual Report . . . 1877,* Bareilly report, 18, OIOC, V/24/2290.

182. Memo, unknown author, n.d. (1908), PRO, CO273/339 (4535).

183. W. A. Forbes, commanding the 5th Division, Benares to C. A. Elliott, Secretary to Government of NWP, 2 July 1870, NAI, Home Department, Public Consultations A, Proceedings, 31 December 1870. With thanks to Ed Moulton for guiding me to this invaluable source.

184. F. O. Mayne, Commissioner, 4th Division to C. A. Elliott, 20 August 1870, NAI, Home Department, Public Consultations A, Proceedings, 31 December 1870.

185. Minute of W. A. Pickering, Protector of Chinese, 14 August 1886, PRO, CO273/140 (17747).

186. W. S. Halsey, Magistrate, Cawnpore to Commissioner of Fourth Division, Allahabad, 27 July 1870, NAI, Home Department, Public, Consultations A, Proceedings 1870, no. 188 & 1 K.W.

187. William Burke, "Memorandum on the Health of Europeans," 7 June 1827, OIOC F/4/1079 (27319).

188. Surgeon Major General W. R. Rice to Edwin W. Collen, Secretary to Government of India, Military Department, 6 June 1893, OIOC, P/4383.
189. Report on the Licensed Brothels in Hong Kong, 1874, PRO, CO129/189 (16884).
190. C. B. H. Mitchell to Joseph Chamberlain, 12 April 1899, PRO, CO273/246 (11454).
191. *Fourth Annual Report... 1877*, Report of Agra, 6, OIOC, V/24/2290; see too Memorandum of J. M. Cuningham, 4 August 1880, f. 461, Ripon Papers, vol. LXXXIV. Diary no. 111. BL, Add. Ms. 43, 574.
192. *Report of the Committee appointed to enquire into the Working of Ordinance XXIII of 1870, commonly called the Contagious Diseases Ordinance*, PRO, CO273/91 (6629).
193. Officer Commanding Mysore Division to Quartermaster General, 3 July 1855, OIOC, P/273/41.
194. Report of the Protector of Chinese for 1883, PRO, CO273/121 (13612).
195. Kamala Visweswaran, "Small Speeches, Subaltern Gender: Nationalist Ideology and Its Historiography," in *Subaltern Studies IX*, ed. Shahid Amin and Dipesh Chakrabarty (Delhi: Oxford University Press, 1996), 90.
196. Florence Nightingale, *Observations by Miss Nightingale on the Evidence contained in Statistical Returns sent to her by the Royal Commission on the Sanitary State of the Army in India*, (1862, n.p.), 6.
197. Warwick Anderson, "'Where Every Prospect Pleases and Only Man Is Vile': Laboratory Medicine as Colonial Discourse," *Critical Inquiry* 18 (1992): 526.
198. Major General H. W. Whitfield, "Sanitation in Hong Kong, 1874," 26 January 1874, PRO, CO129/189 (16884).
199. G. Bidie, Surgeon General with Government of Madras to Chief Secretary, Government of Madras, 16 July 1889, OIOC, P/3656.
200. Newton, *Report of the Yokohama Lock Hospital*, 3, PRO, ADM 125/16 (804).
201. Annual Report of Lock Hospital, Naini Tal, n.d. 1877, OIOC, P/525.
202. Kay J. Anderson, *Vancouver's Chinatown: Racial Discourse in Canada, 1875–1980* (Montreal: McGill-Queen's University Press, 1991), 80.
203. Annual Report of the Colonial Surgeon, 1879, 66, PRO, CO131/11.
204. *Medical and Sanitary Report of the Native Army of Bengal for the Year 1874*, 54, OIOC, V/24/3110. The reference is to the 9th Regiment at Deolee.
205. Lord Curzon to Secretary of State for India, 9 January 1902, OIOC, L/MIL/7/13881. I am indebted to Doug Peers for pointing out to me this common view among British officers in India of Pathan troops.
206. Deputy Surgeon General, Meerut to Surgeon General, Bengal, 30 January 1889, OIOC, P/3477; see too *General Report and Statistics of Venereal Disease Amongst British and Native Troops in India, together with Summary of the Reports on Cantonment Hospitals during the year 1906*, 23 September 1907, 33, OIOC, L/MIL/3/184. Surgeon T. C. Smith to Adjutant, 1–2nd Gurkhas, 22 January 1889, OIOC, P/3477 (2474). Occasional reports claimed the Gurhkas were cleaner and more like the British. One such opinion was expressed in a 1902 report from the Dharmsala medical officer (Punjab), OIOC, L/MIL/7/13922.
207. Comaroff, *Ethnography and the Historical Imagination*, 224; see too Timothy Burke, *Lifebuoy Men, Lux Women: Commodification, Consumption, and Cleanliness in Modern Zimbabwe* (Durham, NC: Duke University Press, 1996).
208. Brenda S. A. Yeoh, *Contesting Space: Power Relations and the Built Environment in Colonial Singapore* (Kuala Lumpur: Oxford University Press, 1996), 93.
209. Kerrie L. Macpherson, *A Wilderness of Marshes: The Origins of Public Health in Shanghai, 1843–1893* (Hong Kong: Oxford University Press, 1987), 38; Carol Benedict, "Framing Plague in China's Past," in *Remapping China: Fissures in Historical Terrain*, ed. Gail Hershatter, Emily Honig, Jonathan N. Lipman, and Randall Stross (Stanford, CA: Stanford University Press, 1996), 31.
210. Minute of General Officer Commanding, Hong Kong, 26 January 1874, PRO, CO131/11.
211. Sanitary Report on the Lock Hospital at Barrackpore for the Year 1870, NAI, Proceedings of the Department of Agriculture, Revenue and Commerce, June 1871.
212. G. Bidie, Surgeon General, Government of Madras to Chief Secretary, Government of Madras, 16 July 1889, OIOC, P/3656.
213. Blair Brown, "The *Pros* and *Cons* of the Contagious Diseases Acts," 85–6.
214. "Lock Hospital Examinations," 118.

215. *Report of the Committee appointed to enquire into the Working of Ordinance XXIII of 1870*, PRO, CO273/91 (6629).
216. "The Sanitary Farce in India," *Indian Medical Journal* 8, no. 12 (June 1888): 257.
217. Henry Britton, *Fiji in 1870, being the Letters of the Argus Special Correspondent* (Melbourne, 1970), 73, quoted in John Young, "Race and Sex in Fiji Re-visited," *Journal of Pacific History* 23, no. 2 (1988): 215.
218. "The Sanitary Farce in India," 256.
219. Copy of Suggestions for the Better Management of Lock Hospitals (1886), QSA, COL/A360 (2815); "Regulations for the General Management of the Brisbane Lock Hospital," *Government Gazette* (1 May 1886): 1613–4.
220. Regulations for the Matron, 1896, PRO, CO129/272 (15263).
221. Rules under Clause 7, Section 19 of Act XXII of 1864, "Note regarding the Principal Duties of the Medical Officer in Charge of the Lock Hospital," OIOC, P/1003.
222. Contagious Disease Act, Bombay Reports, 1883–1887, 22 June 1883, 2, OIOC, V/24/2289.
223. Government of Madras, Military Department, Sanitary Reports and Returns, 1883, 3, OIOC, V/24/304.
224. *Report of the Committee appointed to enquire into the Working of Ordinance XXIII of 1870*, PRO, CO273/91 (6629).
225. Newton, *Report of the Yokohama Lock Hospital*, 4, PRO, ADM 125/16 (804).
226. Ibid., 5, PRO, ADM 125/16 (804).
227. William Burke, "Memorandum on the Health of Europeans," 7 June 1827, OIOC, F/4/1079 (29310).
228. *General Report on the Administration of the Bombay Presidency, 1871–2* (Bombay: Bombay Secretariat Office, 1872), 256, OIOC, V/24/283.
229. Contagious Diseases Act, Bombay Reports, 1883–1887, July 1884, 1, OIOC, V/24/2289; W. M. Clarke, *Report on the Working of the Contagious Diseases Act for December 1st 1869 to December 31st 1870*, n.p., n.d. (1871), PRO, ADM/1/6197.
230. Frank Lenwood reporting to AMSH, 26 January 1911, WL, HJW, India file I-II, 1887–1912, D1/1, file 4.
231. Henry Champly, *The Road to Shanghai: White Slave Traffic in Asia* (London: John Long, 1934), 73.
232. John Cowen, "Extracts from a Report upon Public Prostitution in Singapore," *The Shield* 3rd series. 1, no. 3 (October 1916): 184.
233. Arthur Young to Walter Long, PRO, CO273/457 (60716), quoted in James F. Warren, "Chinese Prostitution in Singapore: Recruitment and Brothel Organisation," in *Women and Chinese Patriarchy: Submission, Servitude and Escape*, ed. Maria Jaschok and Suzanne Miers (London and New Jersey: Zed Books, 1994), 97.
234. Interestingly, R. H. McKie talked in 1942 of the "now gloomy but once electrically brilliant Ginza of Tokyo" in his reminiscences of the Asian sex scene. In this instance, war close to hand did dim the brothel lights to a suitably austere level: *This Was Singapore* (Sydney: Angus and Robertson, 1942), 100.
235. Alfred Keogh, "Introduction", in Officers of the Royal Army Medical Corps, *A Manual of Venereal Diseases* (London: Oxford Medical Publications/Henry Frowde/Hodder and Stoughton, 1907), 2.
236. Paul Gilroy, *The Black Atlantic: Modernity and Double Consciousness* (Cambridge, MA: Harvard University Press, 1993), 188.
237. Uday S. Mehta, "Liberal Strategies of Exclusion," *Politics & Society* 18, no. 4 (1990): 443.
238. Jane M. Jacobs, *Edge of Empire: Postcolonialism and the City* (London and New York: Routledge, 1996), 17.
239. Peter Fitzpatrick, "Passions Out of Place: Law, Incommensurability, and Resistance," in *Laws of the Postcolonial*, ed. Eve Darian-Smith and Peter Fitzpatrick (Ann Arbor: University of Michigan Press, 1999), 48.

Chapter 4

1. Antoinette Burton, *Burdens of History: British Feminists, Indian Women, and Imperial Culture 1865–1915* (Chapel Hill, NC: University of North Carolina Press, 1994), 142.
2. Handwritten minute, probably Frederick Meade, 14 September 1886, PRO, CO273/140 (15227).

3. HC, *SP*, 1887, 347, Edward Stanhope to Governors, Crown Colonies, 25 October 1886, 1. Stanhope (1840–93) was first elected to parliament in 1874. He was under secretary of state for India from 1878 to 1880, and colonial secretary from 1886.
4. Constance B. Backhouse, "Nineteenth-Century Canadian Prostitution Law: Reflections of a Discriminatory Society," *Histoire sociale—Social History* 18, no. 36 (1985): 387–423; John P. S. McLaren, "Chasing the Social Evil: Moral Fervour and The Evolution of Canada's Prostitution Laws, 1867–1917," *Canadian Journal of Law and Society* 1, no. 1 (1986): 125–65.
5. HC, *SP*, 1887, 347, 7.
6. HC, *SP*, 1887, 347, C. B. H. Mitchell to Stanhope, 13 January 1887, 19.
7. HC, *SP*, 1887, 347, Brigade Surgeon H. Knaggs to Brigade Major, 3 December 1886; sent to Henry Holland (Stanhope's successor at the Colonial Office) by Governor Sir H. W. Norman, 29 January 1887.
8. HC, *SP*, 1887, 347, C. J. Irving, Resident Councillor to Colonial Secretary, 19 January 1887, 16.
9. HC, *SP*, 1887, 347, Governor A. E. Hardinge to Henry Holland, 30 April 1887, 27, 45.
10. Memo, George W. Johnson to John Bramston, 21 May 1887; memo, initials illegible, 16 June 1887, PRO, CO273/144 (8517).
11. David J. Pivar, "The Military, Prostitution, and Colonial Peoples: India and the Philippines, 1885–1917," *Journal of Sex Research* 17, no. 3 (1981): 258–9. On Baptist-led protests, see Kenneth Ballhatchet, *Race, Sex and Class Under the British Raj: Imperial Attitudes and Policies and their Critics, 1793–1905* (London: Weidenfeld and Nicholson, 1980), 45–6.
12. Federation File II, 1875–1879, WL, HJW, box 286.
13. Minute Paper, Frederick Meade?, 3 June 1879, PRO, CO129/184 (6690).
14. James Stansfeld, *Lord Kimberley's Defence of the Government Brothel System in Hong Kong* (London: National Association for the Repeal of the Contagious Diseases Acts, 1882). Stansfeld (1820–98) represented Halifax as a Liberal for thirty-six years. He was under secretary at the India Office in 1866 and president of the local government board, 1871 to 1874. He refused the offer of a peerage in the 1890s.
15. Johnson to Meade, 13 September 1886, PRO, CO273/140 (15227); India Secretary Cross to Governor General, 31 August 1887, enclosing a memorandum, 8 February 1887, OIOC, V/6/318, no. 88.
16. Josephine E. Butler, *The Revival and Extension of the Abolitionist Cause: A Letter to the Members of the Ladies' National Association* (London: Dyer Brothers, 1887), 1.
17. Johnson to Meade, 13 September 1886, PRO, CO273/140 (15227).
18. PRO, CO129/184 (4062).
19. The report can be found in OIOC, L/E/6/66 (1054).
20. HC, *SP*, 1883 (200), 13. Memorial, Bishop of Bombay and Others to Governor, Bombay, 30 March 1880.
21. Rao Saheb V. N. Mandlik, *Speech at the Bombay Town Council* (Bombay: Education Society's Press, n.d.? 1880), 1.
22. Ripon to Secretary of State for India, 7 January 1882, OIOC, L/E/7/39 (598). See too Sarvepalli Gopal, *The Viceroyalty of Lord Ripon 1880–1884* (Oxford: Oxford University Press, 1953), 222. George Frederick Samuel Robinson, 1st Marquis of Ripon (1827–1909) was under secretary at the India Office between 1866 and 1868. He served as viceroy from 1880 to 1886, and went on to hold the posts of colonial secretary in 1894 and lord privy seal in 1905.
23. Despatch no. 1, Ripon et al. to Secretary of State for India, 16 January 1882, OIOC, L/E/7/3 (230); also at OIOC, P/1851.
24. Hartington to Ripon, 26 October 1882, OIOC, P/2043. Spencer Compton Cavendish (1833–1908), Marquis of Hartington and 8th Duke of Devonshire from 1891, was appointed Secretary of State for India in 1880, and served two years before moving to the equivalent position at the War Office. His political career began in 1857 when he was appointed Liberal M.P. for Lancashire; his first political appointment was as junior lord of the admiralty in 1863.
25. *Proceedings of the Council of the Governor General of India, 1888* (Calcutta: Office of the Superintendent of Government Printing, 1889), 28, OIOC, V/9/24; Ballhatchet, *Race, Sex and Class*, 50.
26. Paul McHugh, *Prostitution and Victorian Social Reform* (London: Croom Helm, 1980), 223.
27. Hartington to Fergusson, 9 July 1880, OIOC, Mss. Eur. E.214/1, f. 16. James Fergusson (1832–1907) served as governor of Bombay from 1880 to 1885 as well as under secretary for India, 1860–67. He also served as governor of both South Australia (1868–73) and New Zealand (1873–75).

28. HC, *SP*, 1887 (347); 1888 (158); 1889 (59).
29. On Dyer, see Deborah Gorham, "The 'Maiden Tribute of Modern Babylon' Re-Examined: Child Prostitution and the Idea of Childhood in Late-Victorian England," *Victorian Studies* 21 (1978): 357–8. Dyer stood unsuccessfully against William Harcourt on an anti-CD ticket at Derby in the 1885 election.
30. Alfred S. Dyer, *The Black Hand of Authority in India* (London: Dyer Brothers, 1888), 3.
31. Account of B Proceedings, OIOC, P/2958.
32. Telegraph no. 540, 9 July 1886 and no. 699, 7 December 1887, OIOC, Mss. Eur. F.130/14; also at OIOC, L/MIL/7/13814.
33. Dyer, "The Government *versus* the Gospel in India," *The Sentinel* 10 (March 1888) 3: 26. Dyer collected a number of his pamphlets into a booklet in 1888: *Must India Perish Through Britain's Sin? Facts about the Licensing of Impurity by the British Government in India. Five Letters to the Christian Press of Great Britain* (Bombay: Bombay Guardian, 1888).
34. *Licensed Plague Spots: India's Curse and Britain's Shame* (London: Gospel Purity Association, 1888).
35. HC, *SP*, 1888 (197), 17 June 1886.
36. Circular Memoranda, 26 November 1883; 12 July 1884, OIOC, P/3248 (1829).
37. Enclosure no. 1, Dufferin to Roberts, 30 May 1888, OIOC, L/MIL/17/5/1615/8, XXXVII.
38. Richard Assheton, 1st Viscount Cross (1823–1914) was India secretary from 1886 to 1892. First elected as Conservative M.P. for Preston in 1857, Cross served twice as home secretary (1874–80 and 1885–6) and would become lord privy seal in 1895.
39. Frederick Temple Hamilton-Temple Blackwood (1826–1902) was governor general from 1884 to 1888, after which he was appointed ambassador to Italy. His first ministerial appointment had been as under secretary for India under Palmerston from 1864 to 1866.
40. Despatch no. 6, Dufferin et al. to Cross, 27 March 1888, OIOC, P/3248.
41. Cross to Dufferin, 11 May 1888, OIOC, Mss. Eur F.130/12, f. 25. Chapman's actions did not cost him politically in any significant way. Though he left India in 1889, he went on to serve as director of military intelligence at the War Office from 1891 to 1896, before being appointed to the Scots command and a generalship in 1896.
42. Cross to Dufferin, 27 July 1888, OIOC, Mss. Eur F.130/12, f. 45.
43. Josephine E. Butler, *To Mrs. Tanner and Her Sisters* (privately printed, June 1888).
44. J. A. Godley to Sir Donald McKenzie Wallace, 19 April 1888, OIOC, Mss. Eur. F.130/30B, f. 16.
45. HC, *SP*, 1889 (159), Frederick A. Weld to Henry T. Holland, 10 September 1887. Frederick Aloysius Weld (1823–91) governed Western Australia from 1869 to 1875, and took up gubernatorial office at the Straits in 1880.
46. Short-Hand Report of the Proceedings of the Legislative Council, Straits Settlements, 1887, B112, 28 November 1888, PRO, CO275/34.
47. Johnson to John Bramston, 21 May 1887, PRO, CO273/144 (8517); HC, *SP*, 1889 (59), Knutsford to Des Vœux, 12 October 1888.
48. *Hong Kong Gazette*, 18 May 1889, 445–54. George W. Des Vœux (1834–1909) served as governor of Hong Kong from 1887–91, after holding appointments in St. Lucia, Fiji, and Newfoundland.
49. Norman Miners, *Hong Kong Under Imperial Rule 1912–1941* (Hong Kong: Oxford University Press, 1987), 193–4; Henry Lethbridge, "Prostitution in Hong Kong: A Legal and Moral Dilemma," *Hong Kong Law Journal* 8, no. 2 (1978): 154; Frank Welsh, *A History of Hong Kong* (London: Harper Collins, 1993), 265.
50. HC, *SP*, 1889 (159), Clementi Smith to Henry Holland, 30 December 1887.
51. HC, *SP*, 1887 (347), Holland to Governors, Hong Kong and Straits Settlements, 2 July 1887.
52. Short-Hand Report of the Proceedings of the Legislative Council, Straits Settlements, 1887, B108, 28 November 1888, PRO, CO275/34; HC, *SP*, 1890 (242), Enclosure, Lord Knutsford to G. W. Des Vœux, 3 January 1890; James F. Warren, *Ah Ku and Karayuki-San: Prostitution in Singapore 1870–1940* (Singapore: Oxford University Press, 1993), 118; also in his "Prostitution and the Politics of Venereal Disease: Singapore, 1870–98," *Journal of South East Asian Studies* 21, no 2 (1990): 370.
53. Warren, *Ah Ku and Karayuki-San*,118, and in "Prostitution and the Politics of Venereal Disease," 370.
54. Butler to Mary Priestman, 26 July 1895, WL, BALC.
55. John Powell, ed. *Liberal by Principle: The Politics of Wodehouse, 1st Earl of Kimberley, 1843–1902* (London: The Historian's Press, 1996), 167, n. 59.

56. Cross to Connemara, 3 September 1888, OIOC, Mss. Eur. E.243/18, f. 161.
57. Cross to Lord Reay, 10 August 1888, OIOC, Mss. Eur. E.243/18, f. 146.
58. Dufferin to Cross, 1 June 1888, OIOC, Mss. Eur. F.130/11A, f. 85.
59. Miners, *Hong Kong Under Imperial Rule*, 74.
60. G. B. Endacott, *Government and People in Hong Kong 1841–1962: A Constitutional History* (Hong Kong: Hong Kong University Press, 1964), 115–7.
61. For a reassessment of the traditional view of Elgin as a weak governor, see Arnold P. Kaminsky, *The India Office 1880–1910* (New York: Greenwood Press, 1986), 130–4.
62. Telegram, Secretary, Government of Madras Military Department to Secretary, Government of India Military Department, 31 August 1888, OIOC, P/3429.
63. Sir John Strachey, OIOC, C/128, ff. 582–3; reprinted in HC, *SP*, 1888 (22) and at OIOC, L/MIL/7/13820.
64. HC, *SP*, 1888 (220).
65. D. M. Stewart to Dufferin, 18 May 1888, OIOC, Mss. Eur. F.130/30B, f. 45.
66. Ripon to Dufferin, 15 June 1888, OIOC, Mss. Eur. F.130/30B, f. 7.
67. Memorandum, n.d. 1888; Telegram, 7 July 1888, OIOC, L/MIL/7/13826.
68. HC, *SP*, 1890 (241). For details of discussions between the government of India and the India Office, see Arnold P. Kaminsky, "Morality Legislation and British Troops in Late Nineteenth Century India," *Military Affairs* 43 (1979): 79–80.
69. Gorst to Cross, 2 July 1889, OIOC, L/MIL/7/13827.
70. Ballhatchet, *Race, Sex and Class*, 64–5.
71. *The Bengalee*, 21 July 1888, 343, col. 1.
72. "The C.D. Act in Ceylon," *Indian Medical Journal* 8 no. 12 (June 1888): 275.
73. Short-Hand Report of the Proceedings of the Legislative Council, Straits Settlements, 1887, B112, 28 November 1888, PRO, CO275/34.
74. Ibid.
75. Welsh, *A History of Hong Kong*, 264.
76. *QPD*, Legislative Assembly, *Votes and Proceedings*, Eighth Parliament, Report of William Hobbs to Colonial Secretary, 10 March 1879, 1273.
77. *QPD*, Legislative Assembly, Fourth Session of the Ninth Parliament, 1886, vol. 50, 1 October (Brisbane: James C. Beal, Government Printer, 1886), 1045.
78. Ibid., 1052.
79. J. M. C., "Proposed Extension of the Contagious Diseases Act of 1868 to Certain Towns in Queensland"; W. E. Parry-Okeden, Police Commissioner to Under Secretary, Home Department, 18 December 1899, QSA, HOM/J80; Queensland, Legislative Assembly, *Joint Volumes of Papers Presented to the Legislative Council and the Legislative Assembly*, Third Session of the Eighteenth Parliament, 1911–12. vol. 109 (Brisbane: Anthony James Cumming, Government Printer, 1912), 26 September 1911, Hon. C. F. Nielson, 1127.
80. J. Birkbeck Nevins, *Cape of Good Hope re Venereal Diseases* (London: British Committee for the Abolition of State Regulation of Vice in India and throughout the British Dominions, 1895), 10.
81. *State Regulation of Vice in South Africa: Deputation to Sir Henry Loch* (London: F. H. Doulton, 1894), 4. Walter Stowe Bright McLaren (1853–1912) was the independent Liberal M.P. for Crewe from 1886–95 and again from 1910–2.
82. Burton, *Burdens of History*, 142.
83. Report of the Committee of the Friends' Association for Abolishing the State Regulation of Vice for 1886, FHL, vol. K/134.
84. G. W. Johnson to John Bramston, 21 May 1887, PRO, CO273/144 (8517).
85. *Annual Report on the Chinese Protectorate, Singapore and Penang*, (n.p. 1888), PRO, CO273/152 (12665).
86. Cross to Dufferin, 11 May 1888, OIOC, Mss. Eur. F.130/12, f. 25.
87. Report of the Committee of the Friends' Association for Abolishing the State Regulation of Vice for 1887–1888, FHL, vol. K/135.
88. Military Despatch 135, Dufferin et al. to Cross, 27 July 1888, OIOC, L/MIL/3/140.
89. HC, *SP*, 1894 (147), C. B. H. Mitchell to Knutsford, 28 July 1890.
90. Cross to Dufferin, 4 October 1888, OIOC, Mss. Eur. F.130/12, f. 72.
91. Private Telegram, 3 January 1895, PRO, CAB37/38 (1895) no. 4, appendix E.
92. For examples, see HC, *SP*, 1890 (242), 22–7.
93. *Indian Spectator*, 10 June 1888, 466, col. 1; *The Bengalee*, 9 June 1888, 271, cols. 2–3.
94. *The Pioneer*, 7 June 1888, 5; 8 June 1888, 1; 9 June 1888, 5; *Hindoo Patriot*, 17 May 1875, 234.

95. *Report of the Committee appointed to Enquire into the Working of Ordinance XXIII of 1870, commonly called the Contagious Diseases Ordinance*, appendix A, PRO, CO273/91 (6629).
96. Such petitions are mentioned, for instance, in OIOC, P/525 and P/2958; in OIOC, L/MIL/7/13855, and in OIOC, L/E/3/336.
97. Notebook, Copies of Letters from India, 1891–1895, A. Banon, 10 December 1890, WL, HJW, box 77.
98. *Report from Captain Banon addressed to Mr. Stuart for the Committee, 3 April 1891* (London: British, Continental and General Federation for the Abolition of State Regulation of Vice, 1891), marked "Confidential. For the Use of the Committee Only."
99. Notebook, Copies of Letters from India, 1891–1895, William Huntly to Rev J. Dymock, 6 January 1891, WL, HJW, box 77.
100. File I–II, 1887–1912. WL, JEB, India, D1/1, file 1.
101. Butler to Mrs. Tanner and Miss Priestman, 9 March 1891, WL, BALC.
102. Pivar, "The Military, Prostitution, and Colonial Peoples," 259; Ian Tyrrell, *Woman's World, Woman's Empire: The Woman's Christian Temperance Union in International Perspective, 1880–1930* (Chapel Hill, NC: University of North Carolina Press, 1991), 197–8.
103. Elizabeth W. Andrew and Katharine C. Bushnell, *The Queen's Daughters in India* (London: Morgan and Scott, 1899), 48.
104. Manuscript of Indian Journal, 30 March 1892, ff. 1–2, WL, HJW, box 78A.
105. Andrew and Bushnell, *Queen's Daughters*, 42; Indian Report of Katharine Bushnell and Elizabeth Andrew, 12, WL, HJW, box 77.
106. Minute by G. S. White, "Charges against the Indian Cantonment Act, 1889," 1 July 1893, OIOC, Mss. Eur. D.558/49; also at OIOC, L/MIL/7/13843.
107. Burton, *Burdens of History*, 159.
108. Minutes, British Committee of the Continental and General Federation for the Abolition of the State Regulation of Vice, 1890–1893, 16 February 1893, WL, 3/BGF, box 76.
109. Military no. 26, Kimberley to Governor General, 1 April 1894, OIOC, V/6/331; also at OIOC, P/4595 and at OIOC, L/MIL/3/2129 (M11203). John Wodehouse, first Earl of Kimberley (1826–1902) served as under secretary for foreign affairs under Lords Aberdeen and Palmerston. He served briefly as under secretary for India in 1864 before becoming lord lieutenant of Ireland. In 1870 he became colonial secretary for four years, taking the office again in 1880. In 1882, he replaced Hartington at the India Office where he remained until the Liberal administration's defeat in 1885. He was briefly back at the India Office in 1886 and in 1894 became foreign secretary.
110. Lansdowne to Kimberley, 4 July 1893, OIOC, Mss. Eur D.558/6, B40.
111. Kimberley to Lansdowne, 18 August 1893, OIOC, Mss. Eur D.558/6, A49. Kenneth Ballhatchet dubbed Roberts' action an "unmilitary attempt to escape responsibility": *Race, Sex and Class*, 77.
112. Tyrrell, *Woman's World, Woman's Empire*, 200–1.
113. Minutes, British Committee of the Continental and General Federation for the Abolition of the State Regulation of Vice, 1890–1893, 5 August 1892, WL, 3/BGF, box 76.
114. Memo of Lord Elgin, 7 August 1897, NAI, Home Department, Medical, B Proceedings, February 1900, no. 38.
115. Ballhatchet, *Race, Sex and Class*, 69.
116. Tyrrell, *Woman's World, Woman's Empire*, 200–1, 199.
117. Surgeon Major General W. R. Rice to Secretary, Government of India, Military Department, 6 June 1893, OIOC, P/4383 (1431).
118. White, "Charges against the Indian Cantonment Act, 1889," 1 July 1893, OIOC, Mss. Eur. D.558/49; also at OIOC, L/MIL/7/13843.
119. Minutes, British Committee of the Continental and General Federation for the Abolition of the State Regulation of Vice, 1890–1893, Gladstone to Stansfeld, 25 March 1893, WL, 3/BGF, box 76.
120. HC, *SP*, 1894 (146), Lord Knutsford to Smith, 12 August 1891.
121. Minute of G. W. Johnson, 15 December 1891, PRO, CO273/176 (23049).
122. Catherine Hall delineates a similar tension and resentment in colonial Jamaica, where local white colonists also argued that those ruling at a distance could not appreciate local conditions: *Civilising Subjects: Metropole and Colony in the English Imagination, 1830–1867* (Chicago: University of Chicago Press, 2002), 255.
123. Smith to Knutsford, 29 October 1891, PRO, CO273/176 (23049).

124. Henry Holland was raised to the peerage as Baron, later Viscount Knutsford, in 1888; he was colonial secretary from January 1887 until August 1892.
125. Knutsford to Smith, 7 January 1892, PRO, CO273/176 (23049).
126. Minute, 21 October 1880, f. 470, BL, Add. Ms. 43, 574, Diary no. 111.
127. Ballhatchet neatly traces his growing disquiet in chapter 2 of *Race, Sex and Class*.
128. HC, *SP*, 1894 (147), Ripon to Smith and to William Robinson, 17 March 1894.
129. Ibid., Ripon to Sir John B. Thurston, 17 March 1894.
130. Ibid., Ripon to Sir John B. Thurston, 17 March 1894.
131. *Hong Kong Legislative Council Proceedings, 1893–4* (Hong Kong: Noronha and Co., 1894), 55.
132. Ibid., 55–6.
133. Ibid., 56.
134. *Straits Times,* 7 September 1894, PRO, CO273/197 (18487).
135. Clementi Smith to Ripon, 27 April 1893, PRO, CO273/187 (8818).
136. Minute, Johnson to Fairfield, 12 June 1894, PRO, CO129/263 (10161).
137. Tan Jiak Kim at a meeting of the Chinese Advisory Board and the PLK committee, 27 July 1894, quoted in Song Ong Siang, *One Hundred Years' History of the Chinese in Singapore* (Singapore: Oxford University Press, 1984), 281.
138. HC, *SP*, 1889 (159), G. W. Des Vœux to Knutsford, 8 October 1888.
139. *Hong Kong Legislative Council Proceedings, 1890* (Hong Kong: Noronha and Co., 1890), 308.
140. *Hong Kong Legislative Council Proceedings, 1894,* 362.
141. *Report on Voluntary Venereal Hospitals in the Punjab for the Year 1889* (Lahore: Civil and Military Gazette Press, 1890), 3, OIOC, L/MIL/7/13906.
142. Report for Laudour, 1891, n.p. OIOC, L/MIL/7/13911.
143. Medical Report sent to Lord Knutsford, 15 June 1892, PRO, CO273/187 (4922).
144. Minute, G.W. Johnson, 27 May 1893, PRO, CO273/187 (4922).
145. Johnson, 27 May 1893, PRO, CO273/187 (4922).
146. Elgin to Fowler, 9 January 1895, OIOC, Mss. Eur. C.145/2, no. 48.
147. Richard Shannon, *The Crisis of Imperialism 1865–1915* (St. Albans: Paladin, 1986), 265.
148. Ibbetson to Edwin Collen, 6 June 1893, OIOC, P/4383.
149. *Report of the Special Commission appointed to Enquire into the Working of the Cantonment Regulations regarding Infectious and Contagious Diseases* (Simla: Government Printing Office, 1893), 4, s. 9. The report was also included as an appendix to the Russell report.
150. *Report of the Special Commission*, 23, s. 56; 4, s. 9.
151. Ibid., 4, s. 8.
152. Ibid., 35, s. 82.
153. Ibid., 6, s. 13; 6, s. 15.
154. Ibid., 6, s. 15.
155. Ibid., 5, s. 12.
156. Ibid., 5, s. 12.
157. Ibid., 14, s. 35.
158. Ibid., 49, s. 107.
159. Kimberley to Lansdowne, 30 March 1893, OIOC, Mss. Eur. D.558/6, A16.
160. Wilson (1883–1914) was Liberal M.P. for the West Riding constituency of Holmfirth from 1885 until 1912. He was a Home Ruler who opposed the Boer War and was actively involved in opium and temperance campaigns as well as the CD repeal movement.
161. HC, *SP*, 1893 [C.7148]. *Report of the Committee appointed by the Secretary of State for India to Inquire into the Rules, Regulations and Practice in the Indian Cantonments and elsewhere in India with regard to Prostitution and the Treatment of Venereal Diseases,* separate minority report by General Sir D.M. Stewart and Sir J.B. Peile, xxxiii, s. 33.
162. Kaminsky, "Morality Legislation," 80; Lansdowne et al. to Cross, 4 August 1890, OIOC, L/MIL/3/144 (M7665).
163. Report of the Sub-Committee of the Madras Missionary Conference, 19 December 1893, OIOC, L/MIL/7/13853.
164. *Report of the Social Purity Meeting in the Town Hall, Calcutta, November 27, 1893* (n.p., n.d.), in collection of uncataloged pamphlets in the Butler collection at the Women's Library. See too Ballhatchet, *Race, Sex and Class,* 79.
165. Petition to the President, Rangoon Municipality, 19 December 1893, PRO, CO129/265 (977).
166. Army Sanitary Commission Memorandum, 30 August 1893, OIOC, L/MIL/17/1/2132;

OIOC, L/MIL/3/2129, Army Sanitary Commission Memorandum, 11 December 1893, also at OIOC, V/6/331.

167. Godley to Elgin, 2 March 1894, OIOC, Mss. Eur. F.84/29a.
168. Kaminsky, "Morality Legislation," 81.
169. Kimberley to Elgin, 1 March 1894, OIOC, L/MIL/3/2129 (M11203).
170. 27 February 1894, f. 97, OIOC, C/72.
171. 11 October 1893, ff. 186–7, OIOC, C/71.
172. Kimberley to Elgin, 9 March 1894, marked "Private," OIOC, Mss. Eur. F.84/12, A8.
173. J. A. Godley to Elgin, 29 November 1894, OIOC, Mss. Eur. F.84/29a, 119.
174. Philippa Levine, "Rereading the 1890s: Venereal Disease as 'Constitutional Crisis' in Britain and British India," *Journal of Asian Studies* 55, no. 3 (1996): 585–7.
175. Lord Reay to Elgin, 8 February 1895, OIOC, Mss. Eur. F.84/30a, no. 16.
176. Elgin to Sir C. B. Pritchard, 28 December 1894, OIOC, Mss. Eur. F.84/65, no. 233.
177. Kimberley to Elgin, 15 June 1894, OIOC, Mss. Eur. F.84/12, no. 19.
178. Elgin to Kimberley, 2 January 1895, OIOC, Mss. Eur. F.84/13, B1.
179. Butler to Mary Priestman, 15 October 1888, WL, BALC.
180. Geraldine H. Forbes, "The Politics of Respectability: Indian Women and the Indian National Congress," in *The Indian National Congress: Centenary Hindsights*, ed. D. A. Low (Delhi: Oxford University Press, 1988), 55; Levine, "Rereading the 1890s," 605; Meredith Borthwick, *The Changing Role of Women in Bengal, 1844–1905* (Princeton, NJ: Princeton University Press, 1984), 307.
181. Ripon et al. to Hartington, 16 January 1882, OIOC, L/E/7/3 (230).
182. A. P. McDonnell to C. S. Bayley, Officiating Private Secretary to Viceroy, 6 January 1895, OIOC, Mss. Eur. F.84/66, no. 20.
183. Elgin to Fowler, 9 January 1895, OIOC, Mss. Eur. C.145/2, no. 48.
184. *Proceedings of the Council of the Government of India, 1895* (Calcutta: Office of the Superintendent of Government Printing, 1895), 41, Lyon Playfair, 24 January 1895, OIOC, V/9/29; D. M. Stewart, 14 March 1894, f. 13, OIOC, C/129. Elgin noted Playfair as the "most hostile" council member to the new bill: Elgin to Fowler, 30 January 1895, OIOC, C.145/2.
185. *Proceedings of the Council of the Government of India, 1894* (Calcutta: Office of the Superintendent of Government Printing, 1894), 12 July 1894, 344, OIOC, V/9/28.
186. Fowler to Elgin, 13 July 1894, OIOC, Mss. Eur. F.84/2, no. 23.
187. Fowler to Elgin, 20 July 1894, OIOC, Mss. Eur. C.145/3, no. 16; also at OIOC, Mss. Eur. F.84/12, no. 24.
188. Fowler to Elgin, 12 October 1894, OIOC, Mss. Eur. C.145/3, no. 22.
189. Elgin to Fowler, 30 October 1894, OIOC, Mss. Eur. C.145/1, no. 38.
190. Elgin to Hamilton, 10 March 1897, OIOC, Mss. Eur. D.509/4, f. 195.
191. Elgin to Fowler, 7 August 1894, OIOC, Mss. Eur. C.145/1, no. 26.
192. Elgin to Fowler, 16 October 1894, OIOC, Mss. Eur. C.145/1, no. 35.
193. Fowler to Elgin, 23 November 1894, OIOC, Mss. Eur. C.145/3, no. 25.
194. Fowler to Elgin, 30 November 1894, OIOC, Mss. Eur. C.145/3, no. 26; for Godley, see OIOC, no. 19, 29 November 1894, Mss. Eur. F.84/24.
195. Fowler to Elgin, 30 November 1894, OIOC, Mss. Eur. C.145/3, no. 26.
196. Fowler to Elgin, 30 November 1894, OIOC, Mss. Eur. C.145/3, no. 26. The letter quotes Ripon.
197. Minute, G. W. Johnson, 23 June 1893, PRO, CO273/187 (8819).
198. *Straits Settlements Legislative Council Proceedings*, 19 July 1894, Mr. Huttenbach, PRO, CO273/197 (1887).
199. Elgin to Fowler, 23 January 1895, OIOC, Mss. Eur. C.145/2, no. 51.
200. *Proceedings of the Council . . . 1895*, 24 January 1895, 36, Griffith Evans, OIOC, V/9/29. For the judicial opinions, see OIOC, L/P& J/6/392 and HC, *SP*, 1895 (318).
201. John C. Young, Aden to Rev. A. W. Prautch, 24 February 1896, WL, HJW, Regulation File— 1896.
202. Elgin to Hamilton, 8 September 1896, OIOC, Mss. Eur. D.509/2, f. 862. Fears about Russian interest in and movement into India were of long standing in Britain. India Secretary Lord Hartington told a friend that Lord Derby's claim to succeed him at the India Office was undermined by the queen's fear that Derby's indecisiveness would prompt Russia to invade (Powell, *Liberal by Principle*, 161, n. 42). That scare was at its height in the 1890s and early 1900s (Shannon, *Crisis of Imperialism*, 318). John W. Cell points out that, though

it often determined military policy, "the Russian menace to India was frequently imagined," *British Colonial Administration in the Mid-Nineteenth Century: The Policy-Making Process* (New Haven, CT: Yale University Press, 1970), 184.

203. Hamilton to Elgin, 7 July 1897, OIOC, Mss. Eur. C.125/2, f. 194.
204. "The British Army in India," *The Times*, 21 January 1897, OIOC, L/MIL/7/13865.
205. Response to Colonel Lockwood, 25 January 1897, OIOC, L/MIL/7/13860.
206. Circular letter to LNA members from E. A. Lynn, Convener, 1 June 1896, WL, BALC.
207. WL, HJW, box 78 (482).
208. Leppington to Wilson, 11 August 1896, WL, BALC.
209. It is interesting to note that, despite his authoring of this report, Onslow is nowhere mentioned in Arthur Godley, Lord Kilbracken's thorough reminiscences of his many years at the India Office: *Reminiscences of Lord Kilbracken* (London: Macmillan and Co., 1931).
210. Hamilton to Elgin, 30 September 1896, OIOC, Mss. Eur. C.125/1, f. 387.
211. Onslow to Elgin, 26 February 1897, OIOC, Mss. Eur. F.84/27, f. 24.
212. HC, *SP*, 1897, C.-8379, *Report of A Departmental Committee on the Prevalence of Venereal Disease among the British Troops in India*, 9.
213. HC, *SP*, 1897, *Report of A Departmental Committee*, 9, n. 1; 13.
214. Ibid., 10.
215. Ibid., appendix II, Surgeon Major H.R. Whitehead, 21 August 1896.
216. "The British Army in India," *The Times*, 22 January 1897; *The Times*, 15 May 1897 (also at OIOC, L/MIL/7/13866).
217. Army Sanitary Commission: "On the Prevention of Venereal Diseases among British Troops in India in the Years 1894 and 1895," 9 March 1897, OIOC, L/MIL/7/13863; reprinted in HC, *SP*, 1897, C.-8382.
218. HC, *SP*, 1897 (415).
219. Hamilton to Elgin, 30 June 1897, OIOC, Mss. Eur. C.125/2, f. 360.
220. Butler to Mary Priestman, 26 July 1895, WL, BALC.
221. Burton, *Burdens of History*, 139.
222. Elizabeth W. Andrew and Katharine C. Bushnell, *A Fatal Mistake: To The W.C.T.U* (n.p., 1897); idem., *Reply of Dr. Katharine Bushnell and Mrs Elizabeth Andrew to Certain Statements in A Published Letter addressed by Lady Henry Somerset to a Correspondent on the Regulation of Vice in India* (London: Ladies' National Association, 1897).
223. *The Times*, 25 March 1897; reprinted as *The Health of the Army* (London: British Committee of the Federation for the Abolition of State Regulation of Vice, 1897).
224. Hamilton to Elgin, 9 April 1897, OIOC, Mss. Eur. C.125/2, f. 137.
225. Military no. 25, Hamilton to Elgin, 26 March 1897, OIOC, V/6/337; also at OIOC, L/MIL/7/13862.
226. HC, *SP*, 1898, C. 8919.
227. A. E. Havelock to Hamilton, 20 April 1897, OIOC, Mss. Eur. F.123/6.
228. For a discussion of how the Conservatives handled the politics of empire in this period, see E. H. H. Green, *The Crisis of Conservatism: The Politics, Economics and Ideology of the British Conservative Party, 1880–1914* (London: Routledge, 1995), esp. chapter 2.
229. Hamilton to Elgin, 9 April 1897, OIOC, Mss. Eur. C.125/2, ff. 137–41.
230. Military Despatch no. 85, Elgin et al to Kimberley, 29 May 1894, OIOC, L/MIL/3/149.
231. HC, *SP*, 1899, C. 9523, 20; R.S. Gundry, China Association to Chamberlain, 31 May 1897 and C. 9523, 30–2, 30 August 1897; William Adamson, Straits Settlements Association to Chamberlain, 8 November 1897, PRO, CO273/232 (24245); also at WL, HWJ, box H2, file 663A; Henry E. Pollock, Hon. Sec., Navy League, Hong Kong branch to Secretary, Navy League, London, 22 April 1897, sent onto Colonial Office, CO129/279 (17791), (also at OIOC, L/MIL/7/13869); Henry E. Pollock to Major Wilsone Black, 13 May 1897, OIOC, L/MIL/7/13869; William Robinson to Chamberlain, 30 June 1892, PRO, CO129/276 (17234); also in HC, *SP*, 1899, C. 9523, 29.

Chapter 5

1. On Hong Kong, see HC, *SP*, 59 of 1889; *Hong Kong Legislative Council Sessional Papers for 1887, 1889, and 1894*. On the Straits Settlements, see HC, *SP*, 1890 (342); PRO, CO273/247; CO273/236. On India, see OIOC, L/MIL/3/148; P/3477; P/3855; P/4383; L/MIL/7/13863.

2. Norman Miners, *Hong Kong Under Imperial Rule 1912–1941* (Hong Kong: Oxford University Press, 1987), 195; James F. Warren, *Ah Ku and Karayuki-San: Prostitution in Singapore 1870–1940* (Singapore: Oxford University Press, 1993), 123.

3. Lock hospital reports for the first quarter of 1898, PRO, CO273/236; Max F. Simon, Principal Civil Medical Officer, Straits Settlements to Colonial Secretary, 13 April 1899, PRO, CO273/247 (12299).

4. Mian Mir Station Followers' Hospital Report, 1898–9, 2, OIOC, L/MIL/7/13918.

5. 23 October 1899, OIOC, L/MIL/7/13876; also see OIOC, L/MIL/7/13875.

6. HC, *SP,* 1905 [Cd. 2766], *Report on Sanitary Measures in India, 1903–04,* 57. This fall is consistent, too, with the declining rate of alcohol abuse in the British army. See Ken Hendrickson, "A Kinder, Gentler British Army: Mid-Victorian Experiments in the Management of Army Vice at Gibraltar and Aldershot," *War & Society* 14, no. 2 (1996): 30; Alan Ramsay Skelley, *The Victorian Army At Home: The Recruitment and Terms and Conditions of the British Regular 1859–1899* (London: Croom Helm, 1977), 162–3; Edward M. Spiers, *The Army and Society 1815–1914* (London: Longman, 1980), 66–7.

7. Venereal Disease, 1904, British Troops, Military Department Minute Paper, 30 December 1905, OIOC, L/MIL/7/13881.

8. *General Report and Statistics of Venereal Diseases among British and Indian Troops in India during the year 1908* (n.p., 1909), OIOC, L/MIL/7/13887. After 1900, VD among troops in India was tabulated by regiments and batteries as well as by stations, see OIOC, L/MIL/7/13877.

9. See, for instance, Proceeding 130 of Government of Madras Sanitary Proceedings, April 1900, OIOC, P/5883; Memo, Army Sanitary Commission, August 1900, OIOC, P/5884; Military Department Minute Papers for 1902 and 1905, and Army Sanitary Commission memorandum, May 1901, OIOC, L/MIL/7/13881; Army Department, 12 January 1922, OIOC, L/MIL/7/13893; local reports from Cantonment Hospitals 1899–1900, OIOC, L/MIL/7/13919; HC, *SP,* 1912 [Cd. 6373], *Report on Sanitary Measures in India in 1910–11;* HC, *SP,* 1908 [Cd. 5245], *Report on Sanitary Measures in India in 1908–09;* HC, *SP,* 1909 [Cd. 4762], *Report on Sanitary Measures in India in 1907–08.*

10. Warren, *Ah Ku and Karayuki-San,* 118; Lenore Manderson, "Migration, Prostitution and Medical Surveillance in Early Twentieth-Century Malaya," in *Migrants, Minorities and Health: Historical and Contemporary Studies,* ed. Lara Marks and Michael Worboys (London and New York: Routledge. 1997), 57–9; Miners, *Hong Kong Under Imperial Rule,* 195.

11. *Report on Venereal Diseases* (London: HMSO, 1913), iii; 25, WI, RAMC 1212/8.

12. Douglas White and C. H. Melville, *Venereal Disease: Its Present and Future* (n.p., 1911), 5. Melville reiterated this point in "The History and Epidemiology of Syphilis in the More Important Armies," in *A System of Syphilis in Six Volumes:* vol. 6, *Syphilis in Relation to the Public Services,* ed. D'Arcy Power and J. Keogh Murphy (London: Oxford Medical Publications/Henry Frowde/Hodder and Stoughton, 1910), 96; 98.

13. Charles Bell Taylor, *The Soldier and His Masters: From A Sanitary Point of View* (London: Kelvin Glen and Co., 1898), 20.

14. *The Treatment of Venereal Disease and Scabies in the Army: Final Report* (London, HMSO, 1906), 2.

15. On Metchnikoff and Roux, see "Important Medical Discovery," *The Times* (11 May 1906), 4; on syphilis, "The Treatment of Syphilis," *The Times* (6 July 1910), 5; "Preparation 606," *The Times* (13 August 1910), 6; "Preparation 606," *The Times* (19 December 1910), 9. On the Wasserman reaction, see Ilana Löwy, "Testing for a Sexually Transmissible Disease, 1907–1970: The History of the Wassermann Reaction," in *AIDS and Contemporary History,* ed. Virginia Berridge and Philip Strong (Cambridge: Cambridge University Press, 1993: 74–92), and Rudolph H. Kampmeier, "Introduction of Salvarsan," *Sexually Transmitted Diseases* 4, no. 2 (1977): 66–8.

16. Its chemical formula is $C_{12}H_{12}O_2N_2As_2(HCl_2)$. It was marketed as a powder, because the solution was unstable. Neosalvarsan was considerably more stable, and available in solution form, far easier for doctors to administer.

17. John Thorne Crissey and Lawrence Charles Parish, *The Dermatology and Syphilology of the Nineteenth Century* (New York: Praeger, 1981), 361; Charles Clayton Dennie, *A History of Syphilis* (Springfield, IL: Charles C. Thomas, 1962), 111–2; L. W. Harrison, *A Sketch of Army Medical Experience of Venereal Disease during the European War, 1914–18* (London: National Council for Combatting Venereal Disease, 1922), 14–15; J. D. Oriel, *The Scars of Venus: A History of Venereology* (London: Springer-Verlag, 1994), 92; T. E. Osmond, "Venereal Disease

in Peace and War with some Reminiscences of the Last Forty Years," *British Journal of Venereal Diseases* 25 no. 3 (1949): 102.

18. Maurice Gregory, *Supplement to the Solidarity* (London, Social Purity Association, n.d. ?1910/11), 4.

19. D'Arcy Power, "Opening Address with Special Reference to the Treatment of the Disease," *Syphilis: With Special Reference to (a) Its Prevalence and Intensity in the Past and at the Present Day, (b) Its Relation to Public Health, (c) The Treatment of the Disease. A Discussion* (London: Longmans, Green and Co., 1912), 39. See too Crissey and Parish, *Dermatology and Syphilology*, 84. For a discussion of the resistance to pathology, see Christopher Lawrence, "A Tale of Two Sciences: Bedside and Bench in Twentieth-Century Britain," *Medical History* 43(1999): 421–49.

20. Home Secretary's Office to A. Graham Butler, Honorary Secretary, Queensland British Medical Association, 28 March 1918, QSA, HOM/J80.

21. Milton Lewis, *Thorns on the Rose: The History of Sexually Transmitted Diseases in Australia in International Perspective* (Canberra; Australian Government Publishing Service, 1998), 376.

22. Carol Summers, "Intimate Colonialism: The Imperial Production of Reproduction in Uganda, 1907–1925," *Signs* 16, no. 4 (1991): 797.

23. Warwick Anderson, "Where is the Postcolonial History of Medicine?" *Bulletin of the History of Medicine* 72, no. 3 (1998): 524.

24. C. C. Little, Inspector General of Government Hospitals, Burma to Secretary, Government of Burma, 17 April 1901, OIOC, P/6350.

25. Report on Visit of Majors Grigor and Morris to No. 9 Stationary Hospital, France, 20 January 1916, AWM 27 (376/161).

26. Osmond, "Venereal Disease in Peace and War," 101–2, 106.

27. Lesley Hall, "'War always brings it on': War, STDs and the Civilian Population in Britain, 1850–1950," in *Medicine and Modern Warfare*, ed. Roger Cooter, Mark Harrison, and Steve Sturdy (Amsterdam/Atlanta: Rodopi, 1999), 211.

28. J. E. Ross, and S. M. Tomkins, "The British Reception of Salvarsan," *Journal of the History of Medicine and Allied Sciences* 52, no. 4 (1997): 403.

29. Salvarsan was commercially available in Britain from December 1910.

30. David Arnold, "Sex, State, and Society: Sexually Transmitted Diseases and HIV/AIDS in Modern India," in *Sex, Disease, and Society: A Comparative History of Sexually Transmitted Diseases and HIV/AIDS in Asia and the Pacific*, ed. Milton Lewis, Scott Bamber, and Michael Waugh (Westport, CT: Greenwood Press, 1997), 26–7.

31. Military Despatch, 5 July 1923, OIOC, L/MIL/7/13901; HC, SP, 1915 [Cd. 8087], *Report on Sanitary Measures in India, 1913–1914*, 23.

32. HC, SP, 1914. [Cd. 7519], *Report on Sanitary Measures in India, 1912–1913*, 12; *General Report and Statistics of Venereal Diseases amongst British Troops in India during the year 1912*, n.p. 1913, 6, OIOC, L/MIL/7/13893.

33. *Annual Report of Cantonment Hospitals and Dispensaries for the Year 1911* (n.p. 1912), no pagination, OIOC, L/MIL/7/13896.

34. Military Despatch, 5 July 1923, OIOC, L/MIL/7/13901.

35. E. P. Mourilyan, "The Epidemiology of Syphilis in the Royal Navy," in *A System of Syphilis*, 334; Francis H. Welch, "The Prevention of Syphilis," *The Lancet* (12 August 1899): 405; Arthur Powell, "Discussion," in *Syphilis*, 186.

36. E. Montague to Henry J. Wilson, 25 August 1911, WL, JEB, box A6.

37. C. B. Mitchell to Joseph Chamberlain, 10 August 1899; F. Swettenham to High Commissioner, Federated Malay States, 31 July 1899; *Venereal Disease in Perak* (n.d. ?1899); all at PRO, CO273/251 (23660).

38. HC, SP, 1899 [C. 9523], *Correspondence regarding the Measures to be Adopted for Checking the Spread of Venereal Disease*, 115.

39. Diana R. Tibbits, "The Medical, Social and Political Response to Venereal Diseases in Victoria, 1860–1980," (Ph. D. diss., Monash University, 1994), 102.

40. Dr. Baxter Tyrie to Home Secretary, 28 September 1907, QSA, HOM/J80.

41. "The Contagious Diseases Act of 1868," n.d. ?1913, QSA, HOM/J80.

42. *Report of A Sub-Committee of the Burma Branch of the British Medical Association on the Prevalence of Venereal Diseases at Rangoon* (n.d., n.p.); C. C. Little, Inspector General of Government Hospitals, Burma to Secretary, Government of Burma, 17 April 1901, both at OIOC, P/6350.

43. O'Moore Creagh to Helen Wilson, 27 December 1912, WL, HJW, file I–II, 1887–1912, D1/1, file 4.

44. Lucy Bland, *Banishing the Beast: English Feminism and Sexual Morality 1885–1914* (London: Penguin Books, 1995); Anna Davin, "Imperialism and Motherhood," *History Workshop Journal* 6 (1978): 9–65; Frank Mort, *Dangerous Sexualities: Medico-Moral Politics in England since 1830*, 2nd ed. (London: Routledge, 2000).

45. Bland, *Banishing the Beast*, 241–2; Steve Humphries, *A Secret World of Sex: Forbidden Fruit, The British Experience 1900–1950* (London: Sidgwick and Jackson, 1988), 64.

46. "Proposed Scheme for the Diagnosis and Treatment of Venereal Diseases prepared by the Medical Officer of Health in conformity with the Order of the Local Government Board," Liverpool Corporation Health Sub-Committee and Port Sanitary and Hospital Committee, Minutes of Meetings, November 1916, 20–21, LRO, 352 MIN/HEA, II,34/6. Compare the decision taken in Tasmania late in the nineteenth century to transfer Hobart's lock hospital to the women's section of the city jail: see Milton Lewis, "From Blue Light Clinic to Nightingale Centre: A Brief History of the Sydney STD Centre and Its Forerunners. Part I: Venereal Diseases in Europe and in Australia from Colonization to 1945," *Venereology* 1, no. 1 (1988): 4.

47. "The History of the Fight against Venereal Diseases," *British Medical Journal* (12 August 1916): 231; M. A. Crowther, "The Later Years of the Workhouse 1890–1929," in *The Origins of British Social Policy*, ed. Pat Thane (London: Croom Helm, 1978), 43.

48. Frank Mort, "Purity, Feminism and the State: Sexuality and Moral Politics 1880–1914," in *Crises in the British State 1880–1930*, ed. Mary Langan and Bill Schwarz (London: Hutchinson, in association with the Centre for Contemporary Cultural Studies, University of Birmingham, 1985), 222; Judith Allen, *Sex and Secrets: Crimes Involving Australian Women Since 1880* (Melbourne: Oxford University Press, 1990), 109; Bland, *Banishing the Beast*, 109; Stefan Petrow, *Policing Morals: The Metropolitan Police and the Home Office 1870–1914* (Oxford: Clarendon Press, 1994), 145; Bronwyn Dalley, "Lolly Shops 'of the Red-light Kind' and 'Soldiers of the King': Suppressing One-Woman Brothels in New Zealand, 1908–1916," *New Zealand Journal of History* 30, no. 1 (1996): 1.

49. Roger Davidson notes that even the radical policies of the 1916 Venereal Diseases Act did little to lessen the stigma attached to VD: "Venereal Disease, Sexual Morality, and Public Health in Interwar Scotland," *Journal of the History of Sexuality* 5, no. 2 (1994): 273.

50. Rev. F. C. Spurr, *The Red Plague* (Melbourne: J. Kemp, Government Printer, 1911), 7.

51. Helen M. Wilson to Francis Champneys, 17 December 1914, WL, AMSH 311, file 1; Helen M. Wilson, *Sanitary Principles Applied to the Prevention of Venereal Diseases* (London: John Bale, 1911), 5; 4.

52. George Black, *The Red Plague Crusade* (Sydney: William Applegate Gullick, Government Printer, 1916), 9; Philip Fleming, "Fighting the 'Red Plague': Observations on the Response to Venereal Disease in New Zealand 1910–45," *New Zealand Journal of History* 22, no. 1 (1988): 57.

53. Helen M. Wilson to Francis Champneys, 17 December 1914, WL, AMSH 311, file 1.

54. Warren, *Ah Ku and Karayuki-San*, 126.

55. Miners, *Hong Kong Under Imperial Rule*, 196–8.

56. Brenda S. A. Yeoh, "Sexually Transmitted Diseases in Late Nineteenth- and Twentieth-Century Singapore," in *Sex, Disease, and Society*, 181.

57. Report by Acting Protector of Chinese, 1900, PRO, CO273/258 (30403); Inspector General, Police, Straits Settlements, 27 January 1902, PRO, CO273/278 (8861).

58. India Office minute, 1910, OIOC, L/MIL/7/13890.

59. J. Dorgan, "Prevention of Venereal Disease," *Journal of the Royal Army Medical Corps* 11, no. 2 (1908): 124–5.

60. L. W. Harrison, "Some Lessons Learnt in Fifty Years Practice in Venereology," *British Journal of Venereal Diseases* 30 (1954): 184.

61. *Panama Weekly News*, 28 September 1918; internal FO memo, 1 November 1918, PRO, FO 368/198, f. 185731.

62. Major F. G. Cardew, Department Secretary, Government of India, Military Department to Principal Medical Officer, H.M. Forces in India, 20 August 1901, OIOC, L/MIL/7/13920.

63. Cantonment Hospital Reports 1899–1900, Bareilly, OIOC, L/MIL/7/13919.

64. Major F. G. Cardew, Department Secretary, Government of India, Military Department to Principal Medical Officer, India, 20 August 1901, OIOC, P/6392 (1676); also at L/MIL/7/13920.

65. Major W. I. Trotter, Cantonment General Hospital, Bareilly to Oudh and Rohilkhand District Medical Officer, Ranikhet, 13 September 1901, OIOC, L/MIL/7/13920.

66. Lt. Col. H. B. Thornhill to Principal Medical Officer, India, 16 October 1901, OIOC, P/6392 (1676); also at L/MIL/7/13920.

67. James Stuart and J. Morley to India Secretary, 3 November 1910, OIOC, L/MIL/7/13890.

68. India Office Minute, n.d. 1910, OIOC, L/MIL/7/13890.

69. Report of W. Evans, Protector of Chinese, 11 November 1899, PRO, CO273/249 (34493). Reprinted in HC, *SP*, 1906 [Cd. 2903], *Further Correspondence relating to Measures Adopted for Checking the Spread of Venereal Disease*, 13–4.

70. Memorandum, G. W. Johnson, 13 December 1899, PRO, CO273/249 (34493).

71. F. A. Swettenham, Resident General, FMS to Acting High Commissioner, FMS, 6 April 1900, PRO, CO273/261 (15028).

72. Kunal M. Parker, "'A Corporation of Superior Prostitutes:' Anglo-Indian Legal Conceptions of Temple Dancing Girls, 1800–1914," *Modern Asian Studies* 32, no. 3 (1998): 584–5.

73. Ibid., 588. Parker argues (615) that convictions were likelier when the prosecuted was a *devadasi* or temple dancer.

74. *Draft Report of the Committee appointed to consider a Memorial of the Society for the Protection of Children in India* (n.d. ?1907, n.p.), OIOC, P/7891.

75. Sir Harold Stuart, Officiating Secretary to Government of India to Chief Secretary, Government of Bengal, Political Department, 25 August 1908, OIOC, P/7891.

76. Kumar Shri Harbhanji Rawaji, President, Girassia Association to Sir James DuBoulay, Private Secretary to the Viceroy, 8 January 1913, NAI, Home Proceedings Judicial A, July 1913, appendix 8.

77. *Proceedings of the Council of the Governor General in India, 1914* (Calcutta: Office of the Superintendent of Government Printing, 1915), 3, 18 March 1914, Sir Reginald Craddock, OIOC, L/P&J/6/1259 (2894).

78. S. D. Bamber, K. J. Hewison, and P. J. Underwood, "A History of Sexually Transmitted Diseases in Thailand: Policy and Politics," *Genitourinary Medicine* 69, no. 2 (1993): 149.

79. Ordinance XVII of 1903, Malta.

80. Memorandum, 9 December 1902, PRO, CO873/43 (524).

81. Staff Surgeon, Royal Navy to Naval Executive Officer, Wei Hei Wei, 16 April 1903, PRO, CO873/67.

82. Peter Carl Botsman, "The Sexual and the Social: 'Policing Venereal Diseases, Medicine and Morals'" (Ph. D. diss., University of New South Wales, 1987), 364; Allen, *Sex and Secrets*, 75.

83. *Government Gazette*, 25 October, 1913, QSA, A/45284; Lewis, *Thorns on the Rose*, 151.

84. *Government Gazette*, 25 May 1912, QSA, A/45284.

85. Ibid.

86. *Venereal Diseases* (Brisbane, Department of Public Health, 1913).

87. Queensland. *Official Record of the Debates of the Legislative Council and the Legislative Assembly*, 1911–12, 26 September 1911, 1128, vol. 108.

88. B. A. Smithurst, "Historic and Epidemiologic Review of Venereal Disease in Queensland" (MD thesis, University of Queensland, 1981), 92.

89. Ross Patrick, *A History of Health and Medicine in Queensland 1824–1960* (St. Lucia: University of Queensland Press, 1987), 262.

90. Ross Fitzgerald, *From the Dreaming to 1915: A History of Queensland* (St. Lucia: University of Queensland Press, 1982), 217.

91. See, for example, Judith Smart, "Feminists, Labour Women and Venereal Disease in Early Twentieth-Century Melbourne," *Australian Feminist Studies* 15 (1992): 25–40.

92. Rose Scott, *A Law Affecting Women: "The State Regulation of Vice"* (Queensland: WCTU, 1903), 2.

93. See, for example, memorandum on the act in QSA, HOM/J80 which details various petitions in 1906 and 1907; see too letter from J. C. Kirby to ?AMSH, 1 June 1910, on anti-CD organizing in Australia, WL, E1/3.

94. See correspondence between Queensland League of Voters and Queensland Minister for Health and Home Affairs, January 1947 to May 1948, QSA, A/4718.

95. Sub-Inspector to Police Commissioner, 15 December 1897, QSA, POL/J35, 796M.

96. William Gall, Under Secretary, Home Department to Secretary, Brisbane Hospital, 17 February, 1916, QSA, A/4718.

97. Charles Lilley, Acting Medical Superintendent to Under Secretary, Home Secretary's Department, 3 February 1916, QSA, A/4718.
98. Deputy Commissioner of Taxation, Federal Tax Office, Brisbane to Under Secretary, Home Department, 3 August 1918, QSA, A/45284.
99. *The Observer and Evening Brisbane Courier*, 12 December 1911; *Brisbane Daily Mail*, 19 November 1912; *Brisbane Courier*, 19 November 1912, all in QSA A/21955.
100. 21 November 1912, QSA, A/21955.
101. Lenore Manderson, *Sickness and the State: Health and Illness in Colonial Malaya, 1870–1940* (Cambridge: Cambridge University Press, 1996), 182.
102. Copy of a report by T. C. Mugliston, 3 April 1895, PRO, CO273/203 (7714).
103. HC, *SP*, 1906 [Cd. 2903], *Further Correspondence*, H. W. Firmstone, "Report by the Assistant Protector of Chinese, Penang, on the working of Ordinance No. XIII of 1899," n.d. 1900?, 23.
104. Copy of a report by T. C. Mugliston, 3 April 1895, PRO, CO273/203 (7714); E. W. von Tunzelmann, "Report by Acting Colonial Surgeon on the Working, in Singapore, of Ordinance XIII of 1899," 15 January 1900, PRO, CO273/256 (4829).
105. E. O. A. Travers to Colonial Secretary, 29 October 1907, PRO, CO273/335; HC. *SP*, 1923, C. 316-7, PRO, CO275/109; J. G. Butcher, *The British in Malaya 1880–1941: The Social History of A European Community in Colonial South-East Asia* (Kuala Lumpur: Oxford University Press, 1979), 195.
106. E. A. O. Travers to Colonial Secretary, 29 October 1907, PRO, CO273/335; *Report of Venereal Diseases Committee*, CO275/109, *SP*, 1923, C. 316.
107. *Report of Venereal Diseases Committee*, CO275/109, *SP*, 1923, C. 316.
108. Warren D. Barnes, Secretary for Chinese Affairs to British Resident, Perak, 15 May 1905, PRO, CO273/340 (16686); John Anderson, Governor, Straits Settlements to Lord Elgin, Colonial Office, 16 January 1908, PRO, CO273/339 (4535). See too Brendan O'Keefe, "Sexually Transmitted Diseases in Malaysia: A History," in *Sex, Disease, and Society*, 161.
109. *Report of Venereal Diseases Committee*, CO275/109, HC. *SP*, 1923, C. 316; John Anderson to Lord Elgin, 16 January 1908, PRO, CO273/339 (4535).
110. Memo, HBL to C. P. Lucas, 5 November 1908, PRO, CO273/335.
111. E. L. Brockman, Resident General, Selangor to John Anderson, 25 January 1908, PRO, CO273/339 (11053).
112. Manderson, *Sickness and the State*, 185–91.
113. E. L. Brockman to John Anderson, 25 January 1908, PRO, CO273/339 (11053).
114. Colonial Office memoranda in PRO, CO273/160 (13763).
115. George W. Johnson to E. Fairfield, 24 May 1895, PRO, CO273/203 (7714); Johnson to C. P. Lucas, 7 July 1900, PRO, CO273/261 (15028). For details of Johnson's involvement in the repeal campaign, see Alice Johnson, *George William Johnson. Civil Servant and Social Worker* (printed for private circulation, Cambridge, 1927).
116. Lord Ripon to C. B. H. Mitchell, 28 December 1894, PRO, CO882/6 (18487).
117. John Anderson to Lord Elgin, 14 September 1907, PRO, CO273/331 (36323).
118. See, for example, the report by T. C. Mugliston, 3 April 1895, PRO, CO273/203 (7714).
119. In India, civil surgeons but not sanitary officers were permitted private practice. See Mark Harrison, "Towards A Sanitary Utopia? Professional Visions and Public Health in India, 1880–1914," *South Asia Research* 10, no. 1 (1990): 23. Ian Catanach argues that such practice was not actually forbidden to sanitary officers but that it was very limited: see his "Plague and the Tensions of Empire: India 1896–1918," in *Imperial Medicine and Indigenous Societies*, ed. David Arnold (Manchester: Manchester University Press, 1988), 151.
120. The Association for Moral and Social Hygiene certainly knew of the clubs, as is evidenced by their pamphlet, *Moral Problems in Singapore* (London: AMSH n.d. ?1924), probably authored by Alison Neilans.
121. John Anderson to Lord Elgin, 19 September 1907, PRO, CO273/331 (36323). Brendan O'Keefe argues that, nonetheless and despite rulings to the contrary, many such clubs were still extant in the 1920s: "Sexually Transmitted Diseases in Malaysia," 161. These were likely staffed by doctors not associated with the government medical service.
122. HC, *SP*, 1901 [Cd. 844], *Report on Sanitary Measures in India 1899–1900*, 59.
123. For example, Military Despatch 76 of 1901, 30 May 1901, OIOC, L/MIL/3/157.
124. Curzon to Hamilton, 13 June 1901, OIOC, L/MIL/3/157; *Cantonment Code, 1909*, s. 214, OIOC, L/MIL/7/13894; HC, *SP*, 1899 [C. 9448], *Cantonment Act, 1899*, s. 209.

125. For a typical example, see "Report on Secunderabad Station Followers' Hospital 1898–9," 2, OIOC, L/MIL/7/13918.
126. F. G. Cardew, Deputy Secretary to Government of India, Military Department to Quartermaster General in India, 15 November 1900, OIOC, P/5884; Cardew to Government of Burma, Military Department, 20 February 1901, OIOC, P/6118.
127. *Cantonment Manual, 1909* (Calcutta: Army Headquarters, Quartermaster General's Division, 24 January 1909), s. 63, OIOC, L/MIL/7/13891.
128. John Cowen, *Tracts for Rangoon No. 1. 29th Street by Night* (Rangoon: YMCA, ?1914), 1.
129. Social Purity Alliance, *Annual Report 1887–1888* (n.d., n.p.), address of James Stuart, 18.
130. *To The Women of Finchley* (London: Pewtress and Co., n.d. ?1897), n.p.
131. Millicent Garrett Fawcett, *A Speech made at the Croydon Meeting of the General Committee of the National Union of Women Workers, October 1897, by Mrs. Henry Fawcett on the New Rules for Dealing with the Sanitary Condition of the British Army in India* (London: Women's Printing Society, 1897), 11.
132. *The Need for Renewed Agitation in the Abolitionist Movement* (London: Friends' Association for Abolishing State Regulation of Vice, n.d. ?1900), 2.
133. Maurice Gregory, *Facts Used in Japan and Australia in 1911 and 1912* (Perth: V.K. Jones, 1912), 61.
134. Lord Kitchener, *Memorandum to the Troops, 1905* (n.p., 1905), 12–3, WL, HJW, D1/3.
135. *PP*, Cape of Good Hope, *Report of the Select Committee on the Contagious Diseases Acts*, 1906, ix.
136. "Is Empire Consistent with Morality? No! By A Public Servant," *Pall Mall Gazette* 95, no. 6917 (19 May 1887): 3.
137. Katherine Dixon, *An Appeal to the Women of the Empire concerning Present Moral Conditions in Our Cantonments in India* (London: AMSH 1916), 7.
138. Dixon, *An Appeal*, 7. Dixon reiterates the claim in *Mrs. K. Dixon's Work against Regulated Prostitution within the British Empire* (London: Vacher and Sons, [?1919]), 2.
139. Violet Tempest, *Our Army in India* (London: White Slave Abolition Publications, 1913), 3.
140. Cowen, *Tracts for Rangoon No. 1*, 1.
141. Elizabeth W. Andrew and Katharine C. Bushnell, *Heathen Slaves and Christian Rulers* (Oakland, CA: Messiah's Advocate, 1907), iii. In *Recent Researches into the Japanese Slave Trade in California* (n.p., n.d. [1907]), 16, they painted attitudes to women in Japanese society as even worse than in Chinese, lashing out at the "degradation of the unenlightened Oriental woman."
142. Henry J. Wilson to Charlotte Wilson, 3 February 1908, HJW papers, SCA, MD 2605-14.
143. David Brooks, *The Age of Upheaval: Edwardian Politics, 1899–1914* (Manchester: Manchester University Press, 1995), 102.
144. Helen Wilson to Alfred de Meuron, 22 June 1916, WL, IAF, 3/AMS 51.2.
145. Army Sanitary Commission memorandum, 9 March 1897, OIOC, L/MIL/7/13863.
146. Joseph Chamberlain to Governors, Straits Settlements and Hong Kong, 18 February 1898, PRO, CO129/276 (17234). The first woman to hold such a position in Britain was Mona Rawlins, appointed house surgeon at the female London Lock Hospital in 1915; *Annual Report, 1914*, 9, RCS, LLH.
147. Memo, G. W. Johnson, 10 November 1897, PRO, CO129/276 (17234).
148. Military Despatch no. 53, Lord Curzon to Lord Hamilton, 12 April 1900, OIOC, L/MIL/7/13868; also at L/MIL/3/155.
149. Minute of Lord Elgin, 7 August 1897, NAI Proceedings, Home Department, Medical B, February 1900, no. 38.
150. Major General W. Black to J. Chamberlain, 18 November 1898, PRO, CO129/286 (28461).
151. Curzon to Hamilton, 12 April 1900, OIOC, L/MIL/7/13868; also at L/MIL/3/155.
152. J. A. Swettenham to Joseph Chamberlain, 5 August 1898, PRO, CO273/237 (19844).
153. J. M. Atkinson to Colonial Secretary, 2 August 1899, HC. *SP*, 1906 [Cd. 2903]; also at PRO, CO129/292 (25026).
154. Curzon et al. to Lord Hamilton, Military Despatch 139 of 1899, 27 July 1899, OIOC, L/MIL/3/154.
155. J. M. Atkinson to Colonial Secretary, 2 August 1899, HC, *SP*, 1906 [Cd. 2903]; also at PRO, CO129/292 (25026). This question of numbers was put to the test in Uganda in the early 1920s. The elaborate programs to combat venereal diseases there were run almost exclusively

by men. Feminist protesters in Britain took up their cudgels when the only woman doctor in the program resigned in 1921. See Summers, "Intimate Colonialism," 801.

156. Military Despatch 73, 18 May 1897, OIOC, L/MIL/7/13868; also at L/MIL/3/152.

157. A. Fiddes to C. P. Lucas, 26 January 1899, PRO, CO129/294 (1832).

158. Curzon et al. to Lord Hamilton, Military Despatch 53 of 1900, 12 April 1900, OIOC, L/MIL/3/155.

159. Petition noted as held in B Proceedings, October 1881, OIOC, P/1664.

160. For a discussion of this elision of doctors and medical assistants and its meaning, see Alison Bashford, *Purity and Pollution: Gender, Embodiment and Victorian Medicine* (Basingstoke: Macmillan, 1998), 89.

161. Memorandum, Surgeon General W. R. Hooper, 9 November 1899, OIOC, L/MIL/7/13868.

162. Brigadier Surgeon T. Walsh, Rawal Pindi to Deputy Surgeon General A. F. Bradshaw, 5 August 1888, OIOC, P/3474 (3138).

163. George S. White to Surgeon Major General A. F. Bradshaw, 9 August 1893, OIOC, Mss. Eur. F.108/17, f. 40.

164. Frederick Roberts to Surgeon General W. A. Thomson, 23 August 1891, OIOC, L/MIL/17/5/1615/12, CCLXXXV.

165. Philippa Levine, "'Walking The Streets In A Way No Decent Woman Should': Women Police in World War One," *Journal of Modern History* 66 (1994): 34–78.

166. Unknown author, Brisbane Police Department to John Huxham, Assistant Home Secretary, 14 September 1915, QSA, A/45448.

167. Suggestions and Questions about Prostitution in Cantonments, sent by E. Mackenzie, Secretary, LNA, 13 November 1914, OIOC, L/MIL/7/13897.

168. Army Department Despatch 64 of 1915, Austen Chamberlain to Hardinge of Penshurst, 24 June 1915, OIOC, L/MIL/7/13897.

169. A. James Hammerton, *Emigrant Gentlewomen: Genteel Poverty and Female Emigration, 1830–1914* (London: Croom Helm, 1979), 92.

170. Rosemary Hennessy and Rajeswari Mohan, "The Construction of Woman in Three Popular Texts of Empire: Towards a Critique of Materialist Feminism," *Textual Practice* 3, no. 3 (1989): 334.

171. Helen Kanitkar, " 'Real True Boys': Moulding the Cadets of Imperialism," in *Dislocating Masculinity: Comparative Ethnographies,* ed. Andrea Cornwall and Nancy Lindisfarne (Routledge: London, 1994), 185.

172. Errol McDonnell, Consul General, Lourenco Marques to Secretary for the Interior, Pretoria, 7 August 1913, PRO, FO369/611 (42322).

173. Diane Kirkby, *Barmaids: A History of Women's Work in Pubs* (Cambridge: Cambridge University Press, 1997), 123, 128. Kirkby notes earlier attempts at such laws in the 1880s and 1890s as well, all of which failed. See too Peter Bailey, "Parasexuality and Glamour: The Victorian Barmaid as Cultural Prototype," *Gender & History* 2, no. 2 (1990): 148–72.

174. Memorandum of Lord Curzon, 27 August 1902, OIOC, Mss. Eur F.111/279.

175. Letter of Government of Burma to Government of India, 31 July 1902, OIOC, Mss. Eur. F.111/279.

176. Memorandum of Lord Curzon, 24 August 1902, OIOC, Mss. Eur. F.111/279.

177. Kay J. Anderson, *Vancouver's Chinatown: Racial Discourse in Canada, 1875–1980* (Montreal and Kingston: McGill-Queen's University Press, 1991), 159; Constance Backhouse, *Colour-Coded: A Legal History of Racism in Canada, 1900–1950* (Toronto: University of Toronto Press, 2000), chapter 5.

178. Telegram of Viceroy of India to India Secretary, 22 August 1914, OIOC, L/P&J/6/1207.

179. Military Department Minute Paper, 10 November 1897, OIOC, L/MIL/7/13873.

180. *Sixth Annual Report on the Working of the Lock Hospitals in the Northwestern Provinces and Oudh for the year 1879* (Allahabad, n.p., 1880), 17, OIOC, V/24/2290.

181. Grass Cutter's Petition, 1 June 1897, OIOC, P/5248.

182. Colonel P. S. Lumsden to Secretary to Government of India, 4 September 1871, OIOC, P/1003.

183. Lepel Griffin, Officiating Secretary to the Government of the Punjab to Officiating Secretary to the Government of India, 9 June 1877, OIOC, P/1003.

184. Josephine E. Butler, *Personal Reminiscences of A Great Crusade* (London: Horace Marshall and Son, 1896), 1.

185. Report of the Prostitution Committee, 1922, 6, OIOC, V/26/803/4.

186. George Bernard Shaw to Helen Wilson, 26 February 1918, WL, JEB, Papers relating to Army Matters I: 1917–1920.

Chapter 6

1. Lucy Bland, " 'Cleansing the Portals of Life': The Venereal Disease Campaign in the Early Twentieth-Century," in *Crises in the British State 1880–1930*, ed. Mary Langan and Bill Schwarz (London: Hutchinson, in association with the Centre for Contemporary Cultural Studies, University of Birmingham, 1985), 201.

2. Walter H. Long to Dominion Premiers, 19 October 1917, PRO, WO 32/11401/15A.

3. W. G. Macpherson, *History of the Great War Based on Official Documents: Medical Services: General History*, vol. 1, (London: HMSO, 1921), 201.

4. W. G. MacPherson, W. P. Herringham, T. R. Elliott, and A. Balfour, ed. *History of the Great War Based on Official Documents: Medical Services. Diseases of the War*, vol. 2 (London: HMSO, 1923), 118.

5. [A. G. Butler] *The Official History of the Australian Army Medical Services in the War of 1914–1918*: vol. 3, *Special Problems and Services* (Melbourne: Australian War Memorial, 1943), 152; Macpherson et al, *History of the Great War* 2, 118.

6. H. MacDougall, "Sexually Transmitted Diseases in Canada, 1800–1992," *Genitourinary Medicine* 70, no. 1 (1994): 58; Lutz D. H. Sauerteig, "Sex, Medicine and Morality During the First World War," in *War, Medicine and Modernity*, ed. Roger Cooter, Mark Harrison, and Steve Sturdy (Stroud: Sutton Publishing, 1998), 171.

7. L. W. Harrison, *A Sketch of Army Medical Experience of Venereal Disease during the European War, 1914–18* (London: National Council for Combatting Venereal Disease, 1922), 4.

8. Butler, *Official History*, vol. 3, 154.

9. L. W. Harrison, T*he Management of Venereal Disease in the Civil Community* (London: National Council for Combatting Venereal Disease, 1918), 3. For another "war" within a war, that of male homosexuality, see Samuel Hynes, *A War Imagined: The First World War and English Culture* (New York: Athenaeum, 1991), 223–34.

10. D. A. Welsh, "The Enemy in Our Midst: Venereal Disease," in *Proceedings of the University of Sydney Society for Combatting Venereal Diseases* (Sydney: December, 1916), 12.

11. Dennis Winter, *Death's Men: Soldiers of the Great War* (London: Allen Lane, 1978), 46; Bernard Porter, *The Lion's Share: A Short History of British Imperialism 1850–1983* (London: Longman, 1984), 235.

12. Lewis J. Greenstein, "The Nandi Experience in the First World War," in *Africa and the First World War*, ed. Melvin E. Page (Basingstoke: The Macmillan Press, 1987), 81–94; Harry H. Johnston, *The Black Man's Part in the War. An Account of the Dark-Skinned Population of the British Empire: How It Is and Will Be Affected by the Great War; and the Share It Has Taken in Waging That War* (London: Simpkin, Marshall, Hamilton, Kent and Co. 1917), 7; C. L. Joseph, "The British West Indies Regiment 1914–1918," *Journal of Caribbean History* 3 (1971): 94–124; David Killingray, "The Idea of A British Imperial African Army," *Journal of African History* 20 (1979): 421–36; Laura Tabili, *"We Ask for British Justice": Workers and Racial Difference in Late Imperial Britain* (Ithaca, NY: Cornell University Press, 1994), 17; B. P. Willan, "The South African Native Labour Contingent, 1916–1918," *Journal of African History* 19, no. 1 (1978): 61–86.

13. DeWitt C. Ellinwood, "The Indian Soldier, the Indian Army, and Change, 1914–1918," in *India and World War One*, ed. DeWitt C. Ellinwood and S. D. Pradhan (New Delhi: Manohar, 1978), 183. See too Jeffrey Greenhut, "The Imperial Reserve: The Indian Corps on the Western Front, 1914–15," *Journal of Imperial and Commonwealth History* 12, no. 1 (1983): 54–73. Some authorities put the overall figure of Indian participation as high as 1.3 million: Rozina Visram, *Ayahs, Lascars and Princes: Indians in Britain 1700–1947* (London: Pluto Press, 1986), 116. She also says (116) that Indians serving in France numbered 138,000, as does Kusoom Vadgama in *India in Britain: The Indian Contribution to the British Way of Life* (London: Robert Royce Ltd., 1984), 93.

14. S. D. Pradhan, "Indian Army and the First World War," in *India and World War I*, 52, 55.

15. Albert Grundlingh, "The Impact of the First World War on South African Blacks," in *Africa and the First World War*, 55; Bill Nasson, "The Great War in South African Historiography," *Bulletin du Centre de Recherche Historial, Péronne* (June 1993): 9–12; Willan, "The South African Native Labour Contingent," 61; PRO, CO551/117/39492.

16. P. J. Marshall, "1870–1918: The Empire Under Threat," in *The Cambridge Illustrated History of the British Empire*, ed. P. J. Marshall (Cambridge: Cambridge University Press, 1996), 78.
17. David Reynolds, "The Churchill Government and the Black Troops in Britain During World War II," *Transactions of the Royal Historical Society* 5th ser. 35 (1985), 113; Joseph, "The British West Indies Regiment." The American Expeditionary Force used African-American men largely as manual laborers: Arthur E. Barbeau and Florette Henri, *The Unknown Soldiers: Black American Troops in World War I* (Philadelphia, PA: Temple University Press, 1974), 44. For the French use of colonial and immigrant labor, see Tyler Stovall "Colour-blind France? Colonial Workers during the First World War," *Race and Class* 35, no. 2 (1993): 41–55.
18. Angela Woollacott, "'Khaki Fever' and Its Control: Gender, Class, Age and Sexual Morality on the British Homefront in the First World War," *Journal of Contemporary History* 29 (1994): 325–47.
19. Macpherson, *History of the Great War* 1, 184.
20. S. M. Tomkins, "Palmitate or Permanganate: The Venereal Prophylaxis Debate in Britain, 1916–1926," *Medical History* 37 (1993): esp. 382.
21. James W. Barrett, *The Australian Army Medical Corps in Egypt: An Illustrated and Detailed Account of the Early Organisation and Work of the Australian Medical Units in Egypt in 1914–1915* (London: H.K. Lewis and Co. 1918), 129.
22. *Official History of the Australian Army Medical Services*, vol. 1 (Melbourne: Australian War Memorial, 1930), 77.
23. J. D. Oriel, *The Scars of Venus: A History of Venereology* (London: Springer-Verlag, 1994), 200.
24. The contents of such packets are described, for example, in *Instructions to Medical Officers Regarding the Prevention of Venereal Disease* (n.p., 16 September 1918), AWM 25 (267/53), and in Macpherson et al., *History of the Great War* 2, 126.
25. Diana R. Tibbits, "The Medical, Social and Political Response to Venereal Diseases in Victoria, 1860–1980," (Ph. D. diss., Monash University, 1994), 92; Sauerteig, "Sex, Medicine and Morality," 177–8; 180; Robert B. Grubbs, "Venereal Prophylaxis in the Military Service," *Military Surgeon* 25 (1909): 756–71.
26. George Walker, *Venereal Disease in the American Expeditionary Force* (Baltimore, MD: Medical Standard Books, 1922), 6.
27. Angela Booth, *The Prophylaxis of Venereal Disease: A Reply to Sir James Barrett* (Melbourne: Norman Bros. Printers, 1919), 11.
28. Minutes of the Association for Moral and Social Hygiene, 22 September 1916, WL, AMSH, box 42.
29. Mark Harrison, "The British Army and the Problem of Venereal Disease in France and Egypt during the First World War," *Medical History* 39 (1995): 147.
30. B. B. Cubitt, War Office to GOCs of Commands at Home and Districts at Home, 18 March 1916, PRO, WO32/5597.
31. Sergeant Major, R.A.M.C. *With the R.A.M.C. in Egypt* (London: Cassell and Co., 1918), 252; Tomkins, "Palmitate or Permanganate," 387.
32. Assistant Director of Medical Services, AIF to Director of Medical Services, AIF, France, 10 May 1916, AWM 27 (376/160).
33. B. B. Cubitt, War Office to General Officers Commanding, Home and Abroad, 25 May 1918, OIOC, L/MIL/7/13899; B. B. Cubitt, memorandum, 9 August 1917, AWM 27 (376/178).
34. F. A. E. Crew, ed. *The Army Medical Services: Administration*, vol. 2. (London: HMSO, 1955), 232.
35. Irrigation was not confined to soldiers. Hospitalized gonorrhea patients were irrigated with potassium permanganate solution, up to four pints being used as patient toleration grew. They were also subject to silver nitrate injections and prostate massage. See R. J. Silverton, "Report on the Work of the Venereal Section engaged in the Treatment of Venereal Diseases Amongst the Australian and New Zealand Troops in Egypt and Palestine, June 1st 1917 to May 31st 1918," 8, AWM 25 (267/52).
36. *Instructions to A.A.M.C. Orderlies Regarding Prophylactic and Abortive Treatment of Venereal Diseases* (n.d. [?1916]), AWM 25 (267/53).
37. Butler, *Official History: The Western Front*, vol. 2 (Melbourne: Australian War Memorial, 1940), 512.

38. Major B. T. Zwar, No. 2 Australian Stationary Hospital, "Venereal Diseases in Egypt," 23 June 1919, AWM 25 (267/26).

39. Cornelie Usborne, " 'Pregnancy is the Woman's Active Service': Pronatalism in Germany during the First World War," in *The Upheaval of War: Family, Work and Welfare in Europe, 1914–1918*, ed. Richard Wall and J. M. Winter (Cambridge: Cambridge University Press, 1988), 403.

40. Tibbits, "The Medical, Social and Political Response to Venereal Diseases," 95–6.

41. Specimen Lecture to Troops on the Prevention of Disease, OIOC, L/MIL/7/13899; also at AWM 27 (376/196), Part 1.

42. E. T. Burke, "Venereal Disease During the War," *Quarterly Review* 233, no. 463 (April 1920): 309.

43. E. R. Cordner, 51 General Hospital, BEF, 6 January 1917, AWM 27 (376/157), Part 3. Also quoted in *Official History of the Australian Army Medical Services, Special Problems and Services* (Melbourne: Australian War Memorial, 1943), 167.

44. Ettie Rout to Rayner D. Batten, 6 June 1917, AWM 27 (376/163).

45. Richard Davenport-Hines, *Sex, Death and Punishment: Attitudes to Sex and Sexuality in Britain since the Renaissance* (London: Collins, 1990), 227.

46. Joanna Bourke, *Dismembering the Male: Men's Bodies, Britain and the Great War* (Chicago: Chicago University Press, 1996), 85. See too Davenport-Hines, *Sex, Death and Punishment*, 227–8.

47. Director General, Army Medical Services to General Officers Commanding, Home and Abroad, 21 March 1919, OIOC, L/MIL/7/13899.

48. See, for example, the monthly returns of VD and scabies at AWM 27 (376/98), Parts 1 and 2; AWM 27 (376/157), Part 3; and the early treatment reports at AWM 27 (376/187), Parts 2, 3, and 4. For the American Expeditionary Force, see Walker, *Venereal Disease in the American Expeditionary Force*, 23.

49. Usborne, "Pregnancy is the Woman's Active Service," 401.

50. HC, *SP*, 1919, Cmd. 322, *Inter-Departmental Committee on Infectious Diseases in Connection with Demobilisation*, 8.

51. Francis Champneys, 'The Fight Against Venereal Infection: A Reply to Sir Bryan Donkin,' *The Nineteenth Century and After* 82 (November 1917): 1050.

52. Davenport-Hines, *Sex, Death and Punishment*, 194.

53. PRO, WO95/4115 reports VD cases among Britain's black troops. F. W. Weed, "In The American Expeditionary Forces," *Medical Department of the United States Army in the World War*, vol. 6. *Sanitation* (Washington: Government Printing Office, 1926), esp. 953; and Walker, *Venereal Disease in the American Expeditionary Force*, 32 both discuss the compulsory prophylaxis of black American soldiers in the AEF.

54. Macpherson, *History of the Great War* 1, 93.

55. Macpherson et al., *History of the Great War* 2, 125; Walker, *Venereal Disease in the American Expeditionary Force*, 32.

56. H. J. Creedy, War Office to Under Secretary of State for India, 18 September 1919, OIOC, L/MIL/7/13899.

57. David Lloyd George, War Office to Rt. Hon. T. R. Ferens, 8 August 1916, WL, JEB, Papers relating to Army Matters I: 1917–1920.

58. Macpherson et al., *History of the Great War* 2, 126.

59. *The Venereal Problem and The Army* (London: AMSH, 1918), 3.

60. MacDougall, "Sexually Transmitted Diseases in Canada," 57.

61. "The Prophylaxis of Venereal Disease," *Medical Journal of Australia* (22 March 1919): 240–1. Though anonymously penned, the author is James Barrett.

62. Born in Tasmania, Ettie Annie Rout (1877–1936) lived in New Zealand from the age of eight.

63. The Australian High Command seriously considered officially disowning any connection with Rout. See correspondence in AWM 38, Series 5 (3 DRL 6673/149).

64. Jane Tolerton, *Ettie: A Life of Ettie Rout: "Guardian Angel" or "Wickedest Woman"?* (Auckland, NZ: Penguin Books, 1992), 95; Rout to Bryan Donkin, 13 April 1919, 1, AWM 27 (376/174).

65. George Raffan, *Instructions to Medical Officers Regarding the Prevention of Venereal Diseases* (n.p., 16 September 1918), 8, AWM 27 (376/157), Part 2.

66. Rout to Donkin, 13 April 1919, 3, AWM 27 (376/174).

67. Ettie Rout to Anzac Soldiers, Private Memo, 30 April 1919, 2, AWM 27 (376/174). Rout had used the same memorable phrase in a letter to General Richardson at the New Zealand army headquarters in London, 20 December 1918.

68. Ettie A. Rout, *Two Years in Paris* (London: privately printed, 1923), 19.

69. Rout to AIF Headquarters, 27 April 1919; Private Memo from Rout to Anzac Soldiers, "Prevention of VD in Australia," 30 April 1919; Rout to Quarter Master General, 4th Army, British Expeditionary Forces, 13 November 1918, all in AWM 27 (376/174).

70. Ettie Rout, Memo, "Soldier's Toilet Club," 11 August 1918, AWM 38, Series 5 (3 DRL 6673/149). New Zealand public opinion shared Rout's convictions according to Philip Fleming in "Fighting the 'Red Plague': Observations on the Response to Venereal Disease in New Zealand 1910–45," *New Zealand Journal of History* 22, no. 1 (1988): 60.

71. Major General R. W. Birdwood, 27 December 1914, printed letter headed "For Private Circulation Only," AWM 27 (376/173).

72. Addressed to General Sir William Birdwood, n.d. 1917, Bean Collection, AWM 38, Series 5 (3 DRL 8042, Item 76).

73. William Lee Howard, "The Daughters of the Moabites and Our Soldiers," *New York Medical Journal* 107 (1918): 394.

74. Cynthia Enloe, *The Morning After: Sexual Politics at the End of the Cold War* (Berkeley: University of California Press, 1993), 52.

75. Garnet Wolseley, "The Negro As A Soldier," *Fortnightly Review* n.s. 264 (1 December 1888): 689; 697.

76. Shelby Cullom Davis, *Reservoirs of Men: A History of the Black Troops of French West Africa* (1934; reprint, Westport, CT: Negro Universities Press, 1970), 158–9.

77. Letter dated 25 April 1918, 5, PRO, CO 551/117/39492.

78. PRO, CO 551/117/39492, 1.

79. Willan, "The South African Native Labour Contingent," 72; Grundhling, "The Impact of the First World War," 56–7; Weed, *Medical Department of the United States Army,* 953.

80. Willan, "The South African Native Labour Contingent," 81.

81. Mulk Raj Anand, *Across The Black Waters* (London: Jonathan Cape, 1940), 105.

82. 18 June 1918, ff. 60–1, OIOC, L/MIL/5/825.

83. The entire file at OIOC, L/MIL/7/17316 is devoted to correspondence on this issue. See too Gregory Martin, "The Influence of Racial Attitudes on British Policy Towards India during the First World War," *Journal of Imperial and Commonwealth History* 14, no. 2 (1986): 92–7; and Jeffrey Greenhut, "Race, Sex, and War: The Impact of Race and Sex on Morale and Health Services for the Indian Corps on the Western Front, 1914," *Military Affairs* 45, no. 2 (1981): 72–4.

84. Reference Paper, Military, 28 October ?1914, ?H. A. Charles, OIOC, L/MIL/7/17316.

85. *Report on Kitchener's Indian Hospital, Brighton* (n.d. ?1916), 7, OIOC, L/MIL/17/5/2016; Visram, *Ayahs, Lascars and Princes,* 132.

86. N. Manders, *Hints on Health in Egypt* (n.p., n.d), AWM 27 (370/12).

87. *Prevention of Syphilis and Venereal* (n.d. ?1915), AWM 27 (376/181), emphasis in original.

88. Ibid.

89. Diaries and Notes of C. E. W. Bean, 1 January 1915, f. 3, AWM 38 (3 DRL 606), item 2 [4]. For a discussion of Bean's considerable role in mythologizing and romanticizing the role of Australian men in the war, see David Kent, "*The Anzac Book* and the Anzac Legend: C. E. W. Bean as Editor and Image-Maker," *Historical Studies* 21 (1985): 376–90; Annabel Cooper, "Textual Territories: Gendered Cultural Politics and Australian Representations of the War of 1914–1918," *Australian Historical Studies* 25, no. 100 (1993): 403–21, and E. M. Andrews, *The Anzac Illusion: Anglo-Australian Relations during World War I* (Cambridge: Cambridge University Press, 1993), 60–3.

90. Robert Lees, "Venereal Disease in the Armed Forces Overseas," *British Journal of Venereal Diseases* 22, no. 4 (1946): 155.

91. Suzanne Brugger, *Australians and Egypt 1914–1919* (Melbourne: Melbourne University Press, 1980), 61; Alistair Thomson, *Anzac Memories: Living with the Legend* (Melbourne: Oxford University Press, 1994), 31.

92. Barrett, *The Australian Army Medical Corps,* 121. The same figure is given in vol. 1 (76) of the *Official History of the Australian Army Medical Services.*

93. Surgeon General W. D. C. Williams, Director of Medical Services, AIF to Sir George Reid, High Commissioner for Australia, 20 February 1915, AWM 27 (370/55).

94. The IEF in Egypt numbered some 117,000 men. In Mesopotamia, there were about 590,000 IEF troops and in Gallipoli and Salonika a further 9,000. See Ellinwood, "The Indian Soldier," 183.

95. James W. Barrett, *A Vision of the Possible: What the R.A.M.C. Might Become* (London: H.K. Lewis and Co., 1919), 121.

96. Diaries and Notes of C. E. W. Bean, 9–30 January, f. 23, AWM 38 (3 DRL 606), item 2 [4]; Major General R. W. Birdwood, 27 December 1914, printed letter headed "For Private Circulation Only," AWM 27 (376/173).

97. Thomson, *Anzac Memories,* 31; Brugger, *Australians and Egypt,* 42.

98. Diaries and Notes of C. E. W. Bean, 9–30 January 1915, f. 25, AWM 38 (3 DRL 606), item 2 [4].

99. Walter Campbell for General Commander in Chief, Egyptian Expeditionary Force, AIF to Secretary, War Office, 23 April 1917, AWM 22 (80/5/2023).

100. Commandant, Cairo City Police to General Officer Commanding in Egypt, 20 March 1916, AAC, CP78/23, item no. 1914/89/252, file 2.

101. Richard White, "Sun, Sand and Syphilis. Australian Soldiers and the Orient. Egypt 1914," *Australian Cultural History* 9 (1990): 60; Kevin Fewster, "The Wazza Riots, 1915," *Journal of the Australian War Memorial* 4 (1984): 50.

102. Major General James Spens, "Proceedings of a Court of Inquiry assembled at Soldier's Club, Esbekia Gardens," AWM 22 (80/5/2023).

103. Evidence of Bimbashi H. G. F. Archer, Inspector, A Division, Cairo City Police, AWM 10 (4308/5/28).

104. Magnus Hirschfeld, *The Sexual History of the World War* (New York: Cadillac Publishing Co. 1941), 148.

105. Brugger, *Australians and Egypt,* 41.

106. Dr. Sandwith, "Prostitution et maladies vénériennes en Egypte," *Le Conference Internationale pour la Prophylaxie de la Syphilis et des Maladies Vénérienne,* vol. 1, part 1 (1899), 714.

107. *Report of Cairo Purification Committee* (Cairo: Government Press, 1916), 2, WI, RAMC 1212/7.

108. George Harvey to GOC in Chief, Egypt, 20 March 1919, f. 2, AAC, CP 78/23/1914/89/252, file 2.

109. H. Hopkinson, Alexandria City Police Commandant's Office to General Sir J. G. Maxwell, Commanding, 19 March 1916, f. 1, AAC, CP 78/23/1914/89/252, file 2.

110. *Report of the Cairo Purification Committee;* H. Hopkinson, Alexandria City Police Commandant's Office to General Sir J. G. Maxwell, Commanding, 19 March 1916, AAC, CP78/23, f. 1; Barrett, *A Vision of the Possible,* 120. In practice, registered women of all nationalities were examined mostly by colonial doctors and mainly by New Zealanders.

111. Michael Havinden and David Meredith, *Colonialism and Development: Britain and its Tropical Colonies, 1850–1960* (London: Routledge, 1993), 117.

112. Krishan G. Saini, "The Economic Aspects of India's Participation in the First World War," in *India and World War I,* 165.

113. Havinden and Meredith, *Colonialism and Development,* 123.

114. Sugata Bose and Ayesha Jalal, *Modern South Asia: History, Culture, Political Economy* (Delhi: Oxford University Press, 1997; London: Routledge, 1998), 129.

115. Benita Parry, *Delusions and Discoveries: India in the British Imagination, 1880–1930,* 2nd ed. (London: Verso, 1998), 43.

116. Judith M. Brown, "War and the Colonial Relationship: Britain, India, and the War of 1914–18," in *India and World War I,* 29.

117. Ken Inglis, "Men, Women, and War Memorials: Anzac Australia," in *Learning About Women: Gender, Politics, and Power,* ed. Jill K. Conway, Susan C. Bourque, and Joan W. Scott (Ann Arbor: University of Michigan Press, 1989), 36.

118. Carmel Shute, "Heroines and Heroes: Sexual Mythology in Australia 1914–18," in *Gender and War: Australians at War in the Twentieth Century,* ed. Joy Damousi and Marilyn Lake (Melbourne: Cambridge University Press, 1995), 25.

119. In *Ah Ku and Karayuki-San: Prostitution in Singapore 1870–1940* (Singapore: Oxford University Press, 1993), James F. Warren claims that European prostitutes in Shanghai were

also given free passage out of the port (88), something Gail Hershatter does not mention in her exhaustive study of Shanghai prostitution in the twentieth century, *Dangerous Pleasures: Prostitution and Modernity in Twentieth-Century Shanghai* (Berkeley: University of California Press, 1997).

120. Governor Arthur Young to Colonial Secretary Walter H. Long, 13 June 1917, PRO, CO 273/457 (41155). Young repeated the point that the women's passage was paid by government in a letter to Sir George Fiddes, 14 July 1917, PRO, CO 273/457 (36997).

121. Young to Long, 13 June 1917, PRO, CO273/457 (41155).

122. W. F. Rice, Chief Secretary, Government of Burma to Bishop of Rangoon, 28 October 1914, WL, JEB, E2/1; "Report of the Committee appointed by the Local Government to advise on Certain Questions concerning Brothels and Prostitution in Rangoon," November 1917, OIOC, L/P& J/6/1448 (2987).

123. W. H. Tarleton, Commissioner of Police, Rangoon to Chief Secretary, Government of Burma, 14 June 1915, OIOC, L/P& J/6/1448 (2987); OIOC, P/9458.

124. Helen Wilson, WL, IAF Papers, 3/AMS, 51.2.

125. Charles Tarring and Helen Wilson to Colonial Secretary, 18 December 1916, PRO, CO273/452 (60716). The indefatigable Cowen was, only a year later, sending accounts of the sex lives of soldiers behind the lines in France to AMSH office-holders. In addition to descriptions of French brothels, Cowen dwelt on soldiers' use of sexualized language and on the preference for pictures of nude women as wall decoration "from the Head Quarters General Staff to the orderly's billet." John Cowen to Helen Wilson, 1 June 1917, WL, JEB, Papers relating to Army Matters. I: 1917–1920.

126. John Cowen, *Tracts for Rangoon No. 7: Welcome to the Territorials* (Rangoon: YMCA, 1914), 2.

127. W. F. Rice, Chief Secretary to the Government of Burma to Colonial Secretary, Straits Settlements, 29 March 1916, OIOC, L/P& J/6/1448; John Cowen to Helen M. Wilson, 25 February 1915, WL, JEB, box E2/1.

128. John Cowen, "Report of A Visit to the Two Great Brothel Areas of Singapore in the Autumn of 1915," typescript manuscript, PRO, CO273/452 (60716). Cowen published extracts from his report in the abolitionist paper, *The Shield*, 3rd. ser. 1, no. 3 (October 1916): 184–5.

129. Memorandum, Sir A. H. Bodkin, 21 November 1917, OIOC, L/MIL/7/13898.

130. Lieutenant General H. Hudson, Adjutant General to General Officers Commanding in India, 25 September 1917, OIOC, L/MIL/7/13893.

131. Brigadier General H. Barstow to General Officers Commanding in India, 16 January 1917; War Office to Adjutant General in India, 1 August 1917; War Office to Adjutant General in India, 27 September 1917; all in OIOC, L/MIL/7/13893.

132. Lieutenant General H. Hudson, Adjutant General to General Officers Commanding in India, 2 August 1918, OIOC, L/MIL/7/13893; "A Victory in India: The Cantonment System Crumbling," *The Shield* 2, no. 2 (February–March 1918): 79–85; *India and the East* (London: AMSH, n.d. ?1919); *Regulated Prostitution Within the British Empire* (London: AMSH, 1919), 2.

133. Joseph Maxwell, *Hell's Bells and Mademoiselles* (Sydney: Angus and Robertson, 1932), 82, 81.

134. Sir C. Mathews, Sir A. Bodkin, and Guy Stephenson, Director of Public Prosecutions to Home Secretary, n.d. ?1917, PRO, HO 45/10837/331148/18.

135. Deborah Gorham, *Vera Brittain: A Feminist Life* (Oxford: Basil Blackwell, 1996), 92; Angela Woollacott, *On Her Their Lives Depend: Munitions Workers in the Great War* (Berkeley: University of California Press, 1994), 143–6.

136. Arthur Conan Doyle writing to *The Times*, 6 February 1917, quoted in Alison Neilans, "The Protection of Soldiers," *The Shield* 1, no. 4 (March, 1917): 218.

137. *Hansard*, House of Lords, 11 April 1918, vol. 29, no. 17, col. 663.

138. Otto May, *The Prevention of Venereal Disease in the Army* (London: National Council for Combatting Venereal Disease, 1916), 3.

139. *Deputation re Venereal Disease*, 24 October 1918, Mr. McGrath, Prime Minister's Department, Medical, AAC, A458, item I386/4, part 1.

140. Mary Brown, Social Purity Department, South African Woman's Christian Temperance Union to Miss Mason, 13 August 1918, WL, JEB, E1/3.

141. R. K. Webb, *Modern England* 2nd ed. (New York: Harper and Row, 1980), 476. Long (1854–1924) was first elected to Parliament in 1880, representing a considerable number of different

constituencies during his tenure as a Conservative M.P. He was made president of the Local Government Board in 1900, colonial secretary in 1916, and first lord of the admiralty in 1918. He was raised to the peerage in 1921, three years before his death.

142. Memorandum of Walter H. Long to War Cabinet, 6 March 1918, PRO, WO 32/11401/173290.

143. Ramsay MacDonald to Herbert Samuel, n.d. summer 1916, PRO, HO 45/10837/331148.

144. Edith Sellers, "Boy and Girl War-Products: Their Reconstruction," *The Nineteenth Century And After* 84 (October 1918): 704.

145. Maxwell, *Hell's Bells*, 23.

146. Massia Bibikoff, *Our Indians at Marseilles* (London: Smith, Elder and Co., 1915), 6, 5.

147. Alison Neilans to Herbert Samuel, 17 November 1916, WL, AMSH 314.

148. C. K. Francis to Under Secretary, Home Office, 26 January 1916; internal HO Minute, 27 July 1916, PRO, HO 45/10523/140266/3.

149. See Hansard, House of Commons, vol. 93, no. 60, 17 May 1917, 1776–7.

150. Women Police Service, Mary S. Allen to Miss Howes, 30 June 1917, WL, AMSH, box A6.

151. Police Court Rota Sub-Committee, WL, AMSH, box 71.

152. "Venereal Disease in the Army," *The Lancet* (5 February 1916): 306.

153. Lucy Bland, "In The Name of Protection: The Policing of Women in the First World War," in *Women-in-Law: Explorations in Law, Family and Sexuality*, ed. J. Brophy and Carol Smart (London: Routledge and Kegan Paul, 1985), 29–31; Susan R. Grayzel, *Women's Identities at War: Gender, Motherhood, and Politics in Britain and France during the First World War* (Chapel Hill, NC: University of North Carolina Press, 1999), 129–30; Philippa Levine, " 'Walking The Streets In A Way No Decent Woman Should': Women Police in World War I," *Journal of Modern History* 66 (1994): 52–3.

154. HC, *SP*, 1918, 142, Evidence of E. Blackwell, 15 October 1918, q. 130, *Report from Joint Select Committee on the Criminal Law Amendment Bill and Sexual Offences Bill*, 7.

155. PRO, HO 45/10802/307990/7.

156. Grayzel, *Women's Identities at War*, 150.

157. January 1917, PRO, HO 45/10802/307990/15E; 7 September 1916, PRO, HO 45/10802/307990/15D.

158. Suzann Buckley, "The Failure to Resolve the Problem of Venereal Disease among the Troops in Britain During World War I," *War and Society: A Yearbook of Military History* 2 (1977): 72.

159. Walter Long, "Memorandum for the War Cabinet. Venereal Diseases," 6 March 1918, reporting Sir Robert Borden's statement to Imperial War Conference, 24 April 1917, PRO, WO 32/11401/173290.

160. Governor General, New Zealand to Walter Long, 10 February 1918, PRO, WO 32/11401/28A; A. L. Stanley, Deputy to Governor General, Australia to Walter Long, 26 November 1917, PRO, WO 32/11401/29B.

161. In *Making Peace: The Reconstruction of Gender in Interwar Britain* (Princeton, NJ: Princeton University Press, 1993), Susan Kent notes that 40D was introduced "at the height of worries about the German advance" (39).

162. Long to Home Office, Foreign Office, Colonial Office, and Admiralty. n.d, but presumably late February or early March 1918, PRO, WO 32/11401/276.

163. Suzann Buckley and Janice Dickin McGinnis, "Venereal Disease and Public Health Reform in Canada," *Canadian Historical Review* 63, no. 3 (1982): 340.

164. PRO, CO616/78/4328.

165. Andrew Porter, "Introduction: Britain and the Empire in the Nineteenth Century," in *The Oxford History of the British Empire*, vol. 3. *The Nineteenth Century*, ed. Andrew Porter (Oxford: Oxford University Press, 1999), 21.

166. 22 February 1918, PRO, CAB 23/5/WC352 (10).

167. 7 December 1917, PRO, WO32/11401/23A, Inter-Departmental Conference held at the Colonial Office. The idea of masking 40D's gender partiality was put forward by George Cave, a senior Home Office official. See too Ernley Blackwell to Colonial Under Secretary, 18 December 1917, PRO, WO32/11401/25B.

168. Initials illegible but countersigned by C. E. Troup and Secretary of State for Home Affairs, 18 June 1918, PRO, HO 45/10894/359931/53.

169. "Report of Parliamentary Debate on 40D, 19 June 1918," WL, AMSH 311, file 2. The new women's auxiliary services of the war also implemented punishments for VD. Members of the Women's Auxiliary Army Corps and the Women's Royal Air Force who contracted VD were discharged from the service, a luxury the regular army could ill afford given the high

mortality rate among combatants. See memo, T. H. Goodwin, Army Medical Department, 27 March 1918, PRO, WO 32/11402; and "Pregnancy and Venereal Disease in Women of the W.R.A.F." 10 September 1918, AWM 27 (376/178). According to Violet Markham, the War Office also considered excising all mention of cases of VD among servicewomen, Markham to Julia Varley, 6 April 1918, in Helen Jones, *Duty and Citizenship: The Correspondence and Papers of Violet Markham, 1896–1953* (London: The Historian's Press, 1994), 96.

170. Circular Memorandum B/5466, 27 January 1917, AWM 27 (376/202), Part 1.

171. *Report on Kitchener's Hospital*, 7, OIOC, L/MIL/17/5/2016.

172. 26 August 1918, PRO, WO32/4745/4C; HO45/10893/359931, *Evidence of Court of Inquiry on 40D*, 15 October 1918, q. 420.

173. *Evidence to Commission of Inquiry on Regulation 40D*, PRO, HO 45/10893/359931; *Annual Report of the Association for Moral and Social Hygiene, 1918* (London: AMSH, 1919), 10–11.

174. Mrs. A. C. Gotto, NCCVD, *Evidence to Commission of Inquiry . . . 40D*, PRO, HO 45/10893/359931.

175. War Cabinet 465, 28 August 1918, PRO, WO32/4745; also at CAB 23/7 W.C. 465 (4), 28 August 1918.

176. *Commission of Inquiry on 40D*, HO45/10893/359931; *Annual Report of the Association for Moral and Social Hygiene, 1918* (London: AMSH, 1919), 10–11.

177. Extracts from Editorial Notes, Regulation 40D, *The Herald*, 6 April 1918, WL, AMSH 311, file 2.

178. 25 October 1918, PRO, HO 45/10894/359931.

179. Moulton to George Cave, 15 November 1918, PRO, CO616/78/28915.

180. May, *The Prevention of Venereal Disease*, 3. See too Gavin Hart, "The Impact of Prostitution on Australian Troops on Active Service in A War Environment—with Particular Reference to Sociological Factors Involved in the Incidence and Control of Venereal Disease," (MD thesis, University of Adelaide, 1974), 38.

181. A. N. [Alison Neilans]. *A Warning To Men Going Abroad* (London: AMSH, n.d. [1916]). The distribution of the pamphlet by chaplains and the YMCA is described in another of their pamphlets, *The "Maisons Tolérées": An Appeal* (London: AMSH, 1918).

182. Telegram, Military Attaché, Washington DC to Foreign Office, 2 November 1917, PRO, HO 45/10802/307990 (39).

183. Lieutenant Colonel J. M. Y. Stewart to Assistant Director of Medical Services, 5th Australian Division, 30 December 1917, AWM 27 (376/202), Part 2.

184. Beth Bailey and David Farber found much the same at work in the lucrative Hawaiian brothel business in World War Two where the business of black GIs and of local Hawaiians was not welcomed: "Hotel Street: Prostitution and the Politics of War," *Radical History Review* 52 (1992): 54–77.

185. Anand, *Across The Black Waters*, 63.

186. Ibid., 265.

187. Davenport-Hines, *Sex, Death and Punishment*, 226.

188. Report on Visit of Majors Grigor and Morris to No. 9 Stationary Hospital 1916, 20 January 1916, AWM 27 (376/161).

189. Bill Gammage, *The Broken Years: Australian Soldiers in the Great War* (Canberra: Australian National University Press, 1974), 232–44; Thomson, *Anzac Memories*, 44.

190. Surgeon General Howse to General Officers Commanding, AIF, 15 November 1916, AWM 25 (743/14).

191. Circular 8/1/82. "Warrant and N.C.O's who Contract Venereal Disease," 12 October, 1917, AWM 27 (376/196), part 1.

192. Lieutenant Colonel ? (name illegible), Australian Army Medical Corps, memorandum, 24 October 1918, AWM 27 (376/183).

193. Lieutenant Colonel J. M. Y. Stewart to Assistant Director of Medical Services, 5th Australian Division, 30 December 1917, AWM 27 (376/202), Part 2.

194. Confidential Memorandum no. 16, 12 May 1916, AWM 27 (376/184).

195. Central Registry File, AWM 22 (130/1/2008); Hart, "The Impact of Prostitution on Australian Troops," 87.

196. Hinrichsen, "Venereal Disease in the Major Armies," 106; MacDougall, "Sexually Transmitted Diseases in Canada," 58.

197. Minutes of the Association for Moral and Social Hygiene, 18 February 1916, WL, AMSH, box 42.

198. August 1916, PRO, WO32/4745.
199. Wendy Fisher, "Brothels and the Military," *Sabretache* 27 (1986): 24.
200. Report of Metropolitan D Division (Tottenham Court Road), 6 November 1916, PRO, MEPO 2/1714.
201. *Daily Telegraph*, 3 October 1916, cutting contained in PRO, HO45/10837/331148.
202. Diaries and Notes of C. E. W. Bean, 20 February 1915, ff. 50–1, AWM 38 (3 DRL 606), item 2 [4].
203. Lieutenant General H. Hudson, Adjutant General to General Officers Commanding in India, 25 September 1917, OIOC, L/MIL/7/13893.
204. The following all discuss the various strategies used by the British to raise colonial armies in Africa: C. M. Andrew and A. S. Forstner-Kanya, "France, Africa and the First World War," *Journal of African History* 19, no. 1 (1978): 11–23; Greenstein, "The Nandi Experience in the First World War"; Grundlingh, "The Impact of the First World War on South African Blacks"; Killingray, "Military and Labour Policies in the Gold Coast during the First World War," in Page, *Africa and the First World War*, 152–70.
205. Judith Smart, "The Great War and the 'Scarlet Scourge': Debates about Venereal Diseases in Melbourne during World War I," in *An Anzac Muster: War and Society in Australia and New Zealand 1914–18 and 1939–45. Selected Papers*, ed. Judith Smart and Tony Wood (Clayton, VIC: Monash Publications in History) 14, 1992, 58–85; idem. "Sex, the State and the 'Scarlet Scourge': Gender, Citizenship and Venereal Diseases Regulation in Australia during the Great War," unpublished paper (1996).
206. Judith M. Brown, *Modern India: The Origins of An Asian Democracy* (Delhi: Oxford University Press, 1985), 190.
207. Hardinge to Chamberlain, 6 August 1915, quoted in Martin, "The Influence of Racial Attitudes on British Policy Towards India," 103
208. Stephen P. Cohen, *The Indian Army: Its Contribution to the Development of a Nation* (Delhi: Oxford University Press, 1990), 69; David Omissi, *Indian Voices of the Great War: Soldiers' Letters, 1914–1918* (Basingstoke: Macmillan, 1999), 2.
209. Richard Arthur, "An Address delivered to the Officers of the Australian Imperial Force," *Medical Journal of Australia* 20 (May 1916): 413.
210. Arnold White, "Efficiency and Vice," *English Review* 22 (May 1916): 452, 451.
211. Hynes, *A War Imagined*, 222–34.
212. Alice Conklin, *A Mission to Civilize: The Republican Idea of Empire in France and West Africa, 1895–1930* (Stanford, CA: Stanford University Press, 1997), 146; Tyler Stovall, "The Color Line behind the Lines: Racial Violence in France during the Great War," *American Historical Review* 103, no. 3 (1998): 737–69.
213. Association for Moral and Social Hygiene to David Lloyd George, Prime Minister, 19 April 1920, WL, JEB, E1/4. For a full rendering of the colonial troops sent to the Ruhr, see Sally Marks, "Black Watch on the Rhine: A Study in Propaganda, Prejudice, and Prurience," *European Studies Review* 13, no. 3 (1983): 298.
214. Marks, "Black Watch on the Rhine," 297.
215. Keith L. Nelson, "The 'Black Horror on the Rhine': Race as a Factor in Post-World War One Diplomacy," *Journal of Modern History* 42, no. 4 (1970): 613.
216. Claude McKay, *A Long Way From Home,* (New York: Arno Press/New York Times, 1969), 74–5.
217. George Orwell, "As I Please," originally published in *Tribune*, 29 December 1944 and reproduced in *The Collected Essays, Journalism and Letters of George Orwell: As I Please 1943–1945*, vol. 3, ed. Sonia Orwell and Ian Angus (Harmondsworth: Penguin Books, 1970), 348–9.
218. Nelson, "Black Horror," 608–9.
219. Nelson, "The 'Black Horror on the Rhine,'" 615. For an Afro-German reading of the controversy, see May Opitz, Katharina Oguntoye, and Dagmar Schultz, *Showing Our Colors: Afro-German Women Speak Out* (Amherst: University of Massachusetts Press, 1992), 41–9.
220. Medal displayed in a 1996 exhibition entitled "Memoire d'Outre-Mer: Les Colonies et la Première Guerre Mondiale" at Château de Péronne, Somme in France, see *Guardian Weekly*, October 6, 1996.
221. For dissenting views, see the work of socialist and poet McKay, in his *A Long Way From Home*, esp. 74–6; Peter Fryer, *Staying Power: Black People in Britain since 1504* (Atlantic Highlands, NJ: Humanities Press, 1984), 318–21; Robert C. Reinders, "Racialism on the Left: E. D. Morel

and the 'Black Horror on the Rhine,' " *International Review of Social History* 13, no. 1 (1968): 16–17.

222. Marks, "Black Watch on the Rhine," 319; Reinders, "Racialism on the Left," 13–16.

223. Storm Jameson, *Company Parade* (New York: Alfred A. Knopf, 1934), 351–2. I thank Angela Woollacott for bringing this reference to my attention.

224. Draft of a letter from Helen M. Wilson to Yves Guyot, WL, JEB, E1/4. The final version, sent 12 May 1920, expressed the same sentiment.

225. Reinders, "Racialism on the Left," 1.

226. McKay, *A Long Way From Home*, 75.

227. Ibid., 74.

228. E. D. Morel, *The Horror on the Rhine* (London: Union of Democratic Control, 1920), 17.

229. Ibid., 10.

230. E. D. Morel, "Negro Troops in Germany," *Stead's Review* 54, no. 3 (July 1920): 164.

231. Morel's career is detailed in Catherine Ann Cline's biography, *E. D. Morel, 1873–1924: The Strategies of Protest* (Belfast: Blackstaff Press, 1980).

232. Morel, *Horror*, 10–11.

233. Reinders, "Racialism on the Left," 27.

234. Morel in *Labour Leader*, 22 April 1920, quoted in Reinders, "Racialism on the Left," 4.

235. Marks, "Black Watch on the Rhine," 301–10.

236. Page, "Introduction: Black Men in a White Men's War," 15.

237. Hirschfeld, *Sexual History*, 344.

238. Hugh Wansey Bayley, *Triple Challenge, or Wars, Whirligigs and Windmills: A Doctor's Memoirs of the Years 1914 to 1929* (London: Hutchinson, 1935), 331.

239. HC, *SP,* 1919 [Cmd. 322], Inter-Departmental Committee on Infectious Diseases in Connection with Demobilisation, note by the Chairman of the Committee to the Minister of Health on Prophylaxis against Venereal Disease, 10–11.

240. P. M. Ashburn, "Factors Making For A Low Venereal Record in the Army in the United States," *Military Surgeon* 47 (1920): 213.

241. Lieutenant General Shea for Commander in Chief to Under Secretary of State, War Office, 17 September 1925; War Office to Lieutenant General Shea, 18 November 1925, PRO, WO332/5940.

242. S. W. Brown, India Office to Sir C. Jacob, Medical Adviser to Under Secretary of State for India, 23 November 1926, OIOC, L/MIL/7/13906.

243. *The Problem of the "Maisons Tolérées" and the B.E.F. in France (and Elsewhere)* (London: AMSH, 1940).

244. James Marshall, "Prevention of Venereal Disease in the British Army," in *Inter-Allied Conferences on War Medicine 1942–1945*, ed. Henry Letherby Tidy and J. M. Browne Kutschbach (London: Staples Press, 1947), 261.

245. G. L. M. McElligot, "The Prevention of Venereal Disease," in *Inter-Allied Conferences on War Medicine*, 264.

246. Ruth Roach Pierson, "The Double Bind of the Double Standard: VD Control and the CWAC in World War II," *Canadian Historical Review* 52, no. 1 (1981): 44.

247. Samuel Grubbs quoted in Fitzhugh Mullan, *Plagues and Politics: The Story of the United States Public Health Service* (New York: Basic Books, 1989), 73.

248. On the *mui tsai* campaigns, see Maria Jaschok, *Concubines and Bondservants: A Social History* (London: Zed Books, 1988); on genital surgery campaigns, see Susan Pedersen, "National Bodies, Unspeakable Acts: The Sexual Politics of Colonial Policy-Making," *Journal of Modern History* 63, no. 4 (1991): 647–80; on birth control, see Barbara N. Ramusack, "Embattled Advocates: The Debate Over Birth Control in India, 1920–40," *Journal of Women's History* 1, no. 2 (1989): 34–64.

249. For the black soldier in the 1940s, see John Hammond Moore, *Over-Sexed, Over-Paid and Over Here: Americans in Australia, 1941–1945* (St. Lucia: University of Queensland Press, 1981); Annette Palmer, "Black American Soldiers in Trinidad, 1942–44: Wartime Politics in a Colonial Society," *Journal of Imperial and Commonwealth History* 14, no. 3 (1986): 203–18; Harvey Neptune, "White Lies: Race and Sexuality in Occupied Trinidad," *Journal of Colonialism and Colonial History* 2, no. 1 (2001); David Reynolds, "The Churchill Government and the Black Troops in Britain During World War II," *Transactions of the Royal Historical Society* 5th ser. 35 (1985), 113–33; Graham A. Smith, "Jim Crow on the Homefront (1942–1945),"

New Community 8, no. 3 (1980): 317–28; and Christopher Thorne, "Britain and the Black GIs: Racial Issues and Anglo-American Relations in 1942," *New Community* 3, no. 3 (1974): 262–71.

Chapter 7

1. Michael Sturma, *South Sea Maidens: Western Fantasy and Sexual Politics in the South Pacific* (Westport, CT: Greenwood Press, 2002).

2. Jane Caplan, " 'Educating the Eye': The Tattooed Prostitute," in *Sexology in Culture: Labelling Bodies and Desires,* ed. Lucy Bland and Laura Doan (Chicago: University of Chicago Press, 1998), 101.

3. Vern L. and Bonnie Bullough, *Women and Prostitution: A Social History* (Buffalo, NY: Prometheus Books, 1987), 293.

4. Ann Laura Stoler, "Making Empire Respectable: The Politics of Race and Sexual Morality in 20th-century Colonial Cultures," *American Ethnologist* 16, no. 4 (1989): 648.

5. C. B. Mayne, *How Far Past Legislation Has Proved Effective in Securing the Health of the Troops in India, With Suggestions as to Future Legislation on This Important Subject* (London: Horace Marshall, 1897), 12.

6. Clive Moore, "A Precious Few: Melanesian and Asian Women in Northern Australia," in *Gender Relations in Australia: Domination and Negotiation,* ed. Kay Saunders and Raymond Evans (Sydney: Harcourt Brace Jovanovich, 1992), 61; D. C. S. Sissons, "*Karayuki-San:* Japanese Prostitutes in Australia, 1887–1916," Part 1: *Historical Studies* 17 (1977): 323–41; Part 2: *Historical Studies* 17 (1977): 474–88.

7. C. P. Lucas to Frederick Meade, 6 May 1879, PRO, CO129/184 (6690).

8. S. M. Edwardes, *Crime in India* (London: Oxford University Press, 1924), 71. For a similar attitude fifty years earlier, see the comments of W. A. C. Roe, Surgeon General to the Punjab Native Infantry at Rawalpindi, writing to the local Deputy Surgeon General, 27 December 1876, OIOC, PRO, P/1003.

9. Miles Irving, Senior Secretary to Financial Commissioners, Punjab to Revenue Secretary, Government of the Punjab, 9 September 1914, OIOC, L/P&J/6/1259 (2894).

10. S. H. Butler, Secretary to Government, United Provinces to Secretary, Government of India, Home Department (Judicial), 29 January 1904, OIOC, P/7062.

11. T. D. Mackenzie, Acting Chief Secretary to Government of Bombay to Secretary, Government of India, Home Department, 28 January 1888, OIOC, L/MIL/7/13815.

12. S. C. Bayley, Officiating Secretary to Government of Bengal to A. O. Hume, Secretary to Government of India, 19 June 1871, OIOC, P/674.

13. "Resolution on Lock Hospital Reports, British Burma, for the Year 1875," 5, OIOC, V/24/2296.

14. J. Fullarton Beatson, Surgeon General, Indian Medical Department to Officiating Secretary to Government of Bengal, Judicial Department, 16 May 1877, memorandum on the Working of the Contagious Diseases Act on Bengal Proper, OIOC, P/1003.

15. Lieutenant Colonel H. B. Thornhill, Bareilly to Medical Officer, Bareilly, 16 October 1901, OIOC, L/MIL/7/13920.

16. *Annual Report on the Lock Hospitals of the Madras Presidency for the Year 1878* (Madras: Government Press, 1879), 14, OIOC, V/24/2287.

17. *Fourth Annual Report on the Working of the Lock Hospitals in the Northwest Provinces and Oudh for the Year 1877* (Allahabad, n.p, 1878), Agra report, 6–7, OIOC, V/24/2290.

18. Jeffrey Weeks, *Making Sexual History* (Cambridge: Polity, 2000), 132.

19. Susie Tharu and K. Lalita, *Women Writing in India:* vol. 2: *The Twentieth Century* (New York: The Feminist Press, 1993), 9.

20. Registrar General to Acting Colonial Secretary of Hong Kong, 12 September 1882, PRO, CO129/203 (20349).

21. Sander L. Gilman, "Black Bodies, White Bodies: Toward an Iconography of Female Sexuality in Late Nineteenth-Century Art, Medicine, and Literature," in *"Race," Writing, and Difference,* ed. Henry Louis Gates Jr. (Chicago: University of Chicago Press, 1986), 248.

22. Surgeon General, Bengal to Director General, Army Medical Department, 9 June 1884, OIOC, L/MIL/7/13810.

23. For discussion of the gendering of prostitution, see Susan S. M. Edwards, "Sex or Gender: The Prostitute in Law," *British Journal of Sexual Medicine* 9 (1982): 5; and Philippa Levine, "Public and Private Paradox: Prostitution and the State," *Arena*, n.s. 1 (1993): 131–44.
24. Major General E. F. Chapman, Quarter Master General to Secretary to Government of India, Military Department, 6 September 1888, enclosing draft rules, OIOC, P/3473, no. 2907.
25. PP, Cape of Good Hope, *Report of the Select Committee appointed by the Legislative Council on Medical Establishments*, July 1871, vii.
26. Report on the Lock Hospital established at Bangalore, July 1855, 2132, OIOC, P/273/41.
27. Association of Moral and Social Hygiene, Committee of Inquiry into Sexual Morality, evidence of Miss Costin, Women's Training Colony, Newbury, 27 January 1919, WL, AMSH.
28. Cecil Chapman, *The Poor Man's Court of Justice: Twenty-Five Years as a Metropolitan Magistrate* (London: Hodder and Stoughton, 1925), 93.
29. Noah D. Zatz, "Sex Work/Sex Act: Law, Labor, and Desire in Constructions of Prostitution," *Signs* 22, no. 2 (1997): 284.
30. Ashrufa Faruqee, "Conceiving the Coolie Woman: Indentured Labour, Indian Women and Colonial Discourse," *South Asia Research* 16, no. 1 (1996): 74.
31. Francis Hutchins, *The Illusion of Permanence: British Imperialism in India* (Princeton, NJ: Princeton University Press, 1967), 42.
32. Edwardes, *Crime in India*, 84.
33. Major J. B. Hardy, Commanding A Battery, 19th Brigade to Station Staff Officer, Jhansie, 18 May 1870, NAI Home Department, Public Consultation A, Proceedings 1870.
34. Senior Apothecary, Jhansie to Senior Medical Officer, Darjeeling, 18 May 1886, OIOC, L/MIL/7/13903.
35. G. L. M. McElligott, "The Prevention of Venereal Disease," in *Inter-Allied Conferences on War Medicine 1942–1945*, ed. Henry Letherby Tidy and J. M. Browne Kutschbach (London: Staples Press, 1947), 271.
36. T. H. Thornton, Secretary to Government of Punjab to Secretary, Government of India, Department of Revenue, Agriculture and Commerce, 30 June 1873, OIOC, P/1003; see various letters in same file on this topic, 1871–1877.
37. Captain J. C. Garstin, Assistant Commander, Naini Tal to Medical Officer, Lock Hospital, Naini Tal, 18 May 1875, OIOC, P/945.
38. W. A. C. Roe, Surgeon General, Punjab Native Infantry, Rawalpindi to Deputy Surgeon General, 27 December 1876, OIOC, PRO, P/1003.
39. For examples in art, see Helene E. Roberts, "Marriage, Redundancy or Sin: The Painter's View of Women in the First Twenty-Five Years of Victoria's Reign," in *Suffer and Be Still: Women in the Victorian Age*, ed. Martha Vicinus (London: University Paperbacks, 1980), 45–76. For literary examples, see Amanda Anderson, *Tainted Souls and Painted Faces: The Rhetoric of Fallenness in Victorian Culture* (Ithaca, NY: Cornell University Press, 1993).
40. Report on the Lock Hospital established at Bangalore, July 1855, 2132, OIOC, P/273/41.
41. See, for example, Lynda Nead, "Mapping the Self: Gender, Space and Modernity in Mid-Victorian London," *Environment and Planning A* 29 (1997): 659–72; Erika D. Rappaport, "'A New Era of Shopping': The Promotion of Women's Pleasure in London's West End, 1909–1914," in *Cinema and the Invention of Modern Life*, ed. Leo Charney and Vanessa R. Schwarz (Berkeley: University of California Press, 1995), 130–55; Judith R. Walkowitz, *City of Dreadful Delight: Narratives of Sexual Danger in Late-Victorian London* (Chicago: University of Chicago Press, 1992).
42. Conversely, Indrani Chatterjee argues in a recent essay that many prostitute women in colonial India were slave women, bought and sold at whim: "Colouring Subalternity: Slaves, Concubines and Social Orphans in Early Colonial India," in *Subaltern Studies X: Writings on South Asian History and Society*, ed. Gautam Bhadra, Gyan Prakash, and Susie Tharu (Delhi: Oxford University Press, 1999), 66–7. See too Kunal M. Parker, "'A Corporation of Superior Prostitutes:' Anglo-Indian Legal Conceptions of Temple Dancing Girls, 1800–1914," *Modern Asian Studies* 32, no. 3 (1998): 581 on slavery, family, and sex.
43. Raymond Evans, Kay Saunders, and Kathryn Cronin, *Race Relations in Colonial Queensland: A History of Exclusion, Exploitation and Extermination*, 3rd ed. (St. Lucia: University of Queensland Press, 1993), 121.
44. Sanjay Nigam, "Disciplining and Policing the 'Criminals by Birth', Part 2: The Development of a Disciplinary System, 1871–1900," *Indian Economic and Social History Review* 27, no. 3 (1990): 266.

45. Edwardes, *Crime in India*, 85.
46. Deborah Oxley, *Convict Maids: The Forced Migration of Women to Australia* (Cambridge: Cambridge University Press, 1996); Joy Damousi, *Depraved and Disorderly: Female Convicts, Sexuality and Gender in Colonial Australia* (Cambridge: Cambridge University Press, 1997).
47. Major R. C. Temple, Officiating Superintendent to Secretary, Government of India, 30 April 1895, NAI, Home Proceedings, Port Blair, July 1895.
48. Chapman, *The Poor Man's Court*, 92.
49. H. W. Wodehouse to Colonial Secretary, Hong Kong, 27 April 1893, PRO, CO129/259 (12527).
50. William Hill-Climo, "The British Soldier in India and Enthetic Diseases," *United Services Magazine* 15 n.s., (1896–7): 372.
51. Barbara Littlewood and Linda Mahood, "Prostitutes, Magdalenes and Wayward Girls: Dangerous Sexualities of Working Class Women in Victorian Scotland," *Gender & History* 3, no. 2 (1991): 171.
52. *Annual Report of the Administration of the Bengal Presidency* (Calcutta: Bengal Secretariat Office, 1870), 213, OIOC, V/10/34.
53. PP, *Report of the Committee on Homosexual Offences and Prostitution*, Cmd. 247 (1957), s. 234.
54. Police Order, 19 July 1887, PRO, HO 45/9964/X15663.
55. Lauren Benton, "Colonial Law and Cultural Difference: Jurisdictional Politics and the Formation of the Colonial State," *Comparative Studies in Society and History* 41, no. 3 (1999): 569.
56. *The Criminal Law Amendment Bill, 1917* (London, AMSH, 1917).
57. Chrystal Macmillan, *A New Danger: Departmental Orders versus Legislation for Venereal Disease* (n.p., 1919), 214.
58. Carol Smart, "Law and the Control of Women's Sexuality: The Case of the 1950s," in *Controlling Women: The Normal and the Deviant*, ed. Bridget Hutter and Gillian Williams (London: Croom Helm, 1981), 52.
59. Report at Commercial Street Station, 22 May 1902, PRO, MEPO 2/355.
60. F. O. Mayne, Commissioner, 4th Division to C. A. Elliott, Officiating Secretary to Government, Northwest Provinces, 20 August 1870, NAI, Home Department, Public Consultations A, Proceedings, 1870.
61. Author unknown, marginal note in a memo addressed to John Bramston, 17 May 1888, PRO, CO273/152 (7142).
62. *A Doomed Iniquity: An Authoritative Condemnation of State Regulation of Vice from France, Germany and Belgium* (London: Federation for the Abolition of the State Regulation of Vice, 1896), 9.
63. Extract from "Chinese Protectorate Report Summarizing Legislation concerning Brothels and the Protection of Women and Children up to August 1936," 13, RH. Mss. Ind. Ocn. S. 306, box 1, file 6.
64. Committee appointed for framing Rules under Section 19, Act XXII of 1864, 14 August 1865, OIOC, P/438/27, no. 62.
65. Governor of Bengal, 26 July 1880, Ripon Papers, Diary 111, f. 465, BL, Add. Ms. 43,574; also at OIOC, P/1664. The same opinion was expressed some years later by the Chief Secretary to the Government of Madras writing to the Secretary to the Government of India, Home Department, 13 February 1888, OIOC, P/3195. For earlier opinions in the same vein, see Horace A. Cockerell, Secretary, Government of Bengal, Judicial, Political and Appointments Department to Secretary, Government of India, Home Department, 11 July 1878, and Cockerell to Government of India, Home, Revenue and Agriculture Department, 15 October 1879, OIOC, P/1338.
66. Report of Acting Police Magistrate, April 1879, PRO, CO129/203 (20349).
67. Circular Order no. 34, 20 September 1869: "To All Police Officers in Towns and Suburbs," OIOC, P/674.
68. Colman Macaulay, Secretary, Government of Bengal, Municipal Department to Secretary, Government of India, Home Department, 4 January 1888, OIOC, L/MIL/7/13815.
69. *NSWPD* (2nd series), Second Session, 1908, vol. 31.
70. Judith Allen argues, in *Sex and Secrets: Crimes Involving Australian Women since 1880* (Melbourne: Oxford University Press, 1990), that street work in Sydney was more common among older women since their lower price was less attractive to brothel keepers and

pimps (25). Allen also charts a shift from outdoor to indoor prostitution early in the twentieth century, as do a number of U.S. historians (op. cit. 248).

71. Doug J. Porter, "A Plague on the Borders: HIV, Development, and Traveling Identities in the Golden Triangle," in *Sites of Desire, Economies of Pleasure: Sexualities in Asia and the Pacific*, ed. Lenore Manderson and Margaret Jolly (Chicago: University of Chicago Press, 1997), 212–32; Judith Walkowitz, *Prostitution and Victorian Society: Women, Class and the State* (Cambridge: Cambridge University Press, 1980).

72. Porter, "A Plague on the Borders," 223.

73. Elizabeth Van Heyningen, "'Gentoo'—A Case of Mistaken Identity?" *Kronos* 22 (1995): 73–4.

74. Report by Captain Superintendent of Police, F. H. May, 2 February 1895, PRO, CO129/266 (4779).

75. Cecil Chapman, *From the Bench* (London: Hodder and Stoughton, 1932), 107.

76. Frédérique Apffel Marglin, *Wives of the God-King: The Rituals of the Devadasis of Puri* (Delhi: Oxford University Press, 1985), 18; Mrinalini Sarabhai, *The Sacred Dance of India* (Bombay: Bharatiya Vidya Bhavan, 1979), 6; Amrit Srinivasan, "Reform and Revival: The Devadasi and Her Dance," *Economic and Political Weekly* 20, no. 44 (1985): 1870.

77. Lord Salisbury, India Office to Viceroy of India, 31 August 1876, OIOC, L/E/3/643.

78. G. Smith, Surgeon General, Indian Medical Department to Chief Secretary, Government of Madras, 7 February 1878, OIOC, P/1338.

79. Parker, "A Corporation of Superior Prostitutes," 561.

80. Marglin, *Wives of the God-King,* 17. See too Jogan Shankar, *Devadasi Cult: A Sociological Analysis* (New Delhi: Ashish Publishing House, 1990), 16.

81. Marglin, *Wives of the God-King,* 26; Veena Talwar Oldenburg, "Lifestyle as Resistance: The Case of the Courtesans of Lucknow," in *Contesting Power: Resistance and Everyday Social Relations in South Asia,* ed. Douglas Haynes and Gyan Prakash (Berkeley: University of California Press, 1991). The term *nautch* was from the Urdu *naach,* meaning a dance and thus highlighting a central feature of the women's training and performance. See Tharu and Lalita, *Women Writing in India,* 12. Francis Hutchins notes that while evangelicals regarded the *nautch* as indecent, eighteenth-century British residents in India condemned it rather for its dullness: *The Illusion of Permanence,* 102.

82. For a feminist interpretation of the modern Pakistani version of this tradition, particularly among the ethnic *Kanjars,* see Fouzia Saeed, *Taboo! The Hidden Culture of a Red Light Area* (Karachi: Oxford University Press, 2001).

83. Sumanta Banerjee, *Dangerous Outcast: The Prostitute in Nineteenth Century Bengal* (Calcutta: Seagull Books, 1998), 5; Saskia C. Kersenboom-Story, *Nityasumangala: Devadasi Tradition in South India* (Delhi: Motilal Banarsidass, 1987), 207; Maria Mies, *Indian Women and Patriarchy: Conflicts and Dilemmas of Students and Working Women* (New Delhi: Concept Publishing Company, 1980), 72; M. Sundara Raj, *Prostitution in Madras: A Study in Historical Perspective* (Delhi: Konark Publications PVT Ltd., 1993), 126; Shankar, *Devadasi Cult,* 111; K. C. Tarachand, *Devadasi Custom: Rural Social Structure and Flesh Markets* (New Delhi: Reliance Publishing House, 1991), 3.

84. J. H. Oliver, Deputy Commissioner, Gurgaon to Lt. Col. J. E. Cracroft, Commissioner and Superintendent, Delhi Division, 30 May 1872, NAI, Home Department, Judicial Branch, Consultation, July 1873.

85. Edwardes, *Crime in India,* 84.

86. David J. Pivar, "The Military, Prostitution, and Colonial Peoples: India and the Philippines, 1885–1917," *Journal of Sex Research* 17, no. 3 (1981): 264; Parker, "A Corporation of Superior Prostitutes," 562.

87. J. J. Panakal, "Prostitution in India," *Indian Journal of Criminology* 2, no. 1 (1974): 30. See too Neera Desai and Maithreyi Krishnaraj, *Women and Society in India* (Delhi: Ajanta Publications, 1987), 269; Edwardes, *Crime in India,* 86; M. S. Islam, "Life in the Mufassal Towns of Nineteenth-Century Bengal," in *The City in South Asia: Pre-modern and Modern,* ed. Kenneth Ballhatchet and John Harrison (London and Dublin: Curzon Press; Atlantic Highlands, NJ: Humanities Press, 1980), 247; S. D. Punekar and Kamala Rao, *A Study of Prostitution in Bombay* (Bombay: Allied Publishers, 1962), 190.

88. Abha Narain, "Witty Keepers and Royalty," *Times of India* (22 October 1994): n.p; Marglin, *Wives of the God-King,* 10–12.

89. B. R. Patil, "The Devadasis," *Indian Journal of Social Work* 35, no. 4 (1975): 377.

90. Oldenburg, "Lifestyle as Resistance," 33.

91. Major C. Powney Thompson, Deputy Commissioner, Kangra to Registrar, Chief Court, Punjab, 1 June 1911, OIOC, P/8954.

92. *Health Memorandum for British Soldiers in the Tropics,* n.p., ?1919, WL, AMSH Papers, box 313.

93. C. A. Bayly, "The British and Indigenous Peoples, 1760–1860: Power, Perception, and Identity," in *Empire and Others: British Encounters with Indigenous Peoples, 1600–1850,* ed. Martin Daunton and Rick Halpern (Philadelphia, PA: University of Pennsylvania Press, 1999), 21. See too Marilyn Wood, "Nineteenth Century Bureaucratic Constructions of Indigenous Identities in New South Wales," in *Citizenship and Indigenous Australians: Changing Conceptions and Possibilities,* ed. Nicolas Peterson and Will Sanders (Cambridge: Cambridge University Press, 1998), 35–54

94. John Clammer, "The Institutionalization of Ethnicity: The Culture of Ethnicity in Singapore," *Ethnic and Racial Studies* 5, no. 2 (1982): 132.

95. There is a huge literature on caste. See for example Susan Bayly, *Caste, Society and Politics in India from the Eighteenth Century to the Modern Age* (Cambridge: Cambridge University Press, 1999); Ursula Sharma, *Caste* (Buckingham: Open University Press, 1999); Declan Quigley, *The Interpretation of Caste* (Oxford: Clarendon Press, 1993); Veena Das, *Structure and Cognition: Aspects of Hindu Caste and Ritual* 2nd ed. (Delhi: Oxford University Press, 1982); Govind Sadashiv Ghurye, *Caste and Race in India* (Bombay: Popular Prakashan, 1969); Morton Klass, *Caste: The Emergence of the South Asian Social System* (Philadelphia, PA: Institute for the Study of Human Issues, 1980).

96. Satya P. Mohanty, "Drawing The Color Line: Kipling and the Culture of Colonial Rule," in *The Bounds of Race: Perspectives on Hegemony and Resistance,* ed. Dominick LaCapra (Ithaca, NY: Cornell University Press, 1991), 314.

97. Benedict Anderson, *Imagined Communities: Reflections on the Origin and Spread of Nationalism* Revised ed. (London and New York: Verso, 1991), 143.

98. Richard Dyer, *White* (London: Routledge, 1997), 13.

99. Kim F. Hall, *Things of Darkness: Economies of Race and Gender in Early Modern England* (Ithaca, NY: Cornell University Press, 1995), 2.

100. Antoinette Burton, *Burdens of History: British Feminists, Indian Women, and Imperial Culture 1865–1915* (Chapel Hill, NC: University of North Carolina Press, 1994).

101. Ann Laura Stoler, *Race and the Education of Desire: Foucault's* History of Sexuality *and the Colonial Order of Things* (Durham, NC: Duke University Press, 1995), 93.

102. Nancy Leys Stepan and Sander L. Gilman, "Appropriating the Idioms of Science: The Rejection of Scientific Racism," in *The Bounds of Race,* 73.

103. While the idea of extinction may have been extreme, Aboriginal peoples' health was multiply jeopardized by significant changes in diet as a result of the loss of land and lifestyle, by the consumption of alcohol (often tainted), and by narcotics. These factors also inflated mortality rates.

104. B. H. Purcell to Colonial Secretary, 14 November 1892, QSA, COL/A717 (14199).

105. See Daisy Bates, *The Passing of the Aborigines: A Lifetime spent among the Natives of Australia* (London: John Murray, 1944), 12, 22, 67; and *Handbook for Queensland, Australia, By Authority of the Agent General for the Government of Queensland* (London: Lake and Sison, 1893), 17. See also Peter Biskup, *Not Slaves, Not Citizens: The Aboriginal Problem in Western Australia 1898–1954* (St. Lucia: University of Queensland Press, 1973), 15–16; Andrew Markus, *Australian Race Relations 1788–1993* (St. Leonards, NSW: Allen and Unwin, 1994), 107; Evans, Saunders, and Cronin, *Race Relations in Colonial Queensland,* 119. This was also the opinion of powerful British politician, Lord Salisbury. For examples outside Australia, see Karen Jochelsen, "The Colour of Disease: Syphilis and Racism in South Africa, 1910–1950," (D. Phil. diss. Oxford University, 1993), 1. For Fiji, see Margaret Jolly, "Introduction: Colonial and Postcolonial Plots in Histories of Maternities and Modernities," in *Maternities and Modernities: Colonial and Postcolonial Experiences in Asia and the Pacific,* ed. Kalpana Ram and Margaret Jolly (Cambridge: Cambridge University Press, 1998), 7–8.

106. Richard Arthur, *Report on the Existing Facilities for the Treatment of Venereal Diseases in New South Wales, with Recommendations for their Extension and Improvement* (Sydney: Government Printer, 1919), 6.

107. *Kitchener's Memorandum to the Troops, 1905.*

108. *Daily Telegraph*, 30 January 1897, OIOC, L/MIL/7/13867.
109. Robin Gerster, "A Bit of The Other: Touring Vietnam," in *Gender and War. Australians at War in the Twentieth Century*, ed. Joy Damousi and Marilyn Lake (Melbourne: Cambridge University Press, 1995), 229.
110. For example, in Thailand, one word for prostitute translates literally as "venereally diseased woman." See S. D. Bamber, K. J. Hewison, and P. J. Underwood, "A History of Sexually Transmitted Diseases in Thailand: Policy and Politics," *Genitourinary Medicine* 69, no. 2 (1993): 149.
111. See for example Emmanuel Akyeampong, "Sexuality and Prostitution among the Akan of the Gold Coast, c. 1650–1950," *Past and Present* 156 (1997): 144–73; Janet M. Bujra, "Women 'Entrepreneurs' of Early Nairobi," *Revue Canadienne des Etudes Africaines/Canadian Journal of African Studies* 9, no. 2 (1975): 213–34; Tshidiso Maloka, "*Khomo Lia Oela*: Canteens, Brothels and Labour Migrancy in Colonial Lesotho, 1900–40," *Journal of African History* 38 (1997): 101–22; Benedict B. B. Naanen, "'Itinerant Gold Mines': Prostitution in the Cross River Basin of Nigeria, 1930–1950," *African Studies Review* 34, no. 2 (1991): 57–79; Deborah Pellow, "Sexuality in Africa," *Trends in History* 4, no. 4 (1990): esp. 87–92; Charles van Onselen, *Studies in the Social and Economic History of the Witwatersrand 1886–1914*, vol. 1. *New Babylon* (Johannesburg: Ravan Press, 1982); Jay Spaulding and Stephanie Beswick, "Sex, Bondage, and the Market: The Emergence of Prostitution in Northern Sudan, 1750–1950," *Journal of the History of Sexuality* 5, no. 4 (1995): 512–34; Luise White, *The Comforts of Home: Prostitution in Colonial Nairobi* (Chicago: University of Chicago Press, 1990).
112. Noel Loos, *Invasion and Resistance: Aboriginal-European Relations on the North Queensland Frontier 1861–1897* (Canberra: Australian National University Press, 1982), 149.
113. R. W. Connell, *Masculinities* (Berkeley: University of California Press, 1995), 74.
114. Richard Symanski, *The Immoral Landscape: Female Prostitution in Western Societies* (Toronto: Butterworths, 1981), xiv.
115. Rosemary McKechnie and Ian Welsh, "Between the Devil and the Deep Green Sea: Defining Risk Societies and Global Threats," in *The Lesser Evil and the Greater Good: The Theory and Politics of Social Diversity*, ed. Jeffrey Weeks (London: Rivers Oram Press, 1994), 63.
116. Lars D. Ericsson, "Charges against Prostitution: An Attempt at a Philosophical Assessment," *Ethics* 90 (1980): 366.
117. Ibid., 341.

Chapter 8

1. Philip Corrigan and Derek Sayer, *The Great Arch: English State Formation as Cultural Revolution* (Oxford: Basil Blackwell, 1985), 124.
2. Arjun Appadurai, "Number in the Colonial Imagination," in *Orientalism and the Postcolonial Predicament: Perspectives on South Asia*, ed. Carol Breckenridge and Peter van der Veer (Philadelphia, PA: University of Pennsylvania Press, 1993), 314–39; Bernard S. Cohn, "The Census, Social Structure and Objectification in South Asia," in *An Anthropologist Among the Historians and other Essays* (Delhi: Oxford University Press, 1987), 224–54, and introduction to *Colonialism and its Forms of Knowledge: The British in India* (Princeton, NJ: Princeton University Press, 1996); Charles Hirschman, "The Meaning and Measurement of Ethnicity in Malaysia: An Analysis of Census Classifications," *Journal of Asian Studies* 46, no. 3 (1987); 555–82 and "The Making of Race in Colonial Malaya: Political Economy and Racial Ideology," *Sociological Forum* 1, no. 2 (1986): 330–61 See too Ruth Lindeborg on the classifications proposed by missionary Joseph Salter: "The 'Asiatic' and the Boundaries of Victorian Englishness," *Victorian Studies* 37, no. 3 (1994): 395.
3. Sudipta Sen, "Colonial Frontiers of the Georgian State: East India Company's Rule in India," *Journal of Historical Sociology* 7, no. 4 (1994): 376; Lata Mani, *Contentious Traditions: The Debate on Sati in Colonial India* (Berkeley: University of California Press, 1998), 12.
4. Cohn, "The Census, Social Structure and Objectification," 231–2.
5. Cohn, *Colonialism and Its Forms of Knowledge*, 21–2.
6. Gauri Viswanathan, *Masks of Conquest: Literary Study and British Rule in India* (New York: Columbia University Press, 1989), 29.
7. Veena Das, "Gender Studies, Cross-Cultural Comparison, and the Colonial Organization of Knowledge," *Berkshire Review* 21 (1986): 59.

8. Chandra Talpade Mohanty, "Feminist Encounters: Locating the Politics of Experience," *Copyright* 1 (1987): 30.
9. David Ludden, "Orientalist Empiricism: Transformations of Colonial Knowledge," in *Orientalism and the Post Colonial Predicament*, 253.
10. Edward W. Said, *Orientalism* (London: Routledge and Kegan Paul, 1978), 72.
11. Joseph Alter points to similar anxieties around male sexuality in "Celibacy, Sexuality, and the Transformation of Gender into Nationalism in North India," *Journal of Asian Studies* 53, no. 1 (1994): 56.
12. Vinay Lal, "The Incident of the 'Crawling Lane': Women in the Punjab Disturbances of 1919," *Genders* 16 (1993): 46. And see Cheryl McEwan, "Encounters with West African Women: Textual Representations of Difference by White Women Abroad," in *Writing Women and Space: Colonial and Postcolonial Geographies*, ed. Alison Blunt and Gillian Roe (New York: The Guilford Press, 1994), 74.
13. Megan Vaughan, *Curing Their Ills: Colonial Power and African Illness* (Stanford, CA: Stanford University Press, 1991), 11.
14. Nathaniel Caine, *Prostitution: Its Aids and Accessories* (Liverpool: Egerton Smith, 1858); William Greg, "Prostitution," *Westminster Review* 53 (1850): 448–506; Ralph Wardlaw, *Lectures on Female Prostitution: Its Nature, Extent, Effects, Guilt, Causes, and Remedy* (Glasgow: James Maclehose, 1842). Women began writing about prostitution at a slightly later date: Elizabeth Blackwell, *Rescue Work in Relation to Prostitution and Disease* (London, T. Danes, 1881); A. Maude Royden, ed. *Downward Paths: An Inquiry into the Causes which Contribute to the Making of The Prostitute* (London: G. Bell and Sons, 1916); and Helen M. Wilson, *On Some Causes of Prostitution, with Special Reference to Economic Conditions* (London: AMSH, 1916).
15. Robert J. C. Young, *Colonial Desire: Hybridity in Theory, Culture and Race* (London and New York: Routledge, 1995), 98.
16. Henry Champly, *The Road to Shanghai: White Slave Traffic in Asia* (London: John Long, 1934), 73.
17. Kay J. Anderson, *Vancouver's Chinatown: Racial Discourse in Canada, 1875–1980* (Montreal and Kingston: McGill-Queen's University Press, 1991), 168.
18. Harold Meston to Under Secretary, Home Office, 24 September 1902, Colonial Secretary's Office, QSA, COL/143.
19. Ien Ang, "I'm a Feminist But ... 'Other' Women and Postnational Feminism," in *Transitions: New Australian Feminisms*, ed. Barbara Caine and Rosemary Pringle (St. Leonards, NSW: Allen and Unwin, 1995), 70.
20. Gayatri C. Spivak, "The Rani of Sirmur," in *Europe and Its Others*, vol. 1, ed. F. Barker, P. Hulme, M. Iverson, and D. Lozley (Colchester: University of Essex, 1985), 131.
21. José Harris, "Political Thought and the Welfare State 1870–1940: An Intellectual Framework for British Social Policy," *Past and Present* 135 (1992): 119.
22. Ann Laura Stoler, " 'Mixed-bloods' and the Cultural Politics of European Identity in Colonial Southeast Asia," in *The Decolonization of Imagination: Culture, Knowledge and Power*, ed. Jan Nederveen Pieterse and Bhikhu Parekh (London and New Jersey: Zed Books, 1995), 128–29.
23. Hirschman, "The Meaning and Measurement of Ethnicity," and "The Making of Race"; Anderson, *Imagined Communities*, 164; Gyan Prakash, "Writing Post-Orientalist Histories of the Third World: Perspectives from Indian Historiography," *Comparative Studies in Society and History* 32, no. 2 (1990): 387; Sen, "Colonial Frontiers," 378.
24. Hirschman, "The Making of Race," 330.
25. Pamela Scully, "Rape, Race, and Colonial Culture: The Sexual Politics of Identity in the Nineteenth Century Cape Colony, South Africa," *American Historical Review* 100, no. 2 (1995): 335–59.
26. Champly, *The Road to Shanghai*, 147. Lenore Manderson makes a similar point about European differentiation and the swelling Asian mass in *Sickness and the State: Health and Illness in Colonial Malaya, 1870–1940* (Cambridge: Cambridge University Press, 1996), 33.
27. William Hill-Climo, "The British Soldier in India and Enthetic Diseases," *United Services Magazine* 15 n.s., (1896–7): 371.
28. Chandra Talpade Mohanty, "Cartographies of Struggle: Third World Women and the Politics of Feminism," in *Third World Women and the Politics of Feminism*, ed. Mohanty, Ann Russo, and Lourdes Torres (Bloomington: Indiana University Press, 1991), 16.

29. Thomas R. Metcalf, *Ideologies of the Raj*, vol. 3, no. 4, *The New Cambridge History of India* (Cambridge: Cambridge University Press, 1994), 41.

30. John and Jean Comaroff, *Ethnography and the Historical Imagination* (Boulder, CO: Westview Press, 1992), 43.

31. Rana Kabbani, *Europe's Myths of Orient* (Bloomington: Indiana University Press, 1986), 10.

32. Ronald Hyam, "Empire and Sexual Opportunity," *Journal of Imperial and Commonwealth History* 14, no. 2 (1986): 52.

33. Richard Dyer, *White* (London: Routledge, 1997), xiii.

34. Sachiko Sone, "The Karayuki-San of Asia 1868–1938: The Role of Prostitutes Overseas in Japanese Economic and Social Development," *Review of Indonesian and Malaysian Affairs* 26, no. 2 (1992): 53.

35. Peter Biskup, *Not Slaves, Not Citizens: The Aboriginal Problem in Western Australia 1898–1954* (St. Lucia: University of Queensland Press, 1973), 64; Regina Ganter and Ros Kidd, "The Powers of Protectors: Conflicts Surrounding Queensland's 1897 Aboriginal Legislation," *Australian Historical Studies* 25 (1993): 541; W. Ross Johnston, *The Long Blue Line: A History of the Queensland Police* (Brisbane: Boolarong Publications, 1992), 200; William Thorpe, "Archibald Meston and Aboriginal Legislation in Colonial Queensland," *Historical Studies* 21, no. 82 (1984): 62 et seq.

36. Julia F. Solly, *State Regulation of Vice in South Africa: Urgent Appeal* (London: British Committee, International Abolitionist Federation, 1907), n.p.

37. For a discussion of Japanese prostitutes working outside Japan, see Mikiso Hane, *Peasants, Rebels, and Outcastes: The Underside of Modern Japan* (New York: Pantheon, 1982), 218–21, and Sone, "The Karayuki-San of Asia 1868–1938," 44–62.

38. S. M. Edwardes, Commissioner, Bombay Police to Secretary, Government of India, Judicial Department, 2 January 1913, OIOC, L/P& J/6/1207.

39. Frank Lenwood, "The Cantonments at Lucknow, January 26, 1911," WL, HJW, India file I-II, 1887–1912, D1/1, file 4.

40. P. C. B. Ayres, Colonial Surgeon, Hong Kong to Colonial Secretary, 26 April 1893, PRO, CO129/159 (12527).

41. C. C. Smith, Governor, Straits Settlements to Lord Knutsford, Colonial Office, 12 June 1889, enclosing and summarizing a letter from the Acting Principal Civil Medical Officer, PRO, CO273/160 (13763).

42. "Report of Mayor's Speech," *Morning Post* (Cairns), 10 September 1897, Home Secretary's Department, QSA, HOM A/15 (15952); D. Seymour, Police Commissioner, Geraldton (now called Innisfail), to Colonial Secretary, 18 December 1894, QSA, COL/A788 (14408); Sergeant J. Kelly, Childers to Inspector of Police, Maryborough, 25 April 1899, QSA, HOM A/24 (10551); Susan Jane Hunt, *Spinifex and Hessian: Women's Lives in North-Western Australia* (Nedlands, Perth: University of Western Australia Press, 1986), 124. Liesbeth Hesselink notes Dutch colonial approval of the cleanliness of Japanese prostitutes in, "Prostitution: A Necessary Evil, Particularly in the Colonies: Views on Prostitution in the Netherlands Indies," in *Indonesian Women in Focus: Past and Present Notions*, ed. Elsbeth Locher-Scholten and Anke Niehof (Dordrecht: Foris Publications, 1987), 213, 215.

43. Alec Dixon, *Singapore Patrol* (London: George C. Harrap, 1935), 211.

44. R. H. McKie, *This Was Singapore* (Sydney: Angus & Robertson, 1942), 101.

45. G. B. H. Fell, Officiating Secretary to Government of Burma to Secretary, Government of India, Home Department, 7 January 1913, OIOC, L/P& J/6/1207.

46. Quoted in D. C. S. Sissons, "*Karayuki-San:* Japanese Prostitutes in Australia, 1887–1916," Part 2: *Historical Studies* 17 (1977): 479.

47. E. C. S. Shuttleworth, Memorandum: "Extent, Distribution, and Regulation of the 'Social Evil' in the Cities of Calcutta, Madras and Bombay and in Rangoon Town," 1917, OIOC, L/P& J/6/1448 (2987).

48. S. M. Edwardes to Secretary, Government of Bombay, Judicial Department, 2 January 1913, OIOC, L/P& J/6/1207.

49. Sergeant J. Kelly, Childers to Inspector of Police, Maryborough, 25 April 1899, QSA, HOM A/24 (10551).

50. Gail Reekie, "Women, Region and the 'Queensland Difference,'" in *On the Edge: Women's Experiences of Queensland*, (St. Lucia: University of Queensland Press, 1981), 14.

51. R. Simon, Secretary, Government of the Northwest Provinces to E. C. Bayley, Secretary, Government of India, Home Department, 17 March 1869, OIOC, P/436/2 (3945).

52. P. C. B. Ayres to Colonial Secretary, 26 April 1893, PRO, CO129/159 (12527).

53. Hirschman, "The Making of Race," 354.

54. F. Swettenham, Resident General, Selangor to High Commissioner, Federated Malay States, 31 July 1899, PRO, CO 273/251 (23660).

55. S. M. Edwardes, *The Bombay City Police: A Historical Sketch 1672–1916* (London, Bombay, Calcutta and Madras, and Humphrey Milford/Oxford University Press, 1923), 94.

56. John and Jean Comaroff, "Home-Made Hegemony: Modernity, Domesticity, and Colonialism in South Africa," in *African Encounters with Domesticity*, ed. Karen Tranberg Hansen (Brunswick, NJ: Rutgers University Press, 1992), esp. 280; Anne McClintock, *Imperial Leather: Race, Gender, and Sexuality in the Colonial Context* (New York: Routledge, 1995), 207–8. See too Timothy Burke, *Lifebuoy Men, Lux Women: Commodification, Consumption, and Cleanliness in Modern Zimbabwe* (Durham, NC: Duke University Press, 1996).

57. Sergeant F. J. O'Connor, Boulia Sub District to Inspector of Police, 20 December 1898, QSA, COL/144 (12886).

58. C. P. Lucas to F. Meade, 6 May 1879, PRO, CO 129/184 (6690).

59. *Report of Venereal Diseases Committee*, 17 December 1923, PRO, CO275/109, C286.

60. *Seventh Annual Report on the Working of the Lock Hospitals in the Northwest Provinces and Oudh for the Year 1880* (Allahabad, n.p., 1881), 10, OIOC, V/24/2290.

61. *Annual Report on the Military Lock Hospitals of the Madras Presidency for the year 1879* (Madras: Government Press, 1880), 9, OIOC, V/24/2287.

62. Annual Report of Lock Hospital, Naini Tal, 1874, OIOC, P/525.

63. *Report on Voluntary Venereal Hospitals in the Punjab for the Year 1887* (Lahore: Civil and Military Gazette Press, 1888), 3, OIOC, L/MIL/7/13906.

64. Sander L. Gilman, *Inscribing the Other* (Lincoln: University of Nebraska Press, 1991), 20.

65. Inderpal Grewal, *Home and Harem: Nation, Gender, Empire, and the Cultures of Travel* (Durham, NC: Duke University Press, 1996), 47.

66. W. N. Willis, *Western Men with Eastern Morals* (London: Stanley Paul, 1913), 14.

67. Report on Lock Hospitals in British Burma for the Year 1873, Bassein Report, 13, OIOC, V/24/2296.

68. *Annual Medical Report of the Yokohama Lock Hospital for 1869* (Yokohama: *Japan Gazette* Office, 1870), 5, PRO, ADM125/16 (804).

69. J. McNeale Donnelly, Deputy Surgeon General, H.M. Forces, Burma Division to Inspector General of Jails, 18 February 1887, Lock Hospital Reports, Burma 1886–88, OIOC, L/MIL/7/13910.

70. Inspector of Contagious Diseases, Return of Examinations made under CDA, General Correspondence of Colonial Secretary, 1878, QSA CL A/268 (4353).

71. Memorandum of W. E. Parry-Okeden, n.d. 1899, QSA, HOM A/24 (10551).

72. Philippa Levine, "Venereal Disease, Prostitution, and the Politics of Empire: The Case of British India," *Journal of the History of Sexuality* 4, no. 4 (1994): 585–6.

73. Satadru Sen makes a similar point in arguing that the state consciously chose controlled and regulated prostitution over clandestine at the Indian convict settlement at Port Blair: "Rationing Sex: Female Convicts in the Andamans," *South Asia* 30 (1998): 29–59.

74. D. Seymour, Police Commissioner, Geraldton, to Colonial Secretary, 18 December 1894, QSA, COL/A788 (14408).

75. Military Despatch no. 73 of 1879, Lord Elgin et al. to Secretary of State for India, Lord Hamilton, 18 May 1897, OIOC, L/MIL/3/152.

76. See, for example, Lock Hospital reports, Madras 1887–89, OIOC, L/MIL/7/13904; W. H. Tarleton, Commissioner of Police, Rangoon to Chief Secretary to Government of Burma, 1 July 1914, OIOC, L/P& J/6/1448 (2987).

77. See for example *Fourth Annual Report on the Working of the Lock Hospitals in the Northwest Provinces and Oudh for the Year 1877* (Allahabad, n.p., 1878), 68, report for Naini Tal, OIOC, V/24/2290.

78. C. O. Mayne, Commander, Fourth Division to C. A. Elliott, Officiating Secretary to Government of the Northwest Provinces, 20 August 1870, NAI, Home Department, Public Consultations, A, Proceedings no. 188, 1870.

79. Sir Arthur Young to Walter Long, Colonial Office, 13 June 1917, PRO, CO 273/457 (41155).

80. Chandra Talpade Mohanty, "Under Western Eyes: Feminist Scholarship and Colonial Discourses," in *Third World Women and the Politics of Feminism*, 55; Ruth Frankenberg, *White Women, Race Matters: The Social Construction of Whiteness* (Minneapolis: University of

Minnesota Press, 1993), 191–4; Trinh T. Minh-ha, "Difference: A Special Third World Women Issue," *Discourse* 8 (1986–7): 11–38.

81. Sir William Robinson to Joseph Chamberlain, 30 June 1897, PRO, CO 129/276 (17234); Reports of Colonial Surgeons, 1870s and 1880s, CO 129/203 (20349); G. W. Johnson to Mr. Bramston, Colonial Office internal memorandum, 21 May 1887, CO 273/144 (8507); various memoranda, 1893, CO 273/187 (8818).
82. Corrigan and Sayer, *The Great Arch*, 124.
83. *History of the Po Leung Kuk Hong Kong 1878–1968* (Hong Kong: Po Leung Kuk, 1969), 1; Elizabeth Sinn, *Power and Charity: The Early History of the Tung Wah Hospital, Hong Kong* (Hong Kong: Oxford University Press, 1989).
84. G. B. Endacott, *A History of Hong Kong* (London: Oxford University Press, 1958), 246.
85. Henry Lethbridge, *Hong Kong: Stability and Change, a Collection of Essays* (Hong Kong: Oxford University Press, 1978), 83; Sinn, *Power and Charity*, 116; Nigel Cameron, *An Illustrated History of Hong Kong* (Hong Kong: Oxford University Press, 1991), 108.
86. Maria Jaschok and Suzanne Miers, "Women in the Chinese Patriarchal System: Submission, Servitude, Escape and Collusion," in *Women and Chinese Patriarchy: Submission, Servitude and Escape* (London and New Jersey: Zed Books, 1994), 154.
87. "The Po Leung Kuk Society's Home," *China Mail*, 13 November 1895, PRO, CO129/273 (26629).
88. *Hong Kong Legislative Council Sessional Papers, 1893* (Hong Kong: Noronha and Co., 1894), appendix 6, xi. The report gives details only of cases successfully prosecuted; there is no indication of how many other cases the society brought but that did not result in convictions.
89. Elizabeth Sinn, "Chinese Patriarchy and the Protection of Women in Nineteenth-Century Hong Kong," in *Women and Chinese Patriarchy*, 154.
90. Yen Ching-hwang claims it was the first PLK founded, though the evidence to support this claim is blurry: *A Social History of the Chinese in Singapore and Malaya 1800–1911* (Singapore: Oxford University Press, 1986), 257.
91. Annual Report of the Chinese Protectorate, Singapore and Penang, 1887, 3, PRO, CO273/152 (12265).
92. *Proceedings of the Legislative Council of the Straits Settlements, 1898* (Singapore: Government Printing Office, 1899), C. 499–500.
93. Minute Books of Weekly Board, LLH, 1872–1884, 23 May 1878, f. 339, RCS, LLH; H. F. B. Compston, *The Magdalen Hospital: The Story of a Great Charity* (London: Society for the Promotion of Christian Knowledge, 1917), 102–3; Philippa Levine, " 'Rough Usage': Prostitution, Law, and the Social Historian," in *Rethinking Social History: English Society 1570–1920 and Its Interpretation*, ed. Adrian Wilson (Manchester: Manchester University Press, 1993), 282.
94. *Proceedings of the Legislative Council of the Straits Settlements, 1897* (Singapore: Government Printing Office, 1898), n.p.; Rules Governing Po Leung Kuk [Hong Kong] Society Home, 1896, PRO, CO129/272 (15263).
95. *Daily Press*, 21 January 1896, PRO, CO129/271 (3829).
96. Maria Jaschok, *Concubines and Bondservants: A Social History* (London: Zed Books, 1988), 83.
97. Lethbridge, *Hong Kong*, 90; Cameron, *An Illustrated History*, 109.
98. "Annual Report on the Chinese Protectorate for the Year 1897," in *Straits Settlements Annual Reports for the Year 1897* (Singapore: Government Printing Office, 1898), 229, PRO, CO275/55.
99. Minutes of the Po Leung Kuk, *Proceedings of the Legislative Council of the Straits Settlements, 1890* (Singapore: Government Printing Office, 1891), C. 139–40.
100. Edwin Lee, *The British as Rulers: Governing Multi-Racial Singapore 1867–1914* (Singapore: Singapore University Press, 1991), 91–2.
101. James F. Warren, *Ah Ku and Karayuki-San: Prostitution in Singapore 1870–1940* (Singapore: Oxford University Press, 1993), 337.
102. Colonial Office Internal Memorandum initialed by Edward Fairfield, 27 July 1895, PRO, CO273/204 (12722).
103. Sinn, "Chinese Patriarchy," 161.
104. Ibid. 162–3.
105. Memorandum, G. T. Hare, 29 May 1895, PRO, CO 273/204 (12722).

106. Throughout the colonies, the tension between missionary ambition and the rights of local belief were a constant source of friction. Colonial governments and nonmissionary organizations mostly chose to limit conversion tactics seriously. The Lady Dufferin fund aimed at training medical women for work in India, for example, was a strictly nonsectarian body. See Maneesha Lal, "The Politics of Gender and Medicine in Colonial India: The Countess of Dufferin's Fund, 1885–1888," *Bulletin of the History of Medicine* 68 (1994): 36.
107. C. B. H. Mitchell to Colonial Secretary Ripon, 21 June 1895, PRO, CO273/204 (12722).
108. Memo, G. T. Hare, 29 May 1895, PRO, CO 273/204 (12722).
109. Ibid.
110. Memo, George Johnson to Edward Fairfield, 3 July 1895; Edward Fairfield in response, 27 July 1895, PRO, CO273/204 (12722).
111. Song Ong Siang, *One Hundred Years' History of the Chinese in Singapore* (Singapore: Oxford University Press, 1984), 281.
112. Lethbridge, *Hong Kong,* 90.
113. Manderson, *Sickness and the State,* 193.
114. Sinn, "Chinese Patriarchy," 155.
115. C. B. H. Mitchell to Lord Ripon, 21 June 1895, PRO, CO273/204 (12722).
116. *Hong Kong Refuge for Women and Girls* (n.d., n.p. ?1906) bound in BL pamphlet collection, *Hong Kong Charitable Institutions 1903–1907.*
117. *Fifth Annual Report of the Rescue Branch of the Women's Friendly Society* (Calcutta, 1913), 3.
118. Compston, *The Magdalen Hospital,* 200.
119. Good examples of this kind of thinking may be found at CO 129/259 (12527), 1894; CO 273/144, (8517) 1887; QSA COL/144 (1887); NAI Proceedings, Judicial, July 1873. Such thinking was certainly not confined to officialdom; the journalist Henry Champly's work is replete with references to passive and helpless Asian women as are the memoirs of soldiers such as Frank Richards, *Old-Soldier Sahib* (London: Faber and Faber, 1936). Antoinette Burton's *Burdens of History: British Feminists, Indian Women, and Imperial Culture 1865–1915* (Chapel Hill, NC: University of North Carolina Press, 1994) demonstrates how feminist Englishwomen also represented Asian women in this light.
120. *Report of the Committee appointed by the Governor of the Straits Settlements to enquire and report on Certain Measures made by the Secretary of State for the Colonies as to Measures to be Adopted with regard to Contagious Diseases and Brothels with a View to Checking the Spread of Venereal Diseases, 1898* (Singapore: Government Printing Office, 1899), CO 273/237 (19844).
121. Memorandum of C.P. Lucas to F. Meade, 6 May 1879, PRO, CO 129/184 (6690). Jaschok points out in *Concubines and Bondservants* that there was "no uniform Chinese attitude" (83).
122. Report for Year ending 30 June 1902, Western Australia, Aboriginals Department, 6, QSA, COL/143.
123. Minutes of Evidence of Straits Committee on the Prevention of Venereal Diseases, testimony of Dr. Mugliston, July 1899, PRO, CO 882/6.
124. Indrani Chatterjee, "Refracted Reality: The 1935 Calcutta Police Survey of Prostitutes," *Manushi* 57 (1990): 26.
125. Inspector Marrett, Cookstown to Commissioner of Police, Brisbane, 30 June 1898, and Constable James E. Old, Georgetown to Protector of Aborigines, 18 August 1900, both in QSA, COL/143 (11352/08420). See too Ann McGrath, " 'Black Velvet': Aboriginal Women and their Relations with White Men in the Northern Territory, 1910–1940," in *So Much Hard Work: Women and Prostitution in Australian History,* ed. Kay Daniels (Sydney: Fontana/Collins, 1984), 264 et seq., and Su-Jane Hunt, "Aboriginal Women and Colonial Authority: Northwestern Australia 1885–1905," in *In Pursuit of Justice: Australian Women and the Law 1788–1979,* ed. Judy Mackinolty and Heather Radi (Sydney: Hale and Iremonger, 1979), 37.
126. Colonial Office minute, initials illegible, 28 June 1886, PRO, CO 273/139 (6870).
127. See, for example, minute, author unknown (probably Frederick Meade), 9 January 1894; memo of P. C. B. Ayres to Colonial Secretary, Hong Kong, 26 April 1893, PRO, CO129/259 (12527).
128. Kenneth W. Andrew, *Hong Kong Detective* (London: John Long, 1962), 103.
129. Hendrik De Leeuw, *Cities of Sin* (London: Noel Douglas, 1934), 214.
130. J. Russell, Registrar General, Hong Kong to Frederick Stewart, Acting Colonial Secretary, 22 May 1882, PRO, CO129/200.

131. Officiating Magistrate, Benares, to Officer Commanding at Benares, 2 October 1875, OIOC, P/1002.
132. Multra Lock Hospital Report for 1870, NAI, Proceedings of the Department of Agriculture, Revenue and Commerce, Sanitary, June 1871.
133. See the many petitions listed in OIOC, P/525.
134. See for example the petition of Davadassee Mungoo of Madras, 1 September 1866, OIOC, L/E/3/336. The Dutch government was similarly uneasy about how to categorize dancers in the Netherlands Indies: Hesselink "Prostitution: A Necessary Evil," 214.
135. Veena Talwar Oldenburg, *The Making of Colonial Lucknow 1856–1877* (Princeton, NJ: Princeton University Press, 1984), 140.
136. *Report on Voluntary Venereal Hospitals in the Punjab for the Year 1887* (Lahore: Civil and Military Gazette Press, 1888), Rawalpindi report, 2, OIOC, L/MIL/7/13906.
137. M. Sundara Raj, *Prostitution in Madras: A Study in Historical Perspective* (Delhi: Konark Publications PVT Ltd., 1993), 49.
138. W. C. Plowden to M. H. Court, Commissioner, Meerut Division, 18 July 1870, NAI, Home Department, Public Consultation, A Proceedings, 1870.
139. Captain F. Hole, Superintendent of Police, Malabar to Deputy Inspector General of Police, Southern Range, 16 December 1875, OIOC, L/E/3/336.
140. Indian report of Katharine Bushnell and Elizabeth Andrew, typescript copy, 1892, WL, HJW, box 77.
141. Khan Bahadur Khwaja Tasadduq Hussain, Officiating Divisional Judge, Hissar Division to Registrar, Chief Court, Punjab, 17 July 1914, OIOC, L/P& J/6/1259 (2894).
142. Shuttleworth Memorandum, 1917, OIOC, L/P& J/6/1448 (2987).
143. Captain R. G. Briggs, Acting Superintendent, Bellary district to Major H. D. Cloete, Deputy Inspector General of Police, Central Range, 1 December 1875, OIOC, L/E/3/336.
144. India Military Consultations for November 1865, OIOC, P/192/38 (70).
145. Lord Ripon to Lord Hartington, 16 January 1882, OIOC, L/E/7/3 (230) and at OIOC P/1851.
146. Bassein Report, contained in Reports of the Lock Hospitals in British Burma for the year 1881, OIOC, V/24/2297.
147. Extracts of replies to a query from Quartermaster General Stedman, probably dated 1892, OIOC, L/MIL/7/13837.
148. Bassein Report, contained in Reports of the Lock Hospitals in British Burma for the year 1880, OIOC, V/24/2297.
149. Surgeon Major A. Payne, Superintendent of Lock Hospitals to Commissioner of Police, Calcutta, 1 February 1871, OIOC, P/674.
150. Horace A. Cockerell, Secretary to Government of Bengal, Judicial, Political and Appointments Department to Secretary, Government of Bengal, Home Department, 11 July 1878, OIOC, P/1338.
151. Warren, *Ah Ku and Karayuki-San,* 108–9.
152. Harry Ord to Earl of Kimberley, 13 February 1873, PRO, CO273/65 (2546).
153. Registrar General to Acting Colonial Secretary, Hong Kong, 12 September, 1882, PRO, CO129/203 (21149). See also J. Russell, Registrar General to Frederick Stewart, Acting Colonial Secretary, Hong Kong, 22 May 1882, PRO, CO129/200.
154. M. Macauliffe, Deputy Commissioner, Montgomery to Commissioner and Superintendent, Mooltan Division, 27 February 1878, OIOC, P/1338.
155. October 1881, OIOC, P/1664, noted as retained in B Proceedings.
156. Rangoon Town Magistrate, 1876, V/24/2297.
157. C. C. Smith to H. T. Holland, 30 January 1888, HC, *SP,* 59 of 1889, 9.
158. October 1875, OIOC, P/525, noted as retained in B Proceedings.
159. Extract from the Proceedings of the Government of Bengal in the Municipal Department, Darjeeling, 29 April 1884, OIOC, P/2261.
160. PRO, CO129/272 (15263).
161. Even in the more complete records retained by the administrators of British India, these petitions have not survived.
162. For the enquiry following her death, see *Copy of Report of the Commissioners appointed by His Excellency John Pope Hennessy to Inquire into the Working of the Contagious Diseases Ordinance, 1867,* HC, *SP,* 118 of 1880; *Correspondence relating to the Working of the Contagious Diseases Ordinances of the Colony of Hong Kong,* HC, *SP,* [C. 3093] 1881; *Sir John Pope-Hennessy, K.C.M.G., Governor and Commander in Chief of Hong Kong on the Contagious*

Diseases Ordinance in that Colony (London: Frederick C. Banks, 1882); PRO, CO129/179 (491).

163. Surgeon Major A. Payne to Commissioner of Police, Calcutta, 1 February 1871, OIOC, P/674; *Fourth Annual Report . . . 1877*, Allahabad report, 24, OIOC, V/24/2290.

164. Major H. D. Cloete, Deputy Inspector General of Police, Central Range to Lieutenant Colonel C.S. Hearn, Inspector General of Police, Madras, 4 December 1875, OIOC, L/E/3/336.

165. See, for example, report of M. B. Ellis, Officiating Superintendent of Police, Detective Department, Bengal, 11 June 1903, OIOC, OIOC, P/6586.

166. Edward J. Bristow, *Prostitution and Prejudice: The Jewish Fight against White Slavery 1870–1939* (Oxford: Clarendon Press, 1982), 80; Sander L. Gilman, "'I'm Down on Whores': Race and Gender in Victorian London," in *Anatomy of Racism*, ed. David Theo Goldberg (Minneapolis: University of Minnesota Press, 1990), 160 et seq.; Lara V. Marks, *Model Mothers: Jewish Mothers and Maternity Provision in East London 1870–1939* (Oxford: Clarendon Press, 1994), 3; McClintock, *Imperial Leather*, 8.

167. Note by M. W. Fenton, 7 January 1913, OIOC, L/P& J/6/1207.

168. Consul General, Shanghai to Hong Kong Governor, F. J. D. Lugard, 18 November 1908, PRO, CO 129/349 (2486).

169. Willis, *Western Men with Eastern Morals*, 27, 21.

170. Memorandum of Sir F. H. Souther, Commissioner of Police, Bombay, 16 August 1882, OIOC, L/P& J/6/53; F. A. M. Vincent, Commissioner of Police, Bombay to Secretary to Government Bombay, Judicial Department, 24 July 1916, OIOC, L/P& J/6/1416; Susanna Hoe, *The Private Life of Old Hong Kong: Western Women in the British Colony 1841–1941* (Hong Kong: Oxford University Press, 1991), 148.

171. Bristow, *Prostitution and Prejudice*, 191.

172. Bristow, *Prostitution and Prejudice;* Victor A Mirelman, "The Jewish Community Versus Crime: The Case of White Slavery in Buenos Aires," *Jewish Social Studies* 46, no. 2 (1984): 145–68; Lara V. Marks, "Jewish Women and Jewish Prostitution in the East End of London," *Jewish Quarterly* 24, no. 2 (1982): 8.

173. I thank Antoinette Burton for forcing me to push this argument further, and for providing a vocabulary that so perfectly enunciates the point.

174. Officiating Secretary to the Government of Bombay to Secretary, Government of India, Home Department, 7 January 1913, OIOC, L/P& J/6/1207.

175. Hoe, *The Private Life of Old Hong Kong,* 148; Warren, *Ah Ku and Karayuki-San,* 40; Willis, *Western Men with Eastern Morals.*

176. Joan G. Roland, *Jews in British India: Identity In A Colonial Era* (Hanover, NH: University Press of New England), 1989.

177. C. M. Webb, Secretary, Government of Burma to Secretary, Government of India, Home Department, 8 July 1916, OIOC, P/9952, no. 245. In *Jews in British India* (78), Roland claims Jewish elites in India also castigated prostitution as something associated with poor Baghdadi Jews.

178. Charles van Onselen, *Studies in the Social and Economic History of the Witwatersrand 1886–1914*, vol. 1. *New Babylon* (Johannesburg: Ravan Press, 1982); Sueann Caulfield, "The Birth of Mague: Race, Nation, and the Politics of Prostitution in Rio de Janeiro, 1850–1942," in *Sex and Sexuality in Latin America*, ed. Daniel Balderston and Donna J. Guy (New York: New York University Press, 1997), 86–100; Donna J. Guy, "Medical Imperialism Gone Awry: The Campaign against Legalized Prostitution in Latin America," in *Science, Medicine, and Cultural Imperialism*, ed. Teresa Meade and Mark Walker (New York: St. Martin's Press, 1991), 75–94; Donna J. Guy, "White Slavery, Public Health, and the Socialist Position on Legalized Prostitution in Argentina, 1913–1936," *Latin American Research Review* 23, no. 3 (1988): 60–80, Donna J. Guy, *Sex and Danger in Buenos Aires: Prostitution, Family, and Nation in Argentina* (Lincoln: University of Nebraska Press, 1991).

179. Calcutta Vigilance Committee, *Prostitution among Jewesses in India,* 1916, WL, HJW, India D2, file 1.

180. Sir Henry L. Harrison, Calcutta Commissioner of Police to Chief Secretary, Government of Bengal, 6 February 1888, "Traffic in Foreign Prostitution," NAI, Home Department, July 1888, Judicial Proceedings A.

181. A few historians do see a genuine white slave trade coercing Jewish women into sex work, mainly in Argentina and South Africa, and to a lesser extent in India. See for instance Lloyd P. Gartner, "Anglo-Jewry and the Jewish International Traffic in Prostitution, 1885–1914,"

Association for Jewish Studies Review 7/8 (1982–83): 129–78; Nora Glickman, "The Jewish White Slave Trade in Latin American Writings," *American Jewish Archives* 33–4 (1982): 178–89; and Mirelman, "The Jewish Community Versus Crime." Edward Bristow is more skeptical, though he does acknowledge procurers' use of deceit and fear in persuading women to travel east: see his "British Jewry and the Fight Against the International White Slave Traffic, 1885–1914," *Immigrants and Minorities* 2 (1983): 157–8.

182. J. H. Kerr, Chief Secretary, Government of Bengal, Political Department to Secretary to Government of India, Home Department, 28 August 1916, OIOC, L/P& J/6/1416.

183. Calcutta Vigilance Committee, *Prostitution among Jewesses in India,* 1916, WL, HJW, India D2, file 1.

184. WL, HJW, box 78A, 20 February 1892, f. 93.

185. S. M. Edwardes, Commissioner, Bombay Police to Secretary, Government of Bombay, Judicial Department, 2 January 1913, OIOC, L/P& J/6/1207.

186. Gilman, "I'm Down on Whores," 163.

187. A. B. Jordan, Government House, Singapore to Wilson, Colonial Office, 19 September 1931, PRO, CO 129/533/10 (82787).

188. Lord Bishop of Calcutta to Lord Lansdowne, 30 September 1893, OIOC, Mss. Eur. D. 558/25, vol. 2. no. 318; no. 3772 from Government of Bengal, 9 August 1893, NAI, Home Department Proceedings, Police Branch, A Series.

189. Herbert Anderson, Baptist Mission House, Calcutta to Dr. Haridhan Dutt, Calcutta, 18 December 1915, WL, HJW, India D2, file 1; *Fifth Annual Report of the Rescue Branch of the Women's Friendly Society* (Calcutta, 1913), WL, JEB, India box V; S. M. Edwardes, *Crime in India,* 84.

190. Bristow, *Prostitution and Prejudice,* 195.

191. Shuttleworth Memorandum, 1917, OIOC, L/P& J/6/1448 (2987).

192. Evelyn Brooks Higginbotham, "African-American Women's History and the Metalanguage of Race," *Signs* 17, no. 2 (1992): 266.

193. The fiction of Mahasweta Devi mocks this expertise in post-independence India. See the quotation from her work used by Gayatri Chakravorty Spivak, "Woman in Difference: Mahasweta Devi's 'Douloti the Bountiful,' " in *Nationalisms and Sexualities,* ed. Andrew Parker, Mary Russo, Doris Sommer, and Patricia Yaeger (London and New York: Routledge, 1992), 106.

194. Said, *Orientalism,* 207.

195. Partha Chatterjee, *The Nation and Its Fragments: Colonial and Postcolonial Histories* (Princeton, NJ: Princeton University Press, 1993), 223.

196. Metcalf, *Ideologies of the Raj,* 41.

197. Susie Tharu and K. Lalita, *Women Writing in India,* vol. 2: *The Twentieth Century* (New York: The Feminist Press, 1993), 9.

198. Examples might include the many age of consent laws passed in the empire from the 1880s, and laws affecting child marriage and widowhood in India. See among other literature Das's explanation of the new interest in such issues in "Gender Studies, Cross-Cultural Comparison," 64.

199. Frederick Cooper and Ann Laura Stoler, "Tensions of Empire: Colonial Control and Visions of Rule," *American Ethnologist* 16, no. 4 (1989): 610.

Chapter 9

1. Evidence of William Johnston Stuart, Surgeon Major, Bombay Army, 24 January 1865, Skey Committee Report and Minutes of Evidence (1864), 83, PRO, WO33/17A (0274).

2. H. J. C. Turner to H. J. Wilson, Lucknow, 10 August 1910, WL, HJW, INDIA file I-II, 1887–1912, D1/1, file 3.

3. Report on Calcutta lock hospitals for 1875, OIOC, P/525; Sir John Lambert, Commissioner of Police, Calcutta to Chief Secretary to Government of Bengal, 22 May 1894, OIOC, P/4557.

4. Herbert Anderson, Baptist Mission House, Calcutta to Dr. Haridhan Dutt, Nobin Pharmacy, Calcutta, 18 December 1915, WL, HJW, India D2, box II.

5. Deputy Commissioner to Commissioner, Lahore District, 13 December 1912; Chaplain to Deputy Commissioner, 28 November 1912, OIOC, L/P& J/6/1207.

6. G. B. Fell, Officiating Secretary to Government of Burma to Secretary, Government of India, Home Department, 7 January 1913, OIOC, L/P& J/6/1207.

7. Collection of hospital reports for the first quarter of 1898, PRO, CO273/236.

8. Report by Acting Protector of Chinese on the Working of Ordinance XIII of 1899 for the first half of 1900, PRO, CO273/258 (30403).

9. James F. Warren, *Ah Ku and Karayuki-San: Prostitution in Singapore 1870–1940* (Singapore: Oxford University Press, 1993), 87; Sir Arthur Young to Walter Long, Colonial Office, 13 June 1917, PRO, CO273/457 (36997).

10. Antoinette Burton, however, notes that Josephine Butler and other social purity activists largely ignored the white prostitute presence in India, concentrating their rescue efforts instead on Indian women. See *Burdens of History: British Feminists, Indian Women, and Imperial Culture 1865–1915* (Chapel Hill, NC: University of North Carolina Press, 1994), 144.

11. E. C. S. Shuttleworth, memorandum: "Extent, Distribution, and Regulation of the 'Social Evil' in the Cities of Calcutta, Madras and Bombay and in Rangoon Town, 1917," OIOC, L/P& J/6/1448 (2987).

12. Miss E. F. McKenzie, General Secretary, Association of Moral and Social Hygiene to Rt. Rev. Lord Bishop of Rangoon, 14 April 1916, OIOC, L/P& J/6/1448 (2987).

13. Calcutta Vigilance Society, *Prostitution Among Jewesses in India*, 15 March 1916, WL, HJW, India D2, file 1.

14. Ann Laura Stoler, "Making Empire Respectable: The Politics of Race and Sexual Morality in 20th-century Colonial Cultures," *American Ethnologist* 16, no. 4 (1989): 645.

15. Verax, *The Social Evil in South Calcutta* (Calcutta: Calcutta Central Press, 1895), 16.

16. Shuttleworth Memorandum, 1917, OIOC, L/P& J/6/1448 (2987).

17. For a discussion of how this operated for Irish migrants to the United States in the nineteenth century, see Noel Ignatiev, *How the Irish Became White* (London: Routledge, 1995).

18. Theodore W. Allen, *The Invention of the White Race*, vol. 1: *Racial Oppression and Social Control* (London: Verso, 1994), 11.

19. J. Ewing Ritchie, *The Night Side of London* (London: William Tweedie, 1857), 38.

20. Sander Gilman, *The Jew's Body* (London: Routledge, 1991), chapter 4.

21. Philip Howell, "Prostitution and Racialised Sexuality: The Regulation of Prostitution in Britain and the British Empire before the Contagious Diseases Acts," *Environment and Planning D: Society and Space* 18 (2000): 335.

22. "Criminal Women," *Cornhill Magazine* 14 (July–December 1866): 153.

23. G. Kerschener Knight, *The White Slaves of England* (Denham, Buckinghamshire, 1910), 37.

24. Ann Laura Stoler, "Rethinking Colonial Categories: European Communities and the Boundaries of Rule," *Comparative Studies in Society and History* 31, no. 1 (1989): 1.

25. OIOC, L/P& J/6/286 (1614/1890).

26. Satya P. Mohanty, "Drawing the Color Line: Kipling and the Culture of Colonial Rule," in *The Bounds of Race: Perspectives on Hegemony and Resistance*, ed. Dominick LaCapra (Ithaca, NY: Cornell University Press, 1991), 314.

27. Kay Saunders, "Controlling (Hetero)Sexuality: The Implementation and Operation of Contagious Diseases Legislation in Australia, 1868–1945," in *Sex, Power and Justice: Historical Perspectives on Law in Australia*, ed. Diane Kirkby (Melbourne: Oxford University Press, 1995), 5–6.

28. Raelene Frances, "Australian Prostitution in International Context," *Australian Historical Studies* 106 (1996): 129.

29. Commissioner of Police, Brisbane to Under Secretary, Home Department, 4 October 1907, QSA, HOM/J80.

30. In Western Australia, according to Raelene Frances, prostitution was represented as the province of foreign rather than Australian-born women: "Australian Prostitution," 130.

31. Contagious Diseases Act of 1868, Home Secretary's Memorandum, 1911, QSA, HOM/J80.

32. Dr. Baxter-Tyrie, Government Medical Officer, Visiting Prison Surgeon, and Port Health Officer, Cairns to Home Secretary, 28 September 1907, QSA, HOM/J80.

33. H. P. to Editor, *Brisbane Courier*, 23 October 1867 quoted in Enid Barclay, "Queensland's Contagious Diseases Act, 1868—'The Act for the Encouragement of Vice' and some Nineteenth Century Attempts to Repeal It, Part 1," *Queensland Heritage* 2, no. 10 (1965): 31.

34. Henry Champly, *White Women, Coloured Men* (London: John Long, 1936), 181.

35. Rosemary Hennessy and Rajeswari Mohan, "The Construction of Woman in Three Popular Texts of Empire: Towards a Critique of Materialist Feminism," *Textual Practice* 3, no. 3 (1989): 350.

36. Champly, *White Women, Coloured Men*, 283.

37. Ann Laura Stoler, " 'Mixed-bloods" and the Cultural Politics of European Identity in Colonial Southeast Asia," in *The Decolonization of Imagination: Culture, Knowledge and Power*, ed. Jan Nederveen Pieterse and Bhikhu Parekh (London and New Jersey: Zed Books, 1995), 128–48; idem. "Sexual Affronts and Racial Frontiers: European Identities and the Cultural Politics of Exclusion in Colonial Southeast Asia," *Comparative Studies in Society and History* 34, no. 3 (1992): 514–51.

38. Vron Ware, *Beyond the Pale: White Women, Racism and History* (London: Verso, 1992). See too Felicity Nussbaum, "One Part of Womankind: Prostitution and Sexual Geography in *Memoirs of A Woman of Pleasure*," *Differences* 7, no. 2 (1995): 17.

39. Kim F. Hall, *Things of Darkness: Economies of Race and Gender in Early Modern England* (Ithaca, NY: Cornell University Press, 1995), 9.

40. F. J. D. Lugard to Consul General, Shanghai, 26 October 1908, PRO, CO129/349 (2486).

41. Lugard to Earl of Crewe, Colonial Secretary, 14 December 1908, PRO, CO129/349 (2486).

42. Governor General et al. to Marquess of Crewe, India Secretary, 24 July 1913, OIOC, L/P& J/6/1207.

43. W. F. Parry-Okeden, Commissioner of Police, Memorandum, n.d. ?1899, QSA. HOM/A24.

44. Ann Laura Stoler, *Race and the Education of Desire: Foucault's History of Sexuality and the Colonial Order of Things* (Durham, NC: Duke University Press, 1995), 99.

45. *Daily Press*, 30 September 1879; press clipping sent to the Colonial Secretary in a despatch from the Governor, Sir John Pope Hennessy, 21 June 1880, PRO, CO129/188 (12078).

46. Wallace J. Gladwin and R. H. Madden to Viceroy, 28 April 1892, NAI.

47. Minute of Honourable Justice Benson, Madras High Court to Chief Secretary to Government of Madras, 9 January 1913, OIOC, L/P& J/6/1207.

48. Edward R. Henry, Commissioner of Metropolitan Police to F. S. Bullock, Chief, Criminal Investigation Division, Metropolitan Police, 25 November 1905, PRO, MEPO 2/558.

49. Edward J. Bristow, *Prostitution and Prejudice: The Jewish Fight Against White Slavery 1870–1939* (Oxford: Clarendon Press, 1982), 194.

50. Internal Colonial Office memorandum, initialed GG (probably Gilbert Grindle), 29 June 1931, PRO, CO129/533/10.

51. Rev. Joseph Reed, General Superintendent, Wesleyan Church, Bombay, Punjab, and Lucknow Districts to Commander in Chief in India, 24 August 1909, OIOC, L/MIL/7/13891.

52. Catherine Hall, "Rethinking Imperial Histories: The Reform Act of 1867," *New Left Review* 208 (1994): 10.

53. American Embassy Minute, 25 August 1908, PRO, CO129/352 (32116).

54. Elizabeth W. Andrew and Katharine C. Bushnell, *Recent Researches into the Japanese Slave Trade in California* (n.p., n.d. [1907]), 16.

55. Liesbeth Hesselink, "Prostitution: A Necessary Evil, Particularly in the Colonies. Views on Prostitution in the Netherlands Indies," in *Indonesian Women in Focus: Past and Present Notions*, ed. Elsbeth Locher-Scholten and Anke Niehof (Dordrecht: Foris Publications, 1987), 210. Julia Clancy-Smith argues that in French Algeria, European women were servicing the troops as part of colonial policy, though their presence was "rarely admitted" by the authorities. See her "Islam, Gender, and Identities in the Making of French Algeria, 1830–1962," in *Domesticating the Empire: Race, Gender, and Family Life in French and Dutch Colonialism*, ed. Julia Clancy-Smith and Frances Gouda (Charlottesville: University Press of Virginia, 1998), 159.

56. G. B. Fell, Officiating Secretary to Government of Burma to Secretary, Government of India, Home Department, 7 January 1913, OIOC, L/P& J/6/1207.

57. Quoted in Derek Hopwood, *Tales of Empire: The British in the Middle East 1880–1952* (London: I.B. Tauris, 1989), 66.

58. R. C. H. McKie, *This Was Singapore* (Sydney: Angus and Robertson, 1942), 101.

59. McKie, *This Was Singapore*, 101; Wallace J. Gladwin and R. H. Madden, "Horrible Things in Bombay, 1892," WL, HJW, D1/1, file 1; Rev. Joseph Reed, General Superintendent, Wesleyan Church, Bombay, Punjab, and Lucknow Districts to Commander in Chief in India, 24 August 1909, OIOC, L/MIL/7/13891.

60. Alec Dixon, *Singapore Patrol* (London: George C. Harrap, 1935), 210.

61. Bombay Police Commissioner to Secretary to Government, Judicial Department, 11 November 1891, OIOC, L/P& J/6/311 (1082/1891).
62. Short-Hand Report of the Proceedings of the Legislative Council of the Straits Settlements, 1888, B108, PRO, CO275/34.
63. Inspector General of Police, Straits Settlements to Private Secretary to Straits Governor, 27 January 1902, PRO, CO273/278 (8861).
64. Report of J. G. Smith, Superintendent, E Division, Bombay Police, 17 February 1888; Henry L. Harrison, Commissioner of Police, Calcutta to Chief Secretary, Government of Bengal, 6 February 1888, both in OIOC, P/3200.
65. F. C. Gates, Secretary to Chief Commissioner of Burma to Secretary, Government of India, Home Department, 11 April 1894, OIOC, P/4557.
66. Report of M. B. Ellis, Officiating Superintendent of Police, Detective Department, 11 June 1903, OIOC, P/6586.
67. W. J. Clifford, Secretary to the Society for the Protection of Young Children in India to Chief Secretary, Government of Bengal, 14 December 1912, OIOC, L/P& J/6/1207.
68. Memo, J. P. H. to Private Secretary, Governor General, 1 June 1888, NAI, Home Department Proceedings, Judicial, A Series, 1888, nos. 38–9. The Lieutenant Governor of Bengal made the same argument in 1894; see H. J. S. Cotton, Chief Secretary, Government of Bengal to Secretary, Government of India, Home Department, 8 June 1894, OIOC, P/4557.
69. Consul General, Shanghai to F. J. D. Lugard, 18 November 1908, PRO, CO129/349 (2486).
70. Edwardes, *Crime in India*, 94.
71. S.M. Edwardes, Commissioner of Police, Bombay to Secretary to Government, Judicial Department, Government of Bombay, 2 January 1913, OIOC, L/P& J/6/1207.
72. Memorandum from Political Department, Government of Bombay to Secretary of State for India, 11 April 1894, OIOC, L/P& J/6/372 (760/1894).
73. S. M. Edwardes, Commissioner of Police, Bombay to Secretary to Government, Judicial Department, Government of Bombay, 2 January 1913, OIOC, L/P& J/6/1207.
74. Report of Colonial Surgeon, 1 July 1873, CO273/70 (12170).
75. Annual Report of the Colonial Surgeon for 1874, PRO, CO129/189 (13163).
76. Annual Report of Colonial Surgeon, 1874, CO129/203 (20349).
77. *Annual Report of the Administration of the Bengal Presidency* (Calcutta: Bengal Secretariat Office, 1870), 213, OIOC, V/10/34; *Annual Report of the Administration of the Bengal Presidency* (Calcutta: Bengal Secretariat Office, 1872), 207, OIOC, V/10/47.
78. *Annual Report of the Administration of the Bengal Presidency*, 1872, 207, OIOC, V/10/47.
79. *Annual Report of the Administration of the Bengal Presidency* (Calcutta: Bengal Secretariat Office, 1869), 144, OIOC, V/10/32.
80. Secretary, Government of India, Military Department to Secretary, Government of Bengal, 27 November 1876, OIOC, P/1003.
81. Reports on Cantonment Hospitals 1892–1893, OIOC, L/MIL/7/13923.
82. Report of Belgaum Cantonment Hospital, 3, OIOC, L/MIL/7/13919.
83. Report of Northern Protector of Aboriginals, 1900, 21, QSA, COL/142 (04884).
84. Original Journal and Report of Indian Cantonments, 1893 by Mrs. Andrew and Dr. Bushnell, ff. 151-2, handwritten report, WL, HJW, India D1/2.
85. *Rules under Clause 7, Sec. 19 of Act XXII of 1864*, OIOC, P/1003.
86. Norman Miners, *Hong Kong Under Imperial Rule 1912–1941* (Hong Kong: Oxford University Press, 1987), 197.
87. P. C. B. Ayres to Acting Colonial Secretary, 25 September 1882, PRO, CO129/203 (20349).
88. Shuttleworth Memorandum, 1917, OIOC, L/P& J/6/1448 (2987).
89. Hendrik De Leeuw, *Cities of Sin* (London: Noel Douglas, 1934), 121.
90. F. A. M. H. Vincent to Under Secretary, Government of Bombay, Judicial Department, 11 August 1917, NAI, Home Proceedings, Police, 1917, nos. 128–130.
91. Rev. Joseph Reed, General Superintendent, Wesleyan Church, Bombay, Punjab, and Lucknow Districts to Commander in Chief in India, 24 August 1909, OIOC, L/MIL/7/13891.
92. Alfred S. Dyer, *The European Slave Trade in English Girls: A Narrative of Facts* (London: Dyer Brothers, 1880), 6.
93. Amanda Anderson, *Tainted Souls and Painted Faces: The Rhetoric of Fallenness in Victorian Culture* (Ithaca, NY: Cornell University Press, 1993), 1.
94. *SP*, Cd. 3453, Miscellaneous no. 2 (1907), *Correspondence respecting the International Conference on the White Slave Traffic, held in Paris October 1906*, annex 1, F. S. Bullock,

Chief Constable, Criminal Investigation Division, Metropolitan Police, 11, PRO, MEPO2/558. Bullock was head of the first police and Home Office initiative to monitor the white slave trade in early twentieth-century Britain; for Bullock, see Stephan Petrow, *Policing Morals: The Metropolitan Police and the Home Office 1870–1914* (Oxford: Clarendon Press, 1994), esp. 165–7; 172 et seq.

95. Henry L. Harrison, Commissioner of Police, Calcutta to Chief Secretary, Government of Bengal, 6 February 1888, OIOC, P/3200.

96. Frances, "Australian Prostitution," 130, 137. Bronwyn Dalley shows the same fears at work in New Zealand in " 'Fresh Attractions': White Slavery and Feminism in New Zealand, 1885–1918," *Women's History Review* 9, no. 3 (2000): 588.

97. Frederick K. Grittner, *White Slavery: Myth, Ideology, and American Law* (New York: Garland, 1990), 16.

98. Sir John Lambert, Commissioner of Police, Calcutta to Chief Secretary, Government of Bengal, 22 May 1894, OIOC, P/4557. The law to which Lambert refers is the 1885 Criminal Law Amendment Act, 48 & 49 Vic. cap. 69, s.13.

99. HC, *SP*, 1880 (118), *Report of the Commission appointed by His Excellency John Pope Hennessy to inquire into the Working of the Contagious Diseases Ordinance, 1867*, 19.

100. *Report of a Committee appointed by the Governor of the Straits Settlements to Enquire and Report on certain Suggestions made by the Secretary of State for the Colonies as to Measures to be Adopted with regard to Contagious Diseases and Brothels with a View to Checking the Spread of Venereal Diseases*, n.p, PRO, CO273/237 (1898).

101. Internal Colonial Office Memorandum, initialed M, 9 January 1894, PRO, CO129/259 (12527).

102. Sir J. Lambert, Commissioner of Police, Calcutta to Chief Secretary, Government of Bengal, 14 July 1893, NAI, Home Proceedings, Police, A Series, 1893, nos. 50–55.

103. Helen M. Wilson to Marquis of Crewe, India Secretary, 4 March 1913, OIOC, L/P& J/6/1225 (863/1913).

104. Flora Harris, Queensland NCW to Commissioner of Police, 26 January 1917, QSA, A/44696.

105. Ross Barber, "The Criminal Law Amendment Act of 1891 and the 'Age of Consent' Issue in Queensland," *Australia and New Zealand Journal of Criminology* 10 (1977): 101.

106. Frances, "Australian Prostitution," 129.

107. Flora Harris to Premier, Australian Commonwealth, 18 March 1914, QSA, A/4681.

108. Shuttleworth Memorandum, 1917, OIOC, L/P& J/6/1448 (2987).

109. Commissioner of Police, Queensland to Commissioner of Police, South Australia, 1 November 1913, QSA, A/44696.

110. Unknown official, Straits Settlements to Lewis Harcourt, Colonial Secretary, 5 September 1912, PRO, CO273/383 (30649).

111. Internal Home Office memorandum, Geoffrey Lushington, 6 December 1880, PRO, HO45/9546/59343.

112. Champly, *White Women, Coloured Men*, 305.

113. Teresa Billington-Greig, "The Truth About White Slavery," *English Review* 14 (June 1913): 442–3.

114. Mariana Valverde, *The Age of Light, Soap and Water: Moral Reform in English Canada, 1885–1925* (Toronto: McClelland and Stewart Inc., 1991), 79.

115. See, for example, Bristow, *Prostitution and Prejudice;* Guy, *Sex and Danger in Buenos Aires;* Gail Hershatter, *Dangerous Pleasures: Prostitution and Modernity in Twentieth-Century Shanghai* (Berkeley: University of California Press, 1997); Maria Jaschok, *Concubines and Bondservants: A Social History* (London: Zed Books, 1988); Charles Van Onselen, *Studies in the Social and Economic History of the Witwatersrand 1886–1914*. vol. 1. *New Babylon* (Johannesburg: Ravan Press, 1982).

116. LaVerne Kuhnke, *Lives At Risk: Public Health in Nineteenth-Century Egypt* (Berkeley: University of California Press, 1990), 3; Judith Tucker, *Women in Nineteenth-Century Egypt* (Cambridge: Cambridge University Press, 1985), 154.

117. M. Sundara Raj, *Prostitution in Madras: A Study in Historical Perspective* (Delhi: Konark Publications PVT Ltd., 1993), 76; 126.

118. Guy, *Sex and Danger in Buenos Aires*, 3.

119. Carolyn Martin Shaw, *Colonial Inscriptions: Race, Sex, and Class in Kenya* (Minneapolis: University of Minnesota Press, 1995), 8; Stoler, *Race and the Education of Desire*, 11; Valverde, *Age of Light, Soap and Water*, 78.

120. Lori Rotenberg, "The Wayward Worker: Toronto's Prostitute at the Turn of the Century," in *Women at Work: Ontario 1850–1930*, ed. Janice Acton, Penny Goldsmith, and Bonnie Shepard (Toronto: Canadian Women's Educational Press, 1974), 53.
121. Mohanty, "Drawing The Color Line," 325.
122. Hopwood, *Tales of Empire*, 67.
123. Elizabeth Buettner claims that around half of all whites in India were poor: "Problematic Spaces, Problematic Races: Defining 'Europeans' in Late Colonial India," *Women's History Review* 9, no. 2 (2000): 279.
124. See, for instance, Susanna Hoe, *The Private Life of Old Hong Kong: Western Women in the British Colony 1841–1941* (Hong Kong: Oxford University Press, 1991); Henry Lethbridge, *Hong Kong: Stability and Change, A Collection of Essays* (Hong Kong: Oxford University Press, 1978); David Arnold, "European Orphans and Vagrants in India in the Nineteenth Century," *Journal of Imperial and Commonwealth History* 7 (1979): 104–27.
125. *QPD*, 44, 21 November 1884, 1531, quoted in Evans, "Soiled Doves," 8.
126. *QPD*, 6, 1868, 854, speech of Western Wood, M.P., quoted in Barclay, "Queensland's Contagious Diseases Act," 1, 31.
127. Raymond Evans, "The Hidden Colonists: Deviance and Social Control in Colonial Queensland," in *Social Policy in Australia: Some Perspectives 1901–75*, ed. Jill Roe (Stanmore, NSW: Cassell Australia, 1976), 94.
128. Kay Saunders and Helen Taylor, "The Impact of Total War Upon Policing: The Queensland Experience," in *Policing in Australia: Historical Perspectives*, ed. Mark Finnane (Kensington, NSW: New South Wales University Press, 1987), 159; see too Saunders, "Controlling (Hetero)Sexuality," 9.
129. Undated letter, c. 1916, QSA (A/4718).
130. F. E. Drummond Hay, British Consulate General, Rio de Janeiro to Sir Edward Grey, Foreign Office, 23 June 1915, PRO, FO371/2513 (112332).
131. Home Office to Under Secretary of State, Foreign Office, 12 August 1915, PRO, FO371/2513 (112332).
132. Norman Etherington, "Natal's Black Rape Scare of the 1870s," *Journal of Southern African Studies* 15, no. 1 (1988): 36–53; Amirah Inglis, *The White Woman's Protection Ordinance: Sexual Anxiety and Politics in Papua* (New York: St. Martin's Press, 1975); Jock McCulloch, *Black Peril, White Virtue: Sexual Crime in Southern Rhodesia, 1902–1935* (Bloomington: Indiana University Press, 2000); Margaret Strobel, *European Women and the Second British Empire* (Bloomington: Indiana University Press, 1991), 5–6.
133. Stoler, *Race and the Education of Desire*, 132.
134. Bristow, *Prostitution and Prejudice*, 201.
135. Judy Bedford, "Prostitution in Calgary 1905–1914," *Alberta History* 29 (1981): 8; Kay J. Anderson, *Vancouver's Chinatown: Racial Discourse in Canada, 1875–1980* (Montreal and Kingston: McGill-Queen's University Press, 1991), 37.
136. Earl Lewis, "To Turn As On a Pivot: Writing African-Americans into a History of Overlapping Diasporas," *American Historical Review* 100, no. 3 (1995): 704.
137. S. M. Edwardes, Commissioner of Police, Bombay to Secretary to Government, Judicial Department, Government of Bombay, 2 January 1913, OIOC, L/P& J/6/1207.
138. John Cowen, *Public Prostitution in Rangoon: Report to Association of Moral and Social Hygiene*, 9 June 1916, 4, WL, JEB, Rangoon file; W. N. Willis, *Western Men with Eastern Morals* (London: Stanley Paul and Co., 1913), 18.
139. Catherine Hall, " 'From Greenland's Icy Mountains ... to Afric's Golden Sand': Ethnicity, Race and Nation in Mid-Nineteenth Century England," *Gender & History* 5, no. 2 (1993): 216.
140. "A Young Life Ruined," *Australian Star*, 13 October 1905, NSWSA, NSW, 5/5300.
141. Ruth Lindeborg, "The 'Asiatic' and the Boundaries of Victorian Englishness," *Victorian Studies* 37, no. 3 (1994): 388.
142. See for example Laura Tabili, "Women 'of a Very Low Type': Crossing Racial Boundaries in Imperial Britain," in *Gender and Class in Modern Europe*, ed. Laura. L. Frader and Sonya O. Rose (Ithaca, NY: Cornell University Press, 1996), 176, 179 et. seq.
143. Rudyard Kipling, *City of the Dreadful Night* (London: Classic Publishing Company, n.d.), 60.
144. Edward Troup, Home Office to Secretary, NVA, 22 September 1913, WL, NVA, box 102, file S22J.
145. Anderson, *Vancouver's Chinatown*, 37.

146. Guy, *Sex and Danger in Buenos Aires*, 25.
147. For examples of resistance in the form of escapes and protests, see Philippa Levine, "Rough Usage," 266–92.
148. Hall, "Rethinking Imperial Histories," 26.
149. I have borrowed the idea of fallenness as a linear narrative—the downward path—from Anderson, *Tainted Souls*, 9.
150. S. M. Edwardes, Commissioner of Police, Bombay to Secretary to Government, Judicial Department, Government of Bombay, 2 January 1913, OIOC, L/P& J/6/1207.
151. M. W. Fenton, Financial Commissioner, Punjab to Secretary to the Government of India, Home Department, 7 January 1913, OIOC, L/P& J/6/1207.
152. Stoler, *Race and the Education of Desire*, 115.

Chapter 10

1. Mrinalini Sinha, "Giving Masculinity a History: Some Contributions from the Historiography of Colonial India," *Gender & History* 11, no. 3 (1999): 450.
2. John Tosh, *A Man's Place: Masculinity and the Middle-Class Home in Victorian England* (New Haven, CT: Yale University Press, 1999), esp. 111. See too David Alderson's argument that Protestantism was crucial in the construction of nineteenth-century manliness: *Mansex Fine: Religion, Manliness and Imperialism in Nineteenth-Century British Culture* (Manchester: Manchester University Press, 1998), 5.
3. R. W. Connell, *Masculinities* (Berkeley: University of California Press, 1995), 185.
4. Warwick Anderson, "The Trespass Speaks: White Masculinity and Colonial Breakdown," *American Historical Review* 102, no. 5 (1997): 1367. David R. Roediger links whiteness, independence, and masculinity as key factors in the shaping of American masculinity: *The Wages of Whiteness: Race and the Making of the American Working Class* (London: Verso, 1991), 13.
5. Gail Bederman, *Manliness and Civilization: A Cultural History of Gender and Race in the United States, 1880–1917* (Chicago: University of Chicago Press, 1995), 25.
6. C. A. Bayley, *Imperial Meridian: The British Empire and the World 1780–1830* (Harlow, Essex: Longman, 1989), 151.
7. Catherine Hall, "The Economy of Intellectual Prestige: Thomas Carlyle, John Stuart Mill, and the Case of Governor Eyre," *Cultural Critique* 12 (1989): 170.
8. Ann Laura Stoler, *Race and the Education of Desire: Foucault's History of Sexuality and the Colonial Order of Things* (Durham, NC: Duke University Press, 1995), 128–9.
9. Francis G. Hutchins, *The Illusion of Permanence: British Imperialism in India* (Princeton, NJ: Princeton University Press, 1967), 50.
10. Joy Parr, "Gender History and Historical Practice," *Canadian Historical Review* 76, no. 3 (1995): 371.
11. Mrinalini Sinha, *Colonial Masculinity: The "Manly Englishman" and the "Effeminate Bengali" in the Late Nineteenth Century* (Manchester: Manchester University Press, 1995), 21.
12. Judith Allen, " 'Mundane' Men: Historians, Masculinity and Masculinism," *Historical Studies* 22, no. 89 (1987): 627.
13. Marilyn Lake, "Australian Frontier Feminism and the Marauding White Man," in *Gender and Imperialism*, ed. Clare Midgley (Manchester: Manchester University Press, 1998), 123–4.
14. The critical essay for this formulation is Marilyn Lake, "The Politics of Respectability: Identifying the Masculinist Context," *Historical Studies* 22, no. 86 (1986): 116–31. See too Allen, " 'Mundane' Men," 617–28; Patricia Grimshaw, Marilyn Lake, Ann McGrath, and Marian Quartly, *Creating A Nation* (Ringwood, VIC: Penguin Books, 1994), 2; Luke Trainor, *British Imperialism and Australian Nationalism: Manipulation, Conflict and Compromise in the Late Nineteenth Century* (Cambridge: Cambridge University Press, 1994), 5; Richard White, *Inventing Australia: Images and Identity 1688–1980* (Sydney: George Allen and Unwin, 1981). On New Zealand, see Jock Phillips, "Mummy's Boys: Pakeha Men and Male Culture in New Zealand," in *Women in New Zealand Society*, ed. Phillida Bunkle and Beryl Hughes (Auckland: George Allen and Unwin, 1980), 217–43.
15. Catherine Hall, "Imperial Man: Edward Eyre in Australasia and the West Indies 1833–66," in *The Expansion of England: Race, Ethnicity and Cultural History*, ed. Bill Schwarz (London: Routledge, 1996), 133.

16. M. Jacqui Alexander, "Not Just (Any) Body Can Be a Citizen: The Politics of Law, Sexuality and Postcoloniality in Trinidad and Tobago and the Bahamas," *Feminist Review* 48 (1994): 8.

17. John Rosselli makes the point, however, that anxieties over physical weakness were greater in the Bengali than in other Indian communities in the late nineteenth and early twentieth centuries: "The Self-Image of Effeteness: Physical Education and Nationalism in Nineteenth-Century Bengal," *Past and Present* 86 (1980): 133.

18. Hall, "The Economy of Intellectual Prestige," 180.

19. Frances Gouda, "*Nyonyas* on the Colonial Divide: White Women in the Dutch East Indies, 1900-1942," *Gender & History* 5, no. 3 (1993): 327.

20. Report of the Protector of Chinese for 1882, 12 April 1883, PRO, CO273/121 (13612).

21. Maneesha Lal, "The Politics of Gender and Medicine in Colonial India: The Countess of Dufferin's Fund, 1885-1888," *Bulletin of the History of Medicine* 68 (1994): 45. For a full discussion of Indian men's failings as properly masculine, see Sinha, *Colonial Masculinity*.

22. F. O. Mayne, Commissioner, 4th Division to C. A. Elliott, 20 August 1870, NAI, Home Department, Public Consultations A, Proceedings, 31 December 1870.

23. Ania Loomba, *Colonialism/Postcolonialism* (London: Routledge, 1998), 137–8.

24. J. H. Cook, "Pressing Problems in Uganda," *Mercy and Truth* 225 (195): 300, quoted in Megan Vaughan, "Syphilis in Colonial East and Central Africa: The Social Construction of an Epidemic," in *Epidemics and Ideas: Essays in the Historical Perception of Pestilence*, ed. Terence Ranger and Paul Slack (Cambridge: Cambridge University Press, 1992), 274.

25. S. M. Edwardes, *The Bombay City Police: A Historical Sketch 1672–1916* (London, Bombay, Calcutta and Madras: Humphrey Milford/Oxford University Press, 1923), 115–6.

26. C. B. H. Mitchell, Governor, Straits Settlements to Joseph Chamberlain, Colonial Secretary, 12 April 1899, PRO, CO273/246 (134).

27. Edwardes, *The Bombay City Police*, 93.

28. Nancy L. Paxton, "Mobilizing Chivalry: Rape in British Novels about the Indian Uprising of 1857," *Victorian Studies* 36, no. 1 (1992): 7.

29. W. J. Shepherd, *A Personal Narrative of the Outbreak and Massacre at Cawnpore, during the Sepoy Revolt of 1857* (1879; reprint, New Delhi: Academic Books Corporation, 1980), 85.

30. D. E. U. Baker, *Colonialism in an Indian Hinterland: The Central Provinces* (Delhi: Oxford University Press, 1993), 98.

31. See Amirah Inglis, *The White Woman's Protection Ordinance: Sexual Anxiety and Politics in Papua* (New York: St. Martin's Press, 1975). For similar African laws, see Jock McCulloch, *Black Peril, White Virtue: Sexual Crime in Southern Rhodesia, 1902–1935* (Bloomington: Indiana University Press, 2000); Norman Etherington, "Natal's Black Rape Scare of the 1870s," *Journal of Southern African Studies* 15, no. 1 (1988): 36–53; Ros Posel, " 'Continental Women' and Durban's Social Evil, 1899–1905," *Journal of Natal and Zulu History* 12 (1989): 1–13; and Pamela Scully, "Rape, Race, and Colonial Culture: The Sexual Politics of Identity in the Nineteenth Century Cape Colony, South Africa," *American Historical Review* 100, no. 2 (1995): 335–59.

32. Raymond Evans, Kay Saunders, and Kathryn Cronin, *Race Relations in Colonial Queensland: A History of Exclusion, Exploitation and Extermination*, 3rd ed. (St. Lucia: University of Queensland Press, 1993), 216–17.

33. Daisy Bates, *The Passing of the Aborigines: A Lifetime Spent among the Natives of Australia* (London: John Murray, 1944), 12.

34. Lieutenant Colonel De S. Barbow, Officiating Deputy Secretary to Chief Commissioner, Oudh to Secretary, Government of India, Home Department, 3 July 1872, NAI, Home Proceedings, Judicial, July 1873.

35. Internal Colonial Office minute, signature illegible, 28 June 1886, CO273/139 (6870).

36. R. D. Luard, Sub-collector, Pune to R. Mills, Collector, 14 November 1836, quoted in Laurence W. Preston, "A Right to Exist: Eunuchs and the State in Nineteenth-Century India," *Modern Asian Studies* 21, no. 2 (1987): 386.

37. Hutchins, *The Illusion of Permanence*, 69–70. Julia Clancy-Smith explores European opinion about "the social consequences of exaggerated Arab male sexuality symbolized by polygamy and the harem," in her essay, "Islam, Gender, and Identities in the Making of French Algeria, 1830–1962," in *Domesticating the Empire: Race, Gender, and Family Life in French and Dutch Colonialism*, ed. Julia Clancy-Smith and Frances Gouda (Charlottesville: University Press of Virginia, 1998), 162.

38. E. J. Eitel, *Report on Domestic Servitude in Relation to Slavery*, published originally in HC, *SP*, 1882 [Cd.-3185] and reproduced in *Community Problems and Social Work in Southeast Asia*, ed. Peter Hodge (Hong Kong: Hong Kong University Press, 1980), 32.
39. *Report of the Northern Protector of Aborigines for 1900* n.d., n.p., 10, QSA, COL/142 (04884).
40. Internal Colonial Office memo, 1897, probably R. E. Stubbs, PRO, CO 129/276 (17234).
41. Sinha, *Colonial Masculinity*, 19.
42. J. A. Swettenham to Chamberlain, 5 August 1898, PRO, CO 273/237 (19844); *Report of the Committee appointed by the Governor of the Straits Settlements to Enquire and Report on Certain Suggestions made by the Secretary of State for the Colonies as to Measures to be Adopted with regard to Contagious Diseases and Brothels with a view to Checking the Spread of Venereal Diseases, July 1899* (Singapore: Government Printing Office, 1899), PRO, CO 273/237 (19844).
43. Revathi Krishnaswamy, *Effeminism: The Economy of Colonial Desire* (Ann Arbor: University of Michigan Press, 1998), 4.
44. Robert Lees, "Venereal Disease in the Armed Forces Overseas," *British Journal of Venereal Diseases* 22, no. 4 (1946): 155.
45. This is one of Hyam's most commonly-evoked themes in his *Empire and Sexuality: The British Experience* (Manchester: Manchester University Press, 1990).
46. Hanneke Ming found similar assumptions on the Dutch colonial scene: "Barracks-Concubinage in the Indies, 1887–1920," *Indonesia* 35 (1983): 70.
47. Captain W. Morrison to Rev. G. A. Bennetts, 22 March 1897, WL, HJW, box 287, file 1897.
48. Good examples include Alec Dixon, *Singapore Patrol* (London: George C. Harrap and Co., 1935) and R. C. H. McKie, *This Was Singapore* (Sydney: Angus and Robertson, 1942).
49. W. Somerset Maugham, "Neil MacAdam," in *East and West: The Collected Short Stories* (Garden City, NY: Garden City Publishing Co., 1934), 912–55.
50. W. J. Moore, "Memorandum on the Contagious Diseases Acts," October 1886, 1, OIOC, V/24/2289.
51. Joseph S. Alter, "Celibacy, Sexuality, and the Transformation of Gender into Nationalism in North India," *Journal of Asian Studies* 53, no. 1 (1994): 57.
52. Rosalind O'Hanlon, "Issues of Masculinity in North Indian History: The Bangash Nawabs of Farrukhabad," *Indian Journal of Gender Studies* 4, no. 1 (1997): 3.
53. This description of Queensland at mid-century is drawn primarily from Gail Reekie, "Women, Region and the 'Queensland Difference,'" in *On the Edge: Women's Experiences of Queensland* (St. Lucia: University of Queensland Press, 1981), 8–24; and Duncan Waterson and Maurice French, *From the Frontier: A Pictorial History of Queensland to 1920* (St. Lucia: University of Queensland Press, 1987).
54. "G" to Edward Walter Hamilton, 14 February 1887, f. 54^{v}. BL, Add. Ms. 48, 625.
55. Ronald Hyam, "Empire and Sexual Opportunity," *Journal of Imperial and Commonwealth History* 14, no. 2 (1986): 53.
56. Hyam, "Empire and Sexual Opportunity," 35.
57. Ellen Bassano to Melinda Bassano, 23 November 1853, in *Brothers in India: The Correspondence of Tom, Alfred and Christopher Bassano 1841–75*, ed. Mary Doreen Wainwright (London: School of Oriental and African Studies, 1979), 251.
58. Earl of Dufferin to Lord Arthur Russell, 29 June 1888, OIOC, Mss. Eur. F.130/29C, f. 138.
59. Ken Hendrickson, "A Kinder, Gentler British Army: Mid-Victorian Experiments in the Management of Army Vice at Gibraltar and Aldershot," *War & Society* 14, no. 2 (1996): 30.
60. *Soldiers and the Social Evil: A Letter Addressed by Permission to the Rt. Hon. Sidney Herbert, Secretary of State for War, by A Chaplain* (London: Rivingtons and Folkestone: E. Creed, 1860), 5.
61. T. D. Mackenzie, Acting Chief Secretary to Government of Bombay to Secretary, Government of India, Home Department, 28 January 1888, OIOC, L/MIL/7/13815; W. Dick, "A Discussion on the Prevention and Treatment of Syphilis in the Navy And Army," *British Medical Journal* (21 October 1899): 1071.
62. Lees, "Venereal Disease," 155.
63. Abena P. Busia, "Miscegenation as Metonymy: Sexuality and Power in the Colonial Novel," *Ethnic and Racial Studies* 9, no. 3 (1986): 367.
64. Douglas M. Peers, "Contours of the Garrison State: The Army and the Historiography of Early Nineteenth-Century India," in *Orientalism, Evangelicalism and the Military Cantonment in*

Early Nineteenth-Century India: A Historiographical Overview, ed. Nancy Cassels (Lewiston: Edwin Mellen Press, 1991), 90.

65. W. R. Mansfield to John Lawrence, 21 January 1867, OIOC, Mss. Eur. F.90/39, no. 91.
66. David Omissi, *The Sepoy and the Raj: The Indian Army, 1860–1940* (Basingstoke and London: Macmillan, 1994), 193.
67. Hyam, "Empire and Sexual Opportunity," 65.
68. Adjutant General to Secretary to Government of India, Military Department, 18 March 1859, OIOC, P/273/101.
69. Hew Strachan, *The Politics of the British Army* (Oxford: Clarendon Press, 1997), 235, 74.
70. John M. MacKenzie, "Introduction," in *Popular Imperialism and the Military 1850–1950* (Manchester: Manchester University Press, 1992), 1.
71. Joany Hichberger, "Old Soldiers," in *Patriotism: The Making and Unmaking of British National Identity*, vol. 3 *National Fictions*, ed. Raphael Samuel (London: Routledge, 1989), 50.
72. *Lord Kitchener's Memorandum to the Troops*, n.p., 1905, WL, HJW.
73. Graham Dawson, *Soldier Heroes: British Adventure, Empire, and the Imagining of Masculinities* (London: Routledge, 1994), 6.
74. Hamilton to Curzon, 11 October 1900, OIOC, Mss. Eur. C.126/2, f. 373.
75. Lieutenant General M. Beresford, Commanding Mysore Division to Adjutant General, 25 October 1858, OIOC, P273/101.
76. *Saturday Review*, 3 April 1897; *Daily Telegraph*, 30 January 1897; OIOC, L/MIL/7/13867.
77. Frederick S. L. Roberts, to Duke of Cambridge, 24 May 1888, OIOC, L/MIL/17/5/1615/8, no. 36.
78. Earl of Dufferin to Lord Cross, 26 March 1888, OIOC, Mss. Eur. E.243/24.
79. [Blanche Leppington], *The Soldier and His Masters*, n.p., n.d. [1897], reprinted from *Contemporary Review* (January 1897): 2.
80. Connell, *Masculinities*, 54.
81. Walter Hart Blumenthal, *Women Camp Followers of the American Revolution* (Philadelphia, PA: G.S. MacManus, 1952), 20.
82. William Hill-Climo, "The British Soldier in India and Enthetic Diseases," *United Services Magazine* 15 n.s., (1896–7): 371.
83. India and Bengal Despatches, 17 March 1852, OIOC, E/4/814, with thanks to Doug Peers for providing me with a copy of this; *Report on Measures Adopted for Sanitary Improvements in India, from June 1872 to June 1873* (London: HMSO, 1873), 73, OIOC, V/24/3677.
84. Myna Trustram, *Women of the Regiment: Marriage and the Victorian Army* (Cambridge: Cambridge University Press, 1984), 46. Patricia Lin finds Trustram's estimates too conservative; in her work on the army during the Napoleonic Wars, Lin argues that the state bolstered recruitment by providing for soldiers' wives and children in a systematic way. Personal communications with the author, June 1999 and Patricia Y. C. E. Lin, "Extending Her Arms: Military Families and the Transformation of the British State, 1793–1815," (Ph. D. diss., University of California Berkeley, 1997).
85. HC, *SP*, 1898 (81), *Army and Militia: Pamphlets Showing the Conditions of Service in the Army and Militia Respectively*, 23 February 1898, 9. By contrast, 50 percent of warrant officers and NCOs above the rank of sergeant could marry.
86. The disincentives to marriage in the empire were not confined to soldiers, of course; see Margaret Strobel, *European Women and the Second British Empire* (Bloomington: Indiana University Press, 1991), 19–20.
87. *Fourth Annual Report on the Working of the Lock Hospitals in the Northwest Provinces and Oudh for the year 1877* (Allahabad, n.p., 1878), 3, OIOC, V/24/2290. Heather Streets has kindly shared with me an 1893 military report urging that Gurkhas be encouraged to marry to reduce their VD rates, and that women be especially brought from Nepal for this purpose. "Encouragement of Marriage Among Gurkha Sepoys," OIOC, L/MIL/7/7054.
88. *Proceedings of the Council of the Governor General in India, 1864* (Calcutta: Military Orphan Press, 1865), 102, OIOC, V/9/8.
89. A. O. Hume, Memorandum on the Extension of the Lock Hospital System in the Northwest Provinces, 21 December 1870, NAI, Home Department, Public Consultations A, Proceedings 1870, 1 K & W. With thanks to Ed Moulton for sharing this document with me.
90. Surgeon Major G. L. Hinde with 73rd Regiment to Adjutant, 73rd Regiment, 20 May 1875, OIOC, Mss. Eur. F.114/5 (13).

91. Richard S. Hill, *Policing the Colonial Frontier: The Theory and Practice of Coercive Social and Racial Control in New Zealand 1767–1867* (Wellington, New Zealand: Government Printer, 1986), 51.
92. Cynthia Enloe, *The Morning After: Sexual Politics at the End of the Cold War* (Berkeley: University of California Press, 1993), 145. For a perceptive analysis of how military prostitution has long-term effects on prostitution in nonwestern countries, see Robin Gerster, "A Bit of The Other; Touring Vietnam," in *Gender and War: Australians at War in the Twentieth Century,* ed. Joy Damousi and Marilyn Lake (Melbourne: Cambridge University Press, 1995), 228.
93. *Report on Measures Adopted for Sanitary Improvements in India, from June 1871 to June 1872* (London: HMSO, 1872), 70, OIOC, V/24/3676; *Report on Measures Adopted for Sanitary Improvements in India, from June 1872 to June 1873,* 50–3, OIOC, V/24/3677; Memorandum of Army Sanitary Commission, 5, OIOC, P/5648 (12), n.d.; HC, *SP,* 1896 [Cd. 8237], 1; despatch of Lord Elgin et al. to Lord Hamilton, 4 November 1896, OIOC, L/MIL/3/151. For Ceylon figures, see Joseph Chamberlain to Lieutenant Governor, Ceylon, 9 June 1899, PRO, WO 32/6210.
94. HC, *SP,* 1896, 153, 2–3, *Army (Average Numbers at Home and Abroad).*
95. Hendrickson, "A Kinder, Gentler British Army," 24.
96. Neil Cantlie, *A History of the Army Medical Department* (Edinburgh and London: Churchill Livingstone, 1974), 439; Edward M. Spiers, *The Army and Society 1815–1914* (London: Longman, 1980), 59.
97. Printed note, 4 May 1887, in *Roberts in India: The Military Papers of Field Marshal Lord Roberts 1876–1893,* ed. Brian Robson (Stroud, Glos: Alan Sutton for the Army Records Society, 1993), 372.
98. C, *The Army in Its Medico-Sanitary Relations,* (n.p., 1859); Cantlie, *Army Medical Department,* 439; Spiers, *Army and Society,* 56.
99. [Frederick S. L. Roberts], "On the Desirability of Clearly Defining the Principles on which the Administration of the Army in India Should be Based, and of Persevering in the Policy which has Guided the Government of India of Late Years in its Efforts to Strengthen our Military Position in this Country," 1 April 1893, OIOC, L/MIL/17/5/1615/6, no. 374, 1305–6. It was not, of course, only soldiers to whom tropical risk was thought to attach. For a nonmilitary example, see Anderson's discussion (in "The Trespass Speaks") of senior American administrators in the Philippines and the changing status of tropical neurasthenia.
100. George White, Commander in Chief in India to Bishop of Lucknow, 25 August 1896, OIOC, Mss. Eur. F.108/17, f. 118.
101. Minute, H. W. Whitfield, 26 January 1879, PRO, CO129/189 (16884).
102. Leppington, *The Soldier and His Masters,* 2.
103. Charles Allen, ed. *Plain Tales From The Raj: Images of British India in the Twentieth Century* (London: André Deutsch/British Broadcasting Corporation, 1975), 152.
104. Enloe, *The Morning After,* 52; Lawrence James, *Raj: The Making and Unmaking of British India* (New York: St. Martin's Press, 1997), 136–7.
105. Memo, J. G. 14 October 1880, f. 465, BM, Add. Mss. 43, 574, LXXXIV.
106. R. H. Madden and Wallace J. Gladwin to Viceroy, 28 April 1892, NAI, Home Proceedings, Police, B Series, May 1892.
107. Opinion, Acting Attorney General, April 1879, PRO, CO 129/203 (20349).
108. *Fourth Annual Report… 1877,* 76, OIOC, V/24/2290.
109. Hamilton to Curzon, 11 October 1900, OIOC, Mss. Eur. C.126/2, 373. Curzon expresses similar opinions in letters to Hamilton in D.501/2, D.501/3, D.501/4 and P/5910.
110. William Burke, "The Health of Europeans," 7 June 1827, OIOC, F/4/1079.
111. Report on Working of Secunderabad Lock Hospital for 1885, OIOC, P/2958.
112. *Annual Report on the Military Lock Hospitals of the Madras Presidency for the Year 1887* (Madras: Government Press, 1888), 11, OIOC, L/MIL/7/13904; Surgeon General and Principal Medical Officer to Secretary, Government of India, Military Department, 14 May 1877, OIOC, P/1203.
113. Joseph Edmondson, *An Enquiry into the Causes of the Great Sanitary Failure of the State Regulation of Social Vice* (London: British, Continental and General Federation for the Abolition of the State Regulation of Vice, 1897).
114. Frank Richards, *Old-Soldier Sahib* (London: Faber and Faber, 1936), 77.

115. HC, *SP*, 1880 (118), *Copy of Report of the Commissioners appointed by His Excellency John Pope Hennessy to Inquire into the Working of the Contagious Diseases Ordinance, 1867;* HC, *SP*, 1881 [C. 3093], *Correspondence relating to the Working of the Contagious Diseases Ordinances of the Colony of Hong Kong.*
116. Richards, *Old-Soldier Sahib*, 74–5.
117. *Gnanodayamu*, 10 November 1894, 406, *Report on Native Papers Examined by the Translators to the Government of Madras, 1894*, NAI.
118. Strachan, *Politics*, 95.
119. A. J. Arbuthnot, 6 March 1894, OIOC, C/129.
120. Hill-Climo, "The British Soldier in India," 369.
121. Dawson, *Soldier Heroes*, 83.
122. F. P. Gramings, Royal Catholic Bishop of Allahabad to Secretary, Government of India, Army Department, 27 July 1911, OIOC, L/MIL/7/13891.
123. Government of India to Secretary of State for India, 27 March 1888, OIOC, P/3195.
124. Frederick Roberts to Adjutant General in India, 22 October 1882, OIOC, L/MIL/17/5/1615/3, 45. The Army Sanitary Commission claimed that VD rates had risen as a direct consequence of short service, Memorandum, Army Sanitary Commission, 1896, OIOC, P/5648.
125. E. E. Mahon, "A Discussion on the Prevention and Treatment of Syphilis in the Navy and Army," *British Medical Journal* (21 October 1899): 1070.
126. *Twelfth Annual Report on the Working of the Lock Hospitals in the Northwest Provinces and Oudh for the year 1885* (Allahabad, n.p., 1886), 17, OIOC, L/MIL/7/13823; *Fifth Annual Report on the Working of the Lock Hospitals in the Northwest Provinces and Oudh for the year 1878* (Allahabad, n.p., 1879), 22, OIOC, V/24/2290.
127. W. J. Moore, Surgeon General, Memorandum on the Contagious Diseases Act, Bombay, October 1886, 4, OIOC, V/24/2289.
128. Spiers, *Army and Society*, 60; Peter Stanley, *White Mutiny. British Military Culture in India* (New York: New York University Press, 1998), 40; Hew Strachan, *Wellington's Legacy: The Reform of the British Army 1830–54* (Manchester: Manchester University Press, 1984), 65–7; Trustram, *Women of the Regiment*, 25.
129. Hendrickson, "A Kinder, Gentler British Army," 26.
130. Anon., *The Subaltern's Logbook* (London, 1928), ii, 266, quoted in Douglas M. Peers, "Sepoys, Soldiers and the Lash: Race, Caste and Army Discipline in India, 1820–50," *Journal of Imperial and Commonwealth History* 23, no. 2 (1995): 216.
131. Sir Charles Wood, India Secretary to Governor General, 15 August 1863, OIOC, Mss. Eur. F.114/5 (13).
132. Spiers, *Army and Society*, 53.
133. David Arnold, *Colonizing the Body: State Medicine and Epidemic Disease in Nineteenth-Century India* (Berkeley: University of California Press, 1993), 82. Mark Harrison claims the rations for rank and file men included up to a gallon of spirits every twenty days, as well as a daily ration of a quart of beer and one to two drams of rum or arrack: *Public Health in British India: Anglo-Indian Preventive Medicine 1859–1914* (Cambridge: Cambridge University Press, 1994), 62.
134. Curzon to A. Godley, 13 March 1902, OIOC, Mss. Eur. F.111/161, no. 21. Thanks to Derek Blakeley for providing me with a copy of this document.
135. H. J. C. Turner to H. J. Wilson, 10 August 1910, WL, HJW, India, file I-II, 1887–1912, D1/1, file 3.
136. HC, *SP*, 1898 [C.-9025], *East India (Contagious Diseases), No. II*, 4; George White to Bishop of Lucknow, 25 August 1896, OIOC, Mss. Eur. F.108/17, f. 118.
137. Frederick Roberts to Major General Lord Frankfort de Montmorency, 11 March 1890, OIOC, L/MIL/17/5/1615/12, no. 32.
138. *Temperance Chronicle*, 31 January 1908, OIOC, Mss. Eur. F.111/468, Scrapbook, December 1905 to December 1908, vol. 7, unpaginated. Thanks to Derek Blakeley for providing me with a copy of this document.
139. *Annual Report of the Army Temperance Association for the Official Year 1892–3*, n.d. 1036, OIOC, L/MIL/3/1036.
140. George White, "The Defence of India," *Black and White* (1 September 1894): 268, with thanks to Antoinette Burton for drawing my attention to this piece; *Annual Report of the Army Temperance Association for the Official Year 1892–3*, n.d., 18, OIOC, L/MIL/3/1036. Cantlie (376) maintains that what he calls the Army Temperance Society had 20,000 members by the

end of the century. Given the continued complaints about discipline and alcohol well after this time, his claim is not a compelling one.

141. Military Despatch, 9 January 1899, OIOC, L/MIL/7/13881.

142. *Report of Army Health Association for 1894* (n.d., n.p.) 5, OIOC, L/MIL/7/13856. This was a debate which continued well into the twentieth century. Analyzing American soldiers who contracted VD in Italy, Morris Brody ("Men Who Contract Venereal Disease," *Journal of Venereal Disease Information* 29 (1948): 336) correlated STDs and heavy drinking. The Vice Admiral of the British navy did not agree. He argued, on the contrary, that "the tremendous change for the better in the drinking habits of the naval personnel, which has taken place in recent times, has not been associated by (sic) a commensurate fall in the incidence of gonorrhoea." (Sheldon Dudley, "The Prevention of Venereal Disease in the Royal Navy," in *Inter-Allied Conferences on War Medicine 1942–1945*, ed. Henry Letherby Tidy and J. M. Browne Kutschbach [London: Staples Press, 1947], 253.) Gonorrhea was the most prevalent military and civilian STD of the period. In January 1908, the Army Institute Fund was established with a similar mission, to provide wholesome recreation and snack facilities for soldiers: see OIOC, L/MIL/7/13892.

143. War Office memorandum, 28 April 1898, OIOC, L/MIL/7/13872.

144. HC, *SP,* 1898 [C.-9025], *General Order by His Excellency the Commander-in-Chief in India, Dated Simla, 14th July 1897,* 4; Mahon, "Discussion," 1070.

145. *Fourth Annual Report . . . 1877,* 94, OIOC, V/24/2290.

146. Lieutenant General Commanding Forces, Punjab to Principal Medical Officer, 4 December 1897, OIOC, L/MIL/7/13877.

147. Lieutenant Colonel F. H. Whitely, Commanding 2nd Durham Light Infantry to Staff Station Officer, 25 August 1897, OIOC, L/MIL/7/13877.

148. Allen, *Plain Tales,* 40.

149. Notes for Mr. H. J. Wilson on Indian papers sent by Mr. Hallowes, by C. Moore, 22 November 1906, WL, HJW, India file I-II, 1887–1912, D1/1, file 3.

150. Dick, "Discussion," 1071.

151. *Experiences of A Soldier* (1891), NAM, 7008–13, 12.

152. Andrew Davies notes that among the diverse role models available to working-class men, few corresponded to the vision of the authorities: "Youth Gangs, Masculinity, and Violence in Late Victorian Manchester and Salford," *Journal of Social History* 32, no. 2 (1998): 354.

153. Surgeon General and Principal Medical Officer to Secretary, Government of India, Military Department, 14 May 1877, OIOC, P/1203; Cantlie, *Army Medical Department,* 374; Trustram, *Women of the Regiment,* 126.

154. Storks to Skey, 22 October 1865, Skey Committee Report and Minutes of Evidence (1864), appendix no. 2, PRO, WO33/17A (0274).

155. George Newton, *A Medical Report of the Yokohama Lock Hospital for 1869* (Yokohama: *Japan Gazette* Office, 1870), 8, PRO, ADM 125/16 (804); Report of Colonial Surgeon, Hong Kong, PRO, CO129/296 (4718).

156. Circular Memorandum no. 67, 19 August 1876, OIOC, L/MIL/7/13822, and at OIOC, L/MIL/3/980.

157. Circular Memorandum no. 68, 24 November 1880, OIOC, L/MIL/7/13822.

158. Circular Memorandum no. 2, 21 March 1887, OIOC, L/MIL/7/13822.

159. Resolution, Sanitation Department, Naini Tal, 9 May 1877, OIOC, P/1003.

160. *Annual Report on Cantonment Lock Hospitals at Barrackpore and Dum-Dum for 1877* (n.d., n.p.), OIOC, L/MIL/7/13903.

161. Major General G. de C. Morton to Secretary, Government of India, Military Department, 14 May 1897, OIOC, P/5246 (1691); E. H. Collen to Mr. Babington Smith, 18 March 1897, OIOC, Mss. Eur. F.84/50, no. 248.

162. G. Lawson, War Office to Lord Hamilton, 26 July 1897, OIOC, L/MIL/3/2133.

163. Major General G. de C. Morton to Secretary, Government of India, Military Department, 14 May 1897, OIOC, P/5246 (1691); *Fourth Annual Report . . . 1877,* 97, OIOC, V/24/2290. Hendrickson (28) sees the same arguments at work in the metropolitan military environment.

164. Surgeon General and Principal Medical Officer, British Forces in India to Secretary, Government of India, Military Department, 14 May 1877, OIOC, P/1203.

165. Memorandum, W. Taylor, 14 July 1897, PRO, WO32/6210.

166. *Fourth Annual Report . . . 1877,* 97, OIOC, V/24/2290; Surgeon General and Principal Medical Officer to Secretary, Government of India, Military Department, 14 May 1877, OIOC, P/1203.

167. Major General G. de C. Morton to Secretary, Government of India, Military Department, 14 May 1897, OIOC, P/5246 (1691); G. Lawson, War Office to Lord Hamilton, India Office, 26 July 1897, OIOC, L/MIL/3/2133.
168. Cindy Patton, "Critical Bodies," in *Trajectories: Inter-Asia Cultural Studies,* ed. Kuan-Hsing Chen (London: Routledge, 1998), 317.
169. Elgin et al. to Secretary of State for India, 29 December 1898, OIOC, L/MIL/7/13874.
170. Advisory Board for Army Medical Services, *First Report: The Treatment of Venereal Disease and Scabies in the Army* (London: HMSO, 1904), 7. Stoppages were not exclusive to VD sufferers. Hospitalization for other conditions also incurred them.
171. Frederick Roberts to Duke of Cambridge, 15 June 1888, OIOC, L/MIL/17/5/1615/8, no. 39.
172. Skelley, *Victorian Army,* 54; Elgin to Secretary of State for India, 7 March 1894, OIOC, L/MIL/3/149; telegram, Elgin to Secretary of State for India, 16 March 1897, OIOC, Mss. Eur D.508.
173. Captain W. Morrison, to Rev. G. A. Bennetts, 22 March 1897, WL, HJW, box 287, file 1897.
174. Confidential Memorandum, Oliver Newmarch, 25 September 1896, OIOC, L/MIL/17/5/2008.
175. Major General G. de C. Morton to Secretary, Government of India, Military Department, 14 May 1897, OIOC, P/5246 (1691).
176. Arthur Godley to Elgin, 9 July 1897, OIOC, Mss. Eur. F.84/136, 74–5.
177. General Report and Statistics of Venereal Disease among British and Indian Troops in India during the Year 1908, 27 August 1909, 3, OIOC, L/MIL/7/13887.
178. War Office to India Office, 26 July 1897, OIOC, L/MIL/7/13874.
179. Hutchins, *Illusion of Permanence,* 52.
180. Major General W. Galbraith, Commanding Quetta District to Principal Medical Officer, Bombay Command, 4 September 1897, OIOC, L/MIL/7/13877. Rosselli notes that in the 1870s, attempts to foster similar athleticism in the Indian elite had the blessing of the Indian administration: "Self-Image of Effeteness," 139.
181. HC, *SP,* 1898 [C. 9025], 4; *On the Desirability of Clearly Defining the Principles on which the Administration of the Army in India Should be Based,* OIOC, L/MIL/17/5/1615/6. no. 374, 1306.
182. George White, Commander in Chief in India to Bishop of Lucknow, 25 August 1896, OIOC, Mss. Eur. F.108/17, f. 118.
183. Memorandum, Army Sanitary Commission, 11 December 1893, OIOC, V/6/331.
184. George White to Duke of Cambridge, 20 January 1895, OIOC, Mss. Eur. F.108/18, 132.
185. Omissi, *Sepoy and the Raj,* 233.
186. *Rules for the Guidance of Police Officers,* OIOC, P/1003.
187. *Fourth Annual Report... 1877,* 82, OIOC, V/24/2290.
188. Officer Commanding 1st Battalion, 2nd Gurkhas to Deputy Surgeon General, 26 January 1889, OIOC, P/3477; Surgeon General W. Taylor to Government of India, Military Department, 24 July 1900, OIOC, L/MIL/7/13882.
189. *Fifth Annual Report... 1878,* 25, OIOC, V/24/2290. The policy was a long-lived one; the same sentiments are apparent in Military Despatch no. 76 of 1901, 30 May 1901, OIOC, L/MIL/3/157.
190. Persis Charles, "The Name of the Father: Women, Paternity, and British Rule in Nineteenth-Century Jamaica," *International Labor and Working-Class History* 41 (1992): 9; Rana Kabbani, *Europe's Myths of Orient* (Bloomington: Indiana University Press, 1986), 1. See too Inderpal Grewal, *Home and Harem: Nation, Gender, Empire, and the Cultures of Travel* (Durham, NC: Duke University Press, 1996) and Mary Louise Pratt, *Imperial Eyes: Travel Writing and Transculturation* (London: Routledge, 1992).
191. O'Hanlon, "Issues of Masculinity," 16.
192. *Saturday Review,* 26 March 1864, quoted in Trustram, *Women of the Regiment,* 121.
193. Edmund A. Parkes, *A Manual of Practical Hygiene Prepared Especially for Use in the Medical Service of the Army* (London: John Churchill and Sons, 1864), 452.
194. "The Health of the Army in India," *Saturday Review* 3 April 1897, clipping in OIOC, L/MIL/7/13867.
195. Minute of General Officer Commanding, Hong Kong, 26 January 1874, PRO, CO131/11; also at CO129/189 (16884).
196. *Twelfth Annual Report... 1885,* 17, OIOC, L/MIL/7/13823.
197. MacKenzie, "Introduction," 20.

198. C. H. Melville, "The History and Epidemiology of Syphilis in the More Important Armies," in *A System of Syphilis in Six Volumes*, vol. 6: *Syphilis in Relation to the Public Services*, ed. D'Arcy Power and J. Keogh Murphy (London: Oxford Medical Publications/Henry Frowde/Hodder and Stoughton, 1910), 74.

199. Gwyn Harries-Jenkins, *The Army in Victorian Society* (London: Routledge and Kegan Paul/Toronto: University of Toronto Press, 1977), 95.

200. Magnus Hirschfeld notes that in the German army the use of VD exams was not extended to officers: *The Sexual History of the World War* (New York: Cadillac Publishing Co. 1941), 99.

201. Lord Lansdowne to Earl of Kimberley, 18 April 1893, OIOC, Mss. Eur. D.558/6, B26; Lord Dufferin to Lord Cross, 14 May 1888, OIOC, Mss. Eur. F.130/11A, 69^V.

202. 20 September 1893, OIOC, L/MIL/7/13838.

203. Telegram, Secretary of State for India to Viceroy, 29 September 1893, OIOC, L/MIL/7/13851.

204. Enclosures 12 and 13, November 1893, OIOC, L/MIL/3/1036.

205. Quartermaster General, Bombay to Secretary, Government of Bombay, Military Department, 8 January 1894, OIOC, P/4595.

206. Minute Paper, Military Department, 22 November 1893, OIOC, L/MIL/7/13855; Military Despatch 117 of 1894, 3 July 1894, OIOC, L/MIL/3/149.

207. *Report on Measures Adopted for Sanitary Improvements in India from June 1869 to June 1870; Together with Abstracts of Sanitary Reports for 1867 forwarded from Bengal, Madras and Bombay* (London: HMSO, 1870), 78.

208. Major General E. Stedman, Quartermaster General to Secretary, Government of India. Military Department, 30 January 1895, OIOC, P/5016 (1781); Lord Reay to J. J. Frederick, Secretary, Army Sanitary Commission, 17 January 1895, OIOC, L/MIL/3/2130; *General Report and Statistics of Venereal Disease among British and Native Troops in India, together with Summary of the Reports on Cantonment Hospitals during the Year 1906* (n.p. 23 September 1907), 33, OIOC, L/MIL/3/184; W. A. Thomson, Principal Medical Officer to Secretary, Government of India, Military Department, 13 August 1890, P/3939.

209. Lord Lansdowne to Lord Cross, 4 February 1891; Surgeon General W. A. Thompson, Principal Medical Officer, British Troops in India to Secretary, Government of India, Military Department, 13 August 1890, both at OIOC, L/MIL/7/13834.

210. Major General E. Stedman, Quartermaster General to Secretary, Government of India, Military Department, 30 January 1895, OIOC, P/5016 (1781); see too Lord Reay to J. J. Frederick, Secretary, Army Sanitary Commission, 17 January 1895, OIOC, L/MIL/3/2130. Similar arguments were made about the Chinese in the Straits: "The most abandoned criminal never loses the sense of filial piety, and one of the things prisoners feel most is that while in jail they cannot earn money to send home." C. W. S. Kynnersley, "The Prevention and Repression of Crime," *Straits Chinese Magazine* 1, no. 3 (September 1897): 76.

211. E. McKellar, *Medical and Sanitary Report of the Native Army of Bengal for the Year 1873* (Calcutta: Office of the Superintendent of Government Printing, 1874), xv, 41, OIOC, V/24/3110. Other enunciations of this explanation include Lord Reay to J. J. Frederick, Secretary, Army Sanitary Commission, 17 January 1895, OIOC, L/MIL/3/2130; *Medical and Sanitary Report of the Native Army of Madras for the year 1873*, (Madras: Office of the Superintendent of Government Printing, 1875), 6, OIOC, V/24/3099; Lord Lansdowne to Lord Cross, 4 February 1891, OIOC, L/MIL/7/13834.

212. For Madras, see *Medical and Sanitary Reports of the Native Army of Madras . . . 1873*, 6, OIOC, V24/3099, and Omissi, *Sepoy and the Raj*, 64. For Bengal, see McKellar, *Medical and Sanitary Reports of the Native Army of Bengal . . . 1873*, 41, OIOC, V/24/3110.

213. According to Sumit Sarkar, a private in the British infantry in India in 1895 earned twenty-four rupees monthly plus various allowances, while his equivalent in the Indian infantry earned a mere nine rupees: *Modern India 1885–1947*, 2nd ed. (Basingstoke: The Macmillan Press, 1989), 17.

214. Frederick S. L. Roberts to Lord Lansdowne, 18 December 1889, OIOC, Mss. Eur. D.558/17, no. 410.

215. *Sketch of the Medical History of the Native Army of Bombay for the Year 1873* (Bombay: Government Central Press, 1874), 45, OIOC, V/24/3104.

216. *Medical and Sanitary Reports of the Native Army of Bengal for the Year 1872* (Calcutta: Office of the Superintendent of Government Printing, 1874), 48, OIOC, V/24/3109.

217. *General Report and Statistics of Venereal Disease . . . 1906*, 33, OIOC, L/MIL/3/184.

218. *Medical and Sanitary Reports of the Native Army of Bengal for the Year 1872,* 26, OIOC, V/24/ 3109; *Medical and Sanitary Reports of the Native Army of Madras for the Year 1878* (Madras: Office of the Superintendent of Government Printing, 1880), xx, OIOC, V/24/3111; *Medical and Sanitary Reports of the Native Army of Madras for the Year 1873,* 6, OIOC, V24/3099.

219. Colonel J. Emerson to Patna Officiating Magistrate, 11 February 1878, OIOC, V/24/2292.

220. Lionel Caplan, "Martial Gurkhas: The Persistence of A British Military Discourse on 'Race,'" in *The Concept of Race in South Asia,* ed. Peter Robb (Delhi: Oxford University Press, 1995), 260; Indira Chowdhury-Sengupta, "The Effeminate and the Masculine: Nationalism and the Concept of Race in Colonial Bengal," in *Concept of Race;* Stephen P. Cohen, *The Indian Army: Its Contribution to the Development of a Nation* (Delhi: Oxford University Press, 1990), 41; James, *Raj,* 121; Douglas M. Peers, "'Those Noble Exemplars of the True Military Tradition': Constructions of the Indian Army in the Mid-Victorian Period," *Modern Asian Studies* 31 no. 1 (1997): 132.

221. Bernard S. Cohn, "Cloth, Clothes, and Colonialism: India in the Nineteenth Century," in *Colonialism and Its Forms of Knowledge: The British in India* (Princeton, NJ: Princeton University Press, 1996), 123.

222. White, "Defence of India," 267.

223. *Saturday Review* (6 July 1889): 1.

224. Robson, *Roberts in India,* xvii.

225. Ashis Nandy, "The Psychology of Colonialism: Sex, Age, and Ideology in British India," *Psychiatry* 45, no. 3 (1982): 210; Peers, "Those Noble Exemplars", 134.

226. Omissi, *Sepoy and the Raj,* 26–7.

227. See Sinha, *Colonial Masculinity,* 71 for a further discussion of the act.

228. *Saturday Review* (6 July 1889): 1.

229. Garnet Wolseley, "The Negro As A Soldier," *Fortnightly Review* n.s. 264 (1 December 1888): 691, 692, 697.

230. Alter, "Celibacy, Sexuality, and the Transformation of Gender," 56.

231. *Medical and Sanitary Report of the Native Army of Bengal for the Year 1878* (Calcutta: Office of the Superintendent of Government Printing, 1880), 150, OIOC, V/24/3111.

232. *Report on Lock Hospitals in British Burma for the Year 1873* (n.d., n.p.) 3, OIOC, Mss. Eur. F.114/5 (13).

233. Hong Kong, *Report of the Committee constituted in accordance with the directions of His Excellency the Governor of Hong Kong contained in His Excellency's Letter to the Hon. Colonial Secretary* (Hong Kong: Noronha and Co., 1938), 4, HKPRO, C.S.O. 5661/32.

234. Strachan, *Politics,* esp. 104. For a contrary view, see Peter Burroughs "Imperial Defence and the Victorian Army," *Journal of Imperial and Commonwealth History* 15, no. 1 (1986): 55–6.

235. Resolution on the Report on Lock Hospitals in British Burma for the Year 1876, Report on Bassein, 25, OIOC, V/24/2297.

236. J. A. Crawford, Collector of Customs, Calcutta to Junior Secretary to Board of Revenue, Lower Provinces, 30 September 1867, OIOC, P/435/52.

237. John Mordike, *An Army For A Nation: A History of Australian Military Developments 1880– 1914* (North Sydney: Allen and Unwin, 1992), 1.

238. John Bach, *The Australia Station: A History of the Royal Navy in the South West Pacific, 1821–1913* (Kensington: University of New South Wales Press, 1986), 86–7.

239. Queensland, *Official Record of the Debates of the Legislative Assembly: 2nd Session, 9th Parliament 1884,* 44, 21 November 1884, Henry Jordan, 1524. Born in Lincoln, Jordan went first to Australia as a missionary to the Aborigines, and later practiced dentistry. He represented the constituency of South Brisbane in the Legislative Assembly in the 1880s, and had earlier been returned for the East Moreton district.

240. Paul R. Deslandes, "'The Foreign Element': Newcomers and the Rhetoric of Race, Nation, and Empire in 'Oxbridge' Undergraduate Culture, 1850–1920," *Journal of British Studies* 37, no. 1 (1998): 63.

241. Brian L. Blakeley, *The Colonial Office 1868–1892* (Durham, NC: Duke University Press, 1972), 79.

242. Dr. Henry A. Haviland, District Surgeon, Krian to Acting State Surgeon, Taiping, 12 September 1900, PRO, CO 273/263 (38482).

243. Minute, S. C. G. Fox, Acting State Surgeon to Secretary, Straits Settlements Government, 17 September 1900, PRO, CO 273/263 (38482).

244. *Report on Lock Hospitals in British Burma for the Year 1881* (n.d. n.p.) 24, OIOC, V/24/2297; Colin Crisswell and Mike Watson, *The Royal Hong Kong Police (1841–1945)* (Hong Kong: Macmillan, 1982), 77.

245. Elizabeth Sinn, *Power and Charity: The Early History of the Tung Wah Hospital, Hong Kong* (Hong Kong: Oxford University Press, 1989), 27.

246. G. C. Bolton, *A Thousand Miles Away: A History of North Queensland to 1920* (Brisbane: Jacaranda Press, 1963), 71; Donald Denoon, "Temperate Medicine and Settler Capitalism: On the Reception of Western Medical Ideas," in *Disease, Medicine, and Empire: Perspectives on Western Medicine and the Experience of European Expansion,* ed. Roy Macleod and Milton Lewis (London: Routledge, 1988), 125.

247. Bolton, *A Thousand Miles Away,* 135; Waterson and French, *From the Frontier,* 4.

248. Bolton, *A Thousand Miles Away,* 174.

249. Andrew Markus, *Australian Race Relations 1788–1993* (St. Leonards, NSW: Allen and Unwin, 1994), 87.

250. Mark Harrison, "'The Tender Frame of Man': Disease, Climate and Racial Difference in India and the West Indies, 1760–1860," *Bulletin of the History of Medicine* 70 (1996): 92.

251. Alison Bashford, "'Is White Australia Possible?' Race, Colonialism and Tropical Medicine," *Ethnic and Racial Studies* 23, no. 2 (2000): 253; Warwick Anderson, "Geography, Race and Nation: Remapping 'Tropical' Australia, 1890–1930," *Historical Records of Australian Science* 11, no. 4 (1997): 457.

252. David N. Livingstone, "Climate's Moral Economy: Science, Race and Place in Post-Darwinian British and American Geography," in *Geography and Empire,* ed. Anne Godlewska and Neil Smith (Oxford: Blackwell, 1994), 132–54; David Arnold, "White Colonization and Labour in Nineteenth-Century India," *Journal of Imperial and Commonwealth History* 11, no 2 (1983): 138.

253. W. H. Mercer, *A Handbook of the British Colonial Empire* (London: Waterlow and Sons Ltd., 1906), 27.

254. Anderson, "Geography, Race and Nation," 457; Bashford, "Is White Australia Possible?" 255.

255. Warwick Anderson, "Where Every Prospect Pleases and Only Man Is Vile': Laboratory Medicine as Colonial Discourse," *Critical Inquiry* 18 (1992): 512.

256. For a sustained discussion of this issue, see Warwick Anderson, *The Cultivation of Whiteness: Science, Health and Racial Destiny in Australia* (Carlton South: Melbourne University Press, 2002), esp. chapters 3 to 6.

257. Raymond Evans, "The Hidden Colonists: Deviance and Social Control in Colonial Queensland," in *Social Policy in Australia: Some Perspectives 1901–75,* ed. Jill Roe(Stanmore, NSW: Cassell Australia, 1976), 89–90.

258. Grimshaw et al. *Creating A Nation,* 288.

259. Administrator, Straits Settlements to Earl of Kimberley, 21 November 1871, PRO, CO 273/51 (12747).

260. Angus McLaren, *The Trials of Masculinity: Policing Sexual Boundaries 1870–1930* (Chicago: University of Chicago Press, 1997), 27.

261. Ibid., 14.

262. Supreme Court Report, 6 March, n.d., QSA, COL/A251.

263. Memorandum to Commissioner of Police, 18 January, 1878, QSA, COL/A251.

264. Moreton District Police Department, 9 April 1892, QSA, COL/A694 (04330).

265. David Englander, "Booth's Jews: The Presentation of Jews and Judaism in *Life and Labour of the People in London,*" *Victorian Studies* 32, no. 4 (1989): 565.

266. Sir Henry L. Harrison to Chief Secretary, Government of Bengal, 6 February 1888, NAI, Home Judicial Proceedings A, July 1888.

267. Deputy Commissioner to Commissioner, Lahore District, 13 December 1912, OIOC, L/P& J/6/1207; Edwardes, *Bombay City Police,* 85.

268. Bishop of Calcutta to Lord Lansdowne, 30 September 1893, OIOC, Mss. Eur. D.558/25, A318.

269. Rev. John P. Ashton, Secretary, Calcutta Missionary Conference to Private Secretary to Lieutenant Governor, Bengal, 26 April 1894, OIOC, L/P& J/6/398 (950/1895).

270. Edward J. Bristow, "British Jewry and the Fight Against the International White Slave Traffic, 1885–1914," *Immigrants and Minorities* 2 (1983): 153, 158; Hyam, "Empire and Sexual Opportunity," 70.

271. Edward J. Bristow, *Prostitution and Prejudice: The Jewish Fight Against White Slavery 1870–1939* (Oxford: Clarendon Press, 1982), 4. Nora Glickman shows the same anti-Semitism at

work in assessments of the sex trade in Latin America, see her "The Jewish White Slave Trade in Latin American Writings," *American Jewish Archives* 33–4 (1982): 179–80

272. Edwardes, *Bombay City Police*, 85.
273. F. S. Bullock, n.d. 1906, PRO, MEPO 2/558.
274. *Pitfalls for Women* (London: Success Publishing Company, ?1912).
275. John P. Ashton to Chief Secretary to Government of Bengal, June 1893, NAI, Home Proceedings, Police A, December 1893.
276. For example, see the figures for prosecutions in Hong Kong in Philippa Levine, "Modernity, Medicine, and Colonialism: The Contagious Diseases Ordinances in Hong Kong and the Straits Settlements," *Positions* 6, no. 3 (1998): 695.
277. Edwardes, *The Bombay City Police*, 131.
278. Hamilton to Curzon, 24 December 1901, OIOC, Mss. Eur. C.126/4, 462.
279. Internal Colonial Office memorandum, author unknown, 15 June 1887, PRO, CO273/144 (8517).
280. Clancy-Smith, "Islam, Gender, and Identities," 159.
281. Report, H. L. Dowbiggin, Inspector General of Police, n.d., probably 1917, PRO, CO 273/457 (41155).
282. S. H. Butler, Secretary, Government of United Provinces to Secretary, Government of India, Home Department, 29 January 1904, OIOC, P/7062.
283. Norman Chevers, *A Manual of Medical Jurisprudence for Bengal and the North-Western Provinces* (Calcutta: F. Carbery, Bengal Military Orphan Press, 1856), 485–6.
284. Association of Moral and Social Hygiene, Inquiry into Sexual Morality, 1918–1919, q. 1719, WL, AMSH, box 49.
285. Report of the Committee appointed by the Local Government to Advise on Certain Questions Concerning Brothels and Prostitutes in Rangoon, November 1917, OIOC, L/P& J/6/1448 (2987).
286. R. N. Jackson, *Pickering: Protector of Chinese* (Kuala Lumpur: Oxford University Press, 1965), 93.
287. Lai Ah Eng, *Peasants, Proletarians and Prostitutes: A Preliminary Investigation into the Work of Chinese Women in Colonial Malaya* (Singapore: Institute of South East Asian Studies, 1986), 33.
288. Minutes of Evidence of the Straits Committee on the Prevention of Venereal Diseases, 75, PRO, CO882/6.
289. Adjutant General to Lieutenant Generals Commanding Forces in Punjab, Bengal, Madras, Bombay and Burma, 2 June 1904, published in *Our Army in India: Correspondence between the India Office and the British Committee of the International Abolitionist Federation on the Rules, Regulations and Practice in Indian Cantonments with regard to Prostitution and Disease (October 1909 to October 1912)* (London: British Committee of the International Abolitionist Federation, 1912), 62.
290. W. St. John Brodrick to Curzon, 12 November 1889, OIOC, Mss. Eur. F.111/9B. This was, of course, some years before Curzon was appointed viceroy.
291. Hamilton to Curzon, 24 December 1901, OIOC, Mss. Eur. C.126/4, 462.
292. Elgin et al. to Kimberley, 7 March 1894, OIOC, L/MIL/3/149; also at P/4594 (1120) and L/MIL/7/13853. Elgin's predecessor, Lord Lansdowne, had made the same point only four months earlier. In a despatch to the India Secretary, dated 8 November 1893, he expressed a fear that too precipitate an abolition of the existing CD regime "would lead . . . not improbably to the prevalence of far graver forms of immorality." OIOC, L/MIL/3/148.
293. Elgin to Kimberley, 22 May 1894 (and again at 16 October 1894), OIOC, Mss. Eur. F.84/12, B18.
294. Elgin to Hamilton, 8 September 1896, OIOC, Mss. Eur. D.509/2, 867.
295. Thaïs E. Morgan, "Reimagining Masculinity in Victorian Criticism: Swinburne and Pater," *Victorian Studies* 36, no. 3 (1994): 329
296. Eve Kosofsky Sedgwick, *Between Men: English Literature and Male Homosocial Desire* (New York: Columbia University Press, 1985), 89.
297. Bart Moore-Gilbert, "Writing India: Reorienting Colonial Discourse Analysis," in *Writing India 1757–1900: The Literature of British India* (Manchester: Manchester University Press, 1996), 9; Anne McClintock, *Imperial Leather: Race, Gender, and Sexuality in the Colonial Context* (New York: Routledge, 1995).
298. Hall, "Imperial Man," 136.

299. For two examples of men said to be brought low by women, see Kenneth Ballhatchet, *Race, Sex and Class Under the British Raj. Imperial Attitudes and Policies and their Critics, 1793–1905* (London: Weidenfeld and Nicholson, 1980), 124 and 144–48.

300. Despatch, Government of India, Military Department to India Office, 18 May 1888, OIOC, L/MIL/3/139.

301. A. J. Arbuthnot, 21 May 1888, OIOC, C/128, manuscript minutes of dissent by members of the Council of India, 1877–1893.

302. Anderson, "The Trespass Speaks."

303. Edward Said, *Culture and Imperialism* (New York: Alfred A. Knopf, 1993), 137.

304. Surgeon General W. A. Thomson to Secretary to Government of India, Military Department, 13 August 1890, OIOC, P/3939.

305. Joseph Bristow, *Empire Boys: Adventures in a Man's World* (London: Harper Collins Academic, 1991), 225–6. See too McClintock, *Imperial Leather*, 47.

306. Eve Kosofsky Sedgwick, *Epistemology of the Closet* (Berkeley: University of California Press, 1990), 2.

307. Richard Arthur, *Report on the Existing Facilities for the Treatment of Venereal Diseases in New South Wales, with Recommendations for their Extension and Improvement* (Sydney: Government Printer, 1919), 6.

Chapter 11

1. Surendranath Banerjea, *A Nation in Making: Being the Reminiscences of Fifty Years* (1925), quoted in Antoinette Burton, *At the Heart of the Empire: Indians and the Colonial Encounter in Late Victorian Britain* (Berkeley: University of California Press, 1997), 64.

2. Helen Callaway, *Gender, Culture, and Empire: European Women in Colonial Nigeria* (Urbana: University of Illinois Press, 1987), 65.

3. Anne McClintock, *Imperial Leather: Race, Gender, and Sexuality in the Colonial Context* (New York: Routledge, 1995), 36.

4. Catherine Nash, "Remapping the Body/Land: New Cartographies of Identity, Gender, and Landscape in Ireland," in *Writing Women and Space: Colonial and Postcolonial Geographies*, ed. Alison Blunt and Gillian Roe (New York: The Guilford Press, 1994), 228.

5. Susan Morgan, *Place Matters: Gendered Geography in Victorian Women's Travel Books about Southeast Asia* (New Brunswick, NJ: Rutgers University Press, 1996), 11.

6. Anthony D. King, *Global Cities: Post-Imperialism and the Internationalization of London* (London: Routledge, 1990), 43.

7. Simon Ryan, *The Cartographic Eye: How Explorers Saw Australia* (Cambridge: Cambridge University Press, 1996), 4.

8. Kate Teltscher, *India Inscribed: European and British Writing on India 1600–1800* (Delhi: Oxford University Press, 1995), 145.

9. *The Health of the British Army in India* (Army Health Protection Association of India, n.p., n.d. [?1897]), OIOC, L/MIL/7/13869.

10. China Association to Joseph Chamberlain, 23 February 1899, PRO, CO129/296 (4718).

11. Jean and John Comaroff, "Through the Looking-Glass: Colonial Encounters of the First Kind," *Journal of Historical Sociology* 1, no. 1 (1988): 12.

12. Henry Kellett to Annesley, H.M. Consul, Nagasaki, 22 October 1870, PRO, ADM125/16 (804).

13. Lock Hospital Reports for the Year 1889, Nusseerabad, OIOC, L/MIL/7/13909.

14. African historians, however, have persuasively argued that the brothel was an outgrowth of the changing patterns of settlement and labor brought about by colonialism. See, for example, Janet M. Bujra, "Women 'Entrepreneurs' of Early Nairobi," *Revue Canadienne des Etudes Africaines/Canadian Journal of African Studies* 9, no. 2 (1975): 221; Benedict B. B. Naanen, "'Itinerant Gold Mines': Prostitution in the Cross River Basin of Nigeria, 1930–1950," *African Studies Review* 34, no. 2 (1991): 57–79; Jay Spaulding and Stephanie Beswick, "Sex, Bondage, and the Market: The Emergence of Prostitution in Northern Sudan, 1750–1950," *Journal of the History of Sexuality* 5, no. 4 (1995): 512–3; Luise White, "Domestic Labor in a Colonial City: Prostitution in Nairobi, 1900–1952," in *African Women in the Home and the Workforce*, ed. Sharon B. Stichter, and Jane L. Parpart (Boulder, CO: Westview Press, 1988), 139–60.

15. Kenneth W. Andrew, *Hong Kong Detective* (London: John Long, 1962), 90.

16. Quartermaster General in India to General Officer Commanding, Lucknow, 1 May 1911, in Army Despatch to India Secretary, no. 107 of 1911, OIOC, L/MIL/7/13891.
17. Extract from Memorandum included in letter of Quartermaster General in India, 1 May 1911, OIOC, L/MIL/7/13891.
18. E. Waller to Station Staff Officer, OIOC, L/MIL/7/13891.
19. Sub Inspector John Ferguson, Cairns to Inspector Lamond, Cooktown, 24 November 1897, QSA, HOM/A15 (15952).
20. Mr. Tooth to Chief [Colonial] Secretary, Brisbane, 25 May 1899; Sergeant J. Kelly to Inspector of Police, Maryborough, 25 April 1899, QSA, HOM/A24 (10551).
21. James F. Warren, "Chinese Prostitution in Singapore: Recruitment and Brothel Organisation," in *Women and Chinese Patriarchy: Submission, Servitude and Escape,* ed. Maria Jaschok and Suzanne Miers (London and New Jersey: Zed Books, 1994), 91.
22. E. C. S. Shuttleworth, "Extent, Distribution, and Regulation of the "Social Evil" in the Cities of Calcutta, Madras and Bombay and in Rangoon Town," 1917, OIOC, L/P& J/6/1448 (2987).
23. On the Hong Kong phenomenon of the "protected" woman, see Carl T. Smith, "Protected Women in Nineteenth-Century Hong Kong," in *Women and Chinese Patriarchy,* 221–37.
24. Government of Bengal to Secretary of State for India, 7 June 1881, OIOC, P/1664, confirmed in Surgeon General's Report on Contagious Diseases Acts, June 1887, 7, OIOC, V/24/2289.
25. Richard Symanski, *The Immoral Landscape: Female Prostitution in Western Societies* (Toronto: Butterworths, 1981), 9.
26. OIOC, P/438/27, no. 62.
27. Smith, "Protected Women" 226.
28. Gwendolyn Wright makes this point about the *maisons tolérées* in France and its colonies in *The Politics of Design in French Colonial Urbanism* (Chicago: University of Chicago Press, 1991), 33.
29. See, for example, Nicholas Thomas, "Sanitation and Seeing: The Creation of State Power in Early Colonial Fiji," *Comparative Studies in Society and History* 32, no. 1 (1990): 160–1.
30. Annual Report of the Colonial Surgeon, 1879, 66^v, PRO, CO131/11.
31. Brenda S. A. Yeoh, *Contesting Space: Power Relations and the Urban Built Environment in Colonial Singapore* (Kuala Lumpur: Oxford University Press, 1996), 245–6; Veena Oldenburg, *The Making of Colonial Lucknow 1856–1877* (Princeton, NJ: Princeton University Press, 1984), 121.
32. Henry Champly, *The Road to Shanghai: White Slave Traffic in Asia* (London: John Long, 1934), 72.
33. Shuttleworth Report, 1917, OIOC, L/P& J/6/1448 (2987).
34. Health Officer of Madras to Chief Secretary, Government of Fort St. George, 13 December 1872, OIOC, P/674.
35. Judith Walkowitz, *Prostitution and Victorian Society: Women, Class and the State* (Cambridge: Cambridge University Press, 1980); Linda Mahood, *The Magdalenes: Prostitution in the Nineteenth Century* (London: Routledge, 1990), 42 et seq.
36. Joyce Zonana, "The Sultan and the Slave: Feminist Orientalism and the Structure of *Jane Eyre,*" *Signs* 18, no. 3 (1993): 594.
37. Malek Alloula, *The Colonial Harem* (Minneapolis: University of Minnesota Press, 1986); Inderpal Grewal, *Home and Harem: Nation, Gender, Empire, and the Cultures of Travel* (Durham, NC: Duke University Press, 1996); Janaki Nair, "Uncovering the Zenana: Visions of Indian Womanhood in Englishwomen's Writings, 1813–1940," *Journal of Women's History* 2, no. 1 (1990): 8–34; Hanna Papanek and Gail Minault, *Separate Worlds: Studies of Purdah in South Asia* (Columbia, MO: South Asia Books, 1982); Sandhya Shetty, "(Dis)Locating Gender Space and Medical Discourse in Colonial India," *Genders* 20 (1994): 228.
38. Nair, "Uncovering the Zenana," 11.
39. Grewal, *Home and Harem,* 44–5.
40. Philippa Levine, "Consistent Contradictions: Prostitution and Protective Labour Legislation in Nineteenth-Century England," *Social History* 19, no. 1 (1994): 23.
41. Grewal, *Home and Harem,* 44–5.
42. Thomas, "Sanitation and Seeing," 160.
43. Shetty, "(Dis)Locating Gender Space," 208; Antoinette Burton, "Fearful Bodies into Disciplined Subjects: Pleasure, Romance, and the Family Drama of Colonial Reform in Mary Carpenter's *Six Months in India,*" *Signs* 20 (1995): 562. Lenore Manderson makes a parallel observation about colonial condemnations of Malay housing as dark, airless, and pathogenic

in "Shaping Reproductions: Maternity in Early Twentieth-Century Malaya," in *Maternities and Modernities: Colonial and Postcolonial Experiences in Asia and the Pacific*, ed. Kalpana Ram and Margaret Jolly (Cambridge: Cambridge University Press, 1998), 31.

44. Shetty, "(Dis)Locating Gender Space," 209.

45. Paul Scott, *The Day of the Scorpion* (New York: Morrow, 1978), 1.

46. Veena Oldenburg points out that the new European-style residential architecture that began to dominate in India as the nineteenth century wore on made the practice of purdah far harder to maintain, another example of the relationship between the spatial and the cultural: *The Making of Colonial Lucknow*, 124.

47. Nair, "Uncovering the Zenana," 22; Shetty, "(Dis)Locating Gender Space," 208.

48. Shetty, "(Dis)Locating Gender Space," 190; Maneesha Lal, "The Politics of Gender and Medicine in Colonial India: The Countess of Dufferin's Fund, 1885–1888," *Bulletin of the History of Medicine* 68 (1994): 38 et seq.

49. Warwick Anderson "Disease, Race, and Empire," *Bulletin of the History of Medicine* 70 (1996): 62–7; David Arnold, ed., *Imperial Medicine and Indigenous Societies* (Manchester: Manchester University Press, 1988).

50. *Annual Report on the Lock Hospitals of the Madras Presidency for the Year 1878* (Madras: Government Press, 1879), 10, OIOC, V/24/2287.

51. George Newton, *Medical Report of the Yokohama Lock Hospital for 1869* (Yokohama: *Japan Gazette* Office, 1870), 5, PRO, ADM125/16 (804).

52. Annual Report of the Colonial Surgeon, 1874, PRO, CO129/189 (13163).

53. Rules under Clause 7, Section 19 of Act XXII of 1864, rule 21, OIOC, P/1003.

54. *Fourth Annual Report on the Working of the Lock Hospitals in the Northwest Provinces and Oudh for the Year 1877* (Allahabad: n.p., 1878), 96, OIOC, V/24/2290.

55. G. Toynbee, Magistrate of Patna to Commander of Patna Division, 25 February 1878, OIOC, V/24/2292.

56. E. F. S. Chapman, Quartermaster General to Surgeon General of India, 18 October 1887, OIOC, L/MIL/7/13823.

57. Andrew, *Hong Kong Detective*, 93; Marquess of Ripon, Colonial Secretary to Governor C. B. H. Mitchell, 28 December 1894, PRO, CO882/6 (20340).

58. Colonel H. H. Parr, Consideration of Measures for Dealing with Venereal amongst British Troops, 23 March 1897, NAI, Home Proceedings A, Sanitary, May 1897.

59. Statement of Facts as to the Administration of the Indian Cantonment Acts and Regulations, 1892, OIOC, L/MIL/7/13839.

60. Alfred Keogh, "Introduction," *A Manual of Venereal Diseases* (London: Oxford Medical Publications/Henry Frowde/Hodder and Stoughton, 1907), 2.

61. Teltscher, *India Inscribed*, 145.

62. P. J. Marshall, "The White Town of Calcutta under the Rule of the East India Company," *Modern Asian Studies* 43 (2000): 307–32.

63. Dane Kennedy, *The Magic Mountains: Hill Stations and the British Raj* (Berkeley: University of California Press, 1996), 196.

64. Adjutant General to Madras Government, 10 July 1849, OIOC, F/4/2341. I thank Doug Peers for sharing this reference with me.

65. W. C. Macpherson, Officiating Chief Secretary to Government of Bengal to Secretary, Government of India, 15 September 1903, OIOC, P/6818.

66. Lieutenant. W. Lapsley to Principal Medical Officer, Oudh and Rohilkhand District, 7 October 1901, OIOC, P/6392.

67. Secretary, Department of External Affairs, Commonwealth of Australia to Secretary, Attorney General's Department, 25 March 1915, AAC, Series A1/1, item 1933/503.

68. *Women's Journal* 32 (7 September 1901): 36; Edwin Chadwick, *Report on the Sanitary Condition of the Labouring Population of Great Britain* (Edinburgh: Edinburgh University Press, 1965), 199.

69. Chinese Advisory Board, Penang, 18 July 1894, PRO, CO273/197 (18487).

70. Colonel H. R. Drew, General Officer Commanding, Cawnpore to Quartermaster General, Allahabad Division, 10 May 1871, OIOC, Mss. Eur. F.114/5 (13).

71. *Proceedings of the Council of the Governor General of India, 1889* (Calcutta: Office of the Superintendent of Government Printing, 1890), 216, 14 August 1889, comments of commander in chief, OIOC, V/9/25.

72. Report on Venereal Disease, Department of Trade and Customs Committee Concerning Causes of Death and Invalidity in the Commonwealth, 1916, 14, WL, JEB, E1/3.

73. T. Jacob, *Cantonments in India: Evolution and Growth* (New Delhi: Reliance Publishing House, 1994), 1; *Proceedings of the Council of the Governor General of India, 1895* (Calcutta: Office of the Superintendent of Government Printing, 1896), 43, 24 January 1895, OIOC, V/9/29.

74. David Arnold, *Colonizing the Body: State Medicine and Epidemic Disease in Nineteenth-Century India* (Berkeley: University of California Press, 1993), 299.

75. Quartermaster General to Colonel H. K. Burne, Secretary, Government of India, Military Department, 18 June 1875, OIOC, P/945.

76. H. L. Dampier, Officiating Secretary to the Government of Bengal to Secretary, Government of India, Military Department, 19 February 1868, quoting Sir Cecil Beadon, in Government of Bengal Despatch no. 6583, 5 December 1865, OIOC, P/435/52 (379).

77. No. 148 of 1893, Governor General and Council to Earl of Kimberley, India Secretary, 11 July 1893, OIOC, L/MIL/7/13843.

78. QPD. *Votes and Proceedings*, Eighth Parliament, 1879, Report of W. Hobbs, Medical Officer to Colonial Secretary, 10 March 1879, 1273.

79. Queensland, *Debates of the Legislative Council and the Legislative Assembly*, Third Session, Eighteenth Parliament. vol. 108, 13 September 1911, 1127, Hon C. F. Nielson.

80. *New South Wales Legislative Assembly Votes and Proceedings*, Ninth Parliament, vol. 7, 898, Inspector General of Police to Under Secretary, Colonial Secretary's Department, Government of New South Wales, 21 May 1878.

81. Report of Surgeon General of Bombay on Contagious Diseases Act, 1887, 6, OIOC, V/24/2289.

82. R. Simson, Secretary to Government of Northwest Provinces to E. C. Bayley, Secretary, Government of India, Home Department, 17 March 1869, OIOC, P/436/2 (394).

83. Charges against the Cantonment Act 1899, minute, George White, 1 July 1893, OIOC, Mss. Eur. D.558/49; also in OIOC, L/MIL/7/13843.

84. Constable Driscoll, Roma Street Police (Brisbane) to Sub Inspector, Roma Street Police, 14 February 1918, QSA, A/21956.

85. Captain A. M. Muir, Cantonment Magistrate, Secunderabad to First Assistant Resident, Hyderabad, 10 April 1888, OIOC, P/3195.

86. John Cowen, "Report of A Visit to the Two Great Brothel Areas of Singapore in the Autumn of 1915," 10, PRO, CO273/452 (60716), reprinted in an amended and abridged version in *The Shield*, 3rd series, 1, no. 3 (October 1916): 184–5.

87. R. H. Vincent, Acting Commissioner of Police, Bombay to Under Secretary to Government, Judicial Department, 16 May 1894, OIOC, L/P& J/6/375 (1083/1894).

88. Vincent to Under Secretary to Government, Judicial Department, 16 May 1894, OIOC, L/P & J/6/375 (1083/1894).

89. *Annual Report on the Military Lock Hospitals of the Madras Presidency for the Year 1879* (Madras: Government Press, 1880), 9, OIOC, V/24/2287.

90. Mary Anne Jebb, "The Lock Hospitals Experiment: Europeans, Aborigines and Venereal Disease," *Studies in Western Australian History* 8 (1984): 69; Milton Lewis, "Sexually Transmitted Diseases in Australia from the Late Eighteenth to the Late Twentieth Century," in *Sex, Disease, and Society: A Comparative History of Sexually Transmitted Diseases and HIV/AIDS in Asia and the Pacific*, ed. Milton Lewis, Scott Bamber, and Michael Waugh (Westport, CT: Greenwood Press, 1997), 253. Similar resort to containment and isolation were typical in plague-ridden India in the 1890s, and in the Belgian Congo when sleeping sickness hit early in the twentieth century. See Maryinez Lyons, "From 'Death Camps' to *Cordon Sanitaire:* The Development of Sleeping Sickness Policy in the Uele District of the Belgian Congo, 1903–1914," *Journal of African History* 26, no. 1 (1985) 69–91; Mark Harrison, "Towards A Sanitary Utopia? Professional Visions and Public Health in India, 1880–1914," *South Asia Research* 10, no. 1 (1990): 24 et seq.; Rajnarayan Chandavarkar, "Plague, Panic and Epidemic Politics in India, 1896–1914," in *Epidemics and Ideas: Essays in the Historical Perception of Pestilence*, ed. Terence Ranger and Paul Slack (Cambridge: Cambridge University Press, 1992), 203–40.

91. Annual Report of the Chief Protector of Aborigines, 1915, QSA, A/58651. The hospital was not built until the late 1920s.

92. Jebb, "The Lock Hospitals Experiment," 75–6, 79.

93. Report on the Lock Hospitals in British Burma for the Year 1873, OIOC, V/24/2296.

94. Annual Medical Report on the Lock Hospitals, 1877, extracted in Madras Presidency Reports, OIOC, V/24/2287.
95. F. C. Gates, Officiating Chief Secretary to Government of Burma to Secretary, Government of India, Home Department, 19 July 1905, OIOC, P/7326.
96. OIOC, L/MIL/7/13921, 1901–2.
97. Annual Medical Returns of the Civil Hospitals for 1873, *Proceedings of the Legislative Council of the Straits Settlements, 1876* (Singapore: Government Printing Office, 1877), lxxxv; Home Office Correspondence, 1885–1908, QSA, COL/A360 (3279).
98. John Pope Hennessy to Michael Hicks-Beach, Colonial Secretary, 18 March 1879, PRO, CO129/184 (6991).
99. Internal Colonial Office memorandum, George Johnston to Mr. Bramston, 8 June 1894, PRO, CO129/265 (9874).
100. W. E. Parry-Okeden, Commissioner of Police to Under Secretary, Home Department, 14 December 1897, QSA, HOM/A15 (15952).
101. W. C. Macpherson, Officiating Chief Secretary to Government of Bengal to Secretary, Government of India, 15 September 1903, OIOC, P/6818.
102. Lieutenant W. Lapsley to Principal Medical Officer, Oudh and Rohilkhand District, 7 October 1901, OIOC, P/6392.
103. Lansdowne and Council to Lord Kimberley, 8 November 1893, no. 294 of 1893, OIOC, L/MIL/7/13845.
104. Cantonment Hospital Reports, OIOC, L/MIL/7/13921.
105. Quartermaster General, Circular Memorandum no. 14, 9 August 1907, OIOC, L/MIL/7/13890.
106. *General Report and Statistics of Venereal Diseases among British and Indian Troops in India together with a Summary of the Reports on Cantonment Hospitals, 1907,* 14 August 1908, OIOC, L/MIL/7/13887.
107. Cantonment Code, 1909, OIOC, L/MIL/7/13894.
108. Robert Hall, "Aborigines, the Army and the Second World War in Northern Australia," *Aboriginal History* 4, no. 1 (1980): 87.
109. Colonel P. S. Lumsden to Secretary to Government of India, 4 September 1871, OIOC, P/1003.
110. Surgeon Major J. A. Smith to Deputy Surgeon General, Indian Forces, 6 January 1877, OIOC, P/1003.
111. Annual Report of the Colonial Surgeon, 1879, PRO, CO129/203 (20349).
112. Internal Colonial Office Memorandum, G. W. Johnson, 27 October 1887, PRO, CO273/146 (20983).
113. Report of the Sub-Committee of the Madras Missionary Conference, 19 December 1893, OIOC, P/4594.
114. Major General W. Galbraith, Commanding Quetta District to Principal Medical Officer, Bombay Command, 4 September 1897, OIOC, L/MIL/7/13877.
115. Dorgan, "Prevention of Venereal Disease," 124.
116. Sachiko Sone, "The Karayuki-San of Asia 1868–1938: The Role of Prostitutes Overseas in Japanese Economic and Social Development," *Review of Indonesian and Malaysian Affairs* 26, no. 2 (1992): 53; Yamazaki Tomoko, *Sandakan Brothel No. 8: An Episode in the History of Lower-Class Japanese Women* (Armonk, NY: M. E. Sharpe, 1999).
117. Colonel J. Emerson, Cantonment Magistrate, Dinapore to Officer Commanding Dinapore, 28 July 1875, OIOC, P/1003.
118. Court of Judicature, Fort William, Bengal, 2 December 1875, OIOC, P/1003.
119. Circular Memorandum of Quartermaster General, September 1876, opinion of G. C. Paul, Officiating Advocate General, Calcutta, 13 April 1876, OIOC, P/1003.
120. W. S. Halsey to Commander, Fourth Division, Allahabad, 27 July 1870, NAI, Home Proceedings, Public Consultations A.
121. E. F. Chapman, Quartermaster General to Chief Secretary to Government of the Northwest Provinces and Oudh, 18 October 1887, OIOC, L/MIL/7/13823, also at NAI, Home Proceedings, Sanitary Department, January 1888, and at OIOC, P/3248.
122. *Fifth Annual Report on the Working of the Lock Hospitals in the Northwest Provinces and Oudh for the Year 1878* (Allahabad, n.p., 1879), 22, OIOC, V/24/2290.
123. HC, *SP,* 118 of 1880, *Copy of Report of the Commissioners appointed by His Excellency John Pope Hennessy to Inquire into the Working of the Contagious Diseases Ordinance, 1867,* 20.

124. Yeoh, *Contesting Space,* 37; also see Kennedy, *The Magic Mountains,* on the divide at hill stations, 191.

125. James F. Warren, *Ah Ku and Karayuki-San: Prostitution in Singapore 1870–1940* (Singapore: Oxford University Press, 1993), 49.

126. HC, *SP,* 118 of 1880, *Report of the Commissioners . . . to Inquire into the Working of the Contagious Diseases Ordinance,* 21.

127. NSWPD Second Series, Third Session 1908, vol. 31, 3 November 1908, 2153, McGowen, MLA for Redfern.

128. Major W.C. Street, Secretary to Chief Commissioner, British Burma to Officiating Secretary, Government of India, 11 June 1877, OIOC, P/1003.

129. Florence E. Garnham, *A Report on the Social and Moral Condition of Indians in Fiji, Being the Outcome of an Investigation set on Foot by Combined Women's Organisations of Australia* (Sydney: The Kingston Press, 1918), 14

130. Ibid., 17.

131. Neil Smith and Anne Godlewska, "Introduction: Critical Histories of Geography," in *Geography and Empire* (Oxford: Basil Blackwell, 1994), 1–3.

132. Morgan, *Place Matters,* 4.

133. McClintock, *Imperial Leather,* 72.

Epilogue

1. The military vocabulary for medical success has a long history. A cursory glance at the medical history shelves in any library will produce dozens of titles such as *A Destroying Angel: The Conquest of Smallpox in Colonial Boston* (1974); *Sword of Pestilence: The New Orleans Yellow Fever Epidemic of 1853* (1966); *Man Against Disease* (1964); *The Conquest of Epidemic Disease* (1943) and so on, ad nauseam. With the return in the late twentieth century of many diseases hitherto thought eradicated in the west, and with the ongoing nature of AIDS research, the tide of optimism has waned somewhat in recent works. Deborah Lupton, *Medicine as Culture: Illness, Disease and the Body in Western Societies* (London: Sage, 1994), 61–4; Catherine Waldby, *AIDS and the Body Politic: Biomedicine and Sexual Difference* (London: Routledge, 1996), 2–4, 52; and Paula A. Treichler, *How To Have Theory in an Epidemic: Cultural Chronicles of AIDS* (Durham, NC: Duke University Press, 1999), 31–3 all comment on the frequency of the language of warfare in modern medical writings.

2. "Cayman Churches Want Anti-Gay Law," *Associated Press Online* (February 4, 2001); Mark Fineman, "Repeal of Caymans' Anti-Gay Law Strains 'Partnership' With Britain," *Los Angeles Times* (4 March 2001).

3. Manelo Balve, "Angry but Resigned, Islanders Ready for Britain to Scrap Anti-Gay Laws," *Associated Press,* (17 November 2000).

4. M. Jacqui Alexander, "Redrafting Morality: The Postcolonial State and the Sexual Offences Bill of Trinidad and Tobago," in *Third World Women and the Politics of Feminism,* ed. Chandra Talpade Mohanty, Ann Russo, and Lourdes Torres (Bloomington: Indiana University Press, 1991), 136.

5. Evelynn M. Hammonds, "Toward a Genealogy of Black Female Sexuality: The Problematic of Silence," in *Feminist Genealogies, Colonial Legacies, Democratic Futures,* ed. M. Jacqui Alexander and Chandra Talpade Mohanty (New York: Routledge, 1997), 170.

6. Frank Mort, *Dangerous Sexualities: Medico-Moral Politics in England since 1830* 2nd ed. (London and New York: Routledge, 2000), 3–4; Jeffrey Weeks, *Making Sexual History* (Cambridge: Polity, 2000), 133.

7. The few who have acknowledged its centrality are mentioned frequently in this study: Arnold Kaminsky and Kenneth Ballhatchet for India; Norman Miners and Henry Lethbridge for Hong Kong; and James F. Warren for Singapore.

Bibliography

Archival and Manuscript Sources

Australia

Australian Archives, Canberra

Federal papers.

Australian War Memorial, Canberra

World War I official papers.
Papers of C. E. W. Bean

Mitchell Library, New South Wales

Dr. Richard Arthur papers.
Governor's Despatches to the Secretary of State for the Colonies, 1843
Rose Scott papers

Queensland State Archives

Chief Protector of Aboriginals
Colonial Secretary's Office
Governor's Office
Home Secretary's Department
Home Secretary's Office
Police Department. Commissioner's Office
Works Department

Hong Kong

Public Record Office

Colonial Secretary's Office

India

National Archives of India

Home Proceedings
Native Newspaper Reports

United Kingdom

British Library Manuscript Collections, London

Sir Edward Hamilton Correspondence
Henry Campbell-Bannerman papers
Florence Nightingale papers
Lord Ripon papers

Friend's House, London

Friends' Association for Abolishing the State Regulation of Vice papers

Liverpool Record Office

Corporation Health Sub-Committee papers

National Army Museum, London

Lord Frederick Roberts papers
Scotch Military Chaplain, *"Perils in the City": Plain Words to Soldiers about to Move to A City Station*
    Agra: Secunderabad Orphanage Press, n.d. [c. 1850]. Archives 7208–16.
Experiences of A Soldier, 1891. Archives 7008–13.

Oriental and India Office Collections (British Library)

(a) Government of India papers
Administration Reports
Board's Collections
Council of India
India and Bengal Dispatches
Dispatches from Secretary of State
Judicial and Public Department
Military Collections
Military Consultations
Proceedings of Government
Revenue Letters/Statistics and Commerce

(b) European Manuscripts
Cross papers
Curzon papers
Dufferin papers
Elgin papers
Fergusson papers
Hamilton papers
Lansdowne papers
Lawrence papers
Napier papers

Northbrook papers
Roberts papers
White papers

Public Record Office, London

Admiralty papers
Cabinet papers
Colonial Office papers, Ceylon series
Colonial Office papers, Hong Kong series
Colonial Office papers, South Africa series
Colonial Office papers, Straits Settlements series
Colonial Office papers, Wei Hai Wei series
Foreign Office papers
Home Office papers
Metropolitan Police papers
Ministry of Health papers
War Office papers

Rhodes House, Oxford

British and Foreign Anti-Slavery and Aborigines Protection Society papers
MSS. Brit. Emp. s. G. 370
MSS. Brit. Emp. s. 19 6/1
John Pope Hennessy papers, Watts Collection
MSS. Ind. Ocn. 320
MSS. Ind. Ocn. s. 306

Royal College of Surgeons, London

London Lock Hospital and Asylum records

Sheffield City Archives

Henry J. Wilson papers
House of Help records

University College, London

Karl Pearson Collection
Men and Women's Club papers

Wellcome Institute for the History of Medicine

Royal Army Medical Corps Archives
Parkes Pamphlet Collection
Contemporary Medical Archives Centre, Medical Women's Federation, 1897

Women's Library, London

Association for Moral and Social Hygiene papers
British Committee of the International Abolitionist Federation papers
Butler Autograph Letter Collection
International Abolitionist Federation papers
Josephine Butler Collection
Lancashire and Cheshire Association for the Abolition of the State Regulation of Vice papers
National Vigilance Association papers
H. J. Wilson Collection

Printed Primary Materials
Parliamentary Documents/Acts/Official Records
Australia

(a) New South Wales

Legislative Assembly. *Votes and Proceedings*, 1887–1880.
Parliamentary Debates, 1882.
Journal of the Legislative Council of New South Wales, 1899.
Parliamentary Debates, 1906 Crimes (Girls' Protection) Bill.
Parliamentary Debates, 1908.
Votes and Proceedings of the Legislative Assembly during the Second Session of 1908.
Legislative Assembly, *Joint Volumes of Paper Presented to the Legislative Council and the Legislative Assembly*, 1911–12.
Legislative Assembly, *Minutes of Evidence taken before the Select Committee on the Prevalence of Venereal Disease*, 1915.
Police Department. *Annual Reports*, 1863, 1871, 1878, 1883–1902, 1904, 1906, 1908, 1909–12.
Sydney Morning Herald, Report of Proceedings in New South Wales Legislative Assembly, 29 May 1875, 8 December 1875, 13 January 1876, 5 February 1876, 21 February 1876, 23 February 1876, 25 March 1876.

(b) Queensland

Parliamentary Debates, 1867.
Parliamentary Debates, 1868.
Parliamentary Debates, Legislative Assembly, *Votes and Proceedings*, 1879.
Journals of the Legislative Council, 1879.
Official Record of the Debates of the Legislative Assembly, 1884.
Parliamentary Debates, Legislative Assembly, 1884.
Official Record of the Debates of the Legislative Assembly, 1886.
Parliamentary Debates, Legislative Assembly, *Votes and Proceedings*, 1886.
Official Record of the Debates of the Legislative Council and the Legislative Assembly, 1911–1912.
Act. No. 40 *An Act for the Prevention of Contagious Diseases*, 5 February 1868.

(c) South Australia

Proceedings of Parliament. *Final Report of the Royal Commission on the Aborigines*, 1916.

(d) Victoria

Legislative Assembly, *Bills Introduced*, 1878.
Act DCXXXI. *An Act for the Conservation of Public Health*, 2 December 1878.
Act. No. 2858 *An Act relating to Venereal Diseases*, 28 December 1916.

Gibraltar

Ordinance to Make Certain Offences Punishable on Summary Conviction, 1885.

Hong Kong

Hong Kong Government Gazette, 18 May 1889.
Hong Kong Hansard, 1892–93, 1893–94, 1898–99, 1910, 1911, 1914, 1917.
Hong Kong Legislative Council Sessional Papers, 1886, 1887, 1887–88, 1889, 1890, 1891, 1892, 1893, 1894, 1896.
Hong Kong Report of the Committee constituted in accordance with the directions of His Excellency the Governor of Hong Kong contained in His Excellency's Letter to the Hon. Colonial Secretary. Hong Kong: Noronha and Co., 1938.
Hong Kong Report of the Special Committee connected with the Bill for the Incorporation of the Po Leung Kuk, or Society for the Protection of Women and Girls. Hong Kong: Noronha and Co., 1893.

India

(a) India

Proceedings of the Council of the Governor General of India, 1864. Calcutta: Military Orphan Press, 1865.

Proceedings of the Council of the Governor General in India, 1868. Calcutta: Office of the Superintendent of Government Printing, 1869.

Report on Measures Adopted for Sanitary Improvements in India from June 1869 to June 1870; together with abstracts of sanitary reports for 1867 forwarded from Bengal, Madras and Bombay. London: HMSO, 1870.

Report on Measures Adopted for Sanitary Improvements in India, from June 1871 to June 1872. London: HMSO, 1872.

Report on Measures adopted for Sanitary Improvements in India from June 1872 to June 1873. London: HMSO, 1873.

Cantonment Regulations framed under Act XXII of 1864. Calcutta: Superintendent of Government Printing, 1881.

Circular Memorandum No. 21. 17 June 1886.

Cantonment Regulations framed under Act XXII of 1864 and Act III of 1880. Calcutta: Superintendent of Government Printing, 1887.

Proceedings of the Council of the Governor General of India, 1888. Calcutta: Office of the Superintendent of Government Printing, 1889.

Proceedings of the Council of the Governor General of India, 1889. Calcutta: Office of the Superintendent of Government Printing, 1890.

Report of the Special Commission appointed to Enquire into the Working of the Cantonment Regulations regarding Infectious and Contagious Diseases. Simla: Government Printing Office, 1893.

Proceedings of the Council of the Governor-General of India, 1895. Calcutta: Office of the Superintendent of Government Printing, 1896.

Proceedings of the Council of the Governor General of India, 1897. Calcutta: Office of the Superintendent of Government Printing, 1898.

General Report and Statistics of Venereal Disease among British and Native Troops in India, together with Summary of the Reports on Cantonment Hospitals during the Year 1906. 1907.

Cantonment Manual, 1909. Calcutta: Army Headquarters, Quartermaster General's Division, 24 January 1909.

General Report and Statistics of Venereal Diseases among British and Indian Troops in India during the year 1908. 1909.

Annual Report of Cantonment Hospitals and Dispensaries for the Year 1911. N.p. 1912.

General Report and Statistics of Venereal Diseases amongst British Troops in India during the year 1912. 1913.

Proceedings of the Council of the Governor General in India, 1914. Calcutta: Office of the Superintendent of Government Printing, 1915.

(b) Bombay

General Report on the Administration of the Bombay Presidency 1871–2. Bombay: Bombay Secretariat Office, 1872.

Martin, T. E. P. *Sketch of the Medical History of the Native Army of Bombay for the Year 1871.* Bombay: Education Society's Press, 1872.

Sketch of the Medical History of the Native Army of Bombay for the Year 1873. Bombay: Government Central Press, 1874.

Medical History of the European Troops in the Bombay Command for the Year 1885. Bombay: Education Society's Press, 1886.

Report of the Prostitution Committee. Bombay. 19 April 1922.

(c) Bengal

Annual Report of the Administration of the Bengal Presidency. Calcutta: Bengal Secretariat Office, 1868.

Annual Report of the Administration of the Bengal Presidency. Calcutta: Bengal Secretariat Office, 1869.

Annual Report of the Administration of the Bengal Presidency. Calcutta: Bengal Secretariat Office, 1870.

Annual Report of the Administration of the Bengal Presidency. Calcutta: Bengal Secretariat Office, 1872.

Medical and Sanitary Reports of the Native Army of Bengal for the Year 1872. Calcutta: Office of the Superintendent of Government Printing, 1874.

E. McKellar. *Medical and Sanitary Report of the Native Army of Bengal for the Year 1873.* (Calcutta: Office of the Superintendent of Government Printing, 1874).

Medical and Sanitary Report of the Native Army of Bengal for the Year 1874. Calcutta: Office of the Superintendent of Government Printing, 1876.

Medical and Sanitary Report of the Native Army of Bengal for the Year 1878. Calcutta: Office of the Superintendent of Government Printing, 1880.

(d) Madras

Medical and Sanitary Reports of the Native Army of Madras for the Year 1873. Madras: Office of the Superintendent of Government Printing, 1875.

Annual Report on the Lock Hospitals of the Madras Presidency for the Year 1878. Madras: Government Press, 1879.

Annual Report on the Military Lock Hospitals of the Madras Presidency for the Year 1879. Madras: Government Press, 1880.

Annual Report on the Military Lock Hospitals of the Madras Presidency for the Year 1886. Madras: Government Press, 1887.

Annual Report on the Military Lock Hospitals of the Madras Presidency for the Year 1887. Madras: Government Press, 1888.

(e) Northwest Provinces

Fourth Annual Report on the Working of the Lock Hospitals in the Northwest Provinces and Oudh for the Year 1877. Allahabad, 1878.

Fifth Annual Report on the Working of the Lock Hospitals in the Northwest Provinces and Oudh for the year 1878. Allahabad, 1879.

Sixth Annual Report on the Working of the Lock Hospitals in the Northwestern Provinces and Oudh for the year 1879. Allahabad, 1880.

Eighth Annual Report on the Working of the Lock Hospitals in the Northwest Provinces and Oudh for the Year 1881. Allahabad, 1882.

Tenth Annual Report on the Working of the Lock Hospitals in the Northwest Provinces and Oudh for the Year 1883. Allahabad, 1884.

Twelfth Annual Report on the Working of the Lock Hospitals in the Northwest Provinces and Oudh for the year 1885. Allahabad, 1886.

(f) Punjab

Report on Voluntary Venereal Hospitals in the Punjab for the Year 1887. Lahore: Civil and Military Gazette Press, 1888.

Report on Voluntary Venereal Hospitals in the Punjab for the Year 1888. Lahore: Civil and Military Gazette Press, 1889.

Report on Voluntary Venereal Hospitals in the Punjab for the Year 1889. Lahore: Civil and Military Gazette Press, 1890.

South Africa

Parliamentary Papers. Cape of Good Hope. *Report of the Select Committee appointed by the Legislative Council on Medical Establishments.* 1871.

Report of the Select Committee on the Contagious Diseases Act Amendment Bill [C.B. 8–95]. 1895.

Report of the Select Committee on the Contagious Diseases Acts. 1906.

Straits Settlements

Proceedings of the Legislative Council of the Straits Settlements 1875. Singapore: Government Printing Office, 1876.

Proceedings of the Legislative Council of the Straits Settlements, 1876. Singapore: Government Printing Office, 1877.

Report of the Committee appointed to enquire into the Working of Ordinance XXIII of 1870, Commonly called the Contagious Diseases Ordinance. N.p., n.d. [1877].

Annual Report on Chinese Protectorate, Singapore and Penang, 1887. Singapore: Government Printing Office, 1888.

Proceedings of the Legislative Council of the Straits Settlements, 1890. Singapore: Government Printing Office, 1891.

Hare, G. T. *A Text Book of Documentary Chinese Selected and Designed for the Special Use of Members of the Civil Service of the Straits Settlements and the Protected Native States.* Singapore: Government Printing Office, 1894.

Straits Settlements Annual Reports for the Year 1897. Singapore: Government Printing Office, 1898.

Proceedings of the Legislative Council of the Straits Settlements, 1897. Singapore: Government Printing Office, 1898.

Proceedings of the Legislative Council of the Straits Settlements, 1898. Singapore: Government Printing Office, 1899.

Report of the Committee appointed by the Governor of the Straits Settlements to enquire and report on Certain Measures made by the Secretary of State for the Colonies as to Measures to be Adopted with Regard to Contagious Diseases and Brothels with a View to Checking the Spread of Venereal Diseases, 1898. Singapore: Government Printing Office, 1899.

Peacock W. *Annual Report of the Protector of Chinese, Straits Settlements, for the Year 1914.* Singapore: Government Printing Office, 1915.

United Kingdom

(3184) XIX 1863. *Report of the Commissioners appointed to enquire into the Sanitary State of the Army in India.*

An Act for the Prevention of Contagious Diseases at certain Naval and Military Stations. 29 July 1864. 27 & 28 Vic. c. 85.

Skey Committee. *Report and Minutes of Evidence.* 1864.

An Act to amend the Contagious Diseases Act, 1866. 11 August 1869. 32 & 33 Vic. c. 96.

(4031) XXXVII 1867–8. *Report of the Committee appointed to enquire into the Pathology and Treatment of the Venereal Diseases.*

Act No. XXVI of 1868. An Act to enable Municipalities to provide for Lock-Hospitals. [India].

(306) VII 1868–9. *Report from the Select Committee on Contagious Diseases Act (1866) together with the Proceedings of the Committee, Minutes of Evidence.*

(4127) XXXII 1868–9. *Eleventh Report of the Medical Officer of the Privy Council.*

[C. 408 XIX] 1871. *Report of the Royal Commission upon the Administration and Operation of the Contagious Diseases Act.*

(260) 1877. *Workhouse Unions, England and Wales (Diseases). Returns of the General Diseases and Venereal Diseases from the Workhouse of each Union in England and Wales, during the First Week in January 1876.*

(360) 1877. *Navy (Contagious Diseases). Return showing the Number of Cases of Venereal Disease in Her Majesty's Ships and Vessels stationed at Five Home Ports, at which the Contagious Diseases Acts have been and are in operation, and the Number of Cases in Her Majesty's Ships and Vessels at Five Home Ports, at which the Contagious Diseases Acts have never been applied, from the Year 1860 to the Year 1875.*

[C. 2415] 1879. *Report on Sanitary Measures in India in 1877-78.* Vol. XI; *Memorandum of the Army Sanitary Commission on the Report on Lock Hospitals of the Madras Presidency for 1877.*

118 of 1880. *Copy of Report of the Commissioners appointed by His Excellency John Pope Hennessy to Inquire into the Working of the Contagious Diseases Ordinance, 1867.*

[C. 3093] 1881. *Correspondence relating to the Working of the Contagious Diseases Ordinances of the Colony of Hong Kong.*

[C. 3185] 1882. *Correspondence respecting the Alleged Existence of Chinese Slavery in Hong Kong. Report of the Select Committee on the Contagious Diseases Acts.*

(200) 1883. *Copy of, or Extracts from Correspondence between the Government of India and the Secretary of State in Council upon the Subject of the Contagious Diseases Acts and their Repeal.*

1883. *A Bill to provide for the Detention in Certain Hospitals of Persons Affected with Contagious Diseases, and to repeal the Contagious Diseases Acts, 1866 to 1869.*

(247) 1886. *Contagious Diseases Ordinances (British Colonies).*

(20) 1887. *Contagious Diseases Ordinances (British Colonies).*

(196) 1887. *Contagious Diseases Acts (Egypt).*

(347) 1887 *Contagious Diseases Ordinances (Colonies).*

[C. 61. LXII. 903.] 1887. *East India (Contagious Diseases Acts).*

(107) 1888. *East India (Contagious Diseases).*

(158) 1888. *East India (Contagious Diseases).*

(180) 1888. *Despatch to India.*

(220) 1888. *Copy of the Minutes of Dissent by certain Members of the Council of India from the Despatch addressed by the Secretary of State to the Government of India respecting the Contagious Diseases Acts.*

(59) 1889. *Contagious Diseases Ordinances (Colonies).*

(241) 1890. *East India (Cantonments Act).*

(242) 1890. *Contagious Diseases Ordinances (Colonies).*

[C. -5897-14] 1890. *Colonial Possessions. Hong Kong. Further Report on the Blue Book for 1888.*

(339) 1893. *Army (Men Available for India Service).*

[C-7217] 1893. *East India (Cantonments Act).*

Selections from Despatches Addressed to the Several Governments in India by the Secretary of State in Council. London: Eyre and Spottiswoode for HMSO, 1894.

[C. 7148] 1893. *Report of the Committee appointed by Secretary of State for India to Inquire into the Rules, Regulations and Practice in the Indian Cantonments and elsewhere in India with regard to Prostitution and the Treatment of Venereal Diseases.*

(146) 1894. *Contagious Diseases Regulations (Perak and Malay States).*

(147) 1894. *Contagious Diseases Ordinances (Colonies).*

(318) 1895. *East India (Cantonments Act).*

(153) 1896. *Army (Average Numbers at Home and Abroad).*

[Cd. 8237]. 1896. *Report on Sanitary Measures in India in 1894–5.*

(140) 1897. *Army (Average Numbers at Home and Abroad).*

(217) 1897. *Return of the Amount of All Classes of Venereal Disease (including simple Venereal Ulcers) for all Stations where the Act was in force, from 1864 to 1883; And, similar Return for the same Stations, from 1886 to 1895.*

(415) 1897. *East India Contagious Diseases No. 7.*

[C. 8379] 1897. *East India (Contagious Diseases) No. 1. Report of A Departmental Committee on the Prevalence of Venereal Disease among the British Troops in India.*

[C. 8382] 1897. *East India (Contagious Diseases) No. 2. Memorandum by the Sanitary Commission and Correspondence regarding the Prevalence of Venereal Diseases among the British Troops in India.*

[C. 8402] 1897. *East India (Contagious Diseases) No. 3. Representations received by the Secretary of State for India from the Royal College of Surgeons of England and the Royal College of Physicians, relative to the Prevalence of Venereal Disease among the British Troops in India.*

[C. 8401] 1897. *East India (Contagious Diseases) No. 4. Copy of A Despatch to the Government of India regarding the Measures to be Adopted for Checking the Spread of Venereal Diseases among the British Troops in India.*

[C. 8495] 1897. *East India (Contagious Diseases) No. 5. Memorials addressed to the Secretary of State for India on the subject of the Instructions contained in his Despatch of 26th March 1897, for improving the health of the British Troops in India.*

[C. 8538] 1897. *East India (Contagious Diseases) No. 6. Further Correspondence regarding the Measures to be Adopted for Checking the Spread of Venereal Diseases among the British Troops in India.*

[C. 8892] 1898. *Memorial addressed to the Secretary of State for India on the subject of Measures recently Adopted for dealing with Contagious Disease in the Indian Army.*

[C. 8919] 1898. *East India (Cantonment Act and Regulations).*

[C. 9019] 1898. *Army Memorandum.*

[C. 9025] 1898. *East India (Contagious Diseases) No. II.*

[C. 9017] 1898. *East India (Cantonment Regulations).*

(81) 1898. *Army and Military Pamphlets showing the Conditions of Service in the Army and Militia Respectively.*

[C. 9448] 1899. *East India (Cantonment Regulations)*.

[C. 9549] 1899. *Army Sanitary Commission*.

[C. 9523] 1899. *Correspondence regarding the Measures to be Adopted for Checking the Spread of Venereal Disease*.

[Cd. 197] 1900. *The Contagious Diseases Law*.

[Cd. 618] 1901. *Report on Recent Improvements at Gibraltar in respect of Sanitary and Other Matters*.

(249) 1903. *India*.

[Cd. 1850] 1903. *Report on Sanitary Measures in India in 1901–02*.

[Cd. 2175] 1904. *Report of the Inter-Departmental Committee on Physical Deterioration*.

1904. Advisory Board for Army Medical Services. *First Report. The Treatment of Venereal Disease and Scabies in the Army*. London: HMSO.

[Cd. 2298] 1904. *Report on Sanitary Measures in India in 1902–03*.

[Cd. 2766] 1905. *Report on Sanitary Measures in India in 1903–04*.

1906. *The Treatment of Venereal Disease and Scabies in the Army. Final Report*. London: HMSO.

[Cd. 3152] 1906. *Report on Sanitary Measures in India in 1904–05*.

[Cd. 2903] 1906. *Further Correspondence relating to the Measures Adopted for Checking the Spread of Venereal Disease*.

(149) LIX 1907. *Statement exhibiting the Moral and Material Progress and Condition of India during the year 1905–06*.

[Cd. 4314] 1908. *Report on Sanitary Measures in India in 1906–07*.

(38) 1909. *Return to An Address of the House of Commons, 24 June 1908*.

[Cd. 4762] 1909. *Report on Sanitary Measures in India in 1907–08*.

[Cd. 5245] 1910. *Report on Sanitary Measures in India in 1908–09*.

[Cd. 5770] 1911. *Report on Sanitary Measures in India in 1909–10*.

[Cd. 6373] 1912. *Report on Sanitary Measures in India in 1910–11*.

1913. *Report on Venereal Diseases*. London: HMSO.

[Cd. 7113] 1913. *Report on Sanitary Measures in India in 1911–12*.

[Cd. 7519] 1914. *Report on Sanitary Measures in India in 1912–13*.

[Cd. 8087] 1915. *Report on Sanitary Measures in India in 1913–14*.

[Cd. 8189]. 1916. *Final Report of the Commissioners, Royal Commission on Venereal Diseases*.

(142) 1918. *Report from the Joint Select Committee of the House of Lords and the House of Commons on the Criminal Law Amendment Bill and Sexual Offences Bill*.

Hansard: House of Commons,
13 June 1894.
25 April 1917.
17 May 1917.
19 June 1918.
17 October 1918.
28 January 1930.

Hansard: House of Lords,
14 June 1844.
29 July 1855.
11 April 1918.

Primary Non-Official Materials

A Doomed Iniquity: An Authoritative Condemnation of State Regulation of Vice from France, Germany and Belgium. London: Federation for the Abolition of the State Regulation of Vice, 1896.

"A Victory in India: The Cantonment System Crumbling," *The Shield* 2, no. 2 (February–March 1918): 79–85.

A.N. [Neilans, Alison]. *A Warning To Men Going Abroad*. London: Association of Moral and Social Hygiene, n.d. [1916].

Amos, Sheldon. *A Comparative Survey of Laws in Force for the Prohibition, Regulation and Licensing of Vice in England and Other Countries*, London: Stevens and Son, 1877.

Anderson, John. *The Colonial Office List for 1894 comprising Historical and Statistical Information respecting the Colonial Dependencies of Great Britain*. London: Harrison and Sons Ltd., 1894.

————. *The Colonial Office List for 1897 comprising Historical and Statistical Information respecting the Colonial Dependencies of Great Britain.* London: Harrison and Sons Ltd., 1897.

Anderson, John and Sidney Webb. *The Colonial Office List for 1888 comprising Historical and Statistical Information respecting the Colonial Dependencies of Great Britain.* London: Harrison and Sons, Ltd., 1888.

Andrew, Elizabeth W. and Katharine C. Bushnell, *Recent Researches into the Japanese Slave Trade in California.* N.p., n.d. [1907].

————. *Heathen Slaves and Christian Rulers.* Oakland, CA: Messiah's Advocate, 1907.

————. *The Queen's Daughters in India.* London: Morgan and Scott, 1899.

Anon. *Sir John Pope-Hennessy, K.C.M.G., Governor and Commander in Chief of Hong Kong on the Contagious Diseases Ordinance in that Colony.* London: Frederick C. Banks, 1882.

————. *Hong Kong Refuge for Women and Girls,* N.p., n.d., [?1906].

Annual Report of the Army Temperance Association for the Official Year 1892–3, N.p., n.d.

Annual Report of the Association for Moral and Social Hygiene, 1918. London: AMSH, 1919.

Arthur, Richard. "An Address delivered to the Officers of the Australian Imperial Force." *Medical Journal of Australia* 20 (May 1916): 411–14.

————. *Some Aspects of the Venereal Problem.* Sydney: Australasian White Cross League, n.d. [?1916].

————. *Report on the Existing Facilities for the Treatment of Venereal Diseases in New South Wales, with Recommendations for their Extension and Improvement.* Sydney: Government Printer, 1919.

Ashburn, P. M. "Factors Making For A Low Venereal Record in the Army in the United States." *Military Surgeon* 47 (1920): 208–13.

Barrett, James W. *The Australian Army Medical Corps in Egypt: An Illustrated and Detailed Account of the Early Organisation and Work of the Australian Medical Units in Egypt in 1914–1915.* London: H.K. Lewis and Co. 1918.

————. *A Vision of the Possible: What the R.A.M.C. Might Become.* London: H.K. Lewis and Co., 1919.

————. "The Prophylaxis of Venereal Disease," *Medical Journal of Australia* (22 March 1919): 240–1.

Bates, Daisy. *The Passing of the Aborigines. A Lifetime Spent among the Natives of Australia.* London: John Murray, 1944.

Bayley, Hugh Wansey. *Triple Challenge, or Wars, Whirligigs and Windmills. A Doctor's Memoirs of the Years 1914 to 1929.* London: Hutchinson, 1935.

Bibikoff, Massia. *Our Indians at Marseilles.* London: Smith, Elder and Co., 1915.

Billington-Greig, Teresa. "The Truth About White Slavery." *English Review* 14 (June 1913): 428–46.

Black, George. *The Red Plague Crusade.* Sydney: William Applegate Gullick, Government Printer, 1916.

Blackwell, Elizabeth. *Rescue Work in Relation to Prostitution and Disease.* London, T. Danes, 1881.

Blumenthal, Walter Hart. *Women Camp Followers of the American Revolution.* Philadelphia, PA: G.S. MacManus, 1952.

Booth, Angela. *The Prophylaxis of Venereal Disease: A Reply to Sir James Barrett.* Melbourne: Norman Bros. Printers, 1919.

Brody, Morris W. "Men Who Contract Venereal Disease." *Journal of Venereal Disease Information* 29 (1948): 334–7.

Brown, D. Blair. "The *Pros* and *Cons* of the Contagious Diseases Acts as applied in India." *Transactions of the Medical and Physical Society of Bombay* n.s. 11 (1888): 80–97.

Buchanan, David. *An Evil Little Thought of and Seldom Talked Of.* Sydney: Lee and Ross, n.d.

Burdett, Henry. *Hospitals and Asylums of the World: Their Origin, History, Construction, Administration, Management and Legislation.* Vol. 4. London: J. and A. Churchill, 1893.

Burke, E. T. "Venereal Disease During the War." *Quarterly Review* 233, no. 463 (April 1920): 304–16.

Butler, A. G. *The Official History of the Australian Army Medical Services in the War of 1914–1918.* Volume 1: *Gallipoli, Palestine and New Guinea.* Melbourne: Australian War Memorial, 1930. Volume 2: *The Western Front.* Melbourne: Australian War Memorial, 1940. Volume 3, *Special Problems and Services,* Melbourne: Australian War Memorial, 1943.

Butler, Josephine E. *The Revival and Extension of the Abolitionist Cause: A Letter to the Members of the Ladies' National Association.* London: Dyer Brothers, 1887.

————. *To Mrs. Tanner and Her Sisters.* Privately printed, June 1888.

————. *The Present Aspect of the Abolitionist Cause in its Relation to British India.* London: Women's Christian Temperance Union. 1893.

————. *Personal Reminiscences of A Great Crusade.* London: Horace Marshall and Son, 1896.

Byron, George Gordon. *Don Juan*. New York: Random House, 1949.

"C." *The Army in Its Medico-Sanitary Relations [Three Papers reprinted from the Edinburgh Medical Journal]*. 1859.

Caine, Nathaniel. *Prostitution: Its Aids and Accessories*. Liverpool: Egerton Smith, 1858.

Carlyle, Thomas. *Chartism*. London: Chapman and Hall, 1894.

Chadwick, Edwin. *Report on the Sanitary Condition of the Labouring Population of Great Britain*, Edinburgh: Edinburgh University Press, 1965.

Champly, Henry. *The Road to Shanghai: White Slave Traffic in Asia*. London: John Long, 1934.

———. *White Women, Coloured Men*. London: John Long, 1936.

Champneys, Francis. "The Fight Against Venereal Infection: A Reply to Sir Bryan Donkin." *The Nineteenth Century and After* 82 (November 1917): 1044–54.

———. "The Fight Against Venereal Infection: A Further Reply to Sir Bryan Donkin." *The Nineteenth Century and After* 83 (March 1918): 611–8.

Chapman, Cecil. *From the Bench*. London: Hodder and Stoughton, 1932.

———. *The Poor Man's Court of Justice: Twenty-Five Years as a Metropolitan Magistrate*. London: Hodder and Stoughton, 1925.

Chevers, Norman. *A Manual of Medical Jurisprudence for Bengal and the North-Western Provinces*. Calcutta: F. Carbery, Bengal Military Orphan Press, 1856.

Clarke, W. M. *Report on the Working of the Contagious Diseases Act for December 1st 1869 to December 31st 1870*. N.p., n.d. [1871].

"Clinical Notes." *The Indian Medical Journal* n.s. 8, no. 13 (July 1888): 353–4.

Cobbett, William. "Mr. Cobbett's Lecture on Repeal," *Pilot*, 10 November 1834, In *Cobbett in Ireland. A Warning to England*, edited by Denis Knight. London: Lawrence and Wishart, 1984.

Compston, H. F. B. *The Magdalen Hospital. The Story of A Great Charity*. London: Society for the Promotion of Christian Knowledge, 1917.

"Contagious Diseases in China." *The Lancet* (14 November 1868): 645.

"Contagious Diseases on the China Station." *The Lancet* (19 June 1869): 859–60.

Cowen, John. *Tracts for Rangoon No. 1: 29th Street by Day & Night*. Rangoon: YMCA, 1914.

———. *Tracts for Rangoon No. 7: Welcome to the Territorials*. Rangoon: YMCA, 1914.

———. "Extracts from a Report upon Public Prostitution in Singapore." *The Shield* 3rd series. 1, no. 3 (October 1916): 184–5.

"Criminal Women." *Cornhill Magazine* 14 (July–December 1866): 152–60.

Davis, Shelby Cullom. *Reservoirs of Men: A History of the Black Troops of French West Africa*. 1934. Reprint, Westport, CT: Negro Universities Press, 1970.

De Leeuw, Hendrik. *Cities of Sin*. London: Noel Douglas, 1934.

Dick, W. "A Discussion on the Prevention and Treatment of Syphilis in the Navy And Army." *British Medical Journal* (21 October 1899): 1071.

Dixon, Alec. *Singapore Patrol*. London: George C. Harrap, 1935.

Dixon, Katherine. *An Appeal to the Women of the Empire concerning Present Moral Conditions in Our Cantonments in India*. London: Association of Moral and Social Hygiene, 1916.

———. *Regulated Prostitution within the British Empire: The Question of Brothels and State Control (being the substance of addresses given by Mrs. K. Dixon in India, Burma and Singapore. 1918)*. London: Association of Moral and Social Hygiene, 1919.

———. *Mrs. K. Dixon's Work against Regulated Prostitution within the British Empire*. London: Vacher and Sons, [?1919].

Donkin, H. Bryan. "The Fight Against Venereal Infection." *The Nineteenth Century and After* 82 (September 1917): 580–95.

———. "The Fight Against Venereal Infection: A Rejoinder." *The Nineteenth Century and After* 83 (January 1918): 184–90.

Dorgan, J. "Prevention of Venereal Disease." *Journal of the Royal Army Medical Corps* 11, no. 2 (1908): 123–8.

Draft Report of the Committee appointed to consider a Memorial of the Society for the Protection of Children in India. N.p., .n.d. [?1907].

Drysdale, Charles R. *Prostitution Medically Considered with some of its Social Aspects*. London: Robert Hardwicke, 1866.

Dyer, Alfred S. *Slavery Under the British Flag: Iniquities of British Rule in India and in Our Crown Colonies and Dependencies*. London: Dyer Brothers, n.d.

———. "The Government *versus* the Gospel in India." *The Sentinel* 10 (March 1888) 3: 25–8.

———. *Must India Perish Through Britain's Sin? Facts about the Licensing of Impurity by the British Government in India: Five Letters to the Christian Press of Great Britain.* Bombay: Bombay Guardian, 1888.

———. *The Black Hand of Authority in India.* London: Dyer Brothers, 1888.

———. *Repentance or Retribution? A Serious Crisis in India.* London: Dyer Brothers, 1888.

———. *Government versus God in India.* London: Dyer Brothers, 1888.

———. *British Soldiers in India in relation to their Morals and Health.* London: Dyer Brothers; Bombay: Bombay Guardian, 1897.

Edmondson, Joseph. *An Enquiry into the Causes of the Great Sanitary Failure of the State Regulation of Social Vice.* London: British, Continental and General Federation for the Abolition of the State Regulation of Vice, 1897.

Edwardes, S. M. *The Bombay City Police: A Historical Sketch 1672–1916.* London, Bombay, Calcutta and Madras, and Humphrey Milford/Oxford University Press, 1923.

———. *Crime in India.* London: Oxford University Press, 1924.

Elliot, Hugh. "Venereal Prophylaxis: A Layman's View." *The Nineteenth Century and After* 84 (July 1918): 171–9.

Fawcett, Millicent Garrett. *A Speech made at the Croydon Meeting of the General Committee of the National Union of Women Workers, October 1897, by Mrs. Henry Fawcett on the New Rules for Dealing with the Sanitary Condition of the British Army in India.* London: Women's Printing Society, 1897.

Fifth Annual Report of the Rescue Branch of the Women's Friendly Society. Calcutta, 1913.

Gaisford, M. "Some Remarks on the Contagious Diseases Act and Its Working in Indian Cantonments." *Proceedings of the N.W. Provinces and Oudh Branch of the British Medical Association* 2, no. 13 (June 1883): 217–24.

Garnham, Florence E. *A Report on the Social and Moral Condition of Indians in Fiji, Being the Outcome of an Investigation set on Foot by Combined Women's Organisations of Australia.* Sydney: The Kingston Press, 1918.

Gilson, C. L. *Scenes from A Subaltern's Life.* Edinburgh and London: William Blackwood and Sons, 1913.

Godley, Arthur (Lord Kilbracken). *Reminiscences of Lord Kilbracken.* London: Macmillan and Co., 1931.

Gray, David. *The Chinese Problem in the Federation of Malaya.* Malaya: Chinese Secretariat, Federation of Malaya, 1952.

Greg, William. "Prostitution." *Westminster Review* 53 (1850): 448–506.

Gregory, Maurice. *Supplement to the Solidarity.* London, Social Purity Association, n.d. [?1910/11].

———. *Facts Used in Japan and Australia in 1911 and 1912.* Perth: V.K. Jones, 1912.

Grubbs, Robert B. "Venereal Prophylaxis in the Military Service." *Military Surgeon* 25 (1909): 756–71.

Guthrie, G. J. *Observations on the Treatment of Venereal Disease Without Mercury.* London: G. Woodfall, 1817.

Handbook for Queensland, Australia. By Authority of the Agent-General for the Government of Queensland. London: Lake and Sison, 1893.

Harrison, L. W. "Some Lessons Learnt in Fifty Years Practice in Venereology." *British Journal of Venereal Diseases* 30 (1954): 184–190.

———. "Those Were the Days! or Random Notes on Then and Now in VD." *Bulletin of the Institute of Technicians in Venereology* n.d. [?1950s]: 1–7.

———. *A Sketch of Army Medical Experience of Venereal Disease during the European War, 1914–18.* London: National Council for Combatting Venereal Disease, 1922.

———. *The Management of Venereal Disease in the Civil Community.* London: National Council for Combatting Venereal Disease, 1918.

Hill-Climo, William. "The British Soldier in India and Enthetic Diseases." *United Services Magazine* 15 n.s., (1896–7): 369–77.

Health Memorandum for British Soldiers in the Tropics. 1919.

Hill, M. Berkeley. *Syphilis and Local Contagious Disorders.* London: James Walton, 1868.

Hirschfeld, Magnus. *The Sexual History of the World War.* New York: Cadillac Publishing Co. 1941.

Howard, William Lee. "The Daughters of the Moabites and Our Soldiers." *New York Medical Journal* 107 (1918): 394–5.

Hutchinson, Jonathan. *Syphilis.* London: Cassell and Co., 1887.

India and the East. London: Association of Moral and Social Hygiene, n.d. [?1919].

India and the Far East. London: Association of Moral and Social Hygiene, n.d. [?1919].

Instructions to A.A.M.C. Orderlies Regarding Prophylactic and Abortive Treatment of Venereal Diseases. n.d. [?1916].

Instructions to Medical Officers Regarding the Prevention of Venereal Disease. n. p., 16 September 1918.

"Is Empire Consistent with Morality? No! By A Public Servant." *Pall Mall Gazette* 95, no. 6917 (19 May 1887): 2–3.

Jameson, Storm. *Company Parade*. New York: Alfred A. Knopf, 1934.

Johnson, Alice. *George William Johnson: Civil Servant and Social Worker*. Printed for private circulation, Cambridge, 1927.

Johnston, Harry H. *The Black Man's Part in the War: An Account of the Dark-Skinned Population of the British Empire. How It Is and Will Be Affected by the Great War; and the Share It Has Taken in Waging That War*. London: Simpkin, Marshall, Hamilton, Kent and Co., 1917.

Johnstone, R. W. *Report on Venereal Diseases*. London: HMSO, 1913.

Kipling, Rudyard. *City of the Dreadful Night*. London: Classic Publishing Company, n.d.

Kitchener, Horatio. *Memorandum to the Troops, 1905*. N.p. 1905.

Knight, G. Kerschener. *The White Slaves of England*. Denham, Buckinghamshire: The White Slaves Traffic Press, 1910.

Kynnersley, C. W. S. "The Prevention and Repression of Crime." *Straits Chinese Magazine* 1, no. 3 (September 1897): 74–85.

Lawson, Robert. "Observations on the Variation in the Prevalence of Venereal Affections in this Country." *Medical Times and Gazette* (7 January 1871): 7–9.

Lecture delivered by Dr. McLean at the opening of the Military Medical College, Netley, October 1st 1863. N.p., n.d.

[Leppington, Blanche]. *The Soldier and His Masters*. N.p., n.d. [1897].

Licensed Plague Spots: India's Curse and Britain's Shame. London: Gospel Purity Association, 1888.

"Lock Hospital Examinations." *The Indian Medical Journal* n.s. 8, no. 9 (March 1888): 118–9.

"Lock Hospitals." *The Shield* 12, no. 113 (February 1910): 10.

Lowndes, Frederick W. "The Liverpool Lock Hospital, Its Origin and History; Statistics of Recent Years." *Liverpool Medico-Chirurgical Journal* 11 (July 1886): 297–300.

McCosh, John. *Advice to Officers in India*. London: W.H. Allen and Co., 1856.

McElligott, G. L. M. "The Prevention of Venereal Disease." In *Inter-Allied Conferences on War Medicine 1942–1945*, edited by Henry Letherby Tidy and J. M. Browne Kutschbach, 263–5. London: Staples Press, 1947.

———. "Venereal Disease in the Field: Present Policy and Management in the Royal Air Force." In *Inter-Allied Conferences on War Medicine 1942–1945*, edited by Henry Letherby Tidy and J. M. Browne Kutschbach, 272–3. London: Staples Press, 1947.

McKay, Claude. *A Long Way From Home*. 1937. Reprint, New York: Arno Press/*New York Times*, 1969.

McKie, R. H. *This Was Singapore*. Sydney: Angus and Robertson, 1942.

Macmillan, Chrystal. *A New Danger: Departmental Orders versus Legislation for Venereal Disease*. 1919.

Macpherson, W. G. *History of the Great War based on Official Documents. Medical Services. General History*. Vol. 1. London: HMSO, 1921.

MacPherson, W. G., W. P. Herringham, T. R. Elliott, and A. Balfour, ed. *History of the Great War based on Official Documents: Medical Services. Diseases of the War*. Vol. 2. London: HMSO, 1923.

Mahon, E. E. "A Discussion on the Prevention and Treatment of Syphilis in the Navy And Army." *British Medical Journal* (21 October 1899): 1070.

The "Maisons Tolérées": An Appeal. London: Association of Moral and Social Hygiene, 1918.

Manders, N. *Hints on Health in Egypt*. N.p., n.d.

Mandlik, Rao Saheb V. N. *Speech at the Bombay Town Council*. Bombay: Education Society's Press, n.d. [?1880].

Marshall, James. "Prevention of Venereal Disease in the British Army." In *Inter-Allied Conferences on War Medicine 1942–1945*, edited by Henry Letherby Tidy and J. M. Browne Kutschbach, 260–2. London: Staples Press, 1947.

Martindale, Louisa. *The Prevention of Venereal Disease*. London: Research Books Ltd., 1945.

Maugham, W. Somerset. "Neil MacAdam." In *East and West: The Collected Short Stories*. Garden City, NY: Garden City Publishing Co., 1934.

Maxwell, Joseph. *Hell's Bells and Mademoiselles*. Sydney: Angus and Robertson, 1932.

May, Otto. *The Prevention of Venereal Disease in the Army*. London: National Council for Combatting Venereal Disease, 1916.

Mayne, C. B. *How Far Past Legislation Has Proved Effective in Securing the Health of the Troops in India, With Suggestions as to Future Legislation on This Important Subject*. London: Horace Marshall, 1897.

Mercer, W. H. *A Handbook of the British Colonial Empire*. London: Waterlow and Sons Ltd., 1906.

Miller, A. G. "Four and a Half Years' Experience in the Lock Wards of the Royal Edinburgh Infirmary." *Edinburgh Medical Journal* 28 (1882): 385–403.

Morel, E. D. *The Horror on the Rhine*. London: Union of Democratic Control, 1920.

———. "Negro Troops in Germany." *Stead's Review* 54, no. 3 (July 1920): 160–6.

Neilans, Alison. "The Protection of Soldiers." *The Shield* 1, no. 4 (March, 1917): 217–23.

———. *Moral Problems in Singapore*. London: Association of Moral and Social Hygiene, n.d. [?1924]. [authorship uncertain].

Nevins, J. Birkbeck. *Cape of Good Hope re Venereal Diseases*. London: British Committee for the Abolition of State Regulation of Vice in India and throughout the British Dominions, 1895.

Newton, George. *Medical Report of the Yokohama Lock Hospital for 1869*. Yokohama: Japan Gazette Office, 1870.

Nightingale, Florence. *Observations by Miss Nightingale on the Evidence contained in Statistical Returns sent to her by the Royal Commission on the Sanitary State of the Army in India*. N.p., n.d. [1862].

———. *Note on the Supposed Protection Afforded Against Venereal Disease, by Recognizing Prostitution and Putting It Under Police Regulation*. N.p., n.d. [1863].

Officers of the Royal Army Medical Corps. *A Manual of Venereal Diseases*. London: Oxford Medical Publications/Henry Frowde/Hodder and Stoughton, 1907.

Oppert, F. *Hospitals, Infirmaries, and Dispensaries: Their Construction, Interior, Arrangement, and Management with Descriptions of Existing Institutions and Remarks on the Present System of Affording Medical Relief to the Sick Poor*. London: John Churchill and Sons, 1867.

Orwell, George. "As I Please." Originally published in *Tribune*, 29 December 1944. Reproduced in *The Collected Essays, Journalism and Letters of George Orwell: As I Please 1943–1945*. Vol. 3. Edited by Sonia Orwell and Ian Angus, 348–9. Harmondsworth: Penguin Books, 1970.

Osmond, T. E. "Venereal Disease in Peace and War with some Reminiscences of the Last Forty Years." *British Journal of Venereal Diseases* 25 (1949): 101–14.

Our Army in India. Correspondence between the India Office and the British Committee of the International Abolitionist Federation on the Rules, Regulations and Practice in Indian Cantonments with regard to Prostitution and Disease (October 1909 to October 1912). London: British Committee of the International Abolitionist Federation, 1912.

Parkes, Edmund A. *A Manual of Practical Hygiene Prepared Especially for Use in the Medical Service of the Army*. London: John Churchill and Sons, 1864.

Patterson, Alexander. "Statistics of Glasgow Lock Hospital Since Its Foundation in 1805—With Remarks on the Contagious Diseases Acts and on Syphilis." *Glasgow Medical Journal* 6 (December 1882): 401–18.

Pitfalls for Women. London: Success Publishing Company, n.d. [?1912].

Power, D'Arcy and J. Murphy Keogh, eds. *A System of Syphilis in Six Volumes. Syphilis in Relation to the Public Services*. Vol. 6. London: Oxford Medical Publications/Henry Frowde/Hodder and Stoughton, 1910.

Prevention of Syphilis and Venereal. N.p., n.d. [?1915].

Proceedings of the University of Sydney Society for Combating Venereal Diseases. Sydney: December, 1916.

Raffan, George. *Instructions to Medical Officers Regarding the Prevention of Venereal Diseases*. N.p., 16 September 1918.

Regulated Prostitution Within the British Empire. London: Association of Moral and Social Hygiene, 1919.

Reply of Dr. Katharine Bushnell and Mrs. Elizabeth Andrew to Certain Statements in A Published Letter addressed by Lady Henry Somerset to a Correspondent on the Regulation of Vice in India. London: Ladies' National Association, 1897.

Report from Captain Banon addressed to Mr. Stuart for the Committee, 3 April 1891. London: British, Continental and General Federation for the Abolition of State Regulation of Vice, 1891.

Report of Army Health Association for 1894. N.p., n.d.

Report of A Sub-Committee of the Burma Branch of the British Medical Association on the Prevalence of Venereal Diseases at Rangoon. N.p., n.d.

Report of the Cairo Purification Committee. Cairo: Government Press, 1916.

Report of the Social Purity Meeting in the Town Hall, Calcutta, November 27 1893. N.p., n.d.

Report on the Health of the Army for the Year 1914. London: HMSO, 1921.

Report on Kitchener's Indian Hospital, Brighton. N.p., n.d. [?1916].

Richards, Frank. *Old-Soldier Sahib.* London: Faber and Faber, 1936.

Ritchie, J. Ewing. *The Night Side of London.* London: William Tweedie, 1857.

Royden, A. Maude. ed. *Downward Paths: An Inquiry into the Causes which Contribute to the Making of the Prostitute.* London: G. Bell and Sons, 1916.

Rout, Ettie A. *Two Years in Paris.* London: privately printed, 1923.

Routh, C. H. F. *On the Difficulty of Diagnosing the Syphilitic Disease in Women and the Nature of Its Contagion.* London: T. Danks, 1883.

Rumsey, Henry W. *Laws Affecting the Public Health in England.* London, 1870.

Salter, J. *The East in the West or Work Among the Asiatics and Africans in London.* London: S. W. Partridge, 1896.

————. *The Asiatic in England: Sketches of Sixteen Years' Work Among Orientals.* London: Seeley, Jackson and Halliday, 1873.

Sandwith, Dr. "Prostitution et maladies vénériennes en Egypte." *Le Conference Internationale pour la Prophylaxie de la Syphilis et des Maladies Vénérienne.* Vol. 1. Part 1 (1899): 713–25.

Scott, Rose. *A Law Affecting Women: "The State Regulation of Vice".* Queensland: WCTU, 1903.

Sergeant-Major, R.A.M.C. *With the R.A.M.C. in Egypt.* London: Cassell and Co., 1918.

Sellers, Edith. "Boy and Girl War-Products: Their Reconstruction." *The Nineteenth Century And After* 84 (October 1918): 704.

Shepherd, W. J. *A Personal Narrative of the Outbreak and Massacre at Cawnpore, during the Sepoy Revolt of 1857.* 1879. Reprint, New Delhi: Academic Books Corporation, 1980.

Simon, John. *English Sanitary Institutions Reviewed In Their Course of Development, and in Some of their Political and Social Relations.* London: Cassell, 1890.

Sims, J. Marion. "Presidential Address" *Transactions of the American Medical Association* 27 (1876): 100–11.

Social Purity Alliance. *Annual Report 1887–1888.* N.p., n.d.

Soldiers and the Social Evil: A Letter Addressed by Permission to the Rt. Hon. Sidney Herbert, Secretary of State for War, by A Chaplain. London: Rivingtons; Folkestone: E. Creed, 1860.

Solly, Julia F. *State Regulation of Vice in South Africa: Urgent Appeal.* London: British Committee, International Abolitionist Federation, 1907.

Spencer, J. E. and W. L. Thomas. "The Hill Stations and Summer Resorts of the Orient." *Geographical Review* 38, no. 4 (1948): 637–51.

Spurr, F. C. *The Red Plague.* Melbourne: J. Kemp, Government Printer, 1911.

Stansfeld, James. *Lord Kimberley's Defence of the Government Brothel System in Hong Kong.* London: National Association for the Repeal of the Contagious Diseases Acts, 1882.

State Regulation of Vice in South Africa. Deputation to Sir Henry Loch. London: F. H. Doulton, 1894.

Stewart, Alexander P. and Edward Jenkins. *The Medical and Legal Aspects of Sanitary Reform.* 2nd ed. London: R. Hardwicke, 1867.

Syphilis. With Special Reference to (a) Its Prevalence and Intensity in the Past and at the Present Day, (b) Its Relation to Public Health, (c) The Treatment of the Disease. A Discussion. London: Longmans, Green and Co., 1912.

Taylor, Charles Bell. *The Soldier and His Masters: From A Sanitary Point of View.* London: Kelvin Glen and Co., 1898.

Tempest, Violet. *Our Army in India.* London: White Slave Abolition Publications, 1913.

Thackeray, William Makepeace. *Vanity Fair.* New York: Knopf, 1991.

Transactions of the Seventh International Congress of Hygiene and Demography. Volume 11. *Indian Hygiene and Demography.* London: Eyre and Spottiswoode, 1892.

"The C.D. Act in Ceylon." *Indian Medical Journal* 8 (June 1888): 12, 275.

The Criminal Law Amendment Bill, 1917. London, Association of Moral and Social Hygiene, 1917.

The Health of the British Army in India. Army Health Protection Association of India, N.p., n.d. [?1897].

The Health of the Army. London: British Committee of the Federation for the Abolition of State Regulation of Vice, 1897.

"The Health of the Army in India." *Saturday Review* (3 April 1897).

"The History of the Fight Against Venereal Disease." *British Medical Journal* (12 August 1916): 230–1.

The *"Maisons Tolérées": An Appeal.* London: Association of Moral and Social Hygiene, 1918.

The Need for Renewed Agitation in the Abolitionist Movement. London: Friends' Association for Abolishing State Regulation of Vice, n.d. [?1900].

The Problem of the "Maisons Tolérées" and the B.E.F. in France (and Elsewhere). London: Association of Moral and Social Hygiene, 1940.

"The Sanitary Farce in India." *Indian Medical Journal* 8, no. 12 (June 1888): 257.

The Venereal Problem and The Army. London: Association for Moral and Social Hygiene, 1918.

To The Women of Finchley. London: Pewtress and Co., N.p., n.d. [?1897].

Venereal Diseases. Brisbane, Department of Public Health, 1913.

"Venereal Disease in the Army." *The Lancet* 1 (5 February 1916): 305–6.

Verax, *The Social Evil in South Calcutta.* Calcutta: Calcutta Central Press, 1895.

Venereal Disease in Perak. N.p., n.d. [?1899].

Walker, George. *Venereal Disease in the American Expeditionary Force.* Baltimore, MD: Medical Standard Books, 1922.

Wardlaw, Ralph. *Lectures on Female Prostitution: Its Nature, Extent, Effects, Guilt, Causes, and Remedy.* Glasgow: James Maclehose, 1842.

Weed, F. W. "In The American Expeditionary Forces." *Medical Department of the United States Army in the World War. Sanitation.* Vol. 6. Washington: Government Printing Office, 1926.

Welch, Francis H. "The Prevention of Syphilis." *The Lancet* (12 August 1899): 403–6.

Welsh, D. A. "The Enemy in Our Midst: Venereal Disease." In *Proceedings of the University of Sydney Society for Combating Venereal Diseases.* Sydney: December, 1916.

Whitbread, Helena, ed. *I Know My Own Heart: The Diaries of Anne Lister (1791–1840).* London: Virago, 1988.

Williamson, Thomas. *The East India Vade Mecum or, Complete Guide to Gentlemen Intended for the Civil, Military, or Naval Service of the Hon. East India Company.* Vol. 2. London: Black, Parry, and Kingbury, 1810.

Willis, W. N. *Western Men with Eastern Morals.* London: Stanley Paul, 1913.

White, Arnold. "Efficiency and Vice." *English Review* 22 (May 1916): 446–52.

White, Douglas and C. H. Melville. *Venereal Disease: Its Present and Future.* N.p., 1911.

White, George. "The Defence of India." *Black and White* (1 September 1894): 267–8.

Wilson, Helen M. *Sanitary Principles Applied to the Prevention of Venereal Diseases.* London: John Bale, 1911.

———. *On Some Causes of Prostitution, with Special Reference to Economic Conditions.* London: Association of Moral and Social Hygiene, 1916.

Wolseley, Garnet. "The Negro As A Soldier." *Fortnightly Review* n.s. 264 (1 December 1888): 689–703.

Secondary Printed Materials

Akyeampong, Emmanuel. "Sexuality and Prostitution among the Akan of the Gold Coast, c. 1650–1950." *Past and Present* 156 (1997): 144–73.

Alderson, David. *Mansex Fine: Religion, Manliness and Imperialism in Nineteenth-Century British Culture.* Manchester: Manchester University Press, 1998.

Alexander, M. Jacqui. "Not Just (Any) Body Can Be A Citizen: The Politics of Law, Sexuality and Postcoloniality in Trinidad and Tobago and the Bahamas." *Feminist Review* 48 (1994): 5–23.

———. "Redrafting Morality: The Postcolonial State and the Sexual Offences Bill of Trinidad and Tobago." In *Third World Women and the Politics of Feminism,* edited by Chandra Talpade Mohanty, Ann Russo, and Lourdes Torres, 133–52. Bloomington, IN: Indiana University Press, 1991.

Allen, Charles, ed. *Plain Tales From The Raj: Images of British India in the Twentieth Century.* London: André Deutsch/British Broadcasting Corporation, 1975.

Allen, Judith. *Sex and Secrets: Crimes Involving Australian Women Since 1880.* Melbourne: Oxford University Press, 1990.

———. "'Mundane' Men: Historians, Masculinity and Masculinism." *Historical Studies* 22, no. 89 (1987): 617–28.

———. "Policing Since 1880: Some Questions of Sex." In *Policing in Australia: Historical Perspectives,* edited by Mark Finnane, 181–221. Kensington, NSW: New South Wales University Press, 1987.

Allen, Theodore W. *The Invention of the White Race.* Vol. 1. *Racial Oppression and Social Control.* London: Verso, 1994.

Alloula, Malek. *The Colonial Harem.* Minneapolis, MN: University of Minnesota Press, 1986.

Alter, Joseph. "Celibacy, Sexuality, and the Transformation of Gender into Nationalism in North India." *Journal of Asian Studies* 53, no. 1 (1994): 45–66.

Anand, Mulk Raj. *Across The Black Waters.* London: Jonathan Cape, 1940.

Anderson, Amanda. *Tainted Souls and Painted Faces: The Rhetoric of Fallenness in Victorian Culture.* Ithaca, NY: Cornell University Press, 1993.

Anderson, Benedict. *Imagined Communities: Reflections on the Origin and Spread of Nationalism.* Revised ed. London and New York: Verso, 1991.

Anderson, Kay J. *Vancouver's Chinatown: Racial Discourse in Canada, 1875–1980.* Montreal and Kingston: McGill-Queen's University Press, 1991.

Anderson, Warwick. *The Cultivation of Whiteness: Science, Health and Racial Destiny in Australia.* Carlton South: Melbourne University Press, 2002.

———. "Where is the Postcolonial History of Medicine." *Bulletin of the History of Medicine* 72, no. 3 (1998): 522–30.

———. "Geography, Race and Nation: Remapping 'Tropical' Australia, 1890–1930." *Historical Records of Australian Science* 11, no. 4 (1997): 457–68.

———. "Disease, Race, and Empire." *Bulletin of the History of Medicine* 70 (1996): 62–7.

———. " 'Where Every Prospect Pleases and Only Man Is Vile': Laboratory Medicine as Colonial Discourse," *Critical Inquiry* 18 (1992): 506–29.

Andrew, C. M. and A. S. Forstner-Kanya. "France, Africa and the First World War." *Journal of African History* 19, no. 1 (1978): 11–23.

Andrew, Kenneth W. *Chop Suey.* Ilfracombe, Devon: Arthur H. Stockwell, 1975.

———. *Hong Kong Detective.* London: John Long, 1962.

Andrews, Bridie J. "Tuberculosis and the Assimilation of Germ Theory in China, 1895–1937." *Journal of the History of Medicine and Allied Sciences* 51, no. 1 (1997): 114–57.

Andrews, E. M. *The Anzac Illusion: Anglo-Australian Relations during World War I.* Cambridge: Cambridge University Press, 1993.

Ang, Ien. "I'm a Feminist But . . . : 'Other' Women and Postnational Feminism." In *Transitions: New Australian Feminisms,* edited by Barbara Caine and Rosemary Pringle, 57–73. St. Leonards, NSW: Allen and Unwin, 1995.

Appadurai, Arjun. "Number in the Colonial Imagination." In *Orientalism and the Postcolonial Predicament: Perspectives on South Asia,* edited by Carol Breckenridge and Peter van der Veer, 314–39. Philadelphia, PA: University of Pennsylvania Press, 1993.

Arnold, David. "Sex, State, and Society: Sexually Transmitted Diseases and HIV/AIDS in Modern India," In *Sex, Disease, and Society: A Comparative History of Sexually Transmitted Diseases and HIV/AIDS in Asia and the Pacific,* edited by Milton Lewis, Scott Bamber, and Michael Waugh, 19–36. Westport, CT: Greenwood Press, 1997.

———. "Public Health and Public Power: Medicine and Hegemony in Colonial India." In *Contesting Colonial Hegemony: State and Society in Africa and India,* edited by Dagmar Engels and Shula Marks, 131–51. London: British Academic Press/German Historical Institute, 1994.

———. *Colonizing the Body: State Medicine and Epidemic Disease in Nineteenth-Century India.* Berkeley: University of California Press, 1993.

———. "Sexually Transmitted Diseases in Nineteenth and Twentieth Century India." *Genitourinary Medicine* 69, no. 1 (1993): 3–8.

———. "White Colonization and Labour in Nineteenth-Century India." *Journal of Imperial and Commonwealth History* 11, no 2 (1983): 133–58.

———. "European Orphans and Vagrants in India in the Nineteenth Century." *Journal of Imperial and Commonwealth History* 7 (1979): 104–27.

Arnold, David, ed. *Imperial Medicine and Indigenous Societies.* Manchester: Manchester University Press, 1988.

Arya, O. P., A. O. Osoba, and F. J. Bennett. *Tropical Venereology.* 2nd ed. Edinburgh: Churchill Livingstone, 1988.

Aziz, Christine. "A Life of Hell for the Wife of a God." *Guardian Weekly,* (24 September 1995).

Bach, John. *The Australia Station: A History of the Royal Navy in the South West Pacific, 1821–1913.* Kensington: University of New South Wales Press, 1986.

Backhouse, Constance B. *Colour-Coded: A Legal History of Racism in Canada, 1900–1950.* Toronto: University of Toronto Press, 2000.

————. "Nineteenth-Century Canadian Prostitution Law: Reflections of a Discriminatory Society." *Histoire sociale—Social History* 18, no. 36 (1985): 387–423.

Bagchi, Jasodhara. "Colonialism and Socialization: The Girl Child in Colonial Bengal." *RFR/DRF* 22, nos. 3/4 (1993): 23–30.

Bailey, Beth and David Farber. "Hotel Street: Prostitution and the Politics of War." *Radical History Review* 52 (1992): 54–77.

Bailey, Peter. "Parasexuality and Glamour: The Victorian Barmaid as Cultural Prototype." *Gender & History* 2, no. 2 (1990): 148–172.

Baker, D. E. U. *Colonialism in an Indian Hinterland: The Central Provinces.* Delhi: Oxford University Press, 1993.

Ballhatchet, Kenneth. *Race, Sex and Class Under the British Raj: Imperial Attitudes and Policies and their Critics, 1793–1905.* London: Weidenfeld and Nicholson, 1980.

Bamber, S. D., K. J. Hewison, and P. J Underwood. "A History of Sexually Transmitted Diseases in Thailand: Policy and Politics." *Genitourinary Medicine* 69, no. 2 (1993): 148–57.

Banerjee, Sumanta. *Dangerous Outcast: The Prostitute in Nineteenth Century Bengal.* Calcutta: Seagull Books, 1998.

Barbeau, Arthur E. and Florette Henri. *The Unknown Soldiers: Black American Troops in World War I.* Philadelphia, PA: Temple University Press, 1974.

Barber, Ross. "The Criminal Law Amendment Act of 1891 and the 'Age of Consent' Issue in Queensland." *Australia and New Zealand Journal of Criminology* 10 (1977): 95–113.

Bashford, Alison. " 'Is White Australia Possible?' Race, Colonialism and Tropical Medicine." *Ethnic and Racial Studies* 23, no. 2 (2000): 248–71.

————. *Purity and Pollution: Gender, Embodiment and Victorian Medicine.* Basingstoke: The Macmillan Press, 1998.

————. "Quarantine and the Imagining of the Australian Nation." *Health* 2, no. 4 (1998), 387–402.

Barclay, Enid. "Queensland's Contagious Diseases Act, 1868—'The Act for the Encouragement of Vice' and some Nineteenth Century Attempts to Repeal It. Part 1." *Queensland Heritage* 2, no. 10 (1965): 27–34; "Part 2." *Queensland Heritage* 3, no. 1 (1966): 21–9.

Bayly, Susan. *Caste, Society and Politics in India from the Eighteenth Century to the Modern Age.* Cambridge: Cambridge University Press, 1999.

Bayly, C. A. "The British and Indigenous Peoples, 1760–1860: Power, Perception, and Identity." In *Empire and Others: British Encounters with Indigenous Peoples, 1600–1850,* edited by Martin Daunton and Rick Halpern, 19–41. Philadelphia, PA: University of Pennsylvania Press, 1999.

————. *Imperial Meridian: The British Empire and the World 1780–1830.* Harlow, Essex: Longman, 1989.

Bederman, Gail. *Manliness and Civilization: A Cultural History of Gender and Race in the United States, 1880–1917.* Chicago: University of Chicago Press, 1995.

Bedford, Judy. "Prostitution in Calgary 1905–1914." *Alberta History* 29 (1981): 1–11.

Benedict, Carol. "Framing Plague in China's Past." In *Remapping China: Fissures in Historical Terrain,* edited by Gail Hershatter, Emily Honig, Jonathan N. Lipman, and Randall Stross, 27–41. Stanford, CA: Stanford University Press, 1996.

Benton, Lauren. "Colonial Law and Cultural Difference: Jurisdictional Politics and the Formation of the Colonial State." *Comparative Studies in Society and History* 41, no. 3 (1999): 563–88.

Bettley, James. "Post Voluptatem Misericordia: The Rise and Fall of the London Lock Hospital." *London Journal* 10, no. 2 (1984): 167-75.

Bevoise, Ken de. "A History of Sexually Transmitted Diseases and HIV/AIDS in the Philippines," In *Sex, Disease, and Society: A Comparative History of Sexually Transmitted Diseases and HIV/AIDS in Asia and the Pacific,* edited by Milton Lewis, Scott Bamber, and Michael Waugh, 113–38. Westport, CT: Greenwood Press, 1997.

————. *Agents of Apocalypse: Epidemic Disease in the Colonial Philippines.* Princeton, NJ: Princeton University Press, 1995.

Biskup, Peter. *Not Slaves, Not Citizens: The Aboriginal Problem in Western Australia 1898–1954.* St. Lucia: University of Queensland Press, 1973.

Blakeley, Brian L. *The Colonial Office 1868–1892.* Durham, NC: Duke University Press, 1972.

Bland, Lucy. *Banishing the Beast: English Feminism and Sexual Morality 1885–1914.* London: Penguin Books, 1995.

————. " 'Cleansing the Portals of Life': The Venereal Disease Campaign in the Early Twentieth-Century." In *Crises in the British State 1880–1930,* edited by Mary Langan and Bill Schwarz, 192–208. London: Hutchinson and Centre for Contemporary Studies, University of Birmingham, 1985.

————. "In The Name of Protection: The Policing of Women in the First World War." In *Women-in-Law: Explorations in Law, Family and Sexuality,* edited by J. Brophy and Carol Smart, 23–49. London: Routledge and Kegan Paul, 1985.

Bolton, G. C. *A Thousand Miles Away: A History of North Queensland to 1920.* Brisbane: Jacaranda Press, 1963.

Borthwick, Meredith. *The Changing Role of Women in Bengal, 1844–1905.* Princeton, NJ: Princeton University Press, 1984.

Bose, Sugata and Ayesha Jalal. *Modern South Asia: History, Culture, Political Economy.* Delhi: Oxford University Press, 1997; London and New York: Routledge, 1998.

Bourke, Joanna. *Dismembering the Male: Men's Bodies, Britain and the Great War.* Chicago: Chicago University Press, 1996.

Bowen, H. V. "British India, 1765–1813: The Metropolitan Context." In *The Oxford History of the British Empire.* Vol. 2. *The Eighteenth Century,* edited by P. J. Marshall, 530–51. Oxford: Oxford University Press, 1998.

Brantlinger, Patrick. " 'Dying Races': Rationalizing Genocide in the Nineteenth Century." In *The Decolonization of Imagination: Culture, Knowledge and Power,* edited by Jan Nederveen Pieterse and Bhikhu Parekh, 43–56. London and New Jersey: Zed Books, 1995.

Breckenridge, Carol and Peter van der Veer. eds. *Orientalism and the Postcolonial Predicament: Perspectives on South Asia.* Philadelphia, PA: University of Pennsylvania Press, 1993.

Bristow, Edward J. "The German-Jewish Fight Against White Slavery." *Leo Baeck Institute Year Book* 28 (1983): 301–28.

————. "British Jewry and the Fight Against the International White Slave Traffic, 1885–1914." *Immigrants and Minorities* 2 (1983): 152–70.

————. *Prostitution and Prejudice: The Jewish Fight Against White Slavery, 1870–1939.* Oxford: Clarendon Press, 1982.

Bristow, Joseph. *Empire Boys: Adventures In A Man's World.* London: Harper Collins Academic, 1991.

Brooks, David. *The Age of Upheaval: Edwardian Politics, 1899–1914.* Manchester: Manchester University Press, 1995.

Brown, Judith M. *Modern India: The Origins of An Asian Democracy.* Delhi: Oxford University Press, 1985.

————. "War and the Colonial Relationship: Britain, India, and the War of 1914–18." In *India and World War I,* edited by DeWitt C. Ellinwood and S.D. Pradhan, 19–47. New Delhi: Manohar, 1978.

Brown, E. Richard. "Public Health in Imperialism: Early Rockefeller Programs at Home and Abroad." *American Journal of Public Health* 66, no. 9 (1976): 897–903.

Brugger, Suzanne. *Australians and Egypt 1914–1919.* Melbourne: Melbourne University Press, 1980.

Buckley, Suzann "The Failure to Resolve the Problem of Venereal Disease among the Troops in Britain During World War I." In *War and Society: A Yearbook of Military History.* Vol. 2, edited by Brian Bond and Ian Roy, 65–85. New York: Holmes and Meier, 1977.

Buckley, Suzann and Janice Dickin McGinnis. "Venereal Disease and Public Health Reform in Canada." *Canadian Historical Review* 63, no. 3 (1982): 337–54.

Buettner, Elizabeth, "Problematic Spaces, Problematic Races: Defining 'Europeans' in Late Colonial India." *Women's History Review* 9, no. 2 (2000): 277–98.

Bujra, Janet M. "Women 'Entrepreneurs' of Early Nairobi." *Revue Canadienne des Etudes Africaines/Canadian Journal of African Studies* 9, no. 2 (1975): 213–34.

Bullough Vern L. and Bonnie Bullough, *Women and Prostitution: A Social History.* Buffalo, NY: Prometheus Books, 1987.

Burke, Timothy. *Lifebuoy Men, Lux Women: Commodification, Consumption, and Cleanliness in Modern Zimbabwe.* Durham, NC: Duke University Press, 1996.

Burroughs, Peter. "Imperial Defence and the Victorian Army." *Journal of Imperial and Commonwealth History* 15, no. 1 (1986): 55–72.

Burton, Antoinette. *At the Heart of the Empire. Indians and the Colonial Encounter in Late Victorian Britain.* Berkeley, CA: University of California Press, 1997.

————."Who Needs the Nation? Interrogating 'British History' " *Journal of Historical Sociology* 10, no 3 (1997): 231–32.

————."Recapturing *Jane Eyre:* Reflections on Historicizing the Colonical Encounter in Victorian Britain." *Radical History Review* 64 (1996): 58–71.

————."Fearful Bodies into Disciplined Subjects: Pleasure, Romance, and the Family Drama of Colonial Reform in Mary Carpenter's *Six Months in India." Signs* 20 (1995): 545–74.

————. *Burdens of History: British Feminists, Indian Women, and Imperial Culture 1865–1915.* Chapel Hill, NC: University of North Carolina Press, 1994.

————. "The White Woman's Burden: British Feminists and 'The Indian Woman,' 1865–1915." In *Western Women and Imperialism: Complicity and Resistance,* edited by Nupur Chaudhuri and Margaret Strobel, 137–57. Bloomington, IN: Indiana University Press, 1992.

————. "The Feminist Quest for Identity. British Imperial Suffragism and 'Global Sisterhood' 1900–1918." *Journal of Women's History* 3, no. 2 (1991): 46–81.

Busia, Abena P. "Miscegenation as Metonymy: Sexuality and Power in the Colonial Novel." *Ethnic and Racial Studies* 9, no. 3 (1986): 360–72.

Butcher, J. G. *The British in Malaya 1880–1941: The Social History of A European Community in Colonial South-East Asia.* Kuala Lumpur: Oxford University Press, 1979.

Cain, P. J. and A. G. Hopkins. *British Imperialism: Innovation and Expansion, 1688–1914.* Vol. 1. London: Longman, 1993.

Callaway, Helen. *Gender, Culture, and Empire: European Women in Colonial Nigeria.* Urbana, IL: University of Illinois Press, 1987.

Cameron, Nigel. *An Illustrated History of Hong Kong.* Hong Kong: Oxford University Press, 1991.

Camm, J. C. R. and John McQuilton, eds. *Australians: A Historical Atlas.* Broadway, NSW: Fairfax, Syme and Weldon, 1987.

Campbell, Judy. "Smallpox in Aboriginal Australia, 1829–31." *Historical Studies* 20, no. 81 (1983): 536–56.

Cantlie, Neil. *A History of the Army Medical Department.* Edinburgh and London: Churchill Livingstone, 1974.

Caplan, Jane. "'Educating the Eye': The Tattooed Prostitute." In *Sexology in Culture. Labelling Bodies and Desires,* edited by Lucy Bland and Laura Doan, 100–15. Chicago: University of Chicago Press, 1998.

Caplan, Lionel. "Martial Gurkhas: The Persistence of A British Military Discourse on 'Race.'" In *The Concept of Race in South Asia,* edited by Peter Robb, 260–81. Delhi: Oxford University Press, 1995.

Carroll, John M. 'Chinese Collaboration in the Making of British Hong Kong.' In *Hong Kong's History. State and Society Under Colonial Rule,* edited by Tak-Wing Ngo, 13–29. London: Routledge, 1999.

Cassel, Jay. *The Secret Plague: Venereal Disease in Canada, 1838–1939.* Toronto: University of Toronto Press, 1987.

Catanach, I. J. "Plague and the Tensions of Empire: India, 1896–1918." In *Imperial Medicine and Indigenous Societies,* edited by David Arnold, 149–71. Manchester: Manchester University Press, 1988.

Caulfield, Sueann. "The Birth of Mague: Race, Nation, and the Politics of Prostitution in Rio de Janeiro, 1850–1942." In *Sex and Sexuality in Latin America,* edited by Daniel Balderston and Donna J. Guy, 86–100. New York: New York University Press, 1997.

Cell, John W. *British Colonial Administration in the Mid-Nineteenth Century: The Policy-Making Process.* New Haven, CT: Yale University Press, 1970.

Chakravarti, Uma. "Whatever Happened to the Vedic Dasi? Orientalism, Nationalism and a Script for the Past." In *Recasting Women: Essays in Colonial History,* edited by Kumkum Sangari and Sudesh Vaid, 27–87. Delhi: Kali for Women, 1993.

Chandavarkar, Rajnarayan. "Plague, Panic and Epidemic Politics in India, 1896–1914." In *Epidemics and Ideas: Essays in the Historical Perception of Pestilence,* edited by Terence Ranger and Paul Slack, 203–40. Cambridge: Cambridge University Press, 1992.

Chandra, Sudhir. "Whose Laws? Notes on a Legitimising Myth of the Colonial Indian State." *Studies in History* 8, no. 2 (1992): 187–211.

Charles, Persis. "The Name of the Father: Women, Paternity, and British Rule in Nineteenth-Century Jamaica." *International Labor and Working-Class History* 41 (1992): 4–22

Chase, Athol. "'All Kind of Nation': Aborigines and Asians in Cape York Peninsula." *Aboriginal History* 5, no. 1 (1981): 7–19.

Chatterjee, Indrani. "Colouring Subalternity: Slaves, Concubines and Social Orphans in Early Colonial India." In *Subaltern Studies X: Writings on South Asian History and Society,* edited by Gautam Bhadra, Gyan Prakash, and Susie Tharu, 49–97. Delhi: Oxford University Press, 1999.

————. "Refracted Reality: The 1935 Calcutta Police Survey of Prostitutes." *Manushi* 57 (1990): 26–36.

Chatterjee, Partha. *The Nation and Its Fragments: Colonial and Postcolonial Histories.* Princeton, NJ: Princeton University Press, 1993.

———. "Colonialism, Nationalism, and Colonialized Women: The Contest in India." *American Ethnologist* 16, no. 4 (1989): 622–33.

Chew, Dolores F. "The Case of the 'Unchaste' Widow: Constructing Gender in 19th-Century Bengal." *RFR/DRF* 22, no. 3/4 (1993): 31–40.

Ching-hwang, Yen. *A Social History of the Chinese in Singapore and Malaya 1800–1911.* Singapore: Oxford University Press, 1986.

Chowdhury-Sengupta, Indira. "The Effeminate and the Masculine: Nationalism and the Concept of Race in Colonial Bengal." In *The Concept of Race in South Asia,* edited by Peter Robb, 282–303. Delhi: Oxford University Press, 1995.

———. "The Return of the Sati: A Note on Heroism and Domesticity in Colonial Bengal." *RFR/DRF* 22, no. 3/4 (1993): 41–4.

Clammer, John. "The Institutionalization of Ethnicity: The Culture of Ethnicity in Singapore." *Ethnic and Racial Studies* 5, no. 2 (1982): 127–39.

Clancy-Smith, Julia. "Islam, Gender, and Identities in the Making of French Algeria, 1830–1962." In *Domesticating the Empire: Race, Gender, and Family Life in French and Dutch Colonialism,* edited by Julia Clancy-Smith and Frances Gouda, 154–74. Charlottesville, VA: University Press of Virginia, 1998.

Cline, Catherine Ann. *E. D. Morel, 1873–1924: The Strategies of Protest.* Belfast: Blackstaff Press, 1980.

Cohen, Stephen P. *The Indian Army: Its Contribution to the Development of a Nation.* Delhi: Oxford University Press, 1990.

Cohn, Bernard S. *Colonialism and Its Forms of Knowledge: The British in India.* Princeton, NJ: Princeton University Press, 1996.

———. "The Census, Social Structure and Objectification in South Asia." In *An Anthropologist Among the Historians and other Essays,* 224–54. Delhi: Oxford University Press, 1987.

Comaroff, John and Jean. *Ethnography and the Historical Imagination.* Boulder, CO: Westview Press, 1992.

———. "Home-Made Hegemony: Modernity, Domesticity, and Colonialism in South Africa." In *African Encounters with Domesticity,* edited by Karen Tranberg Hansen, 37–74. Brunswick, NJ: Rutgers University Press, 1992.

———. "Through the Looking-Glass: Colonial Encounters of the First Kind." *Journal of Historical Sociology* 1, no. 1 (1988): 6–32.

Conklin, Alice. *A Mission to Civilize: The Republican Idea of Empire in France and West Africa, 1895–1930.* Stanford, CA: Stanford University Press, 1997.

Connell, R. W. *Masculinities.* Berkeley, CA: University of California Press, 1995.

Cooper, Annabel. "Textual Territories. Gendered Cultural Politics and Australian Representations of the War of 1914–1918." *Australian Historical Studies* 25, no. 100 (1993): 403–21.

Cooper, Frederick and Ann Laura Stoler. "Tensions of Empire: Colonial Control and Visions of Rule." *American Ethnologist* 16, no. 4 (1989): 609–21.

Copley, Antony. "Some Reflections by an Historian on Attitudes towards Women in Indian Traditional Society." *South Asia Research* 2 (1981): 22–33.

Corrigan, Philip and Derek Sayer. *The Great Arch: English State Formation as Cultural Revolution.* Oxford: Basil Blackwell, 1985.

Crew, F. A. E. ed. *The Army Medical Services: Administration.* Vol. 2. London, HMSO: 1955.

Crissey, John Thorne and Lawrence Charles Paris. *The Dermatology and Syphilology of the Nineteenth Century.* New York: Praeger, 1981.

Crisswell, Colin and Mike Watson, *The Royal Hong Kong Police (1841–1945).* Hong Kong: Macmillan, 1982.

Crowther, M. A. "The Later Years of the Workhouse 1890-1929." In *The Origins of British Social Policy,* edited by Pat Thane, 36–55. London: Croom Helm, 1978.

Curtin, Philip D. *Disease and Empire: The Health of European Troops in the Conquest of Africa.* Cambridge: Cambridge University Press, 1998.

———. *Death by Migration: Europe's Encounter with the Tropical World in the Nineteenth Century.* Cambridge: Cambridge University Press, 1989.

Dallas, K. M. "The Origins of 'White Australia.'" *Australian Quarterly* 23 (1955): 43–52.

Dalley, Bronwyn. "'Fresh Attractions': White Slavery and Feminism in New Zealand, 1885-1918." *Women's History Review* 9, no. 3 (2000): 585–606.

————. "Lolly Shops 'of the Red-light Kind' and 'Soldiers of the King': Suppressing One-Woman Brothels in New Zealand, 1908–1916." *New Zealand Journal of History* 30, no. 1 (1996): 3–23.

Damousi, Joy. *Depraved and Disorderly: Female Convicts, Sexuality and Gender in Colonial Australia.* Cambridge: Cambridge University Press, 1997.

Daniels, Kay. "Prostitution in Tasmania during the Transition from Penal Settlement to 'Civilized' Society." In *So Much Hard Work: Women and Prostitution in Australian History,* edited by Kay Daniels, 15–86. Sydney: Fontana/Collins, 1984.

Das, Veena. "Gender Studies, Cross-Cultural Comparison, and the Colonial Organization of Knowledge." *Berkshire Review* 21 (1986): 58–79.

————. *Structure and Cognition: Aspects of Hindu Caste and Ritual.* 2nd ed. Delhi: Oxford University Press, 1982.

Davenport-Hines, Richard. *Sex, Death and Punishment: Attitudes to Sex and Sexuality in Britain since the Renaissance.* London: Collins, 1990.

Davidson, Roger. "Venereal Disease, Sexual Morality, and Public Health in Interwar Scotland." *Journal of the History of Sexuality* 5, no. 2 (1994): 267–94.

————. " 'A Scourge to be Firmly Gripped': The Campaign for VD Controls in Interwar Scotland." *Social History of Medicine* 6 (1993): 213–35 .

Davies, Andrew. "Youth Gangs, Masculinity, and Violence in Late Victorian Manchester and Salford." *Journal of Social History* 32, no. 2 (1998): 349–69.

Davin, Anna. "Imperialism and Motherhood." *History Workshop Journal* 6 (1978): 9–65.

Dawson, Graham. *Soldier Heroes: British Adventure, Empire, and the Imagining of Masculinities.* London: Routledge, 1994.

De Silva, P. Ariyaratne and Michael G. Gomez. "The History of Venereal Disease and Yaws (Parangi) in Sri Lanka." *Genitourinary Medicine* 70, no. 5 (1994): 349–54.

Dennie, Charles Clayton. *A History of Syphilis.* Springfield, IL: Charles C. Thomas, 1962.

Denoon, Donald. "Temperate Medicine and Settler Capitalism: On the Reception of Western Medical Ideas." In *Disease, Medicine, and Empire: Perspectives on Western Medicine and the Experience of European Expansion,* edited by Roy Macleod and Milton Lewis, 121–38. London: Routledge, 1988.

Denoon, Donald, with Marivic Wyndham, "Australia and the Western Pacific." In *The Oxford History of the British Empire.* Volume 3. *The Nineteenth Century,* edited by Andrew Porter, 546–72. Oxford: Oxford University Press, 1999.

Desai, Neera and Maithreyi Krishnaraj, *Women and Society in India.* Delhi: Ajanta Publications, 1987.

Deslandes, Paul R. " 'The Foreign Element': Newcomers and the Rhetoric of Race, Nation, and Empire in 'Oxbridge' Undergraduate Culture, 1850–1920." *Journal of British Studies* 37, no. 1 (1998): 54–90.

Dikötter, Frank. *Sex, Culture, and Modernity in China: Medical Science and the Construction of Sexual Identities in the Early Republican Period.* Honolulu, HI: University of Hawaii Press, 1995.

————. "Sexually Transmitted Diseases in Modern China: A Historical Survey." *Genitourinary Medicine* 69, no. 5 (1993): 341–45.

Duara, Prasenjit. *Rescuing History from the Nation: Questioning Narratives of Modern China.* Chicago: University of Chicago Press, 1995.

Durrans, Peter J. "The House of Commons and the British Empire 1868–1880." *Canadian Journal of History* 9, no. 1 (1974): 19–44.

Dyer, Richard. *White.* London and New York: Routledge, 1997.

Edwardes, Allen. *The Jewel in the Lotus: A Historical Survey of the Sexual Culture of the East.* New York: Julian Press, 1959.

Edwards, Susan S. M. "Sex or Gender: The Prostitute in Law." *British Journal of Sexual Medicine* 9 (1982): 5–11.

Ellinwood, DeWitt C. "The Indian Soldier, the Indian Army, and Change, 1914–1918." In *India and World War One,* edited by DeWitt C. Ellinwood and S. D. Pradhan, 177–211. New Delhi: Manohar, 1978.

Elson, Robert E. "International Commerce, The State and Society: Economic and Social Change." In *The Cambridge History of Southeast Asia:* Volume 2. *The Nineteenth and Twentieth Centuries,* edited by Nicholas Tarling, 131–96. Cambridge: Cambridge University Press, 1992.

Endacott, G. B. *Government and People in Hong Kong, 1841–1962. A Constitutional History.* Hong Kong: Hong Kong University Press, 1964.

————. *A History of Hong Kong.* London: Oxford University Press, 1958.

Eng, Lai Ah. *Peasants, Proletarians and Prostitutes: A Preliminary Investigation into the Work of Chinese Women in Colonial Malaya.* Singapore: Institute of South East Asian Studies, 1986.

Engels, Dagmar. *Beyond Purdah? Women in Bengal 1890–1939.* Delhi: Oxford University Press, 1996.

———. "History and Sexuality in India: Discursive Trends." *Trends in History* 4, no. 4 (1990): 15–42.

Englander, David. "Booth's Jews: The Presentation of Jews and Judaism in *Life and Labour of the People in London.*" *Victorian Studies* 32, no. 4 (1989): 551–71.

Enloe, Cynthia. *The Morning After: Sexual Politics at the End of the Cold War.* Berkeley, CA: University of California Press, 1993.

Ericsson, Lars D. "Charges against Prostitution: An Attempt at a Philosophical Assessment." *Ethics* 90 (1980): 335–66.

Etherington, Norman. "Natal's Black Rape Scare of the 1870s." *Journal of Southern African Studies* 15, no. 1 (1988): 36–53.

Evans, David. "Tackling the 'Hidden Scourge': The Creation of Venereal Disease Treatment Centres in Early Twentieth-Century Britain." *Social History of Medicine* 5, no. 3 (1992): 413–33.

Evans, Raymond. "Keeping Australia Clean White." In *A Most Valuable Acquisition: A People's History of Australia Since 1788,* edited by Verity Burgmann and Jenny Lee, 170–88. Melbourne: McPhee Gribble/Penguin, 1988.

———. " 'The Owl and the Eagle': The Significance of Race in Colonial Queensland." *Social Alternatives* 5, no. 4 (1986): 16-22.

———. " 'Don't You Remember Black Alice, Sam Holt?' Aboriginal Women in Queensland History." *Hecate* 8, no. 2 (1982): 7–21.

———. "The Hidden Colonists: Deviance and Social Control in Colonial Queensland." In *Social Policy in Australia: Some Perspectives 1901–75,* edited by Jill Roe, 74–100. Stanmore, NSW: Cassell Australia, 1976.

———. " 'Soiled Doves'. Prostitution and Society in Colonial Queensland—An Overview." *Hecate* 1 (1975): 6–24.

Evans, Raymond, Kay Saunders, and Kathryn Cronin. *Race Relations in Colonial Queensland: A History of Exclusion, Exploitation and Extermination.* 3rd ed. St. Lucia: University of Queensland Press, 1993.

Faruqee, Ashrufa. "Conceiving the Coolie Woman: Indentured Labour, Indian Women and Colonial Discourse." *South Asia Research* 16, no. 1 (1996): 61–76.

Faure, David. ed. *Society.* Hong Kong: Hong Kong University Press, 1997.

Fee, Elizabeth and Dorothy Porter. "Public Health, Preventive Medicine and Professionalization: England and America in the Nineteenth Century." In *Medicine in Society. Historical Essays,* edited by Andrew Wear, 249–75. Cambridge: Cambridge University Press, 1992.

Felstein, Ivor. *Sexual Pollution: The Fall and Rise of Venereal Diseases.* Newton Abbot and London: David and Charles, 1974.

Fessler, A. "Venereal Disease and Prostitution in the Reports of the Poor Law Commissioners, 1834-1850." *British Journal of Venereal Diseases* 27 (1951): 154–57.

Fewster, Kevin. "The Wazza Riots, 1915." *Journal of the Australian War Memorial* 4 (1984): 47–53.

Finch, Lynette. *The Classing Gaze: Sexuality, Class and Surveillance.* St. Leonards, NSW: Allen and Unwin, 1993.

Finnane, Mark and Stephen Garton. "The Work of Policing: Social Relations and the Criminal Justice System in Queensland 1880-1914, Part 2." *Labour History* 63 (November 1992): 43–64.

Finnane, Mark and Clive Moore. "Kanaka Slaves or Willing Workers? Melanesian Workers and the Queensland Criminal Justice System in the 1890s." *Criminal Justice History* 13 (1992): 141–60.

Fisher, Wendy. "Brothels and the Military." *Sabretache* 27 (1986): 22-5.

Fitzgerald, Rosemary. "A 'Peculiar and Exceptional Measure': The Call for Women Medical Missionaries for India in the Later Nineteenth Century." In *Missionary Encounters: Sources and Issues,* edited by Robert A. Bickers and Rosemary Seton, 174–96. Richmond, Surrey: Curzon Press, 1996.

Fitzgerald, Ross. *From the Dreaming to 1915: A History of Queensland.* St. Lucia: University of Queensland Press, 1982.

Fitzpatrick, Peter. "Passions Out of Place: Law, Incommensurability, and Resistance." In *Laws of the Postcolonial,* edited by Eve Darian-Smith and Peter Fitzpatrick, 39–59. Ann Arbor, MI: University of Michigan Press, 1999.

Fitzpatrick, Peter and Eve Darian-Smith. "Laws of the Postcolonial: An Insistent Introduction." In *Laws of the Postcolonial,* edited by Eve Darian-Smith and Peter Fitzpatrick, 1–15. Ann Arbor, MI: University of Michigan Press, 1999.

Fleming, Philip. "Fighting the 'Red Plague': Observations on the Response to Venereal Disease in New Zealand 1910–45." *New Zealand Journal of History* 22, no. 1 (1988): 56–64.

Fluker, J. L. "Personal Reminiscences of a Venereologist before Penicillin." *International Journal of STD & AIDS* 1 (1990): 443–6.

Forbes, Geraldine H. *The New Cambridge History of India*. Vol. 4. *Women in Modern India* Cambridge: Cambridge University Press, 1996.

———. "Managing Midwifery in India." In *Contesting Colonial Hegemony: State and Society in Africa and India*, edited by Dagmar Engels and Shula Marks, 152–72. London: British Academic Press/German Historical Institute, 1994.

———. "The Politics of Respectability: Indian Women and the Indian National Congress." In *The Indian National Congress: Centenary Hindsights*, edited by D. A. Low, 54–97. Delhi: Oxford University Press, 1988.

Frances, Raelene. "Australian Prostitution in International Context." *Australian Historical Studies* 106 (1996): 127–41.

Frankenberg, Ruth. *White Women, Race Matters: The Social Construction of Whiteness*. Minneapolis, MN: University of Minnesota Press, 1993.

Frazer, W. M. *A History of English Public Health 1834–1939*. London: Bailliere, Tindall and Cox, 1950.

Fryer, Peter. *Staying Power: Black People in Britain since 1504*. Atlantic Highlands, NJ: Humanities Press, 1984.

Fuller, J. G. *Troop Morale and Popular Culture in the British and Dominion Armies 1914–1918*. Oxford: Clarendon Press, 1990.

Gammage, Bill. *The Broken Years: Australian Soldiers in the Great War*. Canberra: Australian National University Press, 1974.

Ganter, Regina and Ros Kidd. "'The Powers of Protectors: Conflicts Surrounding Queensland's 1897 Aboriginal Legislation." *Australian Historical Studies* 25 (1993): 536–54.

Gartner, Lloyd P. "Anglo-Jewry and the Jewish International Traffic in Prostitution, 1885–1914." *Association for Jewish Studies Review* 7/8 (1982-83): 129–78.

Gerster, Robin. "A Bit of The Other: Touring Vietnam." In *Gender and War: Australians at War in the Twentieth Century*, edited by Joy Damousi and Marilyn Lake, 223–35. Melbourne: Cambridge University Press, 1995.

Ghurye, Govind Sadashiv. *Caste and Race in India*. Bombay: Popular Prakashan, 1969.

Gilfoyle, Timothy J. "Prostitutes in History: From Parables of Pornography to Metaphors of Modernity." *American Historical Review* 104, no. 1 (1999): 117–41.

Gilman, Sander L. *Inscribing The Other*. Lincoln, NE: University of Nebraska Press, 1991.

———. *The Jew's Body*. London: Routledge, 1991.

———. "'I'm Down on Whores': Race and Gender in Victorian London," in *Anatomy of Racism*, edited by David Theo Goldberg, 146–70. Minneapolis, MN: University of Minnesota Press, 1990.

———. *Sexuality, An Illustrated History: Representing the Sexual in Medicine and Culture from the Middle Ages to the Age of AIDS*. New York: John Wiley and Sons, 1989.

———. "Black Bodies, White Bodies: Toward an Iconography of Female Sexuality in Late Nineteenth-Century Art, Medicine, and Literature." In *"Race," Writing, and Difference*, edited by Henry Louis Gates Jr., 223–61. Chicago: University of Chicago Press, 1986.

Gilroy, Paul. *The Black Atlantic: Modernity and Double Consciousness*. Cambridge, MA: Harvard University Press, 1993.

Glickman, Nora. "The Jewish White Slave Trade in Latin American Writings." *American Jewish Archives* 33–4 (1982): 178–89.

Gopal, Sarvepalli. *The Viceroyalty of Lord Ripon 1880–1884*. Oxford: Oxford University Press, 1953.

Gorham, Deborah. *Vera Brittain: A Feminist Life*. Oxford: Basil Blackwell, 1996.

———. "The 'Maiden Tribute of Modern Babylon' Re-Examined: Child Prostitution and the Idea of Childhood in Late-Victorian England." *Victorian Studies* 21 (1978): 353–79.

Gouda, Frances. "*Nyonyas* on the Colonial Divide: White Women in the Dutch East Indies, 1900–1942." *Gender & History* 5, no. 3 (1993): 318–42.

Grayzel, Susan R. *Women's Identities at War: Gender, Motherhood, and Politics in Britain and France during the First World War*. Chapel Hill, NC: University of North Carolina Press, 1999.

Green, E. H. H. *The Crisis of Conservatism: The Politics, Economics and Ideology of the British Conservative Party, 1880–1914*. London: Routledge, 1995.

Greenhut, Jeffrey. "The Imperial Reserve: The Indian Corps on the Western Front, 1914–15." *Journal of Imperial and Commonwealth History* 12, no. 1 (1983): 54–73.

————. "Race, Sex, and War: The Impact of Race and Sex on Morale and Health Services for the Indian Corps on the Western Front, 1914." *Military Affairs* 45, no. 2 (1981): 71–4.

Greenstein, Lewis J. "The Nandi Experience in the First World War," In *Africa and the First World War*, edited by Melvin E. Page, 81–94. Basingstoke: The Macmillan Press, 1987.

Gregg, Robert. *Inside Out, Outside In: Essays in Comparative History.* Basingstoke, Macmillan; New York, St. Martin's Press: 2000.

Grewal, Inderpal. *Home and Harem: Nation, Gender, Empire, and the Cultures of Travel.* Durham, NC: Duke University Press, 1996.

Grimshaw, Patricia, Marilyn Lake, Ann McGrath, and Marian Quartly. *Creating A Nation.* Ringwood, VIC: Penguin Books, 1994.

Grittner, Frederick K. *White Slavery: Myth, Ideology, and American Law.* New York: Garland, 1990.

Grove, Richard H. "Colonial Conservation, Ecological Hegemony and Popular Resistance: Towards a Global Synthesis." In *Imperialism and the Natural World*, edited by John M. MacKenzie, 15–50. Manchester: Manchester University Press, 1990.

Grundlingh, Albert. "The Impact of the First World War on South African Blacks." In *Africa and the First World War*, edited by Melvin E. Page, 54–80. Basingstoke: The Macmillan Press, 1987.

Guénel, Annick. "Sexually Transmitted Diseases in Vietnam and Cambodia since the French Colonial Period." In *Sex, Disease, and Society: A Comparative History of Sexually Transmitted Diseases and HIV/AIDS in Asia and the Pacific*, edited by Milton Lewis, Scott Bamber, and Michael Waugh, 139–53. Westport, CT: Greenwood Press, 1997.

Guy, Donna J. *Sex and Danger in Buenos Aires: Prostitution, Family, and Nation in Argentina.* Lincoln, NE: University of Nebraska Press, 1991.

————. "Medical Imperialism Gone Awry: The Campaign Against Legalized Prostitution in Latin America." In *Science, Medicine, and Cultural Imperialism*, edited by Teresa Meade and Mark Walker, 75–94. New York: St. Martin's Press, 1991.

————. "White Slavery, Public Health, and the Socialist Position on Legalized Prostitution in Argentina, 1913–1936." *Latin American Research Review* 23, no. 3 (1988): 60–80.

Hall, Catherine. *Civilising Subjects: Metropole and Colony in the English Imagination, 1830–1867.* Chicago: University of Chicago Press, 2002.

————. "Imperial Man: Edward Eyre in Australasia and the West Indies 1833–66." In *The Expansion of England: Race, Ethnicity and Cultural History*, edited by Bill Schwarz, 130–170. London: Routledge, 1996.

————. "Rethinking Imperial Histories: The Reform Act of 1867." *New Left Review* 208 (1994): 3–29.

————. " 'From Greenland's Icy Mountains . . . to Afric's Golden Sand': Ethnicity, Race and Nation in Mid-Nineteenth Century England." *Gender & History* 5, no. 2 (1993): 212–30.

————. "The Economy of Intellectual Prestige: Thomas Carlyle, John Stuart Mill, and the Case of Governor Eyre," *Cultural Critique* 12 (1989): 167–98

Hall, Catherine, Keith McClelland, and Jane Rendall *Defining the Victorian Nation: Class, Race, Gender and the Reform Act of 1867.* Cambridge: Cambridge University Press, 2000.

Hall, Kim F. *Things of Darkness: Economies of Race and Gender in Early Modern England.* Ithaca, NY: Cornell University Press, 1995.

Hall, Lesley A. " 'War Always Brings It On': War, STDs and the Civilian Population in Britain, 1850–1950." In *Medicine and Modern Warfare*, edited by Roger Cooter, Mark Harrison, and Steve Sturdy, 205–23. Amsterdam and Atlanta: Rodopi, 1999.

Hall, Robert. "Aborigines, the Army and the Second World War in Northern Australia." *Aboriginal History* 4, no. 1 (1980): 73–96.

Hammerton, A. James. *Emigrant Gentlewomen: Genteel Poverty and Female Emigration, 1830–1914.* London: Croom Helm, 1979.

Hammonds, Evelynn M. "Toward a Genealogy of Black Female Sexuality: The Problematic of Silence." In *Feminist Genealogies, Colonial Legacies, Democratic Futures*, edited by M. Jacqui Alexander and Chandra Talpade Mohanty, 170–82. New York: Routledge, 1997.

Hane, Mikiso. *Peasants, Rebels, and Outcastes: The Underside of Modern Japan.* New York: Pantheon, 1982.

Hantover, Jeffrey. *Gambling Dens and Licensed Brothels: A Brief History of Cat Street.* Hong Kong: Casey Co. Ltd., 1992.

Harcourt, Freda. "Disraeli's Imperialism, 1866–1868: A Question of Timing." *Historical Journal* 23, no. 1 (1980): 87–109.

Harries-Jenkins, Gwyn. *The Army in Victorian Society.* London: Routledge and Kegan Paul/Toronto: University of Toronto Press, 1977.

Harris, José. "Political Thought and the Welfare State 1870–1940: An Intellectual Framework for British Social Policy." *Past and Present* 135 (1992): 116–41.

Harrison, J. B. "Allahabad: A Sanitary History," In *The City in South Asia: Pre-modern and Modern,* edited by Kenneth Ballhatchet and John Harrison, 166–95. London and Dublin: Curzon Press; Atlantic Highlands, NJ: Humanities Press, 1980.

Harrison, Mark. "'The Tender Frame of Man': Disease, Climate and Racial Difference in India and the West Indies, 1760–1860." *Bulletin of the History of Medicine* 70 (1996): 68–93.

——. "The British Army and the Problem of Venereal Disease in France and Egypt during the First World War." *Medical History* 39 (1995): 133–58.

——. *Public Health in British India: Anglo-Indian Preventive Medicine, 1859–1914.* Cambridge: Cambridge University Press, 1994.

——. "Towards A Sanitary Utopia? Professional Visions and Public Health in India, 1880–1914." *South Asia Research* 10, no. 1 (1990): 19–40.

Harrison, Tom. *Savage Civilization.* New York: Alfred Knopf, 1937.

Havinden, Michael and David Meredith. *Colonialism and Development: Britain and Its Tropical Colonies, 1850–1960.* London: Routledge, 1993.

Hawley, John Stratton, ed. *Sati, the Blessing and the Curse: The Burning of Wives in India.* New York: Oxford University Press, 1994.

Haynes, Douglas Melvin. *Imperial Medicine: Patrick Manson and the Conquest of Tropical Disease.* Philadelphia, PA: University of Pennsylvania Press, 2001.

——. "The Social Production of Metropolitan Expertise in Tropical Diseases: The Imperial State, Colonial Service, and the Tropical Diseases Research Fund." *Science, Technology & Society* 4, no. 2 (1999): 205–38.

——. "Social Status and Imperial Service: Tropical Medicine and the British Medical Profession in the Nineteenth Century." In *Warm Climates and Western Medicine,* edited by David Arnold, 209–26. Amsterdam and Atlanta: Rodopi, 1996.

Heathorn, Stephen. "'Let us remember that we, too, are English': Constructions of Citizenship and National Identity in English Elementary School Reading Books, 1880–1914." *Victorian Studies* 38, no. 3 (1995): 395–427.

Hendrickson, Ken. "A Kinder, Gentler British Army: Mid-Victorian Experiments in the Management of Army Vice at Gibraltar and Aldershot." *War & Society* 14, no. 2 (1996): 21–33.

Hennessy, Rosemary and Rajeswari Mohan. "The Construction of Woman in Three Popular Texts of Empire: Towards a Critique of Materialist Feminism." *Textual Practice* 3, no. 3 (1989): 323–59.

Hershatter, Gail. *Dangerous Pleasures: Prostitution and Modernity in Twentieth-Century Shanghai.* Berkeley, CA: University of California Press, 1997.

Hesselink, Liesbeth. "Prostitution: A Necessary Evil, Particularly in the Colonies: Views on Prostitution in the Netherlands Indies." In *Indonesian Women in Focus: Past and Present Notions,* edited by Elsbeth Locher-Scholten and Anke Niehof, 205–24. Dordrecht: Foris Publications, 1987.

Hichberger, Joany. "Old Soldiers." In *Patriotism: The Making and Unmaking of British National Identity:* Vol. 3 *National Fictions,* edited by Raphael Samuel, 50–63. London: Routledge, 1989.

Higginbotham, Evelyn Brooks. "African-American Women's History and the Metalanguage of Race." *Signs* 17, no. 2 (1992): 251–74.

Hill, Richard S. *Policing the Colonial Frontier: The Theory and Practice of Coercive Social and Racial Control in New Zealand 1767–1867.* Wellington, New Zealand: Government Printer, 1986.

Hinrichsen, Josephine. "Venereal Disease in the Major Armies and Navies of the World." *American Journal of Syphilis, Gonorrhea and Venereal Diseases* 29 (January 1945): 80–124.

Hirschman, Charles. "The Meaning and Measurement of Ethnicity in Malaysia: An Analysis of Census Classifications." *Journal of Asian Studies* 46, no. 3 (1987): 555–82.

——. "The Making of Race in Colonial Malaya: Political Economy and Racial Ideology," *Sociological Forum* 1, no. 2 (1986): 330–61.

History of the Po Leung Kuk Hong Kong 1878–1968. Hong Kong: Po Leung Kuk, 1969.

Hodge, Peter, ed. *Community Problems and Social Work in Southeast Asia.* Hong Kong: Hong Kong University Press, 1980.

Hoe, Susanna. *The Private Life of Old Hong Kong: Western Women in the British Colony 1841–1941.* Hong Kong: Oxford University Press, 1991.

Hopwood, Derek. *Tales of Empire: The British in the Middle East, 1880–1952.* London: I. B. Tauris, 1989.

Howell, Philip, "Prostitution and Racialised Sexuality: The Regulation of Prostitution in Britain and the British Empire before the Contagious Diseases Acts." *Environment and Planning D: Society and Space* 18 (2000): 321–39.

Hughes, Jenny. "A History of Sexually Transmitted Diseases in Papua New Guinea." In *Sex, Disease, and Society: A Comparative History of Sexually Transmitted Diseases and HIV/AIDS in Asia and the Pacific,* edited by Milton Lewis, Scott Bamber, and Michael Waugh, 231–48. Westport, CT: Greenwood Press, 1997.

Humphries, Steve. *A Secret World of Sex: Forbidden Fruit: The British Experience 1900–1950.* London: Sidgwick and Jackson, 1988.

Hunt, Alan, "The Great Masturbation Panic and the Discourses of Moral Regulation in Nineteenth and Early Twentieth Century Britain." *Journal of the History of Sexuality* 8, no. 4 (1998): 575–615.

Hunt, Nancy Rose. *A Colonial Lexicon: Of Birth Ritual, Medicalization, and Mobility in the Congo.* Durham, NC: Duke University Press, 1999.

Hunt, Susan Jane. *Spinifex and Hessian: Women's Lives in North-Western Australia.* Nedlands, Perth: University of Western Australia Press, 1986.

———. "Aboriginal Women and Colonial Authority: Northwestern Australia 1885–1905." In *In Pursuit of Justice: Australian Women and the Law 1788–1979,* edited by Judy Mackinolty and Heather Radi, 32–41. Sydney: Hale and Iremonger, 1979.

Hutchins, Francis G. *The Illusion of Permanence: British Imperialism in India.* Princeton, NJ: Princeton University Press, 1967.

Huttenback, Robert A. *Racism and Empire: White Settlers and Colored Immigrants in the British Self-Governing Colonies, 1830–1910.* Ithaca, NY: Cornell University Press, 1976.

Hyam, Ronald. *Britain's Imperial Century, 1815–1914: A Study of Empire and Expansion.* Basingstoke: The Macmillan Press, 1993.

———. "Concubinage and the Colonial Service: The Crewe Circular (1909)." *Journal of Imperial and Commonwealth History* 14, no. 3 (1986): 170–86.

———. "Empire and Sexual Opportunity." *Journal of Imperial and Commonwealth History* 14, no. 2 (1986): 34–90.

Hynes, Samuel. *A War Imagined: The First World War and English Culture.* New York: Athenaeum, 1991.

Ignatiev, Noel. *How the Irish Became White.* London: Routledge, 1995.

Ingleson, John. "Prostitution in Colonial Java." In *Nineteenth and Twentieth Century Indonesia. Essays in Honour of Professor J. D. Legge,* edited by David P. Chandler and M. C. Ricklefs, 123–40. Clayton, VIC: Centre of Southeast Asian Studies, Monash University, 1986.

Inglis, Amirah. *The White Woman's Protection Ordinance: Sexual Anxiety and Politics in Papua.* New York: St. Martin's Press, 1975.

Inglis, Ken. "Men, Women, and War Memorials: Anzac Australia." In *Learning About Women. Gender, Politics, and Power,* edited by Jill K. Conway, Susan C. Bourque, and Joan W. Scott, 35–59. Ann Arbor, MI: University of Michigan Press, 1989.

Irving, Helen. *To Constitute a Nation: A Cultural History of Australia's Constitution.* Cambridge: Cambridge University Press, 1997.

Islam, M. S. "Life in the Mufassal Towns of Nineteenth-Century Bengal." In *The City in South Asia: Pre-modern and Modern,* edited by Kenneth Ballhatchet and John Harrison, 224–56. London and Dublin: Curzon Press; Atlantic Highlands, NJ: Humanities Press, 1980.

Jacobs, Patricia. "Science and Veiled Assumptions: Miscegenation in W.A. 1930–1937." *Australian Aboriginal Studies* 2 (1986): 15–23.

Jackson, R. N. *Pickering: Protector of Chinese.* Kuala Lumpur: Oxford University Press, 1965.

Jacob, T. *Cantonments in India: Evolution and Growth.* New Delhi: Reliance Publishing House, 1994.

Jacobs, Jane M. *Edge of Empire: Postcolonialism and the City.* London and New York: Routledge, 1996.

James, Lawrence. *Raj: The Making and Unmaking of British India.* New York: St. Martin's Press, 1997.

James, T. E. *Prostitution and the Law.* London: Heinemann, 1951.

Jaschok, Maria. *Concubines and Bondservants: A Social History.* London: Zed Books, 1988.

Jaschok, Maria and Suzanne Miers, "Women in the Chinese Patriarchal System: Submission, Servitude, Escape and Collusion." In *Women and Chinese Patriarchy: Submission, Servitude and Escape,* edited by Maria Jaschok and Suzanne Miers, 1–24. London and New Jersey: Zed Books, 1994.

Jebb, Mary Anne. "The Lock Hospitals Experiment: Europeans, Aborigines and Venereal Disease." *Studies in Western Australian History* 8 (1984): 68–89.

Jeffery, Roger. *The Politics of Health in India.* Berkeley, CA: University of California Press, 1988.

———. "Doctors and Congress: The Role of Medical Men and Medical Politics in Indian Nationalism." In *The Indian National Congress and the Political Economy of India 1885–1985,* edited by Mike Shepperdson and Colin Simmons, 160–73. Aldershot: Avebury/Gower, 1988.

Johnston, W. Ross. *The Long Blue Line: A History of the Queensland Police.* Brisbane: Boolarong Publications, 1992.

Jolly, Margaret. "Introduction: Colonial and Postcolonial Plots in Histories of Maternities and Modernities." In *Maternities and Modernities. Colonial and Postcolonial Experiences in Asia and the Pacific,* edited by Kalpana Ram and Margaret Jolly, 1–25. Cambridge: Cambridge University Press, 1998.

Jones, Helen. ed. *Duty and Citizenship: The Correspondence and Papers of Violet Markham, 1896–1953.* London: The Historian's Press, 1994.

Joseph, C. L. "The British West Indies Regiment 1914–1918." *Journal of Caribbean History* 3 (1971): 94–124.

Kabbani, Rana. *Europe's Myths of Orient.* Bloomington, IN: Indiana University Press, 1986.

Kaminsky, Arnold P. *The India Office 1880–1910.* New York: Greenwood Press, 1986.

———. "Morality Legislation and British Troops in Late Nineteenth Century India." *Military Affairs* 43 (1979): 78–83.

Kampmeier, Rudolph H. "Introduction of Salvarsan." *Sexually Transmitted Diseases* 4, no. 2 (1977): 66–8.

Kanitkar, Helen. " 'Real True Boys': Moulding the Cadets of Imperialism." In *Dislocating Masculinity: Comparative Ethnographies,* edited by Andrea Cornwall and Nancy Lindisfarne, 184–96. Routledge: London, 1994.

Kasturi, Malavika. "Law and Crime in India: British Policy and the Female Infanticide Act of 1870." *Indian Journal of Gender Studies* 1, no. 2 (1994): 169–93.

Kelly, John D. "Gaze and Grasp: Plantations, Desires, Indentured Indians, and Colonial Law in Fiji." In *Sites of Desire, Economies of Pleasure: Sexualities in Asia and the Pacific,* edited by Lenore Manderson and Margaret Jolly, 72–98. Chicago: University of Chicago Press, 1997.

Ken, Wong Li. "Commercial Growth before the Second World War." In *A History of Singapore,* edited by Ernest C. T. Chew and Edwin Lee, 41–65. Singapore: Oxford University Press, 1991.

Kennedy, Dane. *The Magic Mountains: Hill Stations and the British Raj.* Berkeley, CA: University of California Press, 1996.

Kent, David. "*The Anzac Book* and the Anzac Legend: C. E. W. Bean as Editor and Image-Maker." *Historical Studies* 21 (1985): 376–90.

Kent, Susan Kingsley. *Making Peace: The Reconstruction of Gender in Interwar Britain.* Princeton, NJ: Princeton University Press, 1993.

Kersenboom-Story, Saskia C. *Nityasumangala: Devadasi Tradition in South India.* Delhi: Motilal Banarsidass, 1987.

Kiat, Lee Yong. *The Medical History of Early Singapore.* Tokyo: Southeast Asian Medical Information Center, 1978.

Killingray, David. "Military and Labour Policies in the Gold Coast during the First World War." In *Africa and the First World War,* edited by Melvin E. Page, 152–70. London: The Macmillan Press, 1987.

———. "The Idea of A British Imperial African Army." *Journal of African History* 20 (1979): 421–36.

King, Ambrose. "The Life and Times of Colonel Harrison." *British Journal of Venereal Diseases* 50 (1974): 391–403.

———. " 'These Dying Diseases': Venereology in Decline?" *The Lancet* (29 March 1958): 651–7.

King, Anthony D. *Global Cities: Post-Imperialism and the Internationalization of London.* London: Routledge, 1990.

Kiple, Kenneth F., ed. *The Cambridge World History of Human Disease.* Cambridge: Cambridge University Press, 1993.

Kirkby, Diane. *Barmaids: A History of Women's Work in Pubs.* Cambridge: Cambridge University Press, 1997.

Kit-ching, Chan Lau. *China, Britain and Hong Kong, 1895–1945.* Hong Kong: The Chinese University Press, 1990.

Klass, Morton. *Caste: The Emergence of the South Asian Social System.* Philadelphia, PA: Institute for the Study of Human Issues, 1980.

Krishnaswamy, Revathi. *Effeminism: The Economy of Colonial Desire.* Ann Arbor, MI: University of Michigan Press, 1998.

Kuhnke, LaVerne. *Lives At Risk: Public Health in Nineteenth-Century Egypt.* Berkeley, CA: University of California Press, 1990.

Kunitz, Stephen J. *Disease and Social Diversity: The European Impact on the Health of Non-Europeans.* New York: Oxford University Press, 1994.

Lake, Marilyn. "Australian Frontier Feminism and the Marauding White Man." In *Gender and Imperialism,* edited by Clare Midgley, 123–36. Manchester: Manchester University Press, 1998.

———. "The Politics of Respectability: Identifying the Masculinist Context." *Historical Studies* 22, no. 86 (1986): 116–31.

Lal, Maneesha. "The Politics of Gender and Medicine in Colonial India: The Countess of Dufferin's Fund, 1885–1888." *Bulletin of the History of Medicine* 68 (1994): 29–66.

Lal, Vinay. "The Incident of the 'Crawling Lane': Women in the Punjab Disturbances of 1919." *Genders* 16 (1993): 35–60.

Lawrence, Christopher. "A Tale of Two Sciences: Bedside and Bench in Twentieth-Century Britain." *Medical History* 43 (1999): 421–49.

Lee, Edwin. "Community, Family and Household." In *A History of Singapore,* edited by Ernest C. T. Chew and Edwin Lee, 242–67. Singapore: Oxford University Press, 1991.

———. *The British as Rulers: Governing Multi-Racial Singapore 1867–1914.* Singapore: Singapore University Press, 1991.

Lees, Robert. "The 'Lock Wards' of Edinburgh Royal Infirmary." *British Journal of Venereal Diseases* 37 (1961): 187–9.

———. "Venereal Disease in the Armed Forces Overseas." *British Journal of Venereal Diseases* 22, no. 4 (1946): 149–68.

Lethbridge, H. J. *Hong Kong: Stability and Change, A Collection of Essays.* Hong Kong: Oxford University Press, 1978.

———. "Prostitution in Hong Kong: A Legal and Moral Dilemma." *Hong Kong Law Journal* 8, no. 2 (1978): 149–73.

Levesque, Andree. "Prescribers and Rebels: Attitudes to European Women's Sexuality in New Zealand, 1860–1918." In *Women in History: Essays on European Women in New Zealand* edited by Barbara Brookes, Charlotte Macdonald, and Margaret Tennant, 1–12. Wellington, NZ and Sydney: Port Nicholson Press and Allen and Unwin, 1986.

Levine, Philippa. "Battle Colors: Race, Sex, and Colonial Soldiery in World War I." *Journal of Women's History* 9, no. 4 (1998): 104–30.

———. "Modernity, Medicine, and Colonialism: The Contagious Diseases Ordinances in Hong Kong and the Straits Settlements." *Positions* 6, no. 3 (1998): 675–705.

———. "Rereading the 1890s: Venereal Disease as 'Constitutional Crisis' in Britain and British India." *Journal of Asian Studies* 55, no. 3 (1996): 585–612.

———. "'Walking the Streets In a Way No Decent Woman Should': Women Police in World War One." *Journal of Modern History* 66 (1994): 34–78.

———. "Consistent Contradictions: Prostitution and Protective Labour Legislation in Nineteenth-Century England." *Social History* 19, no. 1 (1994): 17–35.

———. "Venereal Disease, Prostitution, and the Politics of Empire: The Case of British India." *Journal of the History of Sexuality,* 4, no. 4 (1994): 579–602.

———. "'Rough Usage': Prostitution, Law, and the Social Historian." In *Rethinking Social History: English Society 1570–1920 and Its Interpretation,* edited by Adrian Wilson, 266–92. Manchester: Manchester University Press, 1993.

Lewis, Earl. "To Turn As On a Pivot: Writing African-Americans into a History of Overlapping Diasporas." *American Historical Review* 100, no. 3 (1995): 756–87.

Lewis, Milton. *Thorns on the Rose: The History of Sexually Transmitted Diseases in Australia in International Perspective.* Canberra: Australian Government Publishing Service, 1998.

———. "Sexually Transmitted Diseases in Australia from the Late Eighteenth to the Late Twentieth Century." In *Sex, Disease, and Society: A Comparative History of Sexually Transmitted Diseases and HIV/AIDS in Asia and the Pacific,* edited by Milton Lewis, Scott Bamber, and Michael Waugh, 249–76. Westport, CT: Greenwood Press, 1997.

———. "From Blue Light Clinic to Nightingale Centre: A Brief History of the Sydney STD Centre and Its Forerunners. Part 1: Venereal Diseases in Europe and in Australia from Colonization to 1945." *Venereology* 1, no. 1 (1988): 3–9.

———. "From Blue Light Clinic to Nightingale Centre: A Brief History of the Sydney STD Centre and Its Forerunners. Part 2: From the Postwar Years to the Present." *Venereology* 1, no. 2 (1988): 45–49.

Lewis, Milton and Scott Bamber. "Introduction." In *Sex, Disease, and Society: A Comparative History of Sexually Transmitted Diseases and HIV/AIDS in Asia and the Pacific*, edited by Milton Lewis, Scott Bamber, and Michael Waugh, 1–17. Westport, CT: Greenwood Press, 1997.

Lindeborg, Ruth. "The 'Asiatic' and the Boundaries of Victorian Englishness," *Victorian Studies* 37, no. 3 (1994): 381–404.

Littlewood, Barbara and Linda Mahood. "Prostitutes, Magdalenes and Wayward Girls: Dangerous Sexualities of Working Class Women in Victorian Scotland." *Gender & History* 3, no. 2 (1991): 160–75.

Livingstone, David N. "Climate's Moral Economy: Science, Race and Place in Post-Darwinian British and American Geography." In *Geography and Empire*, edited by Anne Godlewska and Neil Smith, 132–54. Oxford: Blackwell, 1994.

Loomba, Ania. *Colonialism/Postcolonialism*. London: Routledge, 1998.

———. "Dead Women Tell No Tales: Issues of Female Subjectivity, Subaltern Agency and Tradition in Colonial and Post-Colonial Writings on Widow Immolation in India." *History Workshop Journal* 36 (1993): 209–27.

Loos, Noel. *Invasion and Resistance: Aboriginal-European Relations on the North Queensland Frontier 1861–1897*. Canberra: Australian National University Press, 1982.

Lorimer, Douglas A. "Race, Science, and Culture: Historical Continuities and Discontinuities, 1850–1914." In *The Victorians and Race*, edited by Shearer West, 12–33. Aldershot, Scolar Press, 1996.

Lowe, Kate and Eugene McLaughlin. "Sir John Pope-Hennessy and the 'Native Race Craze': Colonial Government in Hong Kong, 1887–1882." *Journal of Imperial and Commonwealth History* 20, no. 2 (1992): 223–47.

Löwy, Ilana. "Testing for A Sexually Transmissible Disease, 1907–1970: The History of the Wassermann Reaction." In *AIDS and Contemporary History*, ed. Virginia Berridge and Philip Strong, 74–92. Cambridge: Cambridge University Press, 1993.

Ludden, David. "Orientalist Empiricism: Transformations of Colonial Knowledge," In *Orientalism and the Postcolonial Predicament: Perspectives on South Asia*, edited by Carol Breckenridge and Peter van der Veer, 250–78. Philadelphia, PA: University of Pennsylvania Press, 1993.

Luddy, Maria. " 'Abandoned Women and Bad Characters': Prostitution in Nineteenth Century Ireland." *Women's History Review* 6, no. 4 (1997), 485–503.

———. "Women and the Contagious Diseases Acts 1864–1886." *History Ireland* 1, no. 1 (1993): 32–4.

———. "Prostitution and Rescue Work in Nineteenth-Century Ireland." In *Women Surviving: Studies in Irish Women's History in the 19th and 20th Centuries*, edited by Maria Luddy and Cliona Murphy, 51–84. Dublin: Poolberg Press, 1990.

Lupton, Deborah. *Medicine as Culture: Illness, Disease and the Body in Western Societies*. London: Sage, 1994.

Lyons, Maryinez. "Sexually Transmitted Diseases in the History of Uganda." *Genitourinary Medicine* 70, no. 2 (1994): 138–45.

———. "The Power To Heal: African Medical Auxiliaries in Colonial Belgian Congo and Uganda." In *Contesting Colonial Hegemony: State and Society in Africa and India*, edited by Dagmar Engels and Shula Marks, 202–23. London: British Academic Press/German Historical Institute, 1994.

———. "From 'Death Camps' to *Cordon Sanitaire*: The Development of Sleeping Sickness Policy in the Uele District of the Belgian Congo, 1903–1914," *Journal of African History* 26, no. 1 (1985): 69–91.

McCulloch, Jock. *Black Peril, White Virtue: Sexual Crime in Southern Rhodesia, 1902–1935*. Bloomington, IN: Indiana University Press, 2000.

Macdonald, Charlotte. "The 'Social Evil': Prostitution and the Passage of the Contagious Diseases Acts (1869)." In *Women in History: Essays on European Women in New Zealand*, edited by Barbara Brookes, Charlotte Macdonald, and Margaret Tennant, 13–35. Wellington, NZ and Sydney: Port Nicholson Press and Allen and Unwin, 1986.

MacDougall, H. "Sexually Transmitted Diseases in Canada, 1800–1992." *Genitourinary Medicine* 70, no. 1 (1994): 56–63.

MacFarlane, H. and G. E. Aubrey, "Venereal Disease among the Natives of Hong Kong." *The Caduceus* 1, no. 1 (1922): 22–7.

McGrath, Ann. " 'Black Velvet': Aboriginal Women and Their Relations with White Men in the Northern Territory, 1910–1940." In *So Much Hard Work: Women and Prostitution in Australian History,* edited by Kay Daniels, 233–97. Sydney: Fontana/Collins, 1984.

McEwan, Cheryl. "Encounters with West African Women: Textual Representations of Difference by White Women Abroad." In *Writing Women and Space: Colonial and Postcolonial Geographies,* edited by Alison Blunt and Gillian Roe, 73–100. New York: The Guilford Press, 1994.

McHugh, Paul. *Prostitution and Victorian Social Reform.* London: Croom Helm, 1980.

McKechnie, Rosemary and Ian Welsh. "Between the Devil and the Deep Green Sea: Defining Risk Societies and Global Threats" In *The Lesser Evil and the Greater Good: The Theory and Politics of Social Diversity,* edited by Jeffrey Weeks, 57–78. London: Rivers Oram Press, 1994.

MacKenzie, John M. *Popular Imperialism and the Military 1850–1950.* Manchester: Manchester University Press, 1992.

McLaren, Angus. *The Trials of Masculinity: Policing Sexual Boundaries 1870–1930.* Chicago: University of Chicago Press, 1997.

McLaren, John P. S. "Chasing the Social Evil: Moral Fervour and The Evolution of Canada's Prostitution Laws, 1867–1917." *Canadian Journal of Law and Society* 1, no. 1 (1986): 125–65.

Macleod, Roy and Milton Lewis, eds. *Disease, Medicine, and Empire: Perspectives on Western Medicine and the Experience of European Expansion.* London: Routledge, 1988.

McClintock, Anne. *Imperial Leather: Race, Gender, and Sexuality in the Colonial Context.* New York: Routledge, 1995.

Macpherson, Kerrie L. "Conspiracy of Silence: A History of Sexually Transmitted Diseases and HIV/AIDS in Hong Kong" In *Sex, Disease, and Society: A Comparative History of Sexually Transmitted Diseases and HIV/AIDS in Asia and the Pacific,* edited Milton Lewis, Scott Bamber, and Michael Waugh, 85–112. Westport, CT: Greenwood Press, 1997.

———. *A Wilderness of Marshes: The Origins of Public Health in Shanghai, 1843–1893.* Hong Kong: Oxford University Press, 1987.

Mahood, Linda. *The Magdalenes: Prostitution in the Nineteenth Century.* London: Routledge, 1990.

Maloka, Tshidiso. "*Khomo Lia Oela*: Canteens, Brothels and Labour Migrancy in Colonial Lesotho, 1900–40." *Journal of African History* 38 (1997): 101–22.

Manderson, Lenore. "Shaping Reproductions: Maternity in Early Twentieth-Century Malaya." In *Maternities and Modernities: Colonial and Postcolonial Experiences in Asia and the Pacific,* edited by Kalpana Ram and Margaret Jolly, 26–49. Cambridge: Cambridge University Press, 1998.

———. "Migration, Prostitution and Medical Surveillance in Early Twentieth-Century Malaya" In *Migrants, Minorities and Health: Historical and Contemporary Studies,* edited by Lara Marks and Michael Worboys, 49–69. London and New York: Routledge. 1997.

———. "Colonial Desires: Sexuality, Race, and Gender in British Malaya." *Journal of the History of Sexuality* 7, no. 3 (1997): 372–88.

———. *Sickness and the State: Health and Illness in Colonial Malaya, 1870–1940.* Cambridge: Cambridge University Press, 1996.

Mani, Lata. *Contentious Traditions: The Debate on Sati in Colonial India.* Berkeley, CA: University of California Press, 1998.

Marglin, Frédérique Apffel. *Wives of the God-King: The Rituals of the Devadasis of Puri.* Delhi: Oxford University Press, 1985.

Markel, Howard, *Quarantine! East European Jewish Immigrants and the New York City Epidemic of 1892.* Baltimore, MD: Johns Hopkins University Press, 1997.

Markel, Howard and Alexandra Minna Stern. "Which Face? Whose Nation? Immigration, Public Health, and the Construction of Disease at America's Ports and Borders, 1891–1928." *American Behavioral Scientist* 42, no. 9 (1999): 1314–31.

Marks, Lara V. *Model Mothers: Jewish Mothers and Maternity Provision in East London 1870–1939.* Oxford: Clarendon Press, 1994.

———. "Jewish Women and Jewish Prostitution in the East End of London." *Jewish Quarterly* 24, no. 2 (1982): 6–10.

Marks, Sally. "Black Watch on the Rhine: A Study in Propaganda, Prejudice, and Prurience." *European Studies Review* 13, no. 3 (1983): 297–334.

Marks, Shula. "What is Colonial about Colonial Medicine? And What has Happened to Imperialism and Health?" *Social History of Medicine* 10 (1997): 205–19.

Markus, Andrew. *Australian Race Relations 1788–1993.* St. Leonards, NSW: Allen and Unwin, 1994.

————. *Fear and Hatred: Purifying Australia and California 1850–1901.* Sydney: Hale and Iremonger, 1979.

Marshall, P. J. "The White Town of Calcutta under the Rule of the East India Company." *Modern Asian Studies* 43 (2000): 307–32.

————. "The British in Asia: Trade to Dominion, 1700–1765." In *The Oxford History of the British Empire: Vol. 2. The Eighteenth Century,* edited by P. J. Marshall, 487–507. Oxford: Oxford University Press, 1998.

————. "1870–1918: The Empire Under Threat." In *The Cambridge Illustrated History of the British Empire,* edited by P. J. Marshall, 52–79. Cambridge: Cambridge University Press, 1996.

Martin, Gregory. "The Influence of Racial Attitudes on British Policy Towards India during the First World War." *Journal of Imperial and Commonwealth History* 14, no. 2 (1986): 91–113.

May, Dawn. *Aboriginal Labour and the Cattle Industry: Queensland from White Settlement to the Present.* Melbourne: Cambridge University Press, 1994.

Mehta, Uday S. "Liberal Strategies of Exclusion." *Politics & Society* 18 (1990) 4: 427–54.

Merians, Linda E. "The London Lock Hospital and the Lock Asylum for Women." In *The Secret Malady: Venereal Disease in Eighteenth-Century Britain and France,* edited by Linda E. Merians, 128–145. Lexington, KY: University of Kentucky Press, 1997.

Metcalf, Thomas R. *The New Cambridge History of India.* Vol. 4. *Ideologies of the Raj.* Cambridge: Cambridge University Press, 1994.

————. *The Aftermath of Revolt. India, 1857–70.* Delhi: Manohar Publications, 1990.

Meyer, Gregg S. "Criminal Punishment for the Transmission of Sexually Transmitted Diseases: Lessons from Syphilis." *Bulletin of the History of Medicine* 65, no. 4 (1991): 549–64.

Mies, Maria. *Indian Women and Patriarchy: Conflicts and Dilemmas of Students and Working Women.* New Delhi: Concept Publishing Company, 1980.

Miners, Norman. *Hong Kong Under Imperial Rule 1912–1941.* Hong Kong: Oxford University Press, 1987.

Ming, Hanneke. "Barracks-Concubinage in the Indies, 1887–1920." *Indonesia* 35 (1983): 65–93.

Mintz, Sidney W. *Sweetness and Power: The Place of Sugar in Modern History.* New York: Penguin, 1986.

Mirelman, Victor A. "The Jewish Community Versus Crime: The Case of White Slavery in Buenos Aires." *Jewish Social Studies* 46, no. 2 (1984), 145–68.

Mohanty, Chandra Talpade, Ann Russo, and Lourdes Torres. eds. *Third World Women and the Politics of Feminism.* Bloomington, IN: Indiana University Press, 1991.

————. "Feminist Encounters: Locating the Politics of Experience." *Copyright* 1 (1987): 30–44.

Mohanty, Satya P. "Drawing The Color Line: Kipling and the Culture of Colonial Rule." In *The Bounds of Race: Perspectives on Hegemony and Resistance,* edited by Dominick LaCapra, 311–43. Ithaca, NY: Cornell University Press, 1991.

Moore, Clive, "A Precious Few: Melanesian and Asian Women in Northern Australia." In *Gender Relations in Australia: Domination and Negotiation,* edited by Kay Saunders and Raymond Evans, 59–81. Sydney: Harcourt Brace Jovanovich, 1992.

————. *Kanaka: A History of Melanesian Mackay.* Port Moresby: Institute of Papua New Guinea Studies/University of Papua New Guinea Press, 1985.

Moore, John Hammond. *Over-Sexed, Over-Paid and Over Here: Americans in Australia, 1941–1945.* St. Lucia: University of Queensland Press, 1981.

Moore, Robin J. "Imperial India, 1858–1914." In *The Oxford History of the British Empire:* Vol. 3. *The Nineteenth Century,* edited by Andrew Porter, 422–46. Oxford: Oxford University Press, 1999.

Moore-Gilbert, Bart. *Writing India 1757–1900: The Literature of British India.* Manchester: Manchester University Press, 1996.

Morgan, Susan. *Place Matters: Gendered Geography in Victorian Women's Travel Books about Southeast Asia.* New Brunswick, NJ: Rutgers University Press, 1996.

Morgan, Thaïs E. "Reimagining Masculinity in Victorian Criticism: Swinburne and Pater," *Victorian Studies* 36, no. 3 (1993): 315–32.

Mordike, John. *An Army For A Nation: A History of Australian Military Developments 1880–1914.* North Sydney: Allen and Unwin, 1992.

Mort, Frank. *Dangerous Sexualities: Medico-Moral Politics in England since 1830.* 2nd ed. London and New York: Routledge, 2000.

————. "Purity, Feminism and the State: Sexuality and Moral Politics 1880–1914." In *Crises in the British State 1880–1930s,* edited by Mary Langan and Bill Schwarz, 209–25. London: Hutchinson and Centre for Contemporary Studies, University of Birmingham, 1985.

Mullan, Fitzhugh. *Plagues and Politics: The Story of the United States Public Health Service.* New York: Basic Books, 1989.

Murnane, Mary and Kay Daniels. "Prostitutes as 'Purveyors of Disease': Venereal Disease Legislation in Tasmania, 1868–1945." *Hecate* 5 (1979): 5–21.

Naanen, Benedict B. B. " 'Itinerant Gold Mines': Prostitution in the Cross River Basin of Nigeria, 1930–1950." *African Studies Review* 34, no. 2 (1991): 57–79.

Nair, Janaki. *Women and Law in Colonial India: A Social History.* Delhi and Bangalore: Kali for Women and National Law School of India University, 1996.

———. "Uncovering the Zenana: Visions of Indian Womanhood in Englishwomen's Writings, 1813–1940." *Journal of Women's History* 2, no. 1 (1990), 8–34.

Nandy, Ashis. *The Intimate Enemy: Loss and Recovery of Self Under Colonialism.* Delhi: Oxford University Press, 1983.

———. "The Psychology of Colonialism: Sex, Age, and Ideology in British India." *Psychiatry* 45, no. 3 (1982): 197–218.

Narain, Abha. "Witty Keepers and Royalty." *Times of India* (22 October 1994).

Nash Catherine. "Remapping the Body/Land: New Cartographies of Identity, Gender, and Landscape in Ireland." In *Writing Women and Space: Colonial and Postcolonial Geographies,* edited by Alison Blunt and Gillian Roe, 227–50. New York: The Guilford Press, 1994.

Nasson, Bill. "The Great War in South African Historiography." *Bulletin du Centre de Recherche Historial, Péronne* (June 1993): 9–11.

Nead, Lynda. "Mapping the Self: Gender, Space and Modernity in Mid-Victorian London." *Environment and Planning A* 29 (1997): 659–72.

Nelson, Keith L. "The 'Black Horror on the Rhine': Race as a Factor in Post-World War One Diplomacy." *Journal of Modern History* 42, no. 4 (1970): 606–27.

Neptune, Harvey. "White Lies: Race and Sexuality in Occupied Trinidad." *Journal of Colonialism and Colonial History* 2, no. 1 (2001): n.p.

Nigam, Sanjay. "Disciplining and Policing the 'Criminals by Birth', Part 2: The Development of a Disciplinary System, 1871–1900," *Indian Economic and Social History Review* 27, no. 3 (1990): 257–87.

Northrup, David. "Migration from Africa, Asia, and the South Pacific." In *The Oxford History of the British Empire.* Volume 3. *The Nineteenth Century,* edited by Andrew Porter, 88–100. Oxford: Oxford University Press, 1999.

Nussbaum, Felicity. *Torrid Zones: Maternity, Sexuality, and Empire in Eighteenth-Century English Narratives.* Baltimore, MD: The Johns Hopkins University Press, 1995.

———. "One Part of Womankind: Prostitution and Sexual Geography in *Memoirs of A Woman of Pleasure.*" *Differences* 7, no. 2 (1995): 16–40.

O'Connor, P. S. "Venus and the Lonely Kiwi: The War Effort of Miss Ettie A. Rout." *New Zealand Journal of History* 1 (1967): 11–32.

Ogborn, Miles. "This Most Lawless Space: The Geography of the Fleet and the Making of Lord Hardwicke's Marriage Act of 1753." *New Formations (Sexual Geographies)* 37 (1999): 11–32.

———. *Spaces of Modernity: London's Geographies, 1680–1780,* New York: The Guilford Press, 1998.

———. "Law and Discipline in Nineteenth Century English State Formation: The Contagious Diseases Acts of 1864, 1868 and 1869." *Journal of Historical Sociology* 6, no. 1 (1993): 28–55.

O'Keefe, Brendan. "Sexually Transmitted Diseases in Malaysia: A History." In *Sex, Disease, and Society: A Comparative History of Sexually Transmitted Diseases and HIV/AIDS in Asia and the Pacific,* edited by Milton Lewis, Scott Bamber, and Michael Waugh, 155–75. Westport, CT: Greenwood Press, 1997.

O'Hanlon, Rosalind. "Issues of Masculinity in North Indian History: The Bangash Nawabs of Farrukhabad." *Indian Journal of Gender Studies* 4, no. 1 (1997): 1–19.

———. *A Comparison Between Women and Men: Tarabai Shinde and the Critique of Gender Relations in Colonial India.* Madras: Oxford University Press, 1994.

———. "Issues of Widowhood: Gender and Resistance in Colonial Western India." In *Contesting Power: Resistance and Everyday Social Relations in South Asia,* edited by Douglas Haynes and Gyan Prakash, 62–108. Berkeley, CA: University of California Press, 1991.

Oldenburg, Veena Talwar. "Lifestyle as Resistance: The Case of the Courtesans of Lucknow." In *Contesting Power: Resistance and Everyday Social Relations in South Asia,* edited by Douglas Haynes and Gyan Prakash, 23–61. Berkeley, CA: University of California Press, 1991.

———. *The Making of Colonial Lucknow 1856–1877.* Princeton, NJ: Princeton University Press, 1984.

Omissi, David. *Indian Voices of the Great War. Soldiers' Letters, 1914–1918.* Basingstoke: Macmillan, 1999.

———. *The Sepoy and the Raj: The Indian Army, 1860–1940.* Basingstoke: The Macmillan Press, 1994.

Oosterhuis, Harry. "Medical Science and the Modernisation of Sexuality." In *Sexual Cultures in Europe: National Histories,* edited by Franz X. Eder, Lesley A. Hall, and Gert Hekma, 221–41. Manchester: Manchester University Press, 1999.

Opitz, May, Katharina Oguntoye, and Dagmar Schultz. *Showing Our Colors: Afro-German Women Speak Out.* Amherst: University of Massachusetts Press, 1992.

Oriel, J. D. *The Scars of Venus: A History of Venereology,* London: Springer-Verlag, 1994.

Oxley, Deborah. *Convict Maids: The Forced Migration of Women to Australia.* Cambridge: Cambridge University Press, 1996.

Page, Melvin E. "Introduction: Black Men in a White Men's War." In *Africa and the First World War,* edited by Melvin E. Page, 1–27. Basingstoke: The Macmillan Press, 1987.

Palmer, Annette. "Black American Soldiers in Trinidad, 1942–44: Wartime Politics in a Colonial Society." *Journal of Imperial and Commonwealth History* 14, no. 3 (1986): 203–18.

Panakal, J. J. "Prostitution in India." *Indian Journal of Criminology* 2, no. 1 (1974): 29–35.

Panikkar, K. N. "Indigenous Medicine and Cultural Hegemony: A Study of the Revitalization Movement in Keralam." *Studies in History* 8, no. 2, n.s. (1992): 283–308.

Papanek, Hanna and Gail Minault. *Separate Worlds: Studies of Purdah in South Asia.* Columbia, MO: South Asia Books, 1982.

Parker, Kunal M. " 'A Corporation of Superior Prostitutes': Anglo-Indian Legal Conceptions of Temple Dancing Girls, 1800-1914." *Modern Asian Studies* 32, no. 3 (1998): 559–633.

Parr, Joy. "Gender History and Historical Practice." *Canadian Historical Review* 76, no. 3 (1995): 354–76.

Parry, Benita. *Delusions and Discoveries: India in the British Imagination, 1880–1930.* 2nd ed., London: Verso, 1998.

Patil, B. R. "The Devadasis." *Indian Journal of Social Work* 35, no. 4 (1975): 377–89.

Patton, Cindy. "Critical Bodies." In *Trajectories: Inter-Asia Cultural Studies,* edited by Kuan-Hsing Chen, 314–29. London: Routledge, 1998.

Patrick, Ross. *A History of Health and Medicine in Queensland 1824–1960.* St. Lucia: University of Queensland Press, 1987.

———. "Health Administration 1860–1910." In *People, Places and Policies: Aspects of Queensland Government Administration 1859–1920,* edited by Kay Cohen and Kenneth Wiltshire, 246–65. St. Lucia: University of Queensland Press, 1995.

Paxton, Nancy L. "Mobilizing Chivalry: Rape in British Novels about the Indian Uprising of 1857." *Victorian Studies* 36, no. 1 (1992): 5–30.

Pedersen, Susan. "National Bodies, Unspeakable Acts: The Sexual Politics of Colonial Policy-Making." *Journal of Modern History* 63, no. 4 (1991): 647–80.

Peers, Douglas M. "Privates off Parade: Regimenting Sexuality in the Nineteenth-Century Indian Empire," *International History Review* 20, no. 4 (1998): 823–54.

———. "Soldiers, Surgeons and the Campaigns to Combat Sexually Transmitted Diseases in Colonial India, 1805–1860," *Medical History* 42 (1998): 137–60.

———. " 'Those Noble Exemplars of the True Military Tradition': Constructions of the Indian Army in the Mid-Victorian Period." *Modern Asian Studies* 31, no. 1 (1997): 109–42.

———. "Sepoys, Soldiers and the Lash: Race, Caste and Army Discipline in India, 1820–50," *Journal of Imperial and Commonwealth History* 23, no. 2 (1995): 211–47.

Pellow, Deborah. "STDs and AIDS in Ghana." *Genitourinary Medicine* 70, no. 6 (1994): 418–23.

———. "Sexuality in Africa." *Trends in History* 4, no. 4 (1990): 71–96.

Petrow, Stefan. *Policing Morals: The Metropolitan Police and the Home Office 1870–1914.* Oxford: Clarendon Press, 1994.

Phillips, Jock. "Mummy's Boys: Pakeha Men and Male Culture in New Zealand." In *Women in New Zealand Society,* edited by Phillida Bunkle and Beryl Hughes, 217–43. Auckland: George Allen and Unwin, 1980.

Pierson, Ruth Roach. "The Double Bind of the Double Standard: VD Control and the CWAC in World War II." *Canadian Historical Review* 52, no. 1 (1981): 31–58.

Ping, Lee Poh. *Chinese Society in Nineteenth Century Singapore.* Kuala Lumpur: Oxford University Press, 1978.

Pivar, David J. "The Military, Prostitution, and Colonial Peoples: India and the Philippines, 1885–1917." *Journal of Sex Research* 17, no. 3 (1981): 256–69.

Po-Keung, Hui. "Comprador Politics and Middleman Capitalism." In *Hong Kong's History: State and Society under Colonial Rule*, edited by Tak-Wing Ngo, 30–45. London: Routledge, 1999.

Pommerenke, Millicent. *Asian Women and Eros*. New York, Vantage Press, 1958.

Poovey, Mary. "Speaking of the Body: Mid-Victorian Constructions of Female Desire." In *Body/Politics: Women and the Discourses of Science*, edited by Mary Jacobus, Evelyn Fox Keller, and Sally Shuttleworth, 29–46. New York: Routledge, 1990.

Porter, Andrew. "Introduction: Britain and the Empire in the Nineteenth Century." In *The Oxford History of the British Empire*: Volume 3. *The Nineteenth Century*, edited by Andrew Porter, 1–30. Oxford: Oxford University Press, 1999.

Porter, Bernard. *The Lion's Share: A Short History of British Imperialism 1850–1983*. London and New York: Longman, 1984.

Porter, Dorothy and Roy Porter. *In Sickness and In Health: The British Experience 1650–1850*. London: Fourth Estate Press, 1988.

Porter, Doug J. "A Plague on the Borders: HIV, Development, and Traveling Identities in the Golden Triangle." In *Sites of Desire, Economies of Pleasure: Sexualities in Asia and the Pacific*, edited by Lenore Manderson and Margaret Jolly, 212–32. Chicago: University of Chicago Press, 1997.

Posel, Ros. " 'Continental Women' and Durban's Social Evil, 1899–1905." *Journal of Natal and Zulu History* 12 (1989): 1–13.

Powell, John ed. *Liberal by Principle: The Politics of Wodehouse, 1st Earl of Kimberley, 1843–1902.* London: The Historian's Press, 1996.

Pradhan, S. D. "Indian Army and the First World War." In *India and World War I*, edited by DeWitt C. Ellinwood and S. D. Pradhan, 49–67. New Delhi: Manohar, 1978.

Prakash, Gyan. "Writing Post-Orientalist Histories of the Third World: Perspectives from Indian Historiography." *Comparative Studies in Society and History* 32, no. 2 (1990): 383–408.

Pratt, Mary Louise. *Imperial Eyes: Travel Writing and Transculturation*. London: Routledge, 1992.

Punekar, S. D. and Kamala Rao. *A Study of Prostitution in Bombay*. Bombay: Allied Publishers, 1962.

Quigley, Declan. *The Interpretation of Caste*. Oxford: Clarendon Press, 1993.

Raj, M. Sundara. *Prostitution in Madras: A Study in Historical Perspective*, Delhi: Konark Publications PVT Ltd., 1993.

Rajan, Rajeswari Sunder. "The Subject of Sati." In *Interrogating Modernity: Culture and Colonialism in India*, edited by Tejaswani Niranjana, P. Sudhir, and Vivek Dhareshwar, 291–318. Seagull: Calcutta, 1993.

Ramasubbhan, Radhika. "Imperial Health in British India, 1857–1900." In *Disease, Medicine, and Empire: Perspectives on Western Medicine and the Experience of European Expansion*, edited by Roy Macleod and Milton Lewis, 38–60. London: Routledge, 1988.

Ramusack, Barbara N. "Embattled Advocates: The Debate over Birth Control in India, 1920–40." *Journal of Women's History* 1, no. 2 (1989): 34–64.

Rappaport, Erika. D. " 'A New Era of Shopping': The Promotion of Women's Pleasure in London's West End, 1909–1914." In *Cinema and the Invention of Modern Life*, edited by Leo Charney and Vanessa R. Schwartz, 130–55. Berkeley, CA: California, 1995.

Ray, Rajat Kanta. "Indian Society and the Establishment of British Supremacy, 1765–1818." In *The Oxford History of the British Empire*: Volume 2. *The Eighteenth Century*, edited by P. J. Marshall, 508–29. Oxford: Oxford University Press, 1998.

Readings, Bill. *The University in Ruins*. Cambridge, MA: Harvard University Press, 1996.

Reekie, Gail. "Women, Region and the 'Queensland Difference.'" In *On the Edge: Women's Experiences of Queensland*, edited by Gail Reekie, 8–24. St. Lucia: University of Queensland Press, 1981.

Reinders, Robert C. "Racialism on the Left: E. D. Morel and the 'Black Horror on the Rhine.' " *International Review of Social History* 13, no. 1 (1968): 1–28.

Reynolds, David. "The Churchill Government and the Black Troops in Britain during World War II." *Transactions of the Royal Historical Society* 5th ser. 35 (1985): 113–33.

Reynolds, Henry and Dawn May. "Queensland." In *Contested Ground: Australian Aborigines under the British Crown*, edited by Ann McGrath, 168–207. St. Leonards, NSW: Allen and Unwin, 1995.

Robb, Peter, ed. *The Concept of Race in South Asia*. Delhi: Oxford University Press, 1995.

Roberts, Elfed Vaughan, Sum Ngai Ling, and Peter Bradshaw. *Historical Dictionary of Hong Kong and Macau*. Metuchen, NJ and London: The Scarecrow Press, 1992.

Roberts, Helene E. "Marriage, Redundancy or Sin: The Painter's View of Women in the First Twenty-Five Years of Victoria's Reign." In *Suffer and Be Still: Women in the Victorian Age*, edited by Martha Vicinus, 45–76. London: University Paperbacks, 1980.

Robson, Brian, ed. *Roberts in India: The Military Papers of Field Marshal Lord Roberts 1876–1893.* Stroud, Glos: Alan Sutton for the Army Records Society, 1993.

Roediger, David R. *The Wages of Whiteness: Race and the Making of the American Working Class.* London: Verso, 1991.

Roland, Joan G. *Jews in British India: Identity in a Colonial Era.* Hanover, NH: University Press of New England, 1989.

Ross, Elizabeth A. "Victorian Medicine in Penang." *Malaysia in History* 23 (1980): 84–9.

Ross, J. E. and S. M. Tomkins. "The British Reception of Salvarsan." *Journal of the History of Medicine and Allied Sciences* 52, no. 4 (1997): 398–423.

Rosselli, John. "The Self-Image of Effeteness: Physical Education and Nationalism in Nineteenth-Century Bengal." *Past and Present* 86 (1980): 121–48.

Rotenberg, Lori. "The Wayward Worker: Toronto's Prostitute at the Turn of the Century." In *Women at Work: Ontario 1850–1930,* edited by Janice Acton, Penny Goldsmith, and Bonnie Shepard, 33–69. Toronto: Canadian Women's Educational Press, 1974.

Roy, R. Basu. "Sexually Transmitted Diseases and the Raj." *Sexually Transmitted Infections* 74, no. 1 (February 1998): 20–26.

Rozario, Santi. "The *Dai* and the Doctor: Discourses on Women's Reproductive Health in Rural Bangladesh." In *Maternities and Modernities: Colonial and Postcolonial Experiences in Asia and the Pacific,* edited by Kalpana Ram and Margaret Jolly, 144–76. Cambridge: Cambridge University Press, 1998.

Ryan, Simon. *The Cartographic Eye: How Explorers Saw Australia.* Cambridge: Cambridge University Press, 1996.

Saeed, Fouzia. *Taboo! The Hidden Culture of a Red Light Area.* Karachi: Oxford University Press, 2001.

Said, Edward W. "Secular Interpretation, The Geographical Element, and the Methodology of Imperialism," In *After Colonialism: Imperial Histories and Postcolonial Displacements,* edited by Gyan Prakash, 21–39. Princeton, NJ: Princeton University Press, 1995.

———. *Culture and Imperialism.* New York: Alfred A. Knopf, 1993.

———. *Orientalism.* London: Routledge and Kegan Paul, 1978.

Saini, Krishan G. "The Economic Aspects of India's Participation in the First World War." In *India and World War I,* edited by DeWitt C. Ellinwood and S. D. Pradhan, 141–76. New Delhi: Manohar, 1978.

Sarabhai, Mrinalini. *The Sacred Dance of India.* Bombay: Bharatiya Vidya Bhavan, 1979.

Sarkar, Sumit. *Modern India 1885–1947.* 2nd ed., Basingstoke: The Macmillan Press, 1989.

Sarkar, Tanika. "The Hindu Wife and the Hindu Nation: Domesticity and Nationalism in Nineteenth Century Bengal." *Studies in History* n.s. 8, no. 2 (1992): 213–35.

Sauerteig, Lutz D. H. "Sex, Medicine and Morality During the First World War." In *War, Medicine and Modernity,* edited by Roger Cooter, Mark Harrison, and Steve Sturdy, 167–188. Stroud, Glos: Sutton Publishing, 1998.

Saunders, Kay. "Controlling (Hetero)Sexuality: The Implementation and Operation of Contagious Diseases Legislation in Australia, 1868–1945." In *Sex, Power and Justice: Historical Perspectives on Law in Australia,* edited by Diane Kirkby, 2–18. Melbourne: Oxford University Press, 1995.

Saunders, Kay and Helen Taylor. "The Impact of Total War Upon Policing: The Queensland Experience." In *Policing in Australia: Historical Perspectives,* edited by Mark Finnane, 143–69. Kensington, NSW: New South Wales University Press, 1987.

Savage, Gail. " 'The Wilful Communication of a Loathsome Disease': Marital Conflict and Venereal Disease in Victorian England." *Victorian Studies* 34, no. 1 (1990): 35–54.

Schwarz, Bill. "Conservatism, Nationalism and Imperialism." In *Politics and Ideology* edited by James Donald and Stuart Hall, 154–86. Milton Keynes and Philadelphia, PA: Open University Press, 1986.

Scott, Paul. *The Day of the Scorpion.* New York: Morrow, 1978.

Sedgwick, Eve Kosofsky. *Epistemology of the Closet.* Berkeley, CA: University of California Press, 1990.

———. *Between Men: English Literature and Male Homosocial Desire.* New York: Columbia University Press, 1985.

Sen, Satadru. "Policing the Savage: Segregation, Labor, and State Medicine in the Andamans." *Journal of Asian Studies* 58, no. 3 (1999): 753–73.

———. "Rationing Sex: Female Convicts in the Andamans." *South Asia* 30 (1998), 29–59.

Sen, Sudipta. "Colonial Frontiers of the Georgian State: East India Company's Rule in India," *Journal of Historical Sociology* 7, no. 4 (1994): 368–92.

Seton, Malcolm C. C. *The India Office.* London and New York: Putnam's Sons Ltd., 1926.

Scully, Pamela. "Rape, Race, and Colonial Culture: The Sexual Politics of Identity in the Nineteenth Century Cape Colony, South Africa," *American Historical Review* 100, no. 2 (1995): 335–59.

Shankar, Jogan. *Devadasi Cult: A Sociological Analysis.* New Delhi: Ashish Publishing House, 1990.

Shannon, Richard. *The Crisis of Imperialism, 1865–1915.* St. Albans: Paladin, 1986.

Sharma, Ursula. *Caste.* Milton Keynes, Open University Press, 1999.

Shaw, Carolyn Martin. *Colonial Inscriptions: Race, Sex, and Class in Kenya.* Minneapolis, MN: University of Minnesota Press, 1995.

Shetty, Sandhya. "(Dis)Locating Gender Space and Medical Discourse in Colonial India." In *Eroticism and Containment: Genders 20,* edited by Carol Siegel and Ann Kibbey, 188–230. 1994.

Shute, Carmel. "Heroines and Heroes: Sexual Mythology in Australia 1914–18." In *Gender and War: Australians at War in the Twentieth Century,* edited by Joy Damousi and Marilyn Lake, 23–42. Melbourne: Cambridge University Press, 1995.

Siang, Song Ong. *One Hundred Years' History of the Chinese in Singapore.* Singapore: Oxford University Press, 1984.

Sinha, Mrinalini. "Giving Masculinity a History: Some Contributions from the Historiography of Colonial India." *Gender & History* 11, no. 3 (1999): 445–60.

———. *Colonial Masculinity: The "Manly Englishman" and the "Effeminate Bengali" in the Late Nineteenth Century.* Manchester: Manchester University Press, 1995.

———. "Gender in the Critiques of Colonialism and Nationalism: Locating the 'Indian Woman.' " In *Feminists Revision History,* edited by Anne-Louise Shapiro, 246–75. New Brunswick, NJ: Rutgers University Press, 1994.

Sinn, Elizabeth. *Power and Charity: The Early History of the Tung Wah Hospital, Hong Kong.* Hong Kong: Oxford University Press, 1989.

———. 'Chinese Patriarchy and the Protection of Women in Nineteenth-Century Hong Kong.' In *Women and Chinese Patriarchy: Submission, Servitude and Escape,* edited by Maria Jaschok and Suzanne Miers, 141–70. London and New Jersey: Zed Books, 1994.

Sissons, D. C. S. "*Karayuki-San:* Japanese Prostitutes in Australia, 1887–1916. Part 1.:" *Historical Studies* 17 (1977): 323–41. "Part 2." *Historical Studies* 17 (1977): 474–88.

Skelley, Alan Ramsay. *The Victorian Army At Home: The Recruitment and Terms and Conditions of the British Regular 1859–1899.* London: Croom Helm, 1977.

Smart, Carol. "Law and the Control of Women's Sexuality: The Case of the 1950s." In *Controlling Women: The Normal and the Deviant,* edited by Bridget Hutter and Gillian Williams, 40–60. London: Croom Helm, 1981.

Smart, Judith. "The Great War and the 'Scarlet Scourge': Debates about Venereal Diseases in Melbourne during World War I." In *An Anzac Muster: War and Society in Australia and New Zealand 1914–18 and 1939–45. Selected Papers,* edited by Judith Smart and Tony Wood, 58–85. Clayton, Victoria: Monash Publications in History 14, 1992.

———. "Feminists, Labour Women and Venereal Disease in Early Twentieth-Century Melbourne," *Australian Feminist Studies* 15 (1992), 25–40.

Smith, Carl T. "Protected Women in Nineteenth-Century Hong Kong." In *Women and Chinese Patriarchy: Submission, Servitude and Escape,* edited by Maria Jaschok and Suzanne Miers, 221–37. London and New Jersey: Zed Books, 1994.

Smith, F. B. "The Contagious Diseases Acts Reconsidered." *Social History of Medicine* 3, no. 2 (1990): 197–215.

Smith, Graham A. "Jim Crow on the Homefront (1942–1945)." *New Community* 8, no. 3 (1980): 317–28.

Smith, Vincent A. *The Oxford History of India.* 4th ed., Delhi: Oxford University Press, 1958.

Smythe, Donald. "Venereal Disease: The AEF's Experience." *Prologue* 9 (1977): 65–74.

Sone, Sachiko. "The Karayuki-San of Asia 1868–1938: The Role of Prostitutes Overseas in Japanese Economic and Social Development." *Review of Indonesian and Malaysian Affairs* 26, no. 2 (1992): 44–62.

Spaulding, Jay and Stephanie Beswick, "Sex, Bondage, and the Market: The Emergence of Prostitution in Northern Sudan, 1750–1950." *Journal of the History of Sexuality* 5, no. 4 (1995): 512–34.

Spiers, Edward M. *The Army and Society 1815–1914.* London: Longman, 1980.

Spivak, Gayatri C. "Woman in Difference: Mahasweta Devi's 'Douloti the Bountiful.' " In *Nationalisms and Sexualities*, edited by Andrew Parker, Mary Russo, Doris Sommer, and Patricia Yaeger, 96–116. London and New York: Routledge, 1992.

———. "The Rani of Sirmur." In *Europe And Its Others*. Vol. 1., edited by F. Barker, P. Hulme, M. Iverson, and D. Lozley, 128–51. Colchester: University of Essex, 1985.

———. "Can The Subaltern Speak? Speculations on Widow-Sacrifice." *Wedge* 7/8 (1985): 120–30.

Srinivasan, Amrit. "Reform or Conformity? Temple 'Prostitution' and the Community in the Madras Presidency." In *Structures of Patriarchy: State, Community and Household in Modernising Asia*, edited by Bina Agarwal, 175–98. New Delhi: Kali for Women; London: Zed Books, 1988.

———. "Reform and Revival: The Devadasi and Her Dance." *Economic and Political Weekly* 20, no. 44 (1985): 1869–76.

Stanley, Peter. *White Mutiny: British Military Culture in India*. New York: New York University Press, 1998.

Stepan, Nancy Leys and Sander Gilman. "Appropriating the Idioms of Science: The Rejection of Scientific Racism." In *The Bounds of Race: Perspectives on Hegemony and Resistance*, edited by Dominick LaCapra, 72–103. Ithaca, NY: Cornell University Press, 1991.

Sterren, Anke Van Der, Alison Murray, and Terry Hull. "A History of Sexually Transmitted Diseases in the Indian Archipelago." In *Sex, Disease, and Society: A Comparative History of Sexually Transmitted Diseases and HIV/AIDS in Asia and the Pacific*, edited by Milton Lewis, Scott Bamber, and Michael Waugh, 202–30. Westport, CT: Greenwood Press, 1997.

Stockwell, A. J. "British Expansion and Rule in South-East Asia." In *The Oxford History of the British Empire: Volume 3. The Nineteenth Century*, edited by Andrew Porter, 371–94. Oxford: Oxford University Press, 1999.

Stoler, Ann Laura. *Race and the Education of Desire: Foucault's* History of Sexuality *and the Colonial Order of Things*. Durham, NC: Duke University Press, 1995.

———. " 'Mixed-bloods' and the Cultural Politics of European Identity in Colonial Southeast Asia." In *The Decolonization of Imagination: Culture, Knowledge and Power*, edited by Jan Nederveen Pieterse and Bhikhu Parekh, 128–48. London and New Jersey: Zed Books, 1995.

———. " 'In Cold Blood': Hierarchies of Credibility and the Politics of Colonial Narratives." *Representations* 37 (1992): 151–89.

———. "Sexual Affronts and Racial Frontiers: European Identities and the Cultural Politics of Exclusion in Colonial Southeast Asia." *Comparative Studies in Society and History* 34, no. 3 (1992): 514–51.

———. "Carnal Knowledge and Imperial Power: Gender, Race, and Morality in Colonial Asia." In *Gender at the Crossroads of Knowledge: Feminist Anthropology in the Postmodern Era*, edited by Micaela di Leonardo, 51–101. Berkeley, CA: University of California Press, 1991.

———. "Rethinking Colonial Categories: European Communities and the Boundaries of Rule." *Comparative Studies in Society and History* 31, no. 1 (1989): 134–61.

———. "Making Empire Respectable: The Politics of Race and Sexual Morality in 20th-century Colonial Cultures." *American Ethnologist* 16, no. 4 (1989): 634–60.

Stovall, Tyler. "The Color Line behind the Lines: Racial Violence in France during the Great War." *American Historical Review* 103, no. 3 (1998): 737–69.

———. "Colour-blind France? Colonial Workers during the First World War." *Race and Class* 35, no. 2 (1993): 41–55.

Strachan, Hew. *The Politics of the British Army*. Oxford: Clarendon Press, 1997.

———. *Wellington's Legacy: The Reform of the British Army 1830–54*. Manchester: Manchester University Press, 1984.

Strobel, Margaret. *European Women and the Second British Empire*. Bloomington, IN: Indiana University Press, 1991.

Sturma, Michael. *South Sea Maidens: Western Fantasy and Sexual Politics in the South Pacific*. Westport, CT: Greenwood Press, 2002.

———. "Seduction and Punishment in Late Nineteenth Century New South Wales." *Australian Journal of Law & Society* 2, no. 2 (1985): 76–81.

Summers, Carol. "Intimate Colonialism: The Imperial Production of Reproduction in Uganda, 1907–1925." *Signs* 16, no. 4 (1991): 788–807.

Sutphen, Mary P. "Not What, but Where: Bubonic Plague and the Reception of Germ Theories in Hong Kong and Calcutta, 1894–1897." *Journal of the History of Medicine and Allied Sciences* 52, no. 1 (1997): 81–113.

Symanski, Richard. *The Immoral Landscape: Female Prostitution in Western Societies*. Toronto: Butterworths, 1981.

Tabili, Laura. "Women 'of a Very Low Type': Crossing Racial Boundaries in Imperial Britain." In *Gender and Class in Modern Europe*, edited by Laura L. Frader and Sonya O. Rose, 165–90. Ithaca, NY: Cornell University Press, 1996.

———. *"We Ask for British Justice": Workers and Racial Difference in Late Imperial Britain*. Ithaca, NY: Cornell University Press, 1994.

Tapper, Melbourne. *In the Blood: Sickle Cell Anemia and the Politics of Race*. Philadelphia, PA: University of Pennsylvania Press, 1999.

Tarachand, K. C. *Devadasi Custom: Rural Social Structure and Flesh Markets*. New Delhi: Reliance Publishing House, 1991.

Teltscher, Kate. *India Inscribed: European and British Writing on India 1600–1800*. Delhi: Oxford University Press, 1995.

Tharu, Susie and K. Lalita. *Women Writing in India: Volume 2: The Twentieth Century*. New York: The Feminist Press, 1993.

Thomas, Nicholas. "Sanitation and Seeing: The Creation of State Power in Early Colonial Fiji." *Comparative Studies in Society and History* 32, no. 1 (1990): 149–70.

Thompson, Andrew S. "The Language of Imperialism and the Meanings of Empire: Imperial Discourse in British Politics, 1895–1914." *Journal of British Studies* 36, no. 2 (1997): 147–77.

Thomson, Alistair. *Anzac Memories: Living with the Legend*. Melbourne: Oxford University Press, 1994.

Thorne, Christopher. "Britain and the Black GIs: Racial Issues and Anglo-American Relations in 1942." *New Community* 3, no. 3 (1974): 262–71.

Thorpe, Bill. *Colonial Queensland: Perspectives on A Frontier Society*. St. Lucia: University of Queensland Press, 1996.

———. "Archibald Meston and Aboriginal Legislation in Colonial Queensland." *Historical Studies* 21, no. 82 (1984): 52–67.

Tolerton, Jane. *Ettie: A Life of Ettie Rout: "Guardian Angel" or "Wickedest Woman"?* Auckland, NZ: Penguin Books, 1992.

Tomkins, S. M. "Palmitate or Permanganate: The Venereal Prophylaxis Debate in Britain, 1916–1926." *Medical History* 37 (1993): 382–98.

Tomoko, Yamazaki. *Sandakan Brothel No. 8: An Episode in the History of Lower-Class Japanese Women*. Armonk, NY: M.E. Sharpe, 1999.

Tosh, John. *A Man's Place: Masculinity and the Middle-Class Home in Victorian England*. New Haven, CT: Yale University Press, 1999.

Trainor, Luke. *British Imperialism and Australian Nationalism: Manipulation, Conflict and Compromise in the Late Nineteenth Century*. Cambridge: Cambridge University Press, 1994.

Treichler, Paula A. *How To Have Theory in an Epidemic: Cultural Chronicles of AIDS*. Durham, NC: Duke University Press, 1999.

Trocki, Carl A. "Political Structures in the Nineteenth and Early Twentieth Centuries." In *The Cambridge History of Southeast Asia: Volume 2. The Nineteenth and Twentieth Centuries*, edited by Nicholas Tarling, 79–130. Cambridge: Cambridge University Press, 1992.

Myna Trustram. *Women of the Regiment: Marriage and the Victorian Army*. Cambridge: Cambridge University Press, 1984.

Tsai, Jung-Fang. *Hong Kong in Chinese History: Community and Social Unrest in the British Colony, 1842–1913*. New York: Columbia University Press, 1993.

Tyrrell, Ian. *Woman's World: Woman's Empire: The Woman's Christian Temperance Union in International Perspective, 1880–1930*. Chapel Hill, NC: University of North Carolina Press, 1991.

Tucker, Judith. *Women in Nineteenth-Century Egypt*. Cambridge: Cambridge University Press, 1985.

Turnbull, C. M. *A History of Singapore 1819–1988*. 2nd ed. Singapore: Oxford University Press, 1989.

———. *The Straits Settlements 1826–67: Indian Presidency to Crown Colony*. London: The Athlone Press, 1972.

Usborne, Cornelie. " 'Pregnancy is the Woman's Active Service': Pronatalism in Germany during the First World War." In *The Upheaval of War: Family, Work and Welfare in Europe, 1914–1918*, edited by Richard Wall and J. M. Winter, 309–416. Cambridge: Cambridge University Press, 1988.

Vadgama, Kusoom. *India in Britain: The Indian Contribution to the British Way of Life*. London: Robert Royce Ltd., 1984.

Valverde, Mariana. *The Age of Light, Soap and Water: Moral Reform in English Canada, 1885–1925*. Toronto: McClelland and Stewart Inc., 1991.

Van Heyningen, Elizabeth B. " 'Gentoo'—A Case of Mistaken Identity?" *Kronos* 22 (1995): 73–86.

———. "The Social Evil in the Cape Colony 1868–1902: Prostitution and the Contagious Diseases Acts." *Journal of Southern African Studies* 10, no. 2 (1984): 170–91.

Van Onselen, Charles. *Studies in the Social and Economic History of the Witwatersrand 1886–1914: Volume 1. New Babylon.* Johannesburg: Ravan Press, 1982.

Vaughan, Megan. "Health and Hegemony: Representation of Disease and the Creation of the Colonial Subject in Nyasaland." In *Contesting Colonial Hegemony: State and Society in Africa and India,* edited by Dagmar Engels and Shula Marks, 173–201. London: British Academic Press/German Historical Institute, 1994.

———. "Syphilis in Colonial East and Central Africa: The Social Construction of an Epidemic." In *Epidemics and Ideas: Essays in the Historical Perception of Pestilence,* edited by Terence Ranger and Paul Slack, 269–302. Cambridge: Cambridge University Press, 1992.

———. *Curing Their Ills: Colonial Power and African Illness.* Stanford, CA; Stanford University Press, 1991.

Visram, Rozina. *Ayahs, Lascars and Princes: Indians in Britain 1700–1947.* London: Pluto Press, 1986.

Viswanathan, Gauri. *Masks of Conquest: Literary Study and British Rule in India.* New York: Columbia University Press, 1989.

Visweswaran, Kamala. "Small Speeches, Subaltern Gender: Nationalist Ideology and Its Historiography." In *Subaltern Studies IX,* edited by Shahid Amin and Dipesh Chakrabarty, 83–125. Delhi: Oxford University Press, 1996.

Wailoo, Keith. *Dying in the City of the Blues: Sickle Cell Anemia and the Politics of Race and Health.* Chapel Hill, NC: University of North Carolina Press, 2001.

Wainwright, Mary Doreen. *Brothers in India: The Correspondence of Tom, Alfred and Christopher Bassano 1841–75.* London: School of Oriental and African Studies, 1979.

Waldby, Catherine. *AIDS and the Body Politic: Biomedicine and Sexual Difference,* London: Routledge, 1996.

Walkowitz, Judith. *City of Dreadful Delight: Narratives of Sexual Danger in Late-Victorian London.* Chicago: University of Chicago Press, 1992.

———. *Prostitution and Victorian Society: Women, Class and the State.* Cambridge: Cambridge University Press, 1980.

Wallerstein, Immanuel. "Does India Exist?" In *Unthinking Social Science: The Limits of Nineteenth Century Paradigms,* 130–34. Cambridge: Polity Press, 1991.

Ware, Vron. *Beyond the Pale: White Women, Racism and History.* London: Verso, 1992.

Ware, Vron and Les Back, *Out of Whiteness: Color, Politics, and Culture.* Chicago: Chicago University Press, 2002.

Warren, James F. "Chinese Prostitution in Singapore: Recruitment and Brothel Organisation." In *Women and Chinese Patriarchy: Submission, Servitude and Escape,* edited by Maria Jaschok and Suzanne Miers, 77–107. London and New Jersey: Zed Books, 1994.

———. *Ah Ku and Karayuki-San: Prostitution in Singapore 1870–1940.* Singapore: Oxford University Press, 1993.

———. "Prostitution and the Politics of Venereal Disease: Singapore, 1870–98." *Journal of South East Asian Studies* 21, no 2 (1990): 360–83.

———. "Rickshaw Coolie: An Exploration of the Underside of a Chinese City Outside China, Singapore 1880–1940." In *At the Edge of Southeast Asian History,* edited by J. F. Warren, 73–81. Quezon City: New Day Publishers, 1987.

Washbrook, David. "India, 1818–1860: The Two Faces of Colonialism." In *The Oxford History of the British Empire: Volume 3. The Nineteenth Century,* edited by Andrew Porter, 395–421. Oxford: Oxford University Press, 1999.

Waterson, Duncan and Maurice French. *From the Frontier: A Pictorial History of Queensland to 1920.* St. Lucia: University of Queensland Press, 1987.

Watts, Sheldon. *Epidemics and History: Disease, Power, and Imperialism.* New Haven, CT: Yale University Press, 1997.

Waugh, M. A. "Attitudes of Hospitals in London to Venereal Disease in the 18th and 19th Centuries." *British Journal of Venereal Diseases* 47 (1971): 146–50.

Webb, R. K. *Modern England.* 2nd ed. New York: Harper and Row, 1980.

Webster, Anthony. *Gentlemen Capitalists: British Imperialism in South East Asia, 1770–1890.* London and New York: Tauris Academic Studies, 1998.

Weeks, Jeffrey. *Making Sexual History.* Cambridge: Polity, 2000.

Welsh, Frank. *A History of Hong Kong.* London: Harper Collins, 1993.
White, Luise. *The Comforts of Home: Prostitution in Colonial Nairobi.* Chicago: University of Chicago Press, 1990.
———. "Domestic Labor in a Colonial City: Prostitution in Nairobi, 1900–1952." In *African Women in the Home and the Workforce,* edited by Sharon B. Stichter and Jane L. Parpart, 139–60. Boulder, CO and London: Westview Press, 1988.
White, Richard. "Sun, Sand and Syphilis: Australian Soldiers and the Orient: Egypt 1914." *Australian Cultural History* 9 (1990): 49–64.
———. *Inventing Australia: Images and Identity 1688–1980.* Sydney: George Allen and Unwin, 1981.
Whitehead, Judy. "Bodies Clean and Unclean: Prostitution, Sanitary Legislation, and Respectable Femininity in Colonial North India." *Gender & History* 7, no. 1 (1995): 41–63.
Willan, B. P. "The South African Native Labour Contingent, 1916–1918." *Journal of African History* 19, no. 1 (1978): 61–86.
Winter, Dennis. *Death's Men: Soldiers of the Great War.* London: Allen Lane, 1978.
Wolfe, Patrick. "History and Imperialism: A Century of Theory from Marx to Postcolonialism." *American Historical Review* 102, no. 2 (1997): 388–420.
Wood, Marilyn. "Nineteenth Century Bureaucratic Constructions of Indigenous Identities in New South Wales." In *Citizenship and Indigenous Australians: Changing Conceptions and Possibilities,* edited by Nicolas Peterson and Will Sanders, 35–54. Cambridge: Cambridge University Press, 1998.
Woollacott, Angela. " 'Khaki Fever' and Its Control: Gender, Class, Age and Sexual Morality on the British Homefront in the First World War." *Journal of Contemporary History* 29 (1994): 325–47.
———. *On Her Their Lives Depend: Munitions Workers in the Great War.* Berkeley, CA: University of California Press, 1994.
Wright, Gwendolyn. *The Politics of Design in French Colonial Urbanism.* Chicago: University of Chicago Press, 1991.
Wyke, T. J. "Hospital Facilities for, and Diagnosis and Treatment of, Venereal Disease in England, 1800–1870." *British Journal of Venereal Diseases* 49 (1973): 78–85.
Yeoh, Brenda S. A. "Sexually Transmitted Diseases in Late Nineteenth- and Twentieth-Century Singapore." In *Sex, Disease, and Society: A Comparative History of Sexually Transmitted Diseases and HIV/AIDS in Asia and the Pacific,* edited by Milton Lewis, Scott Bamber, and Michael Waugh, 177–202. Westport, CT: Greenwood Press, 1997.
———. *Contesting Space: Power Relations and the Urban Built Environment in Colonial Singapore.* Kuala Lumpur: Oxford University Press, 1996.
———. *Municipal Sanitary Surveillance, Asian Resistance and the Control of the Urban Environment in Colonial Singapore.* Oxford: University of Oxford School of Geography Research Papers, 1991.
Young, John. "Race and Sex in Fiji Re-visited." *Journal of Pacific History* 23, no. 2 (1988): 214–22.
Young, Robert J. C. *Colonial Desire: Hybridity in Theory, Culture and Race.* London and New York: Routledge, 1995.
Zatz, Noah D. "Sex Work/Sex Act: Law, Labor, and Desire in Constructions of Prostitution." *Signs* 22, no. 2 (1997): 280–96.
Zonana, Joyce. "The Sultan and the Slave: Feminist Orientalism and the Structure of *Jane Eyre.*" *Signs* 18, no. 3 (1993): 592–617.

Unpublished Dissertations And Theses

Botsman, Peter Carl. "The Sexual and the Social: Policing Venereal Diseases, Medicine and Morals." Ph. D. diss., University of New South Wales, 1987.
Gamble, John Gill. "The Origins, Administration, and Impact of the Contagious Diseases Acts from a Military Perspective," Ph. D. diss., University of Southern Mississippi, 1983.
Hart, Gavin. "The Impact of Prostitution on Australian Troops on Active Service in A War Environment—with Particular Reference to Sociological Factors Involved in the Incidence and Control of Venereal Disease," MD thesis, University of Adelaide, 1974.

Jochelsen, Karen. "The Colour of Disease: Syphilis and Racism in South Africa, 1910–1950," D. Phil. diss., University of Oxford, 1993.

Kehoe, Jean M. "Medicine, Sexuality and Imperialism: British Medical Discourses Surrounding Venereal Disease in New Zealand and Japan: A Socio-historical and Comparative Study," Ph. D. diss., Victoria University of Wellington, 1992.

Lin, Patricia Y. C. E. "Extending Her Arms: Military Families and the Transformation of the British State, 1793–1815," Ph. D. diss., University of California Berkeley, 1997.

Meduri, Avanthi. "Nation, Woman, Representation: The Sutured History of the Devadasi and Her Dance," Ph. D. diss., New York University, 1996.

Smithurst, B. A. "Historic and Epidemiologic Review of Venereal Disease in Queensland," MD thesis, University of Queensland, 1981.

Tibbits, Diana R. "The Medical, Social and Political Response to Venereal Diseases in Victoria, 1860–1980," Ph. D. diss., Monash University, 1994.

Index

Page number followed by n indicates the numbered note on that page.

Lightning Source UK Ltd.
Milton Keynes UK
UKOW04f1543231014

240536UK00009B/206/P